HISTORY OF
United States Naval Operations
IN WORLD WAR II

★

VOLUME FIFTEEN

Supplement and General Index

HISTORY OF UNITED STATES NAVAL OPERATIONS IN WORLD WAR II

By Samuel Eliot Morison

I *The Battle of the Atlantic*, September 1939 – May 1943

II *Operations in North African Waters*, October 1942 – June 1943

III *The Rising Sun in the Pacific*, 1931 – April 1942

IV *Coral Sea, Midway and Submarine Actions*, May 1942 – August 1942

V *The Struggle for Guadalcanal*, August 1942 – February 1943

VI *Breaking the Bismarcks Barrier*, 22 July 1942 – 1 May 1944

VII *Aleutians, Gilberts and Marshalls*, June 1942 – April 1944

VIII *New Guinea and the Marianas*, March 1944 – August 1944

IX *Sicily – Salerno – Anzio*, January 1943 – June 1944

X *The Atlantic Battle Won*, May 1943 – May 1945

XI *The Invasion of France and Germany*, 1944 – 1945

XII *Leyte*, June 1944 – January 1945

XIII *The Liberation of the Philippines: Luzon, Mindanao, the Visayas*, 1944 – 1945

XIV *Victory in the Pacific*, 1945

XV *Supplement and General Index*

Also

Strategy and Compromise

Part of Pacific Fleet in Eniwetok Lagoon

Before Marianas campaign, May 1944

Two Baltimore Class heavy cruisers are in center foreground; a light cruiser
at left, four Essex Class carriers in rear

HISTORY OF UNITED STATES NAVAL
OPERATIONS IN WORLD WAR II
VOLUME XV

Supplement
and General Index

BY SAMUEL ELIOT MORISON

With Illustrations

An Atlantic Monthly Press Book

LITTLE, BROWN AND COMPANY · BOSTON

1962

ATLANTIC–LITTLE, BROWN BOOKS
ARE PUBLISHED BY
LITTLE, BROWN AND COMPANY
IN ASSOCIATION WITH
THE ATLANTIC MONTHLY PRESS

Published simultaneously in Canada
by Little, Brown & Company (Canada) Limited

PRINTED IN THE UNITED STATES OF AMERICA

Dedicated

to

THE MEN OF THE FLEET

Introduction

BY REAR ADMIRAL ERNEST M. ELLER USN
Director of Naval History

SOME two and a half millennia ago Thucydides, wisest of historians and most readable, set down the first words of an incomparable history. He began to write at the outbreak of the Peloponnesian War because it would be "Great and memorable above any previous war," since Sparta, strongest power on land, was matched against Athens, strongest at sea.

These words of the noblest of historians could be applied to this superb fifteen-volume series of Samuel Eliot Morison's *History of United States Naval Operations in World War II.* In its way it is incomparable, like Thucydides, for the vast cataclysm of World War II had many fateful results like those of the Peloponnesian War.

As a young man I first read Morison's early *Maritime History of Massachusetts* and knew that I had come upon a real historian — one who seeks the truth, tells it in a pattern of significance to destiny, and fills it with the sunlight and shadows that illumine and darken this swift voyage of man.

I met him not long thereafter, but first came to know him when he landed among the "Monks of Makalapa" — a sometime term for Admiral Nimitz's staff, who dwelt at the Makalapa headquarters. He came on board early in his naval writing career, with his crooked London market coronas, his Colombo songs, his Scottish thrift, his Boston charm or haughtiness as the mood served, and his indefatigable application. At that time I was a gunner, but, in the little spare time I had, helped to prepare Admiral Nimitz's war reports and battle analyses. Hence our courses naturally crossed and lay alongside each other for a period. Then, years afterward, through the inscrutable workings of the unknown, I came to my present office. Among the multitude of other duties, it includes responsibility in contracting for, supporting with major staff assistance, clearing the MSS and handling other facets of the Morison series.

In moments of levity during the past five years, Sam Morison has said that he "works" for me. Of course he works for nobody except Clio the Goddess of History, and, in the manner of most men, for his wife. Although we have had several people assisting him, and although several of us have read and commented on drafts of his last five volumes, as did Admiral Heffernan and his staff before us, they are Sam's history. This doesn't mean that drafts don't change — often I have seen nearly every page of a manuscript change repeatedly after it first came to Don Martin, his excellent yeoman here. Many pages go through a dozen revisions. It doesn't mean that he hasn't frequently accepted changes recommended by Captain F. Kent Loomis, my Deputy, Rear Admiral Bern Anderson, tower of strength for years, Dr. K. Jack Bauer, who on several volumes has worked closely and effectively with Sam Morison, and myself as well as many other people — but he has accepted them only when convinced of their validity. Some other suggested changes he has not accepted. Although I have believed from time to time that he erred in so doing, I felt it was honest error and a small spot on a shining and illustrious narration of the greatest sea and overseas war in man's history.

In Thucydides' gripping account of the glory and catastrophe of Athens we find the most godlike people of antiquity rising to greatness by the sea — and ending in disaster through feeble leadership. In Morison's likewise gripping account of the catastrophe and glory of the United States, we find our nation rising from disaster at Pearl Harbor into shining victory through the heroism of countless Americans small and great and the superb leadership at sea of men like Nimitz, Spruance, Halsey, Turner, Hewitt and Blandy; and ashore in combined operations from men like MacArthur and Eisenhower.

What drama lies in this story! Whether one agrees in all details (and I suspect few who know do) anyone who experienced this vast sea-overseas war intimately knows that only Morison of our time, or perhaps since Thucydides, could have caught the vast sweep of this drama and spread it before us like an unfolding sea filled with the sparkle and lights of reality.

How long will these fifteen volumes live? May it be many aeons, for I believe they will live as long as America lives, and this will be only as long as she understands that one of her fundamental strengths and blessings is the sea.

The need for this strength showed in the far-off days of the American Revolution. After years of struggle and frustration, almost in despair Washington said: "In any operations, and under all circumstances, a decisive naval superiority is to be considered as a fundamental principle, and the basis upon which every hope of success must ultimately depend." Repeatedly he had sought the aid of the French Navy; repeatedly plans had fallen through. Victory seemed hopeless. Then like sunlight breaking through clouds he did gain control of the sea for a brief moment of time. In 1781, falling in with Washington's farseeing plan, the French Fleet finally joined; and at last it seemed as if the Divine hand reached down to cause all parts of the puzzle to fall into place at Yorktown.

Thus out of the sea was liberty won. Throughout succeeding generations the United States has gained untold strength from the sea and has often been saved by it. In the strange topsy-turvy years after V-J Day, unbelievably, the nation almost emasculated the Navy, without which World War II could not have been fought and won. Even today, when we have partly rectified this suicidal move, bemused by sputniks, ICBMs and space capsules, America still does not see clearly that her destiny, and the destiny of all men who seek freedom, depend upon the United States' strength at sea. Men everywhere look yearningly to the United States across vast seas that divide or join the free world according to the strength we keep afloat.

Perhaps in years to come, when crises in the storm of the world loom darker even than today, men will read Morison's great series and recall again America's divine heritage of the sea. Perhaps his stirring books will help bring men to their senses, from following one-weapon will-o'-the-wisps and the strange prophets of their era.

"I have but one lamp by which my feet are guided," said Patrick Henry; "and that is the lamp of experience. I know of no way of judging the future but by the past." Perhaps in a grave distant day the Morison series will help men to understand this truth of experience, and to know that though navies change with changing years, the vast influence of the sea does not fade but indeed like a tide in early flood grows ever stronger.

Preface

THIS supplementary volume to my *History of United States Naval Operations in World War II* consists of four distinct parts.

Part I is the story of postwar operations of the Navy in the Pacific, insofar as they were connected with World War II. These include the surrender of outlying Japanese garrisons, the Navy's share in the occupation of Japan proper, minesweeping approaches to Japanese ports, and Operation MAGIC CARPET for the return of armed forces to the United States. Part I, prepared by Rear Admiral Bern Anderson USN (Ret.), was originally intended as an appendix to Volume XIV, from which it was dropped for lack of space.

Part II is a list of all named ships of the United States Navy during World War II, together with their dimensions and armament; all types of landing, beaching and other "lettered" craft; and types of aircraft used by the Navy during the war. Some pertinent statistics are added. Part II is entirely the work of Dr. K. Jack Bauer of my staff.

Part III, to which I have given special attention, is a list of all important errata so far discovered in Volumes I–XIV. In the expectation that new printings of these volumes will be required from time to time, I beg readers to send in any additional errata that they may discover to the Division of Naval History, Navy Department, Washington 25, D. C.

Part IV is a General Index to Volumes I–XIV. This was prepared, under my direction, by the two remaining members of my staff, Dr. Bauer and Mr. Donald R. Martin.

SAMUEL E. MORISON

44 BRIMMER STREET
BOSTON, MASSACHUSETTS
1 April 1961

Contents

Introduction by Rear Admiral Ernest M. Eller USN,
   Director of Naval History   vii

Preface   xi

PART I

OUTLYING SURRENDERS AND EARLY OCCUPATION PROBLEMS
1945–1946

1. Outlying Surrenders	3
2. The Occupation of Japan	6
3. Minesweeping	12
4. Typhoon "Louise," 9–10 October 1945	14
5. Operation MAGIC CARPET	17

PART II

SHIPS AND AIRCRAFT OF THE UNITED STATES NAVY
1940–1945

1. Aircraft Carriers	29
CV Fleet Aircraft Carriers	29
CVL Light Aircraft Carriers	31
CVE Escort Aircraft Carriers	31
2. BB Battleships	33
3. Cruisers	35
CB Large Cruisers	35
CA Heavy Cruisers	35
CL Light Cruisers	36
4. DD Destroyers	38
5. DE Destroyer Escorts	48
6. SS Submarines	54

7. Minecraft 60
   CM Minelayers and CMc Coastal Minelayers 60
   DM Light Minelayers 60
   ACM Auxiliary Minelayers 61
   DMS Fast Minesweepers 61
   AM Minesweepers 62
   AMc Coastal Minesweepers 66
   AMc(U) Underwater Locator Minesweepers 67
   YMS Motor Minesweepers 67
8. Patrol Craft 68
   PG Gunboats 68
   PF Frigates 69
   PR River Gunboats 70
   PY Smaller Converted Yachts 70
   PYc Coastal Yachts 70
   PCE Patrol Craft, Escort 71
   PE Eagle Boats 71
   PCS Patrol Craft, Sweepers (136') 71
   PGM Motor Gunboats 72
   PC Submarine Chasers (Steel Hull) 72
   SC Submarine Chasers (Wooden Hull) 72
9. Motor Torpedo Boats 73
   PT Motor Torpedo Boats 73
   PTC Motor Boat Submarine Chasers 74
10. Auxiliaries 74
   AB Crane Ship 74
   AD Destroyer Tenders 75
   AE Ammunition Ships 75
   AF Store Ships 75
   AG Miscellaneous Auxiliaries 76
   AGC Amphibious Force Command Ships 77
   AGP Motor Torpedo Boat Tenders 78
   AGS Surveying Ships 78
   AH Hospital Ships 78
   AK Cargo Ships 79

Contents xv

AKA Attack Cargo Ships   81
AKN Net Cargo Ships   83
AKS General Stores Issue Ships   83
AN Net-Laying Ships   83
AO Oilers   84
AOG Gasolene Tankers   86
AP Transports   86
APA Attack Transports   89
APB Self-Propelled Barracks Ships   92
APc Coastal Transports   93
APD High-Speed Transports   93
APH Evacuation Transports   95
APL Barracks Ships   95
APM Mechanized Artillery Transport   95
APS Transport Submarine   95
APV Transports and Aircraft Ferries   95
AR Repair Ships   95
ARB Battle-Damage Repair Ships   96
ARG Internal-Combustion-Engine Repair Ships   96
ARH Heavy-Hull Repair Ship   96
ARL Landing-Craft Repair Ships   96
ARS Salvage Vessels   97
ARS(T) Salvage Craft Tenders   98
ARV Aircraft Repair Ships; ARV(A) Aircraft Repair
   Ships (Aircraft); ARV(E) Aircraft Repair Ships
   (Engine)   98
AS Submarine Tenders   98
ASR Submarine Rescue Vessels   98
ATA Auxiliary Tugs   99
ATF Ocean Tugs, Fleet   99
ATO Ocean Tugs, Old   100
ATR Rescue Tugs   100
AV Seaplane Tenders   100
AVC Catapult Lighter   101
AVD Seaplane Tenders (Destroyer)   101

AVP Small Seaplane Tenders 101
AVS Aviation Supply Ships 102
AW Distilling Ships 102
IX Unclassified Vessels 102
11. Landing Ships and Craft 106
LSV Landing Ships, Vehicle 106
LSD Landing Ships, Dock 106
LST Landing Ships, Tank 106
LSM Landing Ships, Medium 106
LSM(R) Landing Ships, Medium (Rocket) 107
LC(FF) Landing Craft, Flotilla Flagships 107
LCI(G) Landing Craft, Infantry (Gunboat) 107
LCI(L) Landing Craft, Infantry (Large) 107
LCI(M) Landing Craft, Infantry (Mortar) 107
LCI(R) Landing Craft, Infantry (Rocket) 108
LCS(L) Landing Craft, Support (Large) 108
LCT Landing Craft, Tank 108
12. Small Landing Craft 108
13. Coast Guard Cutters 109
WPG Cruising Cutters 109
WIX Weather Patrol Ships 110
WPC Patrol Cutters 111
WAG Icebreakers 111
14. United States Naval Combat Aircraft 1941–1945 112
VF Fighters 112
VSB Dive Bombers 112
VT Torpedo Bombers 113
VP Patrol Planes 113
VPB Patrol Bombers 113
VSO, VOS or VS Observation Planes 114
ZNP Patrol Airships (Blimps) 114
15. United States Naval Vessels Transferred to Foreign Nations under Lend-Lease 115
16. Officers and Men on Active Duty, 1 July 1944 to 31 August 1945 116

Contents

PART III

CUMULATIVE ERRATA LIST

121

PART IV

GENERAL INDEX TO VOLUMES I–XIV

151

and

CODE NAMES OF PRINCIPAL OPERATIONS COVERED IN THESE VOLUMES

373

Illustrations

(All photographs not otherwise described are official United States Navy)

Part of Pacific Fleet in Eniwetok Lagoon before Marianas
Campaign, May 1944   *Frontispiece*

*In special section between text pages 22 and 23.
Numbers refer to pages within special section.*

Three Classes of Fleet Aircraft Carriers: 1
Saratoga, Bon Homme Richard, Independence

A "Baby Flattop" and Two "Battlewagons":   2
Escort Carrier *Commencement Bay*, Battleship *Washington*, Battleship *Indiana*

Heavy Cruisers: 3
Salt Lake City; Wichita, with older *Wasp* in background; *Baltimore*

Light Cruisers: 4
Detroit, Nashville, Oakland, Montpelier

Four Older Classes of Destroyers: 5
Schenck, Aylwin, Porter, Drayton

Four Newer Classes of Destroyers: 6
Davis, Dunlap, Roe, Woolsey

Destroyers and Destroyer Escorts: 7
Dyson off Guadalcanal; Destroyer *Waldron*; Destroyer Escorts *Dennis* and *Evarts*

Four Submarines: 8
S-45, Peto, Hake, Snapper

Minecraft: 9
>Minelayer *Tolman*, Minesweeper *Auk*, Motor Minesweeper *YMS-324*

A Frigate, a Yacht, and a Corvette: 10
>Frigate *Asheville*, Converted Yacht *Cythera*, Corvette *Temptress*

Patrol Craft and Submarine Chasers: 11
>Patrol Craft Escort *PCE-898*, Sweeper *PCS-1448*, Submarine Chaser *SC-1036* (wood hull), Submarine Chaser *PC-564* (steel hull)

Auxiliaries: 12–15
>Destroyer Tender *Dixie*, Survey Ship *Bowditch*, Hospital Ship *Consolation*   12
>Attack Cargo Ship *Uvalde*, Fleet Oiler *Guadalupe*, Attack Transport *Leonard Wood*   13
>Barracks Ship *APL-14* ("Ritz Carlton"), Internal Combustion Engine Repair Ship *Mindanao*, Salvage Vessel *Gear*   14
>Submarine Tender *Sperry*, Ocean Tug *Sioux*, Small Seaplane Tender *Duxbury Bay*   15

The Bigger Beaching Craft: 16
>Landing Ship Dock *Gunston Hall*; *LST-332* (Landing Ship Tank) with *LCT-203* (Landing Craft Tank) on deck
>*LST-197* launching *LCT-185*; same, operation completed

Rocket Ship and Big Landing Craft: 17
>Landing Ship Medium, Rocket; Landing Craft Infantry, Large, at Omaha Beach; Landing Craft Support, Large, off Cebu; Landing Craft Control

Small Landing Craft: 18
    LCP(R) (Landing Craft Personnel, Ramped) retrieving UDT swimmers; LVT-1 (Amphtrac); DUKW on beach at Iwo Jima
    LCVP (Landing Craft, Vehicle and Personnel) at Empress Augusta Bay; LCM (Landing Craft, Mechanized) at Bougainville; DUKW going ashore at Noemfoor

The Older Types of Naval Aircraft: 19
    Buffalo fighter, Kingfisher observation (catapult-launched from cruisers or battleships), Devastator torpedo-bomber
    Catalina patrol bomber, Wildcat fighter, Dauntless dive-bomber

Types of Naval Aircraft Developed during the War 20
    Hellcat fighter, Helldiver dive-bomber, Liberator long-range bomber
    Corsair fighter, Avenger torpedo-bomber, Ventura medium bomber

*In a special section between text pages 118 and 119
appear the full color drawings used on the jackets of
this fifteen volume series.*

    I. Air Contact — North Atlantic
    II. Off Fedhala, 8 November 1942
    III. Pearl Harbor, December 7, 1941
    IV. Battle of Midway
    V. U.S. Battleship *Washington* in Night Battle, Guadalcanal
    VI. Divine Services before the Invasion of Bougainville
    VII. Planes Return
    VIII. D-day minus One Bombardment of Saipan
    IX. Assault Wave, Salerno
    X. Escort Carrier and U.S. Destroyer *Charles R. Ware*

XI. The Battle for Fox Green Beach, Omaha
XII. Battle off Samar
XIII. San Fabian Attack Force, Luzon
XIV. D-day plus One, Green Beach Two
XV. Surrender

PART I

Outlying Surrenders and Early Occupation Problems

1945–1946

1. *Outlying Surrenders* [1]

A S already noted in Volume XIV, a few surrenders of Japanese-held islands took place before the formal act of 2 September 1945, on board battleship *Missouri.* But the bulk of this work remained to be done. Japanese armed forces, as estimated in October 1945, amounted to 3,620,000 men. Some were in Japan itself, but the majority were stranded all over Eastern Asia, Indonesia, and the Pacific islands, where the ebb tide of defeat had left them. With a few unimportant exceptions, these men obeyed the Emperor's command to surrender; but they had to be fed, rounded up and shipped home by their former enemies. All available Japanese vessels, including demilitarized warships, were put on the task of repatriation; and, after the first week in November, numerous American amphibious force units, such as the ubiquitous LST, which were unsuited for the MAGIC CARPET return of our own troops to the United States, were assigned to this mission. Most Japanese ground forces on the Asiatic continent surrendered to China, Russia or Great Britain, but the bulk of those in Japan and the islands were taken care of by the United States and Australia.

General Yamashita, still holding out in the mountains of northeastern Luzon, proved to be coöperative.[2] He established communication with Major General W. H. Gill USA on 25 August. There

[1] Cincpac "Report of the Surrender and Occupation of Japan" Feb. 1946; Com Fifth Fleet Report, 11 Nov. 1945; CTF 55 and CTF 56 (Rear Adm. M. L. Deyo) Action Reports of Occupation of Western and Northern Japan 23 Nov. 1945; Fleet Admiral E. J. King *U. S. Navy at War 1941–1945* (1946) 192–95.

[2] See Vol. XIII 210.

followed a courteous exchange of correspondence, in which Yamashita acknowledged receipt of the Emperor's cease-fire order, but said that as yet he had no authority to enter into surrender negotiations. On 2 September he appeared in Baguio with Vice Admiral Okochi and signed the formal surrender of all Japanese forces in the Philippines, now reduced to some 50,000 in number. Since General Gill's 32nd Division had spearheaded General MacArthur's drive in the Buna campaign three years earlier, it was appropriate that he receive the surrender.[3]

The situation in China was full of explosives, the handling of which required delicacy. Shortly before the actual surrender the Japanese withdrew their forces to the Yangtze Valley and to North China, where the Chinese Communists demanded that they receive the Japanese surrender. General Okamura, commander of the North China Area Army, refused, but on 17 August let it be known that he would surrender to Chiang Kai-shek. Unfortunately, the Generalissimo and his Nationalist armies were far distant, in southwest China. A Japanese puppet Chinese government with its own "Peace Preservation Troops" further complicated matters. And although the United States was willing to assist the Nationalist government to reëstablish control over Chinese territory, it was fearful of being involved in a civil war.

As a temporary solution to this dilemma, Fleet Admiral Nimitz ordered Admiral Kinkaid, Commander Seventh Fleet, with III Amphibious Corps under Major General Keller Rockey USMC, to seize and control key areas, such as Shanghai, the Yangtze, Tientsin and Tsingtao, until Nationalist forces could be transported thither to take over. Seventh Fleet also had the task of transporting the occupation troops to South Korea. On 30 September the 1st Marine Division began landing at Taku to take control of the Tientsin region. The 6th Marine Division landed at Tsingtao on 11 October. A few brushes occurred with Communist troops and bandits, but nothing serious. In the meantime Seventh 'Phib (Vice Admiral D. E. Barbey) began to transport Chinese Nationalist troops from southwest

[3] Eichelberger *Jungle Road to Tokyo* pp. 256–59.

China to the northeast and to Manchuria in order to assume control. This movement kept Seventh Fleet busy until well into 1946.

The re-occupation of Hong Kong was strictly a British affair. In order to avoid becoming involved in a political dispute between China and Great Britain over the status of Hong Kong, all United States naval liaison teams were removed from vessels of the British Pacific Fleet before they entered the port. On 30 August a task force, under Rear Admiral C. H. J. Harcourt RN, entered Hong Kong and assumed responsibility for preserving law and order. On 16 September the local Japanese forces surrendered.

Although there had been concern lest isolated Japanese garrisons in Oceania cause trouble, the peaceful surrender of Mili on 22 August set a pattern. On 2 September, Lieutenant General Inoue surrendered the Palaus to Brigadier General F. P. Rogers USMC, island commander at Peleliu. Truk and most of the Caroline Islands, involving some 130,000 Japanese soldiers and sailors, were surrendered the same day to Vice Admiral G. P. Murray in *Portland*. Wake Island, with 1262 emaciated Japanese suffering from malnutrition, surrendered 3 September to Brigadier General L. H. M. Sanderson USMC, in destroyer escort *Levy*.

On 3 September, the Bonin Islands were surrendered by Lieutenant General Yoshio Tachibana, to Commodore John H. Magruder, on board destroyer *Dunlap* off Chichi Jima. The Commodore, at the conclusion of the ceremony, recalled the fact that Commodore Perry had visited Chichi Jima in 1853 and bought land there for a coaling station; now, we had come "to insure that no evil weeds spring up on this real estate to choke the freedom and peace of the future." Actual occupation of the Bonins was postponed until the Japanese garrisons, numbering over 40,000, had been collected for repatriation. Colonel P. M. Rixey USMC then became island commander, and occupied Chichi Jima on 13 December 1945. During the war several American fliers had ditched near that island and had been rescued by the Japanese; but none survived. Japanese explanations of the death of these prisoners aroused suspicion and led to a careful investigation. Through Frederick Savory, a descendant of the original American settlers at Chichi Jima, the deplorable fact was brought out that these aviators had been executed and parts of their bodies eaten by General Tachibana and members of his garrison, yet with no excuse of starvation. The General and another officer were tried at Guam for this outrage, and were executed as war criminals.[4]

Other important island garrisons gave up during September 1945 without incident. Troops in the unoccupied Ryukyus surrendered to General Stillwell at Okinawa on 7 September. Woleai, in the central Carolines, was the last important island to be handed over, on the 19th. All these islands had substantial garrisons, which had to be repatriated to Japan.

A corollary activity was the search by destroyers and destroyer escorts of every habitable island in Oceania for possible Allied prisoners. None were found that had not already been rescued.

Surrenders south of the Line were efficiently handled by the Australians. Some 250,000 Japanese between the Celebes and Ocean Island gave up. The largest group — General Hitoshi Imamura's 80,000 military and 21,000 civilians at Rabaul and New Ireland — surrendered 6 September to Lieutenant General Vernon A. H. Sturdee on board H.M.S. *Glory*. Two days later the Japanese on Bougainville and in Dutch Borneo surrendered. Between 11 and 14 September, the 17,000 remnants of Lieutenant General Hatazo Adachi's New Guinea forces gave up. Far to the east, on 14 September, the 3700-man garrison on Nauru surrendered to Brigadier J. R. Stevenson on H.M.A.S. *Diamantina*.[5]

2. *The Occupation of Japan*

This began with the occupation of the Atsugi airfield near Yokohama by the 11th Airborne Division, and of the Yokosuka naval

[4] Letters from Commo. Magruder, Sept. 1958; Gilbert Cant "Home to Chichi Jima" in *Life* Magazine 24 June 1946 pp. 17–19.
[5] Cdr. G. H. Gill RANVR letter to Dr. K. Jack Bauer, 18 Jan. 1960.

base by a Third Fleet landing force, on 30 August 1945. Vice Admiral Theodore S. Wilkinson, Commander III 'Phib, commanded both landing operations and lifted subsequent echelons of occupation troops. He landed the 1st Cavalry Division at Yokohama, starting at the time of the surrender ceremony on 2 September. At the request of the Japanese high command, the troopers delayed moving into Tokyo for a week. There were hundreds of thousands of Japanese troops in the Tokyo region which the Japanese themselves wished to disarm and demobilize, before Tokyo was physically occupied by our troops, in order to prevent incidents. At 0800 September 8 the 1st Cavalry, unfortunately without horses, made its formal entry into Tokyo. At noon that day General MacArthur raised over the American Embassy the flag which had flown over the Capitol at Washington on Pearl Harbor Day, and in battleship *Missouri* at the surrender.

Other elements of Eighth Army poured into Tokyo Bay, and by the end of September all key points in that Army's zone in Honshu were occupied. Only one fatal incident occurred, when an American soldier accidentally dropped a bomb near a Japanese ammunition dump at the Tateyama airfield. The resulting explosion killed this soldier, injured 53 others, and wounded several Japanese. By 18 September all known Allied prisoners of war in Eighth Army area had been recovered.

Hokkaido and Ominato naval bases, in northern Honshu, were occupied by Vice Admiral Frank J. Fletcher, Commander North Pacific Force, on 6 September. U.S. Navy minecraft under Commander W. A. Nicholson began sweeping Tsugaru Strait on the 8th. As Admiral Fletcher brought only a few Marines up, his was but a token occupation until Eighth Army troops began to disembark on 25 September. By that time he had been relieved by Rear Admiral Francis C. Denebrink, who in turn was relieved by Rear Admiral Morton L. Deyo on 20 October.

On 20 September Admiral Spruance relieved Admiral Halsey, and Third Fleet again became Fifth Fleet, which assumed responsibility for all American naval activities in and around Japan. Admiral Spruance departed a month later and left Vice Admiral Wilkinson in command.

The movement of Sixth Army, lifted by Fifth Fleet into its occupation zone of western Honshu, Kyushu and Shikoku, was delayed by lack of available shipping and extensive mine fields in the Inland Sea and off the harbors. To prepare the way, elements of V Army Air Force and a battalion of infantry flew into Kagoshima in southern Kyushu on 2 September, to establish emergency airfield facilities at Kanoya. Two days later six LSTs began discharging Army units at Takasu, four miles west of Kanoya. These advance parties checked Japanese arrangements for the occupation, investigated beach and dock conditions, and selected troop and supply-dump areas.

Highest priority was assigned to the recovery of prisoners of war. On 11 September a task unit under Rear Admiral F. G. Fahrion in *Wichita*, arrived at Nagasaki for that purpose. Sixth Army supervised the delivery of the POWs from their camps to the port, where they were taken over by the fleet unit for medical care and repatriation. Hospital ship *Haven* acted as station ship, lying at a dock where, in addition to caring for recovered prisoners, her medical contingent made clinical studies of victims of the atomic bomb. By 22 September the evacuation of 9061 prisoners of war to Okinawa had been effected by escort carriers *Chenango* and *Cape Gloucester*, light cruisers *Mobile* and *Biloxi*, and several destroyers.

A similar task unit, with two hospital ships, under Rear Admiral R. S. Riggs, arrived at Wakayama, about 35 miles from Osaka, on 11 September.

"The POWs are streaming out now," wrote Admiral Wilkinson that day to his wife. "We are filling five ships with them, 800 to 1000 to each, and sending other ships to Okinawa to pick up thousands who have been flown this far by air evacuation." Some 10,000 prisoners were supposed to be evacuated here; but by September 15, when this movement was completed, only 2575 had been recovered.

The first occupation in force of western Japan was effected by

Amphibious Group 4, Rear Admiral Reifsnider, lifting the V 'Phib Corps, commanded by Major General H. H. Schmidt USMC. This Corps comprised the 2nd and 5th Marine Divisions, and the 32nd Infantry United States Army. These divisions were brought up from Hawaii, the Marianas, and the Philippines, each moving in separately. Rear Admiral Deyo, commanding the covering force, made a personal reconnaissance of Sasebo on 16 September in *Ralph Talbot*. He found the important naval base to be almost intact, although half the business and residential districts of the city had been wiped out in a raid of 41 B–29s in July.[6] The Admiral removed all restrictions on the operation of Japanese fishermen and small freighters. He was relieved as S.O.P.A. by Vice Admiral Harry W. Hill, who arrived 20 September in amphibious command ship *Auburn*, with General Krueger embarked. The 5th Marine Division commenced landing on the 22nd, under Admiral Reifsnider's direction, and the landing at Nagasaki began on 23 September. Except for one incident everything went smoothly. The skipper of a Japanese coast defense vessel acted in an insolent and provocative manner to a United States Naval inspecting team; but the Japanese authorities, to whom Admiral Deyo reported this, arrested the offender and dismissed him from the Japanese Navy. Admiral Deyo, and other flag officers concerned in the occupation, were impressed by the willing coöperation of Japanese officers, both civil and military, and the apparent lack of resentment or hostility on the part of the populace.

The next important movement was Rear Admiral A. G. Noble's lift of I Corps (Major General I. P. Swift USA) to beaches at Wakayama. This Army corps was to occupy the Osaka-Kobe-Kyoto-Nagoya region of central Honshu. General Swift wished to be landed as close as possible to Osaka, where he planned to establish his headquarters. A study of mine fields, both offensive ones laid by the Allies and defensive ones laid by the Japanese, indicated that it would be highly dangerous, if not impossible, to land near Osaka and Kobe; but that a channel could be swept to Waka-

[6] Rear Adm. Deyo letter to writer 7 Nov. 1945.

yama. That was done, and on 25 September the 33rd Division began landing over the beaches. The unloading of I Corps and of Sixth Army headquarters, later set up at Kyoto, was completed by 8 October.

Hiroshima and Kure were inaccessible because of pressure mines laid by B-29s; but Hiro Wan, a few miles southeast of Kure and free of obstacles, was selected for the landing of the 41st Division and X Corps headquarters. Rear Admiral B. J. Rogers drew this assignment, and the troops began landing 7 October. A special board of inspection and survey was convened to examine the remaining ships of the Japanese Navy in or near Kure and to recommend their final disposition. Suitable units were demilitarized and assigned to the repatriation of Japanese from overseas. Among the ships recovered was U.S.S. *Stewart*, which had been abandoned in Java in 1942.[7] Her name had since been given to another United States destroyer, so on 3 November she was recommissioned without a name but with her original hull number, DD-224, and assigned to the 11th Naval District in San Diego.

The waters around Fukuoka in northern Kyushu, and Shimonoseki in western Honshu, were so heavily studded with pressure mines that occupation by water was out of the question, and General Krueger ordered V 'Phib Corps to occupy Fukuoka overland from Sasebo. An advance party entered the city on 27 September and the 28th RCT entered on the 30th. On 4 October a company occupied Shimonoseki. Other nearby ports, including Senzaki on the northwest coast of Honshu, were taken over by 19 October.

In several camps of Chinese labor units and POWs in northern Kyushu and western Honshu, trouble had developed between the prisoners and Japanese civilians. Marine patrols maintained order and shipping was requested for repatriation of about 6000 Chinese. Matters were further complicated by the large number of Koreans seeking repatriation, and because small ports on the Sea of Japan were jammed with Japanese coming home from Korea. For ten days in October, Koreans were forbidden to buy railway tickets to

[7] See Vol. III 378.

Shimonoseki. By the time the 32nd Division took over, on 24 October, the worst of this bottleneck had been cleared.

The 24th Infantry Division, lifted by Commodore D. L. Ryan's transport flotilla, was landed at Matsuyama, on the northwest coast of Shikoku, on 22 October. Another division of Commodore Ryan's group landed an RCT of the 24th Division at Hiro Wan, for the occupation of the inland city of Okayama. The final debarkation in V 'Phib zone was made by Rear Admiral Noble's group, landing the 25th Infantry Division over the docks in Nagoya on 26 October.

Korea presented a special problem since it had been agreed at the Potsdam Conference that Russia would conduct naval and air operations in that unhappy country north of the 38th parallel, while the Allies operated in the southern half.[8] This was later adopted as a line of demarcation for the occupation. In addition to receiving the surrender of Japanese armed forces, the purpose of the military occupation of Korea was to accomplish complete political, economic and administrative separation from Japan, and to establish Korea as a free and independent nation.

Lieutenant General J. R. Hodge's XXIX Corps — lifted from the Philippines by Vice Admiral Barbey's VII 'Phib — was selected for the occupation of Korea. The first landing point was Jinsen, better known today as Inchon, seaport for Seoul. Rear Admiral I. N. Kiland's amphibious group transported the 7th Infantry Division, which began landing there 8 September. This landing, like the later one in the Korean War, was rendered difficult by the wide range of tides, up to 30 feet. Our troops landed in silence, since the people had been warned to await definite word before making any demonstration; the Japanese police had earlier fired on a group of Korean workers who had formed up to welcome Americans. On 9 September, General Hodge and Admiral Kinkaid went to Seoul, where, in the throneroom of the Japanese governor general's palace, a formal surrender document was signed.

---

[8] At a meeting between the JCS with Russian chiefs on 26 July 1945. There was no question of occupation at that time, only of operations.

Elements of the 40th Infantry Division began arriving at Inchon on 22 September. Next day, a battalion of this division advanced by rail to Pusan, a port on the Strait of Tsushima which was blocked by mines. The final troop movement was the landing of the 6th Infantry Division at Inchon on 17 October. By the end of September, XXIV Corps had satisfactorily occupied its zone. Civilian disturbances against the Japanese and liaison with the Russians along the 38th parallel created serious problems. Owing to the strong local feeling against them, Japanese military and civilians were evacuated by General Hodge as rapidly as facilities permitted. On 22 September, the Russians permitted American evacuation teams to remove 354 British and Australian POWs from their zone to hospital ships at Inchon.

3. *Minesweeping*[9]

Much the most difficult and extensive postwar task that United States naval forces had to cope with was minesweeping. At the cessation of hostilities there were an estimated 100,000 moored mines in Japanese waters. In addition, there were some 12,000 influence mines of several types, the most troublesome being pressure mines laid by B–29s, for which there was no known method of sweeping. Most of these influence mines were set to de-activate themselves in February 1946 — a long time to wait! This huge task of mine clearance was handed to Rear Admiral A. D. Struble, who relieved Rear Admiral A. M. Sharp as Commander Minecraft Pacific Fleet on 30 August 1945.

The most urgent task was to clear channels into the landing ports for occupation troops, or as near to them as possible. Third Fleet minesweepers took charge of clearing enough of Tokyo Bay for the initial entry and formal surrender. Beginning 28 August, a group composed of 23 high-speed and standard minesweepers cleared the

[9] Com Minecraft Pacific Report 29 May 1946; Lt. Cdr. A. S. Lott *Most Dangerous Sea* (1959) chap. xv.

channels and anchorages of Yokohama, Yokosuka and Tokyo proper, in seven days. Only 74 Japanese and three U. S. magnetic mines were found. The same group then swept the Japanese moored-mine fields at Sendai and Chosi, on the northeast coast of Honshu, and opened those ports to navigation.

Twenty-seven minecraft began sweeping a channel through the Kii entrance to the Inland Sea on 11 September. The initial task was to clear a channel for hospital ships to evacuate prisoners of war and for landing the occupation troops for Kobe and Osaka. Clearing of these two harbors was postponed as less urgent. This was the first instance in which Japanese minesweepers operated under the local United States naval task group commander. As in other matters, the Japanese coöperated cheerfully in furnishing details of mine fields, and even helped the actual sweeping.

To clear the way for troops to occupy Kure and Hiroshima it was necessary to sweep a two-mile wide channel for 150 miles through the Bungo Suido and the Inland Sea, to Hiro Wan. Thirty-two American and thirty-three Japanese sweepers, under Commander W. R. Loud, began this mission on 22 September. It was the first operation in which "guinea pigs" were used to dispose of pressure mines. The sacrificial rodents were three large, damaged vessels (U.S.S. *Marathon*, S.S. *Joseph Holt*, S.S. *Pratt Victory*), and LSTs 553 and 768. All were ballasted with empty oil drums, to withstand underwater damage, and had remote controls for a machinery on deck, where their volunteer crews — about 15 for each ship — wore crash helmets and stood on piles of mattresses to take up the shock of an explosion. Four Japanese *Marus* and two old Japanese destroyers joined the herd, and these destroyers were the only ships lost in the sweep.

The sweeping of Ise Wan to clear a channel to Nagoya began on 28 September, and by the end of October the principal Japanese harbors of Honshu were completely cleared. Approaches to Koshi, the only port opened on Shikoku during the first occupation phase, were swept, beginning 8 September. The first channel swept off Kyushu was to Kagoshima, on the southern coast, in preparation for supplying the 1 September airborne landings. This was completed in a week's time. Sweeping at Sasebo began next day, and at Nagasaki on the 10th. Certain fields in the Yellow Sea and Van Diemen Strait south of Kyushu were also taken care of at this time.

After this emergency occupation phase of minesweeping was completed in October, the huge task of opening additional ports, expanding those already opened, and clearing the Inland Sea, commenced. The magnitude of this mission may be indicated by a statistical summary. By the middle of December, there were 510 minesweepers of all types in the Pacific Fleet. Many were operating in the Philippines, Okinawa Gunto and elsewhere; but their major efforts, in conjunction with about 100 Japanese minesweepers, were exerted in Japanese waters. By early March 1946, when the work was so well advanced that Admiral Struble departed, nearly 17,000 square miles of salt water had been swept, with a total catch of 11,982 moored and 62 influence mines. The only loss to the United States Navy was that of minesweeper *Minivet* (Lieutenant R. T. Irvine USNR), which struck a mine northwest of Kyushu on 29 December 1945, losing 31 killed or missing and 5 wounded.

4. *Typhoon "Louise," 9–10 October 1945*

This occupation of Japan was carried out in the typhoon season. A small cyclone which brushed Kyushu on 16 September delayed minesweeping for a day or two and destroyed five YMSs. But typhoon "Louise," which struck Okinawa on 9 October 1945, was a major disaster. This circular storm developed north of Rota in the Marianas on 4 October. Admiral Wilkinson, from his flagship *Mount Olympus* in Tokyo Bay, kept careful watch on all weather reports and diverted approaching echelons of amphibious craft so deftly that all escaped the fury of the storm. Until the evening of 8 October, "Louise" followed a fairly predictable track, which would have taken her between Formosa and Okinawa into the East China Sea. She then began to veer easterly. Okinawa was warned that "Louise" was expected to pass nearby about 1030 October 9. She not only slowed down but increased her intensity. The result was one of the most violent storms that ever hit Okinawa, the center passing less than 15 miles east of the island's southeast coast. There had been some warning, but not enough for ships to get under way and escape the typhoon's terrific violence.

Buckner Bay (as Nakagusuku Wan had been renamed), on the east coast of Okinawa, was jammed with vessels ranging from Victory ships down to landing craft. By 1000 October 9, the wind had risen to 40 knots, the glass had fallen to 29.50 inches, visibility was under 800 yards, seas were rising, and rain was coming down in torrents, liberally mixed with salt spray. By noon visibility was zero, and the wind blew 60 knots from E and NE, raising a sea that broke over moored ships. Small craft were already dragging anchors, and the larger vessels were precariously holding on by running their engines full-speed. By 1400 the wind had risen to 80 knots, with gusts of even greater intensity; the rain, driving horizontally, was more salt than fresh, and even big vessels were dragging anchors under the pounding of 35-foot seas. The bay, blacked out by the heavy overcast and rain, became a scene of indescribable confusion as dragging ships collided, or barely escaped by skillful use of their engines, and disappeared into the murk. Hundreds of vessels were blown ashore; several at a time drifted into a mass of wreckage on the beach, their crews working desperately to maintain watertight integrity and to get a line on anything at hand in order to stop the pounding. Many ships had to be abandoned. Some crews were taken on board other ships; others made their way ashore, where they spent a miserable night in the open or huddled in caves; and many men were drowned.

By 1600 the typhoon reached its peak, with steady winds of 100 knots and gusts up to 120 knots. The glass dropped to 29.15 inches as the center passed, but the winds continued in unabated strength for another two hours. The wind, backing into the N and then NW, began to blow ships off the formerly lee-shore reefs where they had grounded, and right across the bay to the south shore, dragging their anchors the entire way. These wild voyages by help-less, damaged vessels caused another nightmare series of collisions with other drifting ships and shattered hulks, as well as providential escapes.

The shore afforded no sanctuary. Twenty hours of torrential rain soaked everything, made quagmires of roads, and ruined vir-tually all stores, destroying most of the tents and flooding the rest. Some Quonset huts were lifted bodily and moved hundreds of feet; others were torn to bits, the galvanized iron sheets ripped off, the wallboards shredded and the curved supports torn apart. Officers and men, driven from their housing, took shelter in caves and the big Okinawan tombs, and in trenches and ditches in the open fields, to escape the tents, boards and sections of galvanized iron hur-tling through the air. By 2000 the wind had subsided from super-typhoon to mere typhoon strength; but it was not until 1000 Octo-ber 10 that it dropped to 40 knots and the rain began to abate.

Ships of the occupation forces anchored at Amami O Shima also had a rough time, with winds of over 70 knots. All Japan, from Nagasaki to Tokyo, was alerted for the storm, but escaped its full fury. Ships at sea were able to maneuver clear of the worst of "Louise," but some suffered damage from the heavy seas.

Four fifths of all houses and buildings on Okinawa were de-stroyed or rendered uninhabitable, and practically all tentage was blown to ribbons. Food stocks were reduced to ten days' supply. Medical facilities were so generally destroyed that the loan of a hospital ship was requested to support shore activities. Fortunately, considering the extreme violence of the storm, the casualties were low: 36 dead, 47 missing, and approximately 100 men fairly seri-ously injured.

Vice Admiral W. W. ("Poco") Smith, commanding Service Force Pacific Fleet, flew at once to Okinawa and found the dam-age to shipping to be even heavier than he had feared. Twelve ships were sunk, 222 grounded, 32 damaged beyond the ability of the ships' companies to effect repairs. Salvage began promptly. By 19 November, 79 ships had been refloated and 132 were under repair.

The remaining 53, in too bad a state to be restored to duty, were decommissioned, stripped and abandoned. On 14 November Comservpac decided that only ten out of about 90 ships which needed major work were worth complete salvage.

This was the most furious and lethal storm ever encountered by the United States Navy, not excepting the typhoons of December 1944 and June 1945,[10] the famous hurricane at Apia in March of 1889.

5. *Operation* MAGIC CARPET [11]

The sudden cessation of hostilities created the urgent problem of "getting the boys home," and so much political and private pressure was brought to bear as to weaken very seriously the armed forces left in the area. As General George C. Marshall remarked to the writer, "It was not a demobilization; it was a rout"; and the American public paid with the Korean War for its misplaced sentimentality.

The Army recognized as early as 1942 that demobilization would be a major problem, and in mid-1943 a committee representing the Army, Navy, War Shipping Administration, and other interested agencies, went to work on it. For the Army, the problem was complicated by redeployment from Europe to the Pacific and by partial demobilization after the defeat of Germany. Active planning began in the fall of 1944. Since it was assumed that the Pacific war would continue for at least a year after the defeat of Germany in May 1945, the sudden collapse of Japan in August caught the services with their plans still incomplete.

The movement of troops from Europe began shortly after V E

---

10 See Volumes XIII and XIV of this History.

11 Comcardiv 24 (Rear Adm. H. S. Kendall) War Diary, Sept. 1945–Mar. 1946; Joseph Bykofski and Harold Larson *The Transportation Corps: Operations Overseas* (Washington, 1957); Report of the War Shipping Administrator to the President, *The United States Merchant Marine at War* (Washington, 1946); *All Hands*, Sept.–Dec. 1945; Maj. J. C. Sparrow *History of Personnel Demobilization in the United States Army* (Department of the Army pamphlet Washington, 1952).

Day. Even earlier, the War Shipping Administration, anticipating the need for temporary troop lift, began converting Liberty and Victory ships to transports. Conversion consisted of installing bunks in cargo spaces and providing additional sanitary, messing and limited recreational facilities. Eventually, the War Shipping Administration had 546 such vessels engaged in returning overseas troops. Until the Japanese surrender, the Navy did not take part in this movement; the bulk of the troops returned from Europe were in War Shipping Administration ships, augmented by the British *Queens*, Army transports, and other available tonnage. Airlift brought back a limited number from Europe, and also, later, from the Pacific.

As soon as Japan accepted surrender terms, the Navy moved into high gear on the twin problems of reducing its strength to a peacetime fleet and discharging the excess number of sailors. By an "Alnav" of 15 August 1945, it replaced its "computed-age" formula for the release of officers and men to a point system such as the Army had been using in its rotation of troops. Age, length of service and number of dependents established an individual's number of points, which determined his eligibility and priority for discharge. Naval separation centers were established at key cities and training stations throughout the country.

The homeward movement began shortly after the formal Japanese surrender. On 6 September 1945, Task Force 11, consisting of battleships *New Mexico, Idaho, Mississippi* and *North Carolina*, carriers *Monterey* and *Bataan*, and a squadron of destroyers, under Vice Admiral Forrest Sherman, departed Tokyo Bay for the east coast of the United States, calling at Okinawa to embark high-priority "returnees."

The Navy now began to convert suitable combatant ships into temporary transports. Aircraft carriers of all types shifted their planes ashore and had three to five tiers of bunks installed on their hangar decks. These, together with battleships, cruisers, APDs and LSTs, were drawn into a big troop-lift which the Navy called MAGIC CARPET.

On 4 September 1945, Fleet Admiral Nimitz ordered Rear Admiral H. S. Kendall, Comcardiv 24, to report to Commander Service Force at Pearl Harbor for temporary duty in connection with the return of servicemen. On 9 September, he was designated Commander Task Group 16.12, and as such handled the whole of MAGIC CARPET. At that time eight CVEs were assigned to the task group, but by the end of the month 107 ships in all had been assigned, including two hospital ships.

For many of these ships the return from the war zone was to be their last. The Navy, mindful of the rôle it had played in the war against Japan, planned to show its might to the American people on Navy Day, 27 October 1945. In every port, from Seattle to Portland, Maine, naval vessels were on display. In New York, center of this celebration, 47 ships were concentrated, ranging from mighty *Missouri* to patrol craft. President Truman's day began, according to *Newsweek*, "with characteristic briskness at 8 A.M., over bacon and eggs well-seasoned with New York politics." He witnessed the commissioning of the new super-carrier *Franklin D. Roosevelt*, spoke over the air to one million people in Central Park, had lunch on board *Missouri*, and in the afternoon reviewed the Fleet from the bridge of destroyer *Renshaw*.

By October, MAGIC CARPET was operating the world around. The Army, Navy and War Shipping Administration pooled their shipping for the lift, and allocations were made by a Joint Military Transportation Committee in Washington. Most of the Navy's effort was expended in the Pacific. In September only 8241 men were returned by Task Group 16.12 out of a total of 259,856, the balance being lifted by War Shipping Administration ships. In October, however, TG 16.12 lifted 153,593 men out of a total of 446,-715. December of 1945 was the peak month; 695,486 persons of all categories, Army, Navy, Marine Corps and civilians, were returned to the United States from the Pacific. Of these, 370,596 were transported by Rear Admiral Kendall's task group.[12]

During that month the greatest number of vessels were engaged

[12] Figures from Cardiv 24 War Diary.

in the lift — on 15 December 369 ships were assigned to Admiral Kendall. Most of these were amphibious types, including 222 assault transports. A respectable number of combat types were also in the run: six battleships, 18 cruisers and 57 aircraft carriers, 46 of them CVEs. Twelve were hospital ships. By the end of December the demand for shipping fell off rapidly and combat ships were detached from TG 16.12 to resume their place in the peace-time Navy, or head for the boneyard. By 15 March 1946 only 23 vessels remained in the MAGIC CARPET group. Cardiv 24 was then dissolved and Vice Admiral Oscar W. Badger, Commander Service Force, assumed personal command of the task group. By 1 September 1946 demobilization was complete insofar as the Navy was concerned.

Once the demobilization lift got into high gear, shipping was allocated approximately thus: 30 per cent to the Philippines, 30 per cent to the Marianas, 30 per cent to Okinawa and Japan, and the remaining 10 per cent to Hawaii, the South Pacific, Korea and China. Task Group 16.12 was first concerned with returning sailors, but it also carried about 42 per cent of all servicemen and civilians who were sent home by 15 March 1946. From September 1945 to that date, 3,123,394 persons of all categories were returned, and of these the MAGIC CARPET group lifted 1,307,859. Breaking down that number, 501,616 were Army, 679,819 Navy and Coast Guard, 117,686 Marines and 8738 civilians. Between 15 March and 1 September 1946 the total number lifted amounted only to 127,233 of which 89,795 were Navy and Coast Guard.

This combined shipping lift did a remarkable job. It actually got the men home faster than early estimates regarded possible. Yet there was considerable discontent and criticism of the Army for alleged delays. In the United States the public, press and Congress complained about the slowness of the return, especially in the Pacific. There was also much discontent among the troops themselves, especially after the Army announced, early in January 1946, that it was slowing down demobilization owing to replacement problems. When the Southwest Pacific theater was authorized to convert cargo vessels to transports, soldiers volunteered by the hundreds to assist. The results provided rather crude facilities, but the feeling seemed to be "anything to get home." [13] The real bottleneck proved to be transportation within the United States. The railroads did not have the equipment to handle over a million men scheduled to arrive in the United States in December.[14] This was especially true on the Pacific Coast. Rickety old cars were pressed into service, but the situation was so bad that the railroads published advertisements apologizing for the shortage of transportation. The airlines handled as much of the traffic as they could, but there were simply not enough trains or planes to handle the load.

In the Atlantic, naval ships did not get into the MAGIC CARPET lift until mid-October 1945, when carrier *Lake Champlain,* commissioned in the previous June and fitted with 3300 tiered bunks, left Hampton Roads for Southampton. At that time the redeployment of troops from Europe was at its height. In November she was joined by 14 other carriers, several cruisers, and battleship *Washington.* On 20 November 400 ships were engaged in the Atlantic lift, including S.S. *Queen Mary* and seven hospital ships. By January 1946 the bulk of the Atlantic lift was over and the hastily converted ships were returned to their normal use. By the end of February, for all practical purposes, the movement homeward from Europe was completed.

By mid-November 1945, some 29 troop transports were engaged in bringing back more than 200,000 American soldiers and sailors from India and the China-Burma-India theater. This movement was completed by April of 1946.

[13] *The Transportation Corps, Operations Overseas* p. 487.
[14] *Newsweek* 24 Dec. 1945.

Three Classes of Fleet Aircraft Carriers

Saratoga, Bon Homme Richard, Independence

A "Baby Flattop" and Two "Battlewagons"

Escort Carrier *Commencement Bay*, Battleship *Washington*,
Battleship *Indiana*

Destroyers and Destroyer Escorts

(*Top to bottom*) Destroyer *Dyson* off Guadalcanal; Destroyer *Waldron;*
Destroyer Escorts *Dennis* and *Evarts*

7

Four Submarines
(*Top to bottom*) *S–45, Peto, Hake, Snapper*

8

Minecraft

(*Top to bottom*) Minelayer *Tolman*, Minesweeper *Auk*, Motor
Minesweeper *YMS-324*

A Frigate, a Yacht, and a Corvette

(*Top to bottom*) Frigate *Asheville*, Converted Yacht *Cythera*,
Corvette *Temptress*

10

Patrol Craft and Submarine Chasers

(*Top to bottom*) Escort *PCE-898*, Sweeper *PCS-1448*, Submarine Chaser
SC-1036 (wood hull), Submarine Chaser *PC-564* (steel hull)

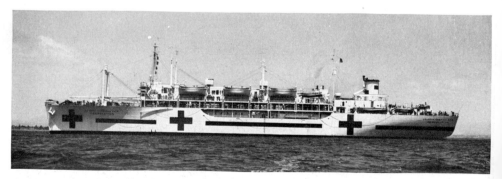

Auxiliaries

(*Top to bottom*) Destroyer Tender *Dixie*, Survey Ship *Bowditch*, Hospital
Ship *Consolation*

12

Auxiliaries

(*Top to bottom*) Attack Cargo Ship *Uvalde*, Fleet Oiler *Guadalupe*,
Attack Transport *Leonard Wood*

13

Auxiliaries

(*Top to bottom*) Barracks Ship *APL-14* ("Ritz Carlton"), Internal
Combustion Engine Repair Ship *Mindanao*, Salvage Vessel *Gear*

14

Auxiliaries

(*Top to bottom*) Submarine Tender *Sperry*, Ocean Tug *Sioux*,
Small Seaplane Tender *Duxbury Bay*

15

The Bigger Beaching Craft

(*Top to bottom*) Landing Ship Dock *Gunston Hall*; *LST–332* (Landing Ship Tank) with *LCT–203* (Landing Craft Tank) on deck. *LST–197* launching *LCT–185*; same, operation completed

Rocket Ship and Big Landing Craft

(*Top to bottom*) Landing Ship Medium, Rocket; Landing Craft Infantry,
Large, at Omaha Beach; Landing Craft Support, Large, off Cebu; Landing
Craft Control

Small Landing Craft

(*Left, top to bottom*) LCP(R) (Landing Craft Personnel, Ramped)
retrieving UDT swimmers; LVT–1 (Amphtrac); DUKW on
beach at Iwo Jima

(*Right, top to bottom*) LCVP (Landing Craft, Vehicle and Personnel)
at Empress Augusta Bay; LCM (Landing Craft, Mechanized) at
Bougainville; DUKW going ashore at Noemfoor

The Older Types of Naval Aircraft

(*Left, top to bottom*) Buffalo fighter, Kingfisher observation
(catapult-launched from cruisers or battleships), Devastator
torpedo-bomber

(*Right, top to bottom*) Catalina patrol bomber, Wildcat fighter,
Dauntless dive-bomber

Types of Naval Aircraft Developed during the War

(*Left, top to bottom*) Hellcat fighter, Helldiver dive-bomber,
Liberator long-range bomber

(*Right, top to bottom*) Corsair fighter, Avenger torpedo-bomber,
Ventura medium bomber

PART II

Ships and Aircraft
of the United States Navy

1940–1945

HERE we list and give principal dimensions, armament, and so on for all vessels serving in the United States Navy and Coast Guard, from the declaration of national emergency on 27 June 1940 to the signing of the Japanese surrender on 2 September 1945. Yard craft, small craft such as the small yachts in the Coast Guard Inshore Patrol, and floating dry docks are excepted. All types of naval combat aircraft which saw action during World War II are included.

Full statistics are shown for combatant vessels, mine, patrol and landing craft: standard displacement, over-all length, extreme beam, maximum draft, rated speed, armament during the period of greatest service, and maximum wartime complement. Propulsion is shown for those vessels not powered by geared turbines.

Space restrictions prevent the inclusion of such detailed information about auxiliaries. Their relative size, however, can be seen from their displacement.

Principal reference works are *Ships Data U. S. Naval Vessels*, editions of 1943, 1945 and 1949; *United States Naval Vessels* (ONI 222–US), 1 September 1945; Comairpac *Index of United States Fleet*, 1 December 1944; and K. Jack Bauer's ms. "Ships of the United States Navy, 1775–1945." Additional information can be found in three unofficial works: *Jane's Fighting Ships*, 1940 and later editions; James C. Fahey *Ships and Aircraft of the United States Fleet*, Victory Edition (1945); and Roger Kafka and Roy L. Pepperburg *Warships of the World*, Victory Edition (1946).

Photographs of several different classes and types of vessels and planes are here shown, but many others, which are in Volumes I–XIV, may be located by consulting the General Index in this volume.

The Navy's system of naming ships is based on rules established by law, custom and tradition, which assign to each type of vessel a particular class or classes of names. Deviations are relatively few, and generally result from reasons of state (such as *Canberra*), merchantmen retaining their names, or other vessels transferred from one class to another.

The following name classifications were used during World War II:

Aircraft Carriers	Famous old ships of U.S.N., and battles
Escort Carriers	Sounds, bays and battles of World War II
Battleships	States of the Union
Large Cruisers	Territories and insular possessions
Cruisers, Gunboats, Frigates	Cities and towns
Destroyers and DEs	Distinguished officers and enlisted men of Navy and Marine Corps, and Secretaries of the Navy, and a few civilians who helped the Navy
Submarines	Fish and other marine creatures
Minelayers	Old monitors of the U. S. Navy
Auxiliary Minelayers	Obstructions
Minesweepers	Birds or abstract qualities, words of action, etc.
Converted Yachts	Precious and semi-precious stones and general words
Destroyer Tenders	Geographical areas of the United States
Ammunition Ships	Volcanoes
Store and Store Issue Ships	Stars
Amphibious Force Flagships	Mountains
Repair Ships and MTB Tenders	Mythological characters
Surveying Ships	Distinguished marine surveyors
Hospital Ships	Peaceful or comforting words
Cargo Ships	Stars, or counties of the United States
Attack Cargo Ships and Attack Transports	Counties of the United States
Aircraft Ferries	Places associated with the history of aviation
Net Tenders	Trees or old monitors
Oilers and Gasoline Tankers	Rivers

Transports	Presidents, "Signers" (of the Declaration of Independence), distinguished generals and admirals, famous women, historic places
Evacuation Transports	Surgeons General of the U. S. Navy
Internal Combustion Engine Repair Ships	Islands
Salvage Vessels	Terms associated with marine salvage
Submarine Tenders	Submarine pioneers and mythological characters
Submarine Rescue Vessels	Birds
Tugs	Indian Tribes
Seaplane Tenders	Aviation pioneers, bays, sounds and straits
Landing Ships, Dock	Homes of famous Americans and famous spots

SHIPS AND AIRCRAFT OF THE UNITED STATES NAVY, 1940–1945

The following symbols and abbreviations will be used:

* Lost in combat or by accident, 27 June 1940–2 September 1945

† Scrapped, sold, reduced to small craft or otherwise disposed of, between the same dates

Comm.—Commissioned

Conv.—Converted

Displ.—Light displacement, i.e., ready for sea but without consumable or variable items, aircraft or crew

kts.—Knots

Reclass.—Reclassified

1. AIRCRAFT CARRIERS

CV Fleet Aircraft Carriers

LEXINGTON Class

33,000 tons; length 901'2"; beam 130'1"; draft 32'6"; speed 34 kts.; armament 16–5"/38 86 planes; complement 3373; turbines with electric motor.

No.	Name	Comm.	No.	Name	Comm.
CV–2	*LEXINGTON	14 Dec. 1927	CV–3	SARATOGA	16 Nov. 1927

Builders: Fore River S. B. Co., Quincy (CV–2) and New York S. B. Co. (CV–3). Converted from battle cruisers.

RANGER

14,500 tons; length 769'; beam 109'6"; draft 24'6"; speed 30 kts.; armament 8–5"/25 72 planes; complement 2461.

CV Fleet Aircraft Carriers: RANGER *(cont'd)*

No.	Name	Comm.
CV-4	RANGER	4 June 1934

Builders: Newport News.

First American carrier built from keel up as such.

YORKTOWN Class

19,800 tons; length 827'4"; beam 114'; draft 28'6"; speed 34 kts.; armament 8–5"/38 85 planes; complement 2919.

| CV-6 | ENTERPRISE | 12 May 1938 | CV-5 | *YORKTOWN | 30 Sept. 1937 |

Builders: Newport News.

WASP

14,700 tons; length 739'; beam 80'9"; draft 20'; speed 30 kts.; armament 8–5"/38 84 planes; complement 1800.

CV-7　*WASP　　　　　25 Apr. 1940

Builders: Bethlehem, Quincy.

HORNET

20,000 tons; length 809'6"; beam 83'3"; draft 21'8"; speed 34 kts.; armament 8–5"/38 81 planes; complement 2072.

CV-8　*HORNET　　　　　20 Oct. 1941

Builders: Newport News.

ESSEX Class, Short-Hull Group

27,100 tons; length 872'; beam 147'; draft 28'7"; speed 33 kts.; armament 12–5"/38 103 planes; complement 3448.

CV-20	BENNINGTON	6 Aug. 1944	CV-12	HORNET	29 Nov. 1943
CV-31	BON HOMME		CV-11	INTREPID	16 Aug. 1943
	RICHARD	26 Nov. 1944	CV-16	LEXINGTON	17 Feb. 1943
CV-17	BUNKER HILL	24 May 1943	CV-18	WASP	24 Nov. 1943
CV-9	ESSEX	31 Dec. 1942	CV-10	YORKTOWN	15 Apr. 1943
CV-13	FRANKLIN	31 Jan. 1944			

Builders: Newport News (CV 9–13); Bethlehem, Quincy (CV 16–18); and New York Navy Yard (CV 20, 31).

ESSEX Class, Long-Hull Group

27,100 tons; length 888'; beam 147'6"; draft 28'7"; speed 33 kts.; armament 12–5"/38 103 planes; complement 3448.

CV-36	ANTIETAM	28 Jan. 1945	CV-15	RANDOLPH	9 Oct. 1944
CV-21	BOXER	16 Apr. 1945	CV-38	SHANGRI-LA	15 Sept. 1944
CV-19	HANCOCK	15 Apr. 1944	CV-14	TICONDEROGA	8 May 1944
CV-39	LAKE CHAM-				
	PLAIN	3 June 1945			

ESSEX Class, Long-Hull Group (*cont'd*)

Builders: Newport News (CV 14–15, 21); Bethlehem, Quincy (CV–19); Philadelphia Navy Yard (CV–36); Norfolk Navy Yard (CV 38–39).

Differ from short-hull group only in having a pointed bow extending beyond the flight deck.

CVL Light Aircraft Carriers

INDEPENDENCE Class

11,000 tons; length 622'6"; beam 109'2"; draft 26'; speed 32 kts.; armament 18–40mm. 33 planes; complement 1569.

No.	'Name	Comm.	No.	Name	Comm.
CVL–29	BATAAN	17 Nov. 1943	CVL–28	LANGLEY	31 Aug. 1943
CVL–24	BELLEAU WOOD	31 Mar. 1943	CVL–26	MONTEREY	17 June 1943
CVL–27	CABOT	24 July 1943	CVL–23	*PRINCETON	25 Feb. 1943
CVL–25	COWPENS	28 May 1943	CVL–30	SAN JACINTO	15 Dec. 1943
CVL–22	INDEPENDENCE	14 Jan. 1943			

Builders: New York S. B. Co.
Converted from light cruisers while building.

CVE Escort Aircraft Carriers [1]

LONG ISLAND

7886 tons; length 492'; beam 102'; draft 25'6"; speed 16 kts.; armament 1–5"/38 2–3"/50 21 planes; complement 1970; diesel engine.

CVE–1   LONG ISLAND   2 June 1941

Builders: 1940 by Sun S. B. & D. D. Co. as merchantman.
Maritime Commission C3–Cargo type. One sister transferred to Britain under Lend-Lease.

BOGUE Class

7800 tons; length 495'8"; beam 111'6"; draft 26'; speed 17 kts.; armament 2–5"/38 28 planes; complement 890–1205.

CVE–18	ALTAMAHA	15 Sept. 1942	CVE–12	COPAHEE	15 June 1943
CVE–20	BARNES	20 Feb. 1943	CVE–13	CORE	10 Dec. 1942
CVE–21	*BLOCK ISLAND	8 Mar. 1943	CVE–25	CROATAN	28 Apr. 1943
CVE–9	BOGUE	26 Sept. 1942	CVE–16	NASSAU	20 Aug. 1942
CVE–23	BRETON	12 Apr. 1943	CVE–31	PRINCE	
CVE–11	CARD	8 Nov. 1942		WILLIAM	9 Apr. 1943

Builders: Seattle-Tacoma S. B. Corp.
Maritime Commission C3–S–A1 type. Twenty-six sisters went to Britain under Lend-Lease.

[1] Carried as Aircraft Carriers, Escort (AVG) until 20 Aug. 1942 and Auxiliary Aircraft Carriers (ACV) until CVE designation established 15 July 1943.

SANGAMON Class

11,400 tons; length 553′; beam 114′3″; draft 32′; speed 18 kts.; armament 2–5″/38; 30 planes; complement 1080.

No.	Name	Comm.	No.	Name	Comm.
CVE–28	CHENANGO	19 Sept. 1942 [2]	CVE–29	SANTEE	24 Aug. 1942 [2]
CVE–26	SANGAMON	25 Aug. 1942 [2]	CVE–27	SUWANNEE	24 Sept. 1942 [2]

Built in 1938 by Federal, Kearny (CVE 26–27) and Sun (CVE 28–29) as merchant tankers.

Converted from oilers; Maritime Commission MC–SO type.

[2] Commissioning date as carrier.

CHARGER

8000 tons; length 492′; beam 102′; draft 25′6″; speed 16 kts.; armament 1–5″/51 4–3″/50 21 planes; complement 970; diesel engine.

CVE–30 CHARGER   Comm. 3 Mar. 1942

Built in 1941 by Sun as merchantman.

Maritime Commission C3–P&C type. Three sisters transferred to Britain under Lend-Lease.

CASABLANCA Class

7800 tons; length 512′3″; beam 108′; draft 22′4″; speed 19 kts.; armament 1–5″/38 28 planes; complement 860; reciprocating engines.

No.	Name	Comm.	No.	Name	Comm.
CVE–99	ADMIRALTY ISLANDS	13 June 1944	CVE–94	LUNGA POINT	14 May 1944
			CVE–91	MAKASSAR STRAIT	27 Apr. 1944
CVE–55	ALAZON BAY [3]	8 July 1943			
CVE–102	ATTU	30 June 1944	CVE–93	MAKIN ISLAND	9 May 1944
CVE–95	*BISMARCK SEA	20 May 1944	CVE–61	MANILA BAY	5 Oct. 1943
CVE–100	BOUGAINVILLE	18 June 1944	CVE–77	MARCUS ISLAND	26 Jan. 1944
CVE–88	CAPE ESPERANCE	9 Apr. 1944	CVE–101	MATANIKAU	24 June 1944
			CVE–63	*MIDWAY [5]	23 Oct. 1943
CVE–57	CORAL SEA [4]	27 Aug. 1943	CVE–59	MISSION BAY	13 Sept. 1943
CVE–58	CORREGIDOR	31 Aug. 1943	CVE–104	MUNDA	8 July 1944
CVE–70	FANSHAW BAY	9 Dec. 1943	CVE–62	NATOMA BAY	14 Oct. 1943
CVE–73	*GAMBIER BAY	28 Dec. 1943	CVE–74	NEHENTA BAY	3 Jan. 1944
CVE–60	GUADALCANAL	25 Sept. 1943	CVE–79	*OMMANEY BAY	11 Feb. 1944
CVE–75	HOGGATT BAY	11 Jan. 1944			
CVE–97	HOLLANDIA	1 June 1944	CVE–80	PETROF BAY	18 Feb. 1944
CVE–76	KADASHAN BAY	18 Jan. 1944	CVE–103	ROI	6 July 1944
			CVE–81	RUDYERD BAY	25 Feb. 1944
CVE–68	KALININ BAY	27 Nov. 1943	CVE–82	SAGINAW BAY	2 Mar. 1944
CVE–69	KAASAN BAY	4 Dec. 1943	CVE–96	SALAMAUA	26 May 1944
CVE–71	KITKUN BAY	15 Dec. 1943	CVE–83	SARGENT BAY	9 Mar. 1944
CVE–98	KWAJALEIN	7 June 1944	CVE–78	SAVO ISLAND	3 Feb. 1944
CVE–56	*LISCOME BAY	7 Aug. 1943	CVE–84	SHAMROCK BAY	15 Mar. 1944
			CVE–85	SHIPLEY BAY	21 Mar. 1944

[3] Renamed CASABLANCA 3 Apr. 1945.
[4] Renamed ANZIO 15 Sept. 1944.
[5] Renamed ST. LO 15 Sept. 1944.

CASABLANCA Class (*cont'd*)

No.	Name	Comm.	No.	Name	Comm.
CVE–86	SITKOH BAY	28 Mar. 1944	CVE–64	TRIPOLI	31 Oct. 1943
CVE–67	SOLOMONS	21 Nov. 1943	CVE–72	TULAGI	21 Dec. 1943
CVE–87	STEAMER BAY	4 Apr. 1944	CVE–65	WAKE ISLAND	7 Nov. 1943
CVE–89	TAKANIS BAY	15 Apr. 1944	CVE–66	WHITE PLAINS	15 Nov. 1943
CVE–90	THETIS BAY	21 Apr. 1944	CVE–92	WINDHAM BAY	3 May 1944

Builders: Kaiser S. B. Co., Vancouver.
Maritime Commission S4–S2–BB3 type.

COMMENCEMENT BAY Class

11,373 tons; length 557'1"; beam 105'2"; draft 32'; speed 19 kts.; armament 2–5"/38 30 planes; complement 1066.

No.	Name	Comm.	No.	Name	Comm.
CVE–115	BAIROKO	16 July 1945	CVE–108	KULA GULF	12 May 1945
CVE–106	BLOCK ISLAND	30 Dec. 1944	CVE–113	PUGET SOUND	18 June 1945
CVE–109	CAPE		CVE–110	SALERNO BAY	19 May 1945
	GLOUCESTER	5 Mar. 1945	CVE–112	SIBONEY	14 May 1945
CVE–105	COMMENCE-		CVE–111	VELA GULF	9 Apr. 1945
	MENT BAY	27 Nov. 1944			
CVE–107	GILBERT				
	ISLANDS	5 Feb. 1945			

Builders: Todd-Pacific Shipyards, Inc., Tacoma.

2. BB BATTLESHIPS

ARKANSAS

26,100 tons; length 562'; beam 106'1"; draft 32'; speed 20.5 kts.; armament 12–12"/50 6–5"/51 10–3"/50 3 planes; complement 1860.

BB–33 ARKANSAS   17 Sept. 1912

Builders: New York S. B. Corp.
Sister-ship WYOMING served as gunnery training vessel.

NEW YORK Class

27,000 tons; length 573'; beam 106'1"; draft 32'3"; speed 20 kts.; armament 10–14"/45 6–5"/51 10–3"/50 3 planes; complement 1264; reciprocating engines.

BB–34 NEW YORK   15 Apr. 1914   BB–35 TEXAS   12 Mar. 1914

Builders: New York Navy Yard (BB–34) and Newport News (BB–35).

NEVADA Class

29,000 tons; length 583'; beam 107'11"; draft 33'6"; speed 20 kts.; armament 10–14"/45 12–5"/51 8–5"/25 3 planes or 10–14"/45 16–5"/38 2 planes; complement 2166; turbine or reciprocating engines.

BB–36 NEVADA   11 Mar. 1916   BB–37 *OKLAHOMA   2 May 1916

Builders: Fore River S. B. Corp., Quincy, Mass. (BB–36) and New York S. B. Corp. (BB–37).

PENNSYLVANIA Class

32,600–33,100 tons; length 608'; beam 106'3"; draft 33'6"; armament 12–14"/45 12–5"'/51 8–5"/25 3 planes or 12–14"/45 16–5"/38 2 planes; complement 2555.

No.	Name	Comm.	No.	Name	Comm.
BB–39	*ARIZONA	17 Oct. 1916	BB–38	PENNSYLVANIA	12 June 1916

Builders: Newport News (BB–38) and New York Navy Yard (BB–39).

NEW MEXICO Class

33,000–33,400 tons; length 624'; beam 106'3"; draft 34'; speed 21.5 kts.; armament 12–14"/50 6–5"/51 8–5"/25 2 planes or 12–14"/50 10–⁴/38 2 planes; complement 1945–2116.

BB–42	IDAHO	24 Mar. 1919	BB–40	NEW MEXICO	20 May 1918
BB–41	MISSISSIPPI	18 Dec. 1917			

Builders: New York Navy Yard (BB–40); Newport News (BB–41); and New York S. B. Corp. (BB–42).

TENNESSEE Class

32,300–32,600 tons; length 624'–624'6"; beam 114'; draft 34'; speed 20 kts.; armament 12–14"/50 12–5"/51 8–5"/25 3 planes or 12–14"/50 16–5"/38 2 planes; complement 2243–2375; turbines with electric drive.

BB–44	CALIFORNIA	10 Aug. 1921	BB–43	TENNESSEE	3 June 1920

Builders: New York Navy Yard (BB–43) and Mare Island Navy Yard (BB–44).

COLORADO Class

31,500–32,500 tons; length 624'; beam 108'1"–114'; draft 33'7"–34'8"; speed 21 kts.; armament 8–16"/45 12–5"/51 8–5"/25 3 planes or 8–16"/45 16–5"/38 2 planes; complement 1968–2182; turbines with electric drive.

BB–45	COLORADO	30 Aug. 1923	BB–48	WEST VIRGINIA	1 Dec. 1923
BB–46	MARYLAND	21 July 1921			

Builders: New York S. B. Corp. (BB–45) and Newport News (BB 46,48).

NORTH CAROLINA Class

35,000 tons; length 729'; beam 108'4"; draft 35'6"; speed 27 kts.; armament 9–16"/45 20–5"/38 3 planes; complement 2339.

BB–55	NORTH CAROLINA	9 Apr. 1941	BB–56	WASHINGTON	15 May 1941

Builders: New York Navy Yard (BB–55) and Philadelphia Navy Yard (BB–56).

SOUTH DAKOTA Class

35,000 tons; length 680'; beam 108'2"; draft 36'2"; speed 27 kts.; armament 9–16"/45 16–20 5"/38 3 planes; complement 2257–2354.

BB–60	ALABAMA	16 Aug. 1942	BB–59	MASSACHUSETTS	12 May 1942
BB–58	INDIANA	30 Apr. 1942	BB–57	SOUTH DAKOTA	20 Mar. 1942

Builders: New York S. B. Co. (BB–57); Newport News (BB–58); Bethlehem, Quincy (BB–59); and Norfolk Navy Yard (BB–60).

IOWA Class

45,000 tons; length 887′3″–887′7″; beam 108′1″–108′2″; draft 37′9″–38′; speed 33 kts.; armament 9–16″/50 20–5″/38 3 planes; complement 2753–2978.

No.	Name	Comm.	No.	Name	Comm.
BB–61	IOWA	22 Feb. 1943	BB–62	NEW JERSEY	23 May 1943
BB–63	MISSOURI	11 June 1944	BB–64	WISCONSIN	16 Apr. 1944

Builders: New York Navy Yard (BB 61, 63); Philadelphia Navy Yard (BB 62, 64).

3. CRUISERS

CB Large Cruisers

ALASKA Class

27,500 tons; length 808′6″; beam 91′1″; draft 32′4″; speed 33 kts.; armament 9–12″/50 12–5″/38 4 planes; complement 2251.

CB–1 ALASKA 17 June 1944 CB–2 GUAM 17 Sept. 1944

Builders: New York S. B. Co.

CA Heavy Cruisers

PENSACOLA Class

9100 tons; length 585′8″; beam 65′3″; draft 22′5″; speed 32.5 kts.; armament 10–8″/55 8–5″/25 2 planes; complement 1113–1135.

CA–24 PENSACOLA 6 Feb. 1930 CA–25 SALT LAKE CITY 11 Dec. 1929

Builders: New York Navy Yard (CA–24) and New York S. B. Co. (CA–25).

NORTHAMPTON Class

9050–9300 tons; length 600′3″; beam 66′1″; draft 24′; speed 32.5 kts.; armament 9–8″/55 8–5″/25 3 planes; complement 1020–1155.

CA–31	AUGUSTA	30 Jan. 1931	CA–30	*HOUSTON	17 June 1930
CA–27	CHESTER	24 June 1930	CA–28	LOUISVILLE	15 Jan. 1931
CA–29	*CHICAGO	9 Mar. 1931	CA–26	*NORTHAMPTON	17 May 1930

Builders: Bethlehem, Quincy (CA–26); New York S. B. Co. (CA–27); Puget Sound Navy Yard (CA–28); Mare Island Navy Yard (CA–29); and Newport News (CA 30–31).

PORTLAND Class

9800–9950 tons; length 610′3″–610′4″; beam 66′1″; draft 24′6″; speed 32.5 kts.; armament 9–8″/55 8–5″/25 3 planes; complement 1229–1382.

CA–35 *INDIANAPOLIS 15 Nov. 1932 CA–33 PORTLAND 23 Feb. 1933

Builders: Bethlehem, Quincy (CA–33) and New York S. B. Co. (CA–35).

Heavy Cruisers (*cont'd*): NEW ORLEANS Class

9375–9975 tons; length 588'2"; beam 61'9"–61'10"; draft 24'4"; speed 32 kts.; armament 9–8"/55 8–5"/25 3 planes; complement 1042–1121.

No.	Name	Comm.	No.	Name	Comm.
CA–34	*ASTORIA	28 Apr. 1934	CA–38	SAN FRANCISCO	10 Feb. 1934
CA–36	MINNEAPOLIS	19 May 1934	CA–37	TUSCALOOSA	17 Aug. 1934
CA–32	NEW ORLEANS	15 Feb. 1934	CA–44	*VINCENNES	24 Feb. 1937
CA–39	*QUINCY	9 June 1936			

Builders: New York Navy Yard (CA 32, 37); Puget Sound Navy Yard (CA–34); Philadelphia Navy Yard (CA–36); New York S. B. Co. (CA–37); Mare Island Navy Yard (CA–38); and Bethlehem, Quincy (CA 39, 44).

WICHITA

10,000 tons; length 608'4"; beam 61'9"; draft 25'; speed 32.5 kts.; armament 9–8"/55 8–5"/38 2 planes; complement 1343.

CA–45	WICHITA	16 Feb. 1939

Builders: Philadelphia Navy Yard.

BALTIMORE Class

13,600 tons; length 673'5"; beam 70'10"; draft 26'10"; speed 33 kts.; armament 9–8"/55 12–5"/38 4 planes; complement 1648–1969.

No.	Name	Comm.	No.	Name	Comm.
CA–68	BALTIMORE	15 Apr. 1943	CA–131	FALL RIVER	1 July 1945
CA–69	BOSTON	30 June 1943	CA–135	LOS ANGELES	22 July 1945
CA–130	BREMERTON	29 Apr. 1945	CA–132	MACON	26 Aug. 1945
CA–70	CANBERRA	14 Oct. 1943	CA–72	PITTSBURGH	10 Oct. 1944
CA–136	CHICAGO	10 Jan. 1945	CA–71	QUINCY	15 Dec. 1943
CA–74	COLUMBUS	8 June 1945	CA–73	ST. PAUL	17 Feb. 1945

Builders: Bethlehem, Quincy (CA 68–74); New York S. B. Co. (CA 130–132); and Philadelphia Navy Yard (CA 135–136).

CL Light Cruisers

OMAHA Class

7050 tons; length 555'6"; beam 55'4"; draft 19'11"–20'10"; speed 35 kts.; armament 10–6"/53 6–8 3"/50 6–21" torpedo tubes; 2 planes; complement 681–823.

No.	Name	Comm.	No.	Name	Comm.
CL–6	CINCINNATI	1 Jan. 1924	CL–5	MILWAUKEE [6]	20 June 1923
CL–10	CONCORD	3 Nov. 1923	CL–4	OMAHA	24 Feb. 1923
CL–8	DETROIT	31 July 1923	CL–7	RALEIGH	6 Feb. 1924
CL–12	MARBLEHEAD	8 Sept. 1924	CL–9	RICHMOND	2 July 1923
CL–13	MEMPHIS	4 Feb. 1925	CL–11	TRENTON	19 Apr. 1924

Builders: Todd S. B. & D. D. Co., Tacoma (CL 4–6); Bethlehem, Quincy (CL 7–8); and Cramp (CL 9–13).

[6] Transferred to U.S.S.R. under Lend-Lease.

BROOKLYN Class

9475–9700 tons; length 608'4"; beam 61'8"–69'6"; draft 24'4"–25'; speed 33 kts.; armament 15–6"/47 8–5"/25 or /38 2 planes; complement 1140–1363.

BROOKLYN Class (*cont'd*)

No.	Name	Comm.	No.	Name	Comm.
CL–47	BOISE	12 Aug. 1938	CL–41	PHILADELPHIA	23 Sept. 1937
CL–40	BROOKLYN	30 Sept. 1937	CL–46	PHOENIX	3 Oct. 1938
CL–48	HONOLULU	15 June 1938	CL–42	SAVANNAH	10 Mar. 1938
CL–43	NASHVILLE	6 June 1938			

Builders: New York Navy Yard (CL 40, 48); Philadelphia Navy Yard (CL–41); New York S. B. Co. (CL 42–43, 46); Newport News (CL–47).

ST. LOUIS Class

10,000 tons; length 608'4"; beam 61'8"; draft 25'10"; speed 32 kts.; armament 15–6"/47 8–5"/38 2 planes; complement 1216.

CL–50	*HELENA	18 Sept. 1939	CL–49	ST. LOUIS	19 May 1939

Builders: Newport News (CL–49) and New York Navy Yard (CL–50).
Modified BROOKLYNS with twin 5" turrets instead of open single mounts.

ATLANTA Class

6000 tons; length 541'6"–541'9"; beam 53'2"; draft 26'6"–26'8"; speed 32–33 kts.; armament 12–16 5"/38 8–21" torpedo tubes; complement 688–820.

CL–51	*ATLANTA	24 Dec. 1941	CL–96	RENO	28 Dec. 1943
CL–97	FLINT	31 Aug. 1944	CL–53	SAN DIEGO	10 Jan. 1942
CL–52	*JUNEAU	14 Feb. 1942	CL–54	SAN JUAN	28 Feb. 1942
CL–95	OAKLAND	17 July 1943	CL–98	TUCSON	3 Feb. 1945

Builders: Federal, Kearny (CL 51–52); Bethlehem, Quincy (CL 53–54); and Bethlehem, San Francisco (CL 95–98).
Anti-aircraft cruisers.

CLEVELAND Class

10,000 tons; length 610'–610'1"; beam 66'3"–66'4"; draft 24'7"–26'6"; speed 32.5 kts.; armament 12–6"/47 12–5"/38 3 planes; complement 1214–1475.

CL–101	AMSTERDAM	8 Jan. 1945	CL–63	MOBILE	24 Mar. 1943
CL–90	ASTORIA	17 May 1944	CL–57	MONTPELIER	9 Sept. 1942
CL–104	ATLANTA	3 Dec. 1944	CL–91	OKLAHOMA CITY	22 Dec. 1944
CL–80	BILOXI	31 Aug. 1943	CL–65	PASADENA	8 June 1944
CL–62	BIRMINGHAM	29 Jan. 1943	CL–102	PORTSMOUTH	25 June 1945
CL–55	CLEVELAND	15 June 1942	CL–82	PROVIDENCE	15 May 1945
CL–56	COLUMBIA	29 June 1942	CL–60	SANTA FE	24 Nov. 1942
CL–105	DAYTON	7 Jan. 1945	CL–66	SPRINGFIELD	9 Sept. 1944
CL–58	DENVER	15 Oct. 1942	CL–67	TOPEKA	23 Dec. 1944
CL–87	DULUTH	18 Sept. 1944	CL–86	VICKSBURG	12 June 1944
CL–81	HOUSTON	20 Dec. 1943	CL–64	VINCENNES	21 Jan. 1944
CL–92	LITTLE ROCK	17 June 1945	CL–103	WILKES-BARRE	1 July 1944
CL–89	MIAMI	28 Dec. 1943			

Builders: New York S. B. Co. (CL 55–60, 103–105); Newport News (CL 62–63, 80–81, 86–87, 101–102); Bethlehem, Quincy (CL 64–67, 82); Cramp (CL 89–92).
Nine sisters were converted to CVL while building.

4. DD DESTROYERS

ALLEN

920 tons; length 315'3"; beam 30'7"; draft 12'9"; speed 30 kts.; armament 4–4"/50 6–21" torpedo tubes; complement 146.

No.	Name	Comm.	No.	Name	Comm.
DD–66	ALLEN	1917			

Builders: Bath.

CALDWELL Class

1020 tons; length 315'6"; beam 31'2"–31'3"; draft 11'6"; speed 30 kts.; armament 4–4"/50 1–3"/23 12–21" torpedo tubes or 3–3"/50; complement 148.

DD–72	CONNER [7]	1918	DD–74	MANLEY	1945 [8]
DD–70	CONWAY [7]	1918	DD–73	STOCKTON [7]	1917

Builders: Norfolk Navy Yard (DD–70); Cramp (DD 72–73); and Bath (DD–74).

[7] Transferred to Great Britain.
[8] Date converted from high-speed transport.

WICKES ("Flush Decker") Class

1060–1090 tons; length 314'5"–315'5"; beam 31'8"–31'9"; draft 12'; speed 35 kts.; armament 4–4"/50 6–21" torpedo tubes or 6–3"/50 6–21" torpedo tubes; complement 149.

DD–132	AARON WARD [9]	1919	DD–134	CROWNINSHIELD [9]	1919
DD–184	ABBOT [9]	1919	DD–116	DENT [11]	1918
DD–128	BABBITT [10]	1919	DD–157	DICKERSON [11]	1919
DD–126	BADGER	1919	DD–185	DORAN [9]	1919
DD–149	BARNEY [10]	1919	DD–117	DORSEY [12]	1918
DD–153	BERNADOU	1919	DD–152	DU PONT [10]	1919
DD–151	BIDDLE [10]	1919	DD–146	ELLIOT [12]	1919
DD–150	BLAKELEY	1919	DD–154	ELLIS [10]	1919
DD–136	BOGGS [11]	1918	DD–78	EVANS [9]	1918
DD–148	BRECKENRIDGE [10]	1919	DD–93	FAIRFAX [9]	1918
DD–131	BUCHANAN [9]	1919	DD–169	FOOTE [9]	1919
DD–106	CHEW	1918	DD–145	GREER	1918
DD–140	CLAXTON [9]	1919	DD–82	GREGORY [11]	1918
DD–155	COLE [10]	1919	DD–133	HALE [9]	1919
DD–85	COLHOUN [11]	1918	DD–141	HAMILTON [12]	1919
DD–167	COWELL [9]	1919	DD–183	HARADEN [9]	1919
DD–109	CRANE	1919	DD–160	HERBERT [11]	1919
DD–164	CROSBY [11]	1919	DD–178	HOGAN [12]	1919

[9] Transferred to Great Britain 1940.
[10] Converted to miscellaneous auxiliary (AG).
[11] Converted to high-speed transport (APD).
[12] Converted to high-speed minesweeper (DMS).

WICKES ("Flush Decker") Class (*cont'd*)

No.	Name	Comm.	No.	Name	Comm.
DD–181	HOPEWELL [9]	1919	DD–159	SCHENCK	1919
DD–179	HOWARD [12]	1920	DD–103	SCHLEY [11]	1918
DD–156	J. FRED TALBOTT [10]	1919	DD–81	SIGOURNEY [9]	1918
DD–130	*JACOB JONES	1919	DD–180	STANSBURY [12]	1920
DD–170	KALK [9]	1919	DD–83	STRINGHAM [11]	1918
DD–138	KENNISON [10]	1919	DD–114	TALBOT [11]	1918
DD–137	KILTY [11]	1918	DD–142	TARBELL	1918
DD–118	LEA	1918	DD–125	TATTNALL [11]	1919
DD–158	*LEARY	1919	DD–162	THATCHER [9]	1918
DD–79	LITTLE [11]	1918	DD–182	THOMAS [9]	1919
DD–90	MC KEAN [11]	1919	DD–135	TILLMAN [9]	1921
DD–175	MACKENZIE [9]	1919	DD–127	TWIGGS [9]	1919
DD–168	MADDOX [9]	1919	DD–144	UPSHUR [10]	1918
DD–161	PALMER [13]	1919	DD–139	WARD [11]	1918
DD–76	PHILIP [9]	1918	DD–115	WATERS [11]	1918
DD–113	RATHBURNE [11]	1918	DD–75	WICKES [9]	1918
DD–89	RINGGOLD [9]	1918	DD–108	WILLIAMS [9]	1919
DD–88	ROBINSON [9]	1918	DD–143	YARNALL [9]	1918
DD–147	ROPER [11]	1919			

Builders: Bath (DD 75–76, 78, 131–134); Fore R. S. B. Corp. (DD 79, 81–83, 85, 161–162, 164, 167–170); Union Iron Works, San Francisco (DD 88–90, 106, 108–109, 175, 178–180); Mare Island Navy Yard (DD 93, 137–141); Cramp (DD 113–118, 142–156); New York S. B. Corp. (DD 125–128, 130, 157–160); Charleston Navy Yard (DD–135); and Newport News (DD 181–185).

[9] Transferred to Great Britain 1940.
[10] Converted to miscellaneous auxiliary (AG).
[11] Converted to high-speed transport (APD).
[12] Converted to high-speed minesweeper (DMS).
[13] Converted to light minelayer (DM).

CLEMSON ("Flush Decker") Class

1190 tons; length 314'5"; beam 31'8"–31'9"; draft 14'1"; speed 35 kts.; armament 4-4"/50 1–3"/23 12–21" torpedo tubes or 6-3"/50 6–21" torpedo tubes; complement 149.

No.	Name	Comm.	No.	Name	Comm.
DD–193	ABEL P. UPSHUR [14]	1920	DD–246	BAINBRIDGE	1921
DD–211	ALDEN	1919	DD–267	BALLARD [19]	1919
DD–258	AULICK [14]	1919	DD–256	BANCROFT [14]	1919
DD–269	BAILEY [14]	1919	DD–213	BARKER	1919

[14] Transferred to Great Britain 1940.
[15] Converted to high-speed transport (APD).
[16] Converted to miscellaneous auxiliary (AG).
[17] Converted to high-speed minesweeper (DMS).
[18] Renamed ALEXANDER DALLAS 22 Mar. 1945.
[19] Converted to seaplane tender (destroyer) (AVD).
[20] Date reconverted from AVP.

CLEMSON ("Flush Decker") Class (*cont'd*)

No.	Name	Comm.	No.	Name	Comm.
DD–248	BARRY [15]	1920	DD–252	MC COOK [14]	1919
DD–215	*BORIE	1920	DD–223	MC CORMICK [16]	1920
DD–197	BRANCH [14]	1920	DD–237	MC FARLAND [15, 19]	1920
DD–232	BROOKS [15]	1920	DD–264	MC LANAHAN [14]	1919
DD–210	BROOME [16]	1919	DD–220	MAC LISH [16]	1920
DD–222	BULMER [16]	1920	DD–191	MASON [14]	1920
DD–206	CHANDLER [17]	1919	DD–274	MEADE [14]	1919
DD–187	DAHLGREN [16]	1920	DD–343	NOA [15]	1921
DD–199	DALLAS [18]	1920	DD–255	OSMUND INGRAM [15, 19]	1919
DD–341	DECATUR	1922	DD–239	OVERTON [15]	1920
DD–219	*EDSALL	1920	DD–218	*PARROTT	1920
DD–265	EDWARDS [14]	1919	DD–230	PAUL JONES [16]	1921
DD–234	FOX [16]	1920	DD–226	*PEARY	1920
DD–196	GEORGE E. BADGER [19]	1920	DD–340	PERRY [17]	1922
DD–260	GILLIS [19]	1919	DD–227	*PILLSBURY	1920
DD–233	GILMER [15]	1920	DD–225	*POPE	1920
DD–247	GOFF	1921	DD–245	*REUBEN JAMES	1920
DD–188	GOLDSBOROUGH [15]	1943 [20]	DD–254	RODGERS [14]	1919
DD–266	GREENE [15, 19]	1919	DD–243	SANDS [15]	1920
DD–231	HATFIELD [16]	1920	DD–190	SATTERLEE [14]	1918
DD–198	HERNDON [14]	1920	DD–268	SHUBRICK [14]	1919
DD–249	HOPKINS [17]	1920	DD–221	SIMPSON [16]	1920
DD–208	HOVEY [17]	1919	DD–207	SOUTHARD [17]	1919
DD–236	HUMPHREYS [15]	1920	DD–224	*STEWART	1920
DD–194	HUNT [14]	1920	DD–240	*STURTEVANT	1920
DD–216	JOHN D. EDWARDS	1920	DD–273	SWASEY [14]	1919
DD–228	JOHN D. FORD [16]	1920	DD–270	THORNTON [19]	1919
DD–235	KANE [15]	1920	DD–339	TREVOR [17]	1922
DD–242	KING	1920	DD–229	*TRUXTUN	1921
DD–263	LAUB [14]	1919	DD–338	WASMUTH [17]	1921
DD–250	LAWRENCE	1920	DD–195	WELBORN C. WOOD [14]	1920
DD–336	LITCHFIELD [16]	1920	DD–257	WELLES [14]	1919
DD–209	LONG [17]	1919	DD–217	WHIPPLE [16]	1920
DD–253	MC CALLA [14]	1919	DD–337	ZANE [17]	1920

Builders: Newport News (DD 186–188, 190–191, 193–199); Cramp (DD 206–211, 213, 215–230); New York S. B. Corp. (DD 231–237, 239–240, 242, 244–250); Bethlehem, Quincy (DD 252–258, 269); Bethlehem, Squantum (DD 263–270, 273–274); and Mare Island Navy Yard (DD 336–343).

[14] Transferred to Great Britain 1940.
[15] Converted to high-speed transport (APD).
[16] Converted to miscellaneous auxiliary (AG).
[17] Converted to high-speed minesweeper (DMS).
[18] Renamed ALEXANDER DALLAS 2 Mar. 1945.
[19] Converted to seaplane tender (destroyer) (AVD).
[20] Date reconverted from AVP.

FARRAGUT Class

1345–1410 tons; length 341'3"; beam 34'2"; draft 16'4"; speed 36.5 kts.; armament 4–5"/38 8–21" torpedo tubes; complement 251.

No.	Name	Comm.	No.	Name	Comm.
DD-355	AYLWIN	1935	DD-350	*HULL	1935
DD-353	DALE	1935	DD-351	MACDONOUGH	1935
DD-349	DEWEY	1934	DD-354	*MONAGHAN	1935
DD-348	FARRAGUT	1934	DD-352	*WORDEN	1935

Builders: Bethlehem, Quincy (DD-348); Bath (DD-349); New York Navy Yard (DD 350, 353); Boston Navy Yard (DD 351, 354); Puget Sound Navy Yard (DD-352); Philadelphia Navy Yard (DD-355).

PORTER Class

1805–1850 tons; length 381'; beam 36'11"; draft 17'9"; speed 37.5 kts.; armament 5–5"/38 8–21" torpedo tubes; complement 294.

DD-363	BALCH	1936	DD-360	PHELPS	1936
DD-361	CLARK	1936	DD-356	*PORTER	1936
DD-358	MCDOUGAL	1936	DD-357	SELFRIDGE	1936
DD-362	MOFFETT	1936	DD-359	WINSLOW	1937

Builders: New York S. B. Co. (DD 356–359); Bethlehem, Quincy (DD 360–363).

MAHAN Class

1450–1500 tons; length 341'4"; beam 35'5"; draft 17'2"; speed 36.5 kts.; armament 4–5"/38 4–8 21" torpedo tubes; complement 251.

DD-370	CASE	1936	DD-367	LAMSON	1936
DD-372	CASSIN	1936	DD-364	*MAHAN	1936
DD-371	CONYNGHAM	1936	DD-377	*PERKINS	1936
DD-365	CUMMINGS	1936	DD-379	*PRESTON	1936
DD-376	*CUSHING	1936	DD-369	*REID	1936
DD-375	DOWNES	1937	DD-373	SHAW	1936
DD-366	DRAYTON	1936	DD-378	SMITH	1936
DD-368	FLUSSER	1936	DD-374	*TUCKER	1936

Builders: United Drydocks, Inc., Mariners Harbor, N. Y. (DD 364–365); Bath (DD 366–367); Federal, Kearny (DD 368–369); Boston Navy Yard (DD 370–371); Philadelphia Navy Yard (DD 372–373); Norfolk Navy Yard (DD 374–375); Puget Sound Navy Yard (DD 376–377); Mare Island Navy Yard (DD 378–379).

DD 372 and 375 completely rebuilt following Pearl Harbor.

GRIDLEY Class

1500 tons; length 340'10"–341'4"; beam 35'5"–35'6"; draft 17'1"; speed 35 kts.; armament 4–5"/38 16–21" torpedo tubes; complement 251.

DD-386	BAGLEY	1937	DD-391	*HENLEY	1937
DD-387	*BLUE	1937	DD-393	*JARVIS	1937
DD-382	CRAVEN	1937	DD-389	MUGFORD	1937
DD-380	GRIDLEY	1937	DD-392	PATTERSON	1937
DD-388	HELM	1937	DD-390	RALPH TALBOT	1937

Builders: Bethlehem, Quincy (DD 380, 382); Norfolk Navy Yard (DD 386–388); Boston Navy Yard (DD 389–390); Mare Island Navy Yard (DD 391–392).

SOMERS Class

1850 tons; length 381'–390'11"; beam 36'7"–36'11"; draft 17'10"–18'; speed 33 kts.; armament 5–6 5"/38 8–21" torpedo tubes; complement 294.

No.	Name	Comm.	No.	Name	Comm.
DD–395	DAVIS	1938	DD–381	SOMERS	1937
DD–396	JOUETT	1939	DD–383	*WARRINGTON	1938
DD–394	SAMPSON	1938			

Builders: Federal, Kearny (DD 381, 383) and Bath (DD 394–396).

FANNING Class

1490 tons; length 341'2"; beam 35'; draft 17'2"; speed 35 kts.; armament 4–5"/38 4–21" torpedo tubes; complement 251.

DD–384	DUNLAP	1937	DD–385	FANNING	1937

Builders: United Drydocks, Inc., Mariners Harbor.

BENHAM Class

1500 tons; length 340'6"–341'4"; beam 35'5"–35'6"; draft 17'3"; speed 34 kts.; armament 4–5"/38 8–21" torpedo tubes; complement 251.

DD–397	*BENHAM	1939	DD–404	RHIND	1939
DD–398	ELLET	1939	DD–405	*ROWAN	1939
DD–399	LANG	1939	DD–406	STACK	1939
DD–400	MCCALL	1938	DD–407	STERETT	1939
DD–401	MAURY	1938	DD–403	TRIPPE	1939
DD–402	MAYRANT	1939	DD–408	WILSON	1939

Builders: Federal, Kearny (DD 397–399); Bethlehem, San Francisco (DD 400–401); Boston Navy Yard (DD 402–403); Philadelphia Navy Yard (DD–404); Norfolk Navy Yard (DD 405–406); Charleston Navy Yard (DD–407); and Puget Sound Navy Yard (DD–408).

SIMS Class

1570 tons; length 347'7"–348'4"; beam 36'1"; draft 17'4"; speed 35 kts.; armament 4–5"/38 8–21" torpedo tubes; complement 251.

DD–411	ANDERSON	1939	DD–415	*O'BRIEN	1940
DD–240	*BUCK	1940	DD–418	ROE	1940
DD–412	*HAMMANN	1939	DD–414	RUSSELL	1939
DD–410	HUGHES	1939	DD–409	*SIMS	1939
DD–417	MORRIS	1940	DD–419	WAINWRIGHT	1940
DD–413	MUSTIN	1939	DD–416	*WALKE	1940

Builders: Bath (DD 409–410); Federal, Kearny (DD 411–412); Newport News (DD 413–414); Boston Navy Yard (DD 415–416); Norfolk Navy Yard (DD 417, 419); Charleston Navy Yard (DD–418).

BENSON Class

1620 tons; length 347'9"–348'4"; beam 36'–36'1"; draft 17'4"–17'6"; speed 33 kts.; armament 4–5"/38 5–21" torpedo tubes; complement 276.

DD–492	BAILEY	1942	DD–599	*BARTON	1942
DD–598	BANCROFT	1942	DD–421	BENSON	1940

BENSON Class (*cont'd*)

No.	Name	Comm.	No.	Name	Comm.
DD-600	BOYLE	1942	DD-459	*LAFFEY	1942
DD-605	CALDWELL	1942	DD-426	*LANSDALE	1940
DD-601	CHAMPLIN	1942	DD-613	LAUB	1942
DD-428	CHARLES F. HUGHES	1940	DD-615	MCLANAHAN	1942
DD-606	COGHLAN	1942	DD-614	MACKENZIE	1942
DD-491	FARENHOLT	1942	DD-425	MADISON	1940
DD-607	FRAZIER	1942	DD-422	MAYO	1940
DD-608	GANSEVOORT	1942	DD-602	MEADE	1942
DD-609	GILLESPIE	1942	DD-603	MURPHY	1942
DD-427	HILARY P. JONES	1940	DD-616	NIELDS	1943
DD-610	HOBBY	1942	DD-617	ORDRONAUX	1943
DD-611	KALK	1942	DD-604	PARKER	1942
DD-612	KENDRICK	1942	DD-460	WOODWORTH	1942

Builders: Bethlehem, Quincy (DD 421–422, 598–601, 616–617); Boston Navy Yard (DD 425–426); Charleston Navy Yard (DD-427); Puget Sound Navy Yard (DD-428); Bethlehem, San Francisco (DD 459–460, 605–611); Bethlehem, Staten I. (DD 491–492, 602–604); and Bethlehem, San Pedro (DD 612–615).

GLEAVES Class

1630 tons; length 347'7"–348'4"; beam 36'–37'; draft 17'5"–17'6"; speed 33 kts.; armament 4–5"/38 5–21" torpedo tubes; complement 276.

No.	Name	Comm.	No.	Name	Comm.
DD-483	*AARON WARD	1942	DD-497	FRANKFORD	1943
DD-624	BALDWIN	1943	DD-637	GERHARDI [21]	1942
DD-640	*BEATTY	1942	DD-423	GLEAVES	1940
DD-453	*BRISTOL	1941	DD-620	*GLENNON	1942
DD-484	BUCHANAN	1942	DD-435	GRAYSON	1941
DD-636	BUTLER [21]	1942	DD-433	*GWIN	1941
DD-493	CARMICK [21]	1942	DD-455	HAMBLETON [21]	1941
DD-463	*CORRY	1941	DD-625	HARDING [21]	1943
DD-632	COWIE [21]	1942	DD-638	HERNDON	1942
DD-618	DAVISON [21]	1942	DD-464	HOBSON [21]	1942
DD-634	DORAN [21]	1942	DD-444	*INGRAHAM	1941
DD-494	DOYLE [21]	1943	DD-621	JEFFERS [21]	1942
DD-485	*DUNCAN	1942	DD-432	KEARNY	1940
DD-635	EARLE [21]	1942	DD-633	KNIGHT [21]	1942
DD-430	EBERLE	1940	DD-486	LANSDOWNE	1942
DD-439	EDISON	1941	DD-487	LARDNER	1942
DD-619	EDWARDS	1942	DD-429	LIVERMORE	1940
DD-454	ELLYSON [21]	1941	DD-438	LUDLOW	1941
DD-457	EMMONS [21]	1941	DD-488	MC CALLA	1942
DD-495	ENDICOTT [21]	1943	DD-496	MC COOK [21]	1943
DD-440	ERICSSON	1941	DD-458	MACOMB [21]	1942
DD-462	FITCH [21]	1942	DD-622	*MADDOX	1942
DD-461	FORREST [21]	1942	DD-434	*MEREDITH	1941

[21] Converted to high-speed minesweeper (DMS).

GLEAVES Class (*cont'd*)

No.	Name	Comm.	No.	Name	Comm.
DD-489	MERVINE [21]	1942	DD-645	STEVENSON	1942
DD-436	*MONSSEN	1941	DD-646	STOCKTON	1943
DD-623	NELSON	1942	DD-443	SWANSON	1941
DD-424	NIBLACK	1940	DD-627	THOMPSON [21]	1943
DD-442	NICHOLSON	1941	DD-647	THORN	1943
DD-431	PLUNKETT	1940	DD-641	TILLMAN	1942
DD-490	QUICK [21]	1942	DD-648	*TURNER	1943
DD-456	RODMAN [21]	1942	DD-628	WELLES	1943
DD-626	SATTERLEE	1943	DD-441	WICKES	1941
DD-639	SHUBRICK	1943	DD-437	WOOLSEY	1941

Builders: Bath (DD 423–424, 429–430, 437–438, 457–458); Federal, Kearny (DD 431–432, 439–440, 453–456, 483–490, 618–623, 645–648); Boston Navy Yard (DD 433–434, 441–442, 461–462, 632–635); Charleston Navy Yard (DD 435, 443–444, 463–464, 640–641); Puget Sound Navy Yard (DD–436); Seattle-Tacoma S. B. Corp., Seattle (DD 493–497, 624–628); Philadelphia Navy Yard (DD 636–637); and Norfolk Navy Yard (DD 638–639).

[21] Converted to high-speed minesweeper (DMS).

FLETCHER Class

2050 tons; length 375'10"–376'7"; beam 39'4"–40'; draft 17'9"; speed 35 kts.; armament 5–5"/38 10–21" torpedo tubes; complement 329.

No.	Name	Comm.	No.	Name	Comm.
DD-629	ABBOT	1943	DD-650	CAPERTON	1943
DD-526	*ABNER READ	1943	DD-550	CAPPS	1943
DD-649	ALBERT W. GRANT	1943	DD-793	CASSIN YOUNG	1943
DD-527	AMMEN	1943	DD-570	CHARLES AUSBURNE	1942
DD-515	ANTHONY	1943	DD-657	CHARLES J. BADGER	1943
DD-569	AULICK	1942	DD-581	CHARRETTE	1943
DD-470	BACHE	1942	DD-667	CHAUNCEY	1943
DD-471	BEALE	1942	DD-451	*CHEVALIER	1942
DD-654	BEARSS	1944	DD-668	CLARENCE K. BRONSON	1943
DD-587	BELL	1943	DD-571	CLAXTON	1942
DD-796	BENHAM	1943	DD-651	COGSWELL	1943
DD-473	BENNETT	1943	DD-658	COLAHAN	1943
DD-662	BENNION	1943	DD*801	*COLHOUN	1944
DD-666	BLACK	1943	DD-582	CONNER	1943
DD-544	BOYD	1943	DD-509	CONVERSE	1942
DD-545	BRADFORD	1943	DD-507	CONWAY	1942
DD-630	BRAINE	1943	DD-508	CONY	1942
DD-546	BROWN	1943	DD-669	COTTEN	1943
DD-518	*BROWNSON	1943	DD-547	COWELL	1943
DD-665	BRYANT	1943	DD-797	CUSHING	1944
DD-660	BULLARD	1943	DD-519	DALY	1943
DD-588	BURNS	1943	DD-659	DASHIELL	1943
DD-529	*BUSH	1943	DD-551	DAVID W. TAYLOR	1943
DD-792	*CALLAGHAN	1943	DD-469	*DE HAVEN	1942

FLETCHER Class (*cont'd*)

No.	Name	Comm.	No.	Name	Comm.
DD-670	DORTCH	1943	DD-653	KNAPP	1943
DD-572	DYSON	1942	DD-448	LA VALLETTE	1942
DD-510	EATON	1942	DD-558	LAWS	1943
DD-631	ERBEN	1943	DD-481	LEUTZE	1944
DD-552	EVANS	1943	DD-675	LEWIS HANCOCK	1943
DD-445	FLETCHER	1942	DD-803	*LITTLE	1944
DD-511	FOOTE	1942	DD-559	*LONGSHAW	1943
DD-554	FRANKS	1943	DD-522	*LUCE	1942
DD-474	FULLAM	1943	DD-534	MCCORD	1943
DD-671	GATLING	1943	DD-677	MCDERMUT	1943
DD-802	GREGORY	1944	DD-678	MCGOWAN	1943
DD-472	GUEST	1942	DD-575	MCKEE	1943
DD-555	HAGGARD	1943	DD-679	MCNAIR	1943
DD-556	HAILEY	1943	DD-676	MARSHALL	1943
DD-642	HALE	1943	DD-680	MELVIN	1943
DD-480	HALFORD	1943	DD-691	MERTZ	1943
DD-583	HALL	1943	DD-595	METCALF	1944
DD-584	*HALLIGAN	1943	DD-535	MILLER	1943
DD-686	HALSEY POWELL	1943	DD-798	MONSSEN	1944
DD-585	HARADEN	1943	DD-560	*MORRISON	1943
DD-573	HARRISON	1943	DD-528	MULLANY	1943
DD-594	HART	1944	DD-576	MURRAY	1943
DD-531	HAZELWOOD	1943	DD-586	NEWCOMB	1943
DD-672	HEALY	1943	DD-449	NICHOLAS	1942
DD-532	HEERMANN	1943	DD-690	NORMAN SCOTT	1943
DD-663	HEYWOOD L. EDWARDS	1944	DD-450	O'BANNON	1942
DD-673	HICKOX	1943	DD-536	OWEN	1943
DD-533	*HOEL	1943	DD-590	PAUL HAMILTON	1943
DD-681	HOPEWELL	1943	DD-498	PHILIP	1942
DD-592	HOWORTH	1944	DD-685	PICKING	1943
DD-475	HUDSON	1943	DD-800	PORTER	1944
DD-674	HUNT	1943	DD-682	PORTERFIELD	1943
DD-476	HUTCHINS	1942	DD-795	PRESTON	1944
DD-652	INGERSOLL	1943	DD-561	PRICHETT	1944
DD-794	IRWIN	1944	DD-477	*PRINGLE	1942
DD-520	ISHERWOOD	1943	DD-446	RADFORD	1942
DD-589	IZARD	1943	DD-688	REMEY	1943
DD-799	JARVIS	1944	DD-499	RENSHAW	1942
DD-447	JENKINS	1942	DD-664	RICHARD P. LEARY	1944
DD-553	JOHN D. HENLEY	1943	DD-500	RINGGOLD	1942
DD-655	JOHN HOOD	1944	DD-562	ROBINSON	1944
DD-574	JOHN RODGERS	1943	DD-804	ROOKS	1944
DD-557	*JOHNSTON	1943	DD-563	ROSS	1944
DD-661	KIDD	1943	DD-564	ROWE	1944
DD-593	KILLEN	1944	DD-465	SAUFLEY	1942
DD-521	KIMBERLY	1943	DD-501	SCHROEDER	1943

FLETCHER Class (*cont'd*)

No.	Name	Comm.	No.	Name	Comm.
DD-596	SHIELDS	1945	DD-530	TRATHEN	1943
DD-643	SIGOURNEY	1943	DD-591	*TWIGGS	1943
DD-502	SIGSBEE	1943	DD-540	TWINING	1943
DD-565	SMALLEY	1944	DD-687	UHLMANN	1943
DD-512	*SPENCE	1943	DD-656	VAN VALKENBURGH	1944
DD-577	SPROSTON	1943	DD-689	WADLEIGH	1943
DD-478	STANLY	1942	DD-516	WADSWORTH	1943
DD-644	STEMBEL	1943	DD-517	WALKER	1943
DD-538	STEPHEN POTTER	1943	DD-466	WALLER	1942
DD-479	STEVENS	1943	DD-567	WATTS	1944
DD-683	STOCKHAM	1944	DD-684	WEDDERBURN	1944
DD-566	STODDARD	1944	DD-578	WICKES	1943
DD-467	*STRONG	1942	DD-597	WILEY	1945
DD-468	TAYLOR	1942	DD-579	*WILLIAM D. PORTER	1943
DD-513	TERRY	1943	DD-568	WREN	1944
DD-514	THATCHER	1943	DD-541	YARNALL	1943
DD-537	THE SULLIVANS	1943	DD-580	YOUNG	1943
DD-539	TINGEY	1943			

Builders: Federal, Kearny (DD 445–448, 465–466, 498–502, 659–661, 666–680); Bath (DD 449–451, 467–469, 507–517, 629–631, 642–644, 650–653, 688–691); Bethlehem, Staten I. (DD 470–471, 518–522, 657–658, 685–687, 796–798); Boston Navy Yard (DD 472–476, 581–586, 662–664); Charleston Navy Yard (DD 477–479, 587–591, 649, 665); Puget Sound Navy Yard (DD 480–481, 592–597); Bethlehem, San Francisco (DD 526–541, 683–684); Bethlehem, San Pedro (DD 544–547, 681–682, 792–795); Gulf S. B. Corp., Chickasaw (DD 550–553, 654–656); Seattle-Tacoma S. B. Corp., Seattle (DD 554–568, 799–803); and Consolidated Steel Corp., Orange, Tex. (DD 569–580).

ALLEN M. SUMNER Class

2200 tons; length 376′–376′6″; beam 40′–41′1″; draft 15′8″; speed 34 kts.; armament 6-5″/38 5-10 21″ torpedo tubes; complement 345.

No.	Name	Comm.	No.	Name	Comm.
DD-752	ALFRED A. CUNNINGHAM	1944	DD-727	DE HAVEN	1944
DD-692	ALLEN M. SUMNER	1944	DD-779	DOUGLAS H. FOX	1944
DD-698	AULT	1944	DD-741	*DREXLER	1944
DD-722	BARTON	1943	DD-696	ENGLISH	1944
DD-756	BEATTY	1945	DD-754	FRANK E. EVANS	1945
DD-744	BLUE	1944	DD-706	GAINARD	1944
DD-704	BORIE	1944	DD-702	HANK	1944
DD-857	BRISTOL	1945	DD-708	HARLAN R. DICKSON	1945
DD-745	BRUSH	1944	DD-748	HARRY E. HUBBARD	1944
DD-697	CHARLES S. SPERRY	1944	DD-700	HAYNSWORTH	1944
DD-730	COLLETT	1944	DD-709	HUGH PURVIS	1945
DD-705	COMPTON	1944	DD-774	HUGH W. HADLEY	1944
DD-695	*COOPER	1944	DD-732	HYMAN	1944
			DD-694	INGRAHAM	1944

ALLEN M. SUMNER Class (*cont'd*)

No.	Name	Comm.	No.	Name	Comm.
DD-776	JAMES C. OWENS	1945	DD-734	PURDY	1944
DD-755	JOHN A. BOLE	1945	DD-757	PUTNAM	1944
DD-753	JOHN R. PIERCE	1944	DD-781	ROBERT K. HUNTING-	
DD-701	JOHN W. WEEKS	1944		TON	1945
DD-724	LAFFEY	1944	DD-747	SAMUEL N. MOORE	1944
DD-759	LOFBERG	1945	DD-707	SOLEY	1944
DD-770	LOWREY	1944	DD-780	STORMES	1945
DD-729	LYMAN K. SWENSON	1944	DD-758	STRONG	1945
DD-731	MADDOX	1944	DD-746	TAUSSIG	1944
DD-733	*MANNERT L. ABELE	1944	DD-699	WALDRON	1944
DD-728	MANSFIELD	1944	DD-723	WALKE	1944
DD-778	MASSEY	1944	DD-703	WALLACE L. LIND	1944
DD-726	*MEREDITH	1944	DD-775	WILLARD KEITH	1944
DD-693	MOALE	1944	DD-777	ZELLARS	1944
DD-725	O'BRIEN	1944			

Builders: Federal, Kearny (DD 692–709); Bath (DD 722–734, 741); Bethlehem, Staten I. (DD 744–748, 752–756); Bethlehem, San Francisco (DD 757–759); Bethlehem, San Pedro (DD 770, 774–776, 857); and Todd-Pacific Shipyards, Inc., Seattle (DD 777–781).

Twelve sisters converted to destroyer-minelayers while building.

GEARING Class

2425 tons; length 390'2"–391'; beam 40'10"–41'2"; draft 18'6"; speed 35 kts.; armament 6–5"/38 5–10 21" torpedo tubes; complement 355.

No.	Name	Comm.	No.	Name	Comm.
DD-807	BENNER	1945	DD-712	GYATT	1945
DD-881	BORDELON	1945	DD-832	HANSON	1945
DD-835	CHARLES P. CECIL	1945	DD-864	HAROLD J. ELLISON	1945
DD-865	CHARLES R. WARE	1945	DD-873	HAWKINS	1945
DD-805	CHEVALIER	1945	DD-785	HENDERSON	1945
DD-866	CONE	1945	DD-875	HENRY W. TUCKER	1945
DD-808	DENNIS J. BUCKLEY	1945	DD-833	HERBERT J. THOMAS	1945
DD-874	DUNCAN	1945	DD-806	HIGBEE	1945
DD-880	DYESS	1945	DD-885	JOHN R. CRAIG	1945
DD-838	ERNEST G. SMALL	1945	DD-713	KENNETH D. BAILEY	1945
DD-711	EUGENE A. GREENE	1945	DD-879	LEARY	1945
DD-830	EVERETT R. LARSON	1945	DD-860	MC CAFFERY	1945
DD-884	FLOYD B. PARKS	1945	DD-784	MC KEAN	1945
DD-742	FRANK KNOX	1944	DD-829	MYLES C. FOX	1945
DD-858	FRED T. BARRY	1945	DD-883	NEWMAN K. PERRY	1945
DD-882	FURSE	1945	DD-859	NORRIS	1945
DD-710	GEARING	1945	DD-877	PERKINS	1945
DD-836	GEORGE K. MAC KENZIE	1945	DD-876	RODGERS	1945
DD-831	GOODRICH	1945	DD-782	ROWAN	1945
DD-783	GURKE	1945	DD-837	SARSFIELD	1945

GEARING Class (*cont'd*)

No.	Name	Comm.	No.	Name	Comm.
DD-743	SOUTHERLAND	1944	DD-878	VESOLE	1945
DD-863	STEINAKER	1945	DD-862	VOGELSGESANG	1945
DD-834	TURNER	1945			

Builders: Federal, Newark (DD 710–713); Bath (DD 742–743, 805–808, 829–838); Todd-Pacific, Seattle (DD 782–785); Bethlehem, San Pedro (DD 858–860); Bethlehem, Staten I. (DD 862–866); and Consolidated Steel, Orange (DD 873–885).

5. DE DESTROYER ESCORTS

EVARTS Class

1140 tons; length 289'5"; beam 35'1"; draft 11'10"; speed 21 kts.; armament 3-3"/50; complement 198; diesel engines with electric drive.

No.	Name	Comm.	No.	Name	Comm.
DE-45	ANDRES	1943	DE-35	FAIR	1943
DE-15	AUSTIN	1943	DE-307	FINNEGAN	1944
DE-10	BEBAS	1943	DE-32	FLEMING	1943
DE-41	BRACKETT	1943	DE-18	GILMORE	1943
DE-13	BRENNAN	1943	DE-37	GREINER	1943
DE-19	BURDEN R. HASTINGS	1943	DE-7	GRISWOLD	1943
DE-260	CABANA	1943	DE-305	HALLORAN	1944
DE-262	CANFIELD	1943	DE-21	HAROLD C. THOMAS	1943
DE-9	CARLSON	1943	DE-528	JOHN J. POWERS	1944
DE-23	CHARLES R. GREER	1943	DE-530	JOHN M.	
DE-265	CLOUES	1943		BERMINGHAM	1944
DE-306	CONNOLLY	1944	DE-301	LAKE	1944
DE-11	CROUTER	1943	DE-20	LE HARDY	1943
DE-303	CROWLEY	1944	DE-39	LOVERING	1943
DE-47	DECKER [22]	1943	DE-302	LYMAN	1944
DE-263	DEEDE	1943	DE-36	MANLOVE	1943
DE-26	DEMPSEY	1943	DE-30	MARTIN	1943
DE-261	DIONNE	1943	DE-529	MASON	1944
DE-48	DOBLER	1943	DE-43	MITCHELL	1943
DE-14	DOHERTY	1943	DE-527	O'TOOLE	1944
DE-44	DONALDSON	1943	DE-304	RALL	1944
DE-49	DONEFF	1943	DE-42	REYNOLDS	1943
DE-27	DUFFY	1943	DE-40	SANDERS	1943
DE-16	EDGAR G. CHASE	1943	DE-31	SEDERSTROM	1943
DE-17	EDWARD C. DALY	1943	DE-256	SEID	1943
DE-34	EISELE	1943	DE-257	SMARTT	1943
DE-264	ELDEN	1943	DE-29	STADTFELD	1943
DE-28	EMERY	1943	DE-8	STEELE	1943
DE-50	ENGSTROM	1943	DE-33	TISDALE	1943
DE-5	EVARTS	1943	DE-258	WALTER S. BROWN	1943

[22] Transferred to China under Lend-Lease.

EVARTS Class (*cont'd*)

No.	Name	Comm.	No.	Name	Comm.
DE–24	WHITMAN	1943	DE–25	WINTLE	1943
DE–22	WILEMAN	1943	DE–6	WYFFELS [22]	1943
DE–259	WILLIAM C. MILLER	1943	DE–38	WYMAN	1943

Builders: Boston Navy Yard (DE 5–11, 256–265, 527–530); Mare Island Navy Yard (DE 13–36, 301–307); Philadelphia Navy Yard (DE 45, 47–50); Puget Sound Navy Yard (DE 37–44).

[22] Transferred to China under Lend-Lease.

RUDDEROW Class

1450 tons; length 306'; beam 36'10"; draft 13'9"; speed 24 kts.; armament 2–5"/38 3–21" torpedo tubes; complement 221; turbines with electric drive.

No.	Name	Comm.	No.	Name	Comm.
DE–709	BRAY [23]	1944	DE–707	JOBB	1944
DE–230	CHAFFEE	1944	DE–580	LESLIE L. B. KNOX	1944
DE–584	CHARLES J. KIMMEL	1944	DE–586	LOUGH	1944
DE–685	COATES	1944	DE–581	MC NULTY	
DE–585	DANIEL A. JOY	1944	DE–582	MERTIVIER	1944
DE–225	DAY	1944	DE–708	PARLE	1944
DE–684	DE LONG [23]	1943	DE–588	PEIFFER	1944
DE–686	EUGENE E. ELMORE	1944	DE–579	RILEY	1944
DE–583	GEORGE A. JOHNSON	1944	DE–224	RUDDEROW	1944
DE–231	HODGES	1944	DE–587	THOMAS F. NICKEL	1944
DE–706	HOLT	1944	DE–489	TINSMAN	1944

Builders: Bethlehem-Hingham (DE 579–589); Bethlehem, Quincy (DE 684–686); Charleston Navy Yard (DE 230–231); Defoe Shipbuilding Co. (DE 706–709); Philadelphia Navy Yard (DE 224–225).

[23] Converted to high-speed transport (APD).

JOHN C. BUTLER Class

1350 tons; length 306'; beam 36'8"; draft 13'4"; speed 24 kts.; armament 2–5"/38 3–21 torpedo tubes; complement 222.

No.	Name	Comm.	No.	Name	Comm.
DE–343	ABERCROMBIE	1944	DE–531	EDWARD H. ALLEN	1943
DE–447	ALBERT T. HARRIS	1944	DE–346	EDWIN A. HOWARD	1944
DE–366	ALVIN C. COCKRELL	1944	DE–404	*EVERSOLE	1944
DE–536	BIVIN	1944	DE–509	FORMOE	1944
DE–368	CECIL J. DOYLE	1944	DE–367	FRENCH	1944
DE–446	CHARLES E. BRANNON	1944	DE–349	GENTRY	1944
DE–421	CHESTER T. O'BRIEN	1944	DE–357	GEORGE E. DAVIS	1944
DE–439	CONKLIN	1944	DE–508	GILLIGAN	1944
DE–438	CORBESIER	1944	DE–444	GOSS	1944
DE–448	CROSS	1945	DE–445	GRADY	1944
DE–405	DENNIS	1944	DE–424	HAAS	1944
DE–422	DOUGLAS A. MUNRO	1944	DE–449	HANNA	1945
DE–353	DOYLE C. BARNES	1944	DE–510	HEYLIGER	1945
DE–423	DUFILHO	1944	DE–533	HOWARD F. CLARK	1944
DE–406	EDMONDS	1944	DE–355	JACCARD	1944

JOHN C. BUTLER Class (*cont'd*)

No.	Name	Comm.	No.	Name	Comm.
DE-410	JACK MILLER	1944	DE-371	PRESLEY	1944
DE-347	JESSE RUTHERFORD	1944	DE-341	RAYMOND	1944
DE-339	JOHN C. BUTLER	1944	DE-403	RICHARD M. ROWELL	1944
DE-370	JOHN L. WILLIAMSON	1944	DE-402	RICHARD S. BULL	1944
DE-360	JOHNNIE HUTCHINS	1944	DE-342	RICHARD W. SUESENS	1944
DE-450	JOSEPH E. CONNOLLY	1945	DE-537	RIZZI	1945
DE-443	KENDALL C. CAMPBELL	1944	DE-345	ROBERT BRAZIER	1944
DE-354	KENNETH M. WILLETT	1944	DE-419	ROBERT F. KELLER	1944
DE-348	KEY	1944	DE-362	ROLF	1944
DE-409	LA PRADE	1944	DE-364	ROMBACH	1944
DE-415	LAWRENCE C. TAYLOR	1944	DE-413	*SAMUEL B. ROBERTS	1944
DE-414	LE RAY WILSON	1944	DE-407	*SHELTON	1944
DE-420	LELAND E. THOMAS	1944	DE-534	SILVERSTEIN	1944
DE-535	LEWIS	1944	DE-411	STAFFORD	1944
DE-356	LLOYD E. ACREE	1944	DE-408	STRAUS	1944
DE-358	MACK	1944	DE-418	TABBERER	1944
DE-351	MAURICE J. MANUEL	1944	DE-369	THADDEUS PARKER	1944
DE-440	MC COY REYNOLDS	1944	DE-350	TRAW	1944
DE-365	MC GINTY	1944	DE-532	TWEEDY	1944
DE-416	MELVIN R. NAWMAN	1944	DE-442	ULVERT M. MOORE	1944
DE-352	NAIFEH	1944	DE-412	WALTER C. WANN	1944
DE-344	*OBERRENDER	1944	DE-361	WALTON	1944
DE-340	O'FLAHERTY	1944	DE-441	WILLIAM SEIVERLING	1944
DE-417	OLIVER MITCHELL	1944	DE-372	WILLIAMS	1944
DE-538	OSBERG	1945	DE-359	WOODSON	1944
DE-363	PRATT	1944			

Builders: Boston Navy Yard (DE 521–538); Consolidated Steel, Orange, Tex. (DE 339–372); Brown Shipbuilding Co., Houston (DE 402–424); Federal, Newark (DE 438–450, 508–510).

BUCKLEY Class

1400 tons; length 306'; beam 36'10"; draft 13'6"; speed 23 kts.; armament 3–3"/50 or 2–5"/38 3–21" torpedo tubes; complement 213; turbines with electric drive.

DE-575	AHRENS	1944	DE-215	BURKE [24]	1943
DE-577	ALEXANDER J. LUKE	1944	DE-53	CHARLES LAWRENCE [24]	1943
DE-66	AMESBURY [24]	1943	DE-158	CHASE [24]	1943
DE-161	BARBER [24]	1943	DE-208	COFER [24]	1944
DE-576	BARR [24]	1944	DE-217	COOLBAUGH	1943
DE-68	BATES [24]	1943	DE-704	CRONIN	1944
DE-69	BLESSMAN [24]	1943	DE-700	CURRIER	1944
DE-790	BORUM	1943	DE-643	DAMON M. CUMMINGS	1944
DE-637	BOWERS [24]	1944	DE-54	DANIEL T. GRIFFIN [24]	1943
DE-51	BUCKLEY	1943	DE-218	DARBY	1943
DE-693	BULL [24]	1943	DE-56	DONNELL [25]	1943
DE-694	BUNCH [24]	1943	DE-666	DURIK	1944

[24] Converted to high-speed transport (APD).
[25] Reclassified unclassified auxiliary (IX).

BUCKLEY Class (*cont'd*)

No.	Name	Comm.	No.	Name	Comm.
DE–702	EARL V. JOHNSON	1944	DE–209	LLOYD [24]	1944
DE–202	EICHENBERGER	1943	DE–680	LOESER	1943
DE–635	ENGLAND [24]	1943	DE–198	LOVELACE	1943
DE–216	ENRIGHT [24]	1943	DE–160	LOY [24]	1943
DE–157	*FECHTELER	1944	DE–796	MAJOR	1944
DE–640	FIEBERLING	1944	DE–791	MALOY	1943
DE–57	FOGG	1943	DE–199	MANNING	1943
DE–633	FOREMAN	1943	DE–699	MARSH	1944
DE–59	FOSS	1943	DE–200	NEUENDORFF	1943
DE–222	FOWLER	1944	DE–205	NEWMAN [24]	1943
DE–677	FRAMENT [24]	1943	DE–701	OSMUS	1944
DE–220	FRANCIS M. ROBINSON	1944	DE–210	OTTER	1944
DE–705	FRYBARGER	1944	DE–642	PAUL G. BAKER	1944
DE–60	GANTNER [24]	1943	DE–698	RABY	1943
DE–639	GENDREAU	1943	DE–156	REEVES [24]	1943
DE–697	GEORGE	1943	DE–153	REUBEN JAMES	1943
DE–62	GEORGE W. INGRAM [24]	1943	DE–695	*RICH	1943
DE–681	GILLETTE	1943	DE–578	ROBERT I. PAINE	1944
DE–679	GREENWOOD	1943	DE–793	RUNELS [24]	1944
DE–795	GUNASON	1944	DE–676	SCHMITT [24]	1943
DE–792	HAINES [24]	1943	DE–214	SCOTT	1943
DE–678	HARMON	1943	DE–799	SCROGGINS	1944
DE–212	HAYTER [24]	1944	DE–154	SIMS [24]	1943
DE–683	HENRY R. KENYON	1943	DE–221	SOLAR	1944
DE–794	HOLLIS [24]	1944	DE–223	SPANGENBURG	1944
DE–703	HOLTON	1944	DE–696	SPANGLER	1943
DE–155	HOPPING [24]	1943	DE–789	TATUM [24]	1943
DE–211	HUBBARD [24]	1944	DE–203	THOMASON	1943
DE–63	IRA JEFFERY [24]	1943	DE–682	*UNDERHILL	1943
DE–219	J. DOUGLAS BLACK-		DE–644	VAMMEN	1944
	WOOD	1943	DE–798	VARIAN	1944
DE–800	JACK W. WILKE	1944	DE–675	WEBER [24]	1943
DE–201	JAMES E. CRAIG	1943	DE–797	WEEDEN	1944
DE–665	JENKS	1944	DE–634	WHITEHURST	1943
DE–204	JORDAN	1943	DE–641	WILLIAM C. COLE	1944
DE–70	JOSEPH E. CAMPBELL [24]	1943	DE–213	WILLIAM T. POWELL	1944
DE–207	KEPHART [24]	1944	DE–638	WILLMARTH	1944
DE–159	LANING [24]	1943	DE–667	WISEMAN	1944
DE–65	LEE FOX	1943	DE 636	WITTER [24]	1943
DE–206	LIDDLE	1943			

Builders: Bethlehem-Hingham (DE 51, 53–54, 56–57, 59–60, 62–63, 65–66, 68–70, 575–578); Bethlehem, Quincy (DE 675–683); Bethlehem, San Francisco (DE 633–644); Charleston Navy Yard (DE 199–213); Consolidated Steel, Orange (DE 789–800); Defoe S. B. Co. (DE 693–705); Dravo Corp., Pittsburgh (DE 665–667); Norfolk Navy Yard (DE 153–161); Philadelphia Navy Yard (DE 214–223).

[24] Converted to high-speed transport (APD).

EDSALL Class

1200 tons; length 306'; beam 36'7"; draft 12'3"; speed 21 kts.; armament 3-3"/50 3-21" torpedo tubes; complement 216; diesel engines.

No.	Name	Comm.	No.	Name	Comm.
DE-147	BLAIR	1943	DE-319	*LEOPOLD	1943
DE-327	BRISTER	1943	DE-325	LOWE	1943
DE-148	BROUGH	1943	DE-249	MARCHAND	1943
DE-390	CALCATERRA	1943	DE-338	MARTIN H. RAY	1944
DE-251	CAMP	1943	DE-320	MENGES	1943
DE-391	CHAMBERS	1943	DE-392	MERRILL	1943
DE-149	CHATELAIN	1943	DE-383	MILLS	1943
DE-398	COCKRILL	1943	DE-240	MOORE	1943
DE-337	DALE W. PETERSON	1944	DE-321	MOSLEY	1943
DE-335	DANIEL	1944	DE-150	NEUNZER	1943
DE-138	DOUGLAS L. HOWARD	1943	DE-322	NEWELL	1943
DE-389	DURANT	1943	DE-330	O'REILLY	1943
DE-129	EDSALL	1943	DE-244	OTTERSTETTER	1943
DE-324	FALGOUT	1943	DE-152	PETERSON	1943
DE-139	FARQUHAR	1943	DE-253	PETTIT	1943
DE-142	FESSENDEN	1943	DE-133	PILLSBURY	1943
DE-328	FINCH	1943	DE-151	POOLE	1943
DE-143	*FISKE	1943	DE-134	POPE	1943
DE-135	FLAHERTY	1943	DE-332	PRICE	1944
DE-334	FORSTER	1944	DE-323	PRIDE	1943
DE-136	*FREDERICK C. DAVIS	1943	DE-382	RAMSDEN	1943
DE-144	FROST	1943	DE-384	RHODES	1943
DE-131	HAMMANN	1943	DE-385	RICHEY	1943
DE-316	HARVESON	1943	DE-254	RICKETTS	1943
DE-393	HAVERFIELD	1943	DE-132	ROBERT E. PEARY	1943
DE-137	HERBERT C. JONES	1943	DE-336	ROY O. HALE	1944
DE-141	HILL	1943	DE-386	SAVAGE	1943
DE-400	HISSEM	1944	DE-255	SELLSTROM	1943
DE-401	*HOLDER	1944	DE-245	SLOAT	1943
DE-252	HOWARD D. CROW	1943	DE-246	SNOWDEN	1943
DE-250	HURST	1943	DE-247	STANTON	1943
DE-145	HUSE	1943	DE-238	STEWART	1943
DE-146	INCH	1943	DE-399	STOCKDALE	1943
DE-140	J. R. Y. BLAKELY	1943	DE-333	STRICKLAND	1944
DE-243	J. RICHARD WARD	1943	DE-239	STURTEVANT	1943
DE-130	JACOB JONES	1943	DE-248	SWASEY	1943
DE-396	JANSSEN	1943	DE-394	SWENNING	1943
DE-317	JOYCE	1943	DE-326	THOMAS J. GARY	1943
DE-241	KEITH	1943	DE-242	TOMICH	1943
DE-318	KIRKPATRICK	1943	DE-387	VANCE	1943
DE-331	KOINER	1943	DE-397	WILHOITE	1943
DE-329	KRETCHMER	1943	DE-395	WILLIS	1943
DE-388	LANSING	1943			

Builders: Brown S. B. Co., Houston (DE 238-255, 382-401); Consolidated Steel Corp., Orange, Tex. (DE 129-152, 316-338).

CANNON Class

1240 tons; length 306'; beam 36'8"; draft 11'8"; speed 21 kts.; armament 3-3"/50 3-21" torpedo tubes; complement 216; diesel engines with electric drive.

No.	Name	Comm.	No.	Name	Comm.
DE–167	ACREE	1943	DE–162	LEVY	1943
DE–101	ALGER 26	1943	DE–750	MCANN 26	1943
DE–168	AMICK	1943	DE–750	MCCLELLAND	1944
DE–169	ATHERTON	1943	DE–163	MCCONNELL	1943
DE–190	BAKER	1943	DE–174	MARTS	1943
DE–739	BANGUST	1943	DE–176	MICKA	1943
DE–166	BARON	1943	DE–770	MUIR	1944
DE–170	BOOTH	1943	DE–769	NEAL A. SCOTT	1944
DE–103	BOSTWICK	1943	DE–188	O'NEILL	1943
DE–104	BREEMAN	1943	DE–164	OSTERHAUS	1943
DE–747	BRIGHT	1944	DE–767	OSWALD	1944
DE–189	BRONSTEIN	1943	DE–165	PARKS	1943
DE–105	BURROWS	1943	DE–175	PENNEWILL 26	1943
DE–99	CANNON 26	1943	DE–177	REYBOLD 26	1943
DE–171	CARROLL	1943	DE–185	RIDDLE	1943
DE–112	CARTER	1944	DE–196	RINEHART	1944
DE–763	CATES	1943	DE–749	ROBERTS	1944
DE–100	CHRISTOPHER 26	1943	DE–197	ROCHE	1944
DE–113	CLARENCE L. EVANS	1944	DE–183	SAMUEL S. MILES	1943
DE–191	COFFMAN	1943	DE–766	SLATER	1944
DE–172	COONER	1943	DE–745	SNYDER	1944
DE–765	EARL K. OLSEN	1944	DE–181	STAUB	1943
DE–768	EBERT	1944	DE–187	STERN	1943
DE–192	EISNER	1944	DE–771	SUTTON	1944
DE–173	ELDRIDGE	1943	DE–186	SWEARER	1943
DE–764	GANDY	1944	DE–102	THOMAS	1943
DE–193	GARFIELD THOMAS	1944	DE–195	THORNHILL	1944
DE–182	GUSTAFSON	1943	DE–748	TILLS	1944
DE–746	HEMMINGER	1944	DS–180	TRUMPETER	1943
DE–178	HERZOG 26	1943	DE–740	WATERMAN	1943
DE–742	HILBERT	1944	DE–741	WEAVER	1943
DE–744	KYNE	1944	DE–184	WESSON	1943
DE–743	LAMONS	1944	DE–194	WINGFIELD	1944

Builders: Dravo Corp., Wilmington (DE 99–105, 112–113); Federal, Newark (DE 162–197); Tampa S. B. Co. (DE 763–771); Western Pipe and Steel Co., San Pedro (DE 739–750).

26 Transferred to Brazil under Lend-Lease.

6. SS SUBMARINES

O Class

521/624 tons; [27] length 172'4"; beam 18'; draft 16'11"; speed 14.5/11 kts.; armament 4–18" torpedo tubes; complement 33; diesel engines/electric motors.

No.	Name	Comm.	No.	Name	Comm.
SS–63	O–2	1918	SS–68	O–7	1918
SS–64	O–3	1918	SS–69	O–8	1918
SS–65	O–4	1918	SS–70	†O–9	1918
SS–67	O–6	1918	SS–71	O–10	1918

Builders: Fore River S. B. Co. (SS 64–65, 67–71); Puget Sound Navy Yard (SS 63).

[27] Surface/submerged.

R Class

530/680 tons; length 186'2"; beam 18'; draft 16'7"; speed 13.5/10.5 kts.; armament 1–3"/50 4–18" torpedo tubes; complement 34; diesel engines/electric motors.

No.	Name	Comm.	No.	Name	Comm.
SS–78	R–1	1918	SS–89	*R–12	1919
SS–79	R–2	1919	SS–90	R–13	1919
SS–80	R–3 [28]	1919	SS–91	R–14	1919
SS–81	R–4	1919	SS–92	R–15	1918
SS–82	R–5	1919	SS–93	R–16	1918
SS–83	R–6	1919	SS–94	R–17 [28]	1918
SS–85	R–8	1919	SS–95	R–18	1918
SS–86	R–9	1919	SS–96	R–19 [28]	1918
SS–87	R–10	1919	SS–97	R–20	1919
SS–88	R–11	1919			

Builders: Fore River S. B. Co. (SS 78–84, 86–91); Union Iron Works (SS 92–97).

[28] Transferred to Great Britain under Lend-Lease.

S–1 Class

850/1062 tons; length 219'3"; beam 20'8"; draft 17'1"; speed 14.5/11 kts.; armament 1–3"/50 or 1–4"/50 4–21" torpedo tubes; complement 50; diesel engines/electric motors.

No.	Name	Comm.	No.	Name	Comm.
SS–105	S–1 [29]	1920	SS–132	*S–27	1924
SS–123	S–18	1924	SS–133	*S–28	1923
SS–125	S–20	1922	SS–134	S–29 [29]	1924
SS–126	S–21 [29]	1923	SS–135	S–30	1920
SS–127	S–22 [29]	1924	SS–136	S–31	1923
SS–128	S–23	1923	SS–137	S–32	1923
SS–129	S–24 [29]	1923	SS–138	S–33	1922
SS–130	S–25 [29]	1923	SS–139	S–34	1923
SS–131	*S–26	1923	SS–140	S–35	1923

[29] Transferred to Great Britain under Lend-Lease.

S–1 Class (*cont'd*)

No.	Name	Comm.	No.	Name	Comm.
SS–141	*S–36	1923	SS–144	*S–39	1923
SS–142	S–37	1923	SS–145	S–40	1923
SS–143	†S–38	1923	SS–146	S–41	1924

Builders: Bethlehem, Quincy (SS 105, 123, 125–134); Bethlehem, San Francisco (SS 135–146).

²⁹ *S–1* Class transferred to Great Britain under Lend-Lease.

S–14 Class

876/1092 tons; length 231′; beam 21′10″; draft 15′; speed 15/10.5 kts.; armament 1–4″/50 4–21″ torpedo tubes; complement 44; diesel engines/electric motors.

No.	Name	Comm.	No.	Name	Comm.
SS–119	S–14	1921	SS–121	†S–16	1920
SS–120	S–15	1921	SS–122	†S–17	1921

Builders: Lake Torpedo Boat Co., Bridgeport, Conn.

S–3 Class

790/1092 tons; length 231′; beam 21′6″; draft 14′9″; speed 15/11 kts.; armament 1–4″/50 5–21″ torpedo tubes; complement 44; diesel engines/electric motors.

No.	Name	Comm.	No.	Name	Comm.
SS–116	S–11	1923	SS–118	S–13	1923
SS–117	S–12	1923			

Builders: Portsmouth Navy Yard.

S–48

1000/1458 tons; length 240′; beam 21′6″; draft 14′5″; speed 14.5/11 kts.; armament 1–4″/50 5–21″ torpedo tubes; complement 51; diesel engines/electric motors.

No.	Name	Comm.
SS–159	S–48	1922

Builders: Lake Torpedo Boat Co., Bridgeport, Conn.

S–42 Class

850/1126 tons; length 225′3″; beam 20′8″; draft 19′5″; speed 14.5/11 kts.; armament 1–4″/50 4–21″ torpedo tubes; complement 51; diesel engines/electric motors.

No.	Name	Comm.	No.	Name	Comm.
SS–153	S–42	1924	SS–156	S–45	1925
SS–154	S–43	1924	SS–157	S–46	1925
SS–155	*S–44	1925	SS–158	S–47	1925

Builders: Bethlehem, Quincy.

B Class

2000/2506 tons; length 341′6″; beam 27′1″; draft 14′7″; speed 19/8 kts.; armament 1–3″/50 6–21″ torpedo tubes; complement 95; diesel engines/electric motors.

No.	Name	Comm.	No.	Name	Comm.
SS–163	BARRACUDA	1924	SS–165	BONITA	1926
SS–164	†BASS	1925			

Builders: Portsmouth Navy Yard.

ARGONAUT

2710/4164 tons; length 381'; beam 33'10"; draft 15'4"; speed 15/8 kts.; armament 2-6"/53 4-21" torpedo tubes; complement 89; diesel engines/electric motors.

No.	Name	Comm.	No.	Name	Comm.
SM-1	ARGONAUT [30]	1928			

Builders: Portsmouth Navy Yard.

[30] Converted to submarine transport (APS).

NAUTILUS Class

2730/3960 tons; length 371'; beam 33'3"; draft 19'7"; speed 17/8 kts.; armament 2-6"/53 10-21" torpedo tubes; complement 100; diesel engines/electric motors.

No.	Name	Comm.	No.	Name	Comm.
SS-167	NARWHAL	1930	SS-168	NAUTILUS	1930

Builders: Portsmouth Navy Yard (SS-167); Mare Island Navy Yard (SS-168).

DOLPHIN

1590/2215 tons; length 319'1"; beam 27'11"; draft 16'6"; speed 17/8 kts.; armament 1-4"/50 6-21" torpedo tubes; complement 77; diesel engines/electric motors.

No.	Name	Comm.
SS-169	DOLPHIN	1932

Builders: Portsmouth Navy Yard.

CACHALOT Class

1110-1130/1650 tons; length 271'10"-274'; beam 24'9"; draft 16'3"; speed 16/8 kts.; armament 1-3"/50 6-21" torpedo tubes; complement 55; diesel engines/electric motors.

No.	Name	Comm.	No.	Name	Comm.
SS-170	CACHALOT	1933	SS-171	CUTTLEFISH	1934

Builders: Portsmouth Navy Yard (SS-170); Electric Boat (SS-171).

PORPOISE Class

1316-1330/1934-1997 tons; length 298'1"-301'; beam 24'11"-25'1"; draft 15'11"-16'11"; speed 19-19.5/8-9 kts.; armament 1-3"/50 6-21" torpedo tubes; complement 73; diesel engines/electric motors.

No.	Name	Comm.	No.	Name	Comm.
SS-176	*PERCH	1936	SS-180	POLLACK	1937
SS-178	PERMIT	1937	SS-181	*POMPANO	1937
SS-177	*PICKEREL	1937	SS-172	PORPOISE	1935
SS-173	PIKE	1935	SS-174	*SHARK	1936
SS-179	PLUNGER	1936	SS-175	TARPON	1936

Builders: Portsmouth Navy Yard (SS 172-173, 179-180); Electric Boat (SS 174-178); Mare Island Navy Yard (SS-181).

SALMON Class

1449/2198 tons; length 308'; beam 26'1"; draft 17'6"-17'7"; speed 21/9 kts.; armament 1-3"/50 8-21" torpedo tubes; complement 75; diesel engines/electric motors.

No.	Name	Comm.	No.	Name	Comm.
SS-182	SALMON	1938	SS-185	SNAPPER	1937
SS-183	SEAL	1938	SS-186	STINGRAY	1938
SS-184	SKIPJACK	1938	SS-187	STURGEON	1938

Builders: Electric Boat (SS 182-184); Portsmouth Navy Yard (SS 185-186); Mare Island Navy Yard (SS-187).

SARGO Class

1450/2350 tons; length 310'6"; beam 27'1"; draft 17'1"–17'3"; speed 20/9 kts.; armament 1–3"/50 8–21" torpedo tubes; complement 78; diesel engines/electric motors.

No.	Name	Comm.	No.	Name	Comm.
SS–192	SAILFISH [31]	1939	SS–195	*SEALION	1939
SS–188	SARGO	1939	SS–196	SEARAVEN	1939
SS–189	SAURY	1939	SS–197	*SEAWOLF	1939
SS–191	*SCULPIN	1939	SS–190	SPEARFISH	1939
SS–194	SEADRAGON	1939	SS–193	*SWORDFISH	1939

Builders: Electric Boat (SS 188–190, 194–195); Portsmouth Navy Yard (SS 191–192, 196–197); Mare Island Navy Yard (SS–193).

[31] Ex-SQUALUS.

TAMBOR Class

1475/2370 tons; length 307'2"; beam 27'3"; draft 16'9"–17'; speed 20/9 kts.; armament 1–3"/50 10–21" torpedo tubes; complement 80; diesel engines/electric motors.

No.	Name	Comm.	No.	Name	Comm.
SS–206	GAR	1941	SS–198	TAMBOR	1940
SS–207	*GRAMPUS	1941	SS–199	TAUTOG	1940
SS–208	*GRAYBACK	1941	SS–200	THRESHER	1940
SS–209	*GRAYLING	1941	SS–201	*TRITON	1940
SS–210	*GRENADIER	1941	SS–202	*TROUT	1940
SS–211	*GUDGEON	1941	SS–203	TUNA	1941

Builders: Electric Boat (SS 198–200, 206–208); Portsmouth Navy Yard (SS 201–202, 209–210); Mare Island Navy Yard (SS 203, 211).

MACKEREL Class

825/1179 tons; length 238'11"; beam 21'8"; draft 13'6"–14'6"; speed 16/9 kts.; armament 1–3"/50 6–21" torpedo tubes; complement 42; diesel engines/electric motors.

No.	Name	Comm.	No.	Name	Comm.
SS–204	MACKEREL	1941	SS–205	MARLIN	1941

Builders: Electric Boat (SS–204); Portsmouth Navy Yard (SS–205).

GATO Class

1526/2424 tons; length 311'8"–311'10"; beam 27'3"; draft 16'10"; speed 20/9 kts.; armament 1–3"/50, 1–4"/50, or 1–5"/23 10–21" torpedo tubes; complement 80; diesel engines/electric motors.

No.	Name	Comm.	No.	Name	Comm.
SS–218	*ALBACORE	1942	SS–225	CERO	1943
SS–219	*AMBERJACK	1942	SS–245	COBIA	1944
SS–240	ANGLER	1943	SS–224	COD	1943
SS–220	BARB	1942	SS–226	*CORVINA	1943
SS–241	BASHAW	1943	SS–246	CROAKER	1944
SS–221	BLACKFISH	1942	SS–247	DACE	1943
SS–222	BLUEFISH	1943	SS–227	*DARTER	1943
SS–242	BLUEGILL	1943	SS–248	*DORADO	1943
SS–223	*BONEFISH	1943	SS–228	DRUM	1941
SS–243	BREAM	1944	SS–230	FINBACK	1942
SS–244	CAVALLA	1944	SS–249	FLASHER	1943

GATO Class (*cont'd*)

No.	Name	Comm.	No.	Name	Comm.
SS–250	*FLIER	1943	SS–265	PETO	1942
SS–251	FLOUNDER	1943	SS–266	POGY	1943
SS–229	FLYING FISH	1941	SS–267	POMPON	1943
SS–252	GABILAN	1943	SS–268	PUFFER	1943
SS–212	GATO	1941	SS–269	RASHER	1943
SS–213	GREENLING	1942	SS–270	RATON	1943
SS–214	GROUPER	1942	SS–271	RAY	1943
SS–215	*GROWLER	1942	SS–272	REDFIN	1943
SS–216	*GUDGEON	1942	SS–273	*ROBALO	1943
SS–217	GUARDFISH	1942	SS–274	ROCK	1943
SS–253	GUNNEL	1942	SS–275	*RUNNER	1942
SS–254	GURNARD	1942	SS–276	SAWFISH	1942
SS–255	HADDO	1942	SS–277	*SCAMP	1942
SS–231	HADDOCK	1942	SS–278	*SCORPION	1942
SS–256	HAKE	1942	SS–235	SHAD	1942
SS–232	HALIBUT	1942	SS–236	SILVERSIDES	1941
SS–257	*HARDER	1942	SS–279	*SNOOK	1942
SS–233	*HERRING	1942	SS–280	STEELHEAD	1942
SS–258	HOE	1942	SS–281	SUNFISH	1942
SS–259	JACK	1943	SS–283	TINOSA	1943
SS–234	KINGFISH	1942	SS–237	*TRIGGER	1942
SS–260	LAPON	1943	SS–284	*TULLIBEE	1943
SS–261	MINGO	1943	SS–282	TUNNY	1942
SS–262	MUSKALLUNGE	1943	SS–238	*WAHOO	1942
SS–263	PADDLE	1943	SS–239	WHALE	1942
SS–264	PARGO	1943			

Builders: Electric Boat (SS 212–227, 240–264); Portsmouth Navy Yard (SS 228–235, 275–280); Mare Island Navy Yard (SS 236–239, 281–284); Manitowoc S. B. Co. (SS 265–274).

BALAO Class

1526/2391–2424 tons; length 311'6"–311'10"; beam 27'3"–27'4"; draft 16'10"; speed 20/10 kts.; armament 1–3"/50, 1–4"/50, or 1–5"/25 10–21" torpedo tubes; complement 80; diesel engines/electric motors.

No.	Name	Comm.	No.	Name	Comm.
SS–308	APOGON	1943	SS–286	BILLFISH	1943
SS–311	ARCHERFISH	1943	SS–322	BLACKFIN	1944
SS–309	ASPERO	1943	SS–324	BLENNY	1944
SS–403	ATULE	1944	SS–325	BLOWER	1944
SS–285	BALAO	1943	SS–326	BLUEBACK	1944
SS–385	BANG	1943	SS–327	BOARFISH	1944
SS–316	*BARBEL	1944	SS–287	BOWFIN	1943
SS–317	BARBERO	1944	SS–330	BRILL	1944
SS–310	BATFISH	1943	SS–331	BUGARA	1944
SS–318	BAYA	1944	SS–332	*BULLHEAD	1944
SS–319	BECUNA	1944	SS–333	BUMPER	1944
SS–320	BERGALL	1944	SS–312	BURRFISH	1943
SS–321	BESUGO	1944	SS–334	CABEZON	1944

BALAO Class (*cont'd*)

No.	Name	Comm.	No.	Name	Comm.
SS–288	CABRILLA	1943	SS–300	MORAY	1945
SS–323	CAIMAN	1944	SS–383	PAMPANITO	1943
SS–289	*CAPELIN	1943	SS–384	PARCHE	1943
SS–336	CAPITAINE	1945	SS–313	PERCH	1944
SS–337	CARBONERO	1945	SS–382	PICUDA	1943
SS–338	CARP	1945	SS–386	PILOTFISH	1943
SS–339	CATFISH	1945	SS–387	PINTADO	1944
SS–328	CHARR	1944	SS–388	PIPEFISH	1944
SS–341	CHIVO	1945	SS–409	PIPER	1944
SS–342	CHOPPER	1945	SS–389	PIRANHA	1944
SS–329	CHUB	1944	SS–390	PLAICE	1944
SS–290	*CISCO	1943	SS–391	POMFRET	1944
SS–343	CLAMAGORE	1945	SS–393	QUEENFISH	1944
SS–344	COBBLER	1945	SS–394	RAZORBACK	1944
SS–345	COCHINO	1945	SS–395	REDFISH	1944
SS–291	CREVALLE	1943	SS–301	RONCADOR	1945
SS–335	DENTUDA	1944	SS–396	RONQUIL	1944
SS–292	DEVILFISH	1944	SS–302	SABALO	1945
SS–293	DRAGONET	1944	SS–381	SAND LANCE	1943
SS–340	ENTEMEDOR	1945	SS–397	SCABBARDFISH	1944
SS–294	*ESCOLAR	1944	SS–399	SEA CAT	1944
SS–361	*GOLET	1943	SS–400	SEA DEVIL	1944
SS–362	GUAVINA	1943	SS–401	SEA DOG	1944
SS–363	GUITARRO	1944	SS–402	SEA FOX	1944
SS–295	HACKLEBACK	1944	SS–405	SEA OWL	1944
SS–364	HAMMERHEAD	1944	SS–406	SEA POACHER	1944
SS–365	HARDHEAD	1944	SS–407	SEA ROBIN	1944
SS–366	HAWKBILL	1944	SS–304	SEAHORSE	1943
SS–367	ICEFISH	1944	SS–315	SÉALION	1944
SS–368	JALLAO	1944	SS–398	SEGUNDO	1944
SS–369	*KETE	1944	SS–408	SENNET	1944
SS–370	KRAKEN	1944	SS–314	*SHARK	1944
SS–371	*LAGARTO	1944	SS–305	SKATE	1943
SS–372	LAMPREY	1944	SS–411	SPADEFISH	1944
SS–296	LANCETFISH	1945	SS–404	SPIKEFISH	1944
SS–297	LING	1945	SS–413	SPOT	1944
SS–298	LIONFISH	1944	SS–414	SPRINGER	1944
SS–373	LIZARDFISH	1944	SS–392	STERLET	1944
SS–374	LOGGERHEAD	1945	SS–415	STICKLEBACK	1945
SS–375	MACABI	1945	SS–306	*TANG	1943
SS–299	MANTA	1944	SS–410	THREADFIN	1944
SS–376	MAPIRO	1945	SS–307	TILEFISH	1943
SS–377	MENHADEN	1945	SS–412	TREPANG	1944
SS–378	MERO	1945			

Builders: Portsmouth Navy Yard (SS 285–291, 308–312, 381–410); Cramp (SS 292–302); Mare Island Navy Yard (SS 304–307, 411–415); Electric Boat (SS 313–345); Manitowoc (SS 361–378).

TENCH Class

1570/2414–2416 tons; length 311'8"; beam 27'2"–27'4"; draft 16'5"; speed 20/9 kts.; armament 1–5"/25 10–21" torpedo tubes; complement 81; diesel engines/electric motors.

No.	Name	Comm.	No.	Name	Comm.
SS–475	ARGONAUT	1945	SS–483	SEA LEOPARD	1945
SS–477	CONGER	1945	SS–485	SIRAGO	1945
SS–478	CUTLASS	1945	SS–417	TENCH	1944
SS–479	DIABLO	1945	SS–418	THORNBACK	1944
SS–482	IREX	1945	SS–419	TIGRONE	1944
SS–480	MEDREGAL	1945	SS–420	TIRANTE	1944
SS–484	ODAX	1945	SS–422	TORO	1944
SS–424	QUILLBACK	1944	SS–423	TORSK	1944
SS–481	REQUIN	1945	SS–421	TRUTTA	1944
SS–476	RUNNER	1945			

Builders: Portsmouth Navy Yard.

7. MINECRAFT

CM Minelayers and CMc Coastal Minelayers

Converted Merchantmen

1400–5300 tons; length 230'6"–386'7"; beam 42'–57'; draft 14'6"–18'6"; speed 12–20 kts.; armament 1–5"/51 or 1–3 3"/50; complement 93–649; turbines or reciprocating engines.

CM–3	†AROOSTOOK	1917	CM–4	OGLALA [34]	1917
CM–8	KEOKUK [32]	1942	CM–11	SALEM [35]	1942
CM–10	*MIANTONOMOH	1941	CMc–3	WASSUC	1941
CM–9	MONADNOCK [33]	1941	CM–12	WEEHAWKEN	1942

[32] Converted to net cargo ship (AKN).
[33] Reclassified auxiliary minelayer (ACM).
[34] Converted to internal combustion engine repair ship (ARG).
[35] Renamed SHAWMUT 15 Aug. 1945.

TERROR [36]

5875 tons; length 454'10"; beam 60'2"; draft 19'7"; speed 20 kts.; armament 4–5"/38; complement 481.

CM–5	TERROR	1942

[36] The Navy's only built-for-the-purpose large minelayer.

DM Light Minelayers

Converted Flush-Decker Destroyers

1190–1215 tons; length 314'4"–314'5"; beam 31'8"–31'9"; draft 12'–15'3"; speed 30 kts.; armament 3–3"/50; complement 146.

DM Light Minelayers (*cont'd*)

No.	Name	Conv.	No.	Name	Conv.
DM-18	BREESE	1931	DM-22	PRUITT [37]	1937
DM-15	*GAMBLE	1930	DM-16	RAMSEY [37]	1930
DM-17	*MONTGOMERY	1931	DM-21	SICARD [37]	1937
DM-20	PREBLE [37]	1937	DM-19	TRACY	1937

Converted from LITTLE and CLEMSON Class destroyers.

[37] Converted to miscellaneous auxiliary (AG).

ROBERT H. SMITH Class

2200 tons; length 376'6"; beam 40'10"; draft 18'8"–18'10"; speed 33 kts.; armament 6–5"/38; complement 363.

No.	Name	Comm.	No.	Name	Comm.
DM-34	AARON WARD	1944	DM-32	LINDSEY	1944
DM-27	ADAMS	1944	DM-23	ROBERT H. SMITH	1944
DM-33	GWIN	1944	DM-25	SHANNON	1944
DM-26	HARRY F. BAUER	1944	DM-30	SHEA	1944
DM-29	HENRY A. WILEY	1944	DM-24	THOMAS E. FRASER	1944
DM-31	J. WILLIAM DITTER	1944	DM-28	TOLMAN	1944

Converted while building from ALLEN M. SUMNER Class destroyers.

ACM Auxiliary Minelayers

640–1054 tons; length 184'6"–188'2"; beam 33'–37'; draft 9'5"–12'6"; speed 12.5–14.5 kts.; armament 1–3"/50 or 1–40mm.; complement 69–102; reciprocating or diesel engines.

No.	Name		No.	Name	
ACM-5	BARBICAN	1945	ACM-7	OBSTRUCTER	1945
ACM-3	BARRICADE	1944	ACM-8	PICKET	1945
ACM-6	BASTION	1945	ACM-2	PLANTER	1944
ACM-4	BUTTRESS	1944 [38]	ACM-9	TRAPPER	1945
ACM-1	CHIMO	1944			

ACM 1–3, 5–9 built for Army as mine planters and ACM-4 converted from PCE. In 1945 minelayer MONADNOCK (CM-9) (*q.v.*) was reclassified auxiliary minelayer.

[38] Converted to miscellaneous auxiliary (AG).

DMS Fast Minesweepers

Converted Flush-Decker Destroyers

1060–1190 tons; length 314'4"–314'5"; beam 31'8"–31'9"; draft 13'4"–14'2"; speed 30 kts.; armament 3–3"/50; complement 149.

No.	Name	Conv.	No.	Name	Conv.
DMS-3	BOGGS [38]	1940	DMS-1	DORSEY	1940
DMS-9	CHANDLER [38]	1940	DMS-4	ELLIOT [38]	1940

[38] Converted to miscellaneous auxiliary (AG).

DMS Fast Minesweepers: Converted Flush-Decker Destroyers
(*cont'd*)

No.	Name	Conv.	No.	Name	Conv.
DMS–18	HAMILTON [38]	1942	DMS–5	*PALMER	1940
DMS–6	HOGAN [38]	1940	DMS–17	*PERRY	1940
DMS–13	HOPKINS	1940	DMS–10	SOUTHARD	1940
DMS–11	*HOVEY	1940	DMS–8	STANSBURY	1940
DMS–7	HOWARD [38]	1940	DMS–16	TREVER [38]	1940
DMS–2	LAMBERTON [38]	1940	DMS–15	*WASMUTH	1940
DMS–12	*LONG	1940	DMS–14	ZANE [38]	1940

Converted from LITTLE and CLEMSON Class destroyers.
[38] Converted to miscellaneous auxiliary (AG).

ELLYSON Class

1630 tons; length 341'; beam 36'1"; draft 17'9"; speed 35 kts.; armament 3–5"/38; complement 272.

No.	Name		No.	Name	
DMS–29	BUTLER	1944	DMS–30	GHERARDI	1944
DMS–33	CARMICK	1945	DMS–20	HAMBLETON	1944
DMS–39	COWIE	1945	DMS–28	HARDING	1944
DMS–37	DAVISON	1945	DMS–26	HOBSON	1944
DMS–41	DORAN	1945	DMS–27	JEFFERS	1944
DMS–34	DOYLE	1945	DMS–40	KNIGHT	1945
DMS–42	EARLE	1945	DMS–36	MCCOOK	1945
DMS–19	ELLYSON	1944	DMS–23	MACOMB	1944
DMS–22	*EMMONS	1944	DMS–31	MERVINE	1945
DMS–35	ENDICOTT	1945	DMS–32	QUICK	1945
DMS–25	FITCH	1944	DMS–21	RODMAN	1944
DMS–24	FORREST	1944	DMS–38	THOMPSON	1945

Converted from GLEAVES Class destroyers.

AM Minesweepers

LAPWING (or Bird) Class

840 tons; length 187'10"; beam 35'5"; draft 15'; speed 14 kts.; armament 2–3"/50; complement 75; reciprocating engine.

No.	Name	Comm.	No.	Name	Comm.
AM–36	*BITTERN	1919	AM–21	LARK [39]	1919
AM–20	BOBOLINK [39]	1918	AM–7	ORIOLE [39]	1918
AM–24	BRANT [39]	1918	AM–2	OWL [39]	1918
AM–40	CORMORANT [39]	1919	AM–16	PARTRIDGE [39]	1919
AM–17	EIDER [40]	1919	AM–46	†PEACOCK	1919
AM–9	*FINCH	1918	AM–15	*QUAIL	1919
AM–43	GREBE [39]	1919	AM–26	RAIL [39]	1918
AM–25	KINGFISHER [39]	1918	AM–3	ROBIN [39]	1918

[39] Converted to ocean-going tug (AT).
[40] Converted to gate vessel (YNg).

AM Minesweepers (*cont'd*)

No.	Name	Comm.	No.	Name	Comm.
AM–30	SEAGULL [39]	1919	AM–52	VIREO [39]	1919
AM–5	*TANAGER	1918	AM–35	WHIPPOORWILL [39]	1919
AM–31	TERN [39]	1919	AM–14	WOODCOCK [39]	1919
AM–13	TURKEY [39]	1918			

[39] Converted to ocean-going tug (AT).

RAVEN and AUK Classes

810–840 tons; length 220'6"–221'2"; beam 32'–32'2"; draft 9'4"–10'9"; speed 17 kts.; armament 1–2 3"/50; complement 105; diesel engine or diesel engine with electric drive.

No.	Name	Comm.	No.	Name	Comm.
AM–340	ARDENT	1944	AM–111	SAGE	1942
AM–57	AUK	1942	AM–381	SCOTER	1945
AM–58	BROADBILL	1942	AM–112	SEER	1942
AM–314	CHAMPION	1943	AM–113	*SENTINEL	1942
AM–59	CHICKADEE	1942	AM–62	SHELDRAKE	1942
AM–315	CHIEF	1943	AM–282	SHOVELER	1945
AM–316	COMPETENT	1943	AM–115	*SKILL	1942
AM–317	DEFENSE	1944	AM–63	*SKYLARK	1942
AM–318	DEVASTATOR	1944	AM–322	SPEAR	1943
AM–341	DEXTROUS	1943	AM–116	SPEED	1942
AM–319	GLADIATOR	1944	AM–384	SPRIG	1945
AM–100	HEED	1943	AM–114	STAFF	1942
AM–101	HERALD	1943	AM–64	STARLING	1942
AM–320	IMPLACABLE	1944	AM–118	STEADY	1942
AM–371	MINIVET	1945	AM–117	STRIVE	1942
AM–102	MOTIVE	1943	AM–383	SURFBIRD	1944
AM–372	MURRELET	1945	AM–119	SUSTAIN	1942
AM–60	NUTHATCH	1942	AM–65	*SWALLOW	1943
AM–103	ORACLE	1943	AM–120	SWAY	1943
AM–56	*OSPREY	1940	AM–121	*SWERVE	1944
AM–61	PHEASANT	1942	AM–122	SWIFT	1943
AM–104	PILOT	1943	AM–123	SYMBOL	1942
AM–105	PIONEER	1943	AM–385	TANAGER	1945
AM–375	POCHARD	1944	AM–386	TERCEL	1945
AM–106	*PORTENT	1943	AM–124	THREAT	1943
AM–107	PREVAIL	1943	AM–125	*TIDE	1943
AM–376	PTARMIGAN	1945	AM–126	TOKEN	1942
AM–108	PURSUIT	1943	AM–387	TOUCAN	1944
AM–377	QUAIL	1945	AM–388	TOWHEE	1945
AM–55	RAVEN	1940	AM–323	TRIUMPH	1944
AM–378	REDSTART	1945	AM–127	TUMULT	1943
AM–109	REQUISITE	1943	AM–128	VELOCITY	1943
AM–110	REVENGE	1943	AM–324	VIGILANCE	1944
AM–379	ROSELLE	1945	AM–389	WAXWING	1945
AM–380	RUDDY	1945	AM–131	ZEAL	1943

Converted Fishermen

314–585 tons; length 122′6″–150′; beam 23′–28′8″; draft 10′11″–14′7″; speed 9–13 kts.; armament 1-3″/23 or 1-3″/50; complement 36; diesel engine.

No.	Name	Comm.	No.	Name	Comm.
AM-71	ALBATROSS [41]	1940	AM-77	†GOLDFINCH	1941
AM-72	BLUEBIRD [41]	1940	AM-79	GOSHAWK [41]	1941
AM-66	†BULLFINCH	1940	AM-73	†GRACKLE	1941
AM-67	†CARDINAL	1940	AM-74	†GULL	1940
AM-68	CATBIRD [41]	1940	AM-133	†HAWK	1942
AM-81	CHAFFINCH	1941	AM-134	†IBIS	1942
AM-69	CURLEW [41]	1940	AM-75	†KITE	1941
AM-132	EAGLE [42]	1942	AM-76	LINNET [41]	1941
AM-70	FLICKER [41]	1940	AM-135	†MERGANSER	1942
AM-80	GOLDCREST	1941			

[41] Converted to unclassified vessel (IX).
[42] Converted to coastal yacht (PYc).

ADROIT Class

295 tons; length 173′9″; beam 23′; draft 6′6″; speed 16 kts.; armament 1-3″/50; complement 65; diesel engines.

No.	Name	Comm.	No.	Name	Comm.
AM-82	ADROIT	1942	AM-91	DYNAMIC	1942
AM-83	ADVENT	1942	AM-92	EFFECTIVE	1942
AM-84	ANNOY	1942	AM-93	ENGAGE	1942
AM-85	CONFLICT	1942	AM-94	EXCEL	1942
AM-86	CONSTANT	1942	AM-95	EXPLOIT	1943
AM-87	DARLING	1942	AM-96	FIDELITY	1942
AM-88	DASH	1942	AM-97	FIERCE	1942
AM-89	DESPITE	1942	AM-98	FIRM	1943
AM-90	DIRECT	1942	AM-99	FORCE	1943

All converted to submarine chasers (PC).

ADMIRABLE Class

625 tons; length 184′6″; beam 33′; draft 10′; speed 15 kts.; armament 1-3″/50; complement 104; diesel engines.

No.	Name	Comm.	No.	Name	Comm.
AM-136	ADMIRABLE [43]	1942	AM-156	CAPTIVATE [43]	1944
AM-137	ADOPT [43]	1942	AM-157	CARAVAN [43]	1944
AM-148	ASTUTE [43]	1944	AM-158	CAUTION [43]	1944
AM-149	AUGURY [43]	1944	AM-159	CHANGE	1944
AM-150	BARRIER [43]	1944	AM-160	CLAMOUR	1944
AM-151	BOMBARD [43]	1944	AM-161	CLIMAX	1944
AM-152	BOND [43]	1943	AM-162	COMPEL	1944
AM-153	BUOYANT	1943	AM-163	CONCISE	1944
AM-154	CANDID [43]	1944	AM-164	CONTROL	1944
AM-155	CAPABLE [43]	1944	AM-165	COUNSEL	1944

[43] Transferred to U.S.S.R. under Lend-Lease.

AM Minesweepers (*cont'd*)

No.	Name	Comm.	No.	Name	Comm.
AM–214	CRAG	1944	AM–263	MEASURE [43]	1944
AM–215	CRUISE	1944	AM–244	METHOD [43]	1944
AM–216	DEFT	1944	AM–265	MIRTH [43]	1944
AM–217	DELEGATE	1944	AM–266	NIMBLE	1944
AM–218	DENSITY	1944	AM–267	NOTABLE	1945
AM–219	DESIGN	1944	AM–268	NUCLEUS [43]	1943
AM–220	DEVISE	1944	AM–269	OPPONENT	1943
AM–221	DIPLOMA	1944	AM–270	PALISADE [43]	1944
AM–222	DISDAIN [43]	1944	AM–271	PENETRATE [43]	1944
AM–223	DOUR	1944	AM–272	PERIL [43]	1944
AM–361	DUNLIN	1945	AM–273	PHANTOM	1944
AM–224	EAGER	1944	AM–274	PINNACLE	1944
AM–225	ELUSIVE	1945	AM–275	PIRATE	1944
AM–226	EMBATTLE	1945	AM–276	PIVOT	1944
AM–232	EXECUTE	1944	AM–277	PLEDGE	1944
AM–233	FACILITY	1944	AM–279	PRIME	1944
AM–234	FANCY [43]	1944	AM–278	PROJECT	1944
AM–235	FIXITY	1945	AM–280	PROWESS	1944
AM–362	GADWALL	1945	AM–281	QUEST	1944
AM–238	GARLAND	1944	AM–282	RAMPART [43]	1945
AM–363	GAVIA	1945	AM–283	RANSOM	1944
AM–239	GAYETY	1944	AM–284	REBEL	1944
AM–364	GRAYLAG	1945	AM–285	RECRUIT	1944
AM–240	HAZARD	1944	AM–286	REFORM	1944
AM–241	HILARITY	1944	AM–287	REFRESH	1944
AM–246	IMPLICIT	1943	AM–294	*SALUTE	1943
AM–247	IMPROVE	1943	AM–295	SAUNTER	1943
AM–242	INAUGURAL	1945	AM–296	SCOUT	1944
AM–248	INCESSANT	1943	AM–297	SCRIMMAGE	1944
AM–249	INCREDIBLE	1944	AM–298	SCUFFLE	1944
AM–250	INDICATIVE [43]	1944	AM–304	SCURRY	1944
AM–251	INFLICT	1944	AM–299	SENTRY	1944
AM–252	INSTILL	1944	AM–300	SERENE	1944
AM–253	INTRIGUE	1944	AM–301	SHELTER	1944
AM–254	INVADE	1944	AM–302	SIGNET	1944
AM–255	JUBILANT	1943	AM–303	SKIRMISH	1944
AM–256	KNAVE	1943	AM–305	SPECTACLE	1944
AM–257	LANCE [44]	1943	AM–306	SPECTOR	1944
AM–258	LOGIC [44]	1943	AM–307	STAUNCH	1944
AM–259	LUCID [44]	1943	AM–308	STRATEGY	1944
AM–260	MAGNET [44]	1944	AM–309	STRENGTH	1945
AM–261	MAINSTAY	1944	AM–310	SUCCESS	1945
AM–262	MARVEL [43]	1944	AM–311	SUPERIOR	1945

Ten sisters were transferred to Russia before commissioning.

[43] Transfered to U.S.S.R. under Lend-Lease.
[44] Transferred to China under Lend-Lease.

AMc Coastal Minesweepers

Converted Vessels

165–270 tons; length 76'6"–136'; beam 19'4"–24'; draft 8'–11'; speed 8.5–14 kts.; armament 1–3"/50, 1–20mm., 2–.30cal. machine guns, or none; complement 15–47; diesel engine.

No.	Name	Comm.	No.	Name	Comm.
AMc–112	AFFRAY	1941	AMc–21	KILDEER [45]	1940
AMc–111	AGILE [45]	1941	AMc–56	KINGBIRD [45]	1940
AMc–23	BLUE JAY [46]	1941	AMc–10	†LONGSPUR	1941
AMc–7	*BUNTING	1941	AMc–2	†MAGPIE	1941
AMc–25	CANARY [46]	1941	AMc–203	MENDRICK	1944 [48]
AMc–16	†CHATTERER	1940	AMc–204	MINAH	1944 [48]
AMc–8	COCKATOO	1941	AMc–28	†MOCKINGBIRD	1941
AMc–14	CONDOR	1941	AMc–18	NIGHTINGALE [47]	1941
AMc–32	†COURSER	1941	AMc–149	NIGHTINGALE [45]	1942
AMc–9	CROSSBILL	1941	AMc–34	†PARRAKEET	1941
AMc–20	*CROW	1941	AMc–57	PHOEBE	1941
AMc–24	EGRET [45]	1941	AMc–17	†PINTAIL	1941
AMc–33	†FIRECREST	1941	AMc–1	†PIPIT	1941
AMc–22	FLAMINGO [45]	1941	AMc–3	†PLOVER	1941
AMc–27	†FRIGATE BIRD	1941	AMc–29	†PUFFIN	1941
AMc–19	†GROSBEAK	1940	AMc–30	REEDBIRD	1941
AMc–12	†GROUSE	1941	AMc–58	RHEA	1941
AMc–6	†HEATH HEN	1941	AMc–35	†ROAD RUNNER	1941
AMc–13	*HORNBILL	1941	AMc–59	RUFF	1941
AMc–26	†HUMMING BIRD	1941	AMc–11	†SANDERLING	1941
AMc–5	KESTREL [45]	1941	AMc–15	†WAXBILL	1940

AMc 203–204 converted from PCSs; others from commercial fishermen.

[45] Converted to unclassified vessel (IX).
[46] Converted to diving tender (YDT).
[47] Converted to patrol vessel (YP).
[48] Conversion date.

ACCENTOR Class

185–205 tons; length 97'1"–98'5"; beam 21'–23'7"; draft 8'11"–10'8"; speed 10 kts.; armament 2–.50cal. machine guns; complement 17; diesel engine.

AMc–36	ACCENTOR	1941	AMc–67	BOLD	1942
AMc–61	ACME	1941	AMc–39	BRAMBLING	1941
AMc–62	ADAMANT	1941	AMc–68	BULWARK	1942
AMc–63	ADVANCE	1941	AMc–40	CARACARA	1941
AMc–64	AGGRESSOR	1941	AMc–41	CHACHALACA	1941
AMc–65	ASSERTIVE	1942	AMc–42	CHIMANGO	1941
AMc–66	AVENGE	1942	AMc–69	COMBAT	1942
AMc–38	BARBET	1941	AMc–70	CONQUEROR	1942
AMc–37	BATELEUR	1941	AMc–71	CONQUEST	1942

AM Minesweepers (*cont'd*)

No.	Name	Comm.	No.	Name	Comm.
AMc-43	COTINGA	1941	AMc-90	MERIT	1942
AMc-72	COURIER	1941	AMc-91	OBSERVER	1942
AMc-44	COURLAN	1941	AMc-51	OSTRICH	1941
AMc-73	DEFIANCE	1941	AMc-92	PARAMOUNT	1941
AMc-74	DEMAND	1941	AMc-93	PEERLESS	1942
AMc-75	DETECTOR	1941	AMc-94	PLUCK	1942
AMc-45	DEVELIN	1941	AMc-95	POSITIVE	1942
AMc-76	DOMINANT	1941	AMc-97	PRESTIGE	1941
AMc-77	ENDURANCE	1941	AMc-98	PROGRESS	1942
AMc-78	ENERGY [49]	1941	AMc-99	RADIANT	1942
AMc-79	EXULTANT [49]	1941	AMc-96	REAPER	1942
AMc-80	FEARLESS [49]	1942	AMc-100	RELIABLE	1941
AMc-81	FORTITUDE [49]	1942	AMc-101	ROCKET	1942
AMc-46	FULMAR	1941	AMc-52	ROLLER	1941
AMc-82	GOVERNOR	1942	AMc-102	ROYAL	1942
AMc-83	GUIDE	1942	AMc-103	SECURITY	1942
AMc-84	HEROIC	1942	AMc-53	SKIMMER	1941
AMc-85	IDEAL	1942	AMc-104	SKIPPER	1942
AMc-86	INDUSTRY	1942	AMc-105	STALWART [50]	1942
AMc-47	JACKAMAR	1941	AMc-106	SUMMIT [50]	1942
AMc-87	LIBERATOR [50]	1942	AMc-54	TAPACOLA	1941
AMc-48	LIMPKIN	1941	AMc-107	TRIDENT	1942
AMc-49	LORIKEET	1941	AMc-55	TURACO	1941
AMc-88	LOYALTY	1942	AMc-108	*VALOR	1942
AMc-50	MARABOUT	1941	AMc-109	VICTOR	1942
AMc-89	MEMORABLE	1942	AMc-110	VIGOR	1942

[49] Converted to diving tender (YDT).
[50] Converted to miscellaneous auxiliary (IX).

AMc(U) Underwater Locator Minesweepers

143–216 tons; length 119′1″–159′; beam 23′8″–32′8″; draft 3′9″–5′8″; speed 10–14 kts.; armament 2–20mm.; complement 21–41; diesel engines.

AMc(U) 1–11   Conv. 1945

AMc(U) 1–6 converted from LCT(6); others from LCI(L).

YMS Motor Minesweepers

207–215 tons; length 136′; beam 24′6″; draft 8′; speed 13 kts.; armanent 1–3″/50; complement 50; diesel engine.

YMS 1–136, 138–140, 143–147, 151, 158–160, 163–166, 169–170, 176–180, 183, 185–186, 191–193, 195–201, 207–208, 215–216, 218–220, 222, 224, 226–228, 231, 235, 237–239, 241–243, 245, 247–251, 259–260, 262–263, 265–276, 281, 283, 285–348, 350–449, 453–473, 475, 477–479, 481

Placed in service 1942–5.

8. PATROL CRAFT

PG Gunboats

990–2000 tons; length 200′5″–328′6″; beam 35′–41′3″; draft 12′1″–14′10″; speed 11–20 kts.; 4–6″/47, 1–5″/38 2–4″/50 1–3″/23, or 1–2 4″/50 1–4 3″/50; complement 180–292; turbines or reciprocating engine.

No.	Name	Comm.	No.	Name	Comm.
PG–21	*ASHEVILLE	1920	PG–18	PADUCAH	1905
PG–51	CHARLESTON	1936	PG–19	SACRAMENTO	1914
PG–17	DUBUQUE	1905	PG–22	TULSA 51	1923
PG–50	*ERIE	1936			

PG 17–18 served as training vessels.

51 Renamed TACLOBAN 27 Nov. 1944.

Converted Yachts

1420–3060 tons; length 226′–333′; beam 34′1″–46′5″; draft 12′8″–18′6″; speed 14.5–16 kts.; armament 2–4″/50, 1–4″/50, 2–3″/50, or 1–4 3″/50; complement 107–135; diesel or reciprocating engines or turbines with electric drive.

No.	Name	Comm.	No.	Name	Comm.
PG–60	BEAUMONT	1942	PG–57	*PLYMOUTH	1942
PG–61	DAUNTLESS	1942	PG–54	*ST. AUGUSTINE	1940
PG–58	HILO 52	1942	PG–59	SAN BERNARDINO	1942
PG–55	JAMESTOWN 52	1941	PG–53	VIXEN	1941
PG–52	NIAGARA 52	1941	PG–56	WILLIAMSBURG	1941
PG–72	NOURMAHAL 53	1942			

52 Converted to motor torpedo boat tender (AGP).
53 Transferred to Coast Guard.

TEMPTRESS (Corvette) Class

900–925 tons; length 205′–205′2″; beam 33′; draft 14′7″; speed 16.5 kts.; armament 1–4″/50 1–3″/50 or 2–3″/50; complement 87–90; reciprocating engine.

No.	Name	Comm.	No.	Name	Comm.
PG–86	ACTION	1942	PG–95	PERT	1943
PG–87	ALACRITY	1942	PG–96	PRUDENT	1943
PG–89	BRISK	1942	PG–67	READY	1942
PG–70	COURAGE	1942	PG–66	RESTLESS	1942
PG–69	FURY	1942	PG–65	SAUCY	1942
PG–92	HASTE	1943	PG–64	SPRY	1942
PG–68	IMPULSE	1942	PG–63	SURPRISE	1942
PG–93	INTENSITY	1943	PG–62	TEMPTRESS	1942
PG–94	MIGHT	1942	PG–71	TENACITY	1942

British and Canadian built Flower Class corvettes. PG 62–71 were formerly HMS *Veronica, Heliotrope, Hibiscus, Arabis, Periwinkle, Calendula, Begonia, Larkspur, Heartsease* and *Candytuft* respectively.

PF Frigates

1430–1445 tons; length 301'6"–303'11" beam 36'6"–37'6"; draft 13'8"; speed 20 kts.; armament 3–3"/50; complement 176–214; reciprocating engines.

No.	Name	Comm.	No.	Name	Comm.
PF–58	ABILENE	1944	PF–20	GULFPORT	1944
PF–7	ALBUQUERQUE [54]	1943	PF–30	HINGHAM	1944
PF–18	ALEXANDRIA	1945	PF–5	HOQUIAM [54]	1944
PF–52	ALLENTOWN [54]	1944	PF–19	HURON	1944
PF–15	ANNAPOLIS	1944	PF–45	HUTCHINSON	1944
PF–1	ASHEVILLE	1942	PF–17	KEY WEST	1944
PF–16	BANGOR	1944	PF–64	KNOXVILLE	1944
PF–55	BATH [54]	1944	PF–34	LONG BEACH [54]	1943
PF–21	BAYONNE [54]	1945	PF–93	LORAIN	1945
PF–59	BEAUFORT	1944	PF–53	MACHIAS [54]	1944
PF–35	BELFAST [54]	1943	PF–61	MANITOWOC	1944
PF–46	BISBEE [54]	1944	PF–94	MILLEDGEVILLE	1945
PF–10	BROWNSVILLE	1944	PF–63	MOBERLY	1944
PF–68	BRUNSWICK	1944	PF–24	MUSKEGON	1943
PF–51	BURLINGTON [54]	1944	PF–49	MUSKOOGEE [54]	1944
PF–50	CARSON CITY [54]	1944	PF–2	NATCHEZ	1942
PF–12	CASPER	1944	PF–71	NEW BEDFORD	1944
PF–60	CHARLOTTE	1944	PF–27	NEWPORT	1944
PF–25	CHARLOTTESVILLE [54]	1944	PF–39	OGDEN [54]	1943
PF–38	CORONADO [54]	1943	PF–43	ORANGE	1944
PF–44	CORPUS CHRISTI	1944	PF–99	ORLANDO	1944
PF–56	COVINGTON	1944	PF–6	PASCO [54]	1944
PF–69	DAVENPORT	1945	PF–67	PEORIA	1944
PF–33	DEARBORN	1944	PF–9	POCATELLO	1944
PF–41	EL PASO	1943	PF–26	POUGHKEEPSIE [54]	1944
PF–28	EMPORIA	1944	PF–13	PUEBLO	1944
PF–40	EUGENE	1944	PF–100	RACINE	1945
PF–70	EVANSVILLE	1944	PF–66	READING	1944
PF–8	EVERETT [54]	1944	PF–48	ROCKFORD [54]	1944
PF–102	FORSYTH	1945	PF–37	SAN PEDRO [54]	1943
PF–47	GALLUP [54]	1944	PF–54	SANDUSKY [54]	1944
PF–62	GLADWYNE	1944	PF–4	SAUSALITO [54]	1944
PF–36	GLENDALE [54]	1943	PF–57	SHEBOYGAN	1944
PF–22	GLOUCESTER [54]	1943	PF–23	SHREVEPORT	1944
PF–11	GRAND FORKS	1944	PF–3	TACOMA [54]	1943
PF–14	GRAND ISLAND	1944	PF–65	UNIONTOWN	1944
PF–31	GRAND RAPIDS	1944	PF–42	VAN BUREN	1943
PF–101	GREENSBORO	1945	PF–32	WOONSOCKET	1944
PF–29	GROTON	1944			

Served as PG 101–102, 111–179, 201–202, and 207–210 until PF classification established in 1945. PF 1–2 were Canadian built of the Royal Navy's "River" Class; the others, modified versions built in American yards by the Maritime Commission (S2-S2-AQ1 type). Twenty-one of the latter went to Britain under Lend-Lease.

[54] Transferred to U.S.S.R. under Lend-Lease.

PR River Gunboats

370–560 tons; length 159'5"–210'9"; beam 27'1"–31'1"; draft 5'1"–5'7"; speed 14.5–16 kts.; armament 2–3"/23 or 2–3"/50; complement 60–80; reciprocating engines.

No.	Name	Comm.	No.	Name	Comm.
PR–7	*LUZON	1928	PR–4	TUTUILA [55]	1928
PR–8	*MINDANAO	1928	PR–3	*WAKE	1927
PR–6	*OAHU	1928			

[55] Transferred to China under Lend-Lease.

PY Smaller Converted Yachts

499–1130 tons; length 170'–245'3"; beam 26'6"–34'; draft 10'4"–16'10"; speed 10–18 kts.; armament 1–2 3"/50; complement 47–127; geared turbines or diesel engine.

PY–24	ALMANDITE	1942	PY–17	JADE [56]	1941
PY–14	ARGUS	1941	PY–28	MARCASITE	1942
PY–22	AZURLITE	1942	PY–29	MIZPAH	1942
PY–23	BERYL	1942	PY–21	RUBY	1941
PY–19	CARNELIAN	1941	PY–13	SIREN	1941
PY–15	CORAL	1941	PY–32	SOUTHERN SEAS	1942
PY–25	CRYSTAL	1942	PY–12	SYLPH	1940
PY–26	*CYTHERA	1942	PY–20	TOURMALINE	1941
PY–31	CYTHERA	1942	PY–18	TURQUOISE [56]	1941
PY–27	GIRASOL	1942	PY–16	ZIRCON	1941
PY–10	ISABEL	1917			

[56] Transferred to Ecuador under Lend-Lease.

PYc Coastal Yachts

75–640 tons; length 99'10"–195'1"; beam 16'–32'; draft 5'6"–14'3"; speed 8–18 kts.; armament 1–4"/50, 1–2 3"/23 or /50, or 1 6-pdr.; complement 24–59; diesel or reciprocating engine.

PYc–28	ABILITY	1942	PYc–1	EMERALD	1941
PYc–4	†AGATE	1941	PYc–35	FELICIA	1942
PYc–21	ALABASTER	1942	PYc–29	†GALLANT	1942
PYc–6	†AMBER	1941	PYc–15	GARNET	1942
PYc–3	AMETHYST	1941	PYc–46	†IMPETUOUS	1943 [57]
PYc–11	ANDRADITE	1942	PYc–24	IOLITE [58]	1942
PYc–7	AQUAMARINE	1941	PYc–41	IOLITE	1942
PYc–45	†BLACK DOUGLAS	1943 [57]	PYc–13	JASPER	1941
PYc–40	†CAPTOR	1942 [57]	PYc–20	JET	1942
PYc–38	CAROLITA	1942	PYc–31	†LASH	1942
PYc–16	CHALCEDONY	1942	PYc–42	LEADER	1942
PYc–27	COLLEEN	1942	PYc–39	MARNELL	1942
PYc–26	CYMOPHANE	1042	PYc–37	MENTOR	1942

[57] Date of conversion.
[58] Converted to patrol vessel (YP).

PYc Coastal Yachts (*cont'd*)

No.	Name	Comm.	No.	Name	Comm.
PYc–9	*MOONSTONE	1941	PYc–49	RETORT	1943 [57]
PYc–22	OLIVIN	1942	PYc–19	RHODOLITE	1941
PYc–5	ONYX	1941	PYc–2	SAPPHIRE	1940
PYc–8	OPAL [59]	1941	PYc–12	SARDONYX	1941
PYc–36	†PARAGON	1942	PYc–43	†SEA SCOUT	1943
PYc–47	†PATRIOT	1943 [57]	PYc–50	†STURDY	1943 [57]
PYc–18	PERIDOT	1942	PYc–10	TOPAZ	1941
PYc–44	PERSEVERANCE	1943	PYc–14	†TRUANT	1941
PYc–48	PERSISTENT	1943 [57]	PYc–30	VAGRANT	1941
PYc–25	PHENAKITE	1942	PYc–51	†VALIANT	1943 [57]
PYc–17	PYROPE	1942	PYc–52	VENTURE	1943 [57]

PYc–40 converted from minesweeper; PYc–45 from an unclassified vessel; and PYc 46–52 from PCs.

[57] Date of conversion.
[58] Converted to patrol vessel (YP).
[59] Transferred to Ecuador under Lend-Lease.

PCE Patrol Craft, Escort

640 tons; length 184′; beam 33′1″; draft 9′5″; speed 15.5 kts.; armament 1–3″/50; complement 99; diesel engines.

PCE 842–860, 867–886, 891–900, 902–904   Comm. 1943–5

PCE 848–860 fitted as rescue vessels (PCER). Fifteen sisters went to Britain under Lend-Lease. PCE–878 converted to auxiliary minelayer (ACM) and PCE 876, 879, and 883 to degaussing vessels (YDG).

PE Eagle Boats

430 tons; length 200′9″; beam 25′9″; draft 13′6″; speed 18 kts.; armament 1–4″/50; complement 68.

PE 19, 32, 38, 48, *56, 57   Comm. 1919

Builders: Ford Motor Co.

PCS Patrol Craft, Sweepers

251 tons; length 136′; beam 24′6″; draft 8′7″; speed 14 kts.; armament 1–3″/50; complement 57; diesel engine.

No.	Comm.
PCS 1376–1392, 1396–1397, 1399–1405, 1413–1414, 1417–1426, 1429–1431, 1441–1442, 1444–1446, 1448–1452, 1455, 1457–1461, 1464–1465	1943–5

PCS 1388, 1404, 1457, and 1458 converted to surveying vessels (AGS), and PCS 1464–1465 became coastal minesweepers (AMc).

PGM Motor Gunboats

95–280 tons; length 110'10"–173'8"; beam 17'–23'; draft 6'6"–10'10"; speed 17.5–20 kts.; armament 1–3"/23 or /50 1–6omm. mortar; complement 28–65; diesel engine.

PGM 1–14, 16–32   Conv. 1942–5

PGM 1–7 converted from SCs and others from PCs. PGM 7, 17 and 18 lost.

PC Submarine Chasers (Steel Hull)

Converted Yachts

35–140 tons; length 85'–120'; beam 15'–24'; draft 4'6"–11'6"; speed 10–17 kts.; armament 1–3"/23 or /50; complement 24; diesel or gasolene engines or turbines with electric drive.

PC 454–458, 460, 509–510, 826   Comm. 1940–1

PC–457 lost; PC 454–456, 458, 460, 509 reclassified coastal yachts (PYc); and PC–510 became a patrol vessel (YP).

Experimental Vessels

270–280 tons; length 169'7"–173'8"; beam 20'9"–22'7"; draft 6'6"–8'7"; speed 18.5–22.5 kts.; armament 2–3"/50; complement 65; diesel engines or geared turbines.

PC 451–452   Comm. 1940–3

PC–452 converted to unclassified vessel (IX).

PC–461 Class

280 tons; length 173'8"; beam 23'; draft 10'10"; speed 18 kts.; armament 1–2 3"/50; complement 65; diesel engines.

No.	Comm.
PC 461–496, 542–627, 776–825, 1077–1087, 1119–1147, 1149, 1167–	1942–4
1188, 1190–1247, 1251–1254, 1256–1265, 1546–1547, 1549, 1563–	
1564, 1569	

PC 469, 558, 1129, and 1260–1261 were war losses. PC–467 transferred to Norway under Lend-Lease; PC 471–475, 480–482, 542–543, 545, 550–551, 556–557, 559, 562, 591, 621, 625–627, 1226–1227, 1235 to France; PC 544, 546, 554, 561, 604–605, 607, 1236 to Brazil; PC–622 to Greece; PC–1234 to Uruguay. PC 468 and 1124 converted to unclassified vessels (IX) and PC–624 to water barge (YW).

PC–1586 Class

295 tons; length 173'8"; beam 23'; draft 11'7"; speed 18 kts.; armament 1–3"/50; complement 65; diesel engines.

PC 1586–1603   Conv. 1944

Converted from minesweepers.

SC Submarine Chasers (Wooden Hull)

Old and Experimental Vessels

75–95 tons; length 110'–111'5"; beam 13'6"–18'4"; draft 6'3"–6'5"; speed 15–17 kts.; armament 1–3"/23; complement 17–28; gasolene or diesel engines.

SC Submarine Chasers (Wooden Hull) (*cont'd*)

No.　　　　　　　　　　　　　　　　　　　　　　　　Comm.

SC 64, 102, †103, *185, 229, 231, 330, 412, 431, †432, 437, †440,　1918–41
449–450, 453

SC–497 Class

95 tons; length 110′10″; beam 17′; draft 6′6″; speed 20 kts.; armament 1–40mm.;
complement 40; diesel engines.

No.　　　　　　　　　　　　　　　　　　　　　　　　Comm.

SC 497–508, 511–521, 523–541, 628–775, 977–1076, 1266–1287, 1289–　1942–4
1375, 1474–1493, 1496–1499, 1502–1508, 1510–1512, 1517

SC 521, 694, 696, 700, 709, 740, 744, 751, 984, 1024, and 1067 were war losses.
SC 644, 757, 1036, 1053, 1056, 1071, 1072, and 1366 were converted to motor gunboats (PGM) and SC–501 to unclassified vessel (IX). The following were transferred under Lend-Lease: to France, SC 497–498, 503, 506–508, 515–517, 519, 522,
524–526, 529–530, 532–535, 638–639, 649, 651, 655, 666, 690–693, 695, 697, 770–771,
977–979, 1029–1030, 1043–1044, 1331, 1335–1337, 1344–1346, and 1359; to U.S.S.R.,
SC 500, 537–538, 634, 643, 646–647, 657, 660–661, 663, 673–675, 685, 687, 713, 719–721,
752, 754, 756, 774, 986, 997, 1007, 1011, 1021, 1031, 1060, 1073–1076, 1283–1287, 1295,
1324, 1364–1365, 1475–1493, 1496–1499, 1502–1508, 1510–1512, 1517; and to Brazil,
SC 762–767, 1289. One SC was transferred to Brazil without commissioning in the
U.S.N.

SC–1466 Class

76 tons; length 111′6″; beam 17′9″; draft 5′3″; speed 16 kts.; armament 1–40mm.;
complement 28; gasolene engines.

SC 1466–1473　　Comm. 1942

Canadian-built units of the British "Fairmile" Class. SC 1466, 1469, and 1471 were
transferred to Mexico under Lend-Lease and SC–1470 became an unclassified vessel (IX). SC–1067 was a war loss.

9. MOTOR TORPEDO BOATS

PT Motor Torpedo Boats

Experimental Vessels

20–35 tons; length 54′–81′; beam 15′–20′; draft 4′; speed 40 kts.; armament 2–4 21″
or 4–18″ torpedo tubes; complement 10–11; gasolene engines.

PT 1–19, 69–70, 564 placed in service 1940–3.

PT 3–7, 9, 10–19 transferred to Britain; PT 1–2 reclassified small boats; and PT 9,
69, 70 were converted to patrol vessels (YP). Note that a replacement PT–6 was
built in 1941.

PT–20 Class

35 tons; length 77′; beam 19′11″; draft 5′6″; speed 40 kts.; armament 2–21″ torpedo tubes; complement 12; gasolene engines.

PT 20–48, 59–68 placed in service 1941–2.

PT 22, 28, 31, 32 were war losses; PT 20, 21, 29, 30, 42, 62, 64, and 65 scrapped.
PT 23–27, 36, 38–40, 45–48, 59, 61, 66 reclassified small boats. Ten sisters were
built for Britain.

PT–71 ("Higgins") Class

35 tons; length 78′; beam 20′8″; draft 5′3″; speed 40 kts.; armament 4–21″ torpedoes; complement 17; gasolene engines.

PT 71–94, 197–254, 265–313, 450–485, 625–660 placed in service 1942–5.

PT 73, 77, 79, 200, 202, 218, 219, 239, 247, 251, 279, 283, 300, 301, and 311 were lost. PT 85–87, 89, 197, 265–276, 289–294 transferred to U.S.S.R.; and PT 88, 90–94, 198, 201, 203–217 to Britain.

PT–95 ("Huckins") Class

34 tons; length 78′; beam 19′5″; draft 5′; speed 41 kts.; armament 4–21″ torpedoes; complement 12; gasolene engines.

PT 95–102, 255–264 placed in service 1942–3.

PT–103 ("Elco") Class

38 tons; length 80′; beam 20′8″; draft 5′; speed 41 kts.; armament 4–21″ torpedoes; complement 17; gasolene engines.

PT 103–196, 314–367, 373–383, 486–563, 565–614, 731–760 placed in service 1942–5.

PT 107, 109–113, 117–119, 121, 123, 133, 135–136, 145, 147, 153, 158, 164–6, 172–173, 193, 337–339, 346–347, 353, 363, 493, 509, and 555 were war losses. PT 498–504, 506–508, 510–521, 552–554, 556, 560–563, and 731–760 went to Russia under Lend-Lease.

PT–368 ("Vosper") Class

33 tons; length 70′; beam 19′; draft 4′9″; speed 41 kts.; armament 2–21″ torpedoes; complement 12; gasolene engines.

PT 368–371, 400–449, 661–718 placed in service 1943–5.

PT 368, 371 were war losses. PT 368–371 were transferred from the Netherlands while building. PT 400–449, 661–687 went to Russia under Lend-Lease. Duplicate the British Vosper boats. Sixteen sisters transferred to Britain under Lend-Lease.

PTC Motor Boat Submarine Chasers

25–27 tons; length 63′–70′; beam 15′3″–20′; draft 3′10″–4′; speed 30–40 kts.; armament 2–4 .50 cal. machine guns; complement 10–11; gasolene engines.

PTC 1–12, 37–66 placed in service 1941–4.

PTC 1–12 transferred to Britain and PTC 37–49, 54–66 to U.S.S.R. under Lend-Lease.

10. AUXILIARIES

AB Crane Ship

No.	Name	Conv.	Displ.
AB–1	CRANE SHIP NO. 1	1920	8275

Converted from battleship KEARSARGE, built 1900.

AD Destroyer Tenders

No.	Name	Comm.	Displ.	No.	Name	Comm.	Displ.
AD-34	ALCOR	1944 [60]	8091	AD-21	MARKAB	1942 [60]	7919
AD-11	ALTAIR	1921	5910	AD-2	MELVILLE	1915	5078
AD-9	BLACK HAWK	1918	5690	AD-17	PIEDMONT	1944	8637
AD-10	†BRIDGEPORT	1917	7175	AD-15	PRAIRIE	1940	9201
AD-16	CASCADE	1943	9813	AD-13	RIGEL [61]	1922	5551
AD-12	DENEBOLA	1921	5628	AD-26	SHENANDOAH	1045	7664
AD-14	DIXIE	1940	9201	AD-18	SIERRA	1944	8637
AD-3	DOBBIN	1924	7938	AD-4	WHITNEY	1924	8042
AD-20	HAMUL	1942 [60]	8560	AD-19	YOSEMITE	1944	8637
AD-22	KLONDIKE	1945	8165				

AD 20-21 converted from cargo ships and AD-34 from a repair ship. AD-16 was a Maritime Commission C3-S1-N2 and AD 20-21, C3-Cargo.

[60] Conversion date.
[61] Converted to repair ship (AR).

AE Ammunition Ships

No.	Name	Comm.	Displ.	No.	Name	Comm.	Displ.
AE-13	AKUTAN	1945	5450	AE-16	MOUNT KATMAI	1945	5450
AE-19	DIAMOND HEAD	1945	5450	AE-2	NITRO	1921	7040
AE-14	FIREDRAKE	1944	5626	AE-18	PARICUTIN	1945	5450
AE-17	GREAT SITKIN	1945	5450	AE-1	PYRO	1920	7040
AE-3	LASSEN	1940	6350	AE-5	RAINIER	1941	6350
AE-8	MAUNA LOA	1943	5450	AE-10	SANGAY	1943	6246
AE-9	MAZAMA	1944	5450	AE-6	SHASTA	1943	6350
AE-4	MOUNT BAKER	1941	6350	AE-15	VESUVIUS	1944	5626
AE-11	*MOUNT HOOD	1944	5604	AE-12	WRANGELL	1944	5626

AE 3-6, 8-9, and 13 were converted from Maritime Commission C2-Cargo hulls; AE-10 was a C1-A; and AE 11-12, 14-19 were C2-S-AJ1 conversions.

AF Store Ships

No.	Name	Comm.	Displ.	No.	Name	Comm.	Displ.
AF-30	ADRIA	1944	3139	AF-29	GRAFFIAS	1944	6313
AF-10	ALDEBARAN	1940	6051	AF-28	HYADES	1943	6313
AF-7	ARCTIC	1921	4997	AF-33	KARIN	1945	3139
AF-31	AREQUIPA	1945	3139	AF-34	KERSTIN	1945	3139
AF-22	ARIEL	1942	7058	AF-35	LATONA	1945	3139
AF-41	ATHANASIA	1945	3139	AF-44	LAURENTIA	1945	3139
AF-42	BONDIA	1945	3139	AF-36	LIOBA	1945	3139
AF-8	BOREAS	1940	4654	AF-45	LUCIDOR	1945	3139
AF-1	BRIDGE	1917	5207	AF-37	MALABAR	1945	3139
AF-18	CALAMARES	1943	7403	AF-21	MERAK	1942	7058
AF-32	CORDUBA	1944	3139	AF-38	MERAPI	1945	3139
AF-23	CYGNUS	1942	7170	AF-12	MIZAR	1942	7098
AF-24	DELPHINIUS	1942	6000	AF-26	OCTANS	1943	7298
AF-43	GORDONIA	1945	3139	AF-46	OCTAVIA	1945	3139

AF Store Ships (*cont'd*)

No.	Name	Comm.	Displ.	No.	Name	Comm.	Displ.
AF-39	PALISANA	1945	3139	AF-15	TALAMANCA	1942	7218
AF-16	PASTORES	1942	7657	AF-13	TARAZED	1941	7218
AF-11	POLARIS	1941	6398	AF-25	TAURUS	1942	6600
AF-20	*PONTIAC	1942	3081	AF-14	URANUS	1941	1432
AF-19	ROAMER	1942	1850	AF-47	VALENTINE	1945	3139
AF-40	SATURN	1945	5088	AF-9	YUKON	1921	4654

AF-40 converted from cargo ship. AF 10-11 were Maritime Commission C2-Cargo vessels; AF 28-29, C2-S-E1; and AF 30-39, 41-47, R1-M-AV3.

AG Miscellaneous Auxiliaries

No.	Name	Comm.	Displ.	No.	Name	Comm.	Displ.
AG-34	ALCOR [62]	1941	8091	AG-75	CUTTYHUNK		
AG-49	ANACAPA	1942	7420		ISLAND	1944	5766
AG-67	ANTAEUS [63]	1943 [64]	5518	AG-26	CUYAHOGA [67]	1935	200
AG-10	ANTARES [65]	1922	4800	AG-91	DAHLGREN	1945 [64]	1190
AG-31	ARGONNE	1940 [64]	8400	AG-80	DU PONT	1944 [64]	1098
AG-76	AVERY ISLAND	1945	5766	AG-104	ELLIOT	1945 [64]	1090
AG-102	BABBITT	1945 [64]	1090	AG-115	ELLIS	1945 [64]	1090
AG-71	BAHAM	1944 [64]	5522	AG-85	FOX	1944 [64]	1190
AG-113	BARNEY	1945 [64]	1090	AG-12	GOLD STAR	1922	4679
AG-68	BASILAN	1944	5371	AG-111	HAMILTON	1945 [64]	1190
AG-29	BEAR	1941	1267	AG-1	†HANNIBAL	1898	2179
AG-73	BELLE ISLE	1944	5766	AG-84	HATFIELD	1944 [64]	1190
AG-66	BESBORO	1943	1716	AG-90	HENRY T.		
AG-114	BIDDLE	1945 [64]	1090		ALLEN	1945 [64]	12,400
AG-19	BOGGS	1945 [64]	1247	AG-105	HOGAN	1945 [64]	1060
AG-30	BOWDITCH [66]	1940	5405	AG-106	HOWARD	1945 [64]	1066
AG-112	BRECKINRIDGE	1945 [64]	1090	AG-77	INDIAN ISLAND	1945	5766
AG-96	BROOME	1945 [64]	1190	AG-81	J. FRED TALBOT	1944 [64]	1090
AG-86	BULMER	1944	1190	AG-33	KAULA	1941	1000
AG-69	BURIAS	1944	5371	AG-83	KENNISON	1944 [64]	1060
AG-35	CALYPSO [67]	1941	370	AG-78	KENT ISLAND	1945	5766
AG-42	CAMANGA	1942	2005	AG-50	†KOPARA	1942	334
AG-108	CHANDLER	1945 [64]	1090	AG-21	LAMBERTON	1945 [64]	1090
AG-74	COASTERS			AG-95	LITCHFIELD	1945 [64]	1190
	HARBOR	1944	5766	AG-118	MCCORMICK	1945 [64]	1190
AG-116	COLE	1945 [64]	1090	AG-87	MacLEISH	1945 [64]	1190

[62] Converted to repair ship (AR).
[63] Converted to hospital ship (AH).
[64] Conversion date.
[65] Converted to general store issue ship (AKS).
[66] Reclassified surveying ship (AGS).
[67] Transferred to Coast Guard.

AG Miscellaneous Auxiliaries (*cont'd*)

No.	Name	Comm.	Displ.	No.	Name	Comm.	Displ.
AG–43	MAJABA [68]	1942	1795	AG–79	SAN CLEMENTE	1944 [64]	8391
AG–44	MALANAO	1943	1077	AG–82	SCHENCK	1944 [64]	1090
AG–36	MANASQUAN [67]	1942	2580	AG–24	SEMMES	1935 [64]	1308
AG–47	MANHASSET [67]	1941	2900	AG–23	SEQUOIA	1933	103
AG–28	MANLEY [69]	1938 [64]	1020	AG–100	SICARD	1945 [64]	1190
AG–124	MAUMEE	1945 [64]	4990	AG–97	SIMPSON	1945 [64]	1190
AG–39	MENEMSHA [67]	1942	2580	AG–107	STANSBURY	1945 [64]	1060
AG–41	MIDWAY [70]	1942	1622	AG–32	SUMNER [66]	1940 [64]	3142
AG–40	MONOMOY [67]	1942	2580	AG–45	TAGANAK	1942	1560
AG–48	MUSKEGET [67]	1942	1800	AG–110	TREVER	1945 [64]	1190
AG–72	PARRIS ISLAND	1944	550	AG–46	TULURAN	1942	1470
AG–125	PATOKA	1945 [64]	5375	AG–103	UPSHUR	1945 [64]	1090
AG–25	POTOMAC	1936	401	AG–16	*UTAH*	1931 [64]	23,033
AG–99	PREBLE	1945 [64]	1190	AG–117	WHIPPLE	1945 [64]	1190
AG–101	PRUITT	1945 [64]	1190	AG–17	WYOMING	1932 [64]	27,243
AG–98	RAMSAY	1945 [64]	1160	AG–109	ZANE	1945 [64]	1190
AG–27	*ROBERT L.			AG–70	ZANIAH	1945 [64]	4000
	BARNES	1918	1630				

AG 16–17 converted from battleships; AG 19, 21, 104–106, 108–109, 111 from high-speed minesweepers; AG 24, 28, 80–87, 91, 95–97, 102–103, 107, 110, 112–118 from destroyers; AG 25–26, 35 from Coast Guard Cutters; AG 31–32, 67 from submarine tenders; AG 70–71 from cargo ships; AG–79 from seaplane tender; AG–90 from attack transport; AG 98–101 from fast minelayers; and AG 124–125 from oilers. AG 68–71, 73–78 were Maritime Commission EC2–S–C1 type and AG–72 converted from a PCE while building.

[64] Conversion date.
[65] Converted to general stores issue ship (AKS).
[66] Reclassified surveying ship (AGS).
[67] Transferred to Coast Guard.
[68] Reclassified unclassified vessel (IX).
[69] Reclassified high-speed transport (APD).
[70] Renamed PANAY 29 May 1943.

AGC Amphibious Force Command Ships

No.	Name	Comm.	Displ.	No.	Name	Comm.	Displ.
AGC–15	ADIRONDACK	1945	7234	AGC–7	MOUNT		
AGC–4	ANCON	1943 [71]	9946		MCKINLEY	1944	7234
AGC–1	APPALACHIAN	1943	7431	AGC–8	MOUNT		
AGC–10	AUBURN	1944	7234		OLYMPUS	1944	7234
AGC–18	BISCAYNE	1943 [71]	1710	AGC–13	PANAMINT	1944	7234
AGC–2	BLUE RIDGE	1943	7431	AGC–3	ROCKY MOUNT	1943	7431
AGC–5	CATOCTIN	1943	7706	AGC–14	TETON	1944	7234
AGC–11	ELDORADO	1944	7234	AGC–9	WASATCH	1944	7234
AGC–12	ESTES	1944	7234				

AGC 1–3, 5 are Maritime Commission C2–S–B1 type and AGC 7–15 C2–S–AJ1. AGC–4 was converted from a transport and AGC–18 from a small seaplane tender.
[71] Conversion date.

AGP Motor Torpedo Boat Tenders

No.	Name	Comm.	Displ.	No.	Name	Comm.	Displ.
AGP-12	ACONTIUS	1944	5236	AGP-1	*NIAGARA	1943 [71]	1333
AGP-14	ALECTO	1945	2179	AGP-10	ORESTES	1944	2028
AGP-16	ANTIGONE	1944	2179	AGP-6	OYSTER BAY	1943	1760
AGP-17	BRONTES	1945	2179	AGP-20	PONTUS	1943 [71]	1490
AGP-15	CALLISTO	1944	2179	AGP-4	PORTUNUS	1943	2028
AGP-18	CHIRON	1945	2179	AGP-11	SILENUS	1944	2028
AGP-13	CYRENE	1944	5236	AGP-5	VARUNA	1943	2028
AGP-2	HILO	1943 [71]	1534	AGP-8	WACHA-		
AGP-3	JAMESTOWN	1943 [71]	1730		PREAGUE	1944	1760
AGP-7	MOBJACK	1943	1760	AGP-9	WILLOUGHBY	1944	1760

AGP 1–3 converted from gunboats and AGP-20 from a LST. AGP 4–5, 10–11, 14–18 converted from LSTs and AGP 6–9 from small seaplane tenders while building. AGP 12–13 were Maritime Commission C1–A type.

[71] Conversion date.

AGS Surveying Ships

No.	Name	Comm.	Displ.	No.	Name	Comm.	Displ.
AGS-9	ARMISTEAD			AGS-10	JOHN BLISH	1945 [71]	273
	RUST	1945 [71]	244	AGS-7	LITTLEHALES	1945 [71]	265
AGS-4	BOWDITCH	1943 [71]	5405	AGS-3	†OCEANOG-		
AGS-11	CHAUVENET	1945 [71]	252		RAPHER	1942	1252
AGS-6	DERICKSON	1944 [71]	244	AGS-1	PATHFINDER	1942	1422
AGS-8	DUTTON	1945 [71]	273	AGS-14	SIMON		
AGS-12	HARKNESS	1945 [71]	265		NEWCOMB	1945 [71]	265
AGS-2	HYDROGRAPHER	1942	907	AGS-5	SUMNER	1943 [71]	3142
AGS-13	JAMES M.						
	GILLIS	1945 [71]	265				

AGS 1–3 transferred from Coast and Geodetic Survey; AGS 4–5 reclassified from miscellaneous auxiliaries; and AGS 6–14 converted from PCs and YMSs.

[71] Conversion date.

AH Hospital Ships

No.	Name	Comm.	Displ.	No.	Name	Comm.	Displ.
AH-13	BENEVOLENCE	1945	11,141	AH-1	RELIEF	1920	7237
AH-9	BOUNTIFUL	1944 [71]	7297	AH-16	REPOSE	1945	11,141
AH-6	COMFORT	1944	6000	AH-18	RESCUE	1945 [71]	5518
AH-15	CONSOLATION	1945	11,141	AH-10	SAMARITAN	1944 [71]	8932
AH-12	HAVEN	1945	11,141	AH-17	SANCTUARY	1945	11,141
AH-7	HOPE	1944	6000	AH-5	SOLACE	1941	6237
AH-8	MERCY	1944	6000	AH-14	TRANQUILLITY	1945	11,141
AH-11	REFUGE	1944 [71]	10,911				

AH 9–11 converted from transports; AH–18 from submarine tender. AH 6–8 were Maritime Commission C1–B type and AH 12–18, C4–S–B2.

[71] Conversion date.

AK Cargo Ships

No.	Name	Comm.	Displ.	No.	Name	Comm.	Displ.
AK-23	ALCHIBA [73]	1941	7293	AK-43	JUPITER [80]	1942	5594
AK-24	ALCYONE [73]	1941	7293	AK-236	LAKEWOOD		
AK-25	ALGORAB [73]	1941	7293		VICTORY	1944	4480
AK-26	ALHENA [73]	1941	7151	AK-229	LAS VEGAS		
AK-27	ALMAACK [73]	1942	7074		VICTORY	1944	4480
AK-47	AQUILA	1944	2054	AK-53	LIBRA [73]	1942	6973
AK-18	ARCTURUS [73]	1940	7476	AK-230	MANDERSON		
AK-51	ARIES	1942 [72]	1881		VICTORY	1944	4480
AK-44	†AROOSTOOK	1941 [72]	4200	AK-31	MARKAB [78]	1941	7919
AK-63	ASTERION [74]	1942	3628	AK-232	MAYFIELD		
AK-98	AURIGA	1943	5006		VICTORY	1944	4480
AK-231	BEDFORD			AK-42	MERCURY [81]	1942	5994
	VICTORY	1944	4480	AK-233	NEWCASTLE		
AK-20	BELLATRIX [73]	1942	5618		VICTORY	1944	4480
AK-28	BETELGEUSE [73]	1941	7476	AK-56	OBERON [73]	1942	7391
AK-227	BOULDER			AK-48	PEGASUS [82]	1941	1758
	VICTORY	1944	4480	AK-46	PLEIADES	1941	2874
AK-234	BUCYRUS			AK-19	PROCYON [73]	1941	8045
	VICTORY	1944	4480	AK-228	PROVO VICTORY	1944	4480
AK-13	CAPELLA	1921	4037	AK-235	RED OAK		
AK-29	DELTA [75]	1941	8975		VICTORY	1944	4480
AK-21	ELECTRA [73]	1942	5618	AK-14	REGULUS	1940	3590
AK-80	ENCELADUS	1943	1677	AK-49	SATURN [83]	1942	5088
AK-22	FOMALHAUT [76]	1942 [72]	4036	AK-15	SIRIUS	1922	4323
AK-52	GEMINI [77]	1942 [72]	1745	AK-16	SPICA	1940	3914
AK-30	HAMUL [78]	1941	8560	AK-55	TITANIA [73]	1942	7047
AK-41	HERCULES	1941	5920	AK-17	VEGA	1921	4323
AK-82	HYDRA [79]	1943	1677				

AK-22 converted from attack cargo ship, and AK-44 from minelayer. AK 18–19, 23–25, 28, 42–43 were Maritime Commission C2–Cargo type; AK 20–21, C2–T; AK-22, C1–A; AK-26, C2–S; AK 27 and 41, C3–E; AK 30–31, C3–Cargo; AK 53 and 55–56, C2–F; AK 80 and 82, N3–M–A1; AK-98, C1–B; AK 228–237, VC2–S–AP2 "Victory."

[72] Conversion date.
[73] Reclassified attack cargo ship (AKA).
[74] Transferred to Coast Guard.
[75] Converted to repair ship (AR).
[76] Reclassified attack cargo ship (AKA) 1943 but reverted to AK 1944.
[77] Converted to transport (AP).
[78] Converted to destroyer tender (AD).
[79] Transferred to Army.
[80] Converted to aviation supply ship (AVS).
[81] Converted to general stores issue ship (AKS).
[82] Converted to unclassified vessel (IX).
[83] Converted to store ship (AF).

AK Cargo Ships (*cont'd*): CRATER Class

4023–4674 tons. Maritime Commission EC2–S–C1 "Liberty" type.

No.	Name	Comm.	No.	Name	Comm.
AK–71	ADHARA	1942	AK–112	GRUMIUM [86]	1943
AK–90	ALBIREO	1943	AK–107	HYPERION	1943
AK–116	ALDERAMIN	1943	AK–221	KENMORE	1944 [85]
AK–109	ALIOTH [86]	1943	AK–128	LEONIS	1943
AK–114	ALKAID	1943	AK–125	LESUTH	1943
AK–110	ALKES	1943	AK–222	LIVINGSTON	1944 [85]
AK–225	ALLEGAN	1944	AK–100	LYNX	1943
AK–127	ALNITAH	1943	AK–101	LYRA	1943
AK–72	*ALUDRA	1942	AK–119	MATAR	1944
AK–226	APPANOOSE	1944	AK–126	MEGREZ	1943
AK–136	ARA	1944	AK–131	MELUCTA	1944
AK–73	ARIDED	1942	AK–123	MENKAR	1944
AK–130	ARKAB	1944	AK–94	MINTAKA	1943
AK–137	ASCELLA	1944	AK–95	MURZIM	1943
AK–124	AZIMECH	1944	AK–105	NAOS	1943
AK–122	BAHAM [84]	1944	AK–139	PAVO	1944
AK–99	BOOTES	1943	AK–129	PHOBOS	1944
AK–106	CAELUM	1943	AK–224	PRINCE GEORGES	1944 [85]
AK–74	CARINA	1942	AK–132	PROPOS	1944
AK–75	CASSIOPEIA	1942	AK–108	ROTANIN	1943
AK–76	CELENO	1943	AK–113	RUTILICUS	1943
AK–77	CETUS	1943	AK–121	SABIK	1943
AK–138	CHELEB	1944	AK–103	SCULPTOR	1943
AK–91	COR CAROLI	1943	AK–133	SEGINUS	1944
AK–70	CRATER	1942	AK–97	*SERPENS	1943
AK–115	CRUX	1944	AK–118	SHAULA	1943
AK–223	DE GRASSE	1944 [85]	AK–140	SITULA	1944
AK–78	*DEIMOS	1943	AK–96	STEROPE	1943
AK–79	DRACO	1943	AK–134	SYRMA	1944
AK–92	ERIDANUS	1943	AK–102	TRIANGULUM	1943
AK–93	ETAMIN [86]	1943	AK–135	VENUS	1944
AK–104	GANYMEDE	1943	AK–120	ZANIAH [84]	1943
AK–111	GIANSAR	1943	AK–117	ZAURAK	1944

[84] Converted to miscellaneous auxiliary (AG).
[85] Date of conversion from transport.
[86] Converted to unclassified vessel (IX).

ALAMOSA Class

2382–3000 tons. Maritime Commission C1–M–AV1 type.

No.	Name	Comm.	No.	Name	Comm.
AK–156	ALAMOSA	1944	AK–161	BEAVERHEAD	1945
AK–157	ALCONA	1944	AK–162	BELTRAMI	1945
AK–158	AMADOR	1944	AK–163	BLOUNT	1945
AK–159	ANTRIM	1944	AK–164	BREVARD	1945
AK–160	AUTAUGA	1944	AK–165	BULLOCK	1945

ALAMOSA Class (*cont'd*)

No.	Name	Comm.	No.	Name	Comm.
AK-166	CABELL	1945	AK-188	HERKIMER	1945
AK-167	CALEDONIA	1945	AK-189	HIDALGO	1945
AK-168	CHARLEVOIX	1945	AK-190	KENOSHA	1945
AK-169	CHATHAM	1945	AK-191	LEBANON	1945
AK-170	CHICOT	1945	AK-192	LEHIGH	1945
AK-171	CLAIBORNE	1945	AK-194	MARENGO	1945
AK-172	CLARION	1945	AK-195	MIDLAND	1945
AK-173	CODINGTON	1945	AK-197	MUSCATINE	1945
AK-174	COLQUITT	1945	AK-198	MUSKINGUM	1945
AK-175	CRAIGHEAD	1945	AK-200	PEMBINA	1945
AK-178	FAIRFIELD	1945	AK-205	POINSETT	1945
AK-179	FARIBAULT	1945	AK-206	PONTOTOC [87]	1945
AK-180	FENTRESS	1945	AK-207	RICHLAND	1945
AK-181	FLAGLER	1945	AK-208	ROCKDALE	1945
AK-182	GADSDEN	1945	AK-209	SCHUYLER	1945
AK-183	GLACIER	1945	AK-210	SCREVEN	1945
AK-184	GRAINGER	1945	AK-211	SEBASTIAN	1945
AK-186	HABERSHAM	1945	AK-213	SUSSEX	1945
AK-187	HENNEPIN	1945	AK-214	TARRANT	1945

[87] Converted to miscellaneous auxiliary (AG).

AKA Attack Cargo Ships

No.	Name	Reclass.	Displ.	No.	Name	Reclass.	Displ.
AKA-6	ALCHIBA	1943	7293	AKA-4	ELECTRA	1943	5618
AKA-7	ALCYONE	1943	7293	AKA-5	FOMAL-		
AKA-8	ALGORAB	1943	7293		HAUT [88]	1943	4036
AKA-9	ALHENA	1943	7151	AKA-12	LIBRA	1943	6973
AKA-10	ALMAACK	1943	7074	AKA-14	OBERON	1943	7391
AKA-1	ARCTURUS	1943	7476	AKA-2	PROCYON	1943	8045
AKA-3	BELLATRIX	1943	5618	AKA-13	TITANIA	1943	7047
AKA-11	BETELGEUSE	1943	7476				

Reclassified from cargo ships. AKA 1–2, 6–8, 11 were Maritime Commission C2–Cargo type; AKA 3–4, C2–T; AKA–5, C1–A; AKA–9, C2–S; and AKA–10, C3–E.

[88] Reclassified cargo ship (AK).

ANDROMEDA Class

6556–7132 tons. Maritime Commission C2–S–B1 type.

No.	Name	Comm.	No.	Name	Comm.
AKA-53	ACHERNAR	1944	AKA-56	ARNEB	1943
AKA-54	ALGOL	1944	AKA-57	CAPRICORNUS	1943
AKA-55	ALSHAIN	1944	AKA-17	CENTAURUS	1944
AKA-15	ANDROMEDA	1944	AKA-18	CEPHEUS	1944
AKA-16	AQUARIUS	1943	AKA-58	CHARA	1944

AKA Attack Cargo Ships: ANDROMEDA Class (*cont'd*)

No.	Name	Comm.	No.	Name	Comm.
AKA-59	DIPHDA	1944	AKA-63	THEENIM	1944
AKA-60	LEO	1944	AKA-19	THUBAN	1943
AKA-95	MARQUETTE	1945	AKA-88	UVALDE	1944
AKA-96	MATHEWS	1945	AKA-20	VIRGO	1943
AKA-97	MERRICK	1945	AKA-89	WARRICK	1944
AKA-98	MONTAGUE	1945	AKA-90	WHITESIDE	1944
AKA-61	MULIPHEN	1944	AKA-91	WHITLEY	1944
AKA-100	OGLETHORPE	1945	AKA-94	WINSTON	1945
AKA-99	ROLETTE	1945	AKA-92	WYANDOT	7944
AKA-62	SHELIAK	1944	AKA-93	YANCEY	1944

ARTEMIS Class

4087 tons. Maritime Commission S4-SE2-BE1 type.

No.	Name	Comm.	No.	Name	Comm.
AKA-21	ARTEMIS	1944	AKA-37	ROXANE	1945
AKA-22	ATHENE	1944	AKA-38	SAPPHO	1945
AKA-23	AURELIA	1944	AKA-39	SARITA	1945
AKA-24	BIRGIT	1944	AKA-40	SCANIA	1945
AKA-25	CIRCE	1944	AKA-41	SELINUR	1945
AKA-26	CORVUS	1944	AKA-42	SIDONIA	1945
AKA-27	DEVOSA	1944	AKA-43	SIRONA	1945
AKA-28	HYDRUS	1944	AKA-44	SYLVANIA	1945
AKA-29	LACERTA	1944	AKA-45	TABORA	1945
AKA-30	LUMEN	1944	AKA-46	TROILUS	1945
AKA-31	MEDEA	1945	AKA-47	TURANDOT	1945
AKA-32	MELLENA	1945	AKA-48	VALERIA	1945
AKA-33	OSTARA	1945	AKA-49	VANADIS	1945
AKA-34	PAMINA	1945	AKA-50	VERITAS	1945
AKA-35	POLANA	1945	AKA-51	XENIA	1945
AKA-36	RENATE	1945	AKA-52	ZENOBIA	1945

TOLLAND Class

6318–6456 tons. Maritime Commission C2-S-AJ3 type.

No.	Name	Comm.	No.	Name	Comm.
AKA-75	ALAMANCE	1944	AKA-68	STOKES	1944
AKA-72	CASWELL	1944	AKA-69	SUFFOLK	1944
AKA-87	DUPLIN	1945	AKA-70	TATE	1944
AKA-74	LENOIR	1944	AKA-71	TODD	1944
AKA-73	NEW HANOVER	1944	AKA-64	TOLLAND	1944
AKA-101	OTTAWA	1945	AKA-76	TORRANCE	1944
AKA-102	PRENTISS	1945	AKA-77	TOWNER	1944
AKA-103	RANKIN	1945	AKA-78	TREGO	1944
AKA-104	SEMINOLE	1945	AKA-79	TROUSDALE	1944
AKA-65	SHOSHONE	1944	AKA-80	TYRRELL	1944
AKA-105	SKAGIT	1945	AKA-106	UNION	1945
AKA-66	SOUTHAMPTON	1944	AKA-81	VALENCIA	1944
AKA-67	STARR	1944	AKA-82	VENANGO	1944

AKA Attack Cargo Ships (*cont'd*)

No.	Name	Comm.	No.	Name	Comm.
AKA-107	VERMILION	1945	AKA-84	WAUKESHA	1944
AKA-83	VINTON	1944	AKA-85	WHEATLAND	1944
AKA-108	WASHBURN	1945	AKA-86	WOODFORD	1944

AKN Net Cargo Ships

No.	Name	Comm.	Displ.	No.	Name	Comm.	Displ.
AKN-1	INDUS	1944	4023	AKN-3	TUSCANA	1944	4023
AKN-4	KEOKUK	1943 [89]	3582	AKN-5	ZEBRA	1944	4023
AKN-2	SAGITTARIUS	1944	4023				

AKN-4 converted from minelayer; others were Maritime Commission EC2-S-C1 "Liberty" conversions.

[89] Conversion date.

AKS General Stores Issue Ships

No.	Name	Comm.	Displ.	No.	Name	Comm.	Displ.
AKS-5	ACUBENS	1944	5244	AKS-6	KOCHAB	1944	4852
AKS-3	ANTARES	1940 [89]	4800	AKS-15	LIGURIA	1944	4852
AKS-1	CASTOR	1941	6365	AKS-7	LUNA	1944	4852
AKS-10	CYBELE	1944	4818	AKS-20	MERCURY	1945 [89]	5994
AKS-11	GRATIA	1944	4852	AKS-2	*POLLUX	1941	6365
AKS-12	HECUBA	1945	4852	AKS-4	POLLUX	1944	6345
AKS-13	HESPERIA	1945	4852	AKS-8	TALITA	1944	4852
AKS-14	IOLANDA	1944	5055	AKS-9	VOLANS	1944	4852

AKS-3 converted from miscellaneous auxiliary; AKS-20 from cargo ship. AKS 1-2 and 20 were Maritime Commission C2-Cargo type; AKS-4, a C2-F; and AKS 5-15 were EC2-S-C1 "Liberties."

[89] Conversion date.

AN Net-Laying Ships

No.	Name	Comm.	Displ.	No.	Name	Comm.	Displ.
AN-58	ABELE	1944	1175	AN-61	CHINABERRY	1944	1175
AN-38	*ALIANTHUS	1944	1100	AN-17	CHINQUAPIN	1941	560
AN-6	ALOE	1941	560	AN-12	CINCHONA	1941	560
AN-40	ANAQUA	1944	1100	AN-50	CINNAMON	1944	1225
AN-7	ASH	1941	560	AN-42	CLIFFROSE	1944	1100
AN-41	BARETTA	1944	1100	AN-78	COHOES	1945	650
AN-39	BITTERBUSH	1944	1100	AN-44	CORKWOOD	1944	1100
AN-8	BOXWOOD	1941	560	AN-45	CORNEL	1944	1100
AN-13	BUCKEYE	1941	560	AN-15	EBONY	1941	560
AN-14	BUCKTHORNE	1941	560	AN-20	ELDER	1941	560
AN-9	BUTTERNUT	1941	560	AN-79	ETLAH	1945	650
AN-47	CANOTIA	1944	1100	AN-16	EUCALYPTUS	1941	560
AN-10	CATALPA	1941	560	AN-18	GUM TREE	1941	560
AN-60	CATCLAW	1944	1175	AN-25	HACKBERRY [90]	1941	560
AN-11	CHESTNUT	1941	560	AN-29	HAZEL	1941	560

[90] Transferred to France under Lend-Lease.

AN Net-Laying Ships (*cont'd*)

No.	Name	Comm.	Displ.	No.	Name	Comm.	Displ.
AN-19	HOLLY	1941	560	AN-30	REDWOOD	1941	560
AN-62	HOPTREE	1944	1175	AN-31	ROSEWOOD	1941	560
AN-5	KEOKUK [91]	1942	3582	AN-32	SANDALWOOD	1941	560
AN-48	LANCEWOOD	1943	1225	AN-43	SATINLEAF	1944	1100
AN-21	LARCH	1941	560	AN-88	SHAKAMAXON	1945	650
AN-22	LOCUST	1941	560	AN-67	SHELLBARK	1944	1175
AN-23	MAHOGANY	1941	560	AN-51	SILVERBELL	1944	1225
AN-81	MANAYUNK	1945	650	AN-68	SILVERLEAF	1944	1175
AN-54	MANCHINEEL	1944	1225	AN-52	SNOWBELL	1944	1225
AN-24	MANGO	1941	560	AN-53	SPICEWOOD	1944	1225
AN-82	MARIETTA	1945	650	AN-69	STAGBUSH	1944	1175
AN-46	MASTIC	1944	1100	AN-80	SUNCOOK	1945	650
AN-26	MIMOSA [90]	1941	560	AN-34	TEABERRY	1942	560
AN-27	MULBERRY	1941	560	AN-35	TEAK	1942	560
AN-83	NAHANT	1945	650	AN-59	TEREBINTH	1943	1196
AN-84	NAUBUC	1944	650	AN-89	TONAWANDA	1945	650
AN-33	NUTMEG	1941	560	AN-55	TORCHWOOD	1944	1225
AN-85	ONEOTA	1945	650	AN-90	TUNXIS	1945	650
AN-28	PALM	1941	560	AN-57	VIBURNUM	1944	1175
AN-49	PAPAYA	1943	1225	AN-91	WAXSAW	1945	650
AN-86	PASSACONAWAY	1945	650	AN-63	WHITEWOOD	1944	1118
AN-87	PASSAIC	1945	650	AN-56	WINTERBERRY	1944	1225
AN-36	PEPPERWOOD [90]	1942	560	AN-92	YAZOO	1945	650
AN-66	PINON	1944	1108	AN-37	YEW [90]	1942	560

[90] Transferred to France under Lend-Lease.
[91] Converted to minelayer (CM).

AO Oilers

No.	Name	Comm.	Displ.	No.	Name	Comm.	Displ.
AO-97	ALLAGASH	1945	5730	AO-30	CHEMUNG	1941	7256
AO-94	ANACOSTIA	1945	5730	AO-31	CHENANGO [93]	1941	7256
AO-51	ASHTABULA	1943	7236	AO-78	CHEPACHET	1943	5730
AO-66	ATASCOSA	1942	6043	AO-34	CHICOPEE	1942	5375
AO-56	AUCILLA	1943	7236	AO-54	CHIKASKIA	1943	7236
AO-45	BIG HORN [92]	1942	4150	AO-63	CHIPOLA	1944	7236
AO-4	BRAZOS	1919	5723	AO-68	CHIWAWA	1942	5650
AO-52	CACAPON	1943	7236	AO-22	CIMARRON	1939	7256
AO-67	CACHE	1942	5730	AO-101	COHOCTON	1945	5730
AO-82	CAHABA	1944	5730	AO-77	COSSATOT	1943	5730
AO-53	CALIENTE	1943	7236	AO-79	COWANESQUE	1943	5730
AO-95	CANEY	1945	5730	AO-3	CUYAMA	1917	5946

[92] Transferred to Coast Guard 1944; reacquired 1945 and converted to unclassified vessel (IX).
[93] Converted to escort aircraft carrier (AVG).

AO Oilers (*cont'd*)

No.	Name	Comm.	Displ.	No.	Name	Comm.	Displ.
AO-55	ELOKOMIN	1943	7236	AO-9	PATOKA [94]	1919	5375
AO-69	ENOREE	1943	5708	AO-44	PATUXENT	1942	6258
AO-70	ESCALANTE	1943	5630	AO-6	*PECOS	1921	5000
AO-80	ESCAMBIA	1943	5730	AO-65	PECOS	1942	5730
AO-32	GUADALUPE	1941	7256	AO-24	PLATTE	1939	7256
AO-35	HOUSATONIC	1942	5375	AO-86	PONAGANSET	1944	5730
AO-1	*KANAWHA	1915	5950	AO-12	RAMAPO	1919	5422
AO-39	KANKAKEE	1942	6013	AO-18	RAPIDAN	1922	5422
AO-27	KASKASKIA	1940	7256	AO-25	SABINE	1940	7256
AO-15	KAWEAH	1921	5450	AO-26	SALAMONIE	1941	7256
AO-81	KENNEBAGO	1943	5730	AO-19	SALINAS	1921	5422
AO-36	KENNEBEC	1942	6013	AO-28	SANGAMON [93]	1940	7256
AO-40	LACKAWANNA	1942	5580	AO-29	SANTEE [93]	1940	7256
AO-16	LARAMIE	1921	5450	AO-11	SAPELO	1920	5422
AO-58	MANATEE	1944	7236	AO-74	SARANAC	1943	5730
AO-57	MARIAS	1944	7236	AO-75	SAUGATUCK	1943	5730
AO-83	MASCOMA	1944	5730	AO-76	SCHUYLKILL	1943	5730
AO-41	MATTAPONI	1942	5882	AO-87	SEBEC	1944	5730
AO-17	MATTOLE	1940	5450	AO-20	SEPULGA	1922	5422
AO-2	MAUMEE [94]	1915	4990	AO-61	SEVERN	1944	7236
AO-40	MERRIMACK	1942	6013	AO-90	SHIKEL-		
AO-73	MILLICOMA	1943	5730		LAMY [96]	1943	3200
AO-59	*MISSIS-			AO-93	SOUBARISSEN	1945	5730
	SINEWA	1943	7190	AO-49	SUAMICO	1942	5730
AO-42	MONONGA-			AO-33	SUWANNEE [93]	1941	7256
	HELA	1942	5882	AO-50	TALLULAH	1942	5730
AO-60	NANTAHALA	1944	7236	AO-62	TALUGA	1944	7236
AO-5	*NECHES	1920	5723	AO-96	TAMALPAIS	1945	5730
AO-47	NECHES	1942	5882	AO-43	TAPPAHAN-		
AO-23	*NEOSHO	1941	6521		NOCK	1942	5882
AO-48	NEOSHO	1942	5580	AO-21	TIPPECANOE	1922	5422
AO-71	NESHANIC	1943	5630	AO-64	TOLOVANA	1945	7236
AO-72	NIOBRARA	1943	5708	AO-88	TOMAHAWK	1944	5730
AO-84	OKLAWAHA	1943	5730	AO-13	TRINITY	1920	5263
AO-85	PAMANSET	1943	5730	AO-46	VICTORIA	1942	4650
AO-89	†PASIG	1943	9783 [95]	AO-38	WINOOSKI	1942	5580

AO 22–33, 51–64 and 97 were Maritime Commission MC–N or T3–S2–A1 type; AO 36–40, 48, and 68–72 were MC–SO or T3–S–A1 type; AO 41–44 and 47, MC–K; AO 49–50, 65, 67, and 73–79 were T2–SE–A1; and AO 80–88, 93–96, and 101, T2–SE–A2.

[93] Converted to escort aircraft carrier (AVG).
[94] Reclassified miscellaneous auxiliary (AG).
[95] Gross tonnage.
[96] Converted to gasolene tanker (AOG).

AOG Gasolene Tankers

No.	Name	Comm.	Displ.	No.	Name	Comm.	Displ.
AOG-6	AGAWAM	1943	1783	AOG-54	NATCHAUG	1945	1764
AOG-23	AMMONUSUC	1944	845	AOG-10	NEMASKET	1944	1783
AOG-14	AROOSTOOK [97]	1943	1007	AOG-55	NESPELEN	1945	1764
AOG-25	CALAMUS	1944	845	AOG-33	OCHLOCKONEE	1944	846
AOG-48	CHEHALIS	1944	1764	AOG-34	OCONEE	1945	846
AOG-49	CHESTATEE	1944	1842	AOG-35	OGEECHEE	1944	846
AOG-50	CHEWAUCAN	1945	1764	AOG-36	ONTONAGON	1944	846
AOG-26	CHIWAUKUM	1944	846	AOG-18	PASQUOTANK	1943	769
AOG-15	CONASAUGA [97]	1943	3100	AOG-1	PATAPSCO	1943	1841
AOG-62	CONEMAUGH	1945	850	AOG-38	PONCHATOULA	1944	846
AOG-7	ELKHORN	1944	1783	AOG-39	QUASTINET	1944	846
AOG-27	ESCATAWPA	1944	846	AOG-3	RIO GRANDE	1943	1841
AOG-8	GENESEE	1944	1783	AOG-40	SACANDAGA	1944	846
AOG-28	GUALALA	1944	846	AOG-19	SAKATONCHEE	1944	769
AOG-16	GUYANDOT [97]	1943	800	AOG-61	SAKONNET	1944	850
AOG-12	HALAWA	1942	1155	AOG-20	SEEKONK	1944	769
AOG-29	HIWASSEE	1944	846	AOG-21	SEQUATCHIE	1944	846
AOG-30	KALAMAZOO	1944	846	AOG-24	*SHEEPSCOT	1944	846
AOG-13	KALOLI	1942	1155	AOG-47	SHIKELLAMY	1943 [98]	3200
AOG-31	KANAWHA	1944	846	AOG-5	SUSQUE-		
AOG-2	KERN	1943	1842		HANNA	1943	1842
AOG-9	KISHWAUKEE	1944	1783	AOG-41	TETONKAHA	1944	846
AOG-63	KLASKANINE	1945	850	AOG-11	TOMBIGBEE	1944	1783
AOG-64	KLICKITAT	1945	1988	AOG-42	TOWALIGA	1944	846
AOG-60	MANOKIN	1944	850	AOG-43	TULAROSA	1945	846
AOG-51	MAQUOKETA	1945	1842	AOG-4	WABASH	1943	1842
AOG-52	MATTABESSET	1945	1842	AOG-44	WAKULLA	1945	846
AOG-17	METTAWEE	1943	769	AOG-46	WAUPACA	1945	846
AOG-65	MICHIGAMME	1945	1988	AOG-22	WAUTAUGA	1944	846
AOG-53	NAMAKAGON	1945	1764	AOG-45	YACONA	1945	846
AOG-66	NANTICOKE	1945	1988	AOG-37	YAHARA	1944	846
AOG-32	NARRAGUAGAS	1944	846				

AOG-47 was converted from an oiler. AOG 17-46 and 60-63 were Maritime Commission T1-M-A2 type while AOG 64-66 were T1-M-BT1.

[97] Transferred to France under Lend-Lease.
[98] Conversion date.

AP Transports

No.	Name	Comm.	Displ.	No.	Name	Comm.	Displ.
AP-124	ADMIRAL C. F.			AP-126	ADM. HUGH		
	HUGHES	1945	9679		RODMAN	1945	9679
AP-123	ADM. E. W.			AP-122	ADM. R. E.		
	EBERLE	1945	9679		COONTZ	1944	9679
AP-125	ADM. H. T.			AP-121	ADM. W. L.		
	MAYO	1945	9679		CAPPS	1944	9679

AP Transports (*cont'd*)

No.	Name	Comm.	Displ.	No.	Name	Comm.	Displ.
AP-120	ADM. W. S.			AP-157	GEN. C. C.		
	BENSON	1944	9679		BALLOU	1945	9943
AP-35	AMERICAN			AP-138	GEN. C. G.		
	LEGION [99]	1941	13,529		MORTON	1944	9943
AP-66	ANCON [100]	1942	9946	AP-142	GEN. C. H.		
AP-76	ANNE				MUIR	1945	9943
	ARUNDEL	1942	7980	AP-156	GEN. D. W.		
AP-174	ARLINGTON	1944	5668		AULTMAN	1945	9943
AP-55	ARTHUR MID-			AP-147	GEN. E. T.		
	DLETON [99]	1942	10,812		COLLINS	1944	9943
AP-11	BARNETT [99]	1941	9432	AP-115	GEN. G. M.		
AP-65	CALVERT [99]	1942	8889		RANDALL	1944	11,828
AP-172	CAPE			AP-130	GEN. G. O.		
	JOHNSON	1944	5668		SQUIER	1943	9877
AP-58	CHARLES			AP-143	GEN. H. B.		
	CARROLL [99]	1942	8889		FREEMAN	1945	9943
AP-31	CHATEAU			AP-144	GEN. H. F.		
	THIERRY [101]	1941	9306		HODGES	1945	9943
AP-5	CHAUMONT [102]	1921	8932	AP-136	GEN. H. L.		
AP-166	COMET	1944	7440		SCOTT	1944	10,034
AP-40	CRESCENT			AP-113	GEN. H. W.		
	CITY [99]	1941	8429		BUTNER	1943	11,828
AP-164	DE GRASSE [103]	1943	4846	AP-145	GEN. HARRY		
AP-67	DOROTHEA L.				TAYLOR	1944	9943
	DIX	1942	6888	AP-176	GEN. J. C.		
AP-52	*EDWARD				BRECKIN-		
	RUTLEDGE	1942	8355		RIDGE	1945	11,828
AP-69	ELIZABETH C.			AP-149	GEN. J. H.		
	STANTON	1942	7980		MCRAE	1944	9943
AP-177	EUROPA	1945	43,407	AP-132	GEN. J. R.		
AP-70	FLORENCE				BROOKE	1944	9877
	NIGHTINGALE	1942	7980	AP-110	GEN. JOHN		
AP-14	FULLER [99]	1940	8789		POPE	1944	10,704
AP-75	GEMINI	1942 [104]	1745	AP-154	GEN. LE ROY		
AP-111	GEN. A. E.				ELTINGE	1945	9943
	ANDERSON	1943	11,828	AP-140	GEN. M. B.		
AP-155	GEN. A. W.				STEWART	1945	9943
	BREWSTER	1945	9943	AP-116	GEN. M. C.		
AP-141	GEN. A. W.				MEIGS	1944	10,786
	GREELY	1945	9943				

[99] Converted to attack transport (APA).
[100] Converted to amphibious force command ship (AGC).
[101] Transferred to the Army.
[102] Converted to hospital ship (AH).
[103] Converted to cargo ship (AK).
[104] Transferred to Brazil under Lend-Lease.

AP Transports (*cont'd*)

No.	Name	Comm.	Displ.	No.	Name	Comm.	Displ.
AP-148	GEN. M. L. HERSEY	1944	9943	AP-105	GEORGE F. ELLIOT	1943	6590
AP-150	GEN. M. M. PATRICK	1944	9943	AP-169	GOLDEN CITY	1944	7440
				AP-8	HARRIS [99]	1941	13,529
AP-133	GEN. O. H. ERNST	1944	10,034	AP-17	HARRY LEE [99]	1940	9989
AP-152	GEN. OMAR BUNDY	1945	9943	AP-1	HENDERSON [102]	1917	7297
				AP-30	HENRY T. ALLEN [99]	1941	12,400
AP-139	GEN. R. E. CALLAN	1944	9943	AP-173	HERALD OF THE MORNING	1944	7440
AP-134	GEN. R. L. HOWZE	1944	10,034	AP-54	†HERMITAGE	1942	15,639
AP-153	GEN. R. M. BLATCHFORD	1945	9943	AP-12	HEYWOOD [99]	1941	8789
AP-137	GEN. S. D. STURGIS	1944	10,034	AP-43	*HUGH L. SCOTT	1942	12,400
AP-131	GEN. T. H. BLISS	1944	9877	AP-27	HUNTER LIGGETT [99]	1941	14,174
AP-112	GEN. W. A. MANN	1943	11,828	AP-34	J. FRANKLIN BELL [99]	1941	13,529
AP-151	GEN. W. C. LANGFITT	1944	9943	AP-167	JOHN LAND	1944	7440
				AP-51	JOHN PENN [99]	1942	8659
AP-146	GEN. W. F. HASE	1944	9943	AP-50	*JOSEPH HEWES	1942	7300
AP-158	GEN. W. G. HAAN	1945	9943	AP-26	JOSEPH T. DICKMAN [99]	1941	13,484
AP-117	GEN. W. H. GORDON	1944	10,786	AP-62	KENMORE [102]	1942	10,911
AP-135	GEN. W. M. BLACK	1944	10,034	AP-162	KENMORE [103]	1943	4846
				AP-28	KENT [101]	1941	5765
AP-118	GEN. W. P. RICHARDSON	1944	10,786	AP-102	LA SALLE	1944	5933
AP-114	GEN. WILLIAM MITCHELL	1944	11,828	AP-73	*LEEDSTOWN	1942	9055
				AP-74	LE JEUNE	1942	12,225
AP-119	GEN. WILLIAM WEIGEL	1945	10,786	AP-25	LEONARD WOOD [99]	1941	13,529
				AP-163	LIVINGSTON [103]	1943	4846
AP-57	GEORGE CLYMER [99]	1942	11,058	AP-71	LYON	1942	7741
				AP-10	MCCAWLEY [99]	1941	9304
AP-13	*GEORGE F. ELLIOTT	1941	7431	AP-64	MONROVIA [99]	1942	8889
				AP-61	MONTICELLO	1941	16,755
				AP-22	MOUNT VERNON	1941	22,559

[99] Converted to attack transport (APA).
[100] Converted to amphibious force command ship (AGC).
[101] Transferred to the Army.
[102] Converted to hospital ship (AH).
[103] Converted to cargo ship (AK).

AP Transports (*cont'd*)

No.	Name	Comm.	Displ.	No.	Name	Comm.	Displ.
AP–20	MUNARGO [101]	1941	18,895	AP–42	*TASKER H.		
AP–16	NEVILLE [99]	1940	8789		BLISS	1942	12,400
AP–24	ORIZABA [104]	1941	7078	AP–60	THOMAS		
AP–38	PRESIDENT				JEFFERSON [99]	1942	10,210
	ADAMS [99]	1941	10,210	AP–59	*THOMAS		
AP–39	PRES. HAYES [99]	1941	10,305		STONE	1942	8475
AP–37	PRES.			AP–77	THURSTON	1942	6932
	JACKSON [99]	1942	10,210	AP–29	U. S. GRANT	1941	10,352
AP–104	PRES. MONROE	1943	7792	AP–21	WAKEFIELD	1941	22,559
AP–103	PRES. POLK	1943	8422	AP–168	WAR HAWK	1944	7440
AP–165	PRINCE			AP–23	WEST POINT	1941	23,179
	GEORGE [103]	1943		AP–7	WHARTON	1939	12,998
AP–33	REPUBLIC [101]	1941	20,110	AP–15	WILLIAM P.		
AP–63	†ROCHAMBEAU	1942	10,748		BIDDLE [99]	1940	8789
AP–32	ST. MIHEIL [101]	1941	8213	AP–6	WILLIAM WARD		
AP–56	SAMUEL				BURROWS	1940	4751
	CHASE [99]	1942	10,812	AP–170	WINGED		
AP–175	STARLIGHT	1944	6363		ARROW	1944	7440
AP–171	STORM KING	1943	5343	AP–9	ZEILIN [99]	1941	13,529
AP–41	STRATFORD	1941	2632				
AP–72	*SUSAN B.						
	ANTHONY	1942	9055				

AP 37–39, 59–60, 103–104 were Maritime Commission C3–A type; AP 40, 58, 64–65, and 105, C3–Delta; AP 55–57, C3–P; AP–67 a C3–E; AP 69–71 and 76, C3–Cargo; AP–77 a C2–F; AP 102, 166, 168–170 were C2–S–B1; AP 110–119, P2–S2–R2; AP 120–126, P2–SE2–R1; AP 130–158, C4–S–A1; AP 162–165, EC2–S–C1 "Liberty"; AP 171 and 175, C2–S–AJ1; and AP 172 and 174, C1–B.

[99] Converted to attack transport (APA).
[100] Converted to amphibious force command ship (AGC).
[101] Transferred to the Army.
[102] Converted to hospital ship (AH).
[103] Converted to cargo ship (AK).
[104] Transferred to Brazil under Lend-Lease.

APA Attack Transports

No.	Name	Comm.	Displ.	No.	Name	Comm.	Displ.
APA–91	ADAIR	1944	7970	APA–21	CRESCENT		
APA–17	AMERICAN				CITY	1943 [105]	8429
	LEGION	1943 [105]	13,529	APA–97	DAUPHIN	1944	7970
APA–25	ARTHUR MID-			APA–1	DOYEN	1943	4351
	DLETON	1943 [106]	10,812	APA–98	DUTCHESS	1944	7970
APA–5	BARNETT	1943 [105]	9432	APA–11	FELAND	1943	4351
APA–94	BAXTER	1943	8355	APA–89	FREDERICK		
APA–32	CALVERT	1943 [105]	8889		FUNSTON	1943	10,967
APA–28	CHARLES			APA–7	FULLER	1943 [105]	8789
	CARROLL	1943 [105]	8889				

[105] Conversion date.
[106] Converted to miscellaneous auxiliary (AG).

APA Attack Transports (*cont'd*)

No.	Name	Comm.	Displ.	No.	Name	Comm.	Displ.
APA-27	GEORGE CLYMER	1943 [105]	11,058	APA-49	ORMSBY	1943	7300
APA-2	HARRIS	1943 [105]	13,529	APA-50	PIERCE	1943	7300
APA-10	HARRY LEE	1943 [105]	9989	APA-19	PRESIDENT ADAMS	1943 [105]	10,210
APA-15	HENRY T. ALLEN [106]	1943 [105]	12,400	APA-20	PRES. HAYES	1943 [105]	10,305
APA-6	HEYWOOD	1943[105]	8789	APA-18	PRES. JACKSON	1943 [105]	10,210
APA-14	HUNTER LIGGETT	1943 [105]	14,174	APA-103	QUEENS	1944	7970
APA-16	J. FRANKLIN BELL	1943 [105]	13,529	APA-26	SAMUEL CHASE	1943 [105]	10,812
APA-90	JAMES O'HARA	1943	10,967	APA-105	SHELBY	1945	7970
APA-23	*JOHN PENN	1943 [105]	8659	APA-51	SHERIDAN	1943	7300
APA-13	JOSEPH T. DICKMAN	1943 [105]	13,484	APA-52	SUMTER	1943	8355
APA-56	LEEDSTOWN	1943	8276	APA-30	THOMAS JEFFERSON	1943 [105]	10,210
APA-12	LEONARD WOOD	1943 [105]	13,529	APA-53	WARREN	1943	8355
APA-4	*MCCAWLEY	1943 [105]	9304	APA-54	WAYNE	1943	8355
APA-31	MONROVIA	1943 [105]	8889	APA-8	WILLIAM P. BIDDLE	1943 [105]	8789
APA-9	NEVILLE	1943 [105]	8789	APA-55	WINDSOR	1943[105]	8276
				APA-3	ZEILIN	1943 [105]	13,529

APA 2-10, 12-21, 23, 25-28 reclassified from transports. APA 1 and 11 were Maritime Commission P1-S2-L2 type; APA 18-20 and 30 were C3-A; APA 21, 28 and 31-32, C3-Delta; APA 25-27, C3-P; APA 49-51, C2-S-B1; APA 52-54 and 94, C2-S-E1; APA 55-56, 91, 97-98, 103 and 105, C3-S-A3; and APA 89-90, C3-S1-A3.

[105] Conversion date.

[106] Converted to miscellaneous auxiliary (AG).

BAYFIELD Class

7845-8593 tons. Maritime Commission C3-S-A2 type.

No.	Name	Comm.	No.	Name	Comm.
APA-92	ALPINE	1944	APA-41	DU PAGE	1943
APA-93	BARNSTABLE	1944	APA-42	ELMORE	1943
APA-33	BAYFIELD	1943	APA-43	FAYETTE	1943
APA-34	BOLIVAR	1943	APA-44	FREMONT	1943
APA-95	BURLEIGH	1944	APA-107	GOODHUE	1944
APA-35	CALLAWAY	1943	APA-108	GOSHEN	1944
APA-36	CAMBRIA	1943	APA-109	GRAFTON	1945
APA-37	CAVALIER	1943	APA-110	GRIGGS	1944
APA-96	CECIL	1944	APA-111	GRUNDY	1945
APA-38	CHILTON	1943	APA-112	GUILFORD	1945
APA-39	CLAY	1943	APA-114	HAMBLEN	1945
APA-40	CUSTER	1943	APA-115	HAMPTON	1945
APA-99	DADE	1944	APA-116	HANOVER	1945

APA Attack Transports (*cont'd*)

No.	Name	Comm.	No.	Name	Comm.
APA-106	HANSFORD	1944	APA-100	MENDOCINO	1944
APA-45	HENRICO	1943	APA-101	MONTOUR	1944
APA-46	KNOX	1943	APA-102	RIVERSIDE	1944
APA-47	LAMAR	1943	APA-113	SITKA	1945
APA-48	LEON	1943	APA-104	WESTMORELAND	1944

GILLIAM Class

4247 tons. Maritime Commission S4–SE2–BD1 type.

No.	Name	Comm.	No.	Name	Comm.
APA-58	APPLING	1944	APA-74	COLUSA	1944
APA-59	AUDRAIN	1944	APA-75	CORTLAND	1945
APA-60	BANNER	1944	APA-76	CRENSHAW	1945
APA-61	BARROW	1944	APA-77	CRITTENDON	1945
APA-62	BERRIEN	1944	APA-78	CULLMAN	1945
APA-63	BLADEN	1944	APA-79	DAWSON	1945
APA-64	BRACKEN	1944	APA-80	ELKHART	1945
APA-65	BRISCOE	1944	APA-81	FALLON	1945
APA-66	BRULE	1944	APA-82	FERGUS	1945
APA-67	BURLESON	1944	APA-83	FILLMORE	1945
APA-68	BUTTE	1944	APA-84	GARRARD	1945
APA-69	CARLISLE	1944	APA-85	GASCONADE	1945
APA-70	CARTERET	1944	APA-86	GENEVA	1945
APA-71	CATRON	1944	APA-57	GILLIAM	1944
APA-72	CLARENDON	1944	APA-87	NIAGARA	1945
APA-73	CLEBURNE	1944	APA-88	PRESIDIO	1945

HASKELL Class

6720–6873 tons. Maritime Commission VC2–S–AP5 "Victory" type.

No.	Name	Comm.	No.	Name	Comm.
APA-127	ALLENDALE	1944	APA-141	BUCKINGHAM	1945
APA-128	ARENAC	1944	APA-142	CLEARFIELD	1945
APA-130	ATTALA	1944	APA-143	CLERMONT	1945
APA-149	AUDUBON	1944	APA-144	CLINTON	1945
APA-131	BANDERA	1944	APA-145	COLBERT	1945
APA-132	BARNWELL	1945	APA-146	COLLINGSWORTH	1945
APA-133	BECKHAM	1944	APA-147	COTTLE	1944
APA-150	BERGEN	1944	APA-148	CROCKETT	1945
APA-225	BINGHAM	1944	APA-159	DARKE	1944
APA-134	BLAND	1944	APA-160	DEUEL	1944
APA-234	BOLLINGER	1944	APA-161	DICKENS	1944
APA-135	BOSQUE	1944	APA-162	DREW	1944
APA-136	BOTETOURT	1945	APA-163	EASTLAND	1944
APA-235	BOTTINEAU	1944	APA-164	EDGECOMBE	1944
APA-137	BOWIE	1944	APA-165	EFFINGHAM	1944
APA-138	BRAXTON	1944	APA-166	FOND DU LAC	1944
APA-139	BROADWATER	1945	APA-167	FREESTONE	1944
APA-236	BRONX	1945	APA-168	GAGE	1944
APA-140	BROOKINGS	1945	APA-169	GALLATIN	1944

APA Attack Transports: HASKELL Class (*cont'd*)

No.	Name	Comm.	No.	Name	Comm.
APA-170	GOSPER	1944	APA-212	MONTROSE	1944
APA-171	GRANVILLE	1944	APA-213	MOUNTRAIL	1944
APA-172	GRIMES	1944	APA-157	NAPA	1944
APA-117	HASKELL	1944	APA-214	NATRONA	1944
APA-118	HENDRY	1944	APA-215	NAVARRO	1944
APA-119	HIGHLANDS	1944	APA-216	NESHOBA	1944
APA-120	HINSDALE	1944	APA-217	NEW KENT	1944
APA-121	HOCKING	1944	APA-158	NEWBERRY	1944
APA-173	HYDE	1944	APA-218	NOBLE	1944
APA-174	JERAULD	1944	APA-187	OCONTO	1944
APA-175	KARNES	1944	APA-219	OKALOOSA	1944
APA-122	KENTON	1944	APA-200	OKANOGAN	1944
APA-176	KERSHAW	1944	APA-188	OLMSTED	1944
APA-177	KINGSBURY	1944	APA-221	ONEIDA	1944
APA-123	KITTSON	1944	APA-189	OXFORD	1944
APA-124	LA GRANGE	1944	APA-222	PICKAWAY	1944
APA-178	LANDER	1944	APA-190	PICKENS	1944
APA-125	LANIER	1944	APA-223	PITT	1944
APA-151	LA PORTE	1944	APA-191	PONDERA	1944
APA-152	LATIMER	1944	APA-224	RANDALL	1944
APA-179	LAUDERDALE	1944	APA-226	RAWLINS	1944
APA-153	LAURENS	1944	APA-227	RENVILLE	1944
APA-180	LAVACA	1944	APA-228	ROCKBRIDGE	1944
APA-195	LENAWEE	1944	APA-229	ROCKINGHAM	1944
APA-196	LOGAN	1944	APA-230	ROCKWALL	1945
APA-154	LOWNDES	1944	APA-192	RUTLAND	1944
APA-197	LUBBOCK	1944	APA-231	ST. CROIX	1944
APA-155	LYCOMING	1944	APA-126	ST. MARY'S	1944
APA-198	MCCRACKEN	1944	APA-232	SAN SABA	1944
APA-199	MAGOFFIN	1944	APA-193	SANBORN	1944
APA-200	MARATHON	1944	APA-194	SANDOVAL	1944
APA-129	MARVIN MCINTYRE	1944	APA-204	SARASOTA	1944
APA-156	MELLETTE	1944	APA-233	SEVIER	1944
APA-201	MENARD	1944	APA-205	SHELBURNE	1944
APA-202	MENIFEE	1944	APA-206	SIBLEY	1944
APA-203	MERIWETHER	1944	APA-208	TALLADEGA	1944
APA-207	MIFFLIN	1944	APA-209	TAZEWELL	1944
APA-211	MISSOULA	1944	APA-210	TELFAIR	1944

APB Self-Propelled Barracks Ships

2189 tons. APB 41-50 converted from LSTs.

APB-49	ACCOMAC	1945 [107]	APB-46	DORCHESTER	1945
APB-50	CAMERON	1945 [107]	APB-47	KINGMAN	1945
APB-45	BLACKFORD	1945	APB-38	MARLBORO	1945

[107] Conversion date.

APB Self-Propelled Barracks Ship (*cont'd*)

No.	Name	Comm.	No.	Name	Comm.
APB-44	PRESQUE ISLE	1945 [107]	APB-42	YAVAPAI	1945 [107]
APB-48	VANDERBURG	1945	APB-43	YOLO	1945 [107]
APB-41	WYTHE	1945 [107]			

[107] Conversion date.

APc Coastal Transports

147–186 tons. Twenty-four sisters went to Britain under Lend-Lease; six to Greece; and one to Ecuador.

APc 1–50, 86–96, 98, 101–103, 108–111   Comm. 1942–3

APD High-Speed Transports

Converted Destroyers

1020–1190 tons. APD-1 reclassified from miscellaneous auxiliary; APD 31–36 from seaplane tenders; and others from destroyers.

No.	Name	Conv.	No.	Name	Conv.
APD-29	*BARRY	1944	APD-15	KILTY [108]	1943
APD-34	BELKNAP	1944	APD-4	*LITTLE	1940
APD-10	BROOKS	1943	APD-5	*MCKEAN	1940
APD-31	CLEMSON [108]	1944	APD-1	MANLEY [108]	1940
APD-2	*COLHOUN	1940	APD-24	*NOA	1943
APD-17	CROSBY	1943	APD-35	OSMOND INGRAM	1944
APD-9	DENT	1942	APD-23	OVERTON	1943
APD-21	*DICKERSON	1943	APD-25	RATHBURNE [108]	1943
APD-33	GEORGE E. BADGER [108]	1944	APD-20	ROPER	1943
APD-11	GILMER	1943	APD-13	SANDS	1943
APD-32	GOLDSBOROUGH [108]	1944	APD-14	SCHLEY [108]	1942
APD-36	GREENE	1944	APD-6	STRINGHAM	1942
APD-3	*GREGORY	1940	APD-7	TALBOT [108]	1942
APD-22	HERBERT	1943	APD-19	TATTNALL	1943
APD-12	HUMPHREYS [108]	1942	APD-16	*WARD	1943
APD-18	KANE	1943	APD-8	WATERS [108]	1942

[108] Converted to destroyer.

Converted Destroyer Escorts

1400–1450 tons. Converted from TE and TEV type destroyer escorts.

APD-46	AMESBURY	1945	APD-47	*BATES	1944
APD-97	ARTHUR L. BRISTOL	1945 [109]	APD-127	BEGOR	1945 [109]
APD-132	BALDUCK	1945 [109]	APD-109	BELET	1945 [109]
APD-57	BARBER	1944	APD-119	BEVERLY W. REID	1945 [109]
APD-39	BARR	1944	APD-48	BLESSMAN	1944
APD-73	BASSETT	1945 [109]	APD-40	BOWERS	1944

[109] Converted while building; commissioning date given.

High-Speed Transports: Converted Destroyer Escorts (*cont'd*)

No.	Name	Conv.	No.	Name	Conv.
APD-139	BRAY	1945	APD-90	KIRWIN	1945 [109]
APD-93	BROCK	1945 [109]	APD-134	KLEINSMITH	1945 [109]
APD-78	BULL	1944	APD-120	KLINE	1944 [109]
APD-79	BUNCH	1944	APD-101	KNUDSON	1944 [109]
APD-133	BURDO	1945 [109]	APD-55	LANING	1944
APD-65	BURKE	1945	APD-45	LEE FOX	1945
APD-136	CARPELLOTTI	1945 [109]	APD-60	LIDDLE	1944
APD-128	CAVALLARO	1945 [109]	APD-63	LLOYD	1944
APD-37	CHARLES LAWRENCE	1944	APD-56	LOY	1944
APD-54	CHASE	1944	APD-105	MYERS	1945 [109]
APD-62	COFER	1944	APD-59	NEWMAN	1944
APD-130	COOK	1945 [109]	APD-71	ODUM	1944 [109]
APD-88	CREAD	1945 [109]	APD-70	PAVLIC	1944 [109]
APD-87	CROSLEY	1944 [109]	APD-96	RAY K. EDWARDS	1945 [109]
APD-38	DANIEL T. GRIFFIN	1944	APD-121	RAYMON W.	
APD-123	DIACHENKO	1944 [109]		HERNDON	1944 [109]
APD-118	DON O. WOODS	1945 [109]	APD-102	REDNOUR	1944 [109]
APD-129	DONALD W. WOLF	1945 [109]	APD-52	REEVES	1944
APD-113	EARHART	1945 [109]	APD-92	REGISTER	1945 [109]
APD-107	EARLE B. HALL	1945 [109]	APD-100	RINGNESS	1944 [109]
APD-41	ENGLAND	1945	APD-115	ROGERS BLOOD	1945 [109]
APD-66	ENRIGHT	1945	APD-89	RUCHAMKIN	1945 [109]
APD-77	FRAMENT	1944	APD-85	RUNELS	1945
APD-42	GANTNER	1945	APD-76	SCHMITT	1945
APD-43	GEORGE W. INGRAM	1945	APD-122	SCRIBNER	1944 [109]
APD-126	GOSSELIN	1944 [109]	APD-50	SIMS	1944
APD-84	HAINES	1944	APD-81	TATUM	1944
APD-108	HARRY L. CORL	1945 [109]	APD-103	TOLLBERG	1945 [109]
APD-80	HAYTER	1945	APD-98	TRUXTUN	1945 [109]
APD-86	HOLLIS	1945	APD-99	UPHAM	1945 [109]
APD-51	HOPPING	1944	APD-111	WALSH	1945 [109]
APD-124	HORACE A. BASS	1944 [109]	APD-106	WALTER B. COBB	1945 [109]
APD-53	HUBBARD	1945	APD-114	WALTER S. GORKA	1945 [109]
APD-112	HUNTER MARSHALL	1945 [109]	APD-131	WALTER X. YOUNG	1945 [109]
APD-44	IRA JEFFERY	1945	APD-125	WANTUCK	1944 [109]
APD-72	JACK C. ROBINSON	1945 [109]	APD-75	WEBER	1944
APD-74	JOHN P. GRAY	1945 [109]	APD-135	WEISS	1945 [109]
APD-94	JOHN Q. ROBERTS	1945 [109]	APD-104	WILLIAM J.	
APD-49	JOSEPH E. CAMPBELL	1944		PATTISON	1945 [109]
APD-117	JOSEPH M. AUMAN	1945 [109]	APD-95	WILLIAM M. HOBBY	1945 [109]
APD-110	JULIUS A. RAVEN	1945 [109]	APD-58	WITTER	1945
APD-61	KEPHART	1944	APD-69	YOKES	1944 [109]
APD-91	KINZER	1944 [109]			

[109] Converted while building; commissioning date given.

APH Evacuation Transports

7791 tons. Maritime Commission C2–S1–A1 type.

No.	Name	Comm.	No.	Name	Comm.
APH–2	PINKNEY	1942	APH–1	TRYON	1942
APH–3	RIXEY	1942			

APL Barracks Ships

1300 tons. Non-self-propelled.
These were unofficially given names such as "Ritz Carlton," "Waldorf," etc.

APL 2–3, 8–15, 17–26, 28–34, 41–48, 53–58   Comm. 1944–5

APM Mechanized Artillery Transport

No.	Name	Reclass.	Displ.
APM–9	LAKEHURST [110]	1942	7450

Reclassified from transport and aircraft ferry.

[110] Transferred to Army.

APS Transport Submarine

No.	Name	Conv.	Displ.
APS–1	*ARGONAUT	1942	2710

Converted from minelaying submarine.

APV Transports and Aircraft Ferries

No.	Name	Comm.	Displ.	No.	Name	Comm.	Displ.
APV–2	HAMMONDS-			APV–1	KITTY HAWK	1941	6861
	PORT	1941	6861	APV–3	LAKEHURST	1942	7450

APV–3 converted to mechanized artillery transport (APM) in 1942; others reclassified cargo ships and aircraft ferries (AKV) in 1943.

AR Repair Ships

No.	Name	Comm.	Displ.	No.	Name	Comm.	Displ.
AR–6	AJAX	1942	9140	AR–1	MEDUSA	1924	8855
AR–10	ALCOR [111]	1941 [112]	8091	AR–3	PROMETHEUS	1913 [112]	6266
AR–12	BRIAREUS	1943	8975	AR–11	RIGEL	1941 [112]	5551
AR–9	DELTA	1942 [112]	8975	AR–4	VESTAL	1913 [112]	6525
AR–21	DIONYSIS	1945	5801	AR–5	VULCAN	1941	9140
AR–7	HECTOR	1943	9140	AR–19	XANTHUS	1945	5801
AR–20	LAERTES	1945	5801				

AR 3–4 converted from colliers; AR–9 from cargo ship; AR–10 from miscellaneous auxiliary; and AR–11 from destroyer tender. AR 19–21 were originally intended for Britain under Lend-Lease. They are modified EC2–S–C1 "Liberties."

[111] Converted to destroyer tender (AD).
[112] Conversion date.

ARB Battle-Damage Repair Ships

1781–2017 tons.

No.	Name	Comm.	No.	Name	Comm.
ARB-1	ARISTAEUS	1943	ARB-2	OCEANUS	1943
ARB-10	DEMETER	1945	ARB-3	PHAON	1943
ARB-11	DIOMEDES	1945	ARB-7	SARPEDON	1945
ARB-12	HELIOS	1945	ARB-8	TELAMON	1945
ARB-5	MIDAS	1944	ARB-9	ULYSSES	1944
ARB-6	NESTOR	1944	ARB-4	ZEUS	1943

Converted from LSTs while building.

ARG Internal-Combustion-Engine Repair Ships

No.	Name	Comm.	Displ.	No.	Name	Comm.	Displ.
ARG-19	BEAVER	1945 [112]	4737	ARG-1	OGLALA	1943 [112]	3746
ARG-6	CEBU	1944	4621	ARG-20	OTUS	1945 [112]	5775
ARG-7	CULEBRA			ARG-5	OAHU	1944	4621
	ISLAND	1944	4621	ARG-10	PALAWAN	1944	5159
ARG-17	HOOPER			ARG-16	KERMIT		
	ISLAND	1945	5159		ROOSEVELT	1945	5159
ARG-8	LEYTE [113]	1944	4621	ARG-11	SAMAR	1945	5159
ARG-2	LUZON	1943	4621	ARG-4	TUTUILA	1944	4621
ARG-3	MINDANAO	1943	4621				
ARG-9	MONA						
	ISLAND	1944	4621				

ARG-1 converted from minelayer and ARG 19-20 from submarine tenders. ARG 2-11 and 16-17 were Maritime Commission EC2-S-C1 "Liberty" type and ARG-20 a C1-B.

[112] Conversion date.
[113] Renamed MAUI 31 May 1945.

ARH Heavy-Hull Repair Ship

No.	Name	Comm.	Displ.
ARH-1	JASON	1944	9140

Converted while building from repair ship.

ARL Landing-Craft Repair Ships

No.	Name	Comm.	No.	Name	Comm.
ARL-1	ACHELOUS	1943	ARL-7	ATLAS	1943
ARL-41	ACHILLES	1944 [114]	ARL-31	BELLEROPHON	1945
ARL-4	ADONIS	1943	ARL-32	BELLONA	1945
ARL-3	AGENOR	1943	ARL-33	CHIMAERA	1945
ARL-29	AMPHITRITE	1945	ARL-10	CORONIS	1944
ARL-2	AMYCUS	1943	ARL-11	CREON	1944
ARL-30	ASKARI	1945	ARL-35	DAEDALUS	1945

[114] Conversion date.

ARL Landing-Craft Repair Ships (*cont'd*)

No.	Name	Comm.	No.	Name	Comm.
ARL-8	EGERIA	1943	ARL-20	PENTHEUS	1945
ARL-9	ENDYMION	1943 [114]	ARL-12	POSEIDON	1944
ARL-36	GORDIUS	1945	ARL-21	PROSERPINE	1945
ARL-37	INDRA	1945	ARL-39	QUIRINUS	1945
ARL-38	KRISHNA	1945	ARL-40	REMUS	1944 [114]
ARL-13	MENELAUS	1945	ARL-22	ROMULUS	1944
ARL-14	MINOS	1944	ARL-23	SATYR	1944
ARL-15	MINOTAUR	1944	ARL-24	SPHINX	1944
ARL-16	MYRMIDON	1944	ARL-26	STENTOR	1944
ARL-17	NUMITOR	1944	ARL-27	TANTALUS	1945
ARL-18	PANDEMUS	1944	ARL-28	TYPHON	1945
ARL-19	PATROCLUS	1944			

Except for ARL 9 and 41 (converted after building) all were converted from LSTs while building.
Two sisters transferred to Royal Navy under Lend-Lease.

[114] Conversion date.

ARS Salvage Vessels

No.	Name	Comm.	Displ.	No.	Name	Comm.	Displ.
ARS-30	ACCELERATE	1945	400	ARS-31	HARJURAND	1942	625
ARS-13	ANCHOR	1943	1089	ARS-40	HOIST	1945	1441
ARS-38	BOLSTER	1945	1441	ARS-8	PRESERVER	1944	1504
ARS-32	BRANT	1942 [114]	855	ARS-14	PROTECTOR	1943	1232
ARS-19	CABLE	1944	1551	ARS-4	*REDWING	1941 [114]	980
ARS-20	CHAIN	1944	1478	ARS-18	*RESCUER	1942	500
ARS-33	CLAMP	1943	1504	ARS-17	RESTORER	1943	1232
ARS-39	CONSERVER	1945	1441	ARS-25	SAFEGUARD	1944	1478
ARS-2	CRUSADER	1941 [114]	980	ARS-26	SEIZE	1944	1342
ARS-21	CURB	1944	1342	ARS-9	SHACKLE	1944	1551
ARS-22	CURRENT	1944	1478	ARS-27	SNATCH	1944	1478
ARS-23	DELIVER	1944	1478	ARS-36	SWIVEL	1943	1232
ARS-3	DISCOVERER	1941 [114]	980	ARS-37	TACKLE [115]	1943	1250
ARS-5	DIVER	1943	1504	ARS-28	VALVE	1944	1232
ARS-6	ESCAPE	1943	1504	ARS-29	VENT	1944	1232
ARS-15	*EXTRACTOR	1944	1232	ARS-1	VIKING	1941 [114]	980
ARS-16	EXTRICATE	1943	1232	ARS-11	WARBLER	1941 [114]	980
ARS-34	GEAR	1943	1504	ARS-35	WEIGHT	1943	1232
ARS-7	GRAPPLE	1943	1504	ARS-12	WILLETT	1941 [114]	980
ARS-24	GRASP	1944	1478				

ARS 1-4 and 11-12 converted from minesweepers; ARS-32 from ocean tug.

[114] Conversion date.
[115] Converted to salvage craft tender — ARS(T).

ARS(T) Salvage Craft Tenders

No.	Name	Comm.	Displ.	No.	Name	Comm.	Displ.
ARS(T)–1	LAYSAN I.	1945	1949	ARS(T)–3	PALMYRA	1945	1949
ARS(T)–2	OKALA	1945	1949	ARS(T)–4	TACKLE	1945 [116]	1250

ARS(T) 1–3 converted while building from LSTs; ARS(T)–4 was an ex-ARS.

[116] Converted to miscellaneous auxiliary (AG).

ARV Aircraft Repair Ships

ARV(A) Aircraft Repair Ships (Aircraft)

ARV(E) Aircraft Repair Ships (Engine)

No.	Name	Comm.	Displ.	No.	Name	Comm.	Displ.
ARV(E)–3	AVENTINUS	1945	1753	ARV(A)–5	FABIUS	1945	1753
ARV(E)–4	CHLORIS	1945	1753	ARV(A)–6	MEGARA	1945	1753
ARV–1	CHOURRE	1944	6225	ARV–2	WEBSTER	1945	6225

The ARV(A)s and ARV(E)s were converted while building from LSTs while ARV 1–2 were Maritime Commission EC2–S–C1 "Liberty" type.

AS Submarine Tenders

No.	Name	Comm.	Displ.	No.	Name	Comm.	Displ.
AS–23	AEGIR	1944	7728	AS–22	EURYALE	1943	8282
AS–21	ANTAEUS [116]	1941	5518	AS–11	FULTON	1941	9734
AS–24	ANTHEDON	1944	7728	AS–13	GRIFFIN	1941	8613
AS–25	APOLLO	1944	7728	AS–3	HOLLAND	1926	8008
AS–10	ARGONNE [116]	1924 [117]	8400	AS–16	HOWARD W.		
AS–5	BEAVER [118]	1918	4737		GILMORE	1944	9734
AS–2	BUSHNELL [116]	1915	3142	AS–18	ORION	1943	9835
AS–15	BUSHNELL	1943	9734	AS–20	OTUS [118]	1941	5775
AS–6	CAMDEN [119]	1917	4218	AS–14	PELIAS	1941	8401
AS–9	*CANOPUS	1922	7750	AS–19	PROTEUS	1944	9835
AS–26	CLYTIE	1945	7728	AS–12	SPERRY	1942	9734

AS–10 converted from transport. AS 13–14 were Maritime Commission C3–Cargo type; AS–20 a C1–B; and AS 23–26, C3–S–A2.

[116] Converted to miscellaneous auxiliary (AG).
[117] Conversion date.
[118] Converted to internal combustion engine repair ship (ARG).
[119] Converted to unclassified vessel (IX).

ASR Submarine Rescue Vessels

No.	Name	Comm.	Displ.	No.	Name	Comm.	Displ.
ASR–7	CHANTICLEER	1942	1653	ASR–11	*MACAW	1943	1584
ASR–3	CHEWINK	1936 [117]	968	ASR–4	MALLARD	1936 [117]	968
ASR–8	COUCAL	1943	1653	ASR–5	ORTOLAN	1936 [117]	997
ASR–2	FALCON	1936 [117]	1051	ASR–12	PENGUIN	1945 [117]	1272
ASR–9	FLORIKAN	1943	1653	ASR–6	*PIGEON	1936 [117]	946
ASR–10	GREENLET	1943	1653	ASR–1	WIDGEON	1936 [117]	1013

ASR 1–6 converted from minesweepers and ASR–12 from an ocean tug.

[117] Conversion date.

ATA Auxiliary Tugs

530–1166 tons. ATA 146, 170 and 172 reclassified from ATR 1944; ATA 173–213 while building. ATA 214–218 converted from net tenders while building. ATA–166 reclassified ocean tug, old (ATO) and ATA–167 returned to Maritime Commission in 1945.

ATA 121–125, 146, 166 (CHETCO), 167 (CHALOT), 170, 172–218 Comm. 1943–5

ATF Ocean Tugs, Fleet

1190–1235 tons. Prior to 15 May 1944 classified as ocean tugs (AT).

No.	Name	Comm.	No.	Name	Comm.
ATF–96	ABNAKI	1943	ATF–105	MOCTABI	1944
ATF–148	ACHOMAWI	1944	ATF–106	MOLALA	1943
ATF–97	ALSEA	1943	ATF–87	MORENO	1942
ATF–67	APACHE	1942	ATF–158	MOSOPELEA	1945
ATF–68	ARAPAHO	1943	ATF–107	MUNSEE	1943
ATF–98	ARIKARA	1944	ATF–88	NARRAGANSETT	1943
ATF–149	ATAKAPA	1944	AT–89	*NAUSET	1943
ATF–150	AVOYEL	1945	AT–64	*NAVAJO	1940
ATF–81	BANNOCK	1943	ATF–157	NIPMUC	1945
ATF–152	CAHUILLA	1945	ATF–159	PAIUTE	1945
ATF–82	CARIB	1943	ATF–108	PAKANA	1943
ATF–151	CHAWASHA	1945	ATF–74	PAWNEE	1942
ATF–66	CHEROKEE	1940	ATF–90	PINTO	1943
ATF–99	CHETCO 120	1944	ATF–109	POTAWATOMI	1944
ATF–83	CHICKASAW	1943	ATF–110	QUAPAW	1944
ATF–153	CHILULA	1945	ATF–111	SARSI	1944
ATF–154	CHIMARIKO	1945	AT–65	*SEMINOLE	1940
ATF–69	CHIPPEWA	1943	ATF–91	SENECA	1943
ATF–70	CHOCTAW	1943	ATF–112	SERRANO	1944
ATF–100	CHOWANOC	1944	ATF–75	SIOUX	1942
ATF–101	COCOPA	1944	ATF–113	TAKELMA	1944
ATF–84	CREE	1943	ATF–114	TAWAKONI	1944
ATF–155	CUSABO	1945	ATF–92	TAWASA	1943
ATF–102	HIDATSA	1944	ATF–93	TEKESTA	1943
ATF–103	HITCHITI	1944	ATF–115	TENINO	1944
ATF–71	HOPI	1943	ATF–116	TOLOWA	1944
ATF–104	JICARILLA	1944	ATF–76	UTE	1942
ATF–72	KIOWA	1943	ATF–117	WATEREE	1945
ATF–85	LIPAN	1943	ATF–118	WENATCHEE	1945
ATF–156	LUISENO	1945	ATF–94	YUMA	1943
ATF–86	MATACO	1943	ATF–95	ZUNI	1943
ATF–73	MENOMINEE	1942			

120 Converted to submarine rescue vessel (ASR).

ATO Ocean Tugs, Old

No.	Name	Comm.	Displ.	No.	Name	Comm.	Displ.
ATO-63	ACUSHNET	1936	604	ATO-136	ORIOLE	1942 [122]	864
ATO-34	ALGORMA	1920	778	ATO-137	OWL	1942 [122]	893
ATO-19	ALLEGHENY	1918	751	ATO-138	*PARTRIDGE	1942 [122]	730
ATO-21	BAGADUCE	1919	751	ATO-33	PINOLA	1920	871
AT-60	BAY			ATO-139	RAIL	1942 [122]	730
	SPRING [121]	1921	501	ATO-140	ROBIN	1942 [122]	730
ATO-131	BOBOLINK	1942 [122]	889	ATO-20	SAGAMORE	1918	749
AT-132	BRANT [123]	1942 [122]	855	ATO-30	SCIOTA	1919	803
ATO-166	CHETCO	1945 [122]	600	ATO-141	SEAGULL	1942 [122]	730
ATO-133	CORMORANT	1942 [122]	858	ATO-12	*SONOMA	1912	972
AT-147	†ESSELIN	1943	800	ATO-28	SUNNADIN	1919	773
AT-55	*GENESEE	1917	668	ATO-27	TATNUCK	1919	848
AT-134	*GREBE	1942 [122]	840	ATO-142	TERN	1942 [122]	730
ATO-37	IUKA	1920	746	ATO-143	TURKEY	1942 [122]	861
ATO-23	KALMIA	1919	775	AT-77	TUSCA-		
ATO-38	KEOSANQUA	1920	815		RORA [124]	1941	427
ATO-24	KEWAYDIN	1919	788	ATO-25	UMPQUA	1919	744
ATO-135	KINGFISHER	1942 [122]	822	ATO-58	UNDAUNTED	1918	625
ATO-168	LARK	1944 [122]	825	ATO-144	VIREO	1942 [122]	730
ATO-29	MAHOPAC	1919	785	ATO-26	WANDANK	1920	764
ATO-39	MONTCALM	1921	815	ATO-169	WHIPPOOR-		
AT-32	*NAPA	1919	757		WILL	1944 [122]	825
ATO-13	ONTARIO	1912	972	ATO-145	WOODCOCK	1942 [122]	862

Prior to 15 May 1944 classified as ocean tugs (AT). ATO 131–145 and 168–169 converted from minesweepers.

[121] Converted to gate vessel (YNg).   [123] Converted to salvage vessel (ARS).
[122] Conversion date.   [124] Reclassified harbor tug (YT).

ATR Rescue Tugs

530–1025 tons. ATR–98 was a war loss and ATR 90, 97, and 99 were reclassified auxiliary tugs (ATA).

ATR 1–16, 21–40, 50–90, 97–99   Comm.   1943–5

AV Seaplane Tenders

No.	Name	Comm.	Displ.	No.	Name	Comm.	Displ.
AV-5	ALBEMARLE	1940	8671	AV-3	*LANGLEY	1937	11,050
AV-10	CHANDELEUR	1942	9031	AV-11	NORTON		
AV-17	CUMBERLAND				SOUND	1945	9106
	SOUND	1944	8510	AV-12	PINE ISLAND	1945	9106
AV-7	CURRITUCK	1944	9106	AV-9	POCOMOKE	1941	7864
AV-4	CURTISS	1940	8671	AV-16	ST. GEORGE	1944	8510
AV-15	HAMLIN	1944	8510	AV-8	TANGIER	1941	7864
AV-14	KENNETH			AV-1	WRIGHT [125]	1921	8391
	WHITING	1944	8510				

AV 9–10 were Maritime Commission C3–Cargo type and AV–10 a C3–S1–B1 AV–3 converted from aircraft carrier.

[125] Converted to miscellaneous auxiliary (AG).

AVC Catapult Lighter

2275 tons. Non-self-propelled.

AVC–1   Comm.   1941

AVD Seaplane Tenders (Destroyer)

1190 tons. Converted from destroyers or small seaplane tenders.

No.	Name	Conv.	No.	Name	Conv.
AVD–10	BALLARD	1940	AVD–13	GREENE [126]	1941
AVD–8	BELKNAP [126]	1940	AVD–6	HULBERT [127]	1940
AVD–1	CHILDS	1940	AVD–9	OSMOND INGRAM [126]	1940
AVD–4	CLEMSON [126]	1940	AVD–14	MCFARLAND [127]	1940
AVD–3	GEORGE E. BADGER [126]	1940	AVD–7	WILLIAM B. PRESTON	1940
AVD–12	GILLIS	1940	AVD–11	THORNTON	1940
AVD–5	GOLDSBOROUGH [126]	1940	AVD–2	WILLIAMSON [127]	1940

[126] Converted to high-speed transport (APD).
[127] Converted to destroyer (DD).

AVG Escort Vessels (Aircraft). *See* CVE Escort Aircraft Carriers

AVP Small Seaplane Tenders

No.	Name	Conv.	Displ.	No.	Name	Conv.	Displ.
AVP–4	AVOCET	1936	904	AVP–1	LAPWING	1936	888
AVP–14	CHILDS [128]	1938	1190	AVP–6	PELICAN	1936	825
AVP–17	CLEMSON [128]	1939	1190	AVP–9	SANDPIPER	1936	887
AVP–8	*GANNET	1936	900	AVP–7	SWAN	1936	860
AVP–16	GEORGE E.			AVP–5	TEAL	1936	900
	BADGER [128]	1938	1190	AVP–3	THRUSH	1936	904
AVP–18	GOLDSBOR-			AVP–20	WILLIAM B.		
	OUGH [128]	1939	1190		PRESTON [128]	1939	1190
AVP–2	HERON	1936	872	AVP–15	WILLIAM-		
AVP–19	HULBERT [128]	1939	1190		SON [128]	1938	1190

AVP 1–9 converted from minesweepers and AVP 14–20 from destroyers.

[128] Reclassified seaplane tender (destroyer) (AVD).

BARNEGAT Class

1766 tons.

No.	Name	Comm.	No.	Name	Comm.
AVP–23	ABSECON	1943	AVP–24	CHINCOTEAGUE	1943
AVP–33	BARATARIA	1944	AVP–36	COOK INLET	1944
AVP–10	BARNEGAT	1941	AVP–25	COOS BAY	1943
AVP–34	BERING STRAIT	1944	AVP–37	CORSON	1944
AVP–11	BISCAYNE [129]	1941	AVP–38	DUXBURY BAY	1944
AVP–12	CASCO	1941	AVP–40	FLOYDS BAY	1945
AVP–35	CASTLE ROCK	1944	AVP–39	GARDINERS BAY	1945

[129] Converted to amphibious force flagship (AGC).

AVP Small Seaplane Tenders (*cont'd*)

No.	Name	Comm.	No.	Name	Comm.
AVP-41	GREENWICH BAY	1945	AVP-29	ROCKAWAY	1943
AVP-26	HALF MOON	1943	AVP-51	SAN CARLOS	1944
AVP-21	HUMBOLDT	1941	AVP-30	SAN PABLO	1943
AVP-13	MACKINAC	1942	AVP-52	SHELIKOF	1944
AVP-22	MATAGORDA	1941	AVP-53	SUISUN	1944
AVP-48	ONSLOW	1943	AVP-31	UNIMAK	1943
AVP-49	ORCA	1944	AVP-32	YAKUTAT	1944
AVP-50	REHOBOTH	1944			

AVS Aviation Supply Ships

No.	Name	Reclass.	Displ.	No.	Name	Reclass.	Displ.
AVS-4	ALLIOTH	1945	4023	AVS-8	JUPITER	1945	5594
AVS-2	FORTUNE	1945	3822	AVS-6	NICOLLET	1945	2411
AVS-3	GRUMIUM	1945	4023	AVS-7	PONTOTOC	1945	2411
AVS-5	GWINNETT	1945	2411	AVS-1	SUPPLY	1945	3450

AVS 1–4 converted from unclassified vessels, AVS 5–7 from miscellaneous auxiliaries; and AVS-8 from a cargo ship.

AW Distilling Ships

No.	Name	Comm.	Displ.	No.	Name	Comm.	Displ.
AW-4	ABATAN	1945	6433	AW-1	STAG	1944	4113
AW-3	PASIG	1944	6433	AW-2	WILDCAT	1944	4113

AW 1–2 were Maritime Commission Z–ET1–S–C3 type "Liberty Tankers" and AW 3–4 were T2–SE–A2 tanker conversions.

IX Unclassified Vessels

IX-131	ABARENDA	1944	4410	IX-57	†ARANER	1942	100
IX-203	AGILE	1944 [130]	190	IX-134	ARAYAT	1944	3481
IX-224	AIDE DE CAMP	1945	170	IX-135	ARETHUSA	1944	4411
IX-171	ALBATROSS	1944 [130]	458	IX-111	ARMADILLO	1943	3665
IX-204	ALLIOTH [131]	1944 [130]	4023	IX-83	†ASHLEY	1942	32
IX-41	AMERICA	1921	146	IX-153	*ASPHALT	1944	5636
IX-132	ANDREW DORIA	1944	4500	IX-108	†ATLANTIDA	1943	4002
IX-109	ANTELOPE	1943	3600	IX-178	BANSHEE	1944	4500
IX-133	ANTONA	1944	4343	IX-199	BARCELO	1944 [130]	80

[130] Conversion date.
[131] Converted to aviation supply ship (AVS).

IX Unclassified Vessels (*cont'd*)

No.	Name	Comm.	Displ.	No.	Name	Comm.	Displ.
IX-161	BARITE	1944	5636	IX-44	*DCH-1	1941 [130]	900
IX-154	BAUXITE	1944	5636	IX-2	DESPATCH	1921 [130]	1700
IX-112	BEAGLE	1943	3665	IX-215	DON MARQUIS	1945	4380
IX-187	BELUSAN	1945	8537	IX-182	DONNELL	1944 [130]	1315
IX-101	BIG CHIEF	1943	600	IX-30	DOVER	1922 [130]	1136
IX-207	BIG HORN	1945	5887	IX-9	DUBUQUE [134]	1922 [130]	936
IX-55	BLACK			IX-58	†DWYN WEN	1942	110
	DOUGLAS [132]	1942	102	IX-103	E. A. POE	1943	3696
IX-65	BLUE DOLPHIN	1942	110	IX-95	†ECHO	1942	340
IX-172	BLUEBIRD	1944 [130]	458	IX-181	EGRET	1944 [130]	185
IX-50	†BOWDOIN	1941	110	IX-79	EL CANO	1942	600
IX-78	BRAVE	1942	110	IX-115	ELK	1943	3665
IX-205	CALLAO	1945	869	IX-173	ETAMIN	1944 [130]	3665
IX-42	CAMDEN	1940 [130]	4218	IX-85	†EUHAW	1942	49
IX-113	CAMEL	1943	3665	IX-221	EUREKA	1945 [130]	275
IX-114	CARIBOU	1943	3665	IX-159	FELDSPAR	1944	5636
IX-152	CARMITA	1944	5636	IX-45	FAVORITE	1921 [130]	1000
IX-136	CARONDELET	1944	4500	IX-192	FLAMBEAU	1945	4500
IX-211	CASTINE	1945 [130]	244	IX-180	FLAMINGO	1944 [130]	175
IX-183	CATBIRD	1944 [130]	505	IX-165	FLICKER	1944 [130]	491
IX-137	CELTIC	1944	6100	IX-90	†FORBES	1942	110
IX-52	CHENG HO	1941	110	IX-146	FORTUNE [131]	1944	3822
IX-206	CHOCURA	1945 [130]	275	IX-43	FREEDOM	1940	60
IX-188	CHOTAUK	1944	4500	IX-54	GALAXY	1941	228
IX-80	CHRISTIANA [133]	1942	386	IX-227	GAMAGE	1945	3381
IX-163	CINNABAR	1944	5636	IX-116	GAZELLE	1943	3665
IX-156	CITY OF			IX-117	GEMSBOK	1943	3665
	DALHART	1944	5093	IX-61	†GEOANNA [135]	1942	90
IX-184	CLIFTON	1945	4600	IX-118	GIRAFFE	1943	3665
IX-144	CLYDE	1944	4800	IX-70	†GLORIA DALTON	1942	75
IX-198	COHASSETT	1944 [130]	1625	IX-195	GOSHAWK	1944 [130]	563
IX-84	CONGAREE	1942	33	IX-106	GREYHOUND	1943	3306
IX-20	CONSTELLATION	1797	1970	IX-174	GRUMIUM [131]	1944 [130]	4023
IX-21	CONSTITUTION	1797	2200	IX-218	GUARDOQUI	1945	6836
IX-164	CORUNDUM	1944	5636	IX-67	GUINIVERE	1943	710
IX-8	CUMBERLAND	1922	1500	IX-225	HARCOURT	1945	3381
IX-170	CURLEW	1944 [130]	505	IX-13	HARTFORD	1858	2900
IX-186	DAWN	1944	4876	IX-14	†HAWK	1921 [130]	200

[130] Conversion date.
[131] Converted to aviation supply ship (AVS).
[132] Converted to coastal yacht (PYc).
[133] Reclassified miscellaneous auxiliary (YAG).
[134] Converted to gunboat (PG).
[135] Transferred to Army.

IX Unclassified Vessels (*cont'd*)

No.	Name	Comm.	Displ.	No.	Name	Comm.	Displ.
IX-48	HIGHLAND LIGHT	1940	30	IX-124	MOOSE	1943	3665
IX-119	IBEX	1943	3665	IX-98	MOOSEHEAD	1943 [130]	901
IX-93	IRENE FORSYTE	1943	200	IX-155	MUSTANG	1944	300
IX-56	IX-56	1942 [130]	110	IX-190	NAUSETT	1945	4378
IX-212	IX-212	1945 [130]	217	IX-33	NEWTON	1922	3400
IX-120	JAGUAR	1943	3665	IX-177	NIGHTINGALE	1944 [130]	160
IX-75	JOHN M.			IX-148	NORTH STAR [136]	1944	1435
	HOWARD	1942	100	IX-110	OCELOT	1943	5093
IX-77	†JUNIATA	1942	300	IX-139	OCTORARA	1944	3677
IX-228	JUSTIN	1945	3381	IX-40	OLYMPIA	1894	4500
IX-71	KAILUA	1943	1027	IX-157	ORVETTA	1944	5093
IX-121	KANGAROO	1943	3665	IX-104	P. H. BURNETT	1943	3432
IX-179	KENWOOD	1944	2000	IX-23	PADUCAH [134]	1922 [130]	936
IX-175	KESTREL	1944 [130]	196	IX-91	PALOMAS	1942	200
IX-194	KILDEER	1944 [130]	214	IX-125	PANDA	1944	3665
IX-176	KINGBIRD	1944 [130]	183	IX-105	PANTHER	1943 [130]	55
IX-122	LEOPARD	1943	3665	IX-222	PEGASUS	1945 [130]	1758
IX-167	†LEYDEN	1944	2500	IX-86	†POCOTALIGO	1942	50
IX-202	LIBERATOR	1945 [130]	170	IX-126	*PORCUPINE	1944	3665
IX-72	LIBERTY BELLE	1942	992	IX-15	PRAIRIE STATE	1924 [130]	7500
IX-162	LIGNITE	1944	5636	IX-169	PRESIDENT		
IX-158	LIMESTONE	1944	5636		WARFIELD	1944	2000
IX-166	LINNET	1944 [130]	389	IX-69	†PURITAN	1942	75
IX-92	†LISTON	1943	75	IX-150	QUARTZ	1944	5636
IX-82	†LUSTER	1942	51	IX-140	QUIROS	1944	5200
IX-102	MAJABA	1943 [130]	1795	IX-127	RACCOON	1944	3665
IX-138	MALVERN	1945	4415	IX-100	RACER	1943 [130]	85
IX-141	MANILENO	1944	4500	IX-76	†RAMONA	1942	90
IX-200	MARATANZA	1944 [130]	75	IX-25	REINA		
IX-197	MARIVELES	1945	4616		MERCEDES	1898	1800
IX-160	MARL	1944	5636	IX-96	RICHARD PECK	1941	2000
IX-189	MARMORA	1944	4329	IX-89	†ROMAIN	1942	63
IX-97	MARTHA'S			IX-94	*RONAKI	1942	300
	VINEYARD	1943	92	IX-81	SABLE	1943	6564
IX-193	MEREDOSIA	1945	4500	IX-87	SALUDA	1942	50
IX-74	METHA NELSON	1942	400	IX-99	†SEA CLOUD	1943	3000
IX-66	MIGRANT	1942	1300	IX-210	SEA FOAM	1945	5000
IX-123	MINK	1943	3665	IX-51	†SEA OTTER I	1941	90

[130] Conversion date.
[131] Converted to aviation supply ship (AVS).
[132] Converted to coastal yacht (PYc).
[133] Reclassified miscellaneous auxiliary (YAG).
[134] Converted to gunboat (PG).
[135] Transferred to Army.
[136] Transferred from Coast Guard.

IX Unclassified Vessels (*cont'd*)

No.	Name	Comm.	Displ.	No.	Name	Comm.	Displ.
IX–53	†SEA OTTER II	1941	740	IX–46	†TRANSFER	1921 [130]	250
IX–39	SEATTLE	1931 [130]	11,000	IX–149	TREFOIL	1944	5636
IX–60	†SEAWARD	1942	100	IX–223	TRIANA	1945	3568
IX–209	SEAWARD	1945 [130]	1490	IX–216	UNICOI	1945	4000
IX–213	SERAPIS	1945	1240	IX–47	VAMARIE	1936	80
IX–68	†SEVEN SEAS	1942	430	IX–191	VANDALIA	1944	4500
IX–142	SIGNAL	1944	5640	IX–62	VILEEHI	1941	90
IX–151	SILICA	1944	5636	IX–145	VILLALOBOS	1944	4500
IX–143	SILVER CLOUD	1944	4352	IX–59	VOLADOR [135]	1942	90
IX–168	SOUTHLAND	1944	1900	IX–28	WHEELING	1921 [130]	700
IX–196	SPARK	1944 [130]	1490	IX–129	WHIPPET	1944	3665
IX–49	SPINDRIFT	1940	30	IX–29	WILMETTE	1913	1802
IX–231	STALWART	1945 [130]	264	IX–88	†WIMBEE	1942	21
IX–201	STERLING	1944 [130]	75	IX–64	WOLVERINE	1942	4152
IX–185	STONEWALL	1944	4600	IX–214	YUCCA	1945	4427
IX–232	SUMMIT	1945 [130]	264	IX–73	†ZACA	1942	110
IX–147	SUPPLY [131]	1944	3450	IX–63	†ZAHMA	1942	100
IX–217	TACKLE	1945 [130]	1250	IX–107	ZEBRA [137]	1943	4023
IX–230	TAPACOLA	1945 [130]	264				

IX 2 and 39–40 were ex-cruisers; IX–8 a former sailing training vessel; IX 9, 23, 28, and 30 ex-gunboats; IX 14, 41, 43, 47–50, 52, 55, 57–63, 65–70, 73–74, 76–79, 82–95, 99 and 224 were converted yachts; IX–15 a former battleship; IX–20 a sailing sloop-of-war; IX–21 a sailing frigate; IX–25 a Spanish-American War prize; IX 44 and 98 were converted from water barges (formerly destroyers); IX–56 from a tug; IX 100 and 105 from SCs; IX–102 from a miscellaneous auxiliary; IX–148 was a Coast Guard Cutter; IX 165–166, 170–172, 175–177, 180–181, 183, 194–195, 202–203, and 230–232 were minesweeper conversions; IX–182 an ex-DE; IX 196, 198, 209 were LST conversions; IX 199–201 ex-YPs; IX–205 was an ex-German prize; IX 206, 211 and 221, ex-PCs; IX–212 a former LCI(G); and IX–217 an ex-salvage tender. IX 64 and 81 were Great Lakes training carriers. IX 103, 107, 109, 173, 204, 215, 223, 225, and 227–228 were Maritime Commission EC2-S-C1 "Liberty" type; IX 111–129, Z-ET1-S-C3 "Liberty Tankers"; and IX 149–154 and 158–164, B7-D1 barges.

[130] Conversion date.
[131] Converted to aviation supply ship (AVS).
[132] Converted to coastal yacht (PYc).
[133] Reclassified miscellaneous auxiliary (YAG).
[134] Converted to gunboat (PG).
[135] Transferred to Army.
[136] Transferred from Coast Guard.
[137] Converted to net cargo ship (AKN).

11. LANDING SHIPS AND CRAFT

LSV Landing Ships, Vehicle

No.	Name	Comm.	Displ.	No.	Name	Comm.	Displ.
LSV–1	CATSKILL	1944	5177	LSV–3	OSAGE	1944	4626
LSV–5	MONITOR	1944	5041	LSV–2	OZARK	1944	5177
LSV–6	MONTAUK	1944	4900	LSV–4	SAUGUS	1945	4626

Converted while building from minelayers (LSV 1–2) or net layers (LSV 3–6).

LSD Landing Ships, Dock

4490–4546 tons.

No.	Name	Comm.	No.	Name	Comm.
LSD–1	ASHLAND	1943	LSD–4	EPPING FOREST	1943
LSD–2	BELLE GROVE	1943	LSD–5	GUNSTON HALL	1943
LSD–16	CABILDO	1945	LSD–6	LINDENWALD	1943
LSD–3	CARTER HALL	1943	LSD–7	OAK HILL	1944
LSD–13	CASA GRANDE	1944	LSD–14	RUSHMORE	1944
LSD–17	CATAMOUNT	1945	LSD–25	SAN MARCOS	1945
LSD–18	COLONIAL	1945	LSD–15	SHADWELL	1944
LSD–19	COMSTOCK	1945	LSD–26	TORTUGA	1945
LSD–20	DONNER	1945	LSD–8	WHITE MARSH	1944

LST Landing Ships, Tank

1490 tons.

LST 1–9, 11–13, 16–61, 66–80, 84, 117–131, 133–134, 137–141, 157–158, 166–179, 181, 197, 201–213, 218–231, 240–247, 261–295, 306–319, 325–327, 331–360, 369–400, 446–488, 491–603, 605–643, 646–649, 651–772, 774–851, 853–857, 859–947, 949–953, 957–961, 964–965, 968–970, 972–975, 978–1035, 1038–1091, 1096–1097, 1101–1110, 1120, 1122–1123, 1126, 1128–1130, 1134–1135, 1138–1142, 1144, 1146, 1148, 1150, and 1152. Comm. 1942–5.

LST 6, 43, 69, 158, 167, 179, 203, 228, 282, 313–314, 318, 333, 342, 348–349, 353, 359, 376, 396, 447–448, 460, 472, 480, 493, 496, 499, 507, 523, 531, 563, 577, 675, 738, 749–750, 808, 906 and 921 were lost; LST 2–5, 8–9, 11–13, 76–77, 79–80, 157, 173, 178, 280, 289, 311, 315, 319, 326, 331, 336–337, 346–347, 351–352, 358, 360, 369, 371, 373, 380–383, 385–386, 394, 538, and 1021 transferred to Britain under Lend-Lease. LST 33, 35–37 went to Greece under Lend-Lease. LST–39 was converted to a covered lighter (YF); LST 129, 278 and 340 to unclassified vessels (IX); LST–201 to motor torpedo boat tender (AGP); LST 231, 453, 455, 513–514, 518 and 1003 to landing craft repair ships (ARL); and LST 575, 676–678, 710 and 928 to barracks ships (APB). Seventy-two additional sisters went to Britain without seeing service in the U.S.N.

LSM Landing Ships, Medium

513–520 tons.

LSM 1–187, 200–400, 413–500   Comm. 1944–5

LSM 12, 15, 20, 59, 135, 149 and 318 lost.

LSM(R) Landing Ships, Medium (Rocket)

760–1187 tons. Converted while building from LSMs.

LSM(R) 188–199, 401–412, 501–528 Comm. 1944–5
LSM(R) 190, 194 and 195 lost.

LC(FF) Landing Craft, Flotilla Flagships

234 tons. Converted from LCI(L).

LC(FF) 367–370, 399, 423–427, 484–486, 503–504, 531–533, 535–536, 569, 571–572, 575, 627–628, 656–657, 679, 775, 782–783, 786, 788–793, 988, 994–995, 998, 1031, 1079–1083. Comm. 1943–4.

LCI(G) Landing Craft, Infantry (Gunboat)

210–230 tons. Converted from LCI(L).

LCI(G) 2, 17–19, 31, 34, 36–37, 39–43, 45–46, 61, 64–70, 73, 76–82, 189–192, 194–196, 220, 233–237, 345–348, 351–356, 365–366, 372–373, 396–398, 401, 403–408, 412–415, 417–422, 428, 437–442, 449–475, 506, 514, 516–517, 528, 530, 534, 538–548, 556, 558–561, 565–568, 570, 573–574, 576–577, 580, 630–633, 638, 658–661, 725–730, 739–742, 744–757, 760, 801–810, 948, 953–962, 964, 975, 1010–1012, 1014–1019, 1023, 1055–1060 and 1088–1089. Conv. 1944–5.

LCI(G) 82, 365, 456, 459, 468, 474 and 494 were lost. LCI(G)–396 was converted to an unclassified vessel (IX); LCI(G) 351–356, 630–633, 638, 658–660, 739–742, 754–757, 760, 801–810, 975, 1010–1012, 1023, 1055–1059 and 1088–1089 to landing craft, infantry (mortar), LCI(M); and LCI(G) 31, 34, and 73 to landing craft, infantry (rocket), LCI(R).

LCI(L) Landing Craft, Infantry (Large)

178–209 tons.

LCI(L) 1–48, 61–136, 161–196, 209–716, 731–780, 784–821, 866–884, 943–1033, 1052–1098. Comm. 1942–4.

Various vessels were converted to LC(FF), LCI(G), LCI(M), and LCI(R). See those types for a list of vessels so converted. LCI(L) 400, 409, 513, 515 and 589 were converted to underwater locator minesweepers, AMc(U). LCI(L) 3–16, 33, 35, 75, 97–136, 161–187, 193, 209–218, 229, 231, 238–318, 374–391, 411, 487–496, 498–502, 505, 507–512 and 537 were transferred to the United Kingdom under Lend-Lease; LCI(L) 521–527, 551, 554, 557, 584–87, 590–593, 665–668, 671–672, 675, 943, 945–946 and 949–950 went to Russia. LCI (L) 1, 20, 32, 85, 91–93, 219, 232, 339, 416, 497, 553, 600, 684 and 1065 were lost.

LCI(M) Landing Craft, Infantry (Mortar)

235 tons. Converted from LCI(L) and LCI(G).

LCI(M) 351–356, 359, 362, 431, 582, 588, 594–596, 630–633, 638, 658–660, 664, 669–670, 673–674, 739–742, 754–757, 760, 801–810, 951–952, 975, 1010–1012, 1023, 1055–1059, 1088–1089. Conv. 1945.

LCI(R) Landing Craft, Infantry (Rocket)

215 tons.

LCI(R) 31, 34 71–74, 224–226, 230–231, 337–338, 340–342, 642–651, 704–708, 762–767, 769–772, 785, 1024, 1026, 1028–1030, 1068–1070, 1077–1078. Conv. 1945. Converted from LCI(L) and LCI(G).

LCS(L) Landing Craft, Support (Large)

123 tons. LCS(L) 7, 15, 26, 33, 49 and 127 lost.

LCS(L) 1–130   Comm.   1944

LCT Landing Craft, Tank

Mark V Type

123 tons.

LCT 1–88, 119–500 placed in service 1942.

LCT 19, 21, 23, 25–28, 30, 35–36, 66, 71, 128, 147, 154, 175, 182, 185, 196–197, 200, 208–209, 215, 220, 241–242, 244, 253, 293–294, 299, 305, 311, 315, 319, 332, 340, 342, 352, 362, 364, 366, 413, 458–459, 486 and 496 lost. LCT–353 was converted to a garbage scow (YG). LCT 2, 4–6, 8–14, 37–57, 73–79, 119–124, 130–131, 135, 138, 150, 186–194, 225–236, 238–243, 246, 261–267, 269–270, 272–273, 275, 281–287, 289, 291–292, 295–297, 301–304, 306–310, 312–313, 331, 334–339, 341, 343–345, 361, 363, 398–399, 402, 420–430, 432–433, 435–442, 444–445, 450, 453–455, 461, 477–480, 483–485, 487–488, 490–491 and 498–500 were transferred to Britain under Lend-Lease.

Mark VI Type

143 tons.

LCT 501–1465 placed in service 1943–4.

LCT 548, 555, 572, 579, 582, 593, 597, 612, 703, 713–714, 777, 823, 961, 963, 983–984, 988, 998, 1029, 1050, 1075, 1090, 1138, 1151, 1181 and 1358 were lost; LCT 843–844, 887–890 converted to underwater locator minesweepers, AMc(U); and LCT 559, 561, 563, 744–745, 1015, 1046–1047, 1163, 1176, 1434–1438, 1442 and 1445 were transferred to the Soviet Union.

12. SMALL LANDING CRAFT

Type	Displ.	Length	No. built
Landing Craft, Control (LCC),			
Mark I	50	56′ ⎫	
Mark II	30	56′ ⎬	99
Landing Craft, Mechanized			
(LCM), Mark II	26	45′	147
Mark III	23	50′	8,631
Mark VI	23	56′	2,718
Landing Craft, Personnel			
(Large) – LCP(L)	5.8	36′8″	2,193

Small Landing Craft (*cont'd*)

Type	Displ.	Length	No. built
Landing Craft, Personnel (Ramp) — LCP(R)	5.8	35'10"	2,631
Landing Craft, Rubber (Large) — LCR(L)	395 lb.	16'	10,123
Landing Craft, Rubber (Small) — LCR(S)	210 lb.	12'5"	8,150
Landing Craft, Support (Small) — LCS(S) Mk. I	9	36'8"	558
Mark II	10	36'8"	
Landing Craft, Vehicle (LCV)	7	36'3"	2,366
Landing Craft, Vehicle, Personnel (LCVP)	9	36'	23,358
Landing Vehicle, Tracked (LVT), Mark I	7.5	21'6"	1,225
Mark II	11	26'1"	2,962
Mark III	12.5	24'2"	2,964
Mark IV	10.4	26'1"	8,350
Landing Vehicle, Tracked (Armored) — LVT(A)			
Mark I	14.6	26'1"	510
Mark II	11.4	26'1"	450
Mark IV	17	26'1"	1,890
Amphibious Trucks			
DUKW	5.8	31'8"	
Jeep	1.6	15'7"	

13. COAST GUARD CUTTERS

WPG Cruising Cutters

No.	Name	Comm.	Displ.	No.	Name	Comm.	Displ.
WPG–164	†AIVIK	1942	251 [138]	WPG–183	MAY-		
WPG–168	†AKLAK	1942	170 [138]		FLOWER	1943	2690
WPG–172	†ALATOK	1942	387 [138]	WPG–171	†NAGAK	1942	176 [138]
WPG–166	†AMAROK	1942	237 [138]	WPG–169	†NANOK	1942	220 [138]
WPG–167	†ARLUK	1942	163 [138]	WPG–170	*NATSEK	1942	225 [138]
WPG–165	†ARVEK	1942	172 [138]	WPG–59	NORTH		
WPG–163	†ATVAK	1942	243 [138]		STAR [139]	1941 [140]	2200
WPG–85	†GRESHAM	1897	1090	WPG–49	NORTH-		
WPG–56	KICKAPOO	1922	840		LAND	1927	2150

[138] Gross tonnage.
[139] Transferred to Navy.
[140] Date acquired from Department of the Interior.

WPG Cruising Cutters (*cont'd*)

No.	Name	Comm.	Displ.	No.	Name	Comm.	Displ.
WPG–122	NOUR-			WPG–54	SHAWNEE	1922	900
	MAHAL	1941 [141]	1969 [138]	WPG–52	TALLA-		
WPG–50	OSSIPEE	1915	908		POOSA	1915	912
WPG–57	PAMLICO	1906	451	WPG–53	UNALAGA	1912	1181

[138] Gross tonnage.
[141] Date acquired from the Navy.

HAIDA Class
1780 tons.

No.	Name	Comm.	No.	Name	Comm.
WPG–45	HAIDA	1921	WPG–47	MOJAVE	1921
WPG–46	MODOC	1922	WPG–48	TAMPA	1921

CHELAN Class
1546 tons. All transferred to Great Britain 1940.

CGC–54	CAYUGA	1932	CGC–46	PONTCHARTRAIN	1928
CGC–48	CHAMPLAIN	1929	CGC–52	SARANAC	1930
CGC–45	CHELAN	1928	CGC–51	SEBAGO	1930
CGC–50	ITASCA	1930	CGC–53	SHOSHONE	1931
CGC–49	MENDOTA	1929	CGC–47	TAHOE	1928

ALGONQUIN Class
1005 tons.

WPG–75	ALGONQUIN	1934	WPG–78	MOHAWK	1934
WPG–76	COMANCHE	1934	WPG–79	ONONDAGA	1934
WPG–77	*ESCANABA	1932	WPG–80	TAHOMA	1934

BIBB or Treasury Class
2216 tons. Converted to amphibious force flagships.

WPG–34	*ALEXANDER		WPG–33	DUANE	1936
	HAMILTON	1937	WPG–35	INGHAM	1936
WPG–31	BIBB	1937	WPG–36	SPENCER	1937
WPG–32	CAMPBELL	1936	WPG–37	TANEY	1936

OWASCO Class
2200 tons.

WPG–41	CHAUTAUQUA	1945	WPG–70	PONTCHARTRAIN	1945
WPG–39	OWASCO	1945	WPG–40	WINNEBAGO	1945

WIX Weather Patrol Ships

No.	Name	Comm.	Displ.	No.	Name	Comm.	Displ.
WIX–207	BIG HORN [142]	1944 [143]	4150	WIX–276	MANHASSET	1943 [143]	2900
WIX–273	MANASQUAN	1943 [143]	2580	WIX–274	MENEMSHA	1943 [142]	2580

Other WIX vessels served as training ships.
[142] Transferred to Navy.
[143] Date acquired from Navy.

WIX Weather Patrol Ships (*cont'd*)

No.	Name	Comm.	Displ.	No.	Name	Comm.	Displ.
WIX–275	MONOMOY	1943 [142]	2690	WAG–48	*MUSKEGET	1942 [142]	1800

[142] Transferred to Navy.

WPC Patrol Cutters

ACTIVE Class

220 tons.

No.	Name	Comm.	No.	Name	Comm.
WPC–125	ACTIVE	1927	WPC–141	HARRIET LANE	1927
WPC–126	AGASSIZ	1927	WPC–142	*JACKSON	1927
WPC–127	ALERT	1927	WPC–143	KIMBALL	1927
WPC–128	*BEDLOE	1926	WPC–144	LEGARE	1927
WPC–129	BONHAM	1927	WPC–146	MCLANE	1927
WPC–130	BOUTWELL	1927	WPC–145	MARION	1927
WPC–131	CAHOONE	1927	WPC–147	MORRIS	1927
WPC–132	CARTIGAN	1927	WPC–148	NEMAHA	1927
WPC–133	COLFAX	1927	WPC–149	PULASKI	1926
WPC–134	CRAWFORD	1927	WPC–150	RELIANCE	1927
WPC–157	CUYAHOGA	1941 [143]	WPC–151	RUSH	1927
WPC–135	DILIGENCE	1927	WPC–152	TIGER	1927
WPC–136	DIX	1927	WPC–153	TRAVIS	1927
WPC–137	EWING	1927	WPC–154	VIGILANT	1927
WPC–138	FAUNCE	1927	WPC–155	WOODBURY	1927
WPC–139	FREDERICK LEE	1927	WPC–156	YEATON	1927
WPC–140	GENERAL GREENE	1927			

[143] Date acquired from Navy.

ARGO Class

334–337 tons.

No.	Name	Comm.	No.	Name	Comm.
WPC–100	ARGO	1933	WPC–109	HERMES	1932
WPC–101	ARIADNE	1934	WPC–110	ICARUS	1932
WPC–102	ATALANTA	1934	WPC–111	NEMESIS	1934
WPC–103	AURORA	1931	WPC–112	NIKE	1934
WPC–104	CALYPSO	1942 [143]	WPC–113	PANDORA	1934
WPC–105	CYANE	1934	WPC–114	PERSEUS	1932
WPC–106	DAPHNE	1932	WPC–115	THETIS	1931
WPC–107	DIONE	1934	WPC–116	TRITON	1934
WPC–108	GALATEA	1933			

WAG Icebreakers

5390 tons. Another icebreaker, MACKINAW (WAG–83), served on the Great Lakes.

No.	Name	Comm.	No.	Name	Comm.
WAG–279	EASTWIND	1944	WAG–280	SOUTHWIND	1943 [143]
WAG–278	NORTHWIND	1943	WAG–281	WESTWIND	1943 [143]

[143] Date acquired from Navy.

14. UNITED STATES NAVAL COMBAT AIRCRAFT
1941–1945 [144]
(*Speeds are in Statute Miles*)

VF Fighters

Brewster F2A–3 "Buffalo." One place; span 35′; length 26′4″; height 12′; one 1200 h.p. Wright R–1820 engine; speed 322 m.p.h.; armament 4–.50cal. fixed machine guns, 200 lb. bombs.

General Motors FM–1 "Wildcat." Duplicates Grumman F4F–4.

FM–2 "Wildcat." One place; span 38′; length 29′1″; height 11′5″; one 1350 h.p. Wright R–1820 engine; speed 326 m.p.h.; armament 4–.50cal. fixed machine guns, 500 lb. bombs.

Goodyear FG–1 "Corsair." Duplicates Vought F4U–1.

Grumman F4F–3 "Wildcat." One place; span 38′; length 28′9″; height 11′10″; one 1200 h.p. Pratt & Whitney R–1830 engine; speed 330 m.p.h.; armament 6–.50cal. fixed machine guns, 200 lb. bombs.

F4F–4 "Wildcat." One place; span 38′; length 28′9″; height 11′10″; one 1200 h.p. Pratt & Whitney R–1830 engine; speed 319 m.p.h.; armament 6–.50cal. fixed machine guns, 200 lb. bombs.

F6F–3 "Hellcat." One place; span 42′10″; length 33′4″; height 11′3″; one 2000 h.p. Pratt & Whitney R–2800 engine; speed 360 m.p.h.; armament 6–.50cal. fixed machine guns, 2000 lb. bombs, or 1 torpedo.

F6F–5 "Hellcat." One place; span 42′10″; length 33′6″; height 13′1″; one 2100 h.p. Pratt & Whitney R–2800 engine; speed 375 m.p.h.; armament 6–.50cal. fixed machine guns, 2000 lb. bombs, or 6 rockets.

Vought F4U–1 "Corsair." One place; span 41′; length 33′5″; height 15′5″; one 2000 h.p. Pratt & Whitney R–2800 engine; speed 399 m.p.h.; armament 6–.50cal. machine guns or 2–20mm. cannon fixed, 2000 lb. bombs or 8 rockets.

VSB Dive Bombers

Canadian Car & Foundry SBW–1 "Helldiver." Duplicates Curtiss SB2C–1.

SBW–3 "Helldiver." Duplicates Curtiss SB2C–3.

Curtiss SB2C–1 "Helldiver." Two place; span 49′9″; length 36′4″; height 15′6″; one 1700 h.p. Wright R–2600 engine; speed 281 m.p.h.; armament 4–.50cal. machine guns or 2–20mm. fixed, 2–30cal. flexible machine guns, 2650 lb. bombs or 1 torpedo.

SB2C–3 "Helldiver." Two place; span 49′9″; length 36′9″; height 13′1″; one 1900 h.p. Wright R–2600 engine; speed 294 m.p.h.; armament 2–20mm. fixed cannon, 2–.30cal. flexible machine guns, 2650 lb. bombs.

SB2C–4 "Helldiver." Two place; span 49′8″; length 36′8″; height 15′1″; one 1900

[144] Excluding obsolete and experimental types which were seldom in action and types flown exclusively by Coast Guard or Marines. This table is based on Buaer "Performance Characteristics – U.S. Navy Service Airplanes;" Technical Air Intelligence Center *Representative Enemy and Allied Aircraft* (Bu. Aero. OpNav–16–V #T303); and AirPac *Air Combat Information Allied Aircraft.*

h.p. Wright R–2600 engine; speed 294 m.p.h.; armament 2–20mm fixed cannon, 2–.30cal. flexible machine guns, 2600 lb. bombs, 8 rockets.

Douglas SBD–1, –2, –3, and –4 "Dauntless." Two place; span 41'6"; length 32'1"; height 13'7"; one 1000 h.p. Wright R–1820 engine; speed 257 m.p.h.; armament 2–.50cal. fixed machine guns, 1–.30cal. flexible machine gun, 1000 lb. bombs.

SBD–5 "Dauntless." Two place; span 41'6"; length 32'6"; height 12'3"; one 1200 h.p. Wright R–1820 engine; speed 252 m.p.h.; armament 2–.50cal. fixed machine guns, 2–.30cal. flexible machine guns, 2250 lb. bombs.

Fairchild (Canada) SBF–1 "Helldiver." Duplicates Curtiss SB2C–1.

Vought-Sikorsky SB2U–3 "Vindicator." Two place; span 41'11"; length 34'; height 14'7"; one 825 h.p. Pratt & Whitney R–1535 engine; speed 240 m.p.h.; armament 2–.50cal. fixed machine guns, 2–.30cal. flexible machine guns, 1000 lb. bombs.

VT Torpedo Bombers

Douglas TBD–1 "Devastator." Three place; span 50'; length 35'; height 15'1"; one 900 h.p. Pratt & Whitney R–1830 engine; speed 221 m.p.h.; armament 1–.50cal. fixed machine gun, 1–.30cal. flexible machine gun, 1200 lb. bombs or 1 torpedo.

General Motors TBM–1 "Avenger." Duplicates Grumman TBF–1.

TBM–3 "Avenger." Three place; span 54'2"; length 40'9"; height 13'9"; one 1800 h.p. Wright R–2600 engine; speed 272 m.p.h.; armament 2–.50cal. fixed machine guns, 1–.50cal. and 1–.30cal. flexible machine guns, 2000 lb. bombs or 1 torpedo.

Grumman TBF–1 "Avenger." Three place; span 54'2"; length 41'; height 16'5"; one 1700 h.p. Wright R–2600 engine; speed 273 m.p.h.; armament 1–.30cal. or 2–.50cal. fixed machine guns, 1–.50cal. and 1–.30cal. flexible machine guns, 1600 lb. bombs or 1 torpedo.

VP Patrol Planes

Lockheed-Vega PV–1 "Ventura." Six place; span 65'6"; length 51'9"; height 14'3"; two 2000 h.p. Pratt & Whitney R–2800 engines; speed 313 m.p.h.; armament 5–.50cal. fixed machine guns, 4–.50cal flexible machine guns, 5000 lb. bombs.

VPB Patrol Bombers

Boeing (Canada) PB2B–2 "Catalina." Duplicates Consolidated PBY–6A.

Consolidated PBY–1 "Catalina." Eight place; span 104'; length 65'2"; height 18'6"; two 900 h.p. Pratt & Whitney R–1830 engines; speed 177 m.p.h.; armament 2–.30cal. and 2–.50cal. flexible machine guns, 4000 lb. bombs.

PBY–3 "Catalina." Eight place; span 104'; length 65'2"; height 18'6"; two 1050 h.p. Pratt & Whitney R–1830 engines; speed 191 m.p.h.; armament 2–.30cal. and 2–.50cal. flexible machine guns, 4000 lb. bombs or 2 torpedoes.

PBY–5 "Catalina." Nine place; span 104'; length 64'; height 19'; two 1200 h.p. Pratt & Whitney R–1830 engines; speed 195 m.p.h.; armament 2–.30cal. and 2–.50cal. flexible machine guns, 4000 lb. bombs or 2 torpedoes.

PBY–5A "Catalina." Amphibian version of PBY–5.

PBY–6A "Catalina." Nine place; span 104'; length 65'; height 17'11"; two 1200 h.p. Pratt & Whitney R–1830 engines; speed 195 m.p.h.; armament 1–.30cal. and 3–.50cal. flexible machine guns, 4000 lb. bombs or 2 torpedoes.

PB2Y–3 "Coronado." Ten place; span 115'; length 79'3"; height 24'8"; four 1200 h.p. Pratt & Whitney R–1830 engines; speed 230 m.p.h.; armament 8–.50cal. flexible machine guns, 12,000 lb. bombs or 2 torpedoes.

PB2Y–5 "Coronado." Ten place; span 115'; length 79'3"; height 27'6"; four 1200 h.p. Pratt & Whitney R–1830 engines; speed 230 m.p.h.; armament 8–.50cal. flexible machine guns, 12,000 lb. bombs or 2 torpedoes.

PB4Y–1 "Liberator." Eleven place; span 110'; length 66'4"; height 17'11"; four 1200 h.p. Pratt & Whitney R–1830 engines; speed 270 m.p.h.; armament 13–.50cal. flexible machine guns, 8000 lb. bombs.

PB4Y–2 "Privateer." Eleven place; span 110'; length 74'7"; height 30'1"; four 1350 h.p. Pratt & Whitney R–1830 engines; speed 237 m.p.h.; armament 12–.50cal. flexible machine guns, 12,800 lb. bombs.

Lockheed PBO–1 "Hudson." Five place; span 65'5"; length 44'5"; height 11'10"; two 1200 h.p. Wright R–1820 engines; speed 275 m.p.h.; armament 7–.30cal. flexible machine guns, 1150 lb. bombs.

Martin PBM–3 "Mariner." Six place; span 118'; length 80'1"; height 24'5"; two 1900 h.p. Wright R–2600 engines; speed 211 m.p.h.; armament 1–.30cal. and 5–.50cal. flexible machine guns, 12,800 lb. bombs or 2 torpedoes.

PBM–5 "Mariner." Nine place; span 118'; length 79'10"; height 27'6"; two 2100 h.p. Pratt & Whitney R–2800 engines; speed 200 m.p.h.; armament 8–.50cal. flexible machine guns, 12,800 lb. bombs or 2 torpedoes.

Naval Aircraft Factory PBN–1 "Nomad." Duplicates Consolidated PBY–6A.

VSO, VOS, or VS Observation Planes
(*These types were used in battleships and cruisers*)

Curtiss SOC–3 "Seagull." Two place; span 36'; length 31'9"; height 14'10"; one 550 h.p. Pratt & Whitney R–1340 engine; speed 164 m.p.h.; armament 1 fixed and 1 flexible .30cal. machine gun, 470 lb. bombs.

SC–1 "Seahawk." One place; span 41'; length 37'8"; height 16'; one 1350 h.p. Wright R–1820 engine; speed 313 m.p.h.; armament 2–.50cal. fixed machine guns, 1300 lb. bombs.

Naval Aircraft Factory SON–1 "Seagull." Duplicates Curtiss SOC–3.

OS2N–1 "Kingfisher." Duplicates Vought-Sikorsky OS2U–3.

Vought-Sikorsky OS2U–3 "Kingfisher." Two place; span 35'11"; length 33'7"; height 15'1"; one 450 h.p. Pratt & Whitney R–985 engine; speed 177 m.p.h.; armament 1 fixed and 1 flexible .30cal. machine gun, 650 lb. bombs.

ZNP Patrol Airships (Blimps)

K–3 class (K 3–13). Eight place; length 250'; volume 415,000 cubic feet; two 400 h.p. Wright R–975 engines; speed 65 m.p.h.; armament 1–.50cal. machine gun, 1200 lb. bombs or depth charges.

K–14 class (K 14–135). Nine place; length 251'; volume 425,000 cubic feet; two 600 h.p. Pratt & Whitney R;1340 engines; speed 65 m.p.h.; armament 1–.50cal. machine gun, 1200 lb. bombs or depth charges. K 74 and 94 lost.

M–1 class (M 1–4). Twelve place; length 294'; volume 725,000 cubic feet; two 600 h.p. Pratt & Whitney R–1340 engines; speed 65 m.p.h.; armament 1–.50cal. machine gun, 2000 lb. bombs or depth charges.

15. UNITED STATES NAVAL VESSELS TRANSFERRED TO FOREIGN NATIONS UNDER LEND-LEASE [145]

	CVE	CL	SS	DE	AM	YMS	PG & PF	PCE	PR	PC	PY & PYc	SC	PT	PTC	AG	AFDL	AN	AOG	AP	APc	AR & ARL	ARS	AT & ATR	LSD	LST	LSM	LCI(L)	Yard Craft	Total
United Kingdom	38	—	9	78	31	150	36	15	—	—	—	—	105	12	—	—	5	—	—	27	4	6	27	4	113	—	220	6	886
U.S.S.R.	—	1	—	—	34	43	28	—	—	—	—	78	205	62	15	—	—	—	—	—	—	—	—	—	—	—	30	4	500
France	—	—	—	6	—	31	—	—	—	32	—	50	—	—	—	—	3	3	—	—	—	—	—	—	—	—	—	20	145
Greece	—	—	—	—	—	—	—	—	—	—	—	—	—	—	—	—	—	—	—	3	—	—	—	—	4	—	—	—	7
Norway	—	—	—	—	—	8	—	—	—	—	—	3	—	—	—	—	—	—	—	—	—	—	—	—	—	—	—	3	14
China	—	—	—	2	4	—	—	2	1	—	—	—	—	—	1	1	—	1	—	—	—	—	—	—	10	8	8	1	39
Brazil	—	—	—	8	—	—	—	—	—	8	—	—	—	—	—	—	—	—	1	—	—	—	—	—	—	—	—	2	19
Ecuador, Mexico, Panama, Peru, & Uruguay	—	—	—	—	—	—	—	—	—	1	3	3	—	—	—	—	—	—	—	1	—	—	—	—	—	—	—	4	12
Total	38	1	9	94	69	232	64	17	1	41	3	134	310	74	16	1	8	4	1	31	4	6	27	4	127	8	258	40	1622

All except 1 AFDL, 1 AG, 1 AOG, 8 LCI(L), 8 LSM, 10 LST, and 1 yard craft for China were delivered before the end of the war.

[145] Excluding LCTs and smaller landing craft. In cases of vessels transferred to two or more countries they have been shown only under the country of first transfer.

16. OFFICERS AND MEN ON ACTIVE DUTY, 1 JULY 1940–31 AUGUST 1945 [146]

	1 July 1940	31 Dec. 1941	30 June 1942	31 Dec. 1942	30 June 1943	31 Dec. 1943	30 June 1944	31 Dec. 1944	31 Aug. 1945
Navy									
Officers, Men	13,162	38,601	67,786	117,268	170,418	212,820	260,143	291,357	316,675
Officers, Women	0	0	0	770	3,827	6,459	7,611	8,744	8,399
Total Officers	13,162	38,601	67,786	118,038	174,245	219,279	267,754	300,101	325,074
Nurses	442	823	1,778	2,907	5,431	7,022	8,399	8,893	10,968
Officer Candidates, Men	2,569	11,452	14,529	35,472	53,661	119,988	104,578	84,627	62,913
Officer Candidates, Women	0	0	0	532	634	484	481	0	12
Total Officer Candidates	2,569	11,452	14,529	36,004	54,295	120,472	105,059	84,627	62,925
Enlisted, Men	144,824	332,274	556,477	1,099,109	1,486,696	1,995,893	2,542,653	2,735,270	2,935,695
Enlisted, Women	0	0	0	3,109	21,083	38,450	57,500	72,864	73,685
Total Enlisted	144,824	332,274	556,477	1,102,218	1,507,779	2,034,343	2,600,153	2,808,134	3,009,380
Total Navy	160,997	383,150	640,570	1,259,167	1,741,750	2,381,116	2,981,365	3,201,755	3,408,347
Marine Corps									
Officers, Men	1,819	4,067	7,138	13,151	21,140	27,588	31,991	34,598	36,851
Officers, Women	0	0	0	0	244	605	797	824	813
Total Officers	1,819	4,067	7,138	13,151	21,384	28,193	32,788	35,422	37,664

Officer Candidates, Men	0	371	702	2,029	1,730	10,573	7,515	5,384	3,741
Officer Candidates, Women	0	0	0	0	86	150	11	1	61
Total Officer Candidates	0	371	702	2,029	1,816	10,723	7,526	5,385	3,802
Enlisted, Men	26,545	70,908	135,688	223,243	284,481	356,533	415,559	414,561	427,017
Enlisted, Women	0	0	0	0	3,313	9,720	16,669	17,012	17,350
Total Enlisted	26,545	70,908	135,688	223,243	287,794	366,253	432,268	431,573	444,367
Total Marine Corps	28,364	75,346	143,528	238,423	310,994	405,169	472,582	472,380	485,833
Coast Guard Officers, Men	1,360	1,854	3,507	5,462	8,104	10,038	11,275	11,697	11,766
Officers, Women	0	0	0	15	235	514	704	918	855
Total Officers	1,360	1,854	3,507	5,477	8,339	10,552	11,979	12,615	12,621
Officer Candidates, Men	145	301	349	992	1,050	1,493	234	480	353
Officer Candidates, Women	0	0	0	0	0	73	64	0	26
Total Officer Candidates	145	301	349	992	1,050	1,566	298	480	379
Enlisted, Men	12,261	25,575	55,142	135,231	142,631	154,251	149,589	147,865	148,629
Enlisted, Women	0	0	0	69	2,956	5,570	7,392	8,911	8,646
Total Enlisted	12,261	25,575	55,142	135,300	145,587	159,821	156,981	156,776	157,275
Total Coast Guard	13,766	27,730	58,998	141,769	154,976	171,939	169,258	169,871	170,275
Grand Total	203,127	486,226	843,096	1,639,359	2,207,720	2,958,224	3,623,205	3,844,006	4,064,455

146 *Annual Report of the Secretary of the Navy*, 10 Jan. 1946 pp. A 14–15.

Jacket Illustrations

The paintings used on the jackets of the fifteen-volume series reproduced in full color. Painting for Volume II owned by S. E. Morison and used by permission of the artist; Volume X by permission of The Mariner's Museum, Newport News, Virginia, and the artist; all others by permission of the Navy Department.

1. *Air Contact — North Atlantic*

by Commander Dwight C. Shepler USNR

Gun crews aboard U.S. Destroyer *Champlin.* Done for the Navy, at sea

II. *Off Fedhala, 8 November 1942*

by Benjamin T. Stephenson

U.S.S. *Brooklyn* firing on Battery Sherki; Higgins boat and LCV carrying tank in foreground

III. Pearl Harbor, December 7, 1941
by Commander Griffith Baily Coale USNR

IV. Battle of Midway

by Commander Griffith Baily Coale USNR

Carrier *Kaga* on fire, June 4, 1942, after attack by American carrier-based dive-bombers

V. U.S. Battleship Washington in Night Battle, Guadalcanal

by Commander Dwight C. Shepler USNR

VI. *Divine Services before the Invasion of Bougainville*

by Lieutenant William F. Draper USNR

VII.   Planes Return

by Lieutenant William F. Draper USNR

VIII.   *D-day minus One Bombardment of Saipan*

by Lieutenant William F. Draper USNR

IX. *Assault Wave, Salerno*
by Lieutenant Mitchell Jamieson USNR

X. *Escort Carrier and U.S. Destroyer* Charles R. Ware

by Thomas C. Skinner

XI. The Battle for Fox Green Beach, Omaha
by Commander Dwight C. Shepler USNR

XII.   Battle off Samar

by Commander Dwight C. Shepler USNR

Counterattack by escort carrier's screen; destroyer *Heermann*, center; battleships *Nagato, Haruna,*
left; salvo from *Yamato*; destroyer *Hoel* sinking, right; cruisers *Tone* and *Chikuma* firing, right rear

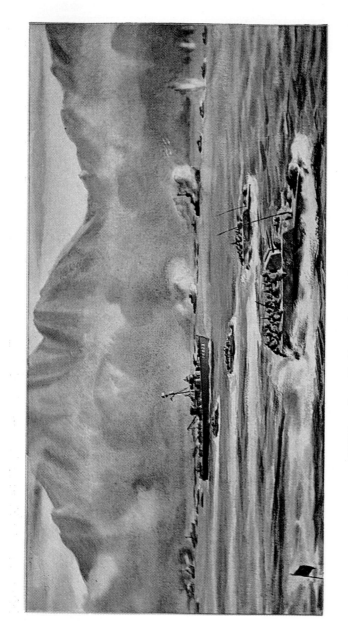

XIII. San Fabian Attack Force, Luzon
by Commander Dwight C. Shepler USNR

XIV. D-day plus One, Green Beach Two

by Lieutenant Mitchell Jamieson USNR

XV. Surrender

by Captain Gerard Richardson USNR

Japanese barge brings surrender party to U.S.S. *Missouri*

Cumulative Errata List

For Vols. I–XIV

S INCE the General Index refers to the latest edition or printing of each volume, it may occasionally mislead readers who possess a first edition or an early printing. We have, therefore, provided this list of all important errata that so far have been detected.

Included are errors of fact, or of opinions which have been revised as a result of better knowledge. Minor errata such as errors in spelling (except of proper names), punctuation, and rephrasing to improve the style are not included. Some errata in this list, especially in Vols. XII–XIV, were discovered too late to be corrected in the latest 1961 printings; but as they will be corrected in future printings, they are here included.

Errata in the volume indexes are not mentioned, since it is presumed that readers will use the General Index.

Volume I: *The Battle of the Atlantic*

Page	Line	
4	8–9 up	Correct score is 57 in service, of which 46 were ready for combat; and 30 of these were 250-tonners.
"	n. 4	*Maass* and *Nürnberg* are correct.
15	2	Correct reading is: 60° W. to lat. 20° N. (Note "to" between "W." and "lat.")
"	n. 26	*Truxtun* is correct.
30	foot	Not "whom Pétain appointed" but "appointed in 1939."
31	1	Not "106" but "112."
32	n. 8	Admiral Spruance's initial: "A."
33	2	Correct reading: ". . . and by Patrol Squadron 51, twelve PBYs under . . . Commander W. J. Mullins, based at San Juan.[9]"

Page	Line	
33	n. 10	Robert did not surrender, but was relieved by a Free French high commissioner 14 July.
34	10	The correct date is 9 September 1940, which was three days after the air assault began.
53	6 up	The correct name is Sir Percy L. H. Noble.
63	4 up	The submarine was *U–69.*
77	13	August 1941 is correct date for Army units' arrival.
79		It was *U–652* that attacked *Greer.*
84	13	Correct place is San Juan, P. R. (not "Port of Spain").
"	n. 18	Add that the Navy prize crew shared the salvage money.
85	1, & n. 21	Cinclant ordered ships darkened 15 July 1941.
90	14 up	The destroyers returned to "Momp" to pick up other convoys.
93		*Kearny* was torpedoed by *U–568; Broadwater* by *U–101.*
94		*Reuben James* was torpedoed by *U–562.*
95	12–15	The explanation is that the Naval War Staff, despite Doenitz's protests, diverted U-boats to escort and weather missions, and merchant vessel concentrations in the Mediterranean.
108	15	Change "naval oilers" to "battleships."
109	add to par. 1:	"Destroyer *Stack* (Lieutenant Commander Isaiah Olch) made two depth-charge attacks which sent *U–132* home for repairs."
109	12	The correct name of this convoy was WS–12X.
126	11 up	Not "fifty" but "25" U-boats.
128	top photo	Taken on *Wichita* (not *Washington*).
129	n. 21	Occasionally a U-boat held up a small freighter to get fresh fruit, but there were no enemy agents.
130	n. 23	Add that *Esso Bolivar* made port owing to fine damage-control by her merchant crew and Navy salvage experts.
133	9 up	*U–754* sank the tugboat and barges.
"	n. 29	*U–552* sank *David H. Atwater.*
134	1	Not "evidence" but "suspicion." *U–126* sank *Hanseat.*
135	11	Not "145-foot" but "165-foot."
"	5–2 up	*U–128* was the first and *U–504* the second U-boat to enter this area.
138	4, 5	*Boutwell* and *Woodbury* were 125-footers, and the other four cutters 165-footers.

Page	Line	
145	16	It was *U–161* (Kapitänleutnant Albrecht Achilles, nicknamed "Ajax") that did all the damage at Castries and Port of Spain.
146	14, 15 up	Not "in March," but "shortly"; and the work was well along in May.
147	10	Not "Cocorite" but "Carenage."
151	9 up	*U–68* sank *Merrimack.*
152	6	Add that *U–504, U–172* and *U–161* were also in the area.
153	11, 12	This submarine was *U–161*, Capt. Achilles.
"	16	Not "three" but "five."
154		Add that *PC–460* accidentally rammed and sank U.S.S. *S–26* off the Canal 25 Jan.
156	15	*Rockefeller* was escorted by Coast Guard Cutter No. 470 and one plane.
181	8	"Nine or more" British ships (not "six to nine").
187	n. 32	Capt. Frankel's middle initial is B.
188	4, 5	There was only one French corvette, but eight British escorts.
200	14 up,	*U–584* operated off Ponte Vedra.
282	n. 15	
213	3 up	*Rathburne* is the correct spelling.
228	11 up	These were not the first sets but a new type.
232	3	McDaniel's rank was Lt. Cdr.
235	4	Not "*Cruising*" but "*Maximum*" speed; delete the †.
240	7 up	This squadron was not Hudsons but Kingfishers.
"	n. 52	Not "Truculent Turtle" but "2-engined Neptune."
249	16	Lt. Neff's initials are H. L.
258	facing	The Trinidad base shown was at Teteron Bay.
265		Delete paragraph beginning "This record," and insert new paragraph:

The very unfortunate sinking of the 2880-ton French submarine *Surcouf* occurred 18 February 1942 about 80 miles north of Cristobal. She was en route to Tahiti and in Bermuda had received onward-routing instructions to the Panama Canal. On a pitch black night, S.S. *Thompson Lykes*, steaming independently, reported striking and running down a partially submerged object which scraped along her side and keel. Her lookouts heard shouts from the water and she carefully searched the area, but found no survivors. Although the evidence is meager and entirely circumstantial, it seems certain

Page	Line	
		that *Surcouf* was then rammed and sunk, for she disappeared about that time and place and none of her officers and men were ever heard from again.
282	12	President Roosevelt proposed this.
283	1	Not "already had a similar machine gun" but "had similar equipment, gear, and . . ."
"	18–26	More details of loss of *Atik* have come in from German sources. *U–123*, Kapitänleutnant Hardegen, did it. After the first torpedo hit her, *Atik* dropped false bulwarks and opened fire, making hits and killing one German. *U–123* closed after dark and sank the disabled ship. There were no survivors.
283	5–7 up	The name of *Asterion's* C.O. was Legwen.
284	2nd para.	Add that *Eagle's* sister ship *Foam* was sunk 17 May 1942 off Nova Scotia by *U–432*, and that *Eagle* remained a Q-ship after her name was changed.
286	9, 10	"Had been persuaded to launch" (not "himself had initiated").
"	14	The correct number lost is 141.
287	n. 18	The correct designation is AMc, and they were minesweepers (not transports).
288	16	*U–432* sank *Foam.*
295	last	The cadets were commissioned Ensign, and many were given active duty in the Navy.
296	n. 14	Correct reading: The total number of merchant seamen in training, 1 Sept. 1942, was 1427; by 31 Dec. 1943, 10,590 more arrived for training; total number of graduates was 6628; 2856 were disenrolled and 2533 were still in training at end of 1943.
326	8–17	Delete "The escort commander . . . January, 1943," and substitute:
		Most of January's attacks were confined to Convoy TM–1, consisting of nine tankers and four British corvettes, bound from Trinidad to Gibraltar, which encountered a wolf-pack of about 9 U-boats. In four days' fighting, between 3 and 10 January, this convoy lost seven tankers. This was the highest percentage of loss inflicted by U-boats on a convoy during the war. Cominch promptly shifted two long-range antisubmarine plane squadrons to North African fields to provide air cover over this dangerous area.
"	2 up	Admiral Davidson's middle initial is A.
332	10 up	Greenspun is the correct spelling.

Page	Line	
333	10, 11	Not "the merchant crew . . . good advantage" but "abandoning ship. A terrific list kept most port lifeboats from being launched."
"	20	Add: "Four Army Chaplains, Rabbi Alexander Goode, Father John P. Washington, Reverend George L. Fox and Reverend Clark V. Poling, gave up their lifebelts to soldiers and went down with the ship."
334	3	Not "904" but "906"; not "299" but "229."
"	n. 36	Not "605" but "677."
336	9, 10 up	Not "ninety" but "thirty" minutes. Not "the seamanship . . . emergency" but "she lacked compartmentation: progressive flooding took charge and she sank stern first."
"	5–8 up	Abandonment was orderly. Nine out of ten lifeboats got into the water, but capsized or were overloaded.
336	2–4 up	Not "sad instances . . . are wanting" but "fortunately the only instances of what could happen to any troop transport torpedoed at night in mid-Atlantic during winter weather."
360	13 up	24 destroyers (not 16).
"	n.	Add: H.M.S. *Audacity* had performed similar duty the previous autumn but was sunk escorting a Halifax–Greenland convoy in December 1941.
361	5, 6	Not "engaged in reconnaissance" but "still chasing the earlier flight of high-level bombers."
"	14, 12 up	"Eight" (not "six") ships; 8 (not 15) torpedo planes.
378	14	*Camaquam* is the correct spelling.
382	2 up	Patrulha and Araujo are the correct spellings.
383	1	Soares is the correct spelling.
384	2 up	Add that *Karin* sank.
397	14	"Motorship" (not "tanker").
397 398	14 up, & 3	Borum is the correct spelling.
398	9 up	The name of the cadet was Edwin O'Hara.
399	4	Raider "J" was armed with one 3-inch and six 5.9-inch guns.
403	2 up	"T–3" not "C–3."
409	7 up	Not "1943. Much" but "1942–43. More."
418		Note that Comdesdiv 60, Cdr. John B. Heffernan, was on board ELLIS.
419		Appendix VI (roster of the Atlantic Fleet) has been added to later printings.

Volume II: *Operations in North African Waters*

Page	Line	
xii	List Ills., &	} The flight deck is *Ranger's*.
31	facing	
10	foot	January (not "the spring").
12	17	April (not "February").
13	n. 18	The U-boat was No. *161*, and the date was 17 July 1942.
17	3 up	Correct number of Americans was 10,000.
34	21, 22	Amphibious Force Atlantic Fleet was an assault force with training responsibilities.
39	center	Under ELLYSON insert: "Desdiv 20, Capt. T. L. Wattles." C.O. of FORREST was Lt. Cdr. M. Van Metre.
42	foot	Add note:

A short time before Task Force 34 sailed, President Roosevelt called General Patton and Admiral Hewitt to the White House. To avoid notice and comment by the press the Army and Navy leaders were admitted at different entrances and brought together by devious routes in the anteroom of the President's office. They discussed the forthcoming operation and the President wished them both "God Speed."

50	8	Not "it meant using" but "he must stay at sea or use."
55	4 up	The correct number is 19,870.
65	last	The correct name of the French general is Charles Mast. (Also on pp. 184–5, 205, 216.)
"	n. 23	Delete "Not to be confused with."
66	n. 26	Gen. Mast was given only the date.
67	7	The name of this general was Henry-Martin.
69		Delete para. beginning "During." Note 29 should read as follows:

At 0130 Greenwich (0230 French) time, half an hour after Michelier had telephoned to him about the leak. In this conversation, according to my French informants, the General, being under duress, ordered the Admiral to take over the Morocco theater command. Michelier had already received an informal warning from Vichy at 0050, and at 0250 (both Greenwich time) he received official notice of the landings at Oran, from Admiral Rioult at that place, in plain language.

Page	Line	
70	4	Michelier was dependent upon Noguès.
71	7	Not "after sunrise" but "almost 0300."
"	n. 30	Correct reading:

The French guarded their own military communication frequencies and did not normally cover other channels or listen to Allied broadcasts.

73	2, 6	*Hogan* was a minesweeper.
78	18	*Palmer* was the ship that knocked them out.
86	14 up	The regiment was the 30th Infantry.
87		Add following note on French chain of command furnished by Service Historique de la Marine:

General Juin was C. in C. of all French forces in North Africa. Under him were three theater commanders: — General Noguès for Morocco, Atlantic side; General Koeltz for the rest of Morocco and Algeria, and General Barre for Tunisia. Under General Noguès were four sector commanders, of which General Henry-Martin commanded the Safi-Mogador, Vice Admiral Michelier the Casablanca, and General Dody the North Morocco sectors. The principle of unity of command over all arms pertained in each sector and in each area; but Michelier was dependent directly on the Admiralty at Vichy in respect of his command over naval vessels.

89	6	The strafing was effective.
96	2, 3 up	Not "exploded" but "penetrated."
"	n. 14	Correct name is Barthes.
97	7	Not "forty-eight" but "about eight" hours.
98	6, 7	Not "The cruisers . . . hits on" but "Around 0745 bombing planes and warships' projectiles sank three . . ."
"	8	Not "possibly" but "also."
99	13	Not "light cruiser . . . until 1000" but "*Milan.* Light cruiser *Primauguet* sortied last, at 0900."
101	n. 27	Correct second sentence is: French sources state that this cruiser opened fire on *Massachusetts* at 0935.
104	7	*Méduse* fired these torpedoes.
"	last	Not "Not over a" but "about three."
106	4	The salvo from *Massachusetts* missed; *Boulonnais* was sunk by a full salvo from *Brooklyn* at 1112.
"	6 up	Not "five" but "three."
"	n. 33	Mordal *La Bataille de Casablanca* is authority for the

		time. The ship on fire at 1109 was *Boulonnais*. The four "hits" by *Massachusetts* turn out to have been near-misses.
		Replace last sentence of note by:
		Prof. R. G. Breckenridge of M.I.T. observes that fluorescin, the dye for green coloration, shows red in the splash when viewed by transmitted light, which may resolve this dilemma.
110	n.	*Méduse* was bombed and damaged by carrier planes on 8 and 9 Nov.
119	5	The volunteers from the Norfolk city (not naval) prison were merchant seamen.
121	n. 11	Last 2 lines should read: We now know that Port Lyautey was alerted by orders from Casablanca received at 0325.
130	9	Correct reading: Destroyer's mission was to land the raiders at Port Lyautey airdrome.
137 143	5 up, & 6	"Nine or ten" (not "Nineteen").
138	5, 6	There were no guns in the old fort.
144	3	Add "The correct course was also given him by *Mervine*."
145	8	*Mervine* gave the "Batter Up!"
148	1, 2	Few men were hit and none killed.
149	n. 22	Add "Col. E. H. Randle USA gave the order."
150	5	Not "the word got through" but "because of a false report" that Gen. Henry-Martin . . .
151	11 up	This plane bombed *Méduse* after she had beached.
154	3, 4 up	Correct reading: "She and other transports served as hospitals for the *Harris* beach party."
155	7–9 up	The Mazagan garrison received the cease-fire order from Casablanca.
162	17	Not "125-mm (4.9-inch)" but "90-mm (3.7-inch)" anti-aircraft batteries.
167	6 up	*Tonnant* was the submarine.
170	3–5	Not "1200" but "400" yards' range.
171	6–13 up	*U–130* approached inside minefield, fired 4 torpedoes from stern and 1 from bow; all 5 made hits on the named transports.
183	13–15	Admiral Esteva would have coöperated with the Allies had they landed at Bône.
184	5, 4 up	Correct date is 29 October, which gave Gen. Charles (not "René") Mast 9 or 10 days.

Page	Line	
187	6	Admiral Fenard was secretary general of French North Africa.
191	n. 4	Add "They landed at Arzeu — see p. 231 below."
208	2–9 up	There is no longer any doubt that Pétain favored the Allied landings. See also p. 219 *n.*
216	12 up	Darlan sent his cease-fire order at 1120, 10 Nov.
219		A new paragraph has been added to later editions, giving more detailed evidence as to Pétain's secret messages to Darlan, which caused the Admiral to order his cease-fire and to coöperate. Reference: Admiral Auphan *Les grimaces de l'histoire* (1951).
225	12	Saint-Grégoire (not "Fort Lamoune") was the objective.
231	8, 22	There were four companies of Rangers.
233	2 up	Add "with the aid of naval gunfire" after "1330."
239	last	The battleship was *Strasbourg*.
240	3	Laborde never received Pétain's orders.
"	16	*Provence* was the battleship (cf. Vol. XI 287).
"	17	Five subs. sortied; 3 joined Allies.
213 241	10 8 up &	The correct spelling is Derrien.
" 242	17–19 & 1–9	There is now no doubt that Admiral Esteva was merely the victim of what Churchill called "the cataract of events."
243	7	Bougie was Anderson's port of debarkation.
245	8 up	The name of No. 41 was *Le Conquérant*.
247	11 up	Capt. Sullivan was then in New York salvaging *Lafayette* (formerly *Normandie*).
260	n. 19	Not "Sir John Cunningham" but "Vice Adm. A. J. Power RN."
263	n. 24	This engine was developed by Packard for aircraft in the 1920's.
274	1–4 up	Correct reading: All were operated by the Royal Navy; the British Flag Officer, Tunisia, had headquarters at Bizerta. The U.S. Navy, however, used a small dry dock at La Goulette in Tunis Bay, and used the French submarine and seaplane base in the inner harbor of Bizerta, as an advanced amphibious base.
275–80		Chapter XII has been so much changed from the first printing that it is not possible to indicate corrections here. The 1961 printing contains these changes.

Volume III: *The Rising Sun in the Pacific*

Page	Line	
Frontispiece		Adm. Hart's middle initial is C.
7	7	Not "Yamamoto" but "Shimada."
14	1–3	The new cabinet formed under General Hayashi lasted until June, when Prince Konoye, who was unable to resist the militarists, became Premier.
17	4–5	Correct reading: An advanced Army unit notified naval authorities that Chinese troops were fleeing the capital in ten ships.
"	15–16	Twelve more planes bombed and nine fighters strafed.
18	n. 15	Add: that the fliers neither recognized *Panay* nor were informed of her presence; they thought they were bombing enemy troops escaping up-river in Chinese merchant ships. (See art. by Cdr. M. Okumiya, who led the dive-bombing attack, in U.S. Nav. Inst. *Proc.* June 1953.)
26		Admirals commanding Second, Fourth and Fifth Fleets were Kondo, Inouye and Hosogaya, respectively.
69	2, 3	The Imperial Conference did this.
71	4 up	This was concluded on 10 Nov. by General Terauchi and Adm. Yamamoto.
76	4 up	"Ozawa's" expeditionary force (not "Kondo's").
80	4 up, 84 9, 86 10	Correct date of Yamamoto's order is 5 Nov.
83	14	The U.S.N. then had eight carriers.
"	18–19	The correct date is 10 September.
84	2 up	There were 27 (not "20") submarines.
85	13–20	Correct numbers of planes are: Total, 423; C.A.P., 30; reserve, 40; 353 attacked (140 Kates, 131 Vals, 79 Zekes); 13 float planes. Of these, 29 were lost.
86	10	The correct date is 5 Nov.
"	12	Not two days "later" but two days "earlier."
"	12 up	Rear Adm. Ugaki is supposed to have made this speech.
87	table	Not "CVL" but "CV"; and not "AKEBONO" but "SAZANAMI."
88	1–15	Carriers *Hiryu* and *Soryu* were 726 ft. long, rated as CV, larger than U.S.S. *Wasp.* The CAs displaced 14,070 and the DDs 1900 tons each.
89	14	The destination was announced at sea, on 2 Dec.
90	14	The fleet sailed at 0600.

The Rising Sun in the Pacific

131

Page	Line	
94	3 up	The commander's name was Itaya.
95	11, 12 16	There were 27 submarines, and 5 joined later. Most of them were long-range.
96	1	Insert "*I–26* and *I–10* broke off, one for the Aleutians, the other to watch Samoa and the Fijis."
98	4–7	Seven were ordered to West Coast to join scouts *I–26* and *I–10*, already there. *I–70*, sunk by *Enterprise*, was not one of these.
101	last, and n.	1364 days of war; the formal surrender V–J Day was 2 Sept. 1945.
103	last	The correct name is Roman L. Brooks.
121	8–9 up	Correct reading: "So impaired by bombing that one gun which did not get the word started a panic of firing . . ." (Delete "Commander Young.")
139	2	The correct date is 1940.
143	1–2	Corrected score is: *Okla., Tenn., W. Va.* & *Calif.* sunk; all but the first raised; *Nev., Md.* & *Penna.* damaged.
146	2	*California* also participated.
155	6–7	Last 2 sentences of para. should read: *Harrison*, overhauled by a Japanese cruiser on 8 December, was run aground to avoid falling into enemy hands. Salvaged and operated as *Kachidoki M*, she was torpedoed by *Pampanito* 12 Sept. 1944.
158	table, *submarines*	The middle initials of Shane, Wallace, Freeman, Stone and Burnside are L.
159	table, *minesweepers*	Lt. Cdr. E. R. J. Griffin commanded the minesweepers; the C.O. of TANAGER was Lt. Cdr. E. A. Roth. Add under tables: "4th Marine Regiment and Navy Yard Marines."
160	4–5 up	Third Fleet included a supporting force of carriers, cruisers and destroyers.
161	table	Add ASAKAZE and MATSUKAZE to Takahashi's force; under Hirose's force there were 9 chasers plus 2 gunboats, plus 9 SCs; replace HAYATAKA by KUMAKAWA under Hara; change "Minclayers" to "Minesweepers" and shift asterisk to No. 19.
162	1st table, 3rd col.	The first line were minesweepers; under them were 9 Subchasers and 6 Transports.
163	1st table 3rd col.	l. 3 should read "5 Transports, 2 PCs"; Under *Co-öperating Army Air Forces*: 48 Reconnaissance, 72 VF, 27 heavy VB planes.
169	9	*Ryujo* was then 100 miles E. of Davao.

Page	Line	
171	10–11 up	52 Zeros and 81 bombers is the correct number.
172	4 up	*Peary* was towed clear by *Whippoorwill*.
174	n.	Add that Rear Adm. Hara's flagship *Natori* was damaged.
176	6	The correct hour is 1340.
"	4–5 up	Nishimura's force comprised 4400 troops in six transports.
177	3 up, 10 up & n.	The correct spelling is Wheless.
180	n.	It now appears *Ashigara* was attacked by Kelly 10 Dec.
181	13 up	Not "Twelve" but "Two" days after the Lingayen Landing . . .
"	7 up	The Lamon Group's escort was a light cruiser, 4 destroyers, and a small craft.
182	9, 10	This happened on the afternoon of the 23rd.
184	8–10	The correct roster of the garrison is 36 naval officers, 6 warrant officers, 5 naval nurses, 230 enlisted men, 153 Marine officers and men, 246 Chamorros.
184	n.	The composition of the enemy force was 4 CA, 4 DD, 4 AM, 2 gunboats, 6 SC and 2 tenders.
190	11	There were almost 100 bombers.
193	4–5	Glassford's force departed Cavite for Balikpapan.
195	n. 5	Add: "S.S. *George G. Henry* stayed; retired with the fleet."
199	2, 3 up	Homma's staff was shaken up, but he was not relieved.
206	3	The submarine was *Spearfish*.
"	10, 11	In addition to *Quail*, *Pigeon*, 3 river gunboats and 2 tugs were left. Bombs sank *Mindanao* and *Pigeon* next day; the others were scuttled.
222		Add note to this effect: "During the three months after 7 Dec. the Japanese reconnoitered Pearl Harbor with planes from the following submarines: *I–7* at dawn 16 Dec.; *I–19* by moonlight 4 Jan.; and *I–9* on night of 23 Feb. 1942.
236	3	These 18 planes were Brewster Buffaloes.
241	19	The correct date is 20 Dec.
242	n. 26	Certain tanks had been water-filled to offset weight of island structure.
243	n. 29	Add that Admiral Fletcher was ordered by Cincpac to fuel when and where he did, because it was then

Page	Line	
		hoped to have Admiral Brown's task force join him, and Brown had to know where to find him.
245	6 up	Abe's first name is Hiroaki.
258	11	The submarine was *I-73*.
262	8 up	Only the Roi attack was unsuccessful.
263	11	The score was transport *Bordeaux M.* and an SC sunk, net tender *Kashima M.*, gunboat *Haya M.*, transport *Nagata M.*, minelayer *Tokiwa* (9240 tons), light cruiser *Katori*, *Kanto M.* (8600 tons) and other vessels damaged; 18 planes destroyed; 90 men, including Rear Adm. Yashiro, killed.
265	18	Canton Island is correct.
267	facing	Lower photo is of *Indianapolis*.
268		Add note to this effect:
		On the night of 5 March two "Emily" flying boats raided Pearl Harbor. Departing Wotje, they refueled from three I-boats at French Frigate Shoals. Army radar stations detected their approach, but poor visibility over Oahu prevented their being spotted. One dropped bombs on a barren hillside six miles east of Pearl; the other dropped hers in the sea.
272	9 up	J. G. Olsen USNR was master of *George G. Henry*.
273	table, *Submarine*	Asterisk: *K-16, *K-17, *K-18; *O-16, *O-17, *O-20. Add that U.S.S. LARK and WHIPPOORWILL operated under R.N.N. till 1 Mar.
"	2 up	J. Ozawa's command was the Southern Expeditionary Fleet.
274	11 up (BASE GROUP)	AK TSUKUSHI MARU is correct spelling (not CHIKUSHI).
276	4 (ESCORT GROUP)	Third in 2nd col. is CL SENDAI (not DD KAWAUCHI).
279	last sentence	Add that Adm. Hart experienced unusual difficulty in carrying out his command functions over forces afloat. (His service base was at Port Darwin, 1200 miles eastward.)
280	11, 12	The correct date is 15 Dec. 1941; "the 11th" means Jan. 1942.
281	1	These 28 planes took off from Davao.
290	10	*Tsuruga* was sunk by *K-18* before midnight.
296	14	The decision was made by Field Marshal Wavell.
297	1	Correct reading: "dispatched seaplane carriers *Chitose* and *Mizuho*" (not "*Zuiho*").

Page	Line	
305	11 up	The correct date is 5 Feb.
308	10, 12 up	Add carrier *Ryujo* and light cruiser *Sendai* to Ozawa's force.
"	7–8 up	Hashimoto commanded the advanced echelon, Capt. Kojima the 14 APs.
315	12 up	This ship was seaplane carrier *Mizuho*.
316	2 up	Correct reading is: "took off for Kendari and Ambon. The three forces, 242 planes strong . . .
317	10 up	The Army transports were anchored.
"	5, 6 up	These ships were the Australian *Manunda*, two Australian sloops, tanker *Benjamin Franklin*, and an Australian troopship.
318	16	Lieutenant Lester A. Wood was in temporary command of *Preston*.
319	4, 5	The length of the attack was 45 minutes.
"	17–21	Not "A Brazilian merchantman" but "Tanker *British Motorist* . . . escaped" (not "were sunk"). The two corvettes and a Norwegian tanker, *Benjamin Franklin*, were hit (not "sunk").
"	22	*Meigs* and *Mauna Loa* were anchored.
"	n. 10	The master's name is Link.
320	2	The score was 8 ships lost and 9 damaged.
321	3 up	Kubo commanded the Bali force.
324	n.	19 (not "33") survivors is correct.
329		*Tromp* was not in this phase of the battle.
333	12 (Division 59, 3rd ship)	W. C. Blinn was C.O. of POPE.
"	1–3 up	Surface Group was: CA ATAGO, MAYA, TAKAO; Destroyers NOWAKI, HAGIKAZE, MAIKAZE, ARASHI.
334	table CARRIER GROUP EASTERN ATTACK GROUP	Add to Carrier Group: CV SHOKAKU & ZUIKAKU, BB KIRISHIMA, CA TONE & CHIKUMA, CL ABUKUMA, and 9 DDs. Under *Destroyer Squadron 2*, KAWAKAZE (not ASASHIO); YAMAKAZE (not AMATSUKAZE). Vice Adm. Ozawa in CA CHOKAI commanded Western Attack Group; Kurita's 4 CA were MOGAMI, MIKUMA, KUMANO & SUZUYA.
335	8	
384	7	Vice Adm. Ozawa commanded this group.
385	7	
335	16	He departed 23 Feb.
"	17–18	Takagi had 3 cruisers and 7 destroyers.
337	8	Add that there were also in Java about 7000 British and Australian and 541 American soldiers.

Page	Line	
341	9	Adm. Helfrich gave the orders.
363	7, 9	*Sea Witch*, Lt. Cdr. J. M. Hatfield, did discharge her planes. *Langley's* planes were Warhawks.
379	4	*Lark, Whippoorwill* and *Tulsa* got through.
384	18	91 VB and 38 VF is correct.
"	2 up	*Hermes* had no planes on board.
389	2	These Army planes were B–17s.
392	3 up	Capt. E. M. Zacharias was C.O. of SALT LAKE CITY.

Volume IV: *Coral Sea, Midway and Submarine Actions*

11	last	Add that it was not under Inouye's command, nor was the 25th A.F. mentioned on p. 14, 8–10.
15	9 up	Middle initial of Adm. Sir John Crace is G.
"	2 up	Doolittle's planes were Mitchells.
18	9, &	
22	5 up,	
29	12,	Correct name of C.O. Support Group is Marumo.
32	15,	
39	last,	
40	3 up	
"	11	Add "and air unit of *Kiyokawa*."
31	8 up	Not "next day" but "too late."
32	8	Takagi, however, had plenty of intelligence by radio.
"	n. 24	Correct time is 0900 May 7.
36	3 up	Correct date is 17 May.
38	2 up	These planes were B–17s.
49	10 up	*Yorktown* planes sighted enemy at 1100.
52	8	"Seventy" planes (not "ninety").
56	table,	
	col. 1	8 VF is correct.
	col. 2	22 VB is correct.
	col. 3	17 VF, 46 VB is correct.
57	1	*Lexington* attack began at 1136.
"	2	*Yorktown* attack over at 1100; *Lexington's* over, 1140.
77	13 up	Not "after nightfall 5" but "at dawn 6" June.
81	3 up	*Yorktown* sailed 30 May.
85	facing	On caption, officer called Lt. Moulton is really Lt. Cdr. S. E. Burroughs.
89	4	"Ichiki" is correct name of Army Detachment.
91	14	Howard H. Good was C.O. of NEW ORLEANS.
"	n. 43	Change "L." to "Lt." W. J. Widhelm.

Page	Line	
92	10	Brockman's middle initial is H.
"	6 up	Kimes's middle initial is E.
"	2 up	Capt. Tyler was not killed.
93	2	Hale's middle initial is H.
112	6	Brockman's middle initial is H.
116	9 up ⎫	*Hornet's* attack group Commander was Cdr. S. C.
117	15 ⎭	Ring.
126	facing	The *Nachi* class is cruiser *Ashigara*.
132	8	The message came from Nagumo at 0847.
136	7 up	Gallaher led the dive-bombers.
176	3	Correct reading is: "Ryujo's, which got through ..."
"	13	They started "shortly after 0807."
178	n. 34	Correct score is 2 VB and 1 VF shot down, 2 VB lost on return flight; *Ryujo* lost 1 VF.
226	3	Munson's middle initial is G.
252	2	Add "and Christmas Island."
"	9 up	Adm. McCain's middle initial is S.
253	9 up	Correct spelling is Chamberlin.
254	8, 9	Seabees and Marines helped the soldiers.
"	3 up	Not "except" but "not even" old Anzac Task Force 44.
265	8 up	Not "eight" but "nine" cargo ships.
"	n. 4	*Lipscomb Lykes* is one ship (not "*Lipscomb, Lykes*"); add *George F. Elliot* and *Barnett*.
267	19	Not "Kenney's" but "Brett's."
276	4	Delete *Salt Lake City*; add CL *San Diego*.
278	last	Delete "in *Chicago*"; insert "augmented by two carrier teams."
281	6, 7	Fletcher *had* been ordered not to do this.
283	6 up	The correct date is 7 August.
285	1	It was sunk by a carrier's Wildcat.
293	4	This hit did considerable damage.
294	3 up	Not "high speed" but "13.5 knots."
295	11	Nine torpedo-bombers passed through.

Volume V: *The Struggle for Guadalcanal*

4	1, 2 up	The NW, not NE, trade winds blow from Nov. to March.
23	13	They were used for short searches only.
24	5	The PBY was sent from tender *Mackinac*, then at Malaita.
25	n. 10	Turner received it about an hour later.

Page	Line	
29	5–8 up	Turner had tactical command of all vessels off Guadalcanal, and Scott of those off Tulagi. The remaining 18 transports (*Elliott* being then on fire and sinking) intended to continue unloading all night.
43	13	It was a shell from *Quincy* that burst in chart room; one of those mentioned on p. 45, l. 12.
115	11	The date of this conference was 28 Sept.
"	3 up	Not while the conferees were talking, but on 4 Sept.
116	9–10	VII 'Phib was authorized 7 Sept.
117	10 up	Not "Almost at that very moment" but "Over three weeks earlier."
"	5 up	MacArthur halted the advance on 17 September.
128	10 up	Not "a few" but "1500" yards.
133	n.	*I-15* was sunk 2 Nov. 1942 by destroyer *McCalla*, south of San Cristobal, not by naval planes 16 Dec.
136		Last two lines should read: "She steamed 2800 miles before a temporary strengthening member let go. Then, despite reduced speed, the hull began to work."
141	1–8 up	Puller operated from destroyer *Monssen*, not *Ballard*.
159	chart	On middle Japanese track, not "1140" but "2340."
184	15	Funafuti was occupied 3 Oct.
190	6 up	This action commenced 20 Oct.
198	3	7th Marines lost 130; 164th Infantry, 78.
204	table	Correct number of Kinkaid's Task Force is 16.
210–11	chart middle left-hand page	ZUIHO was hit at 0740.
215	16	Not "westward" but "eastward."
258	2 up	Adm. Callaghan's middle initial is J.
289	n.	Dale G. Friend is correct.
290–91	chart extreme right	Both times should be "2238" (not "2338"). Track of "Rear DDs" should be of LAMSON.
295	7	First place mentioned should be San Cristobal.
297	12 up	Not "two" but "ten" miles.
324	n. 10	Correct score is: *I-4* sunk by *Sea Dragon* 20 Dec.; *I-18* hit by *Grayback* 2 Jan., sunk 11 Feb. by *Fletcher* and a plane from *Helena*.
335	14	Mt. Austen is 3.2 miles SW of Henderson.
364	5 up	*Stringham* was an APD.
375	middle	Capt. John E. Murray commanded the F5s.

Volume VI: *Breaking the Bismarcks Barrier*

Page	Line	
7	5	The C.C.S. agreed, not at Casablanca, but in May 1943.
48	middle	Identity of these I-boats is uncertain.
68	13 up;	
69	2 & 6 up	This boat has been identified as *I–168*.
70	1	
112	8	Submarine *RO–113* was definitely a victim.
119	6, 7 up	*RO–34* was not sunk then, but by *Strong* on 7 April, off Lark Shoal. (This statement appears wrongly on the last line of the page, in some printings.)
121	16 up	*PC–85* was not in this escort.
"	2 up	Not "PC escort" but "other vessels."
128	5–10 up	Two Bettys and six Zekes took off at 0800 Apr. 18 and arrived over Buin at 0935.
140	3	The correct date is 16th June.
150	17	Not "southwest" but "northwest."
154	12–11 up	*RO–101* was still afloat in September.
166	16, 17	Contact was made at 0106 by *Niizuki's* radar detector and by 0146 the range had closed to 12,000 yds.
167	15–16	Insert: "*Amagiri* took four hits which destroyed her forward radio room and electrical circuits; three duds damaged *Hatsuyuki*."
178	8 up	*Leander* was newer and more powerful than *Omaha*.
179	5–6	Insert: "but *Taylor*, supporting the APDs in Kula Gulf, sank *RO–107*."
187	last	Ainsworth was not worried over any "comeback" but eager to pursue cripples which he supposed had escaped.
195	14 up	Add: "It worked O.K. on *Jintsu*."
229	15	*John Penn* was a transport.
241	last	Walker's middle initial is R.
245	11 up	The correct hour is 2236.
"	2 up	The first group was four destroyers.
297	6 up	The correct spelling is BREESE.
332	13 up	CL *Agano* did not lose her after section.
340	last	Adm. DuBose's middle initial is T.
344	8	*Fuller* was the transport hit.
358	9, 10	Armstrong of *Spence* made this quip.
373	17 & 3 up	Brig. Gen. J. W. Cunningham commanded 112th Cavalry.

Page	Line	
375	14 up	The 1st Marine Tractor Battalion manned these LVTs.
376	8, 9	These landing craft were manned by Army Engineers.
383	2 up	Col. Sumiya commanded troops at beachhead.
416	16 up	C.O. of *St. Louis* was Capt. R. H. Roberts.
417	chart	Delete the south-pointing arrow.
437	14 up	Berkey, not Barbey, was in charge.
440	12, &	Captain Richard M. Scruggs of the LSTs commanded this echelon.
441	11 up	
444	3 up	These guns were ferreted out and destroyed by *Nicholson.*

Volume VII: *Aleutians, Gilberts and Marshalls*

43	2	*Pruitt* was a minelayer.
45	1	Who sank *I-31* is uncertain.
47	n.	Correct title of Commo. Carter's book is *Beans, Bullets and Black Oil.*
57	5, 15	This submarine was *I-24.*
"	20, 21	*I-9* was sunk by *Frazier*, whose C.O. was Lt. Cdr. E. M. Brown. *I-31* went missing.
"	last	Delete any statement about *Tama* here.
58	13–14	*Kunashiri* returned to port and *Wakaba* joined the oilers' screen.
"	16–17	Kimura's evacuation group commenced the 50-mile run, and Kawase remained behind.
79	15–16	The airfield was ready before the end of 1942.
83	6–7 up	The reason Burma never came off was that Churchill opposed it and the C.C.S. killed it at Cairo in Dec. 1943.
86	5 up	The correct date is 15 Aug.
"	facing	O'Hare's plane is a Wildcat.
93	2	Not "battleship" but "destroyers."
94	n. 21	Capt. Jennings's middle initial is F.
116	12	The amphtracs started from San Diego, took on their crews at Samoa.
135		Add note: "*Alcyone* from 21 Nov., and the four merchant ships from 24 Nov., discharged inside the lagoon."
138	3	Not "*Chikuma*" but "*Suzuya.*"
141	n. 8	Note should read: "*I-175* was sunk by DEs *Charrette* and *Fair* 5 Feb. 1944."

Page	Line	
144	8, 19, 21	Make *I–19, I–40;* and *I–40, I–19.*
146ff.		The correct spelling is Jeter A. Isely.
157	n.	Add that Adm. Turner insists that less than 2000 tons were fired, and points out that the island had been frequently bombed from air.
202	10	Add that Capt. Paul S. Theiss was chief of III 'Phib staff.
207	3–7	Spruance commanded Fifth Fleet and Central Pacific Force; Turner commanded the Joint Expeditionary Force (TF 51).
"	12–13 up	Insert that Capt. D. W. Loomis commanded the Reserve Force.
210	14	Not "Southern" but "Northern."
221	5–7	Rear Adm. F. C. Sherman's group (*Bunker Hill*, flag) also took part.
223	3 up, &	Not "*I–21*" but "*I–175.*"
224	3	
"	n. 27	Delete statement about *I–40.*
227	2	Lt. Harvey W. Weeks USMC commanded this party.
239	14	Not "LSTs" but "LSDs."
250	10 up	Not "16th" but "15th."
"	9 up	This was the 109th Seabees.
"	3–8 up	After "Division," correct reading is:
		But the work went slowly, and the runways were not yet flyable when, on 12 February, Japanese planes scored a lucky hit which set off an improperly stowed ammunition dump on Roi. The explosion blasted out a tremendous crater, killed three and wounded 53 Marines, and destroyed large supplies of food and equipment stored nearby. Despite the devastation 16 fighters of Marine Air Group 31 flew in two days later to afford aërial protection. And this was the island whence . . .
254	1	Not "South" but "Gea" Pass.
257	19	Add: "At 0535 destroyer *Colahan* grounded on the reef south of Enubuj, but was later towed clear, somewhat damaged, by tug *Tekesta.*"
258	3–5	Delete sentence "The proper . . . as required."
	10	Not "1000" but "716" rounds.
260	7	Not "beach area" but "secondary defenses in the central part of the island."
261	10–11	Not "stood by for call fire" but "poured gunfire into the beach."

Page	Line	
295	1	Not "Namur" but "Engebi."
300	5	The correct hour is 0930.
318	plate facing	This is a Hellcat (F6F).
337	middle	Capt. S. A. Olsen was C.O. of MIDDLETON; Cdr. C. A. Misson of FELAND; Cdr. G. A. Parsons USNR of MONROVIA.
338	2	Lt. Cdr. J. M. Steinbeck was C.O. of GANSEVOORT.
339	11	Correct spelling is Swensson.
345	18 up	Capt. T. G. Haff was C.O. of SUMTER.

Volume VIII: *New Guinea and the Marianas*

35	chart	Scale of miles should read 100, 200, etc.
39	6	The submarine was *RO–45*.
41	7	*Indiana* should be included with the battleships.
73	13	127th Infantry is correct.
81	10 up	*SC–743* was the control vessel.
175	13	*Bokuyo M.* was the name of this ship.
190	11 up	There were 11 beaches.
221	9 up	Negros is the correct spelling.
230	5	*I–5* disappeared about 19 July.
261	n. 8	Lt. J. H. Trousdale commanded TG 583.
281	17	A bomb magazine exploded.
333	4 up	Correct number of enemy buried is 550.
368	n.	Last word is "Commandos."
383	8	Not "LSMs" but "LCMs."
393	7 up	*SC–1326* is correct.
404	middle	Not "*SC–734(B)*" but "*SC–743*."

Volume IX: *Sicily — Salerno — Anzio*

29	5 up	Not "Beaches" but "Bases."
33	10 up	Not "Ramsay" but "Cunningham."
49	11, 12 up	The correct number of artillery pieces is 22 batteries of 75-mm to 100-mm guns and two of 149-mm.
79	4	Barnes's rank was Commander.
83	7 up	Insert "join *Buck* and" between "to" and "cover."
104 389	9 up, & 3 up	The correct spelling is Faulkner.
108	4 up	Change 1st 4 words to "through the Admiral."
167 393	4 & 7 up	Adm. Willis's middle initial is U.

Page	Line	
194	10, 11	Not "a British small craft" (or, in later printing, "*SC–550*"), but "*SC–530*," escorting one barge.
"	13	The sailors were American.
197	6	Cdr. Rooney's initials are J. B.
209	n. 11	The number of the War Dept. document is 45746.
210	19	The first route started from the port of Messina.
211	chart	The four indicated evacuation routes to Occhio were not used.
235	4 up	The unit was not all Arab, but mixed.
268	11 up	*Woolsey* shot at an observation tower, not Torre di Paestum.
287	15 up	The first colonel's name is Muldrow.
313	5	The convoy was returning to Oran.
347	lower photo facing	Should be credited to Major J. C. Hatlem.
360	16	The officer who took over on 2 Feb. was Capt. Harry Sanders.
366	11	That boat was *U–410*.
"	13	The total loss was 24.
378	3 up	The Germans did not deliberately burn the galleys.

Volume X: *The Atlantic Battle Won*

Page	Line	
3	4 up	Not "49" but "46" U-boats.
16	14	Capt. Canning's middle initial is S.
102	n., last line	Slessor's letter was to Adm. Stark.
124	15	Correct spelling: Hodson.✝
130	8	These were air commanders.
"	14–16	Adm. Hewitt vetoed it; Adm. King concurred.
"	n.	The R.A.F. command at Gib. did revert to Coastal Oct. 1943 (this was deleted in some printings).
134	2 up	It was *Nevada* that the U-boat took for a cruiser.
146	12	ASWORG (Antisubmarine Warfare Operational Research Group) assisted NDRC on FXR.
161	2–4	Avenger piloted by Ensign B. C. Sheela USNR forced *U–402* to dive; Avery's Wildcat sank her.
167	2 up	Delete "all . . . in the dark."
182	10	It was gunboat *Brisk* that bore in.
191	11–13	Adm. Robert did not surrender. On 14 July a High Commissioner appointed by Gen. Giraud arrived in French destroyer *Le Terrible* and took over Martinique.

Page	Line	
194	11 up	Insert at end of paragraph: *U–359*, sixth boat of this group, was sunk 28 July south of Mona Passage by a PBM commanded by Lieutenant (jg) D. C. Pinholster USNR.
213	n. 7	Lt. Cdr. Samuels's middle initial is T.
264	1	*Santa Elena* was an American transport.
282	3 up	*U–515* went down at 1412.
290	n. 22	A fourth, *U–110*, was captured by H.M.S. *Bulldog* in 1940.
293	n.	Three acoustic torpedoes were also salvaged.
311	6 up	*Lark's* stern, not bow, was blasted.
313	4	Not "all but one" but "one another."
324	5–6	Not "augmented by six more" but "together with six R.A.F." squadrons.

Volume XI: *The Invasion of France and Germany*

73	9 up	VIII and IX A.A.F. is correct.
84	16–18	It was Admiral Ramsay who at 2300 June 4 ordered all ships to go, about three hours later, etc.
118	10 up	*Glasgow* was a light cruiser.
141	1	Delete "For two hours they searched in vain, but" and add: "Three LCT had beached at 0830, and" . . .
165	9, 10	Ramsay observed "empty the ships," etc.
216	8	Gen. Hodges' middle initial is H.
239	14	Barnes's vendetta commenced in April.
270	13	Beach Green was about 230 yards long.
271	6–7 up	The 142nd RCT landed by 1512, aided by Cdr. J. P. Graff's 8th Beach Battalion.
277	13 up	In sinking the MTB by gunfire, *Hughes* had the help of *Hilary P. Jones*.
279	8	*Lorraine* was a battleship.
287	7–8 up	These guns had been mounted before the war.
301	8 up	Morlaix had been taken by the Army on 8 August.
302	10	PTs were the first Allied craft to enter Morlaix, but did not liberate it.

Volume XII: *Leyte*

28	n.	*RO–41* was sunk by *Haggard* 22 March 1945.
40	4–5 up	This was routine procedure to evade enemy submarines, not to escape gunfire.
79	3 up	The submarine sunk was *I–41*.
113	3	The 700 ships were under Admiral Kinkaid.

Page	Line	
122	12–13	This was correct; there was a line of mines between these islands.
123	17–18	Correct reading: "despite the considerable number . . ."
160	14–15	This was unknown to Third Fleet.
161	7 & n.	Only *Shinano* (68,000 tons) was bigger than 27,000-ton *Essex* class. *Unryu* and *Katsuragi* were about 20,200; *Amagi*, 24,000 tons.
"	8	Correct spelling is *Ryuho*.
183	11	The torpedoes were fired a minute apart, and the first hit.
184	n. 12	8 of *Princeton's* planes survived.
199	1	Insert "He and" before "His staff."
201	n. 4	Add that the HC fitted no ships present.
207, 209		Page refs. in notes to *War College Analysis* are to an early ms. draft.
224	n.	Delete line 1. Old model radar was responsible for *Pennsylvania's* not getting "on." Delete "now" in line 2.
232	1–6 up	The ships bore N, distant 9000 yards. Target was ships all right, but the torpedoes made erratic runs; at least two were later recovered from Hibuson I.
236	5–6	Delete "probably"; reason was that Oldendorf wished to concentrate in view of the impending battle with Center Force.
"	20	Berkey was pulled out to join Battle Line.
237	4–5 up	Same applied to flag officers.
238	8 up	Shima sent destroyer *Ushio* of his screen to escort *Abukuma*.
"	6 up	Not "27th" but "26th."
239	4–6 up	This ship was probably Kurita's light cruiser *Noshiro* (see p. 311).
241	4	The admiral's correct name is Obdam.
245	2	A.A.F. were there, but had not yet assumed responsibility.
269	6 up	*St. Lo* was not the leading CVE.
275	11	Correct hour is 0800.
281	8	*Kitkun Bay* launched 12 Wildcats and 6 Avengers at this time.
288	12	The two heavy cruisers ceased fire at 0912 and 0917.
292	n. 8	The message, as handed to Admiral Halsey, read WHERE IS RPT WHERE IS TASK FORCE 34 THE WORLD

Page   Line

WONDERS. See E. B. Potter & Admiral Nimitz *Sea Power* (1960) p. 789.

299	n. 17	The last was an intercept either of Kinkaid's orders to Desron 49, or to hospital ship *Mercy*.
308	12	Adm. Felix Stump gave this order.
310	13	The 6th strike was launched from *Natoma Bay* and *Savo Island*.
341	10	*Fujinami* alone was sunk by this strike.
342	9	The destroyers sank *I-46*.
356	3	They sank four destroyers; omit *Kiyoshimo*.
357	16	*Yasoshima* was a cruiser.
369	11–12, 17 up	This submarine, which we have been unable to identify, went down stern first, but apparently was not sunk.
383	13 up	The exec. and 15 others were wounded.
387	8 up	Not "26th" but "96th."
390	6, 17	*Caldwell's* C.O. was Cdr. George Wendelburg.
401	2	The steamer's name was *Shinyo Maru*.
423	last	Cdr. E. B. Ellis USNR was C.O. of ACUBENS.
"	end	Add: Hospital ships MERCY Capt. T. A. Esling USNR, COMFORT Capt. H. F. Fultz.
430	15	No asterisks for SHIMOTSUKI and her C.O.
431	Force C	Correct spelling is YAMASHIRO.

Volume XIII: *The Liberation of the Philippines*

35	9	The 2nd LST crashed was No. 749.
37	n. 25	The last three were 1530-tonners.
81	2 up	The Lt. Cdr.'s name is Plage.
91	15–17	Destroyer escort *CD-3* alone was sunk; destroyer HAMAKAZE and ten other escorts damaged.
104	11	Several destroyers, a DE and *Quapaw* stood by.
146	n. 8	*Newman* was the APD; *Cofer* was around, but not in this fight.
158	16 & table	Omit KONGO (already sunk, see Vol. XII 410), and UNRYU.
306	15 up	BENALLA is the correct spelling.
307	11 up	These were tankers; BIRCH COULIE is one ship.
"	6 up	Delete "escort."
310, last in TG 79.3		Insert ALSHAIN, Lt. Cdr. Strickland.
313	3	OCONTO is the correct spelling.
314	1	Capt. Coward's middle initial is G.
315	8 up	Capt. Debaun's first initial is G.

Page	Line	
316	16 up	The C.O. of HANCOCK is Capt. R. F. Hickey.
317	7	Capt. Porter's middle initial is L.
318	15–16	Cdr. Ailes's first initial is J.
323	15 up	Gen. Arnold's middle initial is H.

Volume XIV: *Victory in the Pacific*

Page	Line	
25	4 up	Sunset was at 1720.
33	5	Sunset was at 1725.
34	n. 3	Place stop after "*New York*." *Chester* was struck a glancing blow by *Estes*.
37	n. 5	Correct reading: The Marines' LVT amphibians again proved themselves at Iwo. Their low speed was no handicap since the equally slow LVT(A)s spearheaded the landings; but the LVTs could land their troops and supplies on dry land despite surf, steep beaches and soft sand.
55	10	Abandon ship was ordered at 1905.
86	n. 6	The British observer's name was Silcock.
97	12–13	Add that Adm. Gardner now took over command of TG 58.2.
115	4 up	Lt. Cdr. E. T. Grace was C.O. of *Halligan*.
116	10	Bjarnson's middle initial is H.
"	last	*Adams* was knocked out same day.
165	10	Tom Hill's middle initial is B.
172	n.	Tailyour is the correct spelling.
204	12 up	Not "Marines" but "Mariners."
211	6–7	*Essex* lost 28 wounded.
220	12 up	Add "On the 7th *PGM-17* was sunk by a mine."
222–23		Add that Capt. C. A. Buchanan in PURDY was O.T.C. of Station no. 1.
221	5	Add "and another unit had to mop up."
238	18	C.O. was Lt. Cdr. C. F. Highfield USNR; Haavik his exec.; both were killed.
245	6–7 up	Insert: "*Mississippi*, whose special assignment was the demolition of Shuri Castle, fired 2289 rounds of 14-inch and 6650 rounds of 5-inch in six weeks."
275	19	*Twiggs* lost 126 officers and men.
279	5	*Curtiss* was hit 20 seconds before *Whiting*.
280	10 up	*Cassin Young* lost 17 killed, 45 wounded.
305	6 up	TG 38.1 is correct.
317	9	The Ulithi attack was on 20 Nov. 1944.

Page	Line	
335	after l. 3	Add:

Last major ship to be damaged was battleship *Pennsylvania.* Vice Admiral Oldendorf had just transferred his flag to her in Buckner Bay, Okinawa on 12 August, when at 2045 a surprise attack was delivered by an enemy airplane. Its torpedo exploded near a propeller, killing 20 men and wounding many others, including the Admiral.

361	last	Tozuka is the correct spelling.
363	14	MacArthur boarded from *Buchanan.*
372	6 up	The correct spelling is Baldauf.
"	5 up	Lt. Cdr. E. T. Grace was C.O. of *Halligan.*
380	18 up	The correct name is LA PORTE.
381	14	Add: "Comdesdiv 126, Capt. C. A. Buchanan, was in HYMAN, later in PURDY."
"	last	Add SOUTHAMPTON Lt. Cdr. L. V. Cooke USNR.
383	middle	Add * to Cdr. Crommelin; Cdr. E. J. Pawka USNR succeeded him.
"	7–8 up	Under ESSEX insert Air Group 83, Cdr. H. T. Utter.
"	5 up	Patriarca is the correct spelling.
386	4	Poindexter is the correct spelling.
387	19	Cdr. Mikkelsen's middle initial is M.
390	2	FRANKLIN was hit 19 March.
392	13–14 up	Insert line after SANDOVAL as follows:
		29 May SHUBRICK air 32 28
"	last	CASSIN YOUNG's wounded numbered 45.

Appendix I

Addenda: The following combat vessels reached Okinawa after 1 April: ALFRED A. CUNNINGHAM (29 June); AULICK (16 May); BLOCK ISLAND (3 May); BRAINE (16 May); CALIFORNIA (17 June); CAPERTON (31 May); CHARLES F. AUSBURNE (16 May); COMPTON (26 April); CONNOLLY (9 April); CROSS (14 June); DAVID W. TAYLOR (30 June); DOUGLAS H. FOX (5 May); DYSON (16 May); FARENHOLT (8 May); FINNEGAN (9 April); FOOTE (16 May); GILBERT ISLANDS (21 May); GILLIGAN (18 April); GRADY (9 April); HALLORAN (9 April); HEMMINGER (14 May); HOGGATT BAY (12 May); INGERSOLL (22 May); LARDNER (8 May); LOUISVILLE (23 May); MANILA BAY (13 June); MANLOVE (2 April); MELVIN R. NAWMAN (3 June); MISSISSIPPI (5 May); MOALE (7 June); NEHENTA BAY (20 May); NEW ORLEANS (22 April); NICHOLSON (1 May); OKLAHOMA CITY (17 June); OLIVER MITCHELL (30 May); RALL (9 April); RALPH TALBOT (26 April); ROBERTS (16 May); ROBERT F. KELLER (30 May); ROWE (22 May); SHIPLEY BAY (7 May); SMALLEY (22 May);

STODDARD (22 May); STORMES (23 May); TATUM (19 May); TAYLOR (17 June); THATCHER (16 May); WALKE (10 May); WATTS (22 May); WILKES (10 May); WOODWORTH (8 May); WREN (22 May).

The following vessels joined Task Force 38 between 1 April and 30 June: ALABAMA (30 April); ABBOT (14 June); AMSTERDAM (21 June); ATLANTA (28 May); BON HOMME RICHARD (6 June); CAPERTON (30 June); COGSWELL (30 June); COWPENS (26 June); DAYTON (16 June); DULUTH (24 May); FRANK KNOX (16 June); HALE (24 June); INGERSOLL (30 June); IOWA (24 April); KNAPP (30 June); LEXINGTON (24 June); MONTEREY (9 May); O'BANNON (28 May); OKLAHOMA CITY (6 June); QUINCY (16 April); RANDOLPH (8 April); ROWE (20 June); SHANGRI-LA (24 April); SMALLEY (20 June); SOUTHERLAND (16 June); STODDARD (20 June); TICONDEROGA (24 May); TOPEKA (5 June); TUCSON (16 June); WADLEIGH (28 May); WATTS (20 June); WREN (20 June).

PART IV

General Index for Volumes I–XIV

THIS INDEX covers Volumes I–XIV, and is based on the latest printing of each volume. It therefore includes corrected references to the changes noted in Part III. The index covers all text, front matter, appendices and illustrations.

Individuals are indexed under the highest rank mentioned in the series.

American aircraft, military units, etc. will be found under their descriptive headings; foreign under their nationality.

Names of warships and code names of operations listed at the end are in SMALL CAPITALS. When two or more warships of the same name appear, foreign vessels have their nationality shown, e.g. HMS, HMAS, HMCS, HMNZS. American vessels are differentiated by commissioning dates.

Names of lettered combat ships, like LSTs and U-boats, and merchantmen are in *italics*.

Code-name operations are listed separately, by volume.

The following abbreviations are used in the index:

A/S — Antisubmarine
A/SW — Antisubmarine warfare
M. — *Maru*
pic., pics. — picture, pictures

S. — Section
S.F. — Sea Frontier
TF — Task Force
T.O. — Task Organization
V., v. — *Victory*

A

A. S. Dunniway, XIII: 324
AARON WARD (1942), IV: 271, V: 87, 166, 182, 205, 226, 232, 237, 248–9, 253–5; sunk, VI: 123
AARON WARD (1944), XIV: 251–3, 376, 391; pic., 294
Abadan, X: 158
Abangarez, X: 381–2
ABATAN, XIV: 161
ABBÉ DESGRANGES, II: 247
ABBOT, VII: 350, VIII: 405, 420, XII: 418, XIII: 305, 315, 322
Abbott, Lt. Cdr. Gordon, XIV: 184, 376
Abbott, Capt. R. W., XIII: 307, 313, XIV: 375
ABC-1 Staff Agreement, I: 46–51, III: 51–3, XI: 4
ABDA Area, map, III: 278; Command, organization, 277–8, 311–13; strategy, 281–2, 292, 297–8; T.O., 271–3; Striking Force, 297–303, 308–11, 320–33, 338–58, 364–5; T.O., 332–3; disintegrates, 336; dissolved, 377
ABDIEL, IX: 235, 314; sunk, 236
Abdill, Capt. E. W., VIII: 407, XIII: 24
Abe, Vice Adm. Hiroaki, III: 245, 253, IV: 88, 132, V: 82, 85, 88, 200, 203, 206–8, 222, 223, 238, 241–2, 251, 258–9, 263
Abe, Vice Adm. Koso, IV: 45, 240–41, V: 258n
Abel, Lt. Cdr. B. M., X: 285–8, 377
Abele, Lt. Cdr. M. L., IV: 217
ABELE, XIV: 377
Abel-Smith, Capt. E. M. C., X: 78
Abemama I., VII: 77, 84, 98, 134n, 154, 179–80, 213, 214n, 308, VIII: 156; landing, VII: 180–82; pic., 175
Abercrombie, Cdr. L. A., V: 296–7, 311, VI: 99
Abercrombie, Lt. W. H., VIII: 414
ABERCROMBIE, XII: 244, 421, XIII: 310, XIV: 375
ABERCROMBIE, HMS, IX: 104, 122, 132, 174, 266, 389, 391
Abernathy, Capt. E. P., III: 159, 272, VI: 297

ABIGAIL, XI: 337
ABNAKI, X: 293
ABNER READ, VII: 63–4, 335, VIII: 127, 406, XII: 415; sunk, 344–5
Abraham Lincoln, X: 381
Abreu, Antonio d', XIII: 255
ABUKUMA, III: 26, 87, 382, IV: 172, VII: 24, 27, 30, 35, 58, XII: 164, 190, 210, 230–32, 431; sunk, 238
Acadia, I: 84
Acate R., IX: 71, 127–9, 145
ACCIAIO, IX: 42
ACHERNAR, XI: 337, 341, XIV: 175, 380, 390
Acheson, Lt. David, XII: 305n
Achilles, Kaptlt. Albrecht, I: 145, X: 180, 224
ACHILLES, XII: 417, 423, XIV: 388
ACHILLES, HMNZS, IV: 254, V: 184, 326, 329–30
Acker, Lt. F. C., I: 421
Ackerman, Lt. Cdr. Edward, XIV: 289
ACONIT, XI: 334
"Acorn" (base), IV: 252, VII: 179
ACREE, VIII: 410, XII: 429
ACTION, I: 13n
ACTIVE, I: 421
ACTIVITY, X: 308
ACUBENS, XII: 423, XIII: 308
Acuff, Capt. J. T., VII: 104, XII: 75, 175, 320, 428, XIII: 55, 60, 63, 67, 70, 73–7, 88–90, 164–5, 169–70, 173, 318
Adachi, Lt. Gen. H., VI: 55, 118n, 255, 390, VIII: 66–7, 72–4
Adair, Ens. David, XIV: 224
Adair, Cdr. Noah, XIV: 332, 384
Adair, Lt. Col. R. D., VIII: 392
ADAIR, XIII: 307, 312; XIV: 378
Adak I., IV: 169, 177, 180, 217–9, VII: 8, 13–15, 25, 28, 44, 47, 63–5
Adams, Cdr. A. B., X: 331
Adams, Capt. A. L., XIII: 230
Adams, Cdr. C. F., XIII: 305, XIV: 111
Adams, Capt. F. M., VIII: 408, IX: 392, XII: 416, XIII: 309, XIV: 380
Adams, Lt. Cdr. J. F., X: 375, 378–9
Adams, Lt. Cdr. R. L., V: 47
Adams, Lt. Samuel, IV: 136

Adams, Sinclair, I: 334n
Adams, Lt. Cdr. W. D., XIV: 386
ADAMS, XIV: 113, 116, 376, 390
Adamson, Lt. Cdr. F. M., I: 420
ADB Conference. *See* Singapore Conference
Addu Atoll, III: 382–3
Adell, Capt. B. B., VIII: 408, XII: 417, XIV: 143, 380
ADHARA, VI: 123, XIV: 386
Adkins, Gunner F. D., IV: 130
ADMIRABLE-class, XIV: 113
ADMIRAL GRAF SPEE, I: 4n
Admiral Halstead, III: 319
ADMIRAL HIPPER, I: 4n, 161, 180, 185, 366–7, X: 57, 237n
ADMIRAL SCHEER, I: 4n, 24, 161, 180, 185, X: 237n
ADMIRAL SIR JOHN LAWFORD, XI: 337
Admiralty Is., VI: 93n, 369–70, 412, 433–4, XII: 114; base, *see* Manus; seizure of, VI: 432–48; casualties, 444, 447; chart, 439; pic., 435
ADMIRALTY ISLANDS, XIV: 386
ADONIS, XI: 336
ADRIA, XIV: 386
ADROIT, VI: 297
ADVENT, VI: 297
Ady, Lt. Howard, IV: 103n
Ægades Is., IX: 168
Ægean, IX: 245, 326, XI: 23n, 224
Æolian Is., IX: 217
Aeolus, I: 288; pic., 280
Aeronautics, Bureau of, I: li, XIII: 52n
Aertsen, Lt. Cdr. G., XII: 195n
AFD–14, XIV: 387
AFDL–32, XIV: 387
Afetna Pt., VIII: 183, 194–8, 203
AFFLECK, X: 372; sunk, X: 337, XI: 304
Africander, I: 364n
Agadir, I: 352, II: 150, X: 129–31
Agaña, VIII: 373n, 378, 398–9
AGANO, VI: 71, 306, 312–13, 321, 328, 332, 341, VII: 44, 326, XIV: 208; sunk, VII: 319
AGASSIZ, I: 306
Agat, VIII: 378, 381, 390–92
Agay, Rade d', XI: 270
AGC. *See* Amphibious Force flagship
AGENOR, VIII: 411, 419
Ageta, Capt. K., XIV: 317
Ageton, Cdr. A. A., XII: 419, XIII: 144–5, 307, 313, XIV: 379
Aggerback, Capt. J. C., V: 374

Agingan Pt., VIII: 194–5, 198–9, 208
Agnew, Lt. Cdr. D. M., IV: 274, V: 194–5, VII: 337, 347
Agnew, Commo. W. G., IX: 167, 235–6
Agrigento, IX: 45, 174–6, 181; pic., 186
Agropoli, XI: 280n
Aguijan I., VIII: 150–51
Agwiworld, III: 221n
AHRENS, X: 284, 289, 377
Aikoku M., VII: 325
Ailes, Cdr. J. W., XIII: 318, XIV: 373
Ailinglapalap Atoll, VII: 312–13
Ailuk Atoll, VII: 313
Ainslie, Lt. Cdr. M. F. R., IX: 387
Ainsworth, Rear Adm. W. L., biog., V: 325n–6n; Comdesron 2, I: 33, 82; Solomons, V: 325–9, 345–7, 352, 372, VI: 106, 113–16, 119–20, 123, 146, 156–9, 209, 213, 415–16; Kula Gulf, 160–63, 166–9, 172, 196, 363–4; Kolombangara, 178–91, 194; Marianas, VIII: 171–3, 180–81, 207, 210, 356, 377–8, 381, 390, 399, 409, 419; Peleliu, XII: 34; Leyte, 145, 419
Air A/S Development Unit, Atlantic Fleet, X: 24, 50–51
Air A/SW, Atlantic, I: 54–6, 101, 118–20, 135, 138–41, 152–6, 237–51, 259, 276–81, 289, 312n, 318–20, 325, 329–30, 338, 345–51, 378–83, 386–90, 401, 415, X: 7, 20, 42–6, 129–32, 144; pics., 112–13; North Africa, II: 245; Mediterranean, X: 252, 259–60, 266; Escort carriers, 279–93, 363–4; South Atlantic, 209–28, 293–9; Bay of Biscay, 87–106; Pacific, III: 217, V: 257; Army-Navy controversy, X: 26–31
Air Bombings, Texts, I: xlix–i
Air Cover and Support, II: 31–2, 88–91, 118, 123, 127–8, 132, 149–52, VII: xxviii–xxix, 43–4, 48, 86, 114, 117–18, 124–5, 130–33, 157–8, 161, 168, 203, 218, 255–60, 267, 279, 289, 299–301, VIII: 82, 98, 110, 186, 192, 205, 326–30, 351–3, 359–61, 365–7, 377–80, 383, 390, 395–401, IX: 16–17, 21–3, 101, 109–10, 121–3, 165, 204–5, 218–20, 247, 250–51, 277–80, 341–4, 351, 364–5, 384, XI: 96, 124, 191, 198–202, 206–10, 256–8, 271, 280, XII: 34, 106–8, 124–6, 133, 143, 149–51, 349–54, XIII: 29–34, 135, 145, 151–2, 178, 194–5, 208, 223, 230, 269–72, XIV: 122, 132–3
Air Forces, Allied, Mediterranean,

IX: 331, 344, 366; Northwest African, II: 277, IX: 16–17, 21–3, 37, 51, 55, 58–60, 94, 101, 120, 123, 149, 172–4, 191–2, 209–10, 214–15, 250–52, 280, 286, 294, 303, 306; Southwest Pacific, IV: 274, VIII: 47, XII: 60, 364, XIII: 17, 22

Air observers, I: 289

Air photography, IV: 267, V: 322, VI: 104–5, 115, 120, 290, 398, 403, 407, VII: 61, 79, 82–3, 96–8, 149–50, 194, 203, 206, 214, 226, 286, 294, 319, VIII: 28–9, 61, 75, 95, 136, 141, 154–5, 158, 164–5, 353–4, 375, 378, IX: 23, XI: 34, 115, XII: 33, XIII: 182, XIV: 11, 102, 131–3, 136, 311

Air-Sea Rescue, I: 249–50, V: 332–3, VI: 397, 404–5, VII: 54, 94, 330, VIII: 49n, 50, 308–9, XII: 26–7, 312–16; pic., VII: 319

Air Search and Reconnaissance, III: 129–30, IV: 16, 22, 30–33, 40, 41n, 45, 48, 87, 96, 102, 136, 145, 148, 149n, 168, 176–7, 269–70, 279–80, V: 12–14, 19, 23–7, 34–5, 80–84, 87–8, 117–18, 130, 150, 200–24, 207–8, 222–4, 238, 260–61, 264, 295–8, 351, 359, 370, VI: 105, 157, 215, 234, 324, 350, 362–3, 412, VII: 34, 202, VIII: 49–50, 61, 101, 106, 119–20, 156, 179, 233–4, 241–2, 245–9, 254–8, 265, 271–2, 284–90, 307–10, 316–17, XI: 73–4, 175, 184, 268, 279, XII: 46, 126–7, 191, 245, 289–90, 293, 321–2, XIV: 18, 119; Night, V: 326–7, 330–32, VI: 183–6, 190, 206–7, 213, 219, 242, 284, 290, 374, 427, 430, VIII: 49n, 127; charts, Pearl Harbor, III: 136; Savo, V: 24; Leyte, XII: 126

Air supply, VI: 176

Air tactics, VI: 398, 401

Aircraft allotment, Army and Navy, I: 240, 245, X: 26–31

Aircraft, A/SW, American and British, types of, I: 240n, 245, 259, 276–81; Adm. King on, 309–10, 319–21, 325, 344–53, 363, 378–80, 386–7, 389–90; statistics, 415, 419–20, X: 26–31, 90–91, 94–104, 108–32, 159–62, 169–72, 189–98, 201–6, 210–26, 231–3, 245, 293–301, 307–10, 319–21, 324–7, 340–41, 345–51, 359, 362–4; statistics, 370–73; T.O., 375–80

Aircraft, Army, I: 135, 138–43, 147, 241–5, 259, 431; III: 305; U.S., B–25 described, VI: 57; B–29 described,

VIII: 7, XIII: 162; F–5 described, VI: 104

Aircraft, Coast Guard, I: 135

Aircraft, losses, Pearl, III: 122–4; North Africa, II: 90; Midway, IV: 131; Guadalcanal, 293; Rabaul, VI: 403–4; Gilberts, VII: 145; Marshalls, 193, 221; Aleutians, 14n; Nauru, 198; Truk, VIII: 38–9; Marianas, 155n; Philippine Sea, 277, 299, 304, 312, 321; Bonins raids, 239, 367n; Mindoro, XIII: 34, 42; Dec. 1944 typhoon, 70–71; South China Sea raid, 169–71, 183; Japan strikes, XIV: 25, 59; Okinawa, 209, 282; June 1945 typhoon, 307

Aircraft, Navy, carrier-borne, I: 195, VII: xxviii, XII: 13, XIII: 21, XIV: 21; land-based, I: 131, 135, 161, 240–48; Avenger, pic., IV: 254, VI: 332, X: 80, XII: 142; Catalina, description, IV: 92n, VIII: 49n; pic., III: 170, IV: 167, V: 307, X: 81; Corsair, VI: 90; pic., 332; Hellcat, 90; pic., 332, VII: 86; Kingfisher, pic., 319; Liberator, VI: 90, VIII: 49n; pic., VI: 332, VII: 262, X: 81; Mariner, pic., I: 388; Ventura, pic., X: 80; SB2U–3, pic., IV: 100; Wildcat, pic., III: 225

Aircraft, Northern Solomons, XIII: 194; Solomons, VI: 99, 234, 239, 243, 288, 290–2, 295, 303, 319, 325, 342–4, 350, 362–3, 369–70, 377, 383, 386, 394–409, 415, 419, 423, 427–34, VIII: 156, 164; South Pacific, IV: 274, XIII: 52n

Aircraft production, XIII: 99

Airfields, Caribbean S.F., chart, I: 238–9; Eastern S. F., chart, X: 179; Gulf S. F., chart, I: 238–9; New Guinea, chart, VI: 29; Solomons, chart, 91; Western Pacific, chart, VII: 153

Airship Wing Two, I: 250

Aitape, VIII: 61–3, 78, 96, XIII: 97; landing, VIII: 54n, 68–74, 83; chart, 71

AIVIK, I: 421

Aiyo M., VI: 56

Ajaccio, Corsica, IX: 306-7

AJAX, VIII: 420, XIV: 387

AJAX, HMS, XI: 257, 339

Aka Shima, Ryukyus, XIV: 120–24; pic., 118

Akagane M., VII: 20

AKAGI, III: 22, 85–8, 93, 276, 334, 382–4, IV: 76, 88, 106, 115, 123–5, 129, 132, X: 37; sunk, IV: 125–6; pic., 127

AKASHI, IV: 88; sunk, VIII: 32
AKATSUKI, IV: 172, V: 194–6, 207, 233, 242; sunk, 254
AKEBONO, III: 274–5, 334, IV: 17, 172, V: 84, XII: 190, 238, 356, 431; sunk, 353
Akebono M., IV: 89, 99
Aki M., VIII: 17
Akibasan M., VII: 220n
AKIGUMO, III: 87, IV: 88, V: 85, 206, 222, VI: 75, 244, 250; sunk, VIII: 19
AKIKAZE, VI: 208, XII: 430; pic., VII: 318
AKISHIMO, VIII: 416, XII: 356, 431; sunk, 353
AKITSUKI, XII: 430; sunk, 325, 334n, 335
AKITSUSHIMA, IV: 292, V: 20, 117–18; pic., 179
Akiyama, Rear Adm. M., VII: 264
Akiyama, Rear Adm. S., VII: 58
Akiyama, Rear Adm. T., VI: 162–3, 166–7, 169, 174
AKIZUKI, V: 85, 151, 197, 207, VIII: 416
AKLAK, I: 62n, 421
AKUTAN, XIV: 386
Akyab, VI: 6, VII: 83
ALABAMA, VII: 85, VIII: 40, 269n, 270, 282n, 415, X: 230, XII: 90, 318, 427, XIII: 54, 316, XIV: 307, 310, 314
Alafoss, I: 77
Alamar, I: 178n
Alameda, Cal., VII: 112, 391
ALAMOSA, XII: 429
ALASKA, I: 28n, VII: 334, XIV: 21, 307, 310, 385–6; class, I: lviii
Alaska Scouts, VII: 42
ALATOK, I: 421
ALBACORE, IV: 228, V: 324, VI: 68–9, 71–3, VIII: 19, 265, 269, 278–81, 285, 415; sunk, XII: 411
ALBACORE, HMS, IX: 393
Alban Hills, pic., IX: 347
Albany, Australia, IV: 219
ALBANY, VII: 152n
ALBATROS, II: 99, 107–10, 248; pic., 174
ALBATROSS, I: 422
Albay Gulf, XIII: 208
ALBEMARLE, I: 420, VII: x
Albert Gallatin, X: 187, 276n
Albert M. Boe, I: 294n
ALBERT T. HARRIS, XIII: 324
ALBERT W. GRANT, VIII: 325, 409, XII: 80, 199, 221–2, 226–30, 234n, 240, 419
Albino Perez, X: 382

Albrook, Panama, X: 201
ALBURY, XI: 335
ALCHIBA, IV: 265n, 273, V: 57, 179–80, 292–3, VI: 297
Alcoa Banner, I: 172
Alcoa Cadet, I: 372
Alcoa Prospector, I: 396
Alcoa Puritan, I: 138
Alcoa Rambler, I: 171n
Alcoa Ranger, I: 191n
Alcorn, Lt. R. C., XIV: 326
ALCYONE, IV: 265n, VII: 135n, 336, VIII: 407, 420, IX: 389, XII: 419, XIII: 139, 311
ALDEBARAN, VII: 110–11, XII: 77n, XIV: 159, 163
ALDEN, III: 160, 272, 331–3, 352, 375
ALDENHAM, XI: 343
ALDERAMIN, XIV: 66n
Alderman, Lt. Cdr. J. C., V: 23, 180–81
Alderman, Lt. Cdr. R. B., XIV: 375
ALDERSDALE, I: 183, 191n
Aldrich, Radarman B. C., XIV: 259n–60n
Aldrich, Cdr. C. W., VII: 335–7, 346, XIV: 379
Aleutian Is., described, IV: 160–65; chart, IV: 164, VII: 6–7; Japanese strategy and plans, IV: 5, 74–6; VII: 4; United States strategy and plans, VI: 6, 156–7, 160–72, 226–7, VII: 4, 8–9; air bases, IV: 163–4, VII: 16, XIII: 164; operations in, IV: 175–84, VII: 3–66; submarine operations, IV: 214–19; T.O., 172–4
ALEX DIACHENKO, XIII: 324
Alexander, A. V., X: 17
Alexander, Gen. Sir H. R., IX: 10, 14, 19, 26–9, 44, 123, 146, 149, 170, 174, 177–81, 195, 206–7, 212–13, 220–21, 239, 246–7, 284, 294–6, 303, 317–18, 323–7, 330, 341, 353, 359, 363–5, 374–5, XI: 229, 296
Alexander, Lt.(jg) J. H., X: 101
Alexander, Capt. R. C., VIII: 414, XII: 347, 427
Alexander Graham Bell, IX: 390
ALEXANDER HAMILTON, sunk, I: 109
Alexander Martin, IX: 390
Alexanderson, Cdr. L. J., VII: 348, VIII: 410, XIV: 378
Alexandria, Egypt, IX: 149–51, 157, 167, 242, 247, X: 250
Algeciras, IX: 44

ALGER, X: 380
ALGÉRIEN, XI: 343
ALGERINE, sunk, II: 212, 284
Algiers, II: 17, 218, 221, 252–4, IX: 15, 19, 33, 61, 124, 149, 168, 182, 208, 231, 247, 251–2, X: 264; landing, II: 181–4, 189–214; landing charts, 188, 196–7, 201
ALGOL, XIII: 307, XIV: 380
ALGOMA, I: 121
ALGONQUIN, I: 330, 421
ALGORAB, II: 26n, 36, VI: 144, XIV: 380
ALHENA, IV: 273, V: 81, VI: 297, VIII: 407, XIII: 307n
Alice, I: 282n
ALISEO, IX: 244
ALKAID, XIV: 66n, 386
ALKES, VII: 348, VIII: 420, XIV: 386
Allan, Cdr. H. C., VII: 346, VIII: 411, XII: 419
Allan, Cdr. R. A., IX: 372–3, XI: 314n, 315
Allan, Lt. Cdr. R. N., XI: 242n
Allan Jackson, I: 131
Allard, D. C., XIII: x, XIV: xi
ALLEGAN, XIV: 386
Allen, Capt. A. C., VII: 340, VIII: 411, XIV: 387
Allen, Capt. A. M. R., III: 53n
Allen, Cdr. B. C., VI: 261, 382, VIII: 55
Allen, Lt. Cdr. C. V., VIII: 404
Allen, Capt. Charles, II: 36, VIII: 410, IX: 389, XII: 418
Allen, Ens. D. M., VII: 294
Allen, Capt. J. L., XIII: 309, 313, XIV: 375
Allen, Lt. Cdr. R. A., II: 264
Allen, Cdr. R. B., VIII: 418, XII: 416, XIV: 383
Allen, Yeoman S. J., VIII: viii
Allen, Maj. Gen. Terry de la M., II: 223, 238, IX: 28, 93, 105, 111, 122, 147, 200, 220, 387
ALLEN, III: 100, 213n, XIV: 88n, 276n
ALLEN M. SUMNER, XII: 371, XIII: 106, 303, 325; class, XIV: 114
ALLENDALE, XIV: 380
ALLENTOWN, XIII: 307n
Allied A/S Survey Board, X: 16; Survey Committee, 307
Allied Control Council, German, XI: 329
Allied Military Government, IX: 368

Allied Naval Forces, Southwest Pacific, VI: 30–32, VIII: 47
Allied Translator and Interpreter Section, III: xi
"Alligator." See LVT
Allison, Lt. Cdr. R. M., XIV: 373
Alliston, Lt. Cdr. J. M., XIII: 304
ALMAACK, II: 192–3, 195n, 199–202, 214, 246n, VII: 345, VIII: 346, 408, 420, XII: 419, XIII: 310
Almirante, Panama, I: 153
ALNWICK CASTLE, X: 311
ALOE, VI: 121, VIII: 419, XIV: 377
ALPINE, VII: 419, XII: 366, 418, XIII: 310, XIV: 175, 380, 390
ALSHAIN, VIII: 419, XII: 418, XIII: 310, XIV: 380
Alsterufer, X: 104, 227
ALTAIR, I: 420, X: 50
ALTAMAHA, V: 291, XII: 428, XIII: 319
Altavilla, IX: 285–6, 296
Altenfjord, I: 185, X: 230
ALUDRA, sunk, VI: 141
Amagai, Cdr. T., IV: 126–7
Amagansett, I: 200
AMAGI, XII: 161, XIII: 158, XIV: 94, 331
AMAGIRI, III: 276, IV: 89, VI: 162, 167–8, 172–3, 211, 341, 353, 356–8
Amami Gunto, XIV: 79, 89
Amami O Shima, XII: 335, XIII: 182, XIV: 4, 58, 129n
Amano, Capt. S., XII: 430
Amapá, X: 216, 218, 223
AMAROK, I: 421; pic., 60
Amato M., XIII: 285
AMATSUKAZE, III: 163, 274, IV: 89, V: 85, 206, 233, 254
AMAZONE, II: 104, 110n
AMBERJACK, V: 179, 196
Ambon I., III: 197, 296–7, 315, VIII: 125, 142, XII: 107
Ambrose Channel, I: 133, X: 76
Ambrosio, Gen., IX: 35
Amchitka I., IV: 215, VII: 25, 34, 44; occupied, 17–18
AMEER, X: 40n
American Food Machinery Corp., VII: 89
AMERICAN LEGION, IV: 266, 272, VI: 297, 303
Ames, Cdr. C. E., I: xv, 258n
Ames, Ens. M. K., I: 395
AMESBURY, XI: 336
AMETHYST, X: 339

Amey, Lt. Col. H. R., VII: 159, 162, 165
AMICK, X: 357
AMMEN, VI: 382, 391, 440–42, VII: 335, VIII: 66, 74, 97, 127, 405, XII: 344, 415, XIV: 259, 381
Ammunition, Gilberts, VII: 111–12; Marshalls, 111–12, 210; Marianas, VIII: 346–7; Normandy, XI: 159, 160n, 161; Leyte, XII: 77, 83, 201–2, 294–5; Okinawa, XIV: 165–6
Ammunition expended, North Africa, II: 285; Shortlands, VI: 321; Buka, 321; Bougainville, 321; Empress Augusta Bay, 321; Komandorskis, VII: 35; Aleutians, 55, 60–61; Kwajalein, 279n; Hollandia, VIII: 82; Saipan, 180, 212n; Sicily, IX: 113, 222n; Surigao Strait, XII: 224, 227n; Leyte, 295; Ormoc, 384; Iwo, XIV: 13, 35n, 73–4; Okinawa, 35n, 138, 165–9, 245–7
Ammunition, replenishment at sea, XIV: 9, 159, 165
Amory, Col. Robert, XIII: xi, 244–5, 250
Amoy, China, XII: 12, XIII: 3, 170, 298
Amphibious assault tactics, VIII: 54–6
Amphibious craft development, VI: 131
Amphibious Force, Atlantic Fleet, II: 19–23; Advance Group, 224–6; XI: 52; Northwest African Waters, IX: 93; Third, VI: 97, 238, 282n, 416, VIII: 161, XII: 14, 17, 32, 113; T.O., VII: 228–9, 297; Fifth, VI: 97, VII: 86–7, 202, XIV: 166; Seventh, VI: 97, 130, 132, 266, 369, 378–80, 389–90, VIII: 47, 53–6, 91, 141, XII: 15–17, 21, 53, 114, XIII: 321; beach parties, VIII: 53; T.O., VI: 261–2; Eighth, IX: 325, 329, 332, 359, XI: 53; Eleventh, XI: 29, 58, 64, 149, 297, 329
Amphibious Force Flagship, described, II: 30–31, VII: 207
Amphibious Group 7, XIII: 94n; Group 9, 187
Amphibious shipping, shortages and transfers, VII: 110, XII: 19
Amphibious training, VI: 131–2, XI: 58–60
Amphibious warfare, history and development, I: liii–lv, II: 19–20, III: 165, 180, 293, 315–16
Amphibious Warfare Section, Cominch, VI: 131
AMPHITRITE, II: 248; sunk, 98

Amphtrac. *See* LVT
AMSTERDAM, XI: 127, 335
Amsterdam I., VIII: 143
AMYCUS, XIII: 306
ANACOSTIA, XIV: 387
Anambas Is., III: 335, 338
Anami, Lt. Gen. K., VIII: 66n, 67, 132
Anami, Gen. S., XIV: 345–6, 348–50
Anapo R., IX: 160
Anatahan I., VIII: 152, 175n
ANCHOR, XIV: 387
Anchorage, Alaska, IV: 174
ANCON, II: 30n, 38, 86, 161, 172, IX: 64–5, 120n, 124, 138, 141–3, 251, 277, 295, 389–91, XI: ix, 63–4, 118–19, 146, 150–52, 156, 335, XIV: 299, 381; pic., XI: 133
ANCYLUS, X: 321
Andaman Is., III: 381, IV: 277; operation canceled, IX: 322
Andersen, Cdr. H. M., IX: 388, XI: 340
Anderson, Capt. A. B., VI: 297, 343
Anderson, Ens. A. W., I: 394
Anderson, Andrew, X: 382
Anderson, Rear Adm. Bern, VI: 15, 130n, 131, 271, VIII: viii, 45n, 64n, 65, 75n, 81, 87, 98, 111–12, 116, 123–4, 135, 404, IX: xiv, X: x, XI: ix–xi, 134, XII: vii, 299n, XIII: ix, XIV: ix, xi
Anderson, Lt. C. A., IX: 102
Anderson, Capt. C. C., VIII: 407, XII: 419, XIII: 311
Anderson, Capt. C. E., pic., VII: 295; mentioned, IV: 165, VII: 179n, 181–2, 228, 304, 341, VIII: 208, XIV: 50
Anderson, Lt. D. E., X: 382
Anderson, Cdr. E. A., XIV: 375
Anderson, Lt. E. G., XII: 421–2, XIII: 306
Anderson, Cdr. E. J., VIII: 408
Anderson, Lt. Cdr. E. L., III: 217, XIII: 317
Anderson, Ens. G., IX: 259
Anderson, Cdr. H. A., VII: 334, 341, VIII: 411, XII: 428, XIII: 318
Anderson, Lt. H. T. E., I: 334n
Anderson, Ens. J. A., II: 273
Anderson, Maj. Gen. J. B., XI: 323
Anderson, Maj. Gen. J. W., II: 23, 27, 33, 37, 59, 87, 157, 162
Anderson, Lt. Gen. K. A. N., II: 190n, 243, 258
Anderson, Lt. N. W., XIII: 308

Anderson, Maj. Gen. O. A., IV: 111n
Anderson, O. C., VII: 334
Anderson, Cdr. P. R., VI: 331, VII: 337, 344, VIII: 405, XII: 416
Anderson, Capt. T. C., VII: 104
Anderson, Capt. W. D., XIV: 373
Anderson, Rear Adm. W. S., IV: 82n-3n
ANDERSON, IV: 19, 59, 60n, 90, V:205, 222, 233, 343, VII: 165, 168, 220, 338, 346, VIII: 405, XII: 345, 416
Andrea, Lt. Cdr. J. P., XIII: 77, 316
ANDREA DORIA, IX: 38
ANDRES, X: 49
Andrew, Cdr. J. D., V: 44-6, XII: 416
ANDREW DORIA, XII: 308
Andrew G. Curtin, X: 305
Andrews, Adm. Adolphus, biog., I: 208n; mentioned, 131, 207-8, 240-41, 254, X: 178-80, 188
Andrews, Cdr. C. H., VIII: 21
Andrews, Capt. C. L., IX: 251n, 300-301, 392
Andrews, Lt. Cdr. E. F., XIII: 308
Andrews, Ens. F. A., V: 167
Andrews, Lt. Gen. Frank, I: 149
ANDROMEDA, IX: 124, 142, 389, 392, XI: 339, XIV: 378
Andrus, Maj. Gen. Clift, IX: 104, 117n, 122
Anegada Passage, X: 195, 198n
"Angau" (Australia–New Guinea Administrative Unit), VI: 28, 42-3, 48
Angaur, Palaus, XII: 32, 46, XIII: 83; landing, XII: 16, 35, 43-7; chart, 45
Angeles, Luzon, XIII: 107
Angelo, Lt. Cdr. A. H., XIV: 373
Angelus, X: 181
ANGLER, VIII: 21-2, XII: 406, 429, XIII: 161, 320
Anglo-American Staff Conversations, I: 38-46, X: 5-6
Angrick, Cdr. F. E., XIV: 379
Ankcorn, Col. C. M., IX: 133, 137n, 144
ANNAMITE, X: 157
ANNAN, X: 329n
ANNE ARUNDEL, II: 36, IX: 139, 389, XI: 335, 339
Anneliese Essberger, I: 384
ANNOY, II: 334
Ansel, Capt. W. C., II: 231, IX: 362, 371, XI: 286, 289, 340
ANSON, X: 231, 308

ANTAEUS, I: 421
ANTARES, III: 96, 137, 240n, IV: 387, XI: 341
Anthéor, France, XI: 269; pic., 284
ANTHONY, VI: 297, 342-3, 415, 421, 427, VIII: 409, 414, 419, XIV: 222, 259-60, 274, 381
ANTHONY, HMS, X: 335, 372
Antiaircraft tactics and doctrine, III: 310, VI: 150
Anti-barge operations, VI: 210, 221, 241-3, 257-8, 273-4, 291, 362, 379, 391, 422, 427-9
Anticline, IX: 390
Anti-Comintern Pact, III: 40, 49
ANTIETAM, XIV: 334n
Antifer, Cap d', XI: 75
Antigua, B.W.I., I: 34, 248
Antigua, XIV: 163
ANTIOPE, II: 110n
Anti-shipping sweeps, XIV: 310, 313, 316, 332
Anti-submarine Development Detachment, I: 251, X: 208, 245, 327, 350
Antisubmarine Measures Unit, X: 22n
"Antisubmarine University," X: 47-51
Antisubmarine Warfare, I: 203, 347; summaries and trends, 157, 198-204, 303-17, 349, 400-409, X: 244-8, 361-4; administration, I: 205-8, X: 12-13; doctrine, I: 219; Marshall and King on, 308-10; tables, 410-15, X: 365-73; vessels, I: 235; X: 32-42; technical developments, 52-4, 82; training, I: 219, 219n, 231-3, 243, VIII: 223, X: 8-9, 47-51; North Atlantic, I: 92-5, 114-35, 154-7, 248-9, 305-6, 317-46, 352-8, X: 65-84, 139-52, 344-56, 361-4; Caribbean, I: 136-54, 346-52, X: 297-8; South Atlantic, I: 378-88, X: 293-9; North Africa, II: 168-71, 174, 250-51; Mediterranean, IX: 40-43, X: 252-73, chart, 254-5; Normandy, 323-4, XI: 72-3; Pacific, III: 97, 115, V: 66-7, 106, 349-50, VIII: 39, 223-30, XII: 51-3; *Monthly Summary*, X: 75n; *Bulletin*, I: 217, VII: 224, X: xii, 24; Operational Research Group (Asworg), I: 218-23, 390, X: 22n, 24, 146, 208, 327; Unit Atlantic Fleet, I: 220-22, 304; A/SW Unit, Boston, 206, 217, X: 22n, 48; weapons, I: 209-12; pic., 211
Antrim, Cdr. R. N., III: 285n, 373

Antwerp, XI: 20, 295–6
ANTWERP, IX: 157, XI: 338
ANZAC Area, chart, III: 278; Force, 261, 359, 387n, IV: 15, 254
Anzio, described, 335–6; pic., IX: 347
ANZIO, XII: 79, XIII: 79, 319, XIV: 18, 59, 120, 244, 314, 318, 373; pic., XIII: 79
Anzio Operation, planning, IX: 317–19, 324–32, rehearsals and movement, 332–4; landing, 333, 335–44, 383; landing, chart, 337; minesweeping, 339–40, 342, 348; pics., 346–7; naval gunfire, 358–64, 383–4; operations ashore, 344–79; map, 357; air attacks, 341, 355, 367–8; unloading, 346–7, 356; logistics, 367; T.O., 395–7; casualties, 343, 380; discussion, 380–84, XI: 223–4
AOBA, III: 26, 185, 245; IV: 17–18, V: 22, 35–7, 44, 59–60, 85, 105, 150–51, 158–64, 168–9, VI: 125, VIII: 118–20, 125, 130–31, XII: 164, 169n, 431; sunk, V: 61n, XIV: 331
Aoki, Cdr. K., XII: 431
Aoki, Capt. T., IV: 124–6
Aola, V: 10, 145
Aosta, Duke of, IX: 244
AOTAKA, III: 274
Aoukasha, Battery, II: 96–8, 106n, 161
APACHE, VI: 295–7, 303, VIII: 419, XII: 416, XIII: 106, 306, 325
APc, VI: 134n; Southwest Pacific, VIII: 55
APc–4, VI: 261, 376; –15, 377; –21, sunk, 376; –46, VIII: 419; –108, VII: 341; –109, 341
APD. *See* Destroyer-transports
APHIS, XI: 250, 282, 338
"Aphrodite," radar decoy, X: 138, 186, 205, 218, 221, 280
Apia, IV: 263n, XIII: 59
Apo I. & Pass, P.I., XIII: 17, 101, 115
APOGON, VII: 187–8, 342, VIII: 24, 155
APOLLO, XI: 159
APPALACHIAN, VII: 233, 237, 249, 345, VIII: 378, 397, 400, 418, XII: 418, XIII: 144, 150, 307
APPANOOSE, XIV: 386
Appledore, XI: 60
Appleman, R. E., *Okinawa: The Last Battle*, XIV: 170n
APPLING, XIII: 307, XIV: 380
Apra, VIII: 350, 375, 396–400
Apulia, IX: 45

AQUARIUS, VII: 346, VIII: 418, XII: 134, 416, XIII: 308, XIV: 378
Aquitania, X: 133
Araki, Capt. D., XII: 430
Aranjo, Cap.-de-Fragata O. de, I: 376n
Araosan M., XIII: 286
ARAPAHO, VII: 306, 341, 345, VIII: 420, XIV: 388
ARARE, III: 87, IV: 89; sunk, IV: 216, VII: 7
ARASHI, III: 333, IV: 88, 122, V: 206, 220n, 339, VI: 39, 214–21
ARASHIO, III: 274, 276, 328–9, IV: 88, 150, V: 234, VI: 56; sunk, 61
Araujo, Cdr. Ernesto de, I: 382
Arawe, New Britain, landing, VI: 372–7
Arbes, Lt. Cdr. J. D., VIII: 413, XII: 425
Arbuckle, Lt. E. C., II: 277, IX: 189–90
Arbuthnot, Vice Adm. Sir Geoffrey, III: 383–4
ARCADIA Conference. *See* Washington Conference, Dec. 1941–Jan. 1942
Archangel, I: 159, 363–5, 373, X: 236
Archdale, Cdr. H., II: 231
Archer, Capt. R. J., XIV: 256, 374, 382
Archer, Cdr. S. M., XIV: 165n
ARCHER, X: 38, 52n, 77, 82
ARCHERFISH, VIII: 30, 415, XII: 161n, 410–11; pic., 407
Archie, Lt. A. S., X: 379–80
ARCHIMEDE, I: 390; sunk, 415
ARCTIC, XIII: 187n
ARCTURUS, I: 76, 421, II: 26n, 38, 60n, 159, 172, IX: 389, 392, XI: 287, 340–41, XIV: 379
ARD–13, XIV: 387; –19, XII: 423; –22, XIV: 387; –27, 387; –28, 387
Ardagh, Lt. Cdr. J. F., XII: 428, XIII: 319
Ardennes, Belgium, XI: 319
ARDENT, XIV: 376
AREQUIPA, XII: 423
ARETHUSA, XII: 423
Argenlieu, Contre-Amiral d', IV: 253
Argentia, I: 34n, 68–9, 75–7, 85, 95, 101, 120, 223, 240, 248, 319–20, X: 111, 152, 329, 355; pic., I: 71, X: 81
Argentina M., VII: 6
ARGENTO, X: 371; sunk, IX: 42–3
Argon, X: 67n
ARGONAUT, IV: 190, 235–7, VII: 77; sunk, IV: 229; pic., 235

ARGONAUT, HMS, II: 189, XI: 341, XIV: 105-7, 388
ARGONAUT Conference. *See* Malta and Yalta Conferences
ARGONNE, III: 100*n*, 104, 119, IV: 280, VIII: 420, XIII: 161*n*
ARGUS, HMS, I: 167, II: 190, 214, X: 37
ARIADNE, XII: 17, 54, 117, 417
ARIAKE, IV: 17, V: 323; sunk, VI: 208, 256
Arias, Dr. Anulfo, I: 150
ARIEL, I: 422
Ariga, Rear Adm. K., XII: 430, XIV: 202, 205-6
Ariizumi, Capt. T., X: 299-300, XIV: 314
ARIKARA, XI: 337, 342, XIV: 190-91, 247, 387
Arima, Rear Adm. M., XII: 101, 166
Arima, Capt. S., VII: 232
Arisio, Gen. Mario, IX: 50, 173
Arison, Capt. R. E., XIII: 245*n*, 247, 322-4
ARISTAEUS, XIV: 387
Arita, Hachiro, III: 36, 43
ARIZONA, I: 206*n*, III: 101*n*, V: 88*n*, X: 51*n*, 200*n*, XI: xv, XII: 119*n*, 244*n*; sunk, III: 103, 106-9; pics., 84, 103, 110
Arizona M., V: 234, 269*n*
ARK ROYAL, X: 213
ARKANSAS, I: 14, 76, 327, 419, II: 176, 193, 247, IX: 92*n*, X: 134, XI: 56, 118-23, 145, 148, 158-60, 167-8, 197-8, 205-10, 238, 268, 271, 284*n*, 336-7, 341, XIII: 94*n*, 176*n*, XIV: 26, 30, 122, 130, 312*n*, 372; pic., XI: 133
ARKHANGELSK, X: 311*n*
Arle, Lt. H. F., VIII: 255
Arles, XI: 286
ARLUK, I: 421
Arlyn, I: 331
ARMADILLO, XIV: 387
Armel, Cdr. L. O., XIV: 375
Arming of merchantmen, I: 80
ARMISTEAD RUST, XIV: 386
Armstrong, Cdr. H. J., IV: 174, VI: 308, 317*n*, 354, 358, VIII: 415, XIV: 376
Armstrong, Capt. J. M., XIII: 133, 303
Armstrong, Capt. R. G., XIV: 381
Armstrong, Cdr. W. W., VI: 113*n*; XIV: 373-4
Army and Navy Petroleum Board, VIII: 344

Army, U.S., available in 1941, I: 47*n*; Hawaiian Army Command, IV: 86; Forces Far East established, III: 153
Army Groups: First, XI: 30; Sixth, 291, 310, 324; Twelfth, 216, 317, 324
Armies, First, XI: 29-30, 70, 158, 168, 190, 195, 198, 216, 295, 323-4, 333; Third, XI: 216, 232, 295-8, 319-21, 324; Fifth, IX: 247, 255, 281, 297, 300, 312, 318-19, 322-8, 332, 344, 358-63, 370, 374, XI: 236, 310-12, 316, 324; Sixth, VI: 15, 274, 374, 380, VIII: 46-7, XII: 15, 56, 154-6, 354, 362, 365, 372-3, 376, 415, XIII: 3*n*, 49, 90, 97, 145, 154-5, 184-5, 193, 197, 207-9, 213, 216, 314*n*; Seventh, IX: 27, 49, 52, 61-4, 72, 123, 147, 170-87, 191, 195-204, 208-9, 218-20, XI: xiv, 233, 236-8, 255, 274, 286, 291, 295, 310-11, 323-4, 338; Eighth, XII: 394, XIII: 49, 189, 207, 210, 213-18, 233-4, 241, 251; XIV: 356-7; Ninth, XI: 321-2; Tenth, XIV: 86, 90, 217, 240, 267, 275, 282
Corps, First, VIII: 63, 403, XIII: 12, 97, 129-30, 135, 145-6, 185, 193, 210, 308; First and Second Phil., III: 199; Second, II: 260, IX: 32, 65, 140, 333, 363, 375-6, 388; Third, IX: 177; Fifth, XI: 29, 64, 105-6, 118, 130, 141, 152, 158-60, 166-8, 189, 324, 335-6; Sixth, IX: 255, 258, 268, 278-95, 302, 327-30, 343, 346-7, 350-53, 356, 360-69, 374-9, 383, 391, 395; XI: 236, 266, 275, 285, 338; Seventh, XI: 29, 107, 156-61, 167, 196-8, 202, 211-13, 333; Eighth, XI: 298, 300-302; Tenth, XII: 56, 114, 130, 139-41, 154, 362-4, XIII: 217, 241, 246, 324; Eleventh, VIII: 72, XII: 21, XIII: 185, 187, 193, 198-9; Fourteenth, V: 340, VI: 364, 425-31, XIII: 12, 94, 117, 125, 128, 135, 146, 185-7, 193-4, 198-9, 310; Nineteenth, XI: 29; Twenty-fourth, VIII: 353, 356, 360; XII: 14-15, 56, 113, 140, 144, 153-6, 363, 393-6, 418; XIII: 4, 185; XIV: 90-91, 108, 128, 171-5, 215, 218, 221, 240-42, 273, 379
Defense Bns., VII: 345
Divisions, American, IV: 248, 253, 263*n*, V: 12, 147-8, 172-4, 189, 192, 231, 285, 288, 334*n*, 335-7, 364, 371, VI: 364-5, 428, XIII: 95, 217, 233, 236-

Army, U.S., (*cont'd*)

7, XIV: 248, 253, 263*n*; 1st Armored, II: 223, 225–30, 259; IX: 329, 356–8, 364–5, 369; 1st Cavalry, VI: 133, 434–48, XII: 114, 130, 139, 153, 362–3, 375, 392–3, 416, XIII: 185, 193–6, 312*n*, XIV: 368; 1st Inf., II: 21–3, 223, 231–5, 238, 259, IX: 28, 61, 93–5, 98, 108, 111–19, 122–5, 147, 171–6, 180, 199–200, 386–7, XI: 110, 122, 130–32, 137–41, 149, 152, 158, 163*n*, 335–6; 2nd Armored, II: 23, 36–9, 128, 152, 157, 161, IX: 28, 108, 111, 176, 181–4, 386, XI: 163*n*; 2nd Inf., XI: 163*n*; 3rd Armored, XI: 163*n*; 3rd Inf., II: 23, 26, 37, 76, 86–7, 157, 162, 173, 178, 271–3, IV: 265, IX: 28–33, 75, 79–90, 171–6, 180–84, 196–8, 203–5, 247, 300, 303–4, 319, 329, 332, 340, 343, 347, 350–54, 358, 361, 365, 369, 386, 395, XI: 236, 241, 254, 258–60, 262–6, 339; 4th Inf., XI: 101*n*, 103, 105, 108, 157, 163*n*, 198, 204, 333; 6th Armored, XI: 299; 6th Inf., VIII: 135, 141–3, XIII: 97, 126, 132–3, 135, 309; 7th Inf., VII: 38, 42–51, 232, 251–81, 285, 334–5, 343, XII: 140, 143–4, 154, 363, 375–9, 387, 418, XIV: 90, 140, 146, 171, 379; 9th Armored, XI: 319; 9th Inf., I: 421, II: 22–3, 36, 39, 116, 123–7, 143–7, 178, 190–93, 198, 209–12, IX: 28, 189, 193, 200, 205–7; XI: 163, 167, 198, 212–15; 11th Airborne, XII: 379, XIII: 189–91, 197–8, 204, 210, XIV: 360–62; 11th Filipino, III: 174, 176, 181; 21st Inf., XIII: 243; 21st Filipino, III: 181; 24th Inf., V: 371, VIII: 63, 75–7, 86–8, 403, XII: 56, 114, 131, 137–40, 151–3, 362–3, 375, 387, 416, XIII: 21, 43, 185, 188, 199, 203, 225, 241, 246, 250, 324; 25th Inf. V: 183, 335–7, 340–43, VI: 222–3, 229, 237*n*, 238, 334*n*, 335–7, 340–43, XIII: 97, 144–5, 306; 27th Inf., VII: 89–91, 114, 122–35, 226–7, 288, 294–300, 336, VIII: 160, 171, 202–9, 330–37, 348, 410, XIV: 90, 175, 217, 220, 242, 381; 28th Inf., XIII: 312*n*; 29th Inf., XI: 110, 121–2, 129–32, 136–40, 151, 158, 160, 163*n*, 335–6; 30th Inf., XI: 163*n*, 168, 322; 31st Inf., XII: 21, 54, XIII: 241, 246, 249, 324; 32nd Inf., VI: 42, 45, 50, 132, 389–90, VIII: 63, 70–72, 96; XII: 56, 363, 375, XIII: 185, 193, 312*n*; 33rd Inf.,

XIII: 312*n*; 34th Inf., II: 190, 193–4, 204–7, IX: 247, 300; 36th Inf., IX: 247, 251, 258, 261–6, 275, 284–6, 378, 391–2, XI: 236, 241, 259, 268–73, 276, 341; pic., IX: 267; 37th Inf., VI: 156*n*, 175, 202, 289*n*, 344, 348, 364, 428–30, XIII: 93–4, 127, 135, 143, 194, 196, 310; 38th Inf., XIII: 185, 188–9, 199, 205; 40th Inf., 94, 96, 127, 135, 217, 229, 231–2, 237, 249, 310, 323; 41st Inf., VI: 50, 137, 258, VIII: 63, 70–72, 79, 82–7, 95–6, 99, 103, 106, 112–16, 135, 403, XIII: 217–18, 222, 241, 313*n*, 321; 43rd Inf., V: 181*n*, VI: 98, 102, 144, 148–9, 155, 177–9, 198–202, 205, 223–4, VIII: 72–3, XIII: 97, 126, 135, 308; 45th Inf., IX: 28, 64, 94, 127, 142–7, 154, 180, 195–6, 247, 258, 280, 285–7, 304, 329, 356, 362–5, 369, 388, 391–2; XI: 236, 241, 249, 258, 264–6, 340; 51st Filipino, III: 182; 66th Inf., XI: 328, 334; 77th Inf., VIII: 160, 371, 374–6, 379, 388–96, 399–400, 419; XII: 56, 372, 375–6, 379, 385–8, 393–5, XIV: 90, 108, 118–19, 126–8, 136, 176, 240, 375; 79th Inf., XI: 163*n*, 198, 212; 80th Inf., XI: 320; 81st Inf., VIII: 348, XII: 16, 34, 41–9, 53, XIV: 90; 82nd Airborne, IX: 93–5, 120–22, 141, 146, 177, 181, 239–40, 291, 296, 304, 353, 392, XI: 89–91, 163*n*; 83rd Inf., XI: 163; 85th Inf., IX: 376; 87th Inf., XI: 320; 88th Inf., IX: 370, 376, 379; 89th Inf., XI: 320; 90th Inf., XI: 162, 163*n*, 167; 93rd Inf., VI: 142, XIV: 360; 96th Inf., XII: 140, 143–4, 154, 286, 363, 375, 387, 419, XIV: 171, 380; 98th Inf., VIII: 348; 101st Airborne, XI: 82*n*, 89–91, 105–6, 163*n*

Engineers, I: 380, IV: 163–4, VI: 36, 262, VII: 15, VIII: 70, 83, 116, 139, 333, 375, IX: 56, 80, 107, 139, 188, 196, 222, 264, 286, 329, 342, X: 210, XI: 140, 161, 262–3, 319–21, XII: 24, 46, 151, 350, XIII: 32, 48; Eng. Amphib. Command, VIII: 52; Eng. Spec. Brigades, VI: 137, 258, VIII: 51–3, 70, 77–8, 85, 137–8, XI: 101*n*, 108, XII: 153, 394, XIII: 204–6, 215, 220, XIV: 174; Eng. Boat and Shore Regiments, VIII: 100, 106, 113, XIII: 244

Paratroops, II: 224, 236, VI: 266, VIII: 139

Rangers, II: 191, 204, 223, 231–2, IX: 28–30, 75, 85, 95–7, 103, 112, 117, 175–6, 258–9, 271–2, 276, 282, 285, 291, 304, 318, 329, 338, 343, 353, 356, XI: 105, 125–9, 136, 144, 158–60, 335, XII: 119–21, 417; pic., II: 273, XI: 132

Shore parties, II: 28, 82, 160–1, 203, XI: 241

Spec. Serv. Force, First, XI: 241

Task Forces, 1st Airborne, XI: 277–8; "Alamo," VI: 133, 379, 434, VIII: 47, 64; "Cyclone," 135; "Reckless," 63; "Typhoon," 141

Army Air Forces, state of in 1941, I: 48n; in A/SW., I: 138–43, 150–53, 207, 237–47, 259, 319, 347, X: 53, 130–32, 260, 362; kills of U boats, I: 156, 350–1, 415, X: 341, 370–3; controversy with Navy, I: 239–46; navigational difficulties, 243; "Horse Trade," X: 26–31; command setup in Pacific, XIV: 9; Trinidad, I: 380–82; Coral Sea, IV: 14, 20, 30, 38, 61; Midway, IV: 85; Alaska, IV: 170–71, 174; New Caledonia, IV: 253; Guadalcanal, V: 70, 138, 257, 260–61, 267, 283–5, 290, 325; Solomons, V: 150, 322; Eastern Sols., V: 105; New Georgia, VI: 146; Rabaul, V: 323–4; Aleutians, VII: 5–6; Sicily, IX: 55–60, 128, 150; Bismarck Sea, VI: 57–62; Bay of Biscay, X: 88–99; Leyte, XII: 125, 344, 347, 368, 387; Mindoro, XIII: 32, 42; Lingayen, XIII: 90; Far East, III: 165, 171, XII: 5, 107, 130, 150, 311, XIII: 163–4, 178, 194, 217, XIV: 278; U. S. Strategic, XI: 35; Transport Command, I: 289, VII: 340, VIII: 349

A/S Command, I: 242–5, 251; X: 19, 26–31

Forces, Individual, First, I: 241–2; Fifth, VI: 55–7, 61, 64, 69, 257, 287–8, 320, 370–73, 376, 383–5, 389, 398, 433–6, VIII: 34–6, 47, 66–7, 92, 96–8, 107, 116, 120, 124, 136, 141–2, 156, XII: 22, 25, 190–91, 238, 345, 393, XIII: 21, 39, 135, 151, 199, 230, XIV: 39, 151; Sixth, I: 153, X: 201; Seventh, IV: 86, 93, VII: 82, 86, 93–8, 118, 287, 307–8, 340, VIII: 156, 164, XII: 55, 60, XIV: 10–12, 68; Eighth, IX: 248, X: 62, 101, 341, XI: 73, 124–6; Ninth, XI: 70, 73, 89, 100, 108, 126, 198, 215; Eleventh,

IV: 164, VII: 5, 14, 17, 21, 39, 54, 61, 65, XIII: 164; Twelfth, II: 280, IX: 22, XI: 233, 239, 280–81; Thirteenth, VIII: 50, 96, 106–7, 110, 143, 156n, 313, XII: 25, 238, 352n, XIII: 223, 230, 286; Fourteenth, XII: 5, 55, 60, 71, 105–7, XIII: 163n, 164, 293, 297; Fifteenth, XI: 244; Twentieth, XII: 55, 60, 71, 94, 105, 163, XIII: 161–4, XIV: 5, 9, 93, 295, 311, 348

Groups, 3rd Bomb't. IV: 20, 275; 11th Bomb't., V: 150, VII: 350; 17th Bomb't., III: 390n; 19th Heavy Bomb't., IV: 20, 275; 22nd Med. Bomb't., 20; 22nd Bomb't., 275; 30th Bomb't., VII: 350; 35th Bomb't., IV: 20; 22nd Bomb't., VII: 350; 318th Bomb't., VIII: 360; 479th Bomber, X: 31; 480th Bomber, 31; 28th Composite, VII: 333; 8th Fighter, IV: 20; 49th Fighter, 20; 343rd Fighter, VII: 333

Squadrons, A/S, 1st, I: 415, X: 88; 2nd, I: 415, X: 88

Squadrons, Bombing, 10th, X: 198n; 13th, VI: 64; 21st, VII: 333; 31st, V: 375; 45th, I: 415; 59th, 415; 63rd, 64th, 65th, VI: 64; 69th, IV: 274, V: 375; 71st, 89th, 90th, VI: 64; 99th, I: 415; 320th, 321st, VI: 65; 396th, I: 415; 403rd, VI: 64; 404th, VII: 333; 405th, VI: 64; 406th, VII: 333; 1st Compron, X: 227n

Squadrons, Fighter, 7th, 8th, 9th, VI: 64; 12th, V: 375; 39th, 40th, VI: 64; 44th, V: 375; 45th, 46th, VII: 350; 67th, V: 74, 375; 68th, 70th, V: 375; 72nd, VII: 350; 339th, V: 375; 531st, VII: 350

Squadrons, Recce. and Photo, 111th Fighter, IX: 267; 8th Photo, VI: 65; 17th Photo, V: 375; 435th, IV: 275

353rd Transport Squadron, VII: 340

Wings, 308th Bomber, XIII: 143; 310th Bomber, 24; 51st Troop Carrier, IX: 150n; 52nd Troop Car., 120

Army-Navy Obstacle Board, XI: 240

ARNEB, XII: 416, XIV: 380

Arnim, Gen. von, II: 243, 258–60

Arno Atoll, VII: 310

Arnold, Maj. Gen. A. V., VII: 251n, 256, 418, XIV: 141, 379

Arnold, Gen. of Army H. H., pic., VI: 18; ASW, X: 27–8, 31, 106; North Africa, II: 12; Casablanca Conf., IX: 6–8; Strategic bombing, V: 185; Halsey-Doolittle raid, III: 390; Guadalcanal, V: 115–17; 1943 strategy, VI: 3; Sicily, IX: 120n; Invasion of Italy, 232; Marianas, VIII: 6; Cross-Channel invasion, XI: 13, 22; Southern France, 229; Leyte, XII: 55; Lingayen, XIII: 161–3; Twentieth Air Force, XII: 105, XIII: 161–3, XIV: 9; Iwo, 7; Okinawa, 87
Arnold, Lt. J. A., XIII: 308
Arnold, Cdr. J. D., VIII: 297–8, 412
Arnold, Capt. J. E., XI: 101, 334
Arnold, Ens. J. S., X: 182
Arnold, Capt. M. E., IV: 127n, 159n, XIV: 373
Arnold, Maj. Gen. W. H., XIII: 217, 233, 323
Arntz, Cdr. G. D., XIV: 387
Aroe Is., XII: 107
AROOSTOOK, XI: 279n
Arpaia, Lt. (jg) W. H., I :333
Arriaga, I: 392
Arrington, Cdr. C. B., XII: 418
Arromanches, XI: 179, 182
Arsuk Fjord, I: 334
Artes, Cdr. J. W., XIV: 186
Arthur, Col. J. M., V: 336
Arthur, Lt. Cdr. T. D., XIV: 387
Arthur, Sqd. Ldr. W. S., VI: 65
ARTHUR MIDDLETON, VII: 159, 337, 347, 419, VIII: 407, XIII: 310, 312, XIV: 378
Arthur Middleton, II: 269
Aruba I., I: 145, 248, 324, 348, 353–4, VIII: 345, X: 196, XII: 82
ARUNDEL, I: 421
Arundel I. landing, VI: 223
ARUNTA, VIII: 73, 97, 127–9, 405, XII: 199, 218, 344, 421, XIII: 103, 304, 325
ARVEK, I: 421
Arzeu, II: 222–4, 231–5, 251, 273–4, IX: 15, 29–32; landing, chart, II: 232
ASAGIRI, III: 276, IV: 89; sunk, V: 109
ASAGUMO, III: 162, 275, 334, 353, IV: 88, V: 84, 151, 234, 239, 273n, 274, 278–9, VI: 56–9, 62, VIII: 120, 131, 416, XII: 190, 209, 216–20, 233, 431; sunk, VI: 63, XII: 237

ASAHI, IV: 221
Asahi M., III: 290
Asaka M., IV: 172, VII: 24, 34
ASAKAZE, III: 161
Asakaze M., VII: 192
Asama M., VIII: 17, XII: 408
Asan, IV: 378–89; pic., 400
ASANAGI, IV: 17; sunk, VIII: 23
ASASHIMO, VIII: 416, XIII: 37n, 158, 431, XIV: 202, 208
ASASHIO, III: 276, 321–4, 328–9, IV: 88, V: 234, VI: 56
ASASHIO-KAGERO class, III: 88
ASCANIA, IX: 395, XI: 340
ASCELLA, XIV: 164
Ascension I., I: 244, 379–80, X: 210, 224–7
Ascherfeld, Lt. Cdr. T. F., V: 135
ASCIANGHI, IX: 168; sunk, 42
"Asdic." *See* "Sonar"
Ashbourne, Capt. Lord, IX: 150, 156, XII: 54, 417
Ashcroft, 1st Lt. W. S., V: 374
Ashe, Capt. G. B., IV: 273, VI: 297
ASHEVILLE (1920), III: 155, 159, 194, 272, 298, IX: 92n; sunk, III: 379
ASHEVILLE (1942), X: 36
Ashford, Cdr. W. H., pic., IV: 85
ASHIGARA, III: 156, 161, 180, 334, 371–2, XII: 103, 164, 190, 230–34, 239–40, 431, XIII: 37, 159; pic., IV: 126
Ashio, VII: 189
ASHIZURI, sunk, VIII: 220
ASHLAND, VII: 90n, 94, 159, 163, 255, 268, 288, 297, 337, 344, VIII: 346, 361, 408, XII: 418, XIII: 311
Ashley, Lt. Cdr. C. A., VIII: 405
Ashley, Cdr. J. H., XII: 429
Ashmun, Capt. G. M., VI: 398
ASHTABULA, VIII: 411, 420, XII: 82–4, 423, XIV: 387
Asia Is., XII: 54
Asiga Bay, VIII: 354, 358
Aslito Field, VIII: 152, 168–9, 178, 206, 208–9; pic., 176. *See also* Isely Field
Aso R., IX: 274
Asosan M., VIII: 20
ASPIRANT, XI: 341
ASPRO, VII: 353, VIII:23, XII: 405
ASSINIBOINE, I: 321–2; pic., 375
Assmann, Vice Adm. Kurt, I: 35, 312, 401; *Deutsche Schicksalsjahre*, X: xiv
ASTERION, I: 282–4
Astor, Capt. Vincent, I: 286n, 287

Astley, Sir Jacob, XIV: 32
ASTORIA (1934), III: 31*n*, 37, 210, 212*n*, 236, 242, IV: 18, 27, 60*n*, 90, 133–5, 153–4, 257, 274, 276*n*, 278, V: 14*n*, 29–30, 32*n*, 41–4, 63*n*; sunk, V: 56–8
ASTORIA (1944), XIII: 54, 316–17, XIV: 21 313, 384, 386
Astrolabe Bay, VI: 389
Asworg. *See* Antisubmarine Warfare, Operational Research Group
At Sea Logistics Service Group, XII: 75–7
ATA-122, XIV: 388; *–124*, 388; *–179*, XIII: 323
Atabrine, V: 289*n*
ATAGO, III: 22, 26, 160–61, 276, 333, IV: 88, 142, V: 84, 206, 233–4, 271–4, 278–80, VI: 323, 328, VIII: 249*n*, 290–91, 416, XII: 162, 430; sunk, XII: 170–72
ATAK, I: 421
ATASCOSA, XII: 428, XIII: 318, XIV: 387
Atenas, I: 394, X: 157
ATHABASKAN, X: 98; sunk, XI: 35
ATHANASIA, XIV: 386
Athenia, I: 9, X: 3
ATHERSTONE, IX: 393, XI: 343
ATHERTON, X: 357, 373
ATHLETE, XI: 341
ATIK, I: 282–3
Atka I., IV: 182–3, VII: 5, 15
Atkeson, Capt. C. L. C., VII: 337, XIII: 307
Atkeson, Cdr. J. C., VII: 23*n*, 32, 348, XII: 427, XIII: 318
Atkins, Cdr. B. K., VI: 61, 136–7, XII: 418, XIII: 307, XIV: 385
Atkins, Capt. J. G., XIV: 372
Atkins, Cdr. N. B., XIV: 377
Atkinson Field, I: 147
ATLANTA (1941), IV: 91, 113*n*, 257, 271, V: x, 86, 92, 98*n*, 106, 205, 226–9, 232, 237, 242–3, 246–7, 250–54; sunk, V: 255–6; class, I: lviii, 28*n*; pic., V: 243
ATLANTA (1944), XIV: 314
Atlantic Conf., I: 69–70, III: 67, X: 6; pic., I: 70
Atlantic Convoy Conf., X: 19–20, 27, 53
Atlantic Narrows, I: 376–7, 383–5, 389–90, X: 226–8, 295; chart, X: 217
Atlantic Ocean, chart, I: 408, X: 368
Atlantic Patrol, I: 81–4
Atlantic Squadron formed, I: 14

Atlantic States, X: 342
"Atlantic Wall," XI: 39–41, 44, 48, 55, 103, 151, XII: 36
Atlas, XI: 334
Atomic bomb, XIV: 320, 333, 339–40, 343–5
ATR-1, IX: 355; *–3*, X: 335; *–31*, XII: 384–5; *–44*, VII: 341, VIII: 420; *–46*, VIII: 420; *–61*, XIII: 306, 309, 322–3; *–80*, XIV: 155, 196; *–86*, XIII: 322
Atrocities, Japanese, X: 276–7, 299–301, XIII: 220
Atsugi, Japan, XIV: 360
"Attack Teacher," I: 216–17
ATTACKER, IX: 250, 393, X: 40*n*, XI: 342
Atterbury, Lt. Cdr. G. R., X: 376
ATTILIO REGOLO, IX: 243
ATTU, XIV: 386
Attu I., IV: 168–70, VII: 6–8, 14, 21, 34, 39–40, 52, 66; pic., 55; description, 41; occupation, IV: 181–3, VII: 13–15, 43; bombardment, 19–20, 43–8, and pic., 31; landing, VI: 227, VII: 37–51, and chart, 45; casualties, 50; pic., 54; T.O., 333–5
ATULE, XII: 333, 408, 429
Atwell, Lt. M. K., V: 223
AUBRETIA, XI: 343
Auboyneau, Contr. Am., XI: 311*n*
AUCILLA, XII: 428, XIII: 318, XIV: 387
Auckland, IV: 254–5, 268, V: 12, XIV: 163
AUDACITY, X: 38
AUDRAIN, XIII: 307, 313, XIV: 380
Augusta, Sicily, IX: 18, 26, 49, 57, 79, 151, 159–63, 171, 213, 252*n*
AUGUSTA, I: 69, 70*n*, 206*n*, 419, II: 31, 37, 43*n*–4*n*, 54*n*, 77, 100, 104–9, 112–13, 158, 162–5, 168, 172, 246, 285, III: 17*n*, 255*n*, V: 293*n*, IX: 92*n*, XI: ix, 71, 150–52, 162, 197, 215, 238, 244, 248, 252–4, 284–5, 288–9, 333, 338, XIV: 344–5; pic., I: 36, II: 45, 93, 113, 174, XI: 100
AUK, I: 422, II: 39, 73, 79*n*, XI: 333, 337–8
AULICK, VIII: 420, XII: 124, 199, 367, 416, XIII: 324
Ault, Cdr. W. B., III: 388, IV: 19, 41
AULT, XIII: 317, XIV: 384; pic., XIV: 158–9
Aurand, Lt. Cdr. E. P., VII: 353, VIII: 302, 413

AURELIA, XIV: 380
AURIGA, VIII: 410, XII: 156, 419, XIII: 309
AURORA, IV: 173
AURORA, HMS, II: 237, 277, IX: 167, 235, 291, XI: 288, 339
Auslander, Lt. (jg) S. E., X: 215–16
Auspach, E. M., XII: 371
Austen, Maj. L., VI: 42n
Austin, Commo. B. L., I: 420, II: 38, VI: 11n, 307–10, 315–18, 354–7
Austin, Cdr. L. B., IV: 272
Austin, Cdr. M. H., VIII: 416
Australia, communications with U.S., III: 220–22, 257, 265; Java, 314–16; invasion threat, 380, IV: 10, 63, 246–7; source of provisions, XII: 81; bases, V: 108, VII: 109; Western, chart, III: 317; Air Force, V: 10–11, 19–20, 25, 60, VI: 52, 58, 64–5, 126, VIII: 47, 70, 139, 406n, X: 371, XII: 24; Army, VI: 37, 46, 136, 258, 261, 269, 272, 389, XII: 25, XIII: 217, 250–60, 263–8, 274–5; Navy, III: 50
AUSTRALIA, III: 261, IV: 19, 22n, 25, 38n, 39, 272, 278, 281, V: 26n, 29–33, 52, VI: 39, 130, 382, VIII: 47, 73, 97, 123–6, 405, XII: 148, 421, XIII: 103, 108, 113, 132–3, 303, 325–6; pic., VIII: 49, XIII: 108–9
Australia Victory, XII: 429, XIII: 319
Avedon, Capt. H., IX: 104n
Avellino, Italy, IX: 291n
AVENGER, I: 360–65, II: 190, VII: 141n, X: 39, 307n; sunk, II: 214, 284

Avery, Lt. Cdr. H. M., X: 161, 295, 376, 380
Avery, Lt. Cdr. J. B., XIII: 309
Aviation, Development of Fleet, I: xlix–liii
Aviation Stores Issue Ships, XII: 77
AVOCET, III: 113, VII: 333
Avola, IX: 18, 151, 157–8, 164
Avranches, XI: 304
Awa M., XIV: 290
Awahou, VI: 121
Awatea, II: 195n, 283
Axtell, Ens. H. A., I: 160
AYANAMI, III: 276, IV: 89, V: 234, 274–6; sunk, 281–2
Ayer, Lt. W. H., VIII: 419, XIV: 381
Ayers, Col. R. C., VII: 296; pic., 294
AYLMER, X: 337
Aylward, Capt. T. C., III: 158, XIV: 378
AYLWIN, III: 104, 114, 213n, IV: 91, 113n, 151n, 276n, VII: 55, 59, 335, 338, 347, VIII: 419, 428, XIII: 73–5, 187n, 318n, 319
Aymeric, X: 77
AYRSHIRE, I: 190–91; pic., 171
AZALEA, XI: 66, 337
Azarigian, Ens. G. J., XII: 422
Azerbaidjan, I: 184
AZIMECH, VIII: 420, XIV: 164
Azores, I: 6, 34, 65–7, 320–21, 358, X: 45–6, 299; A/SW operations, 116–28, 151–2; chart, 120
Azumasan M., IV: 17, V: 177
Azusa M., VIII: 417, XII: 399

B

Baade, Col., IX: 210
Baanga, Solomon Islands, landing, VI: 223
BAARN, IX: 164
Babb, Cdr. R. E., XIV: 383
BABBITT, I: 15*n*, 108, 335, 420, X: 171
Babelthuap, I., Palaus, VIII: 13, 28, XII: 32, 36, 39, 79
Babo, New Guinea, VIII: 89, 219
Babylon, Ens. T. C., X: 381
BACHAQUERO, II: 236
BACHE, VI: 382, 436, 444, VIII: 74, 110, 127, 406, XII: 199, 218–20, 421, XIV: 253, 258, 381, 392
Bachman, Capt. L. A., II: 22, 24, 158*n*, 164, IX: 15, 19*n*, 23*n*, XI: 234
Bacolod, XIII: 232
Bacon, Lt. Cdr. B. E., III: 158
Bacon, Lt. Cdr. H. P., VIII: 405
Bacuit Bay, XII: 239
Bad Neuenahr, XI: 319
Badger, Cdr. N. P., VII: 151*n*
Badger, Rear Adm. O. C., I: 420, XII: 314*n*, 318, 330, 426, XIII: 317, XIV: 12, 313–14, 357, 361
BADGER, I: 16, 420, X: 157, 377
Badoglio, Marshal P., IX: 186–7, 201, 237–42
Badung Strait, III: 320–21; Battle of, 321–30; chart, 323, 326–7
Bagdanovich, Cdr. M. P., II: 39, VI: 331, VII: 339
Bagley, Rear Adm. D. W., IV: 93*n*
BAGLEY, III: 213*n*, IV: 272, V: 29–30, 36–9, 50, 52*n*, 57, VI: 39, 134, 382, VIII: 408, 415, XII: 319, 428, XIII: 305, XIV: 360, 373
Bagnara, IX: 234
Bago, R., XIII: 232
Baguio, XII: 67, XIII: 14–16, 185, 196, 210
Bahamas, I: 34, 242
Bahia, I: 83, 263, 378–9, 386, X: 212, 219, 223
Bahm, Capt. G. H., XIV: 382
Bahr, Kaptlt. Rudolf, X: 81
Baia, Italy, XI: 246

BAIA, X: 214
Bailey, Capt. C. A., IV: 273
Bailey, Maj. Kenneth, V: 141
Bailey, Lt. Cdr. L. S., VII: 341, 348
Bailey, Lt. Cdr. L. W., II: 38, 75, IX: 388
Bailey, Adm. Sir Sidney, I: 41
Bailey, Capt. Vaughn, XII: 428, XIII: 318, XIV: 387
Bailey, Capt. W. O., IV: 273, IX: 127, 133, 389, 392, XI: 130, 335, 341
BAILEY, VII: 23, 29–35, 267, 337, 344, VIII: 409, XIII: 187*n*, 208, 322
"Bailey's Beach," Sicily, IX: 127–30, 133–40, 144; pic., 131
Bailliere, Cdr. L. M., XIV: 378, 380
BAINBRIDGE (1903), IV: 82*n*
BAINBRIDGE (1921), I: 137, 417–18, 421, X: 118, 379
Baines, Lt. Cdr. E. F., XI: 336
Baines, Lt. Cdr. J. B., XI: 335
Baird, Pvt. N. M., VII: 162–3
Bairoko, II: 116, 157, 202–3, 222
"Baitdiv 1." See "Cripdiv 1"
Baka bomb, XIV: 100, 223–5, 255–9; pic., 119
Baker, Air Vice Marshal B. E., X: 102*n*, 104
Baker, Capt. C. A., XI: 207–10, 336, XIV: 372
Baker, Lt. C. S., XIV: 375
Baker, Lt. D. D., XIV: 144
Baker, Cdr. D. M., VI: 382, VIII: 404, XII: 416, XIII: 309
Baker, Lt. Cdr. F. J. T., X: 378
Baker, Capt. F. L., I: 419, XIV: 383
Baker, Lt. Cdr. G. F., XIII: 323
Baker, Lt. Cdr. G. T., X: 377
Baker, Capt. H. D., VIII: 418, XII: 139, 416
Baker, Lt. Cdr. H. W., XIII: 309
Baker, Lt. Harry, VIII: 193
Baker, Cdr. J. E., XIV: 379
Baker, Capt. J. M., VII: 126*n*, 129
Baker, Chief Elect. L. R., VII: 196
Baker, Lt. (jg) P. G., IV: 43
Baker, Maj. R. M., V: 375

Baker, Rear Adm. W. D., I: 100, 205–6, 218, 222, 418, VII: 66, VIII: 239, 415, X: 22*n*, XIII: 54, XIV: 328
Baker, Lt. Cdr. W. G., VII: 347
BAKER, X: 319, 377
Baker I., VII: 94–8, 118, 214
Bakken, Ens. W. E., X: 382
Bakutis, Cdr., F. E., XII: 312–13, 427, XIII: 316
Balabac Strait, XII: 168, XIII: 221, 264, 282
BALAO, VI: 70–71, VIII: 17, XII: 33, XIII: 319, XIV: 290
Balayan, Luzon, XIII: 192, 208–9
Balch, Lt. Cdr., J. B., XIV: 385
BALCH, III: 211*n*, 393, IV: 91, 113*n*, 134, 153*n*, 155, 156, 271, V: 28*n*, 86, 100, VII: 334, VIII: 406
Bald Eagle, XIV: 163
Baldauf, Cdr., L. C., VIII: 411, XII: 429, XIII: 305, XIV: 372
Baldinus, 2nd Lt. Lawrence, V: 104
Baldridge, Lt. Cdr. E. F., XII: 421, XIII: 306
Baldwin, Maj. A. N., VI: 42*n*
Baldwin, Lt. C. A., X: 225
Baldwin, Hanson W., I: 203, 317, IV: 62, XIII: 59*n*, XIV: 74
BALDWIN, X: 157, XI: 123–4, 147, 158, 174, 336, 340, 343
Baler, XIII: 14
Bali, III: 276, 320, 364; Strait, 375
Balikpapan, Borneo, III: 157, 160, 193, 275, 283–4, VI: 76, VIII: 214, XII: 107, XIII: 268–9; pic., 261; Battle of, III: 285–91, and chart, 286–7; Allied Landing, XIII: 217, 267–76, and chart, 273; casualties, 275
Balikpapan, VI: 126
Balintang Channel, XIII: 164–5, 172–3, 179
Ball, Spec. 1st class Elinor M., I: xvii, XIV: ix
Ball, Ens. G. G., III: 126
Ball, Capt. W. W., XIV: 379
Ballale I., VI: 95, 118, 120, 240, 281, 291
Ballantine, Lt. (jg) J. H., X: 118
Ballentine, Capt. J. J., pic., II: 30, VI: 331, 334; VII: 339, 349
BALLARAT, VI: 47
BALLARD, IV: 85, 93, 137*n*, V: 257, VIII: 242*n*, 411, 415
Balliett, Lt. (jg) L. S., X: 112, 162
Ballinger, Ens. S. E., VII: 312

Ballreich, Cdr. C. J., VII: 344, VIII: 419, XIII: 307
Balmer, Wing Cdr. J. R., VI: 65
BALSAM, X: 131, 370
BALTIMORE (1890), II: 286, VII: 17*n*
BALTIMORE (1943), I: 28*n*, VII: 190, 221, 330, 337, 350–52, VIII: 413, XII: 8–11, XIII: 54, 165, 316, XIV: 21, 305, 382, 386; class, I: lviii
Balumis, XIII: 245; pic., 260
Balut I., XIII: 246, 249–50
BAMBOROUGH CASTLE, X: 310
Ban, Rear Adm. M., XII: 431
Banana R., I: 242, 248
BANCKERT, III: 273, 309, 331
BANCROFT, VII: 64, 334, 338, 345, XIII: 208, 322
Banda Sea, III: 316
Bandar-Shapur, X: 158
Bandjermasin, III: 305–7, 362
Bandoeng, III: 339, 350, 377–9
Bandoeng M., V: 324
Bandy, Cdr. J. I., II: 39, V: 353, XIII: 312
Bane, Lt. Cdr. P. A., X: 379–80
BANG, VIII: 23, 278, 415
Bangert, R. W., XI: 287*n*
Bangka Roads, III: 296–7
Bangkok, III: 187, XIII: 164
Bangkok M., VII: 78
BANGOR, XI: 337
BANGUST, VIII: 229, 411, XII: 429, XIII: 319
Banister, Cdr. A. B., XII: 429
"Banister's Beagles," XII: 429
Banka I., air action off, III: 309–11
Banka Str., III: 340
BANKRATE, operation. *See* Marshalls operation
Banks, Cape, IV: 68
BANNER, XIII: 309, 312, XIV: 380
Bannerman, Capt. Graeme, IX: 390
BANNOCK, XI: 337
Bantam, VII: 125, 127*n*
Banten Bay, III: 365–9
Bar Harbor, I: 248, 279–80
Barakoma, VI: 228–33, 237–40, 290–91, 350, 394–6, 399, 402
BARATARIA, XIII: 311
BARB, II: 40, 139–40, VIII: 24, XII: 399–400, XIII: 297–8, 319, XIV: 287, 293–4
Barbara, I: 250
BARBARIGO, I: 380

Barbaro, Capt. J. R., XI: 335, XIV: 378
Barbary Coast, II: 18–19
BARBEL, XII: 429, XIII: 319; sunk, 282
Barber, Lt., R. T., VI: 128
BARBER, X: 283–4, 378
Barbey, Vice Adm. D. E., biog., VI: 131*n*; pics., 132; XII: 70, XIII: 109; mentioned, V: 116, VI: 15, 51, 97, 130–34, 254, 369, VIII: 47, 55–6, IX: 65*n*, XII: 54; New Guinea, VI: 261–3, 269–70, 389–90, VIII: 63–4, 68, 76–81, 85–6, 94, 403; New Brit., VI: 372, 378–83; Admiralties, 434–7; Morotai, XII: 16, 21–6; Leyte, 56, 81, 114, 127–34, 139–40, 155, 314, 376, 415–16; Lingayen, XIII: 6*n*, 7–9, 12, 18, 97, 102, 115–19, 123–6, 130–32, 145–6, 153, 308; Lesser Philippine opns., 199, 208–9, 215–16, 222, 321; Borneo opns., 260, 268, 272–4
Barchet, Capt. S. G., I: 421, XIII: 309
Barclay, Lt. Cdr. K. J., XIII: 319, XIV: 374
BARCOO, XIII: 261*n*, 263
Bard, Lt. Col. E. E., V: 375
Bard, Ralph A., I: 29*n*
Barden, Cdr. H. E., XIV: 387
Bardshar, Cdr. F. A., VIII: 310, XII: 427
Barents Sea, I: 186–9, 413
BARFLEUR, I: 30
Barfleur Cape, XI: 75, 87, 218*n*
Barges, German, IX: 52; Jap., V: 121, 293, 320, 370, VI: 48–9, 208–10, 236, 239–40, 274, 407, VII: 52, VIII: 125–7, 209–12, 324, XII: 26–8, 396; pic., VI: 262; U.S., VII: 106
Bargsten, Kaptlt. Klaus, X: 182
Barham, Lt. Cdr. E. A., VIII: 405
BARHAM, III: 50*n*
Bari, IX: 236, 319–22
Barker, Capt. H. B., VI: 284
Barker, Cdr., N. C., X: 381
Barker, Brig. Gen. R. W., XI: 19
BARKER, III: 160, 272, 298, 310, 320, 332, IV: 276, X: 117, 377
Barkowsky, Lt. Cdr. A. J., VII: 410
Barlow, Wing Cdr. A. A., VI: 65
Barlow, Lt. Cdr. R. C., XIII: 279, 308
Barnard, Cdr. H. A., VII: 341, XII: 27, 420, XIII: 306, XIV: 383
BARNDALE, IX: 397
Barnegat, N. J., I: 133
BARNEGAT, I: 420, II: 37, 44*n*, 129*n*, 131, 245, X: 214, 219

Barnes, Brig. Gen. E. W., VIII: 143
Barnes, Maj. Gen. J. F., III: 271
Barnes, Lt. Cdr. R. C., XII: 420, XIII: 305
Barnes, Lt. Cdr. S. M., II: 263–4, 265*n*, 277, IX: 78–9, 188–90, 213, 300–301, 308, 310, 372, 373*n*, 385, 392, XI: 239, 277, 314–15, 339
Barnes, Lt. Cdr. W. R., XI: 342
BARNES, I: 419, VII: 338, XII: 428
Barnett, Lt. J. T., XIII: 30
Barnett, Lt. M. E., VI: 184
Barnett, Photographer P. T., VI: 327
Barnett, Lt. Cdr. Walter, VIII: 411, XII: 83
BARNETT, IV: 265*n*, 273, IX: 98–100, 109–10, 259*n*, 388, 392, XI: 94, 102, 334, 340, XIV: 378
Barney, Lt. Cdr. W. J., X: 380
BARNEY, I: 84, 142*n*, 145*n*
"BARNEY" Oper., XIV: 292
Barnhart, Lt. Cdr. V. J., XIV: 378
BARNSTABLE, XII: 416, XIII: 309, 312, XIV: 380
Barninger, 1st Lt. C. A., III: 232
Baron, Capt. T. J., XI: 338
BARON, VI: 415, VIII: 410, 420
Barone, Rear Adm. Pietro, IX: 201, 210, 216
Barr, Chief Aviation Electrician C. N., XII: 305
Barr, Cdr. E. L., VI: 74–5, XII: 406, 429, XIII: 285
Barr, Cdr. E. P., XIII: 320
BARR, X: 289–90, 377; XIV: 28, 120, 377
Barracks ships, XIV: 9
BARRACUDA, I: 421
Barrage balloons, VI: 339, 416, IX: 210
Barranquilla, X: 201*n*, 202
Barre, Gen., II: 87*n*
Barrett, Maj. Gen. C. D., VI: 282*n*
Barrett, Capt. J. P. B., IX: 390, XIII: 311
Barrett, Cdr. M. C., IX: 390
BARRICADE, XI: 340
Barrier Forces, X: 344–56; chart, 347
Barringer, Cdr. V. C., II: 40
Barrington, Lt. R. L., XII: 423
Barromey, Cdr. R. J., XII: 418
Barron, Lt. J. P., XIV: 385
Barrowclough, Maj. Gen. H. E., VI: 239, 415, 419
Barrows, Col. R. G., VII: 104

BARRY, I: 15n, 151–2, 390n, X: 122–3, 159–61, 167, 376, XI: 339, XIV, 271, 392; sunk, 279; pic., X: 288
Barthes, Capt., II: 96n
Bartlett, Capt. Bob, I: 62n
Bartlett, Capt. Bradford, VII: 347, VIII: 407
Bartlett, Lt. Cdr. W. R., VII: 344
Bartman, Capt. R. C., XIV: 378
Barton, Maj. Gen. R. O., XI: 333
BARTON (1942), V: 205, 232, 237, 248; sunk, V: 249
BARTON (1943), XI: 129, 206–8, 334, 337, XII: 366n, 377–9, 385, XIII: 26, 105, 109, 304, 312, XIV: 25, 373; pic., XIII: 36
Baruch, Cdr. B. M., Jr., I: 289
Barwise, R. G., XIV: 271n, 276n
Basabua, VI: 33
Base Force, III: 28
BASHAW, VIII: 30, 416, XIII: 285
Basilan I., XIII: 223–4, 226, 245
Basket, Cdr. T. S., XIII: 319
Basore, Lt. H. H., XI: 342
Basra, I: 159
Bass, Lt. H. B., X: 379, XI: 342
Bass, Cdr. R. H., VII: 342
Bass, Gunner R. W., XI: 138n
BASS, I: 421
Bassett, Lt. Cdr. Richard, XIV: 376
BASSETT, XIV: 326
Bastedo, Capt. P. H., I: 15n
Bastia, IX: 244, 306–10, XI: 314
BATAAN, VIII: 36, 174, 238, 250, 292, 311, 412, XIV: 248, 384, 386
Bataan Peninsula, III: 150, 182, XIII: 11, 193, 209; map, III: 202; defense of, 198–204
Bataille, Capit. de Frég., XI: 286
Batan I., III: 161, 174
Batangas Bay, XIII: 11n, 13, 32n, 49–50, 140, 178, 189, 209–10
Batavia, III: 29, 53n, 157, 306, 340, 357, 364, 379, X: 287, 296, 302, XIII: 277
Batchelder, G. L., XIV: 184n
Batchelder, Col. M. J., VIII: 187n, 198
Batcheller, Lt. Cdr. J. H., X: 378
Bates, 1st Lt. C. C., XI: 176n–7n
Bates, Lt. Cdr. F. L., VII: 346, 388
Bates, Lt. Cdr. R. H., XIV: 375
Bates, Rear Adm. R. W., IV: x, 21n, 30n, V: x, 17n, VII: ix, 93n, 329n, 336, X: 28, XII: vii, 165, 198n, 199, 203n, 223n, 290n, 419, XIII: 155,

XIV: 57n, 155, 372; *Battle of Midway*, IV: 69n; *Battle for Leyte Gulf*, XII: vii, 157n
BATES, XI: 334, XIV: 28, 377, 392; sunk, 272
BATFISH, VIII: 367n, XIII: 279–80
Batjan I., VIII: 130, 231, XII: 29
Battalion Landing Team, defined, II: 36n
Battipaglia, IX: 254–6, 260, 278–81, 284–6
Battle, Capt. C. E., I: 110–11
Battle Ensign, defined, II: 71n
Battle Force, U. S., III: 28–9
Battle Line, described, XII: 240–41
BATTLER, IX: 250, 393, X: 40n, 278
Battleship Divisions, Two, VI: 282n, XII: 419; Four, XIII: 317; Five, I: 419; Six, VII: 339, VIII: 415, XIII: 318, XIV: 384; Seven, I: 419, VIII: 415, XII: 426, XIII: 317; Eight, XII: 427, XIII: 316; Nine, VIII: 415, XII: 427, XIV: 385
Battleship Squadron One, XIII: 39n
Bauer, Lt. Cdr. H. F., IV: 273, V: 120
Bauer, Lt. Col. H. W., IV: 274, V: 375
Bauer, Dr. K. J., XII: viii, XIII: x–xi, 158n, XIV: ix, xi
Bauer, Lt. L. H., IV: 271, V: 86
Baum, Lt. Cdr. J. R., XIII: 317
Baum, Cdr. R. J., XII: 426
Baumberger, Cdr. W. H., XIV: 384
Bauxite, I: 251, 253, 308, X: 188, 190
Bawean I., III: 335
Baxter, Lt. A. B., XIV: 377
Baxter, Lt. (jg) D. F., pic., VII: 319; mentioned, 330
Baxter, Lt. Cdr. J. A., XII: 314–16
Baxter, Dr. J. P., X: xiv; *Scientists Against Time*, I: 29n
BAXTER, XII: 419, XIII: 311, XIV: 380
BAYA, XIII: 285–7
Baybay, XII: 63, 373–4
Bayeux, XI: 184
BAYFIELD, XI: ix, 86, 93, 97, 102, 162, 268, 333–4, 341, XIV: 381
Baylis, Lt.(jg) J. S., VI: 61
Bayou Chico, I: 171n
Bays, Lt. Cdr. J. W., II: 37, IX: 389
Bayug, XII: 350, 364, XIII: 18
Beach, Lt. Cdr. E. L., XIV: 293n
Beach Battalions, IX: 349, XI: 241, 271
"Beach Jumpers," IX: 20n–21n, 172
Beach obstacles, Guam, VIII: 380; Normandy, XI: 47, 101, 114, 184–5; sketch,

140; Southern France, 240, 256, 262, 273

Beach parties, II: 28, 160*n*, VI: 418, VIII: 53, 70, IX: 107

Beaches, IX: 31*n*; No. Africa, II: 137; Eniwetok, VII: 295; Sicily, IX: 23-4, 30-31, 72, 98, 106, 152-6; Salerno, 255; Anzio, 339-40; Normandy, XI: 96-7, 111-14; So. France, 259; Tinian, VIII: 354-5; Guam, 375; Leyte, XII: 130-31, 140-41; Lingayen, XIII: 126-7, 130, 141-2; Mindoro, 26

Beaching craft, VIII: 54-6, XI: 52-7, 53*n*, 248-9

Beachmaster, IX: 83, 119

Beachy Head, XII: 241

Beacon Hill, I: 369

BEAGLE, VIII: 420

BEAGLE, HMS, XI: 174

Beakley, Lt. Cdr. W. M., IV: 271, 289, V: 87

BEALE, VI: 382, 390-91, 436, 444, VIII: 66, 127, XII: 199, 218, 421, XIV: 184, 381

BEAR, I: 60, 61-2*n*

Beard, Capt. J. D., XII: 84, 307, 423, XIII: 308

Beardall, Capt. J. R., pic., I: 70

BÉARN, I: 30-31

Beary, Vice Adm. D. B., biog., X: 47*n*, XIV: 158*n*; pic., XIV: 182; mentioned, I: 110-11, IV: xi, V: xi, VI: xii, X: 47-9, XIV: 7-8, 22, 57, 100, 109, 158-60, 168-9, 299, 306-8, 372, 386

Beatty, Capt. F. A., VI: 308

BEATTY, I: 420, II: 40, 146, 285, IX: 113, 141, 146, 389, X: 261; sunk, IX: 313*n*, X: 263

BEAUFORT, IX: 393, 396, XI: 343

Beaufort, Brunei Bay, XIII: 266

Beaufort, N. Car., I: 279

BEAUMARIS, XI: 333

Beaumont, I: 279

Beauregard, Rear Adm. A. T., I: 389

BEAVER, I: 421

BEBAS, XIV: 379

Bechtel, Maj. P. S., V: 375

Beck, Cdr. E. F., XIV: 388

Beck, Cdr. E. L., IV: 19, 91, 271, V: 86, VI: 229, 242

Beck, Lt. Cdr. H. B., XIII: 300*n*

Beck, Lt. (jg) J. R., XII: 422

Beck, Cdr. P. G., XII: 428

Becker, Cdr. A. L., XIII: 287, 320

Becker, Lt. Cdr. C. W., XIV: 247, 372

Beckman, Lt. (jg) J. C., XII: 422

Becton, Cdr. F. J., XII: 334, XIII: 304, XIV: 235-6, 372

BECUNA, XII: 406, XIII: 38*n*

Bedell, Sgt. Henry, III: 232

BEDFORD v., XIII: 307, 386

Bedilion, Cdr. R. W., IV: 174

BEDLOE, X: 327*n*

Beebe, Cdr. M. U., VII: 337, XIV: 382

Beecham, Lt.(jg) R. R., III: 103

Beecher, Capt. W. G., XIV: 386

Beer, Cdr. R. O., XI: 144-5, 336

Bégouën-Demeaux, Capit. de Corv., II: 99, 162

BEGUM, X: 40*n*, 302

Behner, Cdr. H. C., XIV: 386

Behrens, Capt. B. S., VI: 283

Behrens, Capt. W. W., VIII: 415, XII: 98-9, 102, 424

Beibel, Lt. L. F., XIV: 381

Beightler, Cdr. C. S., VII: 347, VIII: 407, XIV: 379

Beightler, Maj. Gen. R. S., VI: 289*n*, 364, 428-30, XIII: 127, 135, 310

Beisang, Lt. R. E., VI: 170

Belben, Capt. G. D., IX: 396

Belden, Jack, IX: 98-9, 106-7

Belem, I: 379, X: 218

BELFAST, X: 237-43

Belfast, Ireland, II: 193, XI: 68, 71, 77-8, 131

Belgian Airman, X: 343

BELKNAP, I: 419, X: 77, 125, 161-2, 375, 378, XII: 422, XIII: 148-9, 304, 326

Bell, Cdr. D. B., XIII: 284, XIV: 293*n*

Bell, Don, XIII: 299

Bell, Lt. Cdr. F. J., IV: 271, V: 86, 180*n*

Bell, Capt. G. A., V: 374

Bell, Cdr. H. B., I: 418, VIII: 413

Bell, Ens. J. J., II: 58, 135*n*, 140, 144-6

Bell, Brig. Gen. M. B., XII: 52-3

Bell, Lt. W. T., XIV: 376

BELL, VII: 349, VIII: 413, XII: 425, XIII: 278-9, 305

Bellairs, Vice Adm. R. M., I: xvi, 45, IX: xv, 315*n*, 380*n*, X: x, xiv, XI: x

BELLATRIX, IV: 266, 272, V: 124-5, 179-80, VII: 337, VIII: 408, IX: 389

BELLE GROVE, VII: 127, 129*n*, 135, 336, 344, VIII: 361, 404, 408, XII: 419, XIII: 309

Belle Isle, Fr., XI: 328

Belle Isle, Strait of, I: 330

BELLEAU WOOD, VII: xxvii, 85, 92, 95, 117, 190–91, 208, 257, 339, 348, 352, VIII: 36, 154*n*, 174, 238, 250, 262, 292, 295, 311–12, 412, XII: 90, 106, 318, 326, 341–2, 346, 360, 428, XIII: 54, XIV: 21, 208, 305, 382, 386
Bellinger, Vice Adm. P. N. L., biog., X: 42*n;* pic., 33; mentioned, I: 251, III: 101, 120, 128, IV: 80, X: 42, 233
Bellinger, Lt. Cdr. W. C. P., XI: 343
Bellingham, I: 191*n*, 365
Bellis, Lt. Cdr. L. J., X: 375
BELLONA, XI: 167–8, 336
Bellows Field, III: 97, 124
BELVOIR, IX: 393, XI: 343
Ben and Josephine, I: 288
Ben F. Dixon, X: 382
Ben Grierson, XIII: 313
Ben H. Miller, X: 381
BEN MY CHREE, XI: 127, 335
Bena Bena, VI: 255, 258, 272
BENALIA, VI: 134, XIII: 306
Bénat, Cap, France, X: 285
Bence, Lt. Cdr. R. L., VII: 341
Bengasi, II: 244, IX: 151
Bengston, Lt. Cdr. R. C., VIII: 406
BENHAM (1914), VI: 211*n*
BENHAM (1939), I: 15*n*, III: 211*n*, 393, IV: 91, 113*n*, 134, 153*n*, 155–6, 271, V: 28*n*, 86, 205, 226, 233, 271, 275–7; sunk, 280–81
BENHAM (1943), VIII: 410, XII: 426, XIII: 316, XIV: 386
Beni Saf, II: 50*n*, 273
Benjamin Franklin, III: 317, 319
Benjamin Harrison, I: 180, 190, 191*n*
Benjamin Huntington, X: 382
Benjes, Lt. A. C., VIII: 412
Benline, Cdr. A. J., XIV: 381
Benn, Maj. Wm., VI: 57
Bennehoff, Capt. O. R., II: 192, 209–10
Bennett, Lt., XI: 335
Bennett, Rear Adm. A. C., II: 16, 225–6, 230, 250–51, 254, XI: 52
Bennett, Cdr. C. H., I: 420
Bennett, Cdr. C. L., VII: 351, XIII: 319, XIV: 291
Bennett, Lt.(jg) H. L., XIII: 41*n*
Bennett, Capt. T. E., IX: 108*n*
Bennett, Lt. Cdr. T. M., XII: 420
Bennett, Cdr. W. C., XII: 428
BENNETT, VI: 297, 360, 415, VIII: 409, 415, XIV: 197, 381, 390
"Bennett's Blazers," T.O., XIII: 319

BENNINGTON (1891), III: 224, VIII: 150
BENNINGTON (1944), XIV: 21, 205, 301, 305, 382, 386
Bennington, XIII: 307
Bennion, Capt. M. S., III: 106–7
BENNION, VIII: 408, XII: 143, 199, 221, 344, 419, XIII: 102, 116, 304, XIV: 18, 227, 373
Benson, Capt. F. W., IV: 273, VI: 144, XII: 417
Benson, Capt. H. H. J., pic., I: 170
Benson, Lt. L. G., VIII: 404, XII: 417, XIII: 307, XIV: 374
Benson, Lt. Cdr. R. H., XII: 416
Benson, Lt. Cdr. R. S., IV: 210–11
Benson, Capt. W. H., XIV: 378
Benson, Cdr. W. L., XI: 334, 342
BENSON, I: 76, 123, 418–20, IX: 385, 391, X: 253, 259–60, 269, 381, XI: 312, 342; class, I: 235, X: 33
BENTINCK, X: 148*n*
Bentley, Lt. Cdr. J. C., VII: 350, XII: 425
Bentley, Lt. W. F., XIV: 380
Bentsen, Hans, X: 382
Beppu Bay, XII: 168
Berdine, Capt. H. S., X: 266
Berg, Lt. H. N., XII: 423
BERGALL, XII: 406, XIII: 284–5
Bergamini, Adm., IX: 242–3, 246
Bergen, Norway, X: 101
Bergen, H. C., X: 382
Berger, Cdr. H. E., VII: 418
Berger, Col. S. S., XII: 33*n*, 39–40
Bergin, Cdr. C. K., XII: 211*n*, 216, 418, XIII: 316, XIV: 382
Bergin, Ens. E. R., VI: 61
Bergquist, Lt. L. C., VII: 310
BERING STRAIT, XIV: 381
Berish, Yeoman R. M., III: xii
Berkey, Rear Adm. R. S., biog., XII: 21*n;* pic., VIII: 49; mentioned, XIII: 108–9; C.O. SANTE FE, VI: 344, VII: 334, 337–8; C. Gloucester, VI: 382; Admiralties, 435–6; New Guinea, VIII: 47, 81, 91, 96–7, 106, 122, 136, 406; Morotai, XII: 21–2; Leyte, 131–2, 421; Surigao Strait, 199–201, 220, 223, 227, 236; Mindoro, XIII: 19, 24–5, 27, 31; Lingayen, 12, 115–18, 133–4, 145, 155, 278, 304; lesser Philippine opns., 177, 188, 199–201, 216–17, 223–6, 234, 322–3; Borneo, 260–1, 264, 272

Berlin, Ens. Theodore, VI: 329
Berlin, Germany, XIV: 324, 326, 329
Bermingham, Lt. Cdr. J. M., III: 196, 272*n*, 319
Bermuda, I: 16, 34*n*, 82–3, 240, 244, 248, II: 43–4, 130, 271*n*-3*n*, X: 28, 49–50, 122, 293, 350; pic., I: 36
BERMUDA, II: 189, 199
BERNADOU, I: 76, 121, 214, 418, II: 40, 138–48, 154, 207, 272*n*, 285, 286*n*, IX: 388, 391, X: 381; at Safi, chart, II: 141; pics., II: 148–9
Bernardelli, Kaptlt., X: 360
Berndtson, Lt. A. H., VI: 210
Berner, Cdr. G. C., XIII: 323
Berner, Cdr. G. R., XIII: 307
Berner, Lt. Cdr. M., XIV: 377
Bernhard, Rear Adm. A. D., I: 419, VII: 306
BERRIEN, XIV: 381
Berry, Lt. Cdr. D. R., XIV: 383
Berry, Capt. R. W., XII: 419, XII: 310
Bertholf, Cdr. C. M., XII: 427, XIII: 318, XIV: 279–80, 373
Besson, Cdr. J. H., VII: 410, XIII: 311
Best, Lt. R. H., III: 392, IV: 91, 124–6
BESUGO, X: 303, XII: 168, 429, XIII: 280–81, 285–6, 320
BETELGEUSE, IV: 273, V: 75, 229, 232, IX: 388, XI: 341, XIV: 379
Bethlehem-Fairfield Yards, I: 294
Béthouart, Gen. Emile, II: 65–71, 86–7, 110, 116
Betio I. *See* Tarawa
Betz, Cpl. F. E., VI: 404–5
Beuzeville, XI: 108
BEVERLEY, I: 335
Bewick, Cdr. J. V., XIV: 374
Bey, Ktradm, Erich, X: 238–43
Beyer, Lt. Cdr. A. F., VII: 341, XII: 263, 421
Beyerly, Cdr. I. F., XIII: 292
Bezemer, K. W. L., III: xiii
Bezzant, Canon J. T., XIV: 213
Biak I., VIII: 37, 50, 89–91, 95–7, 107–8, 141, XIII: 97; action off, VIII: 127–30, and chart, 128; map, 105; air raids on (U.S.), 96–7, 106–7; air raids, (Jap.), 113–14, 119, 132; base, XII: 22, 83, 238, 368
Biak, opn., landing, VIII: 103–16, 220, XII: 3; chart, VIII: 109; Jap., reinf., 118–32; T.O., 403–6; discussion, 145, 316

BIBB, I: 334–5, 343, 421, XIV: 376*n*
Bibilo Hill, VI: 204–6
BICESTER, XI: 343
Bicol Peninsula, XII: 7, 57; XIII: 11*n*, 209
BIDDLE, VII: 236, X: 187
BIDEFORD, X: 95
Bidwell, I: 134
Biebush, Lt. Col. F. C., V: 129; pic., 130
Bieri, Rear Adm. B. H., II: 16, 175*n*, 182, 252, VI: 9
Biesemeier, Rear Adm. Harold, II: 38, 81, IX: 137*n*, 389, XI: 335
"Big Blue Blanket," XIII: 55–7, 88, 107
BIG DRUM Opn., XI: 75
BIG HORN, I: 284–5
Bigart, Homer, XIV: 273
Bigej Islet, VII: 253, 276–7
Bigelow, Lt.(jg) B., X: 382
Biggerstaff, Lt. Cdr. W. E., XIV: 379
Biggs, Capt. B. B., pic., VIII: frontis; mentioned, 345
Bikini Atoll, VII: 79, 313*n*
Biles, Lt. R. C., VII: 418
Bilibid prison, XIII: 196
Bill, Lt. Cdr. D. S., XIII: 319, XIV: 381
BILLFISH, VI: 79–84
Billings, Lt. (jg) R. M., I: 361–3
Billingsley, Boats. Mate, III: 104
Billingsley, Cdr. E. B., XI: 145, 203, 336
BILOXI, VI: 341, VII: 220, 346, 352, VIII: 37, 413, XII: 90, 318, 345, 428, XIII: 54, 318, XIV: 21, 34, 132–3, 240, 373
Binalbagan, XIII: 25
Binford, Cdr. T. H., III: 160, 322–4, 328–9, 333, 343, 351–5, 375, XIV: 382
Binmaley, Luzon, XIII: 135
Birch Coulie, XIII: 307
BIRMINGHAM (1908), V: 325*n*, VII: 101*n*, XIV: 312*n*
BIRMINGHAM (1943), VI: 341, 344, VIII: 197, 335, 409, 414, IX: 28, 74, 88–9, 125*n*, 174–6, 386, XI: 63*n*, XII: 90, 100, 103, 179–82, 427, XIV: 148, 267, 334*n*, 372, 391; pic., IX: 27
Birnbaum, Lt. Cdr. J., VIII: 411
Biros, Lt. Cdr. E. W., VIII: 413
BISBEE, XII: 417
Biscari, IX: 58, 105*n*, 126, 129, 144–6

Biscay, Bay of, Offensive, X: 86–106; chart, 97
BISCAYNE, I: 420, II: 245, IX: 65–6, 74, 83, 89–90, 124, 272–3, 276, 298*n*, 333–4, 341, 359, 386, 393, 395, XI: 265, 340, XIV: 375; pic., IX: 203
Bisceglia, Maj. V. R., XIII: 294
Bishop, Lt. Cdr. C. U., XI: 299*n*
Bishop, Lt. Cdr. N. C., XIV: 387
BISHOPDALE, XII: 423, XIII: 308
BISMARCK, I: 62–4, 69, V: 100*n*, 279*n*, X: 55
Bismarck Archipelago, III: 260, 265, V: 7; chart, VI: 371; Barrier, ix–x, 6, VII: 64, 69–70, 81–4, 222
Bismarck Sea, III: 387, IV: 7; Battle of, VI: 54–65; T.O., 56; chart, 57; pics., 60–61; casualties, 62
BISMARCK SEA, XIII: 304, XIV: 389; sunk, 54–5
Bissell, Lt. Cdr. Howard, XIII: 319
Bisset, Rear Adm. A. W. la T., IX: 393
BITER, II: 223, X: 39, 77–9, 176
Bither, Sgt., III: 397
Bitler, Cdr. W. S., VII: 22*n*, 27
BITTERN, III: 159, 172
Bixby, Cdr. H. L., XII: 423
Bizerta, II: 8–9, 183, 241, 260, 265–6, 274, IX: 23, 31–3, 65–6, 72, 79, 188, 217–18, 235–6, 248, 251–2, 299, 303, X: 251, XI: 246; Lake of, pic., IX: 27
Bjarnason, Cdr. P. H., XIV: 116, 376
Bjork, Maj. D. L., VII: 277
Black, Lt. Cdr. J. D., VII: 339
Black, Lt. K. L., XIII: 309
BLACK, VII: 348, VIII: 405, 419, XII: 418, XIV: 210, 384
Black Cat. *See* Air Search and Reconnaissance
Black Dragon Society, III: 10
BLACK HAWK, III: 154, 160, 272, 320, 332, VII: 334
Black Point, X: 356
BLACK PRINCE, XI: 86, 96, 104–6, 334, XIV: 105, 388
Blackburn, Lt. Cdr. J. T., II: 40, VI: 331–2
Blackburn, Capt. P. P., VII: 341, 347
Blackett, Prof. P. M. S., I: 220–21
Blackett Strait, VI: 119, 209–11, 215, 223, 364; mine field, 111–16; mine field chart 113
BLACKFIN, XIII: 281–4, 320

BLACKFISH, II: 43*n*, VI: 71, 74, VIII: 30, XII: 406, 429
BLACKFLY, X: 372
Blackledge, Capt. A. D., VII: 345
BLACKMORE, IX: 272, 393, XI: 343
Blackowitz, Gen. Obst. J., XI: 239
BLACKPOOL, XI: 337
Blackwell, Lt. Cdr. C. L., II: 37
BLACKWOOD, X: 324
Blair, Lt. G. M., pic., VII: 319; mentioned, VII: 330
Blair, Capt. L. N., VIII: 22
Blair, Lt. W. K., VIII: 273
Blair, Cdr. W. S., XI: 335
BLAIRMORE, XI: 335
"Blair's Blasters," VIII: 22–3
Blake, Adm. Sir Geoffrey, I: 212*n*
Blakely, Cdr. E. N., VIII: 23, XII: 406, 429
BLAKELEY, I: 84, 145*n*, XI: 237*n*
Blakeslee, Cdr. H. W., XIV: 376
Blakeslee, Cdr. V. F., XI: 62
Blakey, Maj. G. A., IV: 93, 137*n*, 141, 145*n*
Blakley, Lt. J. H., XIII: 30
Blamey, Gen. Sir Thomas, VI: 34, 256, VIII: 46–7, XIV: 366
Blanchard, Lt. F. M., XIII: 305*n*, XIV: 373
Blanchard, Cdr. J. W., VIII: 278–80, 415
Blanchard, Lt. Cdr. Theodore, VII: 261*n*, 275*n*, 292, 302, 344, VIII: 410
Blanche, Lt. Cdr. J. B., I: 419, XII: 419
BLANCHE, VI: 293*n*
Blanche Harbor, Treasury Is., VI: 293–5
Bland, Lt. Cdr. J. T., XIII: 309, XIV: 225, 379
Blandy, Rear Adm. W. H. P., biog., XIV: 25*n*–6*n*; pic., 46; Marianas, VIII: 160, 171–2, 410; Peleliu, XII: 34, 44; Ulithi, 47; Iwo, XIV: 7, 25–7, 30–2; Okinawa, 86–8, 101, 108–10, 118–19, 130, 140*n*, 218–20, 371, 373
BLANKNEY, IX: 154, 277, 393, X: 256, 372
Bledsoe, Capt. A. M., XII: 419, XIII: 304
Blee, Lt. Cdr. J. B., XIII: 307
Blehaut, Rear Adm. Louis, II: 240*n*
Blenheim, I: 394–5
Blenman, Lt. Cdr. William, XI: 105, 334
BLENNY, XIII: 285, 288

BLESSMAN, XI: 336, XIII: 304, XIV: 28, 31, 389
Blewitt, Lt. E. J., XIII: 308
Blick, Capt. R. E., XII: 420
Blimps, I: 241n, 250-51, II: 43, X: 182, 187-90, 194, 223-4; Squadron Thirty, X: 189; Forty-one, 223n; Forty-two, 223n; K-34, 187; K-68, 197n, K-74, 125, 194; K-84, 223; K-106, 224n; K-109, XI: 313; K-114, X: 224n; pic., I: 259
Blinn, Cdr. W. C., III: 158, 333, 372-4
Bliss, Cdr. J. B., VII: 341, XIV: 380
Blitch, Lt. Cdr. J. D., VIII: 413, XII: 424
Bloch, Adm. C. C., III: 42, 97, 134, 139, 227-8, 246n
Block, Cdr. A. F., IX: 386
Block, Lt. Col. Edward, VIII: 73
BLOCK ISLAND, I: 419, X: 40, 52, 157, 162, 176, 188, 279-81, 284-7, 371-2, 377; sunk, 289-90
Blockade runners, I: 84, 383-5, 389-90, 398-9, VI: 16, X: 213, 226-8; in Phil. Is., III: 202-3
Blomfield, Lt. A. C., XI: 314-15
Blood, R. S., X: 382
Blood plasma, I: 93
Bloody Marsh, X: 183
Bloody Ridge, Battle of, V: 125-30; map, 127; pics., 131
Blouin, Cdr. F. J., VII: 349, VIII: 415, XIII: 309, 314
Blount, Lt. Cdr. C. E., XII: 416
BLOWER, XIII: 284, 288
BLUE (1937), III: 97, 115, 213n, 243n, IV: 93, 272, V: 29-30, 34-5, 39, 52n, 55; sunk, 81
BLUE (1944), XIII: 81, 316, XIV: 383
Blue Goose, I: 272
BLUE RIDGE, VIII: 63, 135, XII: 131, 156, 314, 415, XIII: 6, 146, 215, 308, 321
BLUEBACK, XIII: 319
BLUEBELL, XI: 337; sunk, X: 312
BLUEBIRD, I: 422
BLUECHER, I: 4n
Bluefield V., XII: 83, 423, XIII: 308
BLUEFISH, VI: 80, VIII: 416, XIII: 288, XIV: 266
BLUEGILL, VI: 74-5, VIII: 17n, 23, XII: 406, 429, XIII: 285-7, 320
"Bluegill Island," XIII: 287
"Bluies," I: 62n; chart, 162
Blumentritt, Gen., XI: 169

Blundon, Cdr. J. P., V: 77
BLYSKAWICA, I: 319
BOADICEA, XI: 337
Boak, Commo. J. E., XII: 115n
BOARFISH, XIII: 281-2, 320
BOBOLINK, III: 104, 112, V: 255-6, 292, 309
Boca Chica, X: 194
Bock, Cdr. B. N., VI: 121, XIV: 378
Bockius, Capt. R. W., XII: 428, XIII: 319
Boddy, Lt. Cdr. C. A., XIII: 318, XIV: 387
Bode, Capt. H. D., III: 110, IV: 19, 67, 272, V: 29-32, 39, 54
Bodell, Lt. S. C., XI: 86n
Bodö, X: 232
Boelhauf, Lt. E. E., XIV: 144
Boettcher, Lt. Cdr. R. R., XIV: 381
Bogan, Rear Adm. G. F., pic., XII: 183; Saipan, VIII: 326, 409; Formosa battle, XII: 12, 86, 90, 93; Luzon strikes, 106, 342, 347-9, 356-8, XIII: 54, 316; Leyte, XII: 108, 133, 150, 339-40, 345-6, 425; Leyte Gulf battle, 175-7, 184, 193-5, 291, 310, 318-20, 329-30; Dec. 1944 typhoon, XIII: 66; Formosa strikes, 87-8, 91, 180-2; South China Sea raid, 165-8; Japan strikes, XIV: 310; Okinawa, 96, 383, 386
"Bogey" defined, VII: xxxvn
Boggs, Maj. C. W., *Marine Aviation in the Philippines*, XIII: xi
BOGGS, IV: 276n
Bogon Islet, VII: 291
BOGUE, X: 20, 40, 51n, 77, 80-81, 109-21, 159, 168-71, 222, 281, 284, 288-9, 298-9, 317n, 325-8, 350-51, 370-73, 375-6; pic., 329; class, 42
Bohn, William, I: 357n
Bohol I., XII: 149, XIII: 18; landing, 217, 228-9, 233, 237-8
Boileau, Cdr. A. R., II: 40
Boisdore, Lt. S. T., XIV: 386
BOISE, III: 31n, 143n, 159, 193, 271, 284, V: 150, 153-8, 162-70, VIII: 47, 97, 108, 123, 126-7, 406, IX: 28, 100-104, 110-18, 125n, 198n, 207, 217, 235-6, 251, 266n, 287, 292-6, 303, 388, 391, XII: 135, 199, 227, 343, 421, XIII: 39, 115-18, 153, 184, 187, 200, 223-5, 234, 261, 264, 278, 303, 322-3; pic., IX: 107
Boisson, Gov. Pierre, II: 5, 8, 240
Boit, Lt. Cdr. J. M., II: 22

Bokuyo M., VIII: 175
Bolger, Capt. J. F., XII: 425
Bolinao, Cape, XIII: 99, 104, 107, 118, 134, 172
BOLIVAR, VII: 346, VIII: 407, 420, XII: 419, XIII: 310
Bolton Castle, I: 191n
"Bombardon" breakwater, XI: 166
Bombay, India, I: 112
Bombing Squadrons, One, VIII: 412; Two, IV: 19, VIII: 412; Three, III: 392, IV: 90, 120n, 270, V: 86, XIII: 315; Four, 317; Five, IV: 19, 90n, VII: 338, 348, XIV: 383; Six, III: 392, IV: 91, 271, V: 86, 375, VII: 339, 349, XIV: 384; Seven, XII: 425, XIII: 316; Eight, IV: 91, V: 205, VIII: 413, XII: 425; Nine, VI: 331, VII: 339, 349, XIV: 385; Ten, V: 204, 233, 268, VII: 324, 348, VIII: 414, XIV: 385; Eleven, XII: 424, XIII: 316; Twelve, VII: 340, 350, XIV: 383; Thirteen, XII: 427; Fourteen, VIII: 413, XII: 424; Fifteen, VIII: 414, XII: 426; Sixteen, VII: 338, VIII: 414; Seventeen, VI: 331, VII: 339, 349, XIV: 382; Eighteen, XII: 425; Nineteen, 426; Twenty, 427, XIII: 316; Eighty, 317; Eighty-one, XII: 349n, XIII: 315; Eighty-two, XIV: 382; Eighty-three, 383; Eighty-four, 384; Eighty-six, 382; Eighty-eight, 385n; One hundred One, VIII: 285n, 415; One hundred Three, X: 100–103, XI: 72, 371; One hundred Five, X: 102, XI: 72; One hundred Six, VIII: 406, 415n; One hundred Seven, X: 212, 216, 220, 224, 227n, 329n, 371–3; One hundred Eight, VII: 340, 350; One hundred Nine, 350, VIII: 230, 354; One hundred Ten, X: 103, 371, XI: 72; One hundred Eleven, X: 102; One Twenty-five, I: 415; One Twenty-seven, X: 209, 212, 219, 371–2; One Twenty-eight, 371; One Twenty-nine, 209, 212, 220, 371; One Thirty, 212, 371; One Thirty-five, VII: 333; One Thirty-Six, 333; One Thirty-seven, 340, 350; One Forty-two, 340, 350; One Forty-three, X: 212; One Forty-five, 212; Two hundred Three, 212
Bombing-Fighting Squadron, Six, XIV: 384; Nine, 385; Ten, 385;

Twelve, 383; Eighty-three, 383; Eighty-six, 382; Eighty-eight, 385n
Bon, Cape, II: 260, IX: 13, 59, 65, 152
BONAISE, II: 252
Bond, Capt. C. A., XIV: 386
Bond, Lt. H. W., VIII: 404
Bône, II: 17, 183, 221, 241–3, 252–4, 262–3, 264n, 266, IX: 242–3, 253; landing, II: 221
BONEFISH, VI: 79–80, VIII: 217–18; lost, XIV: 292
Bonesteel, Maj. Gen. C. H., I: 77
Bonham-Carter, Rear Adm. S. S., I: 168
BONHAM, IV: 173
Bonin, Col. B. von, IX: 173, 202, 218
Bonin, Lt. Cdr. R. A., VIII: 24
Bonin Is., description and history, XIV: 3–6; in strategy, VII: 80, VIII: 157, XII: 5, XIII: 4–5, 159; carrier strikes on, VIII: 238–9, 311–13, 367, XII: 13
Bonis Airfield, VI: 281, 291, 363–4
BONITA, I: 421
Bontier, Lt. Cdr. A. L., XII: 27
Bonvillian, Lt. Cdr. W. D., XIV: 381
Boomer, Sqd. Ldr. K. A., VII: 333
Boone, Lt. C. J., XIV: 223
Boone, Rear Adm. W. F., XI: x, XIV: 385
BOOTES, VIII: 405, XIII: 308
Booth, Lt. Cdr. C. T., II: 39
Bora Bora, III: 258, 265, IV: 251, 263n, VII: 102
Bordeaux, X: 85, 264, 325, XI: 226, 240, 309–10
Bordeaux M., III: 263
Borden, Lt. A. G., X: 379
Borden, Lt. J. J., XIV: 386
BOREAS, VII: 110, VIII: 420
BORIE (1920), I: 15n, 151, 387, 390n, X: 122–4, 159, 200n, 211, 376; sunk, 163–7; pic., 169
BORIE (1944), XIV: 332, 384
Borinquen Field, P. R., I: 110
Bork, Oblt. Helmut, X: 174
Born, Brig. Gen. C. F., I: 148
Borneo, description, XIII: 255–6; map, 260; Japanese invasion, III: 130, 191, 281–91, 294–5; Allied invasion, XIII: 214, 217, 256–76
Borokoe, VIII: 104, 133
Borpop, VI: 422
Borst, Lt. Cdr. L. W., XIV: 386
Borum, Lt. (jg) J. R., I: 397–8

BORUM, XI: 302, 329, 336
Bosnik, VIII: 103–24
Bostock, Air V. Marshal W. D., VI: 64, XIII: 265, 274
BOSTON (1887), II: 286
BOSTON (1943), VII: 221, 350, VIII: 413, XII: 90, 99, 424, 425, XIII: 165, 316, XIV: 21, 313
BOSTON, HMS, IX: 42, XI: 337
Boston, I: 323
Boston, Mass., I: 223, 257, 262, 318–19; Navy Yard, 98, VI: 190n
BOSTWICK, X: 279, 344, 373, 377
Bottom, Capt. J. T., VII: 339, 350, VIII: 405, 420
Botts, Seaman, V: 99
Bou Guedra, II: 150
Bouc, Port de, XI: 285–7, 291
Boucher, Commo. Maitland, X: 237, 243–4
Boud, Lt. Cdr. H. W., VIII: 408
BOUGAINVILLE, XIV: 386
Bougainville I., history and description, V: 4, 7, VI: 228, 279–81; airfields, 90, 99; map, 285; sketch, 298–9; pic., 388; in Jap. strategy, VII: 78, VIII: 12, 66; base, VII: 319, XIII: 94–6
"Bougainville Navy," VI: 364–5, 415, 428, 431
Bougainville Operation. *See* Cape Torokina Operation
Bougie, II: 220–1, 243, 252
Bougnon, Baie de, XI: 258, 264
BOULDER V., XII: 79, 429
Boulogne, XI: 75, 191, 218n
BOULONNAIS, II: 99; sunk, 106, 113
Boulware, Cdr. J. W., VIII: 408, XII: 199, 221, 419
BOUNTIFUL, VIII: 200, 389, 411, XII: 307, XIV: 161, 386
Bourke, Brig. Gen. T. E., VII: 167, XII: 154
Bouscat, Gen. de Div., XI: 281
Boutell, Lt. W. H., XIII: 306, 324
Bouvet, Lt. Col., XI: 253–4, 338
BOUTWELL, I: 138
Boutwood, Capt. J. W., IX: 393
Bouzarea, IX: 15–16, XI: 233
BOWDITCH, VIII: 420, XII: 51, XIV: 119, 127, 386
Bowen, Lt. Cdr. H. G., VIII: 410
Bowen, Col. J. W., IX: 98
Bower, 1st Lt. W. M., III: 392
Bowers, Lt. Cdr. J. M., XIV: 293n

Bowers, Cdr. J. T., IV: 174, VII: 338, 344, VIII: 405
BOWERS, VI: 431n, XII: 423, XIV: 238, 373, 391
Bowes, Lt. Cdr. C. A., XIV: 377
BOWFIN, V: 79–85, XIII: 285, XIV: 292n, 296; pic., XIII: 277
Bowles, Dr. E. L., I: 237n, 243n, X: 26–7
Bowley, Cdr. C. M., XIII: 318, 372
Bowling, Cdr. J. F., X: 332–4, 350, 376
Bowling, Capt. S. S., VIII: 47, 57, XII: 26–8, 203–4, XII: 422, XIII: 247, 324
Bowman, Capt. M. C., IV: 255
Bowman, Capt. R. L., VII: 337, 344, VIII: 405
BOXER, II: 268n, IX: 392, 396
Boyce, Lt. Cdr. T. E., I: 418
Boyd, Chief Torp'man, V: 161, 167
Boyd, Cdr. A. M., X: 379, XI: 341
Boyd, Capt. C. A., VI: 176
Boyd, Lt. Cdr. G. G., XIV: 387
Boyd, Lt. Cdr. G. M., XIV: 374
BOYD, VII: 198, 339, VIII: 239, 413, XII: 425, XIII: 317, XIV: 373
Boyer, Lt. Cdr. R. B., V: 205, 233
Boyington, Maj. Gregory, VI: 396–8
Boykin, Lt. L. M., XIII: 317
Boyle, Cdr. F. D., XIII: 286
BOYLE, II: 38, 54n, 162, 285, IX: 376, 389, XI: 342
Boyum, Lt. J. H., VIII: 413
Bozzoni, Maj. Gen., IX: 210n
Braccetto Pt., IX: 127, 138
Bracht, Lt. Cdr. W. G. von, X: 100
Brackett, Capt. E. E., V: 375
Bradbury, Cdr. H. G., I: 111, 327–8
Bradbury, Cdr. H. W., VI: 297
Braddy, Cdr. R. E., II: 40, 146n, XIII: 316
Bradford, Lt.(jg) G., I: 390
BRADFORD, VII: 144, 326–8, 339, 349, VIII: 413, XIV: 373
Bradley, Maj. Gen. J. L., XII: 419, XIV: 380
Bradley, Maj. Gen. Omar N., II: 260, IX: 32, 65–7, 131, 140–47, 388, XI: 29–30, 37, 69–70, 74, 95, 126, 141, 150–52, 162, 165, 168, 178, 190, 195–8, 216, 295–8, 301, 317, 324, 333; *A Soldier's Story*, xiv
Bradley, Cdr. R. R., XIV: 373
Brady, Capt. J. H., VIII: 408, XII: 418, XIII: 311

Brady, Cdr. P. H., VII: 344, VIII: 223, 418, XII: 421, 429, XIII: 90n, 316, 319
Bragelongue, Cap. de Corv. de, II: 99
Bragg, Lt. H. K., VII: 347
Brainard, Vice Adm. R. M., I: 217, 248, 304–6, 319
Braine, Capt. C. E., I: 419, X: 208
BRAINE, VI: 279, 360–61, 415, VIII: 182, 362n, 409, 414, XII: 418, XIII: 116, 309, 324, XIV: 259–60, 392
Braisted, Capt. F. A., I: 76
BRAKE, sunk, X: 278
Bramston-Cook, Capt. H. E., XIII: 142n, 143
Branco Pt., IX: 127
Brand, Lt. Cdr. S. A., XIV: 377
Brandy, Cdr. J. I., XII: 422
Brannon, Maj. D. D., V: 375
Branson, Cdr. G. C. F., VI: 34n, 51–2, 126
BRANT, IX: 388, XI: 337
Brantingham, Lt. H. J., VI: 210
Brantley, Lt. D. L., XIV: 376
Brantly, Capt. N. D., VI: 382, 384, VIII: 404, XII: 416
Braswell, Chief Radioman W. A., I: 214
Braught, Lt. Cdr. C. F., XIV: 381
Braun, Capt. B. L., VII: 344, VIII: 405, 411, XIV: 382
Braun, Cdr. W. B., XIV: 382
BRAVE, XI: 341
Bray, Lt.(jg) A. F., X: 207n
Brazil, U-boats off, I: 315, 380–81, 385–9, X: 209–23, 295; declares war, I: 376, 381; airfield const'n., 379; chart, X: 217; Air Force, I: 246n, 382–3, X: 209, 214, 219, 371; Navy, I: 376–91, X: 209, 214–15
Brazil M., IV: 212
BRAZOS, IV: 174, VII: 334, XIV: 387
BREAM, XII: 169n, 408, 429, XIII: 286, 320
Breckenridge, R. G., II: 106n
BRECON, IX: 276, 393, 396, XI: 343
BREEMAN, X: 279–81, 377
BREESE, III: 97, 104, 213n, IV: 276n, VI: 112–14, 297, 308, XII: 421, XIII: 109, 113, 306, XIV: 377
Bremen, X: 341, XI: 326–7
Bremer, Lt. Cdr. T. G., X: 381
Bremerhaven, XI: 326–8
Bremerton Navy Yard, III: 145, 260, V: 312
Brenkman, Lt. R. E., XIV: 377

Brennan, Lt. Cdr. J. E., XII: 422, XIII: 109, 306
Brennan, Cdr. Leo, IX: 385
BRENNAN, X: 190
Brereton, Lt. Gen. L. H., III: 156, 173, 176, 189, 271, 336
Brereton, Capt. W. H., XIV: 37, 380
Bresnan, Lt. Cdr. J. A., IX: 387
BRESSAY, XI: 336
Brest, I: 22–3, 81, 85–6, X: 318, 323–5, XI: 46, 107–8, 175, 218, 231, 297, 301–2
BRESTOIS, II: 99, 248; sunk, 106–7
BRETON, VIII: 230, 411, XIV: 374
Brett, Lt. Gen. G. H., III: 271, 277, 336, IV: 20, 267, 274n, X: 200, 203–4
Brett, Lt. Cdr. J. H., IV: 19
Brewer, Capt. C. N., X: 75n, 79
Brewer, Lt. Cdr. C. W., VIII: 266–8, 276, 414, X: 118, 127, 161, 217, 377–8
Brewer, Capt. S. B., V: 86, XIII: 304
Brewington, Cdr. C. W., I: 418
Brewster, Lt.(jg) W. R., II: 146n
Briande, Baie de, XI: 277
BRIAREUS, XIV: 387
BRIDGE, I: 51, VII: 110–11, XIV: 386
Bridget, Cdr. F. J., III: 200
BRIDLINGTON, XI: 337
BRIDPORT, XI: 337
Bridson, Lt. Cdr. G., V: 349–50
Briggs, Capt. J. A., II: 37, 246, XIII: 305
BRIGHT, XIV: 392
BRILLIANT, X: 334–6
Brilliant, I: 397–8
Brind, Rear Adm. E. J. P., XIV: 105, 313, 388
Brindisi, XI: 246
Brindupke, Cdr. C. F., VIII: 31
Bringle, Lt. Cdr. W. F., XI: 342, XIII: 305, XIV: 374
Brink, Lt. Col. F. G., III: 53n
Brinker, Lt. (jg) S. W., XI: 141
Brisbane, IV: 16, 30, 219–20, 225–7, 270, V: 25, VI: 67–71, 435, VII: 102, VIII: 16, 30n, 48, 49n, 55, XII: 399; Conference, VIII: 63
Brisbane M., V: 234, 269n
Briscoe, Capt. R. P., V: 328n, 342, 346, 353, 364–7, 370, VI: 107, 110, 308
BRISK, X: 182, 193
BRISSENDEN, IX: 154, XI: 336
Bristol, Vice Adm. A. L., I: 51, 69, 78n, 85–6, 89–90, 118, 217, 248, 418
Bristol, Cdr. J. M., XII: 417, XIII: 309

Bristol, Rear Adm. M. L., VI: 106*n*, 131*n*
BRISTOL, I: 123, 420, II: 38, 87, 105, 159, 170-2, 285, IX: 72-5, 83, 87-9, 198, 203, 252, 267-8, 299, 314, 386, 391, X: 109; sunk, IX: 313; class, I: 28*n*, 234-5
British Army. *See* Great Britain, Army
British Chancellor, IX: 397
British Chiefs of Staff, 1942 strategy, II: 14-15; Cross-Channel attack, IX: 3-10, X: 10-16; Invasion of Italy, IX: 227-8, 232; Southern France, XI: 28, 223-4, 230-32; 1944 Pacific strategy, XII: 6; Borneo, XIII: 256-8
British Chivalry, X: 276
British Guiana, I: 34
British Joint Intel. Committee, XI: 295
British Motorist, III: 319
British Prestige, X: 181*n*
Britt, Lt. Cdr. J. W., III: 272
Brittain, Commo. T. B., VII: 337, 344, VIII: 419, IX: 64*n*, 385, XII: 139, 416, XIV: 119, 128, 375
Brittin, Lt. B. H., XIV: 384*n*
Britton, Cdr. W. O., VIII: 419, XII: 418
Brixner, Lt. Cdr. Robert, IV: 92
Broach, Cdr. J. C., VIII: 120, 416
BROADBILL, I: 422, XI: 333, 337-8
BROADWATER, I: 92-3
BROADWAY, X: 78
Brock, Lt. Jerome, IX: 274
Brocklebank, W. H., V: 11*n*
BROCKLESBY, IX: 166, 393
Brockman, Lt. Cdr. W. H., IV: 92, 112, 128, 194, 228, 235*n*, V: 348, VII: 334
Brockway, Lt. Cdr. C. W., VI: 122, VIII: 411, XII: 428, XIII: 318
Brodeur, Rear Adm. V. G., X: 19
Brodie, Lt. Cdr. Robert, I: 420, II: 37, 130, IX: 78, 385
Brogger, Cdr. L. C., VIII: 404, XII: 383
Brokas, Lt.(jg) A. X., X: 326
BROKE, II: 207-8, 224, IX: 148*n;* sunk, II: 283
Brolo, pic., IX: 202; landing, 203-5, 207
Bromet, Air V. Mar. G. R., X: 89, 91-2, 95, 98, 101
BRONSTEIN, X: 279-81, 377
BRONZO, captured, IX: 41-2
Brooke, Field Marshal Sir Alan, II: 15*n*, IX: 6-8, 229-30, XI: 11, 16, 23, 69, 295, 298, 318-19, 322, XIII: 256; pic., VI: 18

Brooke, Lt. Cdr. G. M., III: 159
Brooke, Sir James, XIII: 255
Brooke-Popham, Air Ch. Marshal Sir Robert, III: 53-4, 282
Brooketon, XIII: 265
BROOKLYN (1896), II: 286
BROOKLYN (1937), I: 57, 76, 83*n*, 118, 327-9, 419, II: ix, 31*n*, 37, 44-5, 51*n*, 56*n*, 57, 71-7, 100, 104-13, 158, 162*n*, 171, 285, III: 56*n*, 57, VI: 195, IX: 28, 64, 74, 82-3, 88, 110*n*, 174, 342-8, 358, 359*n*, 361*n*, 362, 375-8, 386, 391, 396, X: 253, XI: 238, 257, 276-8, 341; pics., II: 75, 92, 112-13, 174
Brooklyn Navy Yard, III: 306
Brookman, Cdr. H. R., II: 22, IX: 15
Brooks, Lt. B. T., X: 378
Brooks, Lt. H. F., XIII: 304
Brooks, Staff Sgt. J. A., VI: 404-5
Brooks, Commo. J. K., X: 67
Brooks, Ens. R. L., III: 103
Brooks, Lt. Cdr. W. K., XIII: 308
BROOKS, IV: 174, VI: 133, 261, 263, 267, 269*n*, 381, 436, VIII: 404, XII: 422, XIII: 106, 112, 306, 325
Broome, Australia, III: 337, 378
Broome, Cdr. J. E., I: 179
BROOME, I: 15*n*, 418, 421, VI: 47, XIV: 86*n*
Brosin, Kaptlt. H. G., X: 194
Brosset, Gen., XI: 236, 281
Brouillette, Lt. J. P. E., XIII: 221
Broussard, Lt. Cdr. Clarence, I: 76, 418
Brousseau, Lt. Cdr. H. G., VIII: 411, XIV: 373
Browder, Capt. M. E., IV: 279, VIII: 405, 420, XIV: 373
Brown, Cdr. A. C., I: 102*n*, II: 248, XIV: ix
Brown, Capt. A. D., VII: 334, VIII: 415, XII: 426, XIII: 318
Brown, Maj. Gen. A. E., VII: 46-8, 335
Brown, Capt. B. F., VI: 228, XIV: 375
Brown, Lt. Cdr. C. B. X: 378
Brown, Cdr. C. D., XIV: 285
Brown, Capt. C. R., VIII: 410
Brown, Cdr. Chesford, XIII: 311
Brown, Cdr. D. C., XIV: 387
Brown, Lt. Cdr. E. M., VII: 57, 139, 337
Brown, Lt. Cdr. F. E., IV: 20, 225, 275, VII: 53
Brown, Lt. Cdr. Gaylord B., VIII: 273, 276
Brown, Lt. (jg) George B., VIII: 295-6

Brown, Lt. G. E., VII: 189
Brown, Lt. Cdr. H. V., XI: 313
Brown, Lt. J. C., XIII: 308
Brown, Cdr. James H., XII: 415, XIV: 381
Brown, Rear Adm. John H. ("Babe"), XIV: 110
Brown, J. M., IX: 144n
Brown, Col. J. P., V: 107n
Brown, Lt. Col. J. P., pic., IV: 85
Brown, Capt. K. E., VII: 277
Brown, Lt. Col. L. E., VI: 146
Brown, Capt. L. F., VII: 337, 345, VIII: 419
Brown, Lt. L. R., XI: 342
Brown, Cdr. M. H., XI: 94, 333
Brown, Lt. M. R., X: 165
Brown, Lt. Col. N. K., VIII: 187n
Brown, Lt. P. B., X: 164
Brown, Cdr. R. C., XIV: 386
Brown, Lt. (jg) R. W., XII: 210, 422
Brown, Lt. S. V., V: 228
Brown, Lt. Cdr. T. A., VII: 100n, 104
Brown, Lt. V. A., XIV: 377
Brown, Cdr. W. B., XII: 425, XIII: 318
Brown, Capt. W. D., XIV: 384
Brown, Lt. Cdr. W. S., VIII: 415, XII: 428, XIII: 305, XIV: 326
Brown, Vice Adm. Wilson, biog., III: 211n; mentioned, 211, 215, 235-7, 240-43n, 250-52, 260, 265-7, 387-9, IV: 14, XII: 7, 10
BROWN, VII: 144, 339, 349, VIII: 413, XII: 425, XIII: 81-2, 317, XIV: 239
Brown V., XIV: 272
Browne, Cdr. G. H., XII: 429
Browne, Lt. (jg) M. F., VIII: 301
Brownell, Lt. (jg) R. B., X: 103
Browning, Capt. Miles, pic., IV: 85; mentioned, 82, 114, 122, V: 185, VI: 7, 13, 93, 144
Browning, II: 283
BROWNSON, VI: 382; sunk, 385-6
Brownsville, I: 279
Broyles, Lt. N. L., VI: 110
Bruce, Maj. Gen. A. D., VIII: 379, 393n, 396, XII: 56, 376, 379, 393, XIV: 118-21, 241, 375
Bruce, Lt. (jg) J. L., VIII: 276
Bruening, Ktradm., XI: 46
BRUISER, II: 268n, IX: 392, 396
Brumbaugh, Capt. H. B., XIII: 308, 321
Brumby, Cdr. E., VIII: 404
Brunei Bay, XII: 171, 239, 312,

XIII: 258, XIV: 104; landing, XIII: 217, 263-7
Brunelle, A. W., XII: 210
Bruner, Lt. Cdr. F., VII: 333
Brunton, Lt. Cdr. C. E., V: 375
Brush, Capt. Charles, V: 71
Brush, Cdr. F. J., XII: 349n, XIII: 315
Brush, Maj. Gen. Rapp, XIII: 127, 135, 217, 229-32, 310, 323
BRUSH, XIII: 181, 316, XIV: 383
Brussels Conf., III: 15
Bruton, Lt. Cdr. H. C., IV: 204, V: 324
Bryan, Cdr. L. A., IX: 388, XIV: 382
Bryant, Rear Adm. C. F., biog., X: 134n; pic., XI: 141; mentioned, I: 76, 176, 193, 327-8, 419, II: 176, 193, X: 134, XI: 86, 116-19, 125n, 129, 143, 146-8, 198-200, 204-10, 215, 246, 265-7, 336-7, 340
Bryant, Capt. E. H., XII: 406
BRYANT, VIII: 408, XII: 199, 221, 419, XIII: 304, XIV: 237, 373, 391
Bryce, Lt. Cdr. D. G., XIII: 307
BRYTHER, XI: 337
Buchan, Lt. Cdr. R. B., XIV: 385
Buchanan, Cdr. A. E., VIII: 405, XII: 218, 421, XIII: 304
Buchanan, Capt. C. A., XIV: 223, 381
Buchanan, Capt. Pat, IV: 273, V: 232, VII: 335, 346, VIII: 418
BUCHANAN, IV: 274, 289, 291, V: 29, 57, 87, 151-3, 157, 162, 166, 231-2, 236, VI: 144, 149, 182, 421, X: 204n, XIII: 316, 318, XIV: 363
Buchar, Lt. R. J., VIII: 408
Buck, Lt. G. B., X: 380
Buck, Mr. Paul, I: 398
Buck, Cdr. W. A., I: 85n
BUCK, I: xv, 76, 107n, 327, 420, IX: 42-3, 68, 75, 83-4, 88, 386, X: xi, 371, XIV: xii; sunk, I: 312-14; pic., IX: 43
"Bucket brigade," I: 132-3, 254-6, 260n
BUCKEYE, VII: 334
Bucklew, Cdr. Philip, IX: 87, XI: 34n, 132
Buckley, Capt. A. E., XIV: 375
Buckley, Sonarman F. R., VII: 144
Buckley, Lt. F. X., IX: 376
BUCKLEY, X: 285-8, 343, 373, 377; pic., 288
Buckmaster, Capt. Elliott, IV: 19, 55, 90, 135, 154-6
Buckner, Lt. Gen. S. B., pic., VII: 55; mentioned, IV: 162-6, VII: 5, XII: 17,

XIII: 5, XIV: 4, 86–7, 90, 240, 273, 276, 372

Buckner Bay, XIV: 277

"Buco," XI: 27, 163

BUCYRUS V., XIV: 386

Budapest, IX: 44, XI: 227

BUDE, IX: 396

Buderus, Lt. W. H., XII: 284

Buehler, Lt. Howard, XIII: 308

BUFFALO, VII: 101n

"Buffalo." *See* LVT

Buford, Capt. W. P., XII: 425

BUGARA, XIII: 288

Bugsanga R., XIII: 26

Buie, Cdr. P. D., VIII: 257n, 338, 414

Buin, V: 188, 295, 321, 332, 351, VI: 94–5, 160, 190, 207, 220, 362, 425–6, VIII: 219, 224

Buka I., IV: 256, V: 4, 354, VI: 90, 118–20, 280–81, 291–2, 341, 350, 353, 426; bombardment, 363–4, 427

Bulacan R., XIII: 195

Bulkeley, Lt. Cdr. J. D., III: 201, 203, VI: 47, 257, XI: 214–15, 282, 337–8

Bulkley, Cdr. R. J., "History of Motor Torpedo Boats," V: 320n, VI: 41n, VIII: 56n, IX: 188n, XI: 192n, XIII: xii

Bull, Lt. Cdr. C. E., VII: 341, XIII: 310

BULL, XIII: 304, XIV: 28, 377

Bullard, Lt. G. C., VII: 338

Bullard, Lt. Cdr. N. D., XIV: 374

BULLARD, VI: 331, VII: 190, 227, 339, 348, VIII: 405, 410, 420, XIV: 210, 384

BULLDOG, XI: 329

Bullen, Cdr. J. T., XII: 425, XIII: 305

BULLHEAD, sunk, XIII: 288

BULMER, III: 160, 272, 298, 310, 320, 332, X: 117, 377

BULOLO, II: 105n, 190, 194, 195n, IX: 151, 157, 333, 341, 396, XI: 184, 190

Buna-Gona, Japanese campaign to recover, IV: 269, V: 286, VI: 33, 41–50; pic., 41; map, 44

BUNCH, XIV: 378

Bunda Roads, III: 298–9

Bundy, McGeorge, III: 154n; *On Active Service*, X: xiv, XI: xv

Bungo Suido, XII: 168, XIV: 200

BUNKER HILL, VI: 330–36, 346, 411, VII: viii, xxvii, xxix, 117, 138, 157, 197, 208, 219–21, 325, 339, 349, 353, VIII: 32, 37, 154, 174; in Bat. of Phil. Sea, 250, 265n, 268, 271–3, 276, 292, 298–304, 307–8, 413, XII: 12, 50, 90, 103, 106, 182, 425, XIV: 21, 96, 384, 386, 392; crashed, 262–3; pic., VI: 434

Bunkley, Capt. J. W., III: 111n, 112

Bunting, Capt. S. B., I: 208

Bunyan, Cdr. A. V., XII: 416, XIII: 310

BUOYANT, XIV: 375n, 377

Buracker, Capt. W. H., pic., IV: 85; mentioned, VIII: 414, XII: 178, 181–2, 426

Buraku I., V: 332

Burauen, XII: 394

Burch, Lt. Cdr. W. O., IV: 19, 26

Burchett, Lt. Cdr. E. C., I: 420, II: 39

BURDEKIN, XIII: 261n

BURDEN R. HASTINGS, VII: 341, 345, VIII: 229

Burdett, Lt. L. C., X: 381

Burford, Capt. W. P., III: 115, IV: 19, 91, VIII: 415, 419

Burgess, Cdr. E. E., VII: 110

Burgess, Lt. Cdr. K. F., VIII: 410, XIV: 374

Burgess, Ens. W. C., VIII: 310

Burgenland, X: 228

Burgett, Lt. Cdr. W. A., XIII: 309

Burghard, Capt. F. G., XIV: 388

Burhans, Capt. A. D., VII: 338

Buri, XII: 350, 364

Burial at sea, pic., VIII: 401

Burias I., XII: 190

Burke, Rear Adm. Arleigh A., pics., VI: 333, XII: 102; mentioned, VI: 203, 289, 292; Emp. Aug. Bay, 307–18; C. St. George, 353–60; "Little Beavers," 289, 292, 360, 407, 420–21, 427, VIII: 274n, 286n, XII: 196, 222, 424, XIV: 382

Burke, Lt. Cdr. E. J., I: 421, IX: 385

Burke, Cdr. H. J., I: 329, XIV: 98

Burke, Lt. Cdr. R. F., VIII: 184, 359, XIV: 378

Burkhart, Col. E. C., II: 22, 56n, 72n–5n, 78n

BURLEIGH, XIV: 378

BURLESON, XIV: 379

Burlingame, Lt. Cdr. C. C., IV: 194, 204, 227–8

BURLINGTON, XII: 417

Burma, III: 381, VI: 8, VII: 83, XIII: 169; the Road, III: 42, 44, 69, 73n, VI: 6, VII: 80, VIII: 4, XIII: 163n

Burnbaum, Lt. Cdr. J., XIV: 387

Burnett, Capt. H. P., VIII: 409, XII: 419
Burnett, Ens. H. R., V: 95
Burnett, Cdr. P. W., X: 139
Burnett, Vice Adm. R. L., I: 360, 365, X: 237–41
Burnett, Ens. R. W., VIII: 303
Burns, Cdr. E. S., VII: 334, VIII: 404, XII: 417, XIII: 313, XIV: 191, 379
Burns, Col. F. L., VI: 36
Burns, Capt. G. L., VIII: 411, XIV: 380
Burns, Henry, VII: 334
Burns, J. M., *Okinawa: The Last Battle*, XIV: 170*n*
Burns, Lt. J. S., XIII:304*n*
Burns, Lt. Cdr. M. D., X: 212, 227*n*
BURNS (1919), X: 229*n*
BURNS (1943), VII: 219–20, 326–9, 336, 349, VIII: 413, X: 229*n*, XII: 425, XIII: 101, 305
Burnside, Lt. Cdr. J. L., III: 158, 283
BURRFISH, VII: 353, VIII: 23, XII: 33
Burrough, Capt. E. W., II: 39, V: 353, VI: 9
Burrough, Rear Adm. Sir Harold, II: 17, 190, 195*n*, 199, 210, X: 359, XI: 326
Burroughs, Lt. Cdr. S. E., pic., IV: 85
Burrowes, Cdr. Thomas, VII: 335, VIII: 415
Burrows, Lt. Cdr. J. S., XII: 420, XIII: 305, XIV: 374
Burton, Lt. Milby, XI: 299*n*
BURZA, I: 319, 325, 337, 340, 415
Busbey, Capt. L. W., VII: 339, 350, XII: 425
Busck, Cdr. V. K., VI: 416, VIII: 418, XII: 418
Buse, Lt. Col. H. W., VI: 387
Bush, Lt. Cdr. F. M., XIV: 384*n*
Bush, Dr. Vannevar, I: 29, X: 22
BUSH, VI: 382, 391, 436, 438, 441, VIII: 406, XII: 344, 415, XIII: 44, 137, 306, 311, XIV: 381, 390; sunk, 186–90
"Bushido," III: 6, 82
BUSHNELL, VI: 36
Busho M., III: 162
Bushrod Washington, IX: 299, 390
Buskoe, I: 63
Bussey, Lt.(jg) R. Y., XIII: 145–6
Busuanga I., XIII: 221
Butaritari I. *See* Makin I.
Butcher, Capt. H. C., pic., II: 218; mentioned, 16, XI: 231
Butera, IX: 122–4
Butler, Lt. E. F., X: 381
Butler, Capt. F. J., XIV: 388
Butler, J. R. M., XI: x, xiii
Butler, Maj. Gen. W. O., pic., VII: 55; mentioned, IV: 164, 166, 171, 174, 183, VII: 4*n*, 5, 333
BUTLER, IX: 110, 113, 117, 388, XI: 157, 334, 342, XIV: 376, 392
BUTTE, XIV: 380
Butterfield, Capt. H. B., VIII: 410, XII: 428, XIII: 67, 73, 319
Butterfield, Cdr. R. E., VII: 340
BUTTERNUT, VI: 121
BUTTON. *See* Espiritu Santo
Butts, Lt. Cdr. W. S., V: 353
Buxton, Cdr. J. W., XII: 52, 53*n*
Buxton, Lt. Cdr. W. H., X: 379
Buyse, Lt. G. J., XII: 421, XIV: 377
Buzzards Bay, I: 254
BYARD, X: 149
Bye, Capt. Harold, VII: 344, VIII: 419, XII: 416
BYMS–*2022*, sunk, XI: 273
Byrd, Cdr. M. M., XIII: 324
Byrd, Rear Adm. R. E., IV: 252, XIV: 369
Byrd, Lt. T. H., X: 119–21, 375
Byrd, Lt. W. V., XIV: 377
Byrnes, J. F., XIV: 343, 347, 357
Byron D. Benson sunk, pics., I: 134

C

C–*i*, XIV: 86*n*
C. *Francis Jenkins*, XIII: 313
Caballo I., XIII: 199, 200, 204–5
CABANA, VII: 341
Cabanatuan, XIII: 14, 193
CABLE, XII: 423, XIII: 206, 306
CABOT, VII: 208, 321, 349, 352, VIII: 37, 174, 250, 262, 292, 298–9, 303, 413, XII: 90, 93, 100–102, 184–6, 318, 358–60, 425–6, XIII: 52, 54, 316, XIV: 21, 199, 241, 384
Cabras I., VIII: 387, 396; pic., 400
CABRILLA, VI: 85, XII: 405
Cabugan I., XIV: 120
CACAPON, XIII: 318, XIV: 387
CACHALOT, III: 213*n*, IV: 92
CACHE, VIII: 411, XII: 428, XIII: 318, XIV: 387
Cade, Lt.(jg) J. A., XII: 422
CADMUS, IX: 396
Cady, Capt. J. P., VII: 341
CAELUM, VII: 348
Caen, XI: 180–81, 187–9, 216
Caesar Rodney, X: 312
Caffey, Col. B. F., II: 198
Cagayan, Mindanao, XII: 164, XIII: 240, 244
Cagayan Valley, Luzon, III: 176, XIII: 11, 16
Cagger, Lt. G., X: 381
Cagle, Lt. M. W., XIV: 385*n*
Cagliari, XI: 313
CAHABA, VIII: 411, 420, XIV: 387
CAIMAN, XIII: 320
Cain, Lt. Cdr. J. R., VIII: 404, 409
Cairo, IX: 15, 19, 149; Conf., VII: 83, VIII: 7, IX: 322–3, XI: 22–3, XII: 4; Declaration, XIV: 343
CALAMARES, XII: 81, 423
Calcutta, XIII: 163*n*, 164
Calcutta Maru, IV: 201
Calderhead, Lt. Cdr. R. S., I: 419
Caldwell, Lt. Cdr. D. C., XIII: 316
Caldwell, Cdr. H. H., VI: 325–7, VII: 340
Caldwell, Maj. R. M., V: 375
Caldwell, Lt. R. W., IX: 82

Caldwell, Lt. Cdr. S. J., XIV: 379
Caldwell, Cdr. T. F., IV: 271, V: 375, XII: 426, XIII: 318
CALDWELL, VII: 334, 341, 345, XII: 54, 389–92
CALEDON, X: 269–72, XI: 342, 381
Calfee, Lt.(jg) F. I., XIV: 305*n*
Calhoun, Lt. Cdr. C. R., XII: 429, XIII: 73–4, 319
Calhoun, Maj. O. B., V: 374
Calhoun, Capt. William C., VII: 337, 350, VIII: 413, XII: 8–9
Calhoun, Vice Adm. W. L., biog., VII: 103*n;* pic., 103; mentioned, VI: 11*n*, VII: ix, 100*n*, 103–6, 340, VIII: 158, 343, 345, 349, XII: 74, XIV: 168
Calicoan I., XII: 118
CALIENTE, VIII: 411, XII: 428, XIII: 318, XIV: 387
CALIFORNIA, III: 101*n*, 103–4, 111–13, 145, 211*n*, IV: 223*n*, VI: 13*n*, 17*n*, 103*n*, VIII: 180–82, 197, 200–201, 360, 362*n*, 408*n*, 409, 419, IX: 325*n*, X: 200*n*, XII: 119*n*, 163, 199, 202, 224, 228*n*, 295, 343, 419, XIII: 39*n*, 98, 107–9, 113–14, 177–8, 303–4, 325; pics., III: 84, 111
Callaghan, Rear Adm. Daniel J., biog., V: 236*n;* pic., 242; mentioned, IV: 251, 270, 280, V: 227–32, 236–42, 245–8, 253, 258, 285–7, XIV: 280*n*
Callaghan, Lt. Cdr. J. A., I: 421, III: 158
Callaghan, Capt. W. M., VII: 100*n*, 104, XIV: 385
CALLAGHAN, V: 271, VII: 310, VIII: 410, XII: 319, 427, XIII: 318, XIV: 279–80, 373, 392
Callahan, Lt. (jg) G. H., VII: 261*n*, 275*n*
Callahan, Capt. J. W., IV: 272, V: 29, 34*n*, 51, VI: 144, 182, XI: 334, XIII: 306, 317
Callahan, Cdr. M. W., XII: 416, XIII: 310
Callan, Lt. Cdr. P. L., XIV: 374
Callaway, Lt. Cdr. A. W., XIV: 386

CALLAWAY, VII: 236, 345, VIII: 408, XII: 417, XIII: 117, 309, 326
Callis, H. E., X: 381
Calloway, Lt. J. E., XIV: 377
CALM, XI: 341
CALPE, IX: 393, X: 253, 371, XI: 343
Caltagirone, IX: 50–51, 57, 60
Calton, Lt. J. W., II: 147
Calvados Reef, XI: 179–80, 183
Calvert, Cdr. A. P., VI: 145
CALVERT, I: 421, II: 40, 44*n*, 139–42, VII: 336, 346, VIII: 364, 408, IX: 130–31, 389, XII: 418, XIII: 311, 313; pic., II: 149
CALYPSO, X: 185*n*
CAMAQUAM, I: 378
CAMBRIA, VII: 226–8, 285, 288, 347, VIII: 186, 329, 407, XII: 419, XIII: 310, 312, XIV: 378; pic., VII: 278
CAMDEN, XIII: 161*n*
CAMEL, XIV: 379
Camerata, XI: 241
Camerina, IX: 71, 127, 133
Cameron, Lt. Cdr. H. T., XI: 339
Cameron, Cdr. T. F., XI: 337
Camiguin I., III: 174, XII: 106
Caminawit Point, XIII: 26, 29, 32, 46
Cammarata, Coxswain N., IX: 193
Cammarn, Lt. Cdr. I. H., XIII: 307
CAMOCIM, I: 378
Camotes Sea, XII: 353, 368–70, 395, XIII: 12
Camp, Capt. Chauncey, XI: 336
Camp, Cdr. F. C., VII: 411, IX: 388, XII: 429
Camp, Lt. Cdr. W. J., XIII: 312
CAMPANIA, X: 310–11
Campbell, Lt. (jg), III: 293
Campbell, Capt. Colin, VI: 161, 167, 181
Campbell, Lt. Cdr. D. A., pic., X: 328
Campbell, Cdr. E. G., XII: 380–81, 417
Campbell, Lt. Col. F. P., XI: 197, 211
Campbell, Lt. Cdr. G. B., VIII: 412
Campbell, Brig. Gen. H. D., XII: 43*n*
Campbell, Capt. J. C., VII: 337, 344, VIII: 408, XII: 418, XIII: 308
Campbell, Cdr. J. H., XIII: 284
Campbell, Lt. Cdr. R. L., I: 111
Campbell, Ens. S. S., IX: 139*n*
Campbell, Capt. W. S., XI: 335
CAMPBELL, I: xvi, 108, 228, 305, 322, 337–40, 415, 421, X: xi, 269, XI: ix; Convoy UGS-40, 381; pics., I: 281, X: 264
CAMPBELL, HMS, XI: 79

Campfire, I: 374
Camranh Bay, III: 157, 307, 335, IV: 221, XIII: 14, 37, 42, 116, 157–61, 165–6, 168–9, 284–5
Canada, relations with, I: 32, 45–6; Air Force, I: 22, 246, IV: 165*n*, 174*n*, VII: 14, 65, 333, X: 44; Army, IX: 29, 65, 127, 144–5, 150, 154–6, 180, 200, 206, XI: 181, 184–7; First Army, 323; Navy, expansion, I: 13; convoys, 12, 18–19, 58, 85, II: 17, X: 20, 361; Pacific, IV: 165*n*; Sicily, IX: 152, 156; Normandy, XI: 116, 191
Canada V., XII: 423, XIV: 238, 386, 391
Canal Zone. *See* Panama
Canaveral, Cape, I: 135
CANBERRA, VIII: 413, XII: 46, 90, 94–100, 117, 424–5
CANBERRA, HMAS, III: 261, IV: 15*n*, 272, 278, V: 29–32, 35–9, 54, 63*n*; sunk, 55
Canberra M., V: 234, 269*n*
Canham, Col. C. D. W., XI: 130, 139–40
Cann, Lt. Cdr. P. W., IX: 389
Cannes, IX: 365, XI: 234, 278
Canning, Grp. Capt. P. S., X: 16
Cannon, M. H., *Leyte*, XII: viii
CANOPUS, III: 158, 193–5, 198–201, X: 212*n*; scuttled, III: 204; pic., 166
Canton, China, XIII: 171
Canton I., III: 33*n*, 259, 265, IV: 252, 276, V: 340, VII: 82, 89, 95, 98, 118, 211
Canty, Lt. Cdr. J. P., VII: 335–6
Capaccio, IX: 255, 266, 270
Cape Cod Canal, I: 253
Cape Constantine, VII: 341
Cape Engaño, XIII: 12, 107; Battle off, XII: 317–36; T.O., 318–19; chart, 323; pics., 326–7
CAPE ESPERANCE, XII: 428, XIII: 70, 319
Cape Esperance, Battle of, V: 147–171; T.O., 150–51; charts, 155, 159
Cape Fear, VII: 341, 345
Cape Georgia, VII: 347
Cape Gloucester Opn., planning, VI: 370–72, 380–81; rehearsal, 381; landing, 381–9; T.O., 381–2; chart, 380
Cape Isabel, VII: 341, 345
Cape Matapan, Battle of, II: 7
Cape Neddick, X: 210–11

Cape St. George, Battle of, VI: 352–9; T.O., 353–4; chart, 357
Cape San Martin, VII: 341, 347
Cape Stevens, VII: 341, 345
Cape Torokina Opn., plans and prelims., VI: 13–14, 281–4, 289–90; T.O., 297; landing, 296–304; charts, 301, 361; unloading and resupply, 337–45, 348, 351–2, 360–61, 365; perimeter defense, 341–2, 347–8, 360–65, 425–31; numbers and casualties, 297, 337, 430; pics., 253, 299
Cape Verde Is., II: 8, X: 63
CAPEL, X: 337, XI: 304
CAPERTON, VII: 348, VIII: 414, XII: 319, 425, XIII: 318
Capes of Chesapeake, Battle of, VIII: 318, XII: 241
CAPETOWN, XI: 337
Capetown, I: 112, 347
Capira, I: 178, 372
CAPITAINE PAUL LEMERLE, II: 160
Caplan, Lt. Stanley, III: 114, VIII: 419, XII: 422, XIII: 106, 306
Capps, Lt. A. G., XIV: 185
CAPPS, VIII: 411, XII: 428, XIII: 317, XIV: 29, 374
Capri I., IX: 300–301
CAPRICORNUS, XII: 419, XIII: 310, XIV: 380
CAPRIOLO, XI: 282
CAPTOR, I: 284
Carabao I., XIII: 199–200, 206
CARAQUET, HMCS, XI: 116, 335
CARAVELAS, I: 387
Carberry, Lt. Cdr. W. G., VIII: 380, XII: 422, XIV: 378
Carboni, Gen., IX: 240–41
Card, Antha E., I: xvii, III: xii, IV: x, V: xii, VII: x, VIII: viii, IX: xiv, X: x, XI: xi, XII: viii, XIV: ix
CARD, X: 40, 104–27 passim, 149, 159–76 passim, 183, 281, 298, 319, 371–2, 376–7
Cardonia, I: 130n
Cardonnet Bank, XI: 97–8, 108; pics., 100
Carey, Lt. (jg) H. C., X: 214
Carey, Lt. (jg) J. L., VI: 137
Carey, Ens. L. Z., I: 357n
Carey, Lt. Cdr. W. J., XIV: 373
Caribbean, U-boats in, I: 144–54, 257–64, 347–52, 413–14, X: 188–207, 297–8
Caribbean Sea Fron., I: 223, X: 8;
charts, I: 238–9, X: 193; convoys, I: 257–64; patrol of, I: 33n, 68, 84; strength of, I: 242, 248, X: 189
CARIBOU, XII: 423, XIII: 308
Caridad, XII: 390
Cariddi, IX: 212
CARINA, XIV: 391
Carini, Alfred, X: 312–13
CARIOCA, I: 387
Carley, Lt. Cdr. M. J., VIII: 404
Carlill, Capt. S. H., IX: 394
Carlisle, Lt. Cdr. D. G., XI: 342
Carlisle, Capt. H. A., XIII: 308
Carlsen, Oblt. C. P., X: 192–3
Carlson, Capt. C. A., V: 374
Carlson, Cdr. Dan, XIII: 305, XIV: 372
Carlson, Lt. Col. E. F., pics., IV: 235, VII: 167; mentioned, IV: 86, 235–40, V: 290, VII: 77, 158n, 166, 167n
Carlson, Cdr. E. V., XII: 417
Carlson, Lt. J. G., XIV: 386
Carlson, Commo. M. O., VIII: 410, XII: 139, 416, XIII: 310, XIV: 140, 379
CARLSON, X: 193, XIV: 381
Carlton, I: 182, 186, 191n
†Carmichael, Capt. G. K., XII: 425, XIII: 383, XIV: 383
CARMICK, XI: 122, 124, 144–5, 277, 336, 340, 343
Carmody, Lt. (jg) M. D., V: 266n
CARNELIAN, I: 135, 138, 390n
Carnes, Cdr. G. H., XIII: 310
Carney, Adm. Robert B., I: 85n, 217, VI: 13, 279n, VIII: 10n, IX: xvi, XI: xvn, XII: 16, 424, XIV: 361–2; biog., VI: 13n
Caroline Is., III: 7, 60, VII: 70, XII: 4. See also Palaus, Ponape, Truk
CARONDELET, XIII: 308
Caronia, Sicily, IX: 203
Carpender, Vice Adm. Arthur S., IV: 262, VI: 32, 47, 51, 89, 97, 132, 259, 262, 372
Carpenter, Capt. C. L., XIV: 380
Carpenter, F. D., X: 382
Carpenter, Lt. F. G., XIV: 144
Carpenter, Seaman Francis, IX: 131–2
Carpenter, Lt. Cdr. J. H., XIII: 319
Carpenter, Lt. Cdr. J. K., VIII: 411
Carpenter, Lt. J. W., XII: 429
Carpenter, Lt. Cdr. R. E., XIV: 377
Carr, Lt. (jg) G. R., VIII: 267
Carr, Lt. T., VII: 346
Carraway, Ens. H. E., I: 180

Carrier Air Grps.; One, VII: 412; Two, 297, 412; Three, V: 86, XIII: 315; Four, 317; Five, VII: 338, 348, 352, XIV: 383; Six, V: 86, VII: 339, 349, 352, XIV: 384; Seven, V: 87, XII: 425, XIII: 316; Eight, V: 205, VIII: 413, XII: 425; Nine, II: 31–2, 39, VI: 331, VII: 339, 349, XIV: 311n, 385; Ten, V: 204, 233, 283, VII: 348, 352, VIII: 414, XIV: 385; Eleven, XII: 424, XIII: 316; Twelve, VI: 325, VII: 340, 350, XIV: 383; Thirteen, XII: 427; Fourteen, VII: 413, XII: 424; Fifteen, VIII: 414, XII: 426; Sixteen, VII: 338, VIII: 178, 414; Seventeen, VI: 331, VII: 339, 349, 353, XIV: 382; Eighteen, Nineteen, Twenty, XII: 425–7, XIII: 316; Twenty-one, XII: 428; Twenty-two, VI: 331, VII: 339, XII: 424, XIII: 315; Twenty-three, VI: 325, VII: 340, 350, XIV: 385; Twenty-four, VII: 339, 348, 352, VIII: 412, XIV: 374; Twenty-five, VII: 338, 349, 353, VIII: 415, XIV: 374; Twenty-six, XII: 420; Twenty-seven, VIII: 414, XII: 427; Twenty-eight, VIII: 413, XII: 424, XIII: 315; Twenty-nine, XII: 426, XIII: 316, XIV: 384; Thirty, VII: 339, 349, 353, XIV: 382; Thirty-one, VII: 349, 352, VIII: 413; Thirty-two, VII: 350, VIII: 414; Thirty-three, XIV: 373; Thirty-five, VIII: 420; XII: 420; Thirty-seven, VIII: 420, XII: 420; Forty, XIV: 374; Forty-four, XII: 427, XIII: 317; Forty-five, 317, XIV: 382; Forty-six, Forty-seven, 384–5; Fifty, Fifty-one, VIII: 413–14, XII: 428; Sixty, VIII: 420, XII: 420; Sixty-one, 368; Eighty, XIII: 317; Eighty-one, XII: 349n, XIII: 315; Eighty-two, Eighty-three, Eighty-four, Eighty-six, 382–4; Eighty-eight, XIV: 311n, 385n; Night Air Groups, XIII: 87, 165, XIV: 21, 54n; Forty-one, XII: 426, XIII: 318; Ninety, 318, XIV: 383
Carrier Divisions; Three, I: 83; Five, XIII: 316; Twenty-two, VII: 346, VIII: 405, 420; Twenty-four, 378, 405, 420; Twenty-six, XII: 244, 421; Twenty-seven, 244, 420; Twenty-eight, 420; First Car. TF, XIII: 180n

Carrier opns., described by Cdr. Shaw, VII: xxvii–xxxix
Carriers, plane complement, VII: xxviii; changes in aircraft, XIII: 55
Carro, XI: 286
Carroll, Cdr. C. E., IV: 272, V: 29, 50, VII: 339, 348, VIII: 405, 410, 420
Carroll, Lt. Cdr. J. B., VIII: 413, XII: 428, XIII: 305
Carroum, Ens. Jeff, V: 267n
Carson, Capt. J. H., VII: 350
Carson, Lt. Cdr. M. V., I: 154, XII: 421, XIII: 310
CARSON CITY, XII: 417
Carstarphen, Capt. R. J., I: 76
Carter, Capt. Grayson B., VI: 140, 145, 228–31, 237–8, 336–8, 351, 416–17, VII: 348, VIII: 207, 418
Carter, Commo. James B., VI: 11n
Carter, Capt. Jesse H., VI: 259–63, 272–4, 381, 390, 436, 443, XIII: 316, XIV: 382
Carter, Lt. (jg) John H., VII: 341
Carter, Lt. Cdr. U. B., XI: 339, XIV: 379
Carter, Lt. W. B., XIV: 144
Carter, Rear Adm. Worral R., VII: 15n, 100n, 104, 106, 228, VIII: 341n, 343, 420, XII: 51, 75, XIV: 8, 73, 161, 164, 168–9, 372, 387; *Beans, Bullets and Black Oil*, I: lx, VII: 47n, XII: 51n, XIV: 8n
CARTER, X: 349, 378
Carter Braxton, X: 382
CARTER HALL, VI: 374–5, 382, VIII: 77, 403, 419, XII: 416
Carteret, Capt. Philip, VI: 433
Carusi, Cdr. E. C., XI: 336
Caruthers, Lt. Cdr. W. R., I: 421
Carver, Lt. Cdr. L. P., II: 39
Carville, Lt. C. L., II: 200n
Cary, Lt. F. C., VII: 341
Cary, Capt. R. W., IX: 102, 347, 361n, 388, 396
CASA GRANDE, XII: 419, XIII: 311, 314, XIV: 378
CASABIANCA, IX: 305
CASABLANCA, X: 41; class, VII: 141n, X: 42
Casablanca Conf., VI: 3–7, VII: 5, IX: 5–11, X: 16, XI: 18; pic., VI: 18
Casablanca, Morocco, I: 352–5, II: 34, 46; chart, 166, 249; French command at, 68; Battle of, 91–114; charts, 94–5,

102–3; cease fire, 161–5, 186–9; as U.S. base, 174–6, 245–50, IX: 93, X: 127, 279, 282, 289–90, 293, 322; pics., II: 174–5

CASCADE, VII: 341, VIII: 420, XIII: 83, XIV: 387

CASCO, IV: 173, VII: 13, 48, 333, 350, VIII: 255n

Casco Bay, I: 68, 85, 98, 267n, II: 43

Case, Lt. G. F., XIV: 386

CASE (1919), VII: 232n, X: 197n

CASE (1936), III: 104, 231n, IV: 174, V: 335n, VII: 9n, 12, 350, VIII: 415, XII: 51, 425, XIV: 290

Caserta, IX: 328

Casey, Lt. Cdr. V. F., XII: 428

Cashman, Lt. Cdr. W. A., X: 378

Cassady, Capt. J. H., VI: 325, VII: 340, 350

Cassibile, IX: 239, 242

CASSIN, III: 117–19, XII: 425; pic., III: 116

CASSIN YOUNG, VIII: 212, 409, XII: 179–80, 319, 427, XIII: 318, XIV: 186, 190, 222–5, 280, 373, 391–2

Cassino, Monte, IX: 323–4, 330, 333, 360–62, 375

Cassleman, Lt. Cdr. G. W., X: 378–9

Castellammare, IX: 217, 250, 285

Castellano, Gen., IX: 238–9, 242

Castelvetrano, IX: 18, 58, 181–2

Castle, Lt. Cdr. J. H., X: 376

Castle, Lt. Cdr. N. H., XII: 416

CASTOR, XIV: 387

Castries, I: 145

Casualties, in Atlantic, X: 363; Africa, II: 238; Pearl Harbor, III: 107; Wake, 253; Coral Sea and Midway, IV: 60n, 140n, 176; Savo I., V: 60, 63n; Guadalcanal, 372; Central Solomons, VI: 223–4; Bougainville, 322n, 430; Admiralties, 444, 447; Komandorski battle, VII: 33; Aleutians, 19n, 50, 55n, 63–4; Gilberts, 134, 178, 181, 184–6; Marshalls, 255, 277–8, 293, 304; Truk Raid, 330n; New Guinea, VIII: 74, 83, 87–8, 101–2, 133, 140, 144; Marianas, 339, 369, 389, 393, 401n; Philippine Sea battle, 321; Sicily, IX: 179n, 223; Salerno, 285; Anzio, 343, 380; So. France, XI: 264–6; Palaus, XII: 41, 45–6, XIV: 75; Mapia Is., XII: 54; Surigao Str. battle, 240; Samar battle, 316; Leyte, 365, 396–7;

rest of Philippines, XIII: 129, 149–52, 251, 263, 325–6; Borneo, 266–7, 275; Iwo Jima, XIV: 44, 62, 67–9, 75, 389; Okinawa, 208–9, 216, 221, 282, 390–92; in final phases, 318, 327, 335

Caswell, Cdr. G. L., VII: 346, VIII: 405

CASWELL, XIV: 378

Cataisan Pt., XII: 130, 139

Catania, IX: 17, 26, 50, 57–60, 167–87 *passim*, 200, 206–7, 219–20

CATBIRD, X: 199n

Cate, J. L. *See* Craven, Wesley F.

Cater, Capt. C. J., X: 264, XI: 341

Cates, Maj. Gen. C. B., pic., V: 130; mentioned, IV: 286, VIII: 338n, 353, 408n, XIV: 8

Catford, X: 138n

Cathay, II: 195n, 283

Catlett, Lt. W. J., III: 318n

Catmon Hill, XII: 136, 143, 154

CATO, XI: 192

CATOCTIN, XI: ix, 237, 247, 252, 255–7, 274, 311, 338

Caton, Lt. C. E., XIII: 307

CATRON, XIV: 378

CATSKILL, XII: 419, XIII: 310, 312, XIV: 378

CATTERICK, XI: 343

Caufield, Cdr. C. T., VIII: 408, IX: 389, XII: 427

Caughey, Lt. Cdr. W. A., VIII: 408, XII: 418, XIII: 311

Causing, Lt. Col. Juan, XII: 123

Cavalaire, XI: 258–9, 262–4, 282

CAVALIER, VIII: 410, XII: 418, XIII: 189, 278, 308

CAVALLA, VIII: 17n, 241–3, 265, 280–81, 285, 415, XII: 335, 411

Cavallaro, Ens. S. J., IX: 265

Cavenagh, Capt. R. W., VI: 308, 420, VIII: 415, XIII: 309

Cavite, III: 154, 167, 171–2, 193, VII: 102, XIII: 190

Cayenne, X: 191

CAYUGA, I: 60

CD–3, XIII: 91; *CD–9*, XIV: 289; *CD–22*, XII: 430; XIII: 159; *CD–29*, XII: 430, XIII: 159; *CD–30*, XIV: 287; *CD–31*, XII: 430, XIII: 159, XIV: 291; *CD–33*, XII: 430; *CD–42*, XIV: 287; *CD–43*, XII: 430, XIII: 159; *CD–73*, XIV: 291; *CD–132*, XII: 430

Cebu, III: 159, VIII: 219, XII: 57, 107–8, 126, 133, 136, 149, 352, 395, XIII: 18,

Cebu (*cont'd*)
24–6, 44, 234–5; landing, 217, 226, 228–9, 233–7; T.O., 323; pic., 245
CEBU, XIV: 388
Cecil, Capt. Charles P., V: 205, VI: 161, 170–71, 191, 196
CECIL J. DOYLE, XIV: 326–7
Celebes I. and Sea, III: 195–6, XIII: 267, 275
CELENO, VI: 140, XIV: 66n
CENTAURUS, VII: 344, VIII: 405, 419, XIV: 379
"Central Agreement" (Jap.), III: 71–2
Central Pacific Area, IV: 250
Central Pacific Force, VI: 97, VII: 80, 86
Central Shipping Control Agency, VII: 105
Cépet, Cap, XI: 285–9; battery, pic., 285
CEPHEUS, XI: 341, XIV: 379
Ceram I., VI: 30, VIII: 142, XII: 107
CÉRÈS, II: 252
Ceylon, III: 306, 341
Cézembre I., XI: 300–301; pic., 316
Chachao, Mt., VIII: 386, 396
CHAFFEE, XIII: 322
Chalmers, Rear Adm. W. S., *Max Horton*, X: xiv
Chamberlain, Lt. (jg) W. F., X: 81, 295
Chamberlin, Brig. Gen. H. D., IV: 253–4
Chamberlin, Cdr. L. C., XIV: 384
Chamberlin, Maj. Gen. S. J., XII: 57, 377n
Chamberlin, Maj. W. C., VII: 166
Chambers, Lt. Cdr. A. E., X: 380
Chambers, Cdr. G. M., XIII: 317, XIV: 384
Chambers, Lt. Col. J. M., IV: 289, VII: 236n, 239–40, VIII: 363
Chambers, Capt. R. W., IX: 390, XII: 419, XIII: 310, XIV: 378
Chambers, Cdr. T. E., XIV: 225, 376
CHAMBLY, I: 71, X: 143–5
Chamorros, VIII: 149–52, 158, 373, 377, 397–400
CHAMPAGNE, IX: 307
Champe, Lt. J. E., XIII: 295–6
CHAMPION, VIII: 410, XIV: 376
CHAMPLIN, I: 357–8, 415, IX: 378, 389, X: 372, XI: 276, 342
Chance, Lt. R. E., XII: 347, 429
CHANDELEUR, I: 420, XII: 46, XIV: 381

Chandler, Capt. A. D., V: 353, VI: 242, VIII: 228, 404, XIV: 374
Chandler, Lt. Cdr. H. W., V: 309n
Chandler, Rear Adm. Theodore E., biog., X: 204n, XIII: xii; pic., 108; mentioned, I: 84, 419, X: 204–5, XI: 242, 251, 339, XII: 224n–6n, 229, 419, XIII: xii, 39, 43, 103; death, 109
Chandler, Capt. W. D., III: 392
Chandler, Capt. W. W., IV: 91
CHANDLER, VII: 9n, 335, 347–8, VIII: 230, 410, X: 204n, XII: 123, 422, XIII: 112, 306
Chaney, Maj. Gen. J. E., XIV: 65, 68
Chaney, Brig. Gen. S. A., I: 40n
Changchow, XIII: 297–9
Channel Islands, XI: 44, 297–308, 328–9; chart, 305
CHANTICLEER, XII: 239
Chapin, Capt. N. A., XIV: 373
Chapline, Capt. V. D., III: 103n
Chapman, Lt. Cdr. G. H., IV: 93
Chappell, Lt. Cdr. L. H., III: 158, IV: 226–7
Chapple, Cdr. W. G., III: 158, 179, XII: 408, 429
Chapultepec, X: 207n
CHARA, XII: 418, XIII: 311, XIV: 380
Charan Kanoa, Saipan, VIII: 168, 176, 183–211 *passim*, 325–61 *passim*; pics., 176, 193
Charbonnet, Lt. P. N., XIV: 374
CHARGER, I: 419, X: 39, XII: 125n
Charles, Cape, I: 133
CHARLES AUSBURNE, VI: 241, 308, 318, 354–6, 420–21, VIII: 415, XIII: 34, 116, 309, 323–4
CHARLES CARROLL, I: 421, II: 38, 58–62, 172, IX: 133, 137, 259n, 389, 392, XI: 335, 341, XIV: 278
Charles Cotesworth Pinckney, I: 356–7
CHARLES F. HUGHES, I: 75–6, 90, 354, 418–20, XI: 277, 342
Charles Goodnight, XIII: 313
CHARLES J. BADGER, XII: 419, XIII: 311, XIV: 217, 375, 391
CHARLES J. KIMMEL, XIII: 309
CHARLES LAWRENCE, XIV: 379
Charles M. Russell, XIII: 313
Charles Morgan, XI: 171
Charles Piez, IX: 390
CHARLES R. GREER, VII: 341, 348
CHARLES S. SPERRY, XIII: 317, XIV: 384
Charles Willson Peale, X: 214

Charles Wolcott, XIII: 324
CHARLESTON, I: 13n, III: 31n, IV: 165, 173, VII: 48–9, 334, X: 134n
Charleston, S.C., I: 279, X: 184
CHARLOTTE SCHLIEMANN, I: 129n; X: 278
CHARLOTTESVILLE, XIII: 307n
CHARON, XI: 341
CHARR, XIII: 284, 286
CHARRETTE, VII: 223, 326, 338, 349, VIII: 239, 413, XII: 425, XIII: 266, 306
CHARYBDIS, II: 190, IX: 251, 293, 393
Chase, Lt. Cdr. E. N., XIV: 381
Chase, Lt. Cdr. G. P., XIV: 384
Chase, Maj. Gen. W. C., VI: 436–42, XIII: 196, 199
Chase, Lt. William, IV: 103n
CHASE, XIV: 392
CHASER, X: 40n, 307–8
Château d'If, XI: 289
CHATEAU THIERRY, IX: 108, 386
Chatel, Ives, II: 9–10
CHATELAIN, X: 282, 291–2, 354, 378–9
CHATHAM, I: 330–31
CHAUMONT, III: 212
CHAUNCEY, VI: 331, VII: 190, 339, 348, VIII: 405, 410, 420, XII: 418, XIV: 384
Chavasse, Capt. E. H., X: 78
Cheatham, Cdr. B. B., VII: 341, 345, VIII: 409, XII: 390, XIII: 303
CHEBAGUE, X: 329n
Check, Lt. Cdr. L. J., XII: 425, XIII: 316
Chedabucto Bay, I: 24
Chefoo, III: 28, XIV: 354
Chemical Recorder, I: 216–17
CHEMUNG, I: 422, II: 36, 40n, IX: 390
CHENANGO, II: 37, 118, 131, 171, V: 353–4, 359, VII: 288, 301, 338, 346–8, VIII: 405, 420, X: 40, XII: 420, XIII: 272, XIV: 213, 374; pic., II: 174
Cheney, Cdr. W. H., XIV: 377
Chengtu, China, VIII: 8
Chennault, Maj. Gen. C. L., XII: 6, 60, 105
Chennault, Maj. John, IV: 178
CHEPACHET, X: 157, XII: 82, 423, XIII: 308
Cherbourg, XI: 44, 66, 155, 167, 174–6, 189, 212–15, 231–2, 299, 303; bombardment, 195–211; chart, 199; pics., 204–5; minesweeping, etc., 198, 216–18

Cherchel Conf., II: 184
Cheribon M., VII: 14
CHEROKEE, I: 76–7, II: 40, 44n, 138–9, 148, 169, 173–4; pic., 174–5
Cherry Point, I: 156, 249
Cherry Valley, X: 183
Cherwell, Lord, XI: 10n
Chesapeake Bay, I: 132, IX: 127
CHESTER, III: 261, 263, IV: 18, 27, 257, V: 182n, VII: 78, 339, 350, XII: 87, 140n, 425, XIV: 11, 27
CHETCO, VIII: 404
Chevalier, Lt. Jacques, VI: 415, XIV: 377
CHEVALIER, V: 353, VI: 113n, 116n, 156–8, 161, 228, 234–6 244–5; sunk, 248, 250–51
CHEVREUIL, IV: 253
Chew, Lt. Cdr. J. L., VI: 171n, 191–2
CHEW, III: 213n, IV: 276n
CHEWINK, I: 421
Chiang Kai-shek, III: 16, 36–8, 41, 44, 67–9, 73n, 75, 393, VI: 3, 8, IX: 5, XII: 6, 18, XIII: 3n, 290, XIV: 337, 342
CHICAGO (1889), III: 255n, XIV: 86n
CHICAGO (1931), III: 56n, 210, 237, 261, IV: 15, 19, 22, 38–9, 65–7, 272, 276n, 278, 292–3, V: 29–55 passim, 63n–64n, 353–8, VI: 98, VIII: 237n, X: 345n; sunk, V: 359–63, and pic., 339
CHICAGO (1945), XIV: 313
Chicago Tribune, III: 219
Chichagof, Attu, IV: 181, 215, VII: 43
Chichi Jima, VI: 94, VIII: 219, 238–40, 311–13, 354, XIV: 3–6, 10–13, 25–8, 44, 50, 56, 67
CHICKADEE, I: 422, XI: 333, 337–8
CHICKASAW, VII: 347, VIII: 410, XII: 123, 417, XIII: 306, XIV: 387; pic., XIII: 157
Chickering, Lt. Cdr. H. D., XIV: 38n, 237
Chickering, William, XIII: 105
CHICOPEE, I: 422, IX: 390, XII: 428, XIII: 318, XIV: 387
CHIDORI, III: 161, XIV: 286
CHIEF, VII: 345, XIV: 377
Chihaya, Cdr. M., III: xi, 285n, 320n, 333n, VIII: 11n
Chihaya M., V: 293
CHIKASKIA, XII: 428, XIII: 318, XIV: 387

CHIKUMA, III: 87–8, 217, 245, 276, 382, IV: 132, 139, 179n, V: 85, 88, 91, 206, 214, VI: 323, VII: 44, 137, XII: 162, 248, 266–87 *passim*, 310, 431; sunk, 288
Childs, Lt. (jg) R. L., VI: 61
Childs, Lt. Ralph, XII: 422, XIII: 304
CHILDS, III: 159, 173, 194, 272, 293, 337, VIII: 49n, IX: 92n
Chillingworth, Cdr. C. F., IV: 19, 91, 274, VII: 348, VIII: 414
CHILLIWACK, I: 337, 340
CHILTON, XIV: 176, 375
China, relations with U.S. and Japan, III: 4, 7–8, 11, 14–17, 28, 36–42, 66–72; in strategy, VII: 80–82, VIII: 4, XII: 4, XIII: 159; USN Group in, 289–302
"China Incident," III: 14, 49, 69
China V., VIII: 420
CHINCOTEAGUE, VII: 304, XIV: 65
"Chinese landing," V: 57n
Chinigo, Michael, IX: 87
CHINQUAPIN, VIII: 420, XIV: 377
Chinwangtao, III: 155, XIV: 354
Chipman, Lt. Cdr. Briscoe, IX: 387
CHIPOLA, XIV: 387
Chirikof, VII: 46, 334
Chism, Cdr. W. W., XI: 341
Chisman, Lt. H. H., X: 382
CHITOSE, III: 162–3, 182, 245, 274, 297, IV: 18, 89, V: 84, 102–4, 150–51, 171, VIII: 217–18, 247–99 *passim*, XII: 91, 162, 319, 335, 430; sunk, 325–6; pic., 327
CHIYODA, IV: 89, VII: 6, VIII: 217, 247, 263, 294, 298–9, 416, XII: 91, 162, 319, 327–8, 335, 430; sunk, 331
Choate, Lt. A. O., XIII: 304
Chochalousek, Radarman W. G., IV: 129
CHOGEI, XIII: 159
Choiseul I., V: 4, VI: 239–43, 283, 291–3; landing, 295–6
CHOKAI, III: 26, 276, 308, IV: 88, 256, V: 18, 22, 35–50 *passim*, 59, 61n, 85, 104–5, 176, 207, 234, 259, 266, VI: 323, 335, VII: 137–8, VIII: 416, XII: 162, 248, 263–83 *passim*, 430; sunk, 284–5, 288
"Chop Line," X: 20
CHOWANOC, XII: 420, XIII: 119, 306, XIV: 388
Christenson, Cdr. C. H., XII: 423
Christenson, Lt. Cdr. T. B., XIII: 308

Christian, Capt. K. C., XIV: 373
Christian, Lt. (jg) O. R., X: 197
Christiansen, Lt. F. M., VII: 347, VIII: 404, 408, 419, XII: 422
Christie, Cdr. G. L., XIV: 383
Christie, Rear Adm. Ralph W., pic., XIII: 277; mentioned, IV: 16, 20, 187n, 220, 270, 275, VI: 67n, 75–6, 83, VIII: 20, 48, 217–18, 416, XII: 398, 405, 429, XIII: 161, 320
Christie, Cdr. W. B., XII: 417, XIV: 383
Christmas I., III: 265, IV: 15n, 252
Christoph, Capt. K. J., VI: 131
Christopher, Lt. Cdr. T. A., VIII: 406
Christopher Newport, I: 182, 191n
Chung-Hoon, Cdr. G. P., VIII: 419, XII: 417, XIV: 247, 383
Chungking, III: 38–9, XII: 6, XIII: 84, 290, 300–301
Church, Lt. A. B., XII: 423
Church, Lt. Cdr. A. J., XII: 422
Church, Lt. Cdr. F. E., XII: 429
Church, Lt. Cdr. J. H., X: 377
Churchill, Hon. Winston S., pic., VI: 18; strategy, VI: 4–7, XI: 4–5, 8, IX: 221–31, 325, X: 55, XI: 277–9; destroyer-bases deal, I: 33; in Conferences, 69–70, III: 67, VII: 201, IX: 5–7, 322–8, XI: 296; Azores or Iceland, I: 67, 74, X: 45; A/SW, I: 71, 353, X: 11, 17–19, 22n, 29–31, 76, 135–8 (speech), 187; Madagascar, I: 167; N.E.I., III: 312; North Africa, II: 11–15, 218; Guadalcanal, V: 287; Medit. opns., IX: 11–12, 27, 231, 245, 303, 324–8, 353, 363, 367, 381; "light of victory" speech, 230; Italian surrender, 237–8; *Scharnhorst*, X: 243; invasion of Europe, IX: 229n, XI: 11–6, 19–25, 28, 38, 54; Adriatic or Southern France, 221–32, XII: 15; Brit. Pacific Fleet, XIII: 256–7, XIV: 102–3; Rhine crossing, XI: 322; Potsdam Declaration, XIV: 342; *The Second World War*, X: xiv, XI: xiv
CHUYO, VIII: 16n; sunk, VII: 189
Ciano, Count, I: 34, II: 18n
Ciliax, Vice Adm. Otto, I: 165
CIMARRON, I: 110–11, III: 57, 391–3, IV: 91, 97, 152, 272, VII: 341, VIII: 411, XII: 428, XIII: 318, 322, XIV: 387; class, III: 31
CIMETERRE, X: 381
CINCHONA, VIII: 411

CINCINNATI (1894), I: 206*n*, XII: 243*n*
CINCINNATI (1924), I: 83, 377, 380, 383–4, 390*n*, 419, VI: 13*n*, 131*n*, VII: 341, X: 213*n*, XI: 242*n*, 339
Cincpac-Cincpoa Staff, VI: 11; Hqrs. pic., 19
CIRCASSIA, IX: 395
CIRCE, IX: 393
Cisterna, IX: 354–8, 361, 377–8
City of Atlanta, I: 131
CITY OF DALHART, VIII: 420
City of Flint, I: 284, 356, 357*n*
City of Joliet, I: 172–3, 178*n*
City of Omaha, I: 369
City of Rayville, I: 94*n*
Civil Air Patrol, I: 276–81
Civitavecchia, IX: 329, 331
Clagett, Lt. (jg) J. H., V: 339, 367–8
Claggett, Cdr. B. D., VII: 353, VIII: 75, XII: 169–72, 429
Clague, Lt. Cdr. John, VIII: 419, XIII: 306
CLAMP, VII: 341, VIII: 411, 420, XIV: 375, 387
Clan MacTaggart, II: 284
Clancy, Lt. Cdr. A. H., XIV: 384
Clapp, Seaman, V: 99
Clapper, Lt. L. S., XII: 146*n*
Clapper, Raymond, VII: 349*n*
Claremont V., VIII: 420
CLARENCE K. BRONSON, VII: 348, VIII: 414, XII: 319, 331, 427, XIII: 318
Clarey, Cdr. B. A., VIII: 23, 415, XII: 332*n*, 333–4, 408, 429
Clark, Lt. A. A., XII: 421
Clark, Capt. A. Dayton, XI: 24*n*, 26, 165, 177, 337
Clark, Lt. Cdr. Albert H., VIII: 17
Clark, Capt. A. W., RN, I: 45
Clark, Lt. Cdr. D. A., XIV: 382
Clark, Lt. F. C., VII: 345
Clark, Maj. Glen W., VI: 64
Clark, Capt. Guy W., VII: 340, 350, VIII: 413
Clark, Cdr. J. F., XII: 418, XIII: 311, XIV: 380
Clark, Rear Adm. Joseph J., biog., VIII: 238*n*; C.O. *Suwannee*, II: 32, 39, 89; *Yorktown*, VII: 338, 348; Hollandia, VIII: 36–7, 40–41; Marianas, 174–5, 238–40, 367, 378; Philippine Sea battle, 242, 250, 258–60, 272, 286, 313, 412; "Opn. Jocko," 311–13; South China Sea, XIII: 316; Iwo, XIV: 21,

57; Okinawa, 159, 169, 199, 249, 298–9, 382, 386; June 1945 typhoon, 299–301, 308–9
Clark, Capt. J. R., XIII: 310, 313
Clark, Capt. L. M., VII: 299
Clark, Lt. Gen. Mark W., II: 66, 184–5, 215–20, IX: 13, 129*n*, 247; Italy campaign, 269–91 *passim*, 391, XI: 14, 310
Clark, Capt. R. D., XIV: 115
Clark, Lt. Cdr. Robert W., XIV: 383
Clark, Capt. Robley W., XII: 51
Clark, Capt. S. R., I: 76, 418–20, VII: 348, 352
Clark, Lt. Cdr. Sperry, I: 379
CLARK, IV: 93, 276*n*, V: 233
Clark Field, III: 170, 174, 179, XII: 69, 101, 150, 348, XIII: 13–16, 25, 29, 99, 107, 185, 193–4, 209
Clarke, Capt. C. P., RN, XI: 200–201, 211, 336
Clarke, Capt. H. D., VII: 334–6, VIII: 409
Clarke, Capt. R. S., I: 420, XIII: 306, XIV: 374
Clarke, Lt. Cdr. W. E., XIV: 385
Clarke, Capt. W. P. O., II: 22, 28–9, 83*n*, 270
Clarkson, James A., XIII: x
CLAXTON, I: 15*n*, VI: 241, 308, 321, 354, XII: 199, 226, 234, 344–5, 420, XIII: 191, 231, 313, 323–4
Clay, Cdr. D. N., XIV: 377
Clay, Capt. J. P., IX: 395, XI: 275, 342
CLAY, VIII: 407, XII: 419, XIII: 310, 312, XIV: 378
Clayton, Lt. E. P., XIV: 378
Claytor, Lt. Cdr. W. G., XIV: 326–7
Cleague, Lt. Cdr. J., XII: 422
Cleaves, Lt. Col. Haskell N., II: 30
Cleaves, Cdr. W. E., VII: 333
Clemens, Maj. Martin, V: 70, VI: 149
Clement, Lt. Cdr. J. M., I: 421
Clement, Lt. Col. William T., III: 168
Clement Clay, X: 382
Clementson, Cdr. M. K., XIII: 319
CLEMSON, I: 420, VIII: 419, X: 111–13, 168–70, 375, XII: 422, XIII: 304
CLEOPATRA, IX: 167–8
CLEVELAND (1903), XI: 125*n*
CLEVELAND (1942), II: 39, 44, 51, 162*n*, 164, 172, V: 353, VI: 106*n*, 107, 292, 308, 316, VIII: 182, 335, 362, 409, 414, IX: 393, XI: 343, XIII: 219, 244, 272–4, 321–4; class, I: lviii, 28*n*

Clifford, Lt. (jg) E. S. A., II: 265, IX: 309
Clifford, Lt. Cdr. G. M., VII: 337, 344
CLIFFROSE, XIV: 377
Clifton, Cdr. Joseph C., VI: 325n, 326, VII: 340, 350
CLINTON, XI: 339
Cloer, Coxswain C. W., XIV: 236
Cloncurry, Australia, IV: 14, 20, 32
Close, Capt. Forrest, I: 418-20, II: 37, 169n-70n, IX: xiv
Close, Lt. Cdr. R. H., VIII: 415
Cloud, Capt. B. W., IX: 386, XII: 428
Clowes, Maj. Gen. C. A., VI: 37-8
Clusman, Cdr. E. C., XIV: 375
Cluster, Lt. A. P., VI: 146
Clutterbuck, Maj. Gen. W. E., II: 277
Clyde R., XI: 77, 131
Coale, Lt. Cdr. Griffith, I: 98n
Coan, Lt. R. G., VIII: 411
Coast Guard, part of Navy, I: xivn; patrols, neutrality, 16; Greenland, 58-64, 330-34; coastal picket, 268-77; Cutters, 65n, 156, 233-5, XI: 55; Air Squadron 212, I: 249, 415; pics., 280-81
Coastwatchers, V: 11, 22, 139, 323, 337-8, 371, VI: 115, 118-20, 174, 192-3, 211; Solomons, V: 80, 230, 295, VI: 141, 159, 208, 227, 280, 290-96; New Britain, 379, 405; Gilberts, VII: 77; Philippines, VIII: 173, 218, XII: 64; China, XIII: 296-9
Coats, Lt. Cdr. W. B., VII: 334, XII: 429
COBIA, XIII: 287, 320, XIV: 14
Cochran, Cdr. D. E., XIII: 310
Cochran, Lt. Cdr. Drayton, X: 377
Cochran, Capt. Joe B., IV: 274, VIII: 406, IX: xv, XII: 429, XIII: 319
Cochrane, Rear Adm. Edward L., X: 33-4, 41, XIV: 98
Cochrane, Cdr. J. S., XI: 116, 335
Cockell, Cdr. W. A., XII: 429, XIII: 316, 319, XIV: 385
COCKRILL, X: 376
Coco Solo, I: 421, X: 189, 201
Cody, Lt. H. S., X: 381
Coe, Cdr. Benjamin, IV: 274, VIII: 409, XII: 419
Coe, Lt. Cdr. J. W., III: 159, IV: 221
COFER, XII: 383, XIII: 262, 307, 321-3
Coffee, Cdr. D. M., VIII: 404, X: 375, XII: 421, XIV: 381

Coffee, Chief Watertender, V: 132
Coffee Coast Convoys, X: 214
Coffin, Lt. A. P., V: 205n, 233
Coffin, Cdr. C. E., XIV: 378
Coffin, Cdr. H. N., VIII: 406
Coffin Corner, V: 191-2; sketch, 194
COFFMAN, X: 344, 373
COGHLAN, VII: 20-39 passim, 334, 341, 345, VIII: 409, XII: 389-92, XIII: 303
COGSWELL, VII: 348, VIII: 414, XII: 319, 425, XIII: 318
Cohan, Capt. A. M., XIV: 380
Cohen, Lt. Cdr. D. B., XII: 421
Cohen, Capt. M. Y., I: 418
Coie, Lt. J. E., X: 380
Coimbra, I: 130
Coit, Lt. H. G., XIII: 313
COLAC, VI: 47
COLAHAN, VII: 257, 344, VIII: 418, XII: 319, 426, XIII: 316, XIV: 386
Colbert, Lt. Cdr. R. G., X: 377
Colclough, Capt. O. S., XIII: 318, XIV: 384
Cold Bay, Aleutians, IV: 163, 167-83 passim, VII: 5, 38-40, 47n
Cole, Lt., AAF, III: 397
Cole, Lt. B. N., XIII: 306
Cole, C., XIII: 319
Cole, Lt. Cdr. C. C., XIV: 295
Cole, Lt. Cdr. J. E., XIII: 306, XIV: 377
Cole, Lt. (jg) W. H., X: 280
Cole, Capt. William M., V: 232, 250, 297-9, 303, 313, XII: 373-5, 384, 417, XIII: 149, 189, 191, 313, 322, XIV: 387
COLE, I: 214, 418, 420, II: 40, 44n, 138-48, 155, 171-3, 207, 272, IX: 387, 391; at Safi, chart, II: 141; pic., 149
Coleman, Capt. B. M., XIV: 379
Coleman, Cdr. D. B., XIV: 380
Coleman, Cdr. G. S., XIII: 311
Coleman, Cdr. J. W., VII: 344
Coleman, Lt. Robert L., IX: 108
Coleman, Cdr. W. D., XIV: 373
Coleman, Cdr. W. M., XII: 427
Coley, Lt. Cdr. L. E., III: 160
Coley, Lt. (jg) W. H., V: 167
COLHOUN (1918), IV: 273, V: 67; sunk, 109-10
COLHOUN (1944), XIV: 64, 186-90; sunk, 190
Colin P. Kelly Jr., IX: 158-9, X: 382
COLL, XI: 336
Collett, Cdr. J. D., XIII: 316, XIV: 382
Collett, Lt. Cdr. John A., V: 204

COLLETT, XII: 356, XIII: 316, XIV: 248, 382

Colleville, XI: 113, 146, 151–3

Collier, Lt. Roy, XIII: 307

COLLINGWOOD, I: 305

Collins, Lt. C. B., XIV: 383

Collins, Cdr. D. E., VII: 346, VIII: 404, 418, XII: 416, XIII: 309

Collins, Cdr. E. T., XIV: 380

Collins, Maj. Gen. J. Lawton, V: 341–3, 372, VI: 222, XI: 29, 93–5, 156, 167, 195–200, 203–4, 333

Collins, Maj. James F., IV: 93, V: 375

Collins, Commo. John A., RAN, III: 271, 297, 338, VIII: 73–4, 136, 405, XII: 21, 148, 421

Collins, Cdr. W. M., VIII: 413, XII: 425

Collum, Lt. Cdr. W. J., XII: 425

Colombia, X: 204

Colombo, I: 112, III: 336, 381, X: 158

COLOMBO, X: 261, 266, XI: 342

Coloney, Capt. P. R., VII: 334

COLORADO, III: 211n, 213, IV: 82n, V: 88n, 291, VI: 106, VII: 288, 301, 338, 346, VIII: 180, 328, 359–62, 378, 409, 419, X: 47n, 204n, XII: 366–7, XIII: 19, 98, 108–9, 114, 138, 304, XIV: 158n, 240, 245, 372

Colquhoun, Capt. J. S. P., XI: 334

Colthurst, Cdr. A. P., I: 360

COLUMBIA, I: 92n, V: 326, 353, VI: 106n, 241, 292, 308, 346, 415, XII: 119, 199, 227, 237, 366, 417–19, XIII: 19, 108, 126, 244, 269, 304, 325–6; pic., 108–9

Columbia M., VI: 72

Columbia V., XIV: 64

Columbian, I: 395

COLUMBINE, XI: 343

COLUMBUS, XIII: 290n

Colvin, Lt. Cdr., XIII: 34

Colwell, Cdr. J. B., VIII: 415

Coman, Commo. Robert G., I: 421, II: 38, VIII: 47

COMANCHE, I: 58, 331–4, 421

Combat Air Patrol, V: 89, 93–6, 219, VI: 325, 332, VII: 143, 326, VIII: 136, 262–3, 266–74, 312, IX: 192–3, 203–4, 250–51, XIII: 23–61 *passim*, 99, 102–3, 110–52 *passim*, 165, 181, 188, 223, XIV: 133

Combat Information Center, VI: 108n, 161, 311, VII: xxviii

Combat loading, defined, II: 27

Combat Readiness Section, Cincpac, XIV: 165

Combined, defined, II:23n, VI: x

Combined Chiefs of Staff, II: 12–15; A/S warfare, I: 406–7, X: 20–21, 338; decisions and strategy, North Africa, II: 12–15, 245, IV: 258; Casablanca, IX: 5–11; Report, Jan. 1943, VI:3–10; Directives, Feb., IX: 10–11; May, VII: 80–82; Aug., 84, 315n; Dec. 1943, XII: 4; at Casablanca, IX: 5–11, X: 16; Sicily, IX: 19, 27, 55; Italy, 230–33, 248; Cairo Conf., 322–3; Burma, VII: 83, IX: 230, 245; Escort Carriers, X: 39n, 307; Marshalls, VII: 201; Marianas, VIII: 7; invasion of Europe, XI: 3, 18–23, 28, 36–7; Southern France, 221–30; Rhine crossing, XI: 318; British Pacific Fleet Report, XIV:103

Combined Procedures Board, X: 16–17

Combs, Commo. Thomas S., IV: 173, VIII: 47–50, 120, 123, 406, XIII: 315, XIV: 385

Combs, Cdr. W. V., VIII: 404, 418, XII: 416, XIV: 383

COMET, VIII: 407, 420, XII: 419, XIII: 307, 312

Comet, IV: 174

Comfort, Lt. C. W., X: 382

COMFORT, XII: 423, XIV: 110, 244, 386, 391

Cómiso, IX: 19, 57, 126, 129, 143, 291

Comly, Lt. J. A., X: 322, 380

Comly, Capt. S. P., XIII: 307, XIV: 378

Command Areas, map, III: 278

COMMANDANT BORY, XI: 343

COMMANDANT DELAGE, II: 108, 162, XI: 343

COMMANDANT DOMINE, XI: 343

Commandante Lyra, I: 380–81

Commandos, British, IX: 150–52, 158, 162, 177–8, 182–5, 207, 234, 272, 276, 282, 329

Comming, Grp. Cdr. P., I: 259

Communications, A/SW, I: 102–7, 120, 307; N.E.I., III: 342–3; North Africa, II: 30; Solomons battles, V: 88–9, 154–7; Eniwetok, VII: 297; Truk, 328n; Philippine Sea, VIII: 255, 261–2

Comp, Cdr. C. O., XI: 338

COMPETENT, XIV: 377

Compo, Cdr. G. L., I: 419

Composite Squadron One, X: 159, 376;

Composite Squadrons (*cont'd*)
Three, Four, Five, VIII: 410, XII: 421; Six, X: 377, 380; Seven, VII: 344; Eight, X: 290, 379; Nine, 159, 176, 295, 375–6, 380; Ten, Eleven, VIII: 410, XII: 421; Twelve, Thirteen, X: 161, 377–8, XIV: 373; Nineteen, X: 351, 375–6; Twenty, Twenty-one, XII: 420, XIII: 306; Twenty-two, Twenty-five, VI: 331, VII: 338–9; Twenty-seven, XII: 420; Twenty-nine, X: 379; Thirty, VII: 339; Thirty-three through Forty-two, 344–6, VIII: 420, X: 325, 378–9; Forty-four, VII: 344; Fifty-five, Fifty-eight, X: 376–80; Sixty, Sixty-three, VII: 346–8; Sixty-five, VIII: 409, XII: 421; Sixty-six, VII: 347; Sixty-eight, VIII: 409, XII: 421; Sixty-nine, X: 299, 376; Seventy-five, 421; Seventy-six, 420, XIII: 306; Seventy-eight through Eighty-seven, XII: 420, XIII: 304–5, XIV: 373–4; Eighty-eight, XIII: 153*n*, 305, XIV: 374; Ninety through Ninety-four, XIII: 305, XIV: 373–4, 386; Ninety-five, X: 320, 378–9; Ninety-six, XIV: 374; Ninety-seven, 386
Composite Spotting Squadron One, XIII: 305
Compton, K. T., I: 29
Compton, Lewis, I: 29*n*
Compton, Lt. R. N., XIV: 377
Comstock, Capt. L. W., I: 419
Conant, Dr. James B., I: 29, 220
CONCORD (1891), II: 286
CONCORD (1923), III: 265, IV: 223, VII: 152*n*, 232*n*, VIII: 237*n*, XII: 21*n*
CONDOR, III: 96, 137
Cone, Maj. R. A., VII: 6
Coney, Capt. C. E., pic., XII: 70; mentioned, VII: 406, XII: 415
Confesor, Tomás, XIII: 228; quoted, vii
CONFLICT, VI: 121–2, 297
Coningham, Air Vice Marshal Sir A., IX: 22
Conkey, Lt. Cdr. G. L., X: 289, 377
CONKLIN, XII: 53, XIV: 307
Conkling, Lt. R. L., XIII: 313
Conlan, Capt. C. V., VIII: 410, XII: 416, XIII: 309
Conley, Capt. T. F., VII: 338, VIII: 419, XII: 199, 221, 419, XIII: 304
Conlon, Lt. Cdr. E. T., XIV: 380
Conn, Lt. Cdr. J. P., XIV: 384

Connaway, Cdr. Fred, I: 421, VII: 188–9, 342
CONNECTICUT, I: 206*n*, IX: 14*n*
Conner, Cdr. F. S., XII: 429
Conner, Lt. Cdr. R. R., IX: 385, XI: 342
CONNER (1918), X: 204*n*
CONNER (1943), VII: 338, 349, VIII: 240, 413, XII: 366*n*, 370, 425, XIII: 306
Connole, Cdr. D. R., XIV: 289
Connor, Cdr. John, I: 76, 418, X: 158
Connor, Cdr. T. H. W., XIV: 385
Conoley, Maj. O. M., V: 193
Conolly, Vice Adm. Richard L., biog., VII: 232*n*; pics., VIII: 376, IX: 203; Comdesron 6, III: 211*n*, 393; Comlandcrabnaw, II: 273–4, IX: 29–33, 93, 325; Sicily, 28–30, 65–85 *passim*, 89, 124, 142, 166, 177, 224, 386; Salerno, 246, 272–7, 298*n*, 325, 393; Marshalls, VII: 86, 207, 232–50 *passim*, 272, 332, 345; Marianas, VIII: 159, 170–72, 219, 324, 371–401 *passim*, 418; Leyte, XII: 10–14*n*, 140–42, 156, 418; Lingayen, XIII: 97, 130, 144–5, 150, 156, 306
CONQUÉRANT, II: 110*n*, 168, 245
Conrad, Lt. Cdr. C. P., I: 146
Conrad Weiser, X: 382
Conrath, Maj. Gen., IX: 117
Conroy, Col. Gardiner, VII: 90, 126
Consolvo, Lt. Cdr. C. W., VII: 347
CONSTELLATION, I: 419
Construction Battalions. *See* Seabees
Contessa, II: 37, 44*n*, 118–19, 129*n*, 131
Converse, Capt. A. F., X: 258–59, 265, 337, 362, XI: 340
CONVERSE, VI: 308, 317–18, 354, 357, 420, VIII: 240, 415, XIII: 35–6, 132, 323
Convoy and Routing Section, CNO, I: 50, 101, 206–7, 332, X: 22*n*
"Convoy College," VIII: 24, XII: 333, 399, 405–8
Convoy Commodore, I: 18, X: 153–4
Convoy (Atlantic Conference of 1943), X: 19–20; a sample C.C., 155–56
Convoys, definitions and descriptions, I: 17–22, 99–100, X: 153–5; organization, I: 12; U.S.N. prepares for, 44–5, 49–55; U.S. begins, X: 6; air cover, I: 119–20; route chart, 162–3; Adm. King on, 310; system, 404–6; average no. ships, Apr. 1943, 405; Brazilian, 263, 386–90; Central Transatlantic, 109–13, 352–8, X: 108–32; Caribbean, I: 258–9, 347–52; Coastal, 252–7, X: 9;

route chart, I: 254–5; Colliers to France, XI: 303–6; Gulf of Mexico, I: 347; Interlocking, 260–65, X: 9, 246, and chart, I: 261; Mediterranean, 249–73, pic., X: 264; Murmansk, *see* North Russia Run; Northern Transatlantic merchant, I: 12, 18–26, 56–8, 65–102 *passim*, 114, 117–25, 317–26, 334–46, X: 9, 65–84, 133–52; abbreviations, I: 101; charts & tables, 96–7, X: 328; pics., I: 106–7, 128–9, 231, X: 168; Pacific, III: 265; tanker, I: 353, X: 135; troop, I: 22, 118–19, 326–34, 405, X: 133–5, 246; halted, 361 Convoys, individual:

AS–4, I: 381, II: 13*n*; AT–12, I: 118*n*; AT–15, 118; AT–20, 327; AT–23, II: 193; BT–6, I: 387–9, BT–14, X: 211–12; BX–19, I: 257; CU–17, X: 318; CU–21, 318; GN–1, I: 260; GUF–2, II: 247; GUS–3, I: 355; GUS–7A, X: 111; GUS–8, –9, –10, 110, 116–19; GUS–13, 126; GUS–18, 158–9, 162; GUS–23, 168; GUS–24, 171; GUS–37, 282; GUS–38, –39, 256–9; GUS–74, 339

HX–65, –72, –90, –94, I: 23–4; HX–112, 56; HX–126, 65; HX–133, 65; HX–143, 71; HX–150, 86, 90, disposition diagrams, 88; HX–156, 94; HX–159, 108; HX–160, 226; HX–166, 120; HX–179, –183, 119; HX–196, 123; HX–212, 323; HX–217, 325–6, chart, 326–7; HX–218, –219, 325–6; HX–228, X: 77; HX–229, I: 343; HX–233, 344–6; HX–235, X: 77; HX–237, 77–8; HX–239, 81–3; HX–262, 151; HX–322, 337; HX–337, 339; JW–51A, B, I: 366; JW–52, –53, 367–9; JW–54A, X: 236; JW–55B, 237–9; JW–56A, B, 304–6; JW–57, –58, 307–8; JW–60, 310; JW–64, 311; JW–65, 313

KMF–A, II: 191, 195*n*; KMF–O, 191; KMF–1, 195*n*; KMF–5, 254; KMF–25A, X: 261; KMS–A, KMS–O, II: 191; KN–136, I: 260; KN–382, X: 344, MFK–1, II: 284

NA–1, –8, I: 118; NG–376, X: 193; NG–500, I: 260; NK–500, 260

ON–17, X: 152*n*; ON–18, I: 90; ON–41, 107; ON–67, 121–2; ON–68, 123; ON–72, 154; ON–77, 304; ON–103, 306; ON–115, 321; ON–127, 322; ON–154, 325; ON–166, 337–41, and chart, 339; ON–184, X: 79–81; ON–202, –204, –206, –207, 139–51; ON–217, 152*n*; ON–277, 337; ONS–5, 67–76, 79, 192, and chart, 72–3; ONS–6, –7, 77; ONS–18, 139, 142–5; ONS–20, 148–9; ONS–92, I: 102*n*; ONS–102, 228, 305–6; OS–51, X: 131

PQ–8, I: 160; PQ–12, 165; PQ–13, 166; PQ–14, 167*n*; PQ–15, 169; PQ–16, 171–5, 178; PQ–17, 179–92, 358–9, and chart, 176–7; PQ–18, 360–65, X: 307*n*; QP–8, I: 165; QP–11, 168–9; QP–12, 171; QP–13, 178, 181; QP–14, 365; X: 307*n*

RA–53, I: 369–70; RA–54A, –55A, X: 236–8; RA–57, –59, –60, –62, 308–10; RA–64, 311–13; RA–66, 313; RB–1, I: 323

SC–26, I: 56; SC–41, –42, –44, 71, 90; SC–48, 92–3, and pic., 93; SC–52, 95; SC–94, 321–2; SC–95, 105*n*; SC–100, –104, 322–3; SC–107, 324; SC–118, 334–6, and chart, 336–7; SC–121, –122, 341–3; SC–123, –129, –130, X: 77–9; SC–143, 147–8; SC–156, 318; SG–6, I: 330; SG–19, 331; SL–125, 324; SM–2, XI: 263*n*; SN–73, I: 249

TA–18, I: 327; TAG–20, 284; TAW–15, 348–9; TB–1, 387; TF–2, X: 216; TG–4, 350; TJ–1, 389, 215–16; TJ–2, 220; TO–1, I: 351; TS–37, X: 186; TU–2, 134; TU–5, 134; U–2A, XI: 102–3

UC–1, I: 354; UC–6, X: 135; UGF–2, II: 246; UGF–10, X: 261; UGL–2, –3, –4, II: 273*n*; UGS–2, –3, 176, 247; UGS–4, –6, I: 356–8, X: 88*n*; UGS–6A, II: 273*n*; UGS–7A, I: 285; UGS–8, X: 275; UGS–8A, 109–10; UGS–9, 112–14; UGS–10, 116, and chart, 114–15; UGS–11, 117; UGS–12, 119–21; UGS–13, I: 285, X: 122; UGS–14, 125; UGS–15, 127; UGS–19, 159; UGS–20, 161; UGS–21, 155–8;

Convoys, individual (*cont'd*)
   UGS-24, 168; *UGS-36*, 251, 266;
   UGS-37, *-38*, *-39*, 267-8;
   UGS-40, 269-72, 381-2; *UGS-42*,
   -46, *-48*, *-60*, 272-3; *UT-2*,
   -3, 134; *WS-12X*, I: 109-13, and
   T.O., 111
Conway, Lt. Cdr. J. P., XIII: 306
CONWAY, VI: 229-32; V: 353, VI: 297,
   303, 415, 422, 428-9, VIII: 410,
   XII: 370, XIII: 311, 313, 323
Conwell, Cdr. L. C., VI: 331, VII: 339,
   348, VIII: 405, 410, XII: 418, XIV: 384
CONY, VI: 228-30, 242, 295, VIII: 408,
   XII: 199, 237, 370, 416, XIII: 310, 313,
   324
CONYNGHAM, III: 104, 213n, IV: 91, 113n,
   151n, 276n, V: 205, 226, VI: 98n, 260-
   62, 269n, 376, 381, 390, VIII: 408,
   XII: 390-92, XIII: 192, 202, 236, 275,
   313, 322-4
Cook, Capt. A. G., Jr., I: 421, II: 39,
   246, VII: 347
Cook, Vice Adm. Arthur B., biog.,
   X: 197n; mentioned, I: 83, 110-11,
   X: 197, 297, XI: 146
Cook, Lt. Cdr. B. E., XIV: 385
Cook, Lt. (jg) C. C., X: 382
Cook, Lt. Cdr. Charles O., VI: 169-70
Cook, Lt. Cdr. Duncan, II: 192
Cook, Lt. Cdr. F. E., XII: 426
Cook, Ens. George C., IV: 220
Cook, Cdr. L. B., VIII: 408, XII: 419
Cooke, Rear Adm. Charles M., I: 116,
   III: 118, VI: 9, IX: 7, XI: 54-6,
   XII: 291
Cooke, Rear Adm. Henry D., X: 134
Cooke, Lt. Cdr. L. V., XIV: 381
Cooke, Capt. William R., III: 393;
   VI: 228, 237, 242
Cookson, Col. F. E., IX: 130
COOLBAUGH, XII: 244, 304-5 420,
   XIII: 307
Cooley, Rear Adm. T. R., VIII: 415,
   XII: 427, XIII: 318, XIV: 384
Coolidge, Lt. Cdr. J. W., VI: 228,
   X: 381
Cooper, Capt. G. R., VII: 335, 349,
   VIII: 413
Cooper, Lt. Cdr. J. E., III: 158, 290, 333,
   V: 297
Cooper, Cdr. J. W., II: 39, VIII: 408,
   XII: 419
Cooper, Capt. T. V., I: 111, 418,

   VII: 346, VIII: 418, XII: 416,
   XIII: 308, XIV: 378
Cooper, Capt. W. G., V: 151, 162, 168,
   232, XII: 419
COOPER, XII: 371; sunk, 371-2
COPAHEE, IV: 180n, VIII: 411
Copeland, Brig. Gen. J. E., VII: 334
Copeland, Lt. Cdr. R. G., VII: 347
Copeland, Lt. Cdr. R. L., XIV: 384
Copeland, Lt. Cdr. R. W., XII: 262, 270,
   421
Copeman, Cdr. T. H., VII: 339, 349,
   413, XII: 425, XIII: 317
Copping, Cdr. B. S., X: 376
CORAL, I: 138
Coral Sea, IV: 6-7, 16; Jap. and U.S.
   Forces, 17-20; Tulagi strike, 21-7;
   Battle of, 28-64, 74; aircraft losses, 56;
   charts, 8-9, 12, 23, 36, 47, 50, 54; pics.,
   52-3, 60-61
CORAL SEA, VII: 337, 344, VIII: 207, 405,
   420
CORBESIER, XII: 53
Corbet-Singleton, Cdr. C. H., IX: 339n
Corbett, Maj. Gen. Charles H., XI: 29
Corbett, Sir Julian, VI: vii, VIII: 383,
   XII: 59
Corbin, Cdr. C. T., XIV: 387
Corbus, Lt. Cdr. J., I: 421
Cordiner, Cdr. D. L. L., XII: 417,
   XIII: 309, XIV: 383
CORE, I: 419, X: 40, 117-18, 125-8, 161-
   2, 176, 192, 198n, 222, 328-9, 350-51,
   370-73, 377-8
Corey, Cdr. H. G., VI: 262, XII: 421
CORKWOOD, XIV: 127, 377
Corlett, Maj. Gen. Charles H., pics.,
   VII: 55, 278; mentioned, 62, 251, 256-
   7, 265-75, 279, 343
Corman, Cdr. H., XIV: 387
Cormier, Lt. (jg) R. L., X: 122
Corn, Capt. W. A., VII: 334-6
"Corncobs," XI: 26, 72
CORNELIAN, XI: 337
Cornelius Gilliam, X: 382
Cornelius Hartnett, I: 367-8
Cornell, Lt. Cdr. W. G., VII: 57,
   XIV: 379
Cornell, Seaman, V: 133
Cornwall, Lt. Col. (New Zealand),
   VI: 414
Cornwall, U.S. Bases in, XI: 58-61
CORNWALL, III: 383
Cornwallis, X: 331

Cornwell, Capt. D. S., XIV: 374
Coron Bay, XII: 311–12
CORONADO, VIII: 404
Corpus Christi, Texas, I: 248, 279, X: 189; oil field, I: 253
CORREGIDOR, VII: 337, 344, VIII: 405, 420
Corregidor I., III: 167, 172, 194, 204–6, IV: 220, XIII: 11, 99, 205; map, 190; landing, 202–4; pic., 196
Corrie, Lt. (jg) O. W., II: 150n
Corrigan, VI: 103
Corrigan, Flight Lt. J. A., VI: 159
CORRY (1921), XIV: 86n
CORRY (1942), I: 420, II: 39, X: 279–80, 377, XI: 88, 106–8, 334; sunk, 96
Corsica, IX: 215, 242, 304–8, XI: 246
Cortner, Cdr. C. E., VII: 345, VIII: 411, XII: 419, XIII: 305
Corvettes, I: 13, 125n
CORVINA, VII: 187, 342; sunk, 188
CORVUS, XIV: 380
Cory, Lt. G. L., VI: 266
Cosgrove, Lt. Cdr. C. R., VIII: 411, XII: 428, XIII: 318, XIV: 387
"Cossac," XI: 18–21, 25–7; plan, 221
COSSATOT, XIV: 387
Costello, Lt. Cdr. R. W., XIV: 376
Costet, Capit. de Frég., II: 99
Cota, Brig. Gen. N. D., XI: 139–40
Cote, Lt. J. J., XIII: 91n, 157
Cotentin Peninsula, XI: 20–21, 44, 48, 93, 190, 195–6, 215
Cotten, Cdr. J. H., XII: 419, XIII: 311, XIV: 375
COTTEN, VII: 338, 348, VIII: 414, XII: 31, 331, 427, XIII: 318
Cottingham, Lt. R. B., VII: 349, VIII: 415
COTTON, X: 313
Couble, Cdr. A. J., VIII: 408
Coughlin, Lt. (jg) P. E., IX: 133n
COURAGE, I: 387, 390n
COURAGEOUS, X: 4
Couronne, La, XI: 286–7
Courseulles, XI: 188
Courten, Adm. de, IX: 244
Courtney, Rear Adm. C. E., I: 16
Courtney, Maj. H. D., VII: 333
Courts of Inquiry, Dec. 1944 typhoon, XIII: 82–4; 1945 typhoon, XIV: 307–8; *Indianapolis,* 327
Cousins, Cdr. A. P., VIII: 403, XII: 416, XIII: 310
Coveney, W. J., X: 382

Cover, Lt. Cdr. C. L., XII: 428, XIII: 318, XIV: 387
COWANESQUE, XIII: 98, 308, 325, XIV: 387
Coward, Capt. Jesse G., IV: 271, V: 87, 232, 245, VII: 345, VIII: 409; Surigao battle, XII: 199–222 *passim,* 232, 237, 418; Philippines, XIII: 21, 314; pic., XII: 215
COWDRAY, II: 198–9, 212
Cowdrey, Capt. R. T., VI: 294
COWELL, VII: 338, 349, VIII: 413, XII: 425, XIII: 317, XIV: 256
COWICHAN, XI: 335
COWIE, I: 420, II: 40, IX: 113, 141, 146, 389
COWPENS, VII: xxvii, 92, 116, 141, 190–91, 208, 326, 330, 338, 349, 353, VIII: 36, 174, 238, 250, 268, 273, 414, XII: 90, 100–102, 309, 424–5, XIII: 54, 70, 181, 315, XIV: 21
Cox, Lt. (jg) Clifford C., X: 195
Cox, Lt. R. D., XI: 334
Cox, Lt. (jg) W. N., XIII: 39
Cox, Cdr. W. R., VIII: 409, XII: 211n, 418, XIII: 307, XIV: 385
Coxe, Lt. Cdr. A. B., VI: 113n
Coye, Cdr. J. S., I: 421, VI: 70, VIII: 22, XII: 429
Cozumel I., I: 151
Crace, Rear Adm. J. G., III: 266, 388–9, IV: 15–16, 19, 22–5, 29, 37–46, 62, 65
Craig, Col. Edward A., VI: 347
Craig, Lt. Cdr. E. F., XII: 427
Craig, Lt. Cdr. J. R., VI: 107
Craig, Capt. Kenneth, X: 345, 349, 378
Craig, Lt. Cdr. V. H., VII: 341, XIII: 104, 162n, 305
Craig, Lt. W. D., XIV: 375
Craig, Capt. Wyatt, IV: 174, 176, VII: 337
Craighill, Lt. Cdr. R. R., V: 47
Craighill, Cdr. R. S., XII: 374, 417
Crafts, Lt. Cdr. D. A., XIII: 313
Cram, Lt. Col. Jack, V: 177
Cramer, Lt. H. C., XII: 100, 429
Cramer, Lt. Cdr. R. H., VIII: 230, 411
Crandell, Capt. P. S., XIII: 307, XIV: 380
Crane, Lt. R. H., I: 421
Cras, Med. en Chef Hervé, XI: x, 146n
Craven, Capt. F. S., III: 392, IV: 173
Craven, Wesley F., *Army Air Forces in*

Craven, Wesley F. (cont'd)
  World War II, VII: 3n, X: xiv,
  XI: xiii, XII: viii, XIII: xi
CRAVEN, III: 211n, VI: 98n, 214–16,
  VII: 350, VIII: 413
Craw, Col. Demas T., II: 125, 133–4
Crawford, Capt. D. S., XIII: 6
Crawford, Capt. J. G., VIII: 415,
  XII: 426, XIII: 317
Creasy, Adm. Sir George E., XI: xi, 19,
  69
Creath, Lt. Cdr. R. F., XIII: 313
CREE, XIV: 387
Creehan, Capt. E. P., I: 418, V: 213–14,
  220–21, XIV: 380
Creelman, Lt. B. W., XI: 315
Creighton, Cdr. L. W., I: 421, II: 38,
  IX: 268, 361–2, 386, XI: 340, 343
Crenshaw, Capt. J. S., VI: 145
Crenshaw, Capt. Russell S., I: 135n
Cresap, Lt. Cdr. J. B., XII: 419,
  XIII: 311, XIV: 375
CRESCENT CITY, IV: 273, V: 231, 352,
  VI: 98n, 297, 303n, VIII: 418, XII: 417,
  XIII: 94n
Cresswell, Lt. Col. L. B., V: 72
Creswell, Sqd. Ldr. R., VI: 65
CRETE, IX: 396, XI: 343
Cretin, Cape, VIII: 63, 135
CREVALLE, VIII: 21–2, XIV: 292n
Crichton, Cdr. C. H., VII: 349
"Cripdiv 1," XII: 95–106; pic., 102
Cripps, Sir Stafford, X: 18
Crisbecq, XI: 157, 167
Crist, Lt. H. M., XI: 299n, 300
Crist, Cdr. L. E., II: 106n
Crist, Capt. M. E., X: 295, 380
Crist, Lt. T. C., VIII: 380
Cristobal, I: 152
Crittenden, Lt. Cdr. J. L., VII: 333
CROAKER, VIII: 17n
CROATAN, I: 419, X: 40, 125–6, 283–4, 320–
  22, 345–50, 372–3, 378; pic., X: 41
Crocker, Lt. D. S., VII: 223, 411
Crockett, Lt. H. M., VI: 327
Crockett, Lt. L. D., X: 196, 197n
Crocodile, Camp, VI: 282, 298
Croisette, Cap, XI: 289
Crommelin, Cdr. C. L., VII: 192n, 338,
  XIV: 383
Crommelin, Capt. Henry, I: 420, II: 39,
  VII: 338, 344, VIII: 405, 419, XII: 416
Crommelin, Capt. J. G., VII: 141n
Crommelin, Lt. Cdr. Richard G.,
  XIV: 312, 385n

Cromwell, Capt. John P., pic., VII: 198;
  mentioned, 188–9, 342
Cronin, Capt. J. C., XI: 342, XIII: 305,
  XIV: 18, 374
Crooked Island Passage, X: 190, 193
CROOME, IX: 396
Crosby, Lt. J. R., X: 351, 378
CROSBY, VI: 142, 145, 152, 156n, 295,
  381, 415, VIII: 404, XII: 120, 382, 417,
  XIII: 26n, 307
CROSLEY, XIV: 378
Cross, Lt. Cdr. H. E., X: 376
Cross, Cdr. J. G., VIII: 411
Cross, Cdr. R. C., XIII: 281
Cross, Lt. T. W., VIII: 419
Crouch, Cdr. E. M., III: 160, 378
Crouch, Maj. W. L., VIII: 336
Crouter, Cdr. M. H., V: 231
CROUTER, XIV: 381
Crowe, Lt. Col. H. P., VII: 159, 166,
  VIII: 193
Crowe, Lt. R. H., XIV: 377
Crowell, Lt. R. B., VII: 333
Crowl, Philip A., XIII: 127n; U.S. Ma-
  rines and Amphibious War,
  VII: 146n, VIII: 186n
Crowley, Cdr. John D., IV: 174,
  VIII: 416
Crowley, Lt. R. E., XIV: 377
CROWLEY, XII: 429, XIII: 71, 319
Crudele, Chief Signalman, VI: 248
Cruise, Capt. E. A., VII: 306, 347,
  VIII: 306
Cruiser Division Two, I: 383n, 419,
  VII: 340; Four, V: 231, XII: 419,
  XIII: 39n; Five, V: 205, VII: 339,
  XIV: 11–12; Six, I: 206n, III: 212n,
  236, IV: 91, VIII: 415, XII: 424,
  XIII: 316; Seven, I: 419; Eight, 83n,
  419; Nine, VI: 161, 181, XII: 419;
  Ten, VIII: 413, XII: 113n, 424,
  XIII: 316; Twelve, V: 353, VI: 289,
  308, VIII: 414, XII: 419, XIII: 274,
  304; Thirteen, VI: 289, 340–41,
  VII: 352, VIII: 413, XII: 427,
  XIII: 318; Fourteen, VIII: 415,
  XII: 426, XIII: 318, XIV: 382; Fifteen,
  VI: 435; Sixteen, XIV: 385; Seven-
  teen, XIII: 317, XIV: 384; Twenty-
  one, XII: 431
Cruising Club of America, I: 268–9
Crutcher, Capt. C. R., II: 38, 64n, 83n
Crutchfield, Lt. R. R., X: 343
Crutchley, Rear Adm. V. A. C., pic.,
  VIII: 49; mentioned, IV: 269, 272–4,

278–81, V: 15, 22, 25–35, 52, 63, 64n, VI: 39, 51, 130, 380–83, 390, 444, VIII: 47, 76, 91, 96–7, 106, 122–30, 136, 220, 405
CRUX, XII: 423
Cruz, Pt., Guadalcanal, pic., V: 18
CRYSTAL, IV: 93
CS-13, X: 190, 370
Cuba, Navy, I: 208–9, X: 190; U.S. bases, I: 244. *See* Guantanamo
Cubs, bases, IV: 252; Cub One, V: 67–8
Culbert, Ens., II: 216
Culbert, Hon. Frederick P., II: 6n
Culebra I., II: 20, 267
Culhane, Maj. Tom, pic., VII: 167; mentioned, 164
Culin, Col. F. L., VII: 42, 46–8
Cullinan, Cdr. Ralph, XII: 79, XIII: 319, XIV: 374
Cullins, Cdr. T. O., XI: 340
Culver, Capt. B. K., VIII: 418, XII: 418, XIII: 310, XIV: 380
CUMBERLAND, I: 181
Cumming, Col. S. C., VII: 236n, 273
Cummings, Lt. Col. G. I., II: 79n
CUMMINGS (1913), II: 21n, IX: 14n
CUMMINGS (1936), III: 104, 213n, V: 335n, VII: 350, 425
Cunha, Lt. Cdr. G. D. M., XII: 349n, XIII: 315
Cunningham, Adm. of the Fleet Sir Andrew B., biog., IX: 13n; pics., II: 218, IX: 162; Admiral King on, 13–14; C. Matapan, II: 6–7, X: 252; C. in C. Med., II: 12, 16, 32 ("not afford to wait"), 182–3 ("snap into Bizerta"), 202–3 ("must be trained seamen"), 209, 218, 226 ("Gallic fervour"), 277; Sicily, IX: 13–14; messages, 19, 66; Malta HQ, 29, 79n, 101, 124; on Admiral Kirk, 143; on merchant marine, 159; on British landings, 165–8; on naval gunfire, 206–9; on evacuation, 212–13, 216; Taranto landing, 235–6; on Italian surrender, 239, 244, 253; Salerno, 246–9, 293, 297; First Sea Lord, XI: 69; Southern France, 231; dispatch on Montgomery quoted, IX: 206–7; *Sailor's Odyssey*, 216n, 152
Cunningham, Civil Eng. A. C., VII: 101, 106
Cunningham, Cdr. C. C., XII: viii
Cunningham, Lt. Cdr. C. R., XIII: 306, XIV: 376

Cunningham, Adm. Sir John, IX: x, 149, 323–4, 327–8, 350, 359–60, X: 252, 258–9, 264, XI: 222, 236, 247, 311; pics., IX: 283, XI: 244
Cunningham, Brig. Gen. J. W., VI: 373
Cunningham, Cdr. W. S., III: 228–9n, 243, 248–9, 252–4n
Cupero, Pharmacist J. E., XII: 316
Curaçao, I: 147, 248, 263–4, 324, 347, 353, X: 196, VIII: 345
CURLEW, X: 199n
Curran, Lt. J. A., VI: 157
Curran, Joseph, I: 298, 300
CURRENT, XII: 104, XIV: 387–8
CURRIER, XI: 343
Currin, Lt. Col. M. S., VI: 152
CURRITUCK, VIII: 50–51, XIII: 118, 311
Curry, Capt. Duncan, XIV: 386
Curry, Cdr. R. R., X: 342
Curtin, Cdr. J. F., XI: 334
Curtin, Hon. John, IV: 63
Curtin, Cdr. N. R., XI: 334
Curtis, Lt. Cdr. A. D., VI: 297, XIV: 376
Curtis, Capt. L. H., VII: 341, 345, XIV: 375
Curtis, Cdr. R. W., XIII: 316, 318
CURTISS, III: 113–15, IV: 252n, 263n, 270, V: 205, 344, VI: 139n, VII: 98, 118, 211, 340, 350, XIV: 279
Curts, Capt. M. E., XII: 419, XIII: 126, 304
CUSHING (1915), X: 189n
CUSHING (1936), V: 205, 232, 237, 241, 244, 254; sunk, 251, 256
CUSHING (1944), XII: 319, 426, XIII: 316, XIV: 386
Custer, 1st Sgt. S. A., V: 68–9
CUSTER, VII: 347, VIII: 410, XII: 418, XIII: 311, XIV: 380
Cutler, Lt. P., X: 381
Cutler, Capt. Roger W., VI: 339, 415–19, VIII: 419, XIII: 311, 314, XIV: 380
Cutter, Lt. Cdr. S. D., VIII: 17, 415
CUTTLEFISH, IV: 92, 99n, 205; pic., 206
Cutts, Capt. E. F., I: 421
CUYAMA, VII: 334, XIV: 387
Cuyo East Pass, XII: 311
CYANE, IV: 173
CYCLOPS, I: 126, 130
Cyclops Mts. and airfield, VIII: 60, 76, 86
CYGNET, X: 313
Cynthia Olsen, III: 221n
CYRENE, XIII: 308

D

Dabney, Cdr. T. B., XIII: 320
DACE, VII: 353, VIII: 75, XII: 169–74, 183, 429
Dadavata, VI: 141
DADE, XIV: 379
Dagupan, XIII: 153, 155
Dagupan R., XIII: 130–32
DAHLGREN, I: 138–9, 143, 347, 420, X: 194
Dahlquist, Maj. Gen. J. E., XI: 236, 268, 272, 276, 341
Daietsu M., XIII: 282
Daigen M. No. 3, VI: 74
Dairen, XIV: 355
Daisy Moller, X: 276
Dakar, II: 7–9, 43–7, 91, 110–11, 160, 163*n*, 218, 240, X: 209, 280, 296, 306
Dalap I., VII: 226–8, 305
Dale, Lt. Cdr. J. R., XII: 308–9, 420
Dale, Cdr. R. H., VII: 339, 349
DALE, III: 104, 213*n*, IV: 271, V: 28*n*, 86, VII: 23, 31, 35, 335–7, 346, VIII: 419, XII: 428, XIII: 319
DALLAS, I: 86, 136, 418, 420, II: 37, 122*n*, 123–5, 129–33, 272*n*, 285, IX: 388, 391, X: 381; pic., II: 131
Dallis, Lt. Cdr. P. A., XIV: 377
DALMATIA, XI: 337
Dalton, Lt. Cdr. C. M., I: 420, VII: 337, 344
Dalton, Lt. Cdr. G. F., XIII: 305
DALY, VI: 382, 386, 436, 444, VIII: 66, 127, 406, XII: 199, 218–20, 421, XIV: 239, 373
Damage Control, VII: xxix, XIV: 98–9; Jap., VIII: 281–2
Damon, Lt. Cdr. A. H., V: 157*n*
DAMON M. CUMMINGS, XIV: 381
Damortis, XIII: 145, 154
Dampier Strait, VI: 254, 260, 271–4, 369–70, 382–3
Dana, Lt. (jg) Paul, VIII: 178
DANAË, II: 252, III: 340
Danckwerts, Rear Adm. V. H., I: 45, III: 57*n*
DANDALO, IX: 168
Daniel, Commo. C. S., I: 195

Daniel, Capt. H. C., IV: 91, V: 205, XIV: 383
Daniel, Capt. J. C., XIV: 381
Daniel, Lt. Cdr. T. S., III: 159
Daniel Morgan, I: 188, 190, 191*n*
DANIEL T. GRIFFIN, X: 318, XIV: 191, 377
Daniel Webster, IX: 390
Daniels, Josephus, I: xxxv
Dannenberg, Cdr. J. Y., VII: 345, VIII: 408
Danz, Lt. L. F., IX: 389
Dao Channel, XII: 50
Dapitan, XII: 238
Darby, Lt. Col. W. O., II: 191*n*, IX: 112, 272, 329, 338, 342
DARBY, XIII: 307
Darden, 1st Lt. J. H., X: 130
Darden, Capt. T. F., XIII: 246
DARING, VI: 297
Darlan, Adm. J. L. F., pic., II: 218; mentioned, 4, 7–11, 50*n*, 67, 133, 155, 164–6, 185–7, 206–55 *passim*; "deal," 215–19; killed, 255, IX: 13
Darrit I., VII: 226–8
Darroch, Lt. Cdr. J. W., XIII: 319
Dart R., pic., XI: 68
DARTER, VII: 353, XII: 169–73, 183, 406, 429; sunk, 173–4
Dartmouth, Eng., XI: 58, 64, 86, 318
Darwin, III: 177, 197, 212, 268, 277–9, 282, 298, 303*n*, 314–20, 330, IV: 20, 75, 79, 83, VIII: 28, 86, 97, XIII: 256
DASH, I: 422
DASHER, II: 223, X: 39, 307*n*
DASHIELL, VII: 153, 158, 168, 338, VIII: 405, 419, XII: 417, XIII: 24, 32, 141, 309, XIV: 383
Dashing Wave, VII: 341
Dasol Bay, XII: 311, 357
Daubin, Rear Adm. F. A., I: 421
Daunis, Cdr. S. S., XI: 311, 338
DAUPHIN, I: 337, 340*n*, 342
Davao, town and gulf, III: 159, 163, 169, 281–2, 296, 304, IV: 224, VIII: 13, 66, 88, 107, 119–20, 145, 218–19, XII: 300, XIII: 25, 29, 236, 239, 246, 250, 268

Davenport, Cdr. R. M., XIV: 285
Davey, Lt. (jg) K. L., VII: 341
David, Lt. (jg) A. L., X: 292–3
David, Fireman James F., VII: 27
David Campbell, IX: 390
David Dudley Field, XIII: 150, 313, 326
David H. Atwater, I: 133
David McKelvey, I: 138
David Taylor Experimental Model Basin, I: 220
David W. Branch, VII: 334
David W. Field, VII: 334
DAVID W. TAYLOR, VIII: 230, 411, XII: 428, XIII: 317, XIV: 12
Davidson, Lt., III: 246
Davidson, Lt. Cdr. C. O., VIII: 410
Davidson, Brig. Gen. G. H., XI: 233
Davidson, Rear Adm. L. A., biog., IX: 191*n*; pic., 42; CTF-37, I: 326; Comcrudiv 8, 419; North Africa, II: 33, 39, 50, 54, 135, 138–9, 149–52; Sicily, IX: 105*n*, 175, 191–217 *passim*, 389; Salerno, 235, 266, 303, 391; Anzio, 362, 375–7; Southern France, XI: 215, 238, 248, 251–4, 284–9, 311, 338
Davidson, Lt. L. G., X: 382
Davidson, Lt. Cdr. W. B., V: 44
Davies, Capt. G. O. C., XI: 342
Davies, Lt. Cdr. T. D., X: 220
Davis, Rear Adm. A. C., IV: 271, V: 86, 99–100, XIV: 372
Davis, Signalman C. L., VI: 273
Davis, Cdr. George F., V: 306, XIII: 106, 304
Davis, Rear Adm. Glenn B., I: 419, V: 233, 270*n*, 280–82, VI: 146, VII: 339, 348, 353, VIII: 415, XII: 427, XIII: 83, 316
Davis, Cdr. H. J., XIV: 375
Davis, Capt. James K., XIII: 307
Davis, Cdr. James W., IV: 20, 225, VI: 71–2, VIII: 21
Davis, Lt. Cdr. John, I: 419
Davis, Lt. Cdr. John K., XI: 329, 336
Davis, Cdr. J. R., I: 418
Davis, Maj. L. K., V: 374
Davis, Capt. N. B., XIII: 19, 32, 37*n*, 39*n*, 40, 46, 50, 189
Davis, Lt. (jg) Nelson, XII: 422
Davis, Lt. P. J., XIII: 317
Davis, Capt. R. K., IX: 175
Davis, Capt. R. O., V: 353, 357, 362
Davis, Lt. Cdr. Ray, IV: 271, V: 86, 375

Davis, Lt. Cdr. S. N., XIV: 388
Davis, Vernon E., XIV: xi
Davis, Capt. W. V., XIV: 374
DAVIS, I: 15*n*, 84, 377, 390*n*, 420, X: 213*n*
Davison, Rear Adm. R. E., pic., XII: 183; mentioned, VII: 344, VIII: 405, XII: 13, 86, 90–94, 100–108, 133, 150, 175–6, 184, 193–5, 291, 318–28, 339–46, 427, XIV: 21–2, 44, 52, 94–6, 99, 203, 248, 383
DAVISON, I: 420, IX: 389
Dawes, Lt. Cdr. R. A., VIII: 406
Dawkins, Lt. (jg) Marion, X: 226
Dawley, Maj. Gen. E. J., IX: 247, 285–6, 325, 391
DAWSON, VII: 333
Day, Lt. Cdr. B. E., VII: 338, 346
Day, Cdr. D. H., VIII: 84, 111, XIII: 323
Day, Cdr. D. P., XIII: 322
DAY, XIII: 208, 309
Dayton, Cdr. M. T., VIII: 413, XII: 425, XIII: 304
DAYTON, XIV: 314
Dealey, Cdr. S. D., I: 321, VIII: 19, 33, 220, 416
Dean, Capt. C. W., VII: 347, VIII: 407, XII: 419, XIII: 310, XIV: 378
Dean, Capt. F. H., IV: 273, V: 231, VI: 144
Dean, Chief Boatswain William A., XIV: 229
Dean, Lt. Cdr. William A., Jr., VII: 339, VIII: 412
DeBaun, Cdr. G. H., IV: 20, 30, XIII: 315
De Bay, Lake, XIII: 190
DeBold, Lt. J. K., XII: 422, XIII: 304
Deboyne I., IV: 42, 61
DeCarre, Brig. Gen. Alphonse, V: 340*n*, 343
DECATUR, I: 15*n*, 92, 420, X: 171–3, 266, 376, XII: 118*n*
Dechaineux, Capt. E. F. V., VIII: 405, XII: 148, 421
Decker, Lt. Cdr. A. T., VI: 331, VII: 339, 349
Decker, Capt. B. W., VI: 146
DECKER, X: 381; pic., 40
DeCoudras, Lt. Cdr. D. A., XIV: 374
Dededo, VIII: 373
DEEDE, VII: 348
Deer Lodge, I: 169, 375, 392–3
Dees, Capt. R. E., VII: 339, 350
DEFENSE, XIV: 184, 197, 376, 390

De Freitas, Lt. P. F. M., VII: 333
DeGarmo, Lt. Cdr. E. E., XIV: 382
De Gaulle, Gen. Charles, I: 31, 167, II: 4, 8–9, 66, 258, VI: 94*n*, IX: 13, 305, 308, XI: 233, 310
Degen, Horst, I: 155
DE GRASSE, VII: 348, VIII: 410
DeHaven, Col. L. G., VIII: 187*n*
DEHAVEN (1942), V: 342, 345–6, 364; sunk, 366
DEHAVEN (1944), XIII: 316, XIV: 382
DEIMOS, sunk, VI: 141
Deits, Lt. Cdr. D. W., XIV: 377
DeKay, Cdr. R. D., VIII: 405, XIII: 307
De Kieffer, Lt. Cdr. E. L., XIII: 308
De Laborde, Adm., II: 218, 240
De la Guardia, Pres., I: 150
Delaney, Lt. (jg) W. E., XIV: 208
DeLany, Capt. W. S., IV: 270, V: 86, VI: 11*n*
Delate, Ens. T. E., I: 375*n*
DeLattre de Tassigny, Gen., XI: 233, 236, 275, 281–4, 291, 323, 338
De Laureal, Lt. Cdr. H. H., XIII: 304
DELAWARE, XIV: 86*n*
Delaware-Chesapeake Canal, I: 253–4
Del Brazil, IV: 265*n*
Delgado, Alférez de Fragata M. R., X: 190
DELHI, II: 223, IX: 358, X: 267, 393, XI: 342
Delisle, X: 374
DELIVER, XIV: 387
DeLong, Cdr. E. R., VII: 350
DELTA, IX: 390
Del Valle, Brig. Gen. P. A., pic., V: 130; mentioned, 126–8, 144, 174, 226, VIII: 419, XIV: 245, 378
De Meester, Cdr. J. B., III: 322, 325
Dement, Lt. J. S., XIII: 306
Demetropolis, Cdr. George, XIV: 384
Dempo, II: 192, 195*n*, 200, 213–14
Dempsey, Lt. J. C., III: 158, 307
Dempsey, Lt. Gen. Sir Miles, IX: 151, XI: 29, 69, 181, 190, 195
DEMPSEY, VII: 341, 348
DENBIGH CASTLE, X: 311
DENEBOLA, I: 420, XIV: 88*n*
Denebrink, Rear Adm. F. C., pic., II: 112; mentioned, I: 327–8, 419, II: ix, 37, 104, 112, X: 48
Denfeld, Rear Adm. L. E., I: 15*n*, 53–4, 85, XIV: 112, 385
Denig, Capt. J. L., VII: 248

Denman, Lt. (jg) K. W., XII: 422
Denmark Strait, I: 82, 161, 168
Dennett, Lt. Cdr. E. V. E., IV: 271, V: 86, VII: 335
Dennis, Cdr. S. H., IX: 388, XI: 335
DENNIS, XII: 244, 263, 266–9, 304, 421, XIV: 374
Denniston, Lt. Cdr. R., XII: 424
Denny, Cdr. J. B., VII: 54, 334, XIII: 316
Denny, Capt. M. M., XIV: 388
DENSITY, XIV: 377
Dent, Lt. Magruder, VII: 345, VIII: 410
DENT, I: 213, IV: 174, VI: 142–5, 148, 156*n*, 193–4, 228, 381, 389*n*, VIII: 404, 419
Denton, Lt. Cdr. W. T., VII: 341, 348
DENVER, VI: 13*n*, 106*n*, 107, 292, 308, 313, 322, 337, 346, XII: 119–22, 166, 199, 227, 236–7, 366, 417–19, XIII: 19, 115, 187, 219, 246, 269, 304, 321, 324; pic., VI: 61
Deprez, Capt. de V., XI: 336
Deptford, XI: 61
Depth charges, I: 210–11, II: 127, X: 52
De Preneuf, Capit. de Corv., II: 99
Deragon, Lt. Cdr. W. N., VIII: 415
DERBYSHIRE, IX: 396
Derevyanko, Lt. Gen. K., XIV: 366
DeRivera, Cdr. H. L., XII: 428, XIII: 318, XIV: 387
Derna, II: 19, 242
Derrien, Vice Adm. E.-L., II: 241, 243
Derry Cunahy, XI: 190
DE RUYTER, III: 273, 299–305, 308, 322, 332–3, 342, 345–8, 351, 354–7
DERWENTDALE, IX: 392
DE SCHELDE, XI: 308
DESIGN, XIV: 377
Desolation Pt., XII: 121
DESPITE, I: 422
Dessez, Capt. J. H. S., III: 195, 242
De Sticca, Capt., II: 71*n*
Destroyers, number available, I: lxi, 235; "short-legged," 87, 107, 321; as patrol ships, 134–5, 139; as escorts and A/S vessels, 234; training centers, 307–8
Destroyer Escorts, I: lviii, 66, 205, 234, 406, X: 32–6, 245; number authorized and built, X: 35–6
Destroyer–Naval Bases Deal, I: 26, 33–6, X: 5
Destroyer Squadrons, One, III: 237, IV: 257, XII: 429, 431, XIII: 73, 319;

Two, I: 32, 82, IV: 257, V: 233, VIII: 405, XII: 417, XIII: 309; Three, III: 56*n*; Four, III: 242, IV: 130, XII: 389, 425; Five, 373, 417, XIII: 313; Six, III: 211*n*, 393, IV: 257, V: 86, XII: 428; Seven, I: 76, 418-20, IX: 391; Eight, I: 57, 111, 168, 420, II: 91, IX: 187, 391, XI: xv; Nine, I: 57, 83, 420; Ten, I: 420, II: 39, X: 258; Eleven, I: 83, 420; Twelve, V: 87, VI: 181, 419-20, VIII: 415; XII: 425; pic., VI: 434; Thirteen, I: 420, II: 38, 77-8, IX: 391; Fourteen, VII: 23; Fifteen, I: 420, II: 40; Sixteen, IX: 389, X: 264; Seventeen, IX: 193, 388; Twenty-one, V: 353, VI: 161, XII: 295*n*, 417, XIII: 304; Twenty-two, VI: 337, 420, 428, XII: 369, XIII: 310; Twenty-three, VI: 292, 308, 353-4, 420, VIII: 415, XIII: 309; Twenty-four, XII: 217, 421; Twenty-five, 416; Twenty-seven, I: 420; Twenty-nine, III: 160, 272; Thirty, I: 418, 420; Thirty-one, 100, 418, 420; Forty-five, VI: 297, 420-21; Forty-six, VII: 349, 353, XII: 425; Forty-seven, XIII: 318; Forty-eight, VII: 350, VIII: 405, XII: 418; Forty-nine, 295*n*, 419, XIII: 311; Fifty, VII: 348, 352, VIII: 414, XII: 426-7, XIII: 318; Fifty-one, XII: 429, XIII: 305; Fifty-two, VII: 349, 353, VIII: 413, XII: 426; Fifty-four, XII: 203, 211, 418, XIII: 316; Fifty-five, XII: 427, XIII: 318; Fifty-six, VIII: 408, XII: 199, 221, 387, 419, XIII: 304; Fifty-seven, XII: 107*n*; Sixty, 366*n*, 371, XIII: 304; Sixty-one, 316

Destroyer-Transports, Guadalcanal, V: 67; Cape Torokina, VI: 337; Admiralties, 437; Southwest Pacific, VIII: 54; Sansapor, 143; Saipan, 184; Morotai, XII: 22; Peleliu, 34; Leyte, 120, 123; Ormoc, 379; Mindoro, XIII: 31; Cebu, 233; Mariveles, 199; Iwo, XIV: 27
Desusino, Monte, IX: 78, 86, 88
DETROIT, III: 113-14, 212, VII: 15, 18, 39, 334, X: 204*n*, 229*n*, XII: 254*n*, XIII: 180*n*, XIV: 8, 160, 386
Deutermann, Cdr. H. T., VII: 348
Deutermann, Cdr. W. V., XII: 377, XIII: 189, 217, 321-3
Deutsch, Lt. Col., II: 149*n*

Deuve, Capt., II: 138*n*, 144
De Valera, Eamon, I: 54*n*, X: 45
Devaney, T. F., XI: 287*n*
DEVASTATOR, XI: V 376
Devereux, Maj. J. P. S., III: 227-34, 246-8, 252-3
Devers, Lt. Gen. J. L., IX: 365, XI: 229, 291, 310, 324
DEVICE, XIV: 377
DEVILFISH, XIV: 289
DEVONSHIRE, IX: 393
Devonshire, Eng., U.S. Bases in, XI: 58-63
DEVOSA, XIV: 378
De Vos, Cdr. P. L., XVI: 383
De Vries, Lt. Cdr. W. M., III: 333
Dewar, Capt. A. C., I: xvi
De Welden, Felix, XIV: 61
DEWEY, III: 104, 159, 213*n*, IV: 19, 274, VII: 18, 48, 309, 335-6, 347, VIII: 413, XII: 429 XIII: 73-5, 319
DEWEY dry dock, III: 155; scuttled, 204
DeWitt, Maj. Gen. J. L., VII: 20, 62
Dexter, Lt. Cdr. D. H., V: 16
Dexter, Cdr. E. B., XIII: 109, 304, XIV: 373
Dexter, R. J., X: 382
DEXTROUS, IX: 396, XI: 340
Deyo, Rear Adm. Morton L., biog., XIV: 88*n*; pic., XI: 52; Comdesron 11, I: 83, 86-7, X: 6; Comdeslant, I: 356; C.O. Indianapolis, VII: 9; Normandy, XI: 70-71, 86, 93-6, 106-7, 157, 161, 168, 171, 196-215 passim, 334, 337; Southern France, 268-71, 276-8, 284, 341; Leyte, XII: 427; South China Sea, XIII: 318; Okinawa, XIV: 88, 108-10, 121, 130-33, 140, 149, 181-2, 203-4, 220, 226-7, 245, 267, 372
DIADEM, X: 308, XI: 185
Dial, Lt. N. M., III: 159
Diamond Shoals, I: 156, 249
DIANTHUS, I: 322, 337-41, 345
Dichter, Lt. Cdr. M. M., XIV: 379
Dick, Rear Adm. Royer M., II: 215, IX: 213*n*
Dicken, Chief Signalman R. J., IV: 34
Dickens, Yeoman H. C., IV: x
DICKERSON, I: 16*n*, 215, 420, VI: 415, VIII: 404, 409, XIII: 304, XIV: 176, 376, 390; sunk, 176-7
Dickey, Capt. F. C., IV: 21*n*, XII: 425
Dickey, Lt. Cdr. G. D., II: 225, 229
Dickey, Col. W. E., XIV: 374

Dickie, Lt. Cdr. P. T., XIV: 377
Dickinson, Lt. C. E., III: 121, 217
DIDO, IX: 167, 329, 358, 361n, 375, 378, XI: 253–4, 338
Diego Suarez, IV: 68
Diehl, Cdr. H. T., XIV: 376
Dieppe, II: 14n, IX: 30, XI: 39
Dierdorff, Capt. R. A., II: 38, III: 225, IX: 388, 392, XI: 340
Dierksen, Kaptlt. Reiner, X: 190–91
Dietrich, Lt. E. P., VIII: 410
Dietrich, Cdr. W. F., IV: 272
Dietz, C., X: 381
Diffley, Lt. Cdr. F. M., XIV: 378
Dill, Field Marshal Sir John, pics., I: 70, VI: 18; mentioned, II: 12, XI: 12n, 13
Dillard, Lt. R. W., VI: 265
Dillon, Lt. Cdr. E. J., VII: 246n
Dillon, Capt. W. M., VII: 350, VIII: 414
DILWARA, XI: 340
Dimmick, Cdr. J. B., XIII: 316, XIV: 382
DiNapoli, J. F., XII: viii, XIII: x
Dinagat I., XII: 118–21
DIONNE, VII: 341
DIPHDA, XIII: 307, 312, XIV: 380
DIPLOMA, XIV: 377
DIRECT, I: 422
Direction-finder, III: 215. *See also* High-frequency direction-finder
Dirks, Cdr. J. A., XII: 418
Diver, Ens. W. S., XII: 422
DIVER, XI: 337
Dix, Capt. J. P., XIII: 307, XIV: 380
DIXIE, XIV: 387
Dixie Arrow, pic., I: 135
Dixon, Cdr. D. P., XIII: 304, XIV: 373
Dixon, Lt. Cdr. R. E., IV: 19, 42, 48–9
Dixon, Lt. (jg) W. A., X: 325–6
Djar, Cape, VIII: 81, 87
Djidjelli, II: 220, 252
Djoeata, Cape, XIII: 262
DOBBIN, III: 104, 116, IV: 65–6, V: 36n, XII: 140n
Dobbs, Lt. Cdr. W. A., X: 296, 379
DOBLER, X: 381
Dobodura, VI: 42–3, 46, 49, 56, 125, 255, 259–60, 266, 286, 328, 376, 381
Dobson, Lt. Cdr. C. J., XIV: 382
Dockum, Cdr. D. G., XIII: 188, 311
Dodd, Capt. Harold, I: 376n, 389n, IV: 173, X: 213
Dodds, Lt. Cdr. C. R., XIII: 312

Dodds, Capt. S. B., XI: 275
Dodge, Capt. F. R., IX: 375, XI: 341
Dodge, Cdr. H. B., VII: 342, 351–3
Dody, Gen., II: 87n
Doe, Cdr. H., XIV: 375
Doe, Maj. Gen. Jens A., VIII: 63, 72, 96, 403, XIII: 217–18, 222–4, 241, 322
Doebler, Cdr. H. J., VIII: 405
Doenitz, Grossadm. Karl, I: 4–5, 22–3, 26n; C. in C. Navy, 316–17; methods of warfare, 8–10, 35, 95, X: 57n; *Laconia* order, 58n; North Atlantic, I: 126, 137, 157, 321–4, X: 71–9 *passim*, 108, 139, 144–52, 178–80, 249, 331–50 *passim*; Biscay, 90–99; North Russia, I: 164, X: 236–8, 305; tonnage concept, I: 198–9, 400–404, X: vii, 58–63, 140, 274, 361; and Luftwaffe, I: 246, 316, X: 59, 95, 98, 101; Caribbean, I: 311, 348, X: 298, 190–91, 198–9; Central Atlantic, 108, 111, 115–16, 124, 130–32, 168, 176–7, 283–4; South Atlantic, I: 311, 385, X: 209–11, 220–22, 227, 295–6; fueling, I: 312, X: 122, 160, 284; strategy and tactics, I: 318, 402, X: 83–4, 92, 119, 149–50, 162, 249, 318; Med., IX: 44–5, X: 252, 264; advises Italian Navy, IX: 36–8; Sicily, IX: 201; mining offensive, X: 184; Indian Ocean, X: 275–304 *passim*; Snorkel, X: 318; Normandy, X: 319–25, XI: 43, 107; Spitzbergen raid, X: 231; surrender, XI: 308, 324–5, 327, 329, 358–9; conclusions, I: 157, 198–9, 401–2, X: 358–60; quoted, I: 72, X: vii, 83–4, 119, 128, 132, 198, 246, 284, 332; Fuehrer, 358–60; "Essay on the War at Sea" quoted, I: 3n; X: xiv
Doherty, Lt. J. A., XI: 299n
Dolan, Col. W. C., I: 247n
Dollman, Genoberst., XI: 45, 49, 103, 113, 153, 159
DOLPHIN (1885), I: 208n
DOLPHIN (1932), III: 104, 213n, 261, IV: 92
Domingoes, J. A., X: xi, XI: xi
Dominica Passage, X: 198n, 199, 201
Donaho, Cdr. G. R., IV: 92, XII: 399
Donahue, Lt. F. M., XIV: 377, 381
"Donald Duck Navy," I: 231–2
Donaldson, Yeoman, H. M., III: xii, XIV: ix
DONALDSON, XII: 429, XIII: 319
Donbass, I: 189

Dongon Pt., XIII: 40, 42
Donnell, Ens. J. G., IX: 259
Donnell, Lt. Cdr. R. H., XIII: 306, 322
Donohue, Cdr. T. F., XIV: 115, 376
Donovan, Capt. J. F., XIII: 317, XIV: 382
Donovan, Seaman L. O., II: xix, XIV: ix
Donovan, Maj. Gen. W. J., I: 54n, IX: 341, XIII: 293
Doolittle, H. A., II: 241-2
Doolittle, Maj. Gen. James H., pic., III: 394; mentioned, II: 224, 390-98, IX: 21; Tokyo Raid, III: 389-98
Dooman, Hon. E. H., III: xii, 85n
Doorman, Rear Adm. K. W. F. M., III: 271, 299-301, 305-12, 320-24, 332, 335, 338-58
DORADO, sunk, X: 199, XII: 414n
Dorado, I: 274n
DORAN, I: 420, II: 40, 285, IX: 136, 389
Dorchester, I: 331-4
Dore, Lt. Cdr. J. F., XIII: 311
DORIA, IX: 38
Dorling, Rear Adm. J. W. S., I: 65, X: 34
Dornin, Cdr. M. E., VII: 350, VIII: 405
DORNOCK, XI: 333
DOROTHEA L. DIX, II: 40, 139-43, 154, IX: 389, XI: 335, 341; pic., II: 149
DORSETSHIRE, I: 111-12, III: 383, IX: 158
DORSEY, IV: 276n, VI: 297, VII: 37n, VIII: 420, XIII: 306, XIV: 31, 134, 376
DORTCH, VII: 348, VIII: 414, XII: 319, 427, XIII: 318, XIV: 25
Dos Hermanos, XIII: 25
Dose, Cdr. R. G., VIII: 350
Doty, Lt. (jg) S. E., X: 81, 160
Douala, X: 209
Dougherty, Lt. Cdr. J. E., XIV: 381
Dougherty, Lt. (jg) T. A., II: 106n
Doughty, Capt. Leonard, IX: 189, 244, 295
Douglas, Capt. A. H., III: 213, 252
Douglas, Air Chief Marshal Sir Sholto, X: 324
DOUGLAS, X: 157n
DOUGLAS A. MUNRO, XIII: 262
DOUGLAS H. FOX, XIV: 259
DOUGLAS L. HOWARD, X: 322, 379-80
Douglas-Pennant, Commo. C. E., XI: 181, 184, 190
DOUR, XIV: 377
Douw, Cdr. V. P., VIII: 344, XII: 420, XIII: 317-18, XIV: 249, 385

Dow, Lt. Cdr. L. J., V: 93n
Dowd, Lt. Cdr. F. S., VII: 341
Downes, Lt. A. M., XIV: 378
Downes, Capt. W. M., VI: 146, XIII: 264, 303
DOWNES, III: 117-19, XII: 425; pic., III: 116
Downing, Cdr. A. A., XIII: 310, XIV: 381
Dowty, Lt. (jg) N. T., X: 280
DOYEN, VII: 337, 346, VIII: 407, 420, XII: 419, XIII: 310
Doyle, Capt. A. K., I: 419, VII: 334, XII: 424, XIII: 316, XIV: 382
Doyle, Capt. F. R., I: 135n
Doyle, Capt. J. H., pic., VII: frontispiece; mentioned, XIV: 384
Doyle, Capt. T. J., I: 421
Doyle, Capt. W. E., III: 158, 193, 272
Doyle, Cdr. W. T., V: 157n
DOYLE, XI: 123, 146, 336, 343
Draemel, Rear Adm. Milo F., III: 114, 212, 215-16, 251
DRAGON, III: 340, XI: 192
Drane, Lt. Cdr. W. M., X: 80, 111, 375
DRAYTON, III: 210n, V: 294, 297-9, 308-11, 326, 345, VI: 98n, 262, 382, 390, 436, XII: 373-4, 417, XIII: 262, 309, 322-3
Drea, Lt. Cdr. A. R., XIV: 381
Dresbach, Lt. (jg) J. W., X: 197
Dressling, Lt. Cdr. R. J., XI: 312, 315-16, 338
DREW, XIV: 375
Drewes, Maj. H. C., VII: 167
"Drews," XI: 58-60, 217
Drexler, Cdr. L. A., XIII: 307
DREXLER, XIV: 374, 392; sunk, 260-61
Driniumor R., Battle of, VIII: 72-4
"Drone" boats, VII: 245, VIII: 166, XI: 192, 241, 256, 271, 277
Dropp, Lt. A. H., I: 421
Drotning, Lt. Cdr. O. B., IV: 93
Drum, Lt. Gen. H. A., I: 241
DRUM, IV: 203, 212, 275n, VI: 69, XII: 406, 429
DRUMHELLER, X: 78
Drury, Capt. M. J., XIV: 380
Dry, Lt. Cdr. M. H., VII: 342, 351-3
Dryer, Lt. R. C., IX: 389
DUANE, I: 60, 305, 345, 421, X: 205, XI: 259, 262, 339
Dublon I., VII: 316-18, 320, 324, 331, VIII: 38

Du Bose, Lt. E. A., II: 263*n*, IX: 309, 372–3, XI: 279
DuBose, Rear Adm. Laurance T., IV: 90, 271, V: 86, 205, 231, 247, 253, VI: 289, 340, 344–5, 348, VII: 116, 243, 337, 346, 352, VIII: 367, 413, IX: 386, XII: 100–103, 318, 326–8, 331–2, 425, 427
DUCA D'AOSTA, IX: 198, 243
DUCA DEGLI ABRUZZI, IX: 243
Ducat, Lt. Cdr. J. R., XIII: 318, XIV: 387
Duchein, Maj. Charles, VII: 248
DUCHESS OF BEDFORD, IX: 269, 392
Duckworth, 1st Lt. W. G., II: 140
Dudley, Capt. J. R., X: 161–2, 378
Dudley, Lt. Cdr. R. W., X: 376
Dudley, Capt. Roy, VI: 262
Due Rocchi, Punta, IX: 86, 88; pic., 82
Dufek, Capt. G. J., X: 350–51, 355, 376
Duff, Lt. Cdr. H. C., X: 353–5, 378
Duffield, Lt. Cdr. M. D., XIV: 376
DUFFY, VII: 341, 345
DUFILHO, XIV: 326
Dugan, Capt. P. F., VII: 337, 347, VIII: 410, XIII: 263
Dugan, Capt. T. B., VIII: 415, XIII: 34–5, 144, 309, 323–4
Duggan, R., XI: 335
DUGUAY-TROUIN, XI: 341
DUILIO, IX: 38
Duke, Lt. Cdr. C. E., IV: 92
Duke of York I., VI: 402, 420–21
DUKE OF YORK, I: 181, II: 189, X: 231, 237–43, XIV: 333, 361, 369
Dukw, VII: 89*n*, 183*n*, VIII: 53–4; described, IX: 32; pics., VII: 270, IX: 347, XI: 269; Arawe, VI: 375–6; Kwajalein, VII: 252, 256; Sicily and Italy, IX: 32, 84, 88, 99, 106, 140, 204, 264–9, 300, 332, 339–44, 356, 369; New Guinea, VIII: 81, 106, 110–12; Marianas, 184, 195, 209, 356, 363, 383, 389; Normandy, XI: 139, 147, 303; Leyte, XII: 127, 142; Lingayen, XIII: 127; Okinawa, XIV: 17
Dulag, XII: 63, 124, 135, 140–44, 151, 154, 341, 350, 365, 379, XIII: 18, 23, 43, 258; charts, 132, 141; pic., 142–3
DULUTH, XIV: 305
DULVERTON, IX: 393
Dumaguete, XIII: 232, 237–8
Dumaran I., XIII: 221

Dumas, Ens. H. F., XII: 422
"Dumbo," V: 332–3. *See also* Air-Sea Rescue
Dummer, Lt. Col. H. W., IX: 75
Dunboyne, I: 168, 172, 372
Duncan, Lt. Cdr. C. K., VI: 331, VII: 340, 349
Duncan, Adm. Donald B., III: 389*n*, 390, VII: 339, IX: xvi
Duncan, Capt. J. H., VIII: 406, XII: 421, XIII: 304
DUNCAN (1913), XIV: 88*n*
DUNCAN (1942), V: 151–3, 156–8, 161–3, 166; sunk, 166–8; pic., 147
DUNCAN, HMS, X: 67–70, 148
Dunckel, Brig. Gen. William C., XIII: 21, 24, 26–8, 31, 38, 49
Dundon, Lt. Cdr. J. M., XIV: 143
Dunkeswell, X: 73, 94, 100, 103
Dunkirk, X: 5, XI: 328–9
Dunlap, Cdr. S. B., VIII: 406
DUNLAP, III: 211*n*, IV: 276, VI: 214–18, VII: 350, XII: 425
Dunleavy, J. J., XI: 287*n*
Dunn, Rear Adm. C. A., VII: 103
Dunn, Lt. (jg) C. A., Jr., VIII: 258*n*, 299*n*
Dunn, Cdr. H. A., VIII: 410, XII: 416, XIII: 309
Dunn, Capt. J. B., pic., X: 128; mentioned, 119, 168–70
Dunn, Brig. Gen. Ray A., IX: 150*n*
Dunn, Capt. W. A., X: 213*n*
Dunne, Lt. Cdr. A. D. S., XI: 336
Dunstan, Lt. Cdr. T. K., XIV: 377
Dunstan, Capt. T. S., X: 378
Dunston, Lt. C. E., XIV: 377
Duntroon, VI: 36
DU PAGE, VII: 346, VIII: 418, XII: 416, XIII: 143–4, 308, 326
Duplessis-Casso, Capt. de C., XI: 336
DUPONT, I: 214, 418, 420, VII: 232*n*, X: 168–70, 375–6
Du Port, Batterie, II: 77–8, 98, 100
Dupuy, Lt. R. F., VI: 303
DUQUESNE, XI: 309
Durgin, Rear Adm. Calvin T., biog., XI: 279*n*; pic., 284–5; mentioned, I: 419, II: 32, 39, XI: xv*n*, 239, 279, 342, XIII: 12, 105, 110, 119, 151, 155, 278, 304, XIV: 26, 44, 54–6, 59, 107, 119, 132, 161, 211–13, 373
Durgin, Cdr. E. R., I: 57, 76, 98, 418, 420, II: 38, 61, 74, IX: 68, 386, 391

Durham V., XII: 83, 198, 201*n*, 423, XIII: 308
Durney, Lt. Cdr. J. J., XIV: 377
Durrant, Lt. Cdr. D. A., XIV: 386
Duryea, Lt. H. E., IV: 174
Dussault, Capt. G. A., VII: 338
Dutch Harbor, III: 32, IV: 160*n*, 163, 165, 167–74, 181–2, 214–17, VII: 5, 16, 47*n*, 102; raid, IV: 77, 175–80
Dutra, Contra-almirante A. S., I: 383, X: 209
Dutton, Lt. Cdr. W. T., VIII: 410
DuVal, Cdr. M. P., XIV: 379
Duvall, Cdr. W. H., I: 420, II: 37, X: 256–7, 268

Dwyer, Lt. Cdr. Carl, XIII: 319, XIV: 287
Dybdal, Lt. Cdr. V. A., XIII: 262, 309
Dyer, Capt. G. C., XIII: 316–17, XIV: 384
Dyer, Capt. W. L., XIII: 311, 313
Dyess, Lt. Col. A. J., VII: 249, 306
Dykers, Cdr. T. M., VI: 84
Dyment, Lt. H. E., X: 94
DYNAMIC, I: 422
Dynastic, I: 372
Dyson, Cdr. G. R., VII: 350
DYSON, VI: 241, 308, 354, 421, VIII: 240, 415, XII: 429, XIII: 316, 319, 323, XIV: 279

E

E. A. Burnett, XIII: 313
Eaden, Lt. Cdr. D., XI: 342
Eagle, Capt. C. R., VII: 100*n*, 104, 110–11
EAGLE (1898), IX: 14*n*
EAGLE (1942), I: 282–4
EAGLE, HMS, I: 196; pic., 210
Eagle, X: 214
Eagle Boats, I: 229
Eagles, Maj. Gen. W. W., IX: 362, 364, XI: 236, 264–5, 340
Eagleton, Lt. Cdr. W. L., XIII: 319, XIV: 387
Eaker, Lt. Gen. Ira C., IX: 323
Eareckson, Col. W. O., VIII: 82
Earle, Col. E. P., VII: 45, 49
Earle, Capt. Ralph, IV: 93, VI: 297, 343, 360, 413–15, 420–21
EARLE, I: 355–6, 420, IX: 142, 389
Earlston, I: 191*n*
Early, Capt. A. R., III: 237, IV: 19, 91, VIII: 413, XII: 424
Easley, Lt. Col. J. W., VIII: 369
Eason, Lt. V. V., VII: 324*n*, VIII: 297, 302–3
East China Sea, VIII: 38, XIV: 80; sub. patrols, IV: 201–2
East Coast Sound School, I: 138–9, 206*n*, 214–15, 347
Eastabrook, Cdr. W. S., VIII: 409
EASTBOURNE, XI: 337
Eastern Sea Frontier, I: 71*n*, 126–35, 207–8, 223, 241, 248, 255–7, 413, X: 91, 178–88, 331, 342–4; chart, 179
Eastern Solomons, Battle of, V: 80–106; chart, 82, 93; T.O., 84–7
Eastern Sun, I: 138
EASTLAND, XIV: 375
Eastman, Cdr. G. L., XIV: 387
Eastwood, Lt. Cdr. J. A., XIV: 377
Eaton, Lt. Cdr. J. B., XII: 422
Eaton, Capt. J. W., II: 265*n*
Eaton, Capt. M. E., VI: 297
EATON, VI: 229–32, 242, 337, 415, 429, VIII: 410, XII: 370, XIII: 311, 313, 323–4

Ebb, Lt. L. F., XII: 163*n*
Ebb, I: 288
Eberbach, Lt. Heinz, XI: 284
EBERLE, I: 86–7, 384, 420, II: 37, 120–22, 285, XI: 285, 339
Ebert, Lt. Cdr. W. G., VI: 69–70
Ebeye Islet, VII: 75, 193, 219, 232, 253, 257–8, 273–6, 306
E-Boats. *See* Germany, Navy, Motor torpedo boats
Ebon Atoll, VII: 312–13
Eccles, Rear Adm. Henry E., III: 160, 321*n*, 329*n*, 333, 343, VII: 100*n*, 103, 104*n*, VIII: 341*n*, XII: 74*n*, XIV: 156*n*, 162*n*, 265
Eccles, Capt. J. A. S., XIV: 388
ECHO, I: 196, IX: 42, 394
Eck, Kaptlt. Heinz, X: 300
Eckelmeyer, Cdr. E. H., IX: 395, XI: 340
ECLIPSE, IX: 42, 394
Eddins, Lt. (jg) J. A., XII: 422
Eddy, Lt. Cdr. I. C., IV: 20
Eddy, Lt. Cdr. J. F., XIV: 377
Eddy, Maj. Gen. M. S., I: 421, II: 22, IX: 200
Eddy, Lt. Col. W. A., II: 65
Edelston, Rear Adm. J. H., XIV: 105, 388
EDENSHAW, IX: 397
Eder, Lt. Cdr. W. E., XII: 426, XIII: 316, XIV: 384
Edgar, Commo. C. D., I: 76, II: 191–6, 199, 209, 212–15, IX: 388, 392, XI: 29, 77, 150–51, 336, 339
Edge, Cdr. L. L., XIV: 292*n*
EDGECOMBE, XIV: 380
Edgigen I., VII: 234
EDINBURGH, I: 168–9
Edinburgh Field, Trinidad, X: 190; pic., I: 259
Edison, Charles A., I: 14, 29
EDISON, I: 121–22, 152, 420, II: 38, 77, 162, 285, IX: 83–5, 252, 268, 348, 351, 358, 361*n*, 389, 391, 396, X: 253, XI: 342

Edlu II, I: 273–4
Edmands, Lt. Cdr. A. C., VII: 338, XIV: 383
EDMONDS, XII: 420, XIII: 305, XIV: 374
Edo, Rear Adm. H., XII: 319, 430
Edsall, Cdr. W. R., VIII: 409, 420, XIII: 318
EDSALL, III: 160, 272, 332–3, 361, 378; sunk, 378
Edson, Col. M. A., pic., VII: 167; mentioned, IV: 273, 288–90, V: 124–30, 140, 144, VII: 173
Edson, Cdr. S. R., II: 22
Edward H. Crockett, X: 310
Edward N. Westcott, XIII: 150, 313, 326
Edward P. Costigan, IX: 390
EDWARD RUTLEDGE, I: 358, 421, II: 26*n*, 38, 168, 172–3; pic., 165; sunk, 171–3, 284
Edwards, Cdr. D. S., XIV: 384
Edwards, Ens. G. E., X: 295
Edwards, Lt. Cdr. H. L., I: 418
Edwards, Lt. J. W., XII: 423
Edwards, Cdr. John E., VII: 49, XIII: 181, 316, XIV: 383
Edwards, Capt. R. A. B., XIV: 388
Edwards, Capt. R. D., I: 214, II: 39, 79, XIV: 113*n*
Edwards, Capt. R. J., USMC, VII: 277
Edwards, Lt. Cdr. Richard, XII: 96
Edwards, Vice Adm. Richard S., I: 116, X: 19, 45
EDWARDS, V: 353, 362, VI: 331, VII: 44, 335, 340, XII: 383–5, 392, XIII: 45, 303
Edwin L. Drake, X: 311
Efate I., IV: 246–54, 263*n*, 270, 279, V: 12–14, 318, 353, 359, VI: 94*n*, 298, VII: 90, 99, 102, 110, 114–16, 210, VIII: 172
EFFECTIVE, I: 422
Effingham, I: 166
EFFINGHAM, XIV: 379
EGERIA, XII: 420, XIII: 306, 309, XIV: 185, 375
Eggert, Lt. J. R., VIII: 261
EGGESFORD, XI: 343
EGLANTINE, I: 325
EGRET, X: 98
Ehrman, John, *Grand Strategy*, XI: xiii
Eichelberger, Lt. Gen. Robert L., pic., VI: 41; mentioned, VI: 46, 49, 132, 136; Marianas, VIII: 63, 75–9, 85–7, 94, 133, 403, XII: 394; Philippines,

XIII: 187, 192, 214–50 *passim*, 321, XIV: 356, 362; *Our Jungle Road to Tokyo*, VIII: 59*n*, XIII: xi
EICHENBERGER, VIII: 406, XIII: 101, 308
Eikel, Lt. Cdr. Robert, VII: 310–12
Einmo, Lt. Cdr. A. S., VII: 334, XII: 423
EISELE, VIII: 410, XIV: 374
Eisenhower, General of the Army D. D., pics., II: 218, IX: 203, XI: 52; Com. U.S. Mil. Forces Europe, II: 12, XI: 7–8, 14–16; North Africa, II: 16, 70–73, 115; and Giraud, 66, 186; Darlan deal, 164–6, 215–20, IX: 13, II: 175, 181–2, 185–6, 192, 203, 239, 252–5; on unity of command, 181; Supreme Commander, Med., II: ix, xii, 33; Pantelleria, 275–7; Sicily, IX: xvi, 10, 15–19, 29, 55, 68, 110, 118, 121–3, 143, 149, 188, 223; Italy, 229–42, 246–52, 293–7, 303, 317–18, 322–5, 380, XI: 311; Ægean Is., IX: 245; Corsica, XI: 305; Supreme Commander, Europe, IX: 323; X: 345, 358, XI: 3, 22–3, XIII: 5; planning OVERLORD, XI: 27–30, 36–8, 65, 68–72; D-day decided, 70–83; Normandy, 159, 211; Southern France, 55, 222, 229–33; later European operations, 291, 295–8, 308, 318, 323, 328–30; *Crusade in Europe*, IX: viii, XI: xv
Ekholm, Mr. August, VII: 334
Ekstrom, Capt. C. E., XII: 420, XIII: 103, 305
El Alamein, 2nd Battle of, II: 13*n*, 186, 258
El Aouina, II: 242
El Capitan, I: 190, 191*n*
El Fraile I., XIII: 199, 205; pic., 197
El Oriente, I: 371–2
EL PASO, XII: 418
Elb, Cdr. Aloysius, XIV: 386
ELDEN, VIII: 420, XII: 429
Eldena, I: 168, 172
Elder, Cdr. H. M., XII: 428, XIV: 387
Elder, Lt. Cdr. R. D., XIV: 376
Elder, Lt. (jg) R. M., V: 101
ELDER, VII: 258
ELDORADO, XIV: 61, 65, 132, 187, 204, 372
Eldridge, Frank R., V: 16*n*
Eldridge, Lt. Cdr. John, IV: 271, V: 87
Eleazar Wheelock, XI: 336
ELECTRA, I: 421, II: 26*n*, 36, 133, 173–4, III: 188, 272, 333–50 *passim*, IV: 265*n*, VII: 347, VIII: 407, XII: 416, XIII: 309, 313; pic., II: 174

Electric Boat Co., I: 229, II: 261–3
Elihu B. Washburne, X: 214
Elihu Yale, IX: 363
ELISTIN, I: 370
ELIZABETH C. STANTON, II: 38, 161, 172, IX: 98, 388, 392, XI: 340
Elizabeth Kellogg, X: 202
Elizabeth City, X: 185, 343
ELK, VIII: 420, XIV: 379
Elkins, Lt. Cdr. J. S., XIV: 385*n*
Eller, Cdr. D. T., VII: 219, 336, 349, VIII: 413
Eller, Rear Adm. Ernest M., VII: ix, 111, 121*n*; Director of Naval History, XI: xi, XII: viii, XIII: x, XIV: x; data on logistics, 157*n*, 165*n*
Eller Islet, VII: 277
ELLESMERE, XI: 337
ELLET, I: 15*n*, III: 211*n*, 393, IV: 91, 113*n*, 151*n*, 274, V: 55, 86, VI: 193, VII: 242, 346, VIII: 405, 415, XII: 51
Ellice Is., VII: 76–80, 94, 116, 211, 309
ELLIOT, VII: 9*n*, 12, 335
Elliott, Capt. John, VII: 52*n*
Elliott, Dr. Robert M., I: 224
Ellis, Coxswain C. M., V: 120*n*
Ellis, Cdr. E. B., XII: 423, XIII: 308
Ellis, Maj. H. A., XIV: 384
Ellis, Capt. N. W., XII: 428
Ellis, Lt. Cdr. R. A. L., XI: 313*n*, 338
Ellis, Cdr. Robert B., X: 259, 377, XI: 342
Ellis, Cdr. William E., II: 37, XII: 425
ELLIS, I: 76, 86–8, 107, 214, 350, 418, X: 381
Ellison, Lt. Cdr. T. B., XIV: 383
Ellison, Lt. (jg) W. D., VIII: 195–6
Ellsberg, Capt. Edward, II: 251
Ellwood, Cal., IV: 165*n*
ELLYSON, I: 420, II: 39, 167, X: 258–9, XI: 160, 202–3, 284, 337, 340, XIV: 135, 195, 279, 376
Elmira V., XII: 429, XIII: 308
Elmore, Lt. Cdr. E. E., V: 45
ELMORE, VII: 346, VIII: 418, XII: 134, 416, XIII: 309, XIV: 380
Elrod, Capt. H. T., III: 231, 234, 248
Elsey, Cdr. G. M., XI: ix, 125*n*, XIV: ix
Ely, Cdr. G. E., XII: 428, XIII: 318, XIV: 387
Ely, Col. L. B., II: 22, 56*n*
Ely, Col. W. J., XII: 14
Embargoes, III: 35–6, 56–64
Embick, Lt. Gen. S. D., I: 45, VIII: 8*n*

Embree, Cdr. R. A., II: 163, XIV: 383
EMDEN, I: 4*n*
EMERALD, I: 138
Emerson, Lt. A. C., IV: 133
Emidio, III: 221*n*
ÉMILE BERTIN, I: 30, IX: 378, XI: 271, 276, 288, 341
Emirau I., VI: 370, 419, 423–4, VIII: 154*n*, 156, XII: 107, XIII: 153
Emmerman, Kaptlt. Carl, X: 218, 221
Emmet, Capt. R. R. M., I: 421; many commands, II: 27*n*; in operation TORCH, 20–28, 33, 37–41, 58, 74–8, 109, 157–9, 160*n*, 168
Emmons, Maj. Gen. D. C., I: 40, IV: 80*n*
Emmons, Ens. J. W., VI: 61
EMMONS, I: 134, 359, 420, II: 40, X: 258, 372, XI: 123, 145–6, 202–3, 336, 340, XIV: 193, 376, 390; sunk, 193–5; pic., XI: 148
Emory, Cdr. C. D., I: 76, 418, V: 252, VII: 334
EMPEROR, XI: 342
Empire Alliance, X: 381
EMPIRE ANN, XI: 340
EMPIRE ANVIL, XI: 118–19, 137, 335
Empire Byron, I: 191*n*
EMPIRE CHARMAIN, IX: 392
Empire Housman, X: 152*n*
EMPIRE GAUNTLET, XI: 102, 334
EMPIRE JAVELIN, X: 337, XI: 19, 136, 304, 335
Empire Lawrence, Meteor, Moon, Purcell, I: 174, 178*n*, 371, IX: 41
EMPIRE SPITFIRE, XI: 340
Empire Stalwart, Tide, Trader, I: 187–8, 340, X: 382
Empress Augusta Bay, VI: 281–4, 292, 299, XIII: 94; charts, VI: 309, 311, 314, 316; landings, 296–304, VII: 109, 137; Battle of, VI: 305–22; T.O., 306–8; casualties, 322*n*
Empress of Asia, I: 86
EMPRESS OF SCOTLAND, I: 329, X: 133
Emrick, Lt. Cdr. P. E., VI: 331, VII: 339
ENCOUNTER, III: 272, 333, 338, 349, 357, 364–5, 371–2
ENDICOTT, XI: 249, 282, 338
Endo, Vice Adm. Y., VIII: 67, 88–9
ENGAGE, I: 422
Engebi I., VII: 75, 221, 283, 287, 301, 306; landing, 289–93; pic., 279; chart, 290

ENGLAND, Submarine hunt, VII: 224–8, 230, and chart, 226, X: 332, XIV: 268–9, 373, 392
English, Lt. D. K., XIV: 373
English, Capt. R. A. J., pic., V: 244; mentioned, II: 22, 25, 28n, IX: 15, 23n, XI: ix, 233
English, Rear Adm. Robert H., III: 117, IV: 92, 97, 157n; Comsubpac, 199n, 202, 210
ENGLISH, XIII: 167–8, 317, XIV: 384
Engman, Lt. W. J., XIII: 316
Eniwetok Atoll, VI: 286, VII: 137–8, 282–304; strategic importance, 70, 202; U.S. capture of, recce. and planning, 79, 206, 213, 285–9, 295–6; strikes and raids on, 218–21; landing, 294–300, 316; T.O., 343; naval gunfire, 288–9, 296–8, 301–3; minesweeping, 289–90; casualties, 304; U.S. base, 75, 306, 321, VIII: 41, 145–389 passim, XII: 13, 34, 47, 75, 398, XIV: 54, 162; charts, VII: 284, 290, 295; pics., 244–5
Enloe, Lt. (jg) G. A., V: 200
Enna, IX: 49–51, 116, 171, 180–1
ENNERDALE, XI: 340
Ennubirr, Ennuebing, Ennugarret, Ennumennet, Ennylabegan Islands, VII: 234–9, 252, 255–7, 274
Enogai Pt., VI: 176, 202–3
ENOREE, II: 263, XIII: 318, XIV: 387
Enright, Cdr. J. F., I: 421, XII: 410
Ensey, Cdr. Lot, I: 420, XIII: 316, XIV: 382
ENTERPRISE, I: liii, II: 31, III: 31; Ops., Dec. '41–Feb. 1942, 98, 120–21, 211–12, 216–18, 228, 235, 241, 259–68, VII: 75; raid on Tokyo, III: 392–7, IV: 15, 62; Midway, 82–3, 97, 101–3, 112–52 passim, 157, 182–4; Guadalcanal, 257, 271, 285, 293–5, V: 14, 28n, 58, 74, 183–4, 189, 228, 233, 236n, 259–61, 264–9, 283, 291, VI: 106; E. Solomons, V: 80–206 passim; Sta. Cruz, 200–204, 207–19, 224; Rennell I., 352, 359–61; Gilberts, VII: 91, 116–17, 130, 133, 143, 213, 339; Marshalls, 190–92, 208, 220, 242, 257, 348; Truk, 324–6, 352, VIII: 154n; Hollandia, 37; Marianas, 174–6, 179; Philippine Sea, 250, 256, 268, 271, 283–307 passim, 414; Formosa and Luzon, XII: 90, 106; Leyte Gulf, 186, 190, 243n, 254n, 312, 318–20, 341, 427; Lingayen, XIII: 54, 87, 318; South China Sea, 165, 170–71; Iwo Jima, XIV: 21, 52, 55–6; Okinawa, 210, 222, 248, 263, 383, 386, 392; strikes on Japan, 94, 100; pics., III: 266, IV: 85, V: 99, 195
ENTERPRISE, HMS, X: 104, XI: 95, 104–6, 161–2, 198, 201, 334, 337
Enubuj Islet, VII: 252–7, 260, 264, 274–7
ÉPERVIER, II: 228, 237, 251
Eppelman, Capt. G. H., VIII: 408, XII: 416, XIII: 308, XIV: 379
EPPING FOREST, VII: 244, 345, VIII: 418, XII: 416, XIII: 308, 314, XIV: 141–4, 380
ERBEN, VII: 190, 339, 350, VIII: 405, 420, XII: 418, XIV: 384
Erck, Cdr. C. F., I: 421
EREBUS, IX: 234, XI: 104, 107, 334
Erickson, Seaman Frederick, VI: 265
Erickson, Lt. Cdr. J. L., XII: 425, XIII: 316
Ericsson, Lt. Cdr. H. M., VIII: 406
ERICSSON, I: 86–7, 420, II: 37, 285, IV: 265, X: 356–7, 371, 377, XI: 284, 339
ERIE, I: 13n, 151, 284
Erie, III: 31n
ERNE, I: 417
Erskine, Maj. Gen. G. B., VIII: 407, XIV: 8
Erskine, Lt. (jg) J. M., X: 196
Erskine Phelps, VI: 121–2
Erwin, Capt. M. C., VIII: 418, XIII: 307
ESCABURT, XI: 252
ESCALANTE, XIV: 387
ESCAMBIA, XII: 428, XIV: 387
ESCANABA, I: 331–4, 421
ESCAPE, X: 327
ESCATAWPA, XIV: 387
Escort Carriers, development and description, I: liii, 80n, V: 73, X: 37–42; controversy with R.N., 39n; A/S W, I: 117, 278–83, 318, 360, 384, 401, X: 16, 20, 77–82, 117, 245, 278–93, 362–3, XII: 242–3; Groups, T.O. X: 375–80; score of, I: 176, X: 176; North Russia, I: 307–10, X: 307–13; amphib. and logistic support, V: 291, 353–4, 359, VII: 89, 108, XII: 75–9, 92, 243, XIII: 172, XIV: 9, 158, 198; training, XII: 245n; North Africa, II: 89–90, 150–52, 155, 168; Gilberts & Marshalls, VII: 114–17, 139–40, 161, 168, 237n, 249, 252, 288–9, 299–301; New Guinea and Marianas, VIII: 68–70, 203, 206–7,

Escort Carriers (*cont'd*)
326, 360; Salerno, IX: 247, 250, 277, 286; Southern France, XI: 279–81, and pics., 284–5; Morotai and Palaus, XII: 22, 25–7, 34, 39, 45; Leyte, 121, 125, 149, 206*n;* Battle off Samar, 242–316; Mindoro, XIII: 8, 33; Lingayen Gulf, 8, 98–104, 113, 117–19, 134, 144, 155–6, 178; Balikpapan, 272–4; Iwo, XIV: 44, 59, 65; Okinawa, 92, 132–6, 161

Escort of convoy, defined, I: 17; vessels for, 26, 65–6, 233–7, 405–6, X: 3–5, 115; Iceland, I: 78–80; Atlantic, 84–93; diagrams of, 88–9, 91, 355; instructions, 100, 225; table of, 235

Escort vessels, Japanese. *See CD*

Escort-Fighting Squadrons, II: 37–40, 39

Escort-Scouting Squadrons, II: 37, 39–40, V: 353, 375

Eshelman, Boatswain Walter, X: 175

ESKIMO, IX: 157, 162, 164

Eskridge, Cdr. I. E., XII: 416, XIII: 308, XIV: 378

Eslick, Lt. Cdr. M., XII: 425

Esling, Capt. T. A., XII: 423, XIV: 386

Espe, Capt. Carl F., VII: 349, 353, XII: 425

Esperance, Cape, V: 121, VIII: 171; Battle of, *see* Cape Esperance

Espiritu Santo, IV: 252*n,* 254, 263*n,* 270, 279, V: 14, 23, 70, 113–363 *passim,* VI: 90, 103–6, 112, 298, 330, 412, VII: 99, 102, 110–11, 117, 210, XIV: 89, 163; air raids on, VI: 139*n,* 240–41; pic., IV: 254–5

ESSEX, Class, I: lviii, 28*n,* VI: 10, 335*n,* VII: xxvii, 85, 116; the carrier, II: 32, VI: 330–5, 346, VII: xxvii, 85, 92, 117, 138, 157, 190–92, 208, 219, 325, 339, 349, 352, VIII: 154, 174, 237*n,* 238–40, 250, 266–9, 273, 276, 360, 414, XII: 12, 90, 177, 180, 184–6, 254*n,* 318–59 *passim,* 426, XIII: 52–4, 87, 317, XIV: 21, 24*n,* 197, 200, 203–4, 211, 383, 386; Track chart against Truk, VII: 322–3; pics., 87, XII: 78

Esslinger, Cdr. R. J., XIV: 375

Esso Augusta, I: 417

Esso Baton Rouge, I: 354

Esso Bolivar, Buffalo, Gettysburg, Harrisburg, I: 130*n,* X: 182, 207*n,* 298

Estabrook, Cdr. W. S., XII: 418, XIII: 307

Estep, Lt. Cdr. G. M., VIII: 418–19, XIV: 134, 376

Estes, Ens. G. C., V: 106

ESTES, XIV: 44, 106, 110

Esteva, Admiral, II: 8, 65*n,* 183, 217–18, 241–2

ETAMIN, VI: 382, 445, VIII: 69–71, 404

Eten I., VII: 318, 320, 324, VIII: 38

Etheridge, Cdr. Walker, XIV: 384

Etna, Mt., IX: 157, 173, 178–80, 202, 206

ETTRICK, II: 204, 233; sunk, 214, 284

Eubank, Col. E. L., III: 337*n*

EUCALYPTUS, VII: 334

Euerle, Cdr. G. A., XIV: 375

EUGENE, XII: 418

EUGENE E. ELMORE, X: 284, 289, 377, XIII: 313–14

EUGENIO DI SAVOIA, IX: 194, 243

EUROPA, XI: 328

European Advisory Committee, XI: 325

European War, effect on Pacific, III: 40–47

EURYALUS, IX: 167, 293, 393, XIV: 105, 388

Euster, Lt. Tilden, XII: 47*n*

Evans, Sub-Lt. A. R., VI: 115

Evans, Cdr. D. S., II: 22, 24

Evans, Cdr. Ernest E., pic., XII: 279; mentioned, VII: 346, VIII: 223, 419, XII: 255–7, 263, 267, 273–4, 282, 421

Evans, Cdr. G. B., XIV: 388

Evans, Cdr. M. J., X: 82, 142–4

Evans, Lt. Philip C., I: 337*n*

Evans, Lt. Cdr. T. C., I: 15*n*

Evans, T. E., X: 382

Evans, Lt. T. R., XI: 269

Evans, Capt. W. A., XIII: 311

EVANS (1918), XIV: 86*n*

EVANS (1943), VIII: 411, XII: 429, XIII: 317, XIV: 256–7, 374, 392

EVARTS, X: 381

EVEA, IX: 397

EVERSOLE, XII: 164, 244, 306, 314, 420; sunk, 306–7

EVERTSEN, III: 273, 333, 339, 364–5, 370

Evins, Lt. Cdr. R. C., VIII: 410

Ewa airfield, III: 122–3

Ewe, Loch, I: 160, 179, 366–9, X: 236, 309

Ewen, Rear Adm. Edward C., V: xi, XII: 195, 426, XIII: 318, XIV: 106

Ewoldt, Lt. Cdr. L. E., XIII: 316

EXCEL, I: 422

Exceller, II: 192, 195*n*, 202, 212–14
EXECUTE, XIV: 377
Executive, I: 369
EXETER, III: 272, 306–8, 332, 338, 342–3*n*, 351–2, 364–5, 371–2
Exeter, Eng., XI: 60–3
EXMOOR, IX: 162, 393
Exmouth Gulf, III: 320, 330–32, 337, 377, VI: 75

EXPLOIT, I: 422
Export, II: 133
Expositor, I: 169, 71*n*
EXPRESS, III: 188, 190
Exterminator, I: 178
EXTRACTOR, sunk, XIV: 288
Eyth, Lt. Cdr. George, XIII: 318
Ezaki, Col. Y., VI: 437, 439
Ezra Meeker, IX: 386

F

F-lighters, IX: 189–90, 197, 210–14, 300, 372–3, XI: 314–16
Fabian, Cdr. L. M., XIV: 387
Fabre, Lt. (jg) J. M., VI: 228
FACILITY, XIV: 377
Fahle, Cdr. R. S., XII: 425
Fahrion, Rear Adm. Frank G., pic., IV: 166; mentioned, XIV: 110, 372
Fahy, Lt. Cdr. E. J., VIII: 415
Fahy, Cdr. J. S., VIII: 403
Fain, Ens. E. M., III: 112
FAIR, VII: 223–4, 411, XIV: 379
Fairbanks, Lt. Cdr. Douglas E., XI: 250, 338
Fairbanks, Helen R., XI: 322n
Fairchild, Maj. Gen. M. S., VIII: 8n
Fairfax, Lt. Cdr. E. G., XIII: 316
Fairfield City, I: 188, 191n
Fais I., VIII: 367, XII: 52–3; pic., 79
Faisi, V: 105, 369
FALCON, I: 421
Falconara Pt., IX: 86–8
Faldella, Gen. Emilio, IX: 52
Falk, H. A., XIII: 44
FALKE, sunk, XI: 191
Fallon, Capt. J. J., VII: 347, VIII: 418
Falmouth, Eng., XI: 52, 58
Falmouth, Mass., I: 279–80
FAME, I: 325
Fancourt, Capt. H. L. S., II: 208
FANNING (1912), VI: 13n
FANNING (1937), III: 211n, 393, IV: 276, VII: 350, XII: 425, XIV: 12
FANSHAW BAY, VIII: 207, 409, XII: 27, 244–78 *passim*, 302–3, 421, XIV: 250, 373; pic., XII: 302
Farallon de Pajaros, VIII: 149
FARENHOLT, IV: 271, V: 28n, 87, 136, 151–8, 161–3, VI: 144, 149–51, 325, 420–21, VIII: 419
Farewell, Cape, I: 323
Fargo, Lt. Cdr. A. W., XIII: 40–41, 265
Farley, Lt. Cdr. E. T., VII: 345–7, 404, XII: 417, XIII: 307
Farley, Lt. Cdr. J. P., VIII: 410, XIV: 374

Farley, Cdr. L. C., I: 285
Farley, Lt. Cdr. P. G., VIII: 420, XII: 420
Farmer, Ens. C. D., VIII: 283, 297n
Farmer, Lt. Cdr. C. S., XIII: 309
Farncomb, Commo. H. B., IV: 19, 272, V: 29, XI: 342, XIII: 201, 275, 303
FARNDALE, IX: 393, XI: 343
Farnham, Lt. Cdr. D. W., XIII: 305
FARQUHAR, X: 355, 379–80
FARRAGUT, III: 31n, 104, 213n, IV: 19, 37n, 38, 271, V: 86, 110, VII: 44, 61, 335, 338, 346–7, XII: 429, XIII: 319; Class, III: 22n, XIII: 71
Farrar, Capt. M. T., VIII: 419
Farrell, Col. E. J., V: 191
Farrell, Capt. L. B., XIV: 387
Farrell, Cdr. R. M., XIII: 285, XIV: 289
Farrington, Lt. J. S., V: 375
Farrington, Lt. Cdr. R. F., VI: 325n, VII: 340
Farrow, Cdr. Henry, XIV: 377
Farrow, 2nd Lt. W. G., III: 392, 397
Farwell, Lt. R. E., XII: 382, 417
Fassarai I., XII: 49
Fast Carrier Forces, Pacific Fleet, XII: 12, 19, 74–6, 87. *See also* TF–38, TF–58
Faulkner, Lt. C. W., V: 338, 368
Faulkner, Maj. Cecil, VI: 65
Faulkner, Capt. G. V. B., IX: 104, 389
FAULKNOR, IX: 394
FAUNCE, I: 421
Fauzon, II: 248
Fawkes, Capt. G. B. H., IX: 72
Fay, Lt. Cdr. E. B., VII: 345, VIII: 229
FAYETTE, VII: 344, VIII: 419, XII: 416, XIII: 308
Fear, Cape, I: 255
Fechteler, Adm. William M., biog., VIII: 64n; pic., 48; Admiralties, VI: 436–8; Gilberts, VII: 339; Hollandia, VIII: 64–5, 81–6, 404; Wakde-Sarmi, 95–6; Biak, 103–4, 108, 111, 114, 125; Noemfoor, 135–6; Sansapor, 141–3; Morotai, XII: 21; Leyte, 130–31,

135, 416; Lingayen, XIII: 115, 126, 130, 309; other Philippines, 178, 189–92, 209, 215–20, 233, 321
FECHTELER, sunk, X: 257
Fedhala, II: 33–4, 41, 46, 51; landing, 55–87; charts, 57, 166, 172; pics., 75, 82–3, 175; unloading, 157–61, 171; base, 245–6
Fegen, Capt. E. S. F., I: 24
Feilbach, Lt. Cdr. H. O., VII: 346, VIII: 420, XII: 420
FELAND, VII: 337, 344, VIII: 407, 420, XII: 418, XIII: 308
Feldt, Cdr. E. A., *The Coastwatchers*, V: 11n
Felix, Lt. Cdr. D. T., VIII: 255n
Fellows, Lt. Cdr. J. B., V: 232, VI: 145, 182
Felmly, Lt. L. M., XIII: 302
Fels, Lt. Cdr. J. R., VII: 347, VIII: 410
Felt, Capt. H. D., IV: 270, V: 86, 88–90, XIV: 374
Felter, Lt. (jg) W. A., X: 127
Fenard, Vice Adm. Raymond, II: 187, 209
FENCER, X: 40n, 160n, 308
Fenno, Lt. Cdr. F. W., IV: 92, 194, 199–200
Fenski, Oblt. Horst, X: 256–7
Fenton, Lt. Cdr. C. R., IV: 19
Ferebee, Maj. T. W., XIV: 344
Ferguson, Lt. Cdr. E. F., VII: 338, 346
Ferguson, Lt. E. R., XIV: 377
Ferguson, Lt. Cdr. J. N., II: 122n, VIII: 404
Fernald, Capt. J. M., VII: 345, VIII: 418
Fernando Noronha, X: 224
Fernbrook, X: 382
Ferrall, Lt. Cdr. W. E., III: 158, V: 324
Ferrell, Lt. Cdr. F. P., XII: 428, XIII: 319, XIV: 387
Ferris, Capt. F. F., VI: 297, VIII: 418
Ferriter, Lt. Cdr. C. A., III: 159
Ferry, Lt. Col. G. F., V: 337, 371n
Fertig, Col. W. W., pic., XIII: 260; mentioned, 240–41
FESSENDEN, X: 257, 296, 329n, 379
Fiala, Cdr. R. P., VII: 345, VIII: 409, XII: 418, XIII: 307, XIV: 385
Fick, Capt. H. F., VIII: 405, X: 115, 118–19, 379
Fickenscher, Lt. E. R., VIII: 410, XII: 421
Fidel, Lt. Cdr. J. A., XIII: 316

Fieberling, Lt. L. K., IV: 92
FIEBERLING, XIV: 379, 390
Field, Lt. Cdr. B. P., IX: 389, XI: 342
Field, James A., *The Japanese at Leyte Gulf*, XII: ix
Field, Capt. W. L., XII: 419, XIII: 310
Fielding, Capt. C. F., X: 213n
FIERCE, I: 422
Fife, Rear Adm. James, biog., XIII: 281n; mentioned, III: 193, 303n, IV: 222, VI: 67, 142, VII: 353, XIII: 281–3, 286, 320n
Fighting Squadron One, VII: 338n, VIII: 412; Two, IV: 19, VII: 339, VIII: 412; Three, IV: 90, 120, XIII: 315; Four, 317; Five, IV: 270, V: 86, VII: 338, 348, XIV: 383; Six, III: 392, IV: 91, 120, 271, V: 86, VI: 331, VII: 338–9, 349, XIV: 384; Seven, XII: 425, XIII: 316; Eight, IV: 91, VIII: 413, XII: 425; Nine, II: 39, 88, VI: 331, 339, 349, XIV: 385; Ten, V: 204, 233, 268, VII: 348, VIII: 414, XIV: 385; Eleven, XII: 424, XIII: 316; Twelve, VII: 340, 350, XIV: 383; Thirteen, XII: 427; Fourteen, VIII: 413, XII: 424; Fifteen, VIII: 268, 414, XII: 426; Sixteen, VII: 338, VIII: 414; Seventeen, VI: 331–2, XIV: 382; Eighteen, VI: 331, VII: 339, 349, XII: 425; Nineteen, Twenty, 426–7, XIII: 316; Twenty-one, XII: 428; Twenty-two, VI: 331, VII: 339, XII: 424, XIII: 315; Twenty-three, VII: 340, 350, XIV: 385; Twenty-four, VII: 339, 348, VIII: 412; Twenty-five, VII: 338, 349, VIII: 415; Twenty-seven, 414, XII: 427; Twenty-eight, VIII: 413, XII: 424, XIII: 315; Twenty-nine, X: 379, XII: 426, XIII: 316, XIV: 384; Thirty, VII: 339, XIV: 382; Thirty-two, VII: 350; Thirty-three, VI: 331–3; Thirty-five, Thirty-seven, VII: 346, VIII: 420; Forty-one, II: 39, 88–9; Forty-two, IV: 19, 90; Forty-four, XIII: 317; Forty-five, 317, XIV: 382; Forty-six, 385; Fifty, Fifty-one, VIII: 413–14; XII: 428; Sixty, VII: 346, VIII: 420; Seventy-one, IV: 271, V: 87; Seventy-two, 205; Eighty, XIII: 317; Eighty-one, XII: 349n, XIII: 315; Eighty-two, XIV: 382;

Fighting Squadrons (*cont'd*)
Eighty-three, Eighty-four, Eighty-six, 382–4; Eighty-eight, 316, 334, 385*n*
Night (VFN) Squadrons, Forty-one, XII: 426, XIII: 318; Seventy-six, Seventy-seven, VII: 352–3, VIII: 412–14; Ninety, XIII: 318, XIV: 383; One Hundred-One, VII: 352, VIII: 414
Fighter-director, V: 87, 92–6, 107, 210–11, 223, 360, VI: 303, VIII: 116, 261–2, 274, IX: 102, 250, 277–8, 340, 351, 355, 396*n*, X: 266, XII: 22, XIII: 102
Fiji Is., IV: 6, 257–9, 263*n*, 265, 281, V: 183*n*, 291, 369, VII: 109, 112; troops, VI: 431*n*
Fike, Lt. Col. C. L., V: 74–5
Filippe de Neve, IX: 390
Fina Susu, Mt., VIII: 193, 197–9
FINBACK, IV: 92, 210, 213, VIII: 250*n*, 254, 278, 415
Finch, Radioman J. H., X: 112
FINCH, sunk, III: 205
Fines, Lt. Cdr. C. A., IX: 391
Fink, Capt. C. K., XIII: 316, XIV: 382
Finley, Col. G. S., VI: 446
Finn, Lt. Col. R. W., I: 243*n*
FINNEGAN, XIV: 18
Finney, R. T., IX: xvi
Finnie, Lt. (jg) R. J., X: 131
Finschhafen, VI: 96, 136, 255–7, 261, 369, VIII: 71, 137, XII: 22, XIII: 97, 154, 208; bombardment, VI: 260; landing, 269–71; counter-landing, 274
Fioravanzo, Rear Adm. G., IX: xvi
Fire control. *See* Naval Gunfire Control
FIREDRAKE, XIV: 167*n*, 386
Fire fighting, I: 329, XIV: 98–9
FIRM, I: 422
Firth, Capt. C. L., IX: 394
Firth, Cdr. M. W., XIII: 313
Firth, Robert, VI: 192
Fischer, Lt. Cdr. C. F., X: 212
Fischler, Rear Adm. P. K., XIII: 176*n*, XIV: 372
Fish, Lt. Col. James, VII: 50
Fisher, Rear Adm. Douglas B., XIV: 105, 388
Fisher, Wing Cdr. G. H., V: 375
Fishermen Observers, I: 286–8
Fiske, Capt. L. S., I: 419, II: 36, VIII: 349, 420
FISKE, X: 322, 380
Fiss, Lt. Col. G. R., I: 349
Fitch, Vice Adm. Aubrey W., pics., IV: 29, XII: 191; post-Pearl Harbor opns., III: 213, 236–7, 252, IV: 14–16, 19; assistance, III: 242*n*, Coral Sea, IV: 19–30, 37–8, 53, 81; Midway, 156–7, 257; Comairsopac, V: 166, 184, 200–205, 228, 232, 261, 359, 374, VI: 90, 104–5, 139, 146, 281, 290, VII: 96; on *Franklin,* XIV: 97
Fitch, Cdr. H. W., II: 39
Fitch, Cdr. R. A., X: 381
FITCH, I: 420, II: 39, X: 231, XI: 89, 95, 334, 341
Fitts, Lt. Cdr. W. M., VII: 333
Fitts, Cdr. W. W., VIII: 409, XII: 418, XIII: 309, XIV: 260
Fitz, Capt. H. C., I: 123, X: 24, XIII: 318, XIV: 96, 383
FitzGerald, Cdr. P. H., V: 297, VIII: 401
Fitzpatrick, Lt. J. R., V: 353
Fitzpatrick, Capt. T. B., VII: 335, 337, VIII: 405, XIII: 307
Fitzsimmons, C. H., VI: xii
Fitzsimmons, Lt. Cdr. J. P., V: 375
Fitzwilliam, Cdr. A. E., XIII: 313
FIXITY, XIV: 377
Flachsenhar, Cdr. J. J., XIII: 167–8, 320
FLAHERTY, X: 282, 353–5, 378–9
Flanagan, Commo. H. C., IV: 273, VI: 297, VII: 346, VIII: 407, 420, XII: 419, XIV: 37, 381
FLASHER, XII: 406
Flatley, Cdr. J. H., V: 204, 233, 268, 361–2, XII: 196
Fleck, Lt. Cdr. F. E., XI: 342
Fleck, Cdr. T. M., VIII: 406
Fleet, Lt. John, VIII: 382
Fleets of U.S. Navy:
Asiatic, III: 28–9, 53, 58, 152–4, 278–9; T.O., 158–60, 271–3
Atlantic, I: 14, 51, 57, 82, III: 57; T.O., I: 419–22; Op Plans, 74, 78, 82, 83*n*–4*n*, *Administrative History of,* X: xii–xiii
Pacific, established, III: 47; movements and strength 1941, 56–8; training, 132–3; opns. Jan.–May '42, chart, 264; expansion in 1943, VI: 5, VII: 91; weather central, XIII: 60
United States, III: 28–31, 38, 42–3, 46; renamed Pacific Fleet, 47
Third, VI: 89, 97, VIII: 161, XII: 16, 55–7, 60, 71, 74–80, XIII: 52–92,

160, 163, 176, XIV: 20, 357, 361;
T.O.s, XII: 90, 424–9, XIII: 315–
19; pic., XIV: 366
Fourth, I: 377, 328n, 390, X: 208–28,
293–6; strength, 208–9
Fifth, VI: 97, 401, 434, VII: 86, 99,
XIV: 20; T.O.s, VII: 336–53,
VIII: 407–15, XIV: 272–88
Seventh, VI: 89, 97, 130, 255, 370–72,
433, VIII: 47–51, 110, 116, 217,
IX: 327, XII: 5, 55, 60, 74, 80–85,
123, 126, XIII: 38, 50, 90, 155–6,
208, 214, 233–4; T.O.s, VIII: 403–
6, XII: 415–23, XIII: 321
Eighth, II: 255, X: 251–2, XI: 236–8
Tenth, I: 244–5, 409, X: 12–31, 115,
245, 278, 284, 295, 332–3, 345, 349,
356
Twelfth, XI: 57, 329
Fleet Air Wing Seven, X: 100, 324, 359;
pic., 328; Nine, 46; Ten, VIII: 49n;
Eleven, 189, 197; Fifteen, 129; Six-
teen, I: 378, 386, X: 209, 212, 222;
Seventeen, VIII: 50, 406, XII: 25
Fleet Airship Wing Four, X: 223; Five,
X: 223
Fleet problems, I: lii–liii, III: 13, 29, 38,
42–3
Fleet Train, I: lvi–lvii, III: 28, VII: 100–
102; see Logistics, Service Squadrons
FLEETWOOD, X: 105n
Fleming, Cdr. M. K., VIII: 123,
XIII: 312
Fleming, Capt. R. W., XIII: 105, 304
Fleming, Capt. Richard E., IV: 145, 149
FLEMING, VIII: 410, XIV: 374
Flenniken, Cdr. J. A., XIV: 381
Fletcher, Vice Adm. Frank J., biog.,
III: 236n; pic., IV: 28; post-Pearl Har-
bor opns., III: 212, 236, 241–4, 247,
251–4, 259–66, 387; Coral Sea, IV: 14–
18, 21–31, 40–49, 58–60; Midway, 84–
5, 90, 94, 97, 101–4, 112, 122, 131–6,
141, 153–4, VIII: 254; Guadalcanal,
IV: 257, 268–70, 280–81, 290–92, V: 14,
23, 27–8, 53, 110–12; Eastern Solo-
mons Battle, 80, 83, 86–90, 102–6;
North Pacific Force, VII: 66, 86,
XIV: 357
Fletcher, Cdr. F. O., XIII: 303
Fletcher, Capt. W. B., IV: 273, V: 232,
VI: 144
FLETCHER, V: 205, 226, 232, 237, 248–50,
253, 256, 294–311 passim, 326–8, 344n,

364–7, VI: 107, 116, VII: 190, 339, 346,
VIII: 127–30, 405, XII: 23, 377, 387,
416, XIII: 27n, 200, 261, 304, 321–2;
Class, I: lviii, 28n, 234–5
FLICKER, I: 390n, 422
FLIER, VIII: 416
Flinders, Capt. Matthew, IV: 6–7
Flint, Lt. Cdr. R. L., VII: 338
FLINT, XIII: 318, XIV: 21, 385–6
Flittie, Lt. W. J., VI: 61
Floating dry docks, VIII: 350, XII: 80
Flood, Chief Signalman C. A., VI: 191
FLORENCE NIGHTINGALE, II: 36, IX: 130,
389, XI: 341
FLORES, IX: 156, 207, 251n, 266, 392, 396
Flores Sea, III: 299–300
FLORIDA, V: 325n, VI: 282n, IX: 14n,
XIV: 25n
Florida I., Solomons, IV: 282, V: 6, 66,
181, 339, VI: 102; chart, V: 8–9; pic.,
IV: 255
Florida, U.S., "dim-out," I: 129–30; see
also Gulf Sea Frontier
Florida, Strait of, X: 192, 207n
Florida M., VI: 125
FLOUNDER, X: 302, 329n, XIII: 282–3
Floyd, Cdr. W. O., IX: 23n, 75, 86–8,
387, 395, XI: 340
Fluckey, Cdr. E. B., XII: 399, XIII: 297–
8, 319, XIV: 294
Fluegel, Cdr. F. C., VII: 337, VIII: 408,
XII: 416, XIII: 309
FLUELLEN, II: 283
FLUSSER (1909), IX: 14n
FLUSSER (1936), III: 210n, VI: 261, 267,
270, 381–4, 390, 436, 443, XII: 344,
373–4, 384–5, 417, XIII: 236, 248–9,
313, 322–4
FLUTTO, IX: 41
Fly, Cdr. W. A., IX: 389, XI: 339
FLY, IX: 393, 396
FLYING FISH, IV: 92, 212, VIII: 23, 231,
241–3, 415, XIV: 292n
Flynn, Capt. C. W., IV: 272, V: 52n, 87
Flynn, Lt. Cdr. J. E., X: 376
Flynn, Cdr. J. F., XI: 341
Flynn, Lt. R. B., XIII: 35
Flynn, Lt. W. T., pic., X: 184; men-
tioned, 181
Foam, I: 284, 288
Fogde, Lt. (jg) F. D., X: 113
FOGG, X: 331–2
Foggia, IX: 58, 232, 302–3
Folbots, IX: 69, 72, 152, 338

Foley, Cdr. J. F., XI: 336
Foley, Cdr. R. J., V: 348*n*, VI: 73, VII: 353
Folger, Lt. Cdr. E. C., I: 421
Foltz, C. E., X: 382
Foltz, Ens. R. E., VIII: 270
FOMALHAUT, IV: 273, V: 81, VIII: 410, XIII: 307, XIV: 386
FOND DU LAC, XIV: 380
Fonda, Lt. Cdr. T. C., VIII: 407, XII: 419
Fonick, Lt. Cdr. T. R., XII: 422, XIII: 306
Fontana, Maj. P. J., V: 375
Foochow, XIII: 298
FOOTE, VI: 241-2, 308, 316-22, 338, XIII: 35, 309
Forbes, Lt. A. C., VI: 228
Forbes, Cdr. Alexander, I: 62*n*
Forbes, Lt. Cdr. F. Murray, XI: ix
Forbes, Lt. Cdr. G. W., XIII: 288
FORBIN, XI: 311, 343
FORCE, I: 422
Forces françaises de l'intérieure (F.F.I), XI: 34, 38, 226, 235, 263, 286, 298, 302
Ford, Ens., III: 106
Ford, Lt. Cdr. Joel C., IX: 251*n*, 298, 389, 392
Ford, Lt. Cdr. L. M. D., VIII: 412
Ford, Lt. Cdr. R. S., II: 38, IX: 385
Ford, Ens. T. J. F., III: 106
Ford, Lt. W. R., X: 216, 225
Ford, Lt. Cdr. Walter C., IV: 19
Ford, Lt. William, I: 386
Ford I., III: 32; pic., 102
FOREMAN, XIV: 373, 390
FORFAR, I: 24
Forman, Ens. A. L., V: 310*n*
Fórmia, IX: 370, 375
FORMIDABLE, II: 189, 382, IX: 167, 251, 393, XIV: 249, 265, 388
FORMOE, XIII: 263
Formosa, III: 26, 166-70, VIII: 4, 157, XII: 165, 344, XIII: 56, 102, 151, 158-61, 163-4, 170, 172, 176, 179-82, XIV: 17, 80, 89; in strategy, XII: 4-5, 10-12, 17-18, 66, XIII: 3-5; strikes on, XII: 50, 57, XIII: 88-90; air battle, XII: 92-109; Strait, XII: 402-4, XIII: 38, 297
Forney, Lt. Col. E. H., VI: 428
Forney, Lt. (jg) R. H., X: 124
Fornick, Lt. Cdr. T. R., XII: 208

Forrest, Lt. Cdr. G. O., XIII: 307, XIV: 380
FORREST, I: 420, II: 39, X: 281, 379, XI: 333-4, 340-41, XIV: 373, 376, 392
Forrestal, Hon. James V., pic., XIV: 366; mentioned, I: 29, III: 142, V: 117, 263, VII: viii, 101, X: 35, XI: 252, 274, XIV: 61, 231, 273, 308, 339, 347
Forrestel, Capt. Emmet P., pic., VIII: frontispiece
Forrester, Lt. Cdr. R. R., XIV: 377
Forshew, Cdr. J. H., X: 380
Forster, Capt. O. M., II: 40, 139*n*, 142*n*
Forsyth, Capt. J. E., XI: 216*n*
Forsythe, Commo. H. C. C., X: 79
Forsythe, Col. J. D., IX: 261
Fort, Rear Adm. George H., IV: 271, V: 86, VI: 121, 145-6, 294, 415, 418, XII: 34, 43*n*, 44
Fort Bellingham, X: 305
Fort Lee, X: 302
Fort Michipicoten, X: 381
Fort Pierce, Fla., VIII: 166, XI: 240
FORT WILLIAM, XI: 335
Fortaleza, I: 379, X: 209, 212, 219, 223
FORTUNE, XII: 77
Fos, Golfe de, XI: 285-6
Foskett, Capt. J. H., IX: 148*n*
Foss, Lt. Cdr. Eugene N., XIV: 193-4, 195*n*, 376
Foss, Lt. Cdr. H. O., VII: 347, XII: 420
Foss, Maj. J. J., V: 340
Foster, Cdr. E. L., VII: 350, XIV: 377
Foster, Lt. Cdr. E. P., XIV: 381
Foster, Capt. F. F., VI: 204*n*, 339
Foster, Yeoman H. E., I: xvii, 62*n*
Foster, Lt. Cdr. H. P., VIII: 411
Foster, Capt. J. G., XIV: 374
Foster, Cdr. J. L., VIII: 405, XII: 416, XIII: 304
Foster, Cdr. John, IV: 122*n*
Foster, Lt. Cdr. R. C., XIII: 307
Foster, Cdr. W. M., I: 420, XIII: 30, 304
Fougier, Gen., IX: 57
FOUGUEUX, II: 99; sunk, 101, 113
Fowler, Ens. R. E., VIII: 267
Fowler, Cdr. R. L., V: 161, XII: 254, 279-81, 285, 308-9, 421
Fowler, Lt. (jg) W. S., X: 112, 162
FOWLER, X: 339, 373
Fowlkes, Col. B. C., VIII: 113
Fox, Lt. Cdr. D. H., V: 205, 232

Fox, Lt. F. M., XIV: 135
Fox, Rev. George L., I: 333
Fox schedule, I: 103–5
"Foxer" gear, X: 146, 159, 256, 285, 320, 351, 353
Foyle, Lough, I: 54, X: 339
Foyt, Lt. Cdr. R. C., XIV: 387
Frakes, Lt. Cdr. D. R., IX: 389
France, Capt. A. F., VII: 334–6
France, Capt. W. C., XIV: 177, 375
France, relations with U.S., in Caribbean, I: 30–33, X: 192; in Morocco, II: 3–11, 215–20; chain of command in N. Africa, 87; Army, IX: 306–7, 333, 375, XI: 101*n*, 233, 236–8, 250–53, 270, 281, 338; First Army, XI: 233, 291, 310, 323; Navy in 1922–1941, I: lxi, X: 4; Fleet problem, II: 3–5, 11; Toulon Fleet, 240; in Pacific, IV: 253. *See also* North Africa and Southern France ops.
Francis, Cdr. D. L., XIV: 375, 378
FRANCIS M. ROBINSON, X: 288–9, 376
Francis M. Smith, X: 382
Francis Parkman, IX: 386
Francis Scott Key, I: 169, 171*n*
Franco, Gen. Francisco, I: 67, II: 7, 188, IX: 13, 87
Frank, Lt. L. B., XII: 420
Frank, Cdr. N. J. F., VIII: 228, 404, XII: 417
Frankel, Capt. S. B., I: 158*n*, 172, 178, 187*n*, 373–5, X: 306
FRANKFORD, XI: 145, 156, 174, 277, 335–6, 337, 343
Franklin, Lt. Charles H., V: 375
Franklin, Lt. G. P., XII: 419
Franklin, Cdr. J. G., XII: 416, XIV: 383
FRANKLIN, VII: xxix, X: 109*n*, XII: 13, 90, 94, 106, 166, 169*n*, 182–90 *passim*, 318, 325–8, 341–2, 346, 360, 427, XIII: 31, 54, XIV: 21, 160, 248, 383; hits on, XII: 94, 101; crippled, XIV: 95–100; casualties, 390; pic., 103
Franklin MacVeagh, VII: 334
FRANKS, VII: 140, 273, 334, 337, 347, VIII: 223–4, 419, XII: 244, 287, 421, XIII: 316, 318, XIV: 385
Fraser, Adm. Sir Bruce, X: 231–2, 237–41, XIII: 105, 257, XIV: 103–6, 333, 361, 366, 369
Fraser, Cdr. G. K., XIV: 381
Fraser, Lt. N. E., XI: 127

Fraser, Cdr. T. E., I: 418, IV: 19, V: 233, 276
Fratello, Monte, IX: 197–9, 202
FRAZIER, V: 353, VII: 57, 139, 168, 334, 337, 344, XIII: 303
Fredendall, Maj. Gen. L. R., II: 17, 223, 237
Frederick, Maj. Gen. R. T., XI: 248*n*, 277–8
FREDERICK, XI: 63*n*
FREDERICK C. DAVIS, IX: 347, 355, 395–6, X: 351–53, 378, XI: 343; pic., X: 360
Frederick Douglass, X: 140–42
FREDERICK FUNSTON, VIII: 407, 420, IX: 389, 392, XII: 419, XIII: 311
FREDERICK LEE, I: 421
Fredericks, Lt. Col. C. G., VII: 280*n*
Freeland, Lt. Frank, V: 320
Freeman, Lt. C. L., III: 158
Freeman, Cdr. J. S., IV: 273, V: 292
Freeman, Lt. R. M., VIII: 414
Freeman, Wing Cdr. T. O., VI: 396
Freeman, Gunner W. R., XI: 138*n*
Freese, Lt. Cdr. J. B., IX: 387
Freese, Lt. J. L., XIV: 325
FREESTONE, XIV: 380
Freetown, Sierra Leone, I: 263, X: 209
Freiburghouse, Cdr. L. F., XIV: 115, 120, 376
Fréjus, Golfe de, XI: 235, 256, 266–7, 270–73, 275; pic., 284–5
Fremantle, I: 112, III: 303*n*, 305, 359, 379, IV: 206–8, 219–20, VI: 65, 75–6, 82, 85, VIII: 16, 20–21, 24, 48, 217, X: 302, XII: 174, 399, XIII: 286, XIV: 104
FREMONT, VIII: 410, XII: 34, 416, XIII: 309
French, Lt. Cdr. L. C., XII: 427
French, Cdr. R. H., X: 342, 379
FRENCH, XIV: 66*n*, 326
French Frigate Shoals, IV: 70, 76, 85, 93–4
Frerks, Oblt., X: 123
Freseman, Capt. W. L., XI: 206–8, 334, 337, XII: 350*n*, 371, 377, 385, XIII: 105, 109, 304, 312, XIV: 373
Freuler, Capt. H. C., III: 246
Freund, Cdr. B. W., VI: 331, VII: 339, 348, VIII: 405, 410, XIV: 384
Frey, Lt. Cdr. C. W., X: 378
Frey, Lt. (jg) H. W., VI: 329
Friend, Col. Dale G., VI: 102
Fries, Gen. Walter, IX: 198–9

Frigates, I: 13, X: 36, 37n
Frink, Maj. Gen. J. L., VIII: 47
Frisbie, Col. J. W., VI: 385
Frisco, Capt. L., VII: 337, VIII: 405, XII: 416
Fritzsche, Capt. E. H., XI: 130, 335
FROBISHER, XI: 192
Froccaro, 2nd Lt. C. J., X: 130–31
FRONDEUR, II: 99, 248; sunk, II: 107
Frost, Cdr. L. H., I: 79, 420, V: 353, VI: 228
FROST, X: 283–4, 320–22, 348, 378
Frundt, Lt. Cdr. W. G., XII: 428, XIII: 318, XIV: 387
Fryatt, Lt. (jg) H. E., X: 114, 161–2
FS–154, –173, –174, –364, XIII: 307n
FUBUKI, III: 276, 365–6, IV: 89, V: 151, 161n; sunk, 162–3; class, III: 22
Fuchida, Mitsuo, *Midway,* IV: xi
Fuehrer Conferences, I: 5n, X: xiv
Fueling, I: 321, VI: 324; South Pacific bases, IV: 263n; in port, VI: 353, 421, VIII: 122, 126, IX: 286, XII: 306; at sea, I: 107–10, II: 47, III: 237, 243, IV: 22, 30–31, 37, VII: 9, 61, 107–8, 114–18, 228, 320, VIII: 29–30, 38, 221, 231–2, 243, 309–11, XII: 76, 92, 104–6, 118, 175, 193, 329–30, 339, XIII: 55, 60–66, 76–7, 84, 88–9, 107, 116–17, 165, 169–73, 180, XIV: 9, 22, 57, 159–60, 165, 213, 250, 307; pics., II: 45, XII: 78
Fuetsch, Cdr. B. A., VII: 335, VIII: 409
Fujikawa M., VII: 325
FUJINAMI, VI: 328, VIII: 416, XII: 431; sunk, 341
Fujisan M., IV: 172
Fujita, Rear Adm. R., III: 162n, 274–5, 280, IV: 89
Fukudome, Vice Adm. S., VIII: 13, XII: 68–9, 91–3, 100–104, 161n, 165, 187, 432, XIII: 15, 152
Fukuoka, Capt. T., XII: 431
FULLAM, VI: 297, 360, 413, 415, 420, VIII: 409, 415, 419, XIV: 374

Fuller, Lt. Cdr. H. D., VIII: 403
Fuller, Maj. Gen. Horace H., VIII: 63–5, 81–3, 95, 103, 106, 113–15, 123–5, 133, 403
FULLER, I: 76, IV: 266, 272, V: 124–5, VI: 297, 344, VIII: 408, XII: 416, XIII: 308, 312, XIV: 378
Fullinwider, Capt. E. G., VIII: 413, XIV: 378
Fulp, Cdr. J. D., XIV: 285
Fulton, Lt. Cdr. R. L., VII: 350, VIII: 413
FULTON, IV: 155n
Fultz, Capt. H. F., XII: 423
Fumi Maru No. 2, IV: 18
FUMITSUKI, III: 161, VI: 125, 244, 412, VII: 330; sunk, 325–6
Funafuti, IV: 246, V: 184, VI: 94n, VII: 78–98 *passim,* 106, 110, 118, 208, 211, 226
Funk, Lt. Cdr. H. N., XII: 420
Funk, Lt. Col. R. D., IX: 287
Funke, Capt. Frederick, XIV: 374
Furer, Rear Adm. Julius A., I: ix, 29
FURIOUS, II: 223
Furlong, Rear Adm. William R., III: xii, 100–101, 109–10, 116, 125–6, 143, IV: 81n
Furlow, Cdr. C. M., VIII: 419, XII: 418, XIII: 308
Furnas, Electrician T. R., VII: 141
Furtwangler, Lt. A. S., XIV: 377
FURUTAKA, III: 26, 245, IV: 18, V: 35–7, 40, 45, 50–53, 60, 61n, 85, 105, 150–68 *passim;* sunk, 61n
FURY, IX: 394
FUSO, III: 26, IV: 89, VII: 137, 222, 319, VIII: 118–20, XII: 162–3, 190–91, 209–33 *passim,* 431; sunk, 217, 220n
Fusselman, Cdr. R. D., XIV: 381
FUYO, sunk, VI: 75
FUYUZUKI, XIII: 158, XIV: 202
Fyfe, Cdr. J. K., XIII: 279–80
Fyffe, Lt. J. B., X: 380
Fyne, Loch, II: 193

G

Gabbert, Cdr. J. S. C., VIII: 413, XII: 425, XIII: 305
Gabel, Lt. (jg) R. W., XIV: 135
Gabès, II: 242, 258–9
GABILAN, XII: 429, XIII: 282, 286, 320
Gadd, Ens. P. R., XII: 207, 422
Gaëta, town and gulf, IX: 310, 317, 324, 333, 370, 375–6, 381, XI: 241
Gaffey, Maj. Gen. H. J., II: 155, IX: 28, 386
Gaffi, IX: 79–84
Gage, Cdr. N. D., XIII: 320
GAGE, XIV: 378
Gaida, Aviation Mech. B. P., III: 264
Gainard, Cdr. J. A., I: 284
Gaines, Cdr. R. K., V: 204, 209, 233
Gairdner, Maj. Gen. C. H., IX: 15–17
GAIRSAY, XI: 192
Galantin, Cdr. I. J., XII: 429
Galapagos Is., X: 201n
GALATEA, I: 138
Gale, Cdr. Winsor C., VII: 27
Galer, Capt. R. E., V: 374
Gali, VI: 391
GALILEI, X: 290n
Gallagher, Lt. Cdr. J. M., XIV: 381
Gallaher, Cdr. A. R., VIII: 415
Gallaher, Capt. J. F., IX: 389, X: 185, 186n
Gallaher, Lt. W. E., IV: 91, 124–6, 136
Gallery, Rear Adm. Dan V., pic., X: 289; mentioned, 201, 281–3, 290–93, 379; *Clear the Decks!*, xv
Gallery, Cdr. P. D., VIII: 404, XII: 416, XIII: 309
Gallery, Cdr. W. O., VIII: 406
Gallmeier, 1st Lt. C. F., X: 94
Gallodoro, Monto, IX: 75, 86–8; pic., 82
Galloway, Lt. (jg) G. R., IX: 259, 264
GALLUP, XII: 417
Gallup polls, III: 18, 39n, 59–61
Galveston, I: 262, II: 271n
Galvin, Ens. J. R., VIII: 33
Gambacorta, Cdr. F. M., XIII: 319
GAMBIA, XIV: 105, 212, 313, 333, 388
GAMBIER BAY, VIII: 207, 360, 410, XII: 244, 253, 272, 276–80, 287, 306,
313–15, 421; pic., 247, 278; sunk, 282–4
Gamble, Lt. (jg) L. H., V: 319, 339, 349, 367
GAMBLE, III: 104, 213n, IV: 276n, V: 67, 85n, VI: 112–14, 297, 308, XIV: 31, 114, 389
Gamet, Capt. W. N., XIII: 310, 375
Gammelgard, Lt. Cdr. P. N., XIII: 307
Gander, I: 320, X: 28, 71
Gandy, Lt. (jg) D. W., XIV: 27
GANDY, X: 318–19, 372
GANNET, I: 15n
Gano, Cdr. R. A., VI: 308, 354
Ganongga, VI: 239
Ganse, Gen., II: 243
GANSEVOORT, VII: 334, 338, XII: 418, XIII: 46–7
GANYMEDE, VIII: 404, XII: 423
GAR, III: 213, IV: 229, VIII: 30, 415
Garapan, town and roads, VIII: 152, 200, 208, 242n, 254, 286, 329
GARDENIA, II: 283
Gardes, Lt. Cdr. A. W., XII: 307, 420
Gardiner, Col. W. T., IX: 240
Gardner, Lt. Cdr. E. R., I: 86
Gardner, Lt. Cdr. F. H., III: 393, IV: 91, 274, V: 86
Gardner, Rear Adm. M. B., V: 25n, VII: 348, 352, VIII: 414, X: 28, XIII: 87, 165, 318, XIV: 21, 97
Gardner, Cdr. R. N., XIV: 387
Gardner Pinnacles, IV: 85, 93
Gare Loch, I: 53, 160
Garfield, Lt. W. E., XII: 203n
Garigliano R., IX: 324, 333, 374–5
GARLAND, I: 178n
Garling, II: 283
Garnett, Lt. P. W., I: 421
Garretson, Maj. F. E., VIII: 363
Garrett, Lt. Cdr. F. B., XIII: 77, 319
Garrison, Cdr. M. E., VIII: 17–18
Garrison, Lt. P. B., XII: 280
Garsian, Radioman Leon, XII: 146n
Garton, Lt. Cdr. N. F., IV: 173
Gary, Lt. (jg) D. A., XIV: 98
GASCOYNE, XII: 422, XIII: 102, 306

Gash, Lt. R. W., VI: 171*n*
Gasmata, IV: 256, VI: 56, 372
Gasolene, shortage of, I: 267–8; pipelines, XI: 26, 218, XIV: 70
Gatch, Capt. T. L., I: 419, V: 200, 204, 218, 233, 279
Gates, Hon. Artemus L., I: 29*n*
Gates, Lt. Cdr. B. V., XIV: 374
Gates, Capt. H. K., XIII: 83, XIV: 387
GATESHEAD, XI: 336
GATINEAU, X: 139, 142
GATLING, VII: 348, VIII: 414, XII: 179, 182, 427, XIII: 81, 318
GATO, IV: 92, V: 348, VI: 72–4, 280–83, VII: 353, XIII: 285, XIV: 289
Gatzenmeier, Isabel J., V: x, VII: viii
Gauger, Lt. W. R., VII: 265
Gavin, Col. J. M., IX: 94
Gavutu, IV: 287–92, V: 11, 16; pic., 289
Gay, Ens. G. H., IV: 120
Gay, Brig. Gen. H. S., pic., II: 218; mentioned, 109
GAYETY, XIV: 377
Gayler, Cdr. N. A. M., XIV: 383
Gaylord, Lt. (jg) E. C., X: 169
GAZELLE, VI: 293*n*, VII: 347
Gea Islet, VII: 252–4, 257
GEAR, VIII: 420, XIV: 387
Gebelin, Lt. Cdr. A. L., XI: 147, 333, 336
Geelvink Bay, VIII: 60, 86, 103, XII: 107, XIII: 97; chart, VIII: 105
Gehres, Capt. L. E., IV: 166, 173, 177, 182–3, VII: 5, 8, 333, XIV: 95–7, 383
Geiger, Maj. Gen. Roy S., biog., V: 75*n*; pic., VIII: 377; Guadalcanal, V: 75, 113, 176–7, 198, 228, 372–4; Bougainville, VI: 282, 348, 352, 364; Guam, VIII: 159, 170, 374–9, 383, 392, 418; Palaus, XII: 32–4, 44; Okinawa, XIV: 86, 89, 108, 241, 276, 279, 378
Geiselman, Capt. E. H., VII: 334
Geissert, Lt. Cdr. F. A., XIV: 386
Gela, IX: 18, 45, 49–51, 61–87 *passim;* landings, 28, 31, 92–125; unloading, 105–9, 123; tank fight, 109–19; charts, 96, 114–15; pic., 106–7
Gellhorn, Lt. Cdr. George, XII: 284
Gelling, Lt. Cdr. W. E., XI: 335
GEMSBOK, VII: 347
Genda, Cdr. Minoru, IV: 76, 138
Gendreau, Lt. Cdr. E. A. M., XIV: 379
GENDREAU, XIV: 379
GENERAL G. O. SQUIER, XI: 341
GENERAL GREENE, I: 64*n*

General Electric Motors, III: 145, I: 229–31
Genereaux, Cdr. E. C., VIII: 419
GENESEE, XIV: 387
Genoa, IX: 260, 365, XI: 312–16
Genthner, Cdr. E. G., XIV: 387
Gentner, Lt. Cdr. W. E., X: 212
Gentry, Lt. E. H., XIV: 376
Gentry, Cdr. K. M., IV: 174, VII: 349
Gentry, Lt. Cdr. W. W., XIV: 376
Genyo M., IV: 88, VIII: 295, 417
George, Lt. Col. A. M., V: 337, 371
George, Lt. Cdr. F. J., XIV: 386
George VI, King, pic., I: 170; mentioned, X: 243, XI: 69–71
GEORGE, VIII: 224–8, XIII: 319
GEORGE A. JOHNSON, XIII: 313
GEORGE A. MC NULTY, XIII: 314
George Ade, X: 327
GEORGE CLYMER, I: 421, II: 36, 120–24, 129, VI: 297, 300, VIII: 419, XII: 418, XIV: 378; pic., VI: 253
GEORGE E. BADGER, I: 419, X: 111, 117–19, 168–70, 375, XII: 422, XIII: 304, XIV: 374
GEORGE F. ELLIOT (1943), VIII: 408, XII: 419, XIII: 311, 312
GEORGE F. ELLIOTT (1941), IV: 265*n*, 273, V: 29, 34; sunk, 16, 295–6
George G. Henry, III: 195*n*, 272, 331
George H. Dern, X: 382
George Matthews, IX: 390
George Taylor, XIII: 313
George Washington, X: 183
GEORGES LEYGUES, II: 240*n*, XI: 118, 122, 149, 159–60, 265, 311, 336, 340
GEORGIA, X: 197*n*
Gerbini, IX: 18, 26, 57–8
Gerhardt, Maj. Gen. C. H., XI: 130*n*, 151, 336
Gerlach, Oblt. Wilhelm, X: 320–21
German, Cdr. J. P., XII: 417
Germany, strategy, I: 5–6, IX: 44–7, X: 63; priority as enemy, I: 46–8, VI: 3; relations with Japan, III: 40–42, 45–8, IV: 197, XI: 42; intelligence, X: 59; radar, IX: 70, X: 87–9, 99

  Agents. *See* Saboteurs
  Air Force. *See* Luftwaffe
  Army, II: 242–4, 258–60, IX: 47, 50, 94–376 *passim*, XI: 45, 89–187 *passim*, 239
  Armies and Groups, First & G, XI: 239; Seventh, 41, 45, 49, 89, 103,

113, 153, 159, 186, 297–8; Southwestern, 382; Tenth, IX: 260, 361, 366n; Fourteenth, 350, 361, 366; Fifteenth, XI: 41, 45, 49, 190; Nineteenth, 239

Coast defense batteries, Sicily, IX: 175, 212–13, 216; Italy, 265–8, 276–7, 340–42, XI: 311; Normandy, 43–4, 88, 94–5, 101, 104–6, 142–9, 157, 161, 171, 183–4, 196–7, 202–10; Southern France, 240, 251, 264–5

Navy, policy, I: 1–10, 34–5; in 1939, 4; Northern waters, 161–92, X: 230–31, 236–43; Mediterranean, IX: 39–40, XI: 314; Normandy, 183; motor torpedo boats, II: 264–6, 278, IX: 39–40, 78, 169, 193n, 244, 298–9, 310, 372, XI: 46, 65–6, 87, 107, 155–6, 174–5, 191–2, 277, 306, 311–12; submarines, *see* U-boats; blockade runners and raiders I: 84, III: 50–51, X: 213, 226–8, 275–8

Germershausen, Cdr. W. J., I: 421, XIV: 292n

Gerow, Maj. Gen. L. T., I: 45, XI: 29, 134n, 141, 152, 335

Gertrude, I: 278

Gervais de Lafond, Contre-Am., II: 71n, 99, 109

Getting, Capt. F. E., IV: 272, V: 29, 38, 54

Gex, Lt. Cdr. V. E., X: 378

GHERARDI, IX: 191, 197, 388, XI: 203, 334, 342, XIV: 193, 376

Ghormley, Vice Adm. Robert L., biog., IV: 250n; pic., 278; London mission, I: 40–45; Guadalcanal, IV: 250–55, 262–70, 278–81, 292, V: 12–14, 17, 27, 58, 64n, 80, 108–10, 114–17, 139, 148, 178, 182–3, 236; Com. Naval Forces Germany, XI: 325–8, 329n

Giambattista, Cdr. F. D., X: 283, 320–21, 348–50, 362, 378

Giammarino, Col. Giuseppe, IX: xvi

Gibbs, Cdr. R. H., I: 183, 420, II: 36, IX: 385

Gibraltar, I: 347, II: 31, 187, 199, 215, 225, 236–7, 263, 271n–2n, 273, IX: 13, 38, 168, 242, X: 103, 129, 157–8, 250–51, 269, 273

Gibson, Capt. F. S., VIII: 411, XII: 428, XIV: 387

Gibson, Lt. Cdr. J. E., VI: 416, 418

Giens Peninsula, XI: 285

Giffen, Vice Adm. Robert C. ("Ike"), pics., I: 128, 170; mentioned, 82, 168, 181, 185n, 419, II: 36, 44, 48, 91–2, 96–7, 100–101, 110, 247, V: 352–63, VI: 106n, VII: 55–6, 59–61, 260n, 334–6, 344, 353, X: 297

Gift, Lt. R. P., VIII: 298–9, 413, XII: 424, XIII: 315

Gifu M., IV: 223–4

Gilbert, Capt. E. L., V: 374

Gilbert, Cdr. W. C., IV: 93

GILBERT ISLANDS, XIII: 272

Gilbert Is., history and description, VII: 69–70, 76–7; Jap. occupation, III: 240, 257; operation, VI: 289, 324, 330, VII: 82–99, 105–86; submarines, 187–9; Jap. countermoves, 136–45, 213–14; T.O., 336–42; chart, 115; pics., 86–7

Giles, Capt. D. T., III: 184n, 186

Gili Gili, VI: 35–9, 53, 56, 126

Giliberty, Lt. F. R., XII: 419, XIII: 311

Gilkeson, Cdr. F. B., XIV: 373

Gill, Cdr. G. H., IV: 65n, XIII: 255n

Gill, Lt. (jg) W. C., IV: 173

Gill, Maj. Gen. William H., VIII: 72–3, XII: 56, 67

Gillan, Capt. M. J., II: 40, VI: 241

Gillespie, Capt. J. J., II: 205

Gillespie, Lt. W. R., X: 296

GILLESPIE, VI: 444, VII: 20, VIII: 116, 126n, 403

Gillette, Commo. Norman C., I: 180, 359, 419, II: 36, 101n, 106, XIV: 328–9

Gillette, Cdr. N. C., Jr., XIII: 311

Gillette, Lt. Cdr. W. B., XIV: 381

GILLIAM, XIII: 307, 312, XIV: 378

GILLIGAN, XIII: 146–7, 310, 326

Gillis, Lt. Cdr. J. A., XI: 336, XIV: 380

GILLIS, IV: 173, 176, 182–3, VII: 5, 8, 333, XIV: 380

GILMER, IV: 173, VI: 133n, 261–3, 267, 269n, 381, 444, VIII: 404, XIV: 124, 377

Gilmore, Lt. Cdr. H. W., IV: 92, 215–16, 228–9, V: 348n

Ginder, Capt. J. K. B., IV: 19, XII: 417, XIII: 304

Ginder, Rear Adm. Samuel P., VII: 208, 218–21, 286–9, 319, 339, 350, VIII: 32, 239

Gingrich, Vice Adm. John E., IX: xvi, XIV: 97, 304, 382

Ginisi plain, IX: 71, 75
Gioia Tauro, IX: 217
GIRAFFE, XIV: 387
Giraud, Gen. Henri, pic., II: 218; mentioned, II: 66–8, 185–6, 215–20, 255, IX: 13, 129n, X: 191
Gironde R., XI: 297
GIULIO CESARE, IX: 244
GIUSEPPE GARIBALDI, IX: 198, 243
Gizo Strait, VI: 213–15, 230, 239
Gjedsted, Lt. Cdr. C. B., XIII: 319
GLADIATOR, XIV: 226, 376
GLADIOLUS, I: 93
Gladisch, Adm. Walter, I: 401
Gladstone, Capt. G. V., XIV: 388
GLASGOW, X: 104, XI: 118, 122, 149, 158–60, 167–8, 198–204, 211, 336–7
Glass, Cdr. R. P., VII: 334
Glassford, Vice Adm. William A., II: 240, 152–4, 158, 173, 193, 240, 271–303 *passim*, 322–78 *passim*, XIII: 268
Gleason, Lt. C. T., XII: 210, 233, 422
GLEAVES, I: 76, 90, 123, 418, 420, IX: 193, 194n, 295, 313, 348, 385, 391, 396, X: 257–9, 372, XI: 312, 338
Gleim, Cdr. Fritz, VIII: 410
Gleis, Lt. S. N., X: 381
GLENDALE, VIII: 405
Glenfinlas, II: 284
GLENGYLE, IX: 393, 396
GLENNON, XI: 105, 110–17, 157, 334, 388; sunk, 171–3
Glenwright, Lt. Cdr. C. H., XIV: 387
Glick, Cdr. J. A., II: 38, IX: 73, 313
Glidden, Capt. E. G., IV: 110, V: 374
Glide bombs, IX: 243, 283, 290–91, 296, 299, 303, 314, 344, 355, 359, 363, 366, X: 98, 262–3, 269, 351
Glober, Maj. G. E., V: 375
Globokar, Lt. (jg) Raymond, XII: 281n
GLOIRE, II: 105, 240n, 316, 339, XI: 257, 311
GLORIOUS, X: 4, 37
Glosten, Capt. E. R., XIV: 375
GLOUCESTER, II: 286
Gloucester, Cape, VI: 63, 258, 378–9, 387, VIII: 156, XIII: 94; pic., VI: 388. *See also* Cape Gloucester opn.
Glover, Capt. C. D., I: 419, XII: 427
Glover, Rear Adm. Robert Q., biog., XII: 80n; mentioned, XII: 80–81, 423, XIII: 308
Glutting, Capt. P. R., II: 38, 84n, IX: 389

GNEISENAU, I: 4n, 161n
Godefroy, Adm., II: 217, 239
Godfrey, Capt. V. S., XI: 339
Godfrey, Capt. Vincent H., XI: 327
Godolphin, Capt. F. R. B., XIII: 194
Godsey, Lt. Cdr. H. M., X: 378
Godt, Ktradm. Eberhard, X: 62n, 78, 112, 222–3, 276, 332n, 358n, 362n, 363
Godthaab, I: 60
Goebbels, Dr. Joseph, X: 246
Goering, Reichsmarschall Hermann, I: 7, 34, 316, IX: 59, 95, 98, 101, 182–3, X: 56, 59, 95, 98, 101, 264, XI: 47, 156
Goettge, Col. F. B., pic., V: 130; mentioned, 69
GOFF, I: 15n, 151, 390n, X: 122, 159, 166–7
Goheen, Lt. Col. R. F., XIII: 194
Gold, Capt. P. D., XIV: 169
Gold, removal of, III: 203, X: 280–81
GOLD STAR, III: 159, 272
GOLDEN CITY, VIII: 419, XII: 418, XIII: 308
GOLDFINCH, I: 422
GOLDSBOROUGH, I: 420, VIII: 408, X: 161, 378, XII: 123, 422, XIII: 146, 307
Goldsmith, Cdr. F. O., II: 40
Goldstein, Dr. Harry, I: 228
Goldwaite Capt. Robert, XIV: 374
Golinkin, Cdr. J. W., VIII: 411, XIV: 387
Gomes, Brig. Gen., I: 383
Gona, IV: 269, VI: 41, 45–6, 49
Good, Lt. Col. G. F., VII: 78
Good, Rear Adm. Howard H., IV: 18, 91, V: 205, 233
Good, Lt. Cdr. Romer F., VII: 337, 345, XII: 368, 421, XIII: 306
Good, Capt. Roscoe F., XIII: 318, XIV: 48, 384
Good Hope, Cape of, I: 112, 159, 315, 385
Goodall, Lt. Henry W., III: 200
GOODALL, sunk, X: 313
Goode, Rabbi Alexander, I: 333
Goode, Cdr. J. B., VII: 341
Goodenough I., VI: 38–9, 373–4, 380–81, 389, VIII: 63
Goodfellow, Lt. Cdr. W. P., XI: 336
Goodhue, Lt. Cdr. N. M., X: 380
GOODHUE, XIV: 176, 375, 390
Goodman, Lt. C. M., XIII: 309
Goodney, Capt. W. K., XII: 46

Goodnough, Capt. J. C., XIV: 375, 380
Goodwin, Capt. E. S. L., XI: xi
Goodwin, Capt. H. H., VIII: 410
Goorigian, Lt. Cdr. R., XII: 428, XIV: 387
"Gooseberry" breakwaters, XI: 26, 165, 188, 192
Gordinier, Cdr. V. F., VI: 145, 182
Gordon, Lt. Cdr. H. W., I: 420, II: 40, IX: 389
Gordon, Capt. O. L., III: 332, 371–2
Gordon, Ens. R. T., V: 101
Gore, Lt. T., IX: 388
GORGO, X: 252, 370
Gorgon, VI: 126
Gorham, Lt. Cdr. J. A., XIII: 309
GORIZIA, IX: 37
Gorry, Cdr. W. A., I: 421
GOSS, XIII: 104, 305, XIV: 374
Goto, Rear Adm. A., III: 185, 245, 253, IV: 11–42 *passim*, 61, V: 85, 150–71 *passim*
Goto, Maj. U., XII: 44 5
Gouin, Capt. M. E. A., XIV: 386
Gould, Cdr. F. G., VI: 214, 331, VII: 340, XIII: 313–14
Gould, R. A., XIV: xi
Gould, Lt. Cdr. R. K., X: 377–80
Gourcock, X: 313
Gowen, Col. J. K., XI: 69n
Goyo M., IV: 18
Gozo I., IX: 22n, 56, 65, 165
Grabenhorst, Lt. Cdr. C. L., XIV: 376
Graber, Cdr. G. W., VII: 347
Grabowsky, Lt. Leon, pic., XIV: 183; mentioned, 184, 373
Grace, Lt. Cdr. E. T., XIV: 115, 372
GRACKLE, I: 422
Grady, Lt. J. B., I: 421
Grady, Chief T. F., IX: xiii
GRADY, XIII: 319
Graef, Kaptlt. Adolph, X: 123–4
Graf, Cdr. F. A., VIII: 408, XII: 416, XIII: 308
Graf, Commo. H. W., XIII: 150, 307, 312
Graff, Cdr. J. P., pic., XIII: 261; mentioned, XI: 271, XIII: 324
Graff, Lt. Cdr. V. B., XIII: 309
Gragg, Lt. Cdr. J. B., I: 420
Graham, Maj. Gen. D. A. H., IX: 271, 275, XI: 181
Graham, Capt. H. R., XI: 342

Graham, Lt. Cdr. R. W., XII: 421, XIII: 147, 311, XIV: 375
Graham, Lt. Cdr. W. A., I: 76
Graham, Lt. Cdr. William W., IV: 272, V: 36n, 52n
GRAMPUS, VI: 107
Granat, Capt. W., VII: 388, 346, VIII: 409
Grand Bank of Newfoundland, I: 16n, 154
Grandcamp, XI: 218n
Grand Cayman I., I: 140, 153, 242
Grande I., Luzon, XIII: 188–9
GRANITE II Plan, XII: 7
Granstrom, Lt. Cdr. D. M., VII: 346, VIII: 409, 418, XIV: 376
Grant, Lt. Cdr. A. G., VI: 145
Grant, Lt. Cdr. E., III: 159
Grant, Capt. H. T. W., XI: 334
Grant, Lt. Cdr. M. A., VII: 338
Grant, Capt. V. F., VII: 305–6
Grantham, Cdr. E. B., VIII: 409, XII: 419, XIII: 310
Granum, Capt. A. M., XII: 306, 415, XIII: 303
Granville, XI: 298, 303–8, 328
GRAPH, I: 72n, X: 290n
GRAPPLE, VIII: 419, XIII: 45, 306, XIV: 388
Grasmere, Lt. R. H., XIII: 308
GRASP, XIII: 306
Grassie, Capt. H. J., XIV: 373
Grattan, 1st Lt. Henry, X: viii
Graves, Capt. E. D., II: 36
Graves, Capt. T. J., V: 375
Gray, Mr. A., X: 382
Gray, Commo. Augustine H., pic., XIV: 159; mentioned, II: 36, 118–20, 123, VII: 104, 107, 340, VIII: 345, XII: 75n, 82, XIV: 156–8, 168
Gray, Capt. C. W., VII: 334, XIII: 261–2, 275
Gray, Cdr. J. P., XIV: 379
Gray, Cdr. James S., III: 392, IV: 91, 120–22, XIII: 316
Gray, 1st Lt. R. M., III: 392
Gray, Lt. Cdr. Richard, VIII: 420, XII: 424
Gray, Cdr. S. F., X: 269n, 381
Gray, Cdr. T. A., III: 173
GRAYBACK, IV: 228n, V: 324, 327–8, VI: 107; sunk, VIII: 17
Graybill, Capt. M. W., XIV: 379
GRAYLING, IV: 92, 151, VI: 85

GRAYSON, III: 393, IV: 271, V: 28n, 86, 102–5, 180, VI: 98n, 242, VIII: 403, XII: 425
Great Britain, and naval limitation, I: xxxv–xlii; at war, 1939–41, 9–11, 17–26, 33–72, X: 4–6; U.S. bases in, I: 53–4, 119, XI: 57–64
  Aircraft, carrier-borne, I: 165–6, 194–7, 363, XIV: 105; land-based, X: 87–106; losses, XIV: 250
  Armies; First, II: 190n, 221, 243, 258; Second, XI: 29, 181, 190, 195, 323, 327; Eighth, II: 242–4, 258–9, IX: 3, 19, 27n, 28, 52, 119, 148–80 *passim*, 202–20 *passim*, 223, 233, 255, 284, 302–3, 318–30 *passim*, 344, 359–61, 374, XI: 310; Army in general, II: 190–94, 203–4, 220–21, 277–8, IX: 150–296 *passim*, 332–43, 352–96 *passim*, XI: 181–7
  Royal Air Force, I: 12, 22, 25, 40, 243–6, 259, 383–5, IV: 275, VII: 209, IX: 56, 249, X: 4, 9, 12, 17–46 *passim*, 78–106 *passim*, 131, 135, 147–8, 198n, 209, 258, 275, 324, 349, 357n, 361, 370–73, XI: 35, 42, 72–3, 191
  Royal Navy, strength 1922–41, I: lxi, 11–12, III: 58; escort of convoy, I: 18–26, II: 17; Escort Groups, X: 75, 309, 337–40; loan of trawlers, II: 131; gunfire support, IX: 165–6; Fleets; Eastern, III: 382, 385, V: 184, VIII: 154n, X: 226, XII: 61; Pacific, XIII: 256–8, XIV: 102–7, 211–14, 249–50, 264–5, 314–16, 388; Lettered Forces, "A" & "B," IX: 150–51, 157; "H," I: 167–8, II: 189, 251, IX: 167, 251; "N," 150, 156; "Q," 42, 167–8, 217; "V," 150, 251, 306; "W," I: 195; "Z," IX: 167–8; Mine Flotillas, XI: 79, 116, 198; Motor torpedo boats, II: 264n, IX: 41, 174, 300, XI: 34–5, 66, 311, 337; Support Groups, X: 70, 77–9; ships built for, in U.S., XI: 344–5
Great Sitkin I., VII: 15
GREBE, III: 104
Greber, Capt. C.F., XII: 420, XIII: 306
Green, Sgt. C. E., VII: 299
Green, Cdr. T. C., VI: 382, VIII: 403, XIV: 380
Green Is., VI: 15, 370, 406, 418, VIII: 156; landings, VI: 402, 413–18; T. O., 415–16; chart, 417

Greenacre, Cdr. A. J., IV: 271, V: 87, VI: 443, XII: 428
Greenamyer, Lt. Cdr. L. K., VII: 335
Greenburg V., XIV: 386
Greene, Cdr. R. O., VIII: 164n
Greene, Cdr. T. W., XI: 337
GREENE, I: 419, X: 77, 111, 119, 161, 375, 378, XI: 339, XIV: 374
Greenfield, Col. Kent R., III: xiii, V: x, IX: xv, XI: 5–7
Greening, Capt. C. R., III: 392
Greenland, occupation of, I: 58–60; bases and patrol, I: 61–3, 81, 421; pics., 60, X: 44; chart, I: 162–3; convoys to, 330–35; German weather stations, XI: 49n
Greenlee, Cdr. D. G., XIV: 378
GREENLING, IV: 204, 208, 212, 275n, V: 324, 348, VI: 293, VIII: 375
Greenman, Capt. W. G., I: 14, 15n, IV: 274, V: 29, 41–4, 56–7, VII: 104
Greenock, I: 194, 359, II: 214
Greenslade, Rear Adm. John W., I: 32, 146
Greenspun, Capt. Joseph, I: 332
Greenup, Cdr. F. W., XIII: 280, 320
GREENWOOD, XIII: 307; pic., X: 40
Greer, Lt. (jg) G. A., X: 381
Greer, Lt. Cdr. J. D., I: 420
Greer, Capt. Marshall R., I: 419, X: 117–18, 126, 307, 377, XII: 425; pic., X: 129
GREER, I: 79–80, 92–3, 143, 342–3, 418–20, X: 6; pics., I: 93, 129
Gregg, Ens. H. A., XII: 422
Gregor, Cdr. O. F., IV: 271, V: 87, 232, 249, IX: 395, XI: 339
Gregory, Capt. J. W., III: 158
GREGORY (1918), IV: 273, V: 67; sunk, 118–20; chart, 119
GREGORY (1944), XIV: 191, 197–8, 391
Gregson, Cdr. C. M., XIV: 380
GREINER, VII: 341
Gremonini, Lt., pic., IX: 43
GRENADIER, IV: 92, 203, 229–30
Grenadier, I: 272
Grenville M. Dodge, X: 382
Gretton, Cdr. Peter W., X: 65n, 67–90, 148–51
Grew, Hon. Joseph C., III: xii, 12, 15–17, 35–7, 41, 45, 60–62, 68, 72, XIV: 338–40
Grey, Lt. Cdr. E. J., XIII: 307
Grey, Lt. Cdr. J. R., XIV: 374

Greytak, Lt. Cdr. J. J., IV: 174, VI: 331, VII: 337, 344, VIII: 405
GRIDLEY, III: 211n, IV: 173, VI: 193, 213, VII: 9n, 337, 350, VIII: 413, XII: 319, 342, 428, XIII: 305
Griffin, Lt. Cdr. E. R. J., III: 159
Griffin, Lt. (jg) H. E., XIII: 42
Griffin, Lt. J. J., XIV: 194
Griffin, Col. Raphael, VIII: 187n
Griffin, Rear Adm. Robert M., VI: 423, VII: 55-6, 59-61, 139-40, 336, 344
Griffin, Lt. Cdr. Terry, XI: 34n
Griffin, Ens. W. F., VI: 229
GRIFFIN, IV: 20, 200
Griffith, Lt. Col. Samuel B., V: x, 129, 141, VI: 103, 175
Griffith, Lt. Cdr. W. T., I: 421, VI: 80-84
Griggs, Cdr. Gale E., pic., IV: 85; mentioned, VII: 144, 339, VIII: 404
Griggs, Capt. J. B., XIV: 372, 385
Grills, Lt. N. G., X: 194
Griner, Maj. Gen. G. W., VIII: 335n, 410n, XIV: 381
Griswold, Lt. B. H., II: 22
Griswold, Maj. Gen. Oscar W., VI: 198-203, 206, 223, 279n, 364, 425n, 426-31, XII: 361, XIII: 94-6, 117, 125, 146, 310
Gritta, Capt. P. B., VII: 254, 255n
Groesbeck, Capt. B., pic., IV: 85
Groff, Cdr. R. H., XIV: 379
Grondin, R. P., IX: xv
Gross, Cdr. R. L., XIII: 320
Grosscup, Ens. B. M., XII: 422
Grosskopf, Capt. H. L., XIV: 30, 40
Grote, Lt. W. G., XIII: 309
Grotenrath, Lt. J. C., I: 173
GROUPER, IV: 92, 126n, V: 324, VI: 67n
Groverman, Cdr. W. H., VI: 228, XIV: 382
Groves, Lt. Cdr. C. W., XIV: 388
Grow, Capt. B. E., XI: 342
Grow, Capt. H. B., XIV: 360
GROWLER, IV: 92, 215-16, 228-9, V: 348, VII: 7, VIII: 415, XII: 400; sunk, 411
Grube, Cdr. J. F. IX: 388, XI: 341
Grumble, Lt. W. E., X: 102
GRUMIUM, XII: 77, XIV: 381
Gruner, Lt. Cdr. W. P., VII: 319, 353
GRUNION, IV: 217, VII: 12; lost, 7
GUADALCANAL, X: 41, 201, 281-3, 290-93, 298, 371-2, 379

Guadalcanal I., IV: 256, 261, 267, 286, V: 4, 10, 32, VI: 22-3, 120, XII: 376, XIII: 97, 144; charts, V: 8-9, 195, 365; pics., 18-19, 178, VI: 102; as U.S. base, VI: 90, 94, 100-103, 140, 282, 294, 298, 339, VIII: 160, 170, 374, 380, XIII: 153, XIV: 111; Jap. evacuation of, V: 333, 342, 364-71
Guadalcanal, Naval Battle of, V: 227-85, XII: 241; Cruiser Night Action, V: 235-58, charts, 240-43, 255; Battleship Action, 270-85, chart, 274-5; air attacks, chart, 265; discussion, 285-7; T.O., 231-5; pic., 283
Guadalcanal-Tulagi Opn., planning, IV: 259-70, 278-9, V: 12-15; command, IV: 268-9; approach and landings, 281-7, V: 15-16; chart, IV: 283; pic., 254-5; opns. ashore, V: 65-78, 123-30, 140-46, 188-98, 289-90, 333-7, 340-44; maps, 68, 190, 336, 339; naval gunfire support, IV: 284-5, V: 138, 173, 182, 191, 226-7, 337, 341-4; air raids and bombardments, IV: 292-6, V: 70, 84, 104, 118-27, 149-50, 171-7, 194, 197, 262-3, 347-8, 366-8, VI: 120-22, 229, 328n; pic., 240, V: 243; supply and reinforcement, 18, 67-75, 80-82, 104-30 *passim*, 148-9, 169-72, 176-80, 189, 226-93 *passim*, 316-63 *passim;* pic., 283; discussion, 371-3
GUADALUPE, IV: 93, 152, V: 312, VII: 9, 47n, 334, 341, VIII: 411, XII: 428, XIII: 318, XIV: 387
Guadeloupe, I: 30
GUAM, I: 28n, XIV: 307, 310, 385-6
Guam, history and description, VIII: 149-51; strategic importance, III: 32-4, 225, VII: 70; fall of, III: 184-6; U.S. recovery of, planned, VIII: 8-9, 157-9, 162-4, 197, 241, 371, 375; Jap. reinforcements, 17, 167, 175; landings, 160-61, 382-98; charts, 372, 384-5; air and naval gunfire support, 377-83, 393-9; unloading, 388-91; opns. ashore, 398-400; numbers & casualties, 401n; T.O., 418-20; discussion, 401-2; as forward base, 349, XII: 75, 80, 398, XIII: 153, XIV: 158, 162-4, 248, 267-357 *passim;* weather central, XIII: 83, XIV: 298-9; Cincpac HQ moves to, XIII: 156
Guantanamo, I: 33n, 248-9, 256-66, 324, X: 189, 199

GUARDFISH, IV: 209–10, V: 348, VI: 73, 284, 298, VII: 222, 351, VIII: 19, 24, XIII: 319, XIV: 228

GUAVINA, XIII: 284

GUDGEON, III: 104, 213n, 258, IV: 74n, 92, 126n, 208, 227, 230, V: 177, VI: 77–9, 85; lost, VIII: 24

Guerrillas, Borneo, VIII: 22; China, XIII: 291–6, 299; Philippines, IV: 230, VI: 78, 85, VIII: 21–2, XII: 27, 64–7, 123, 392, 395, XIII: 16–18, 40, 50, 114, 188, 207, 210, 214, 225, 229–32, 237, 240–42, 249; pic., 260; Solomons, VI: 141–2, 159

Guest, Harold R., XI: 287n

GUEST, VI: 297, 360–61, 413, 415, VIII: 409, 415, 419, XIV: 374

Gugegwe Islet, VII: 253, 276–7

Guggenberger, Kaptlt. Fritz, X: 213, 218–19

Guimaras I., VIII: 241, XIII: 231; Strait, VIII: 221, 231–2

Guinhandang, Mt., XII: 133–6, 151

Guinea, Gulf of, I: 315, 323

GUINEVERE, I: 267; pic., 280

GUITARRO, XII: 184, 357, 406–8, 429, XIII: 320

Guiuan, XII: 350

Gulbranson, Capt. C., I: 76, 111, II: 38

Gulf Belle, Penn, Prince, I: 138, 397, IX: 40

Gulf Sea Frontier, I: 135–44, 198, 233, 248, 346–7, 413, X: 8, 91, 189; charts, I: 140–41, 238–9

Gulftrade, I: 133

GULL, I: 422

Gummer, Cdr. E. G., XIV: 386

Gunn, Cdr. F. A., XII: 408

Gunn, Lt. Cdr. J. M., X: 376

Gunn, Maj. Paul I., VI: 57

GUNNEL, II: 39, 54n

Gunnell, Capt. P. M., VII: 341, XII: 428, XIII: 319

GUNSTON HALL, VII: 244, 346, VIII: 404, 418, XII: 416, XIII: 309, XIV: 380

Gurda, Ens. M. A., X: 211

GURNARD, VIII: 21, 90, 218, XIII: 320

Gurnette, Lt. Cdr. B. L., IX: 385, XI: 338

GUSTAFSON, X: 295, 342–3, 373, 380

Guthrie, Lt. H. A., XII: 429

Guthrie, Lt. Cdr. R. A., V: 205, 233

GUYSBOROUGH, XI: 333

Guzzoni, Gen. Alfredo, IX: 48, 51, 69, 103, 110, 119, 171–3, 183, 195, 201, 209

GWIN (1941), I: 82, III: 393, IV: 90, 154–5, 271, V: 28n, 172, 180, 232–3, 259, 271, 275–7, 281, VI: 145, 149, 156n, 158, 182, 191–3, 224; sunk, 189

GWIN (1944), XIV: 256, 376

Gwinn, Lt. (jg) Wilbur C., XIV: 325–7

Gyoten M., VII: 319n

H

H. T. Dodge, XIII: 307
Haaf, Capt. T. G., VIII: 408
Haavik, Lt. Cdr. S. A., XIV: 238
Habecker, Lt. Cdr. F. S., IX: 391, XII: 419
Hachijo Jima, XIV: 52
HACKLEBACK, XIV: 200, 203
HADDO, VIII: 22, 416
HADDOCK, IV: 210, XII: 333-4, 429, XIV: 296
Haddon, Lt. Cdr. E. J., VII: 347
Hadley, Cdr. H. W., IV: 273, V: 118-20
Haff, Capt. T. G., VII: 345, IX: 390
Hagan, I: 142
Hagberg, Lt. O. E., I: 421
Hagen, Lt. R. C., XII: 272-5, 282
HAGGARD, VII: 267, 344, 347, VIII: 223-4, 418, XII: 28, 244, 287, 421, XIII: 318, XIV: 112, 243, 249, 385, 391
Haggart, Capt. R. S., VII: 337, 346
HAGIKAZE, III: 333, IV: 88, V: 70, VI: 214-16, 221; sunk, 218-19
Hagoromo M., IV: 17-18
Hague, Cap de la, XI: 308
HAGURO, III: 26, 274-5, 296, 334-71 *passim*, IV: 17, 88, 179*n*, V: 84, VI: 305-8, 312-13, 321, VII: 44, VIII: 118-20, 130-32, 282, 287, 300, 416, XII: 162, 248, 258-85 *passim*, 288, 431, XIII: 159
Hagushi beaches, XIV: 90-91, 108; roadstead, 236-8, 256, 259, 269, 272
Haha Jima, VIII: 239, 313, 354, XIV: 10-12, 25, 44, 50
Hai Tan Strait, XIII: 297-8
HAIDA, IV: 173
HAIDA, HMCS, XI: 35
Haifa, IX: 158, 242
Haight, Capt. S. M., XIII: 310
HAILEY, VII: 302, 344, 347, VIII: 223-4, 418, XII: 244, 287, 421, 429, XIII: 90*n*, 316, 319, XIV: 386
Hainan I., III: 26, 37-8, XIII: 161, 171, 281, 285
Haines, Capt. J. M., IV: 236, VI: 67*n*, VIII: 48, X: 24, XIII: 304*n*, XIV: 373

Haines, Maj. J. P., VII: 335
Haines, Lt. M. W., XII: 391, 422
Haines, Lt. Cdr. N. S., VII: 333
Haines, Lt. Cdr. P. B., XIV: 384
Haines, Lt. R. A., V: 310*n*
HAINES, XI: 340, 343
Haines, VIII: 420
Hains, Cdr. Hamilton, VIII: 224-8, X: 332
Haiti, II: 43
HAKAZE, V: 348
HAKE, VIII: 120, 416, XII: 411
"Hakko Ichiu," III: 3-18, 45, 65, 81-2, IV: 4
Hakozaki M., XIV: 290
Hakuju M., XIV: 293
Hakusan M., IV: 173
HALBERT, III: 213*n*
Hale, Lt. Cdr. Fletcher, VIII: 410, XII: 416, XIII: 311
Hale, Lt. Cdr. H. D., I: 419
Hale, Lt. Cdr. P. G., I: 418
Hale, Cdr. S. C., XIV: 378
Hale, Group Capt. W. A. O., VIII: 139
Hale, Maj. Gen. W. H., IV: 93, 159*n*, VII: 82-3, 118, 211, 340, 350, X: 30, XII: 60, XIV: 10
HALE (1919), IX: 325*n*
HALE (1943), VII: 190, 339, 350, VIII: 405, 420, XII: 304, 418, XIV: 211, 384
Haleiwa, III: 124
Haley, Lt. Cdr. S. M., VIII: 414, XII: 427
Haley, Lt. Cdr. T. B., I: 420
HALF MOON, VIII: 50*n*, 406, XII: 422, XIII: 45, 312
Halfon, Lt. Cdr. Sam, XIV: 377
HALFORD, VI: 415, 418, VIII: 409, 415, XII: 199, 221, 420, XIII: 306, 311
HALIBUT, IV: 213, 217-18, XII: 333-4, 429
HALIFAX, I: 349
Halifax, I: 12-24, 110, 160, 256-62, 318-19, 329, X: 184-5
Halkon, Mt., XIII: 17-18
Hall, Capt. A. G., XII: 418, XIII: 308

Hall, Lt. Cdr. C. E., IX: 387
Hall, Lt. C. G., X: 377
Hall, Lt. C. O., XII: 429
Hall, Maj. Gen. C. P., VIII: 72–4, XII: 21–3, XIII: 187
Hall, Cdr. F. S., X: 282, 290, 350–55, 360, 378–9
Hall, Capt. G. B. H., XIII: 318, XIV: 383
Hall, Rear Adm. John L., biog., IX: 92n; pics., II: 93, 164, IX: frontispiece; North Africa, II: 21–2; Moroccan Sea Frontier, 82, 176, 245–7; Sicily, IX: 28, 31, 61, 65, 92–3, 100–16, 118–19, 123–6, 224, 387; Salerno, 246–51, 258, 266, 269, 298, 391; Anzio, 325; Normandy, XI: xi, 24, 29, 33n, 37, 52–8, 63–4, 67, 77, 110–64 *passim*, 179, 215, 297, 335; Okinawa, XIV: 86, 108, 140, 147, 174, 379
Hall, Lt. Cdr. K. R., XIV: 387
Hall, Cdr. Madison, VI: 181, VII: 339, XIV: 252–3
Hall, Lt. Col. R. K., V: 192
Hall, Lt. R. N., XIV: 377
Hall, Lt. Cdr. S., XI: 342
Hall, Lt. (jg) T. C., XII: 422
HALL, VII: 257, 275, 309, 344, VIII: 411, XII: 385, 429, XIII: 305, XIV: 135, 246, 372
HALLIGAN, VII: 345, VIII: 411, XII: 419, XIII: 104, 305, XIV: 372, 390; sunk, 115–16
Hallmark, 2nd Lt. D. E., III: 392, 397
HALLORAN, XII: 429, XIV: 392
Hallowell, Lt. Roger H., XII: 369, XIII: 265
Halma, X: 374
Halmahera I., VIII: 90, 95, 107, 141–2, XII: 19–20, 26–8, 107, XIV: 360
Halsey, Capt. T. E., XIV: 388
Halsey, Flt. Adm. William F., biog., III: 211n; pics., IV: 85 (with staff), V: frontispiece; XII: 103, XIV: 366; post-Pearl Harbor opns., III: 211, 214–17, 241, 252, 259–68; raid on Tokyo, 390–98; Coral Sea, IV: 15–16, 62; Comsopac, V: 183, VII: 197; Nouméa HQ, V: 185–7; Guadalcanal campaign, 201–372 *passim*; Central Solomons, VI: 13–15, 89, 93–8, 110–304 *passim*; orders to Burke, 353; Green I., 413–14; Rabaul, 324, 333, 419–22; Emirau, 423; Admiralties, 433–4; strategy, VIII: 10n, XII: 12–15; Com. Third Fleet, VIII: 161; A/S warfare, 224; Escort Carriers, X: 37; Palaus, XII: 33–4, 47; Formosa battle, 86–109 *passim*; message, 109, 117; Leyte battle, 12, 15, 55–60, 71–2, 105–6, 125, 137, 159–60, 170, 290–96, 339–55, 360, 424, 187; the great decision, 193–6, 289–90; inquiry from Nimitz, 292; Cape Engaño battle, 317–22, 331, 335; Samar battle, 309, 329–30; Luzon strikes, XIII: 52–8, 87–90, 315; Dec. 1944 Typhoon, 63–87; South China Sea raid, 92, 157–8, 161–74, 281; Lingayen, 106–7; Formosa raid, 179–82; relieved by Spruance, XIV: 20, 87n; relieves Spruance, 169, 266, 272; June 1945 Typhoon, 299, 308–9; strikes on Japan, 310, 316, 332–4; occupation, 357, 360; surrender ceremony, 363–9; quoted, VI: 96, 329–30, XII: 53, 90n, 183, XIV: 308–9
HALSEY POWELL, VIII: 409, XII: 319, 426, XIII: 316, 318, XIV: 99, 390
HALSTEAD, XI: 191
Hamacheck, Lt. (jg) R. E., VI: 61
HAMAKAZE, II: 88, III: 87, V: 206, 370, VI: 37, 162, 174, 181, 234–6, VIII: 416, XII: 186, 431, XIII: 91, 158, XIV: 202, 205; sunk, 208
Haman, Lt. Cdr. C. W., I: 420
HAMANAMI, XII: 311, 431; sunk, 353
Hamberger, Cdr. D. C. E., I: 420, VI: 308, 354
HAMBLETON, I: 134, 352, 420, II: 37, 169, 170n, 172, 248, X: 258–9, 372, XI: 174, 204, 284, 337, 341, XIV: 113, 376
Hamblett, Cdr. C. B., XIII: 307, XIV: 378
Hamblin, Cdr. F. D., IX: 390, XII: 429
Hamilton, Lt. D., XII: 422
Hamilton, Capt. J. H., III: 229
Hamilton, Capt. J. L., X: 98
Hamilton, Rear Adm. L. H. K., I: 180–85
Hamilton, Lt. M. J., I: 421
Hamilton, Maj. Pierpont M., II: 125, 133
Hamilton, T/Sgt. W. J., III: 231
Hamilton, Capt. W. V., XIV: 384
Hamilton, Lt. Cdr. Weldon L., IV: 19, 41–2
Hamilton, Commo. William H., X: 100, 103–4, 324, XI: 72; pic., X: 328

General Index

HAMILTON, I: 15n, 421, II: 40, 139, VI: 440, 444, VII: 346, VIII: 69, 404, 410, 419, XII: 422, XIV: 31

HAMLIN, XII: 49, XIV: 65, 126, 381

HAMMANN, IV: 19, 27, 28n, 59, 60n, 90, 155; sunk, 156

HAMMERHEAD, VIII: 25, XII: 406, XIII: 285-7

Hammitt, Lt. Cdr. F. M., I: 419

Hammond, Cdr. D. T., I: 421, XIII: 319, XIV: 288

Hammond, Lt. Col. H. O., VII: 246n

Hammond, Lt. Cdr. K. G., XIII: 317

Hammond, Capt. Paul, I: 211

Hampshire, Wing Cdr. K. M., VI: 65

Hampton, Lt. Cdr. I. M., VII: 339

Hampton Roads, I: 254, 256, 355, II: 43, 111, 133, 174-6, 193, 246, 271n, X: 114, 122, 125-6, 161, 168, 176, 288-90, 343, 346

HAMUL, I: 76, 420, X: 49-50, XIV: 387

Hanada, Capt. T., XII: 431

HANCOCK (1902), V: 325n

HANCOCK (1944), XII: 90, 106, 294, 309, 358-9, 425, XIII: 52, 54, 57, 67, 70, 91, 182, 315-16, XIV: 21, 44, 96, 99, 205, 209, 384, 390

Hancock Pt., Me., X: 330

Hand, Lt. Cdr. C. F., XIV: 271

Handley, Lt. (jg) Coit, XI: 139-40

Handly, Capt. Albert, XIII: 118, 305

Haneken, Col. H. H., XII: 37

Haney, Brig. Gen. H. H., XIII: 217-18, 221, 321

Hangchow, XIII: 302

Hank, Lt. Cdr. W. E., IV: 271, V: 151, 232

HANK, XIV: 211, 384

Hankinson, Lt. W. O., XIV: 377

Hankow, XIII: 295-7, 300, 302

Hanlon, Capt. B. H., XIII: 304, XIV: 26, 30, 119, 377, 384

Hanna, Lt. R. M., III: 247

Hannan, Lt. K. H., VIII: 411

Hanneken, Lt. Col. H. H., V: 144, 191-3

Hannett, Lt. Cdr. G. W., XII: 419, XIII: 311

Hannon, Lt. Cdr. E. R., IV: 20, 275

Hanoi, III: 29, 44

Hansa Bay, VIII: 8, 10, 66

Hanseat, I: 134

Hansen, Cdr. H. G., VII: 340, XII: 428, XIII: 319, XIV: 387

Hansen, Cdr. H. J., XII: 417, XIII: 309

Hansen, Sgt. H. O., pic., XIV: frontispiece

Hansen, Maj. Herman, XIV: 382

Hansen, Cdr. J. R., XIV: 254-5, 372

Hansen, Lt. Cdr. Samuel, XII: 266, 421

Hansen, Cdr. Sigurd, VII: 341, XIV: 374

Hanson, Rear Adm. Edward W., IV: 173, VII: 338, 349, 353, VIII: 305n, 415, XII: 427, XIII: 317

Hanson, Lt. N. R., XIV: 377

Hanson, Capt. R. E., VII: 347, VIII: 408

Hanson, Lt. R. M., VI: 402

Hara, Rear Adm. C., VII: 317

Hara, Rear Adm. K., III: 161-2, 174n, 178

Hara, Maj. M., VI: 141

Hara, Rear Adm. Tadaichi, IV: 4, 11, 17; Coral Sea, 24, 33-7, 44-5, 50; Guadalcanal, V: 82, 85, 206

Harada, Rear Adm. K., XIII: 234

HARADEN, VII: 238-9, 346, VIII: 411, XII: 295n, 419, XIII: 24

Harcourt, Rear Adm. C. H. J., IX: 276, 282, 393

Hard, Lt. George, VII: 179n, 180

Hardegen, Kaptlt., I: 283

Hardenburg, Cdr. H. T., X: 363n

HARDER, VIII: 19, 22, 33, 220, 416

Hardesty, Capt. F. A., VII: 340, VIII: 411, XII: 423, XIII: 310, 322

HARDHEAD, VIII: 17n, XII: 160n, 313, 411, XIII: 280, 286, 320

Hardin, Capt. D. W., XIII: 313

Hardin, Lt. Cdr. J. T., I: 218n

Harding, Maj. Gen. E. F., VI: 47

HARDING (1919), XI: 140n

HARDING (1943), XI: 123, 129, 146, 158, 277, 336, 343, XIV: 238, 376, 391

Hardison, Capt. O. B., V: 204, 207, 217, 233, 264

Hardy, Cdr. R. J., VIII: 409, XII: 420, XIII: 306, 311

Hardy, Maj. Gen. T. T., XI: 146

HARDY, HMS, X: 306

Hare, Lt. (jg) F. F., X: 215

Hargraves, Lt. A. L., XI: 333

HARJURAND, I: 330, 331n

Harkness, Lt. Albert, I: 102n, III: xii, 147n, VI: 27n, XIV: x

Harlan, Lt. Cdr. J. L., VII: 344, VIII: 408

Harlan, Cdr. R. S., XIV: 225, 379

Harlfinger, Cdr. F. J., VIII: 20, XII: 335, 406, 429

Harmer, Lt. Cdr. R. E., VII: 352, VIII: 414

Harmon, Maj. Gen. E. N., II: 23, 33, 39, 147–55, 162, 177–8, IX: 356–8, 364

Harmon, Lt. L. E., X: 102, 104

Harmon, Lt. Gen. M. F., VI: 7, 98, 205–6, 228, 364, XII: 17, XIII: 5, XIV: 4, 9

Harmon, Cdr. W. L., XIV: 384

HARMON, XIII: 307

HAROLD C. THOMAS, VII: 341, 347

Harold L. Winslow, X: 310

Harper, Cdr. J. F., XIII: 304, XIV: 254, 373

Harper, Lt. Cdr. J. S., III: 104

Harper, Lt. Cdr. R. M., XIII: 311

Harper, Lt. Cdr. T. E., XIII: 319, XIV: 286

Harral, Lt. B. J., I: 421

Harrell, Lt. Cdr. N., VIII: 406, XIII: 308

Harrell, Lt. R. B., XIV: 377

Harries, Lt. Cdr. J. L., XI: 217

Harriet Monroe, XIII: 313

Harrill, Rear Adm. William K., biog., VIII: 238n; mentioned, I: 111, VIII: 174–5, 238–42, 249–50, 258, 265, 272, 282–3, 414, XIV: 360

Harriman, Hon. W. Averell, pic., I: 70; mentioned, X: 18

Harris, Air Chief Marshal Sir Arthur, XI: 35–6

Harris, Cdr. D. A., III: 272n, VII: 344, VIII: 223, 418, XII: 421, XIII: 318

Harris, Lt. Cdr. D. L., XIII: 305

Harris, Capt. Dale, VIII: 411

Harris, Lt. Cdr. F. J., VIII: 403, 419

Harris, Lt. G. C., VIII: 75

Harris, Cdr. G. L., III: 160

Harris, Col. Harold D., XII: 37

Harris, Cdr. M. H., IX: 388, X: 345, 349, 377–8

Harris, Col. N. D., pic., VII: frontispiece

Harris, Cdr. P. V. R., XII: 423

HARRIS, II: 40, 139–43, 153–4, IV: 253, VII: 181, 335–7, 344, VIII: 410, XII: 131–3, 416, XIII: 310, XIV: 143n, 380; pic., II: 149

Harrison, Capt. B. R., I: 111, 420, IX: 389, XIV: 237, 373

Harrison, Capt. Drayton, VII: 346, VIII: 418, XII: 416, XIII: 309

Harrison, Lt. Cdr. H. W., VI: 331, VII: 339, 349

HARRISON, VII: 337, 344, VIII: 404, 418–19, XII: 416, XIV: 383

Harriss, Cdr. G. L., III: 272, XIV: 375

Harrold, Lt. Cdr. C., XIV: 379

HARRY E. HUBBARD, XIV: 257

HARRY F. BAUER, XIV: 274, 377, 392

HARRY LEE, I: 421, II: 26, 44n, VII: 337, 344, VIII: 405, 419, IX: 389, XIII: 310

Hart, Col. F. A., VIII: 187n, 247–9

Hart, Lt. Cdr. J. E., XIV: 385n

Hart, Cdr. J. G., VIII: 410, XII: 419, XIII: 309

Hart, Lt. Col. Joseph, VII: 126

Hart, Lt. Cdr. L. E., XI: 102, 334

Hart, Adm. Thomas C., biog., III: 151n; pic., frontispiece; C. in C. Asiatic Fleet, 55, 57n, 74, 151–8; on outbreak of war, 168–73, 179, 188, 193–8, XIII: 160; War Order, III: 170; in N.E.I., 271, 277–9, 282–5, 292, 296–8; relieved, 304–13

HART, XIV: 373

Hartigan, Lt. Cdr. C. C., XII: 429, XIII: 319

HARTLAND, II: 207, 224–7, 230, 237, 251–2; sunk, II: 228–9, 283

Hartlebury, I: 191n

Hartley, Lt. Cdr. Barnard, XIV: 379

Hartley, Capt. Henry, I: 76, II: 36, IX: 389, XII: 425

Hartman, Capt. C. C., pic., X: 265; mentioned, I: 420, II: 40, X: 261, 264, 362

Hartman, Lt. Cdr. I. S., IV: 275, VII: 53

Hartmann, Lt. Cdr. H. G., XIII: 319

Hartt, Cdr. B. A., IX: 389

Hartt, Cdr. W. H., IV: 274

Hartwig, Capt. G. R., IV: 19, V: 205, 233, 381, XIV: 275

HARUKAZE, III: 161, 368, XIII: 179

HARUNA, III: 26, 161, 180, 276, 382, IV: 88, 111, 128n, V: 173–4, 199, 206, 234, VII: 44, 137, VIII: 298, 309, 416, XII: 162–3, 186, 248, 251, 259–60, 267, 281, 431, XIII: 158; sunk, XIV: 331

HARUSAME, III: 162, 334, IV: 88, V: 84, 197, 206–7, 234, 242, VIII: 125, 416; sunk, 126, 220

HARVARD, VI: 106n

Harvard Sound Laboratory, I: 220

Harvey, Lt. Cdr. H. O., VII: 338

Harvey, Lt. J. A., X: 382

Harwich, XI: 77, 182
Harwood, Lt. B. L., V: 90
Harwood, Capt. C. W., I: 111, II: 38, IX: 388
Hashimoto, Col., III: 16
Hashimoto, Lt. Cdr. M., XIV: 321–2, 328–30
Hashimoto, Vice Adm. S., III: 276, 308, IV: 89, V: 234, 273–6, VIII: 416, XII: 431
HASKELL, XIII: 307, XIV: 380
Haskins, Cdr. E. D., XII: 406, 429
Hasset, H. J., VII: 334
HATAKAZE, III: 161, 368, VIII: 20; sunk, XIII: 171
Hatcher, Lt. Cdr. M. T., VII: 340, 350
Hatfield, Lt. Cdr. J. M., III: 363
Hatfield, Lt. Cdr. J. S., XIV: 374
Hathaway, Cdr. A. T., V: 194n, XII: 259, 271, 304, 421, XIV: 385
Hathorn, Lt. Cdr. V. L., VII: 350
HATSUHARU, III: 274, IV: 172, VII: 14, XII: 356, 431
HATSUKAZE, III: 163, 274, 334, IV: 89, V: 85, 206, 339, VI: 306, 312; sunk, 315, 318, 322n
HATSUSHIMO, III: 274–6, 329, IV: 172, VII: 24, 31, 35, 417, XII: 431; XIII: 158, XIV: 202
HATSUTAKA, XIII: 287
HATSUYUKI, III: 276, IV: 89, V: 118, 151, 158, 161–4, 168–9, 234, VI: 162, 167–8, 172, 206
HATSUZAKURA, XIV: 361
HATSUZUKI, VIII: 416, XII: 332, 335, 430; sunk, 331
Hatteras, Cape, I: 130, 133, 156, 255
Hauck, Lt. Cdr. P. F., VIII: 409
Hauer, Radio Tech. F. R., X: 175
Haughen, Ens. E. S., XII: 422
Haughian, Lt. (jg) M. A., XIII: 192
Hauser, Gen. Wolf, IX: 352
Haussler, Lt. Cdr. G. A., XIV: 387
Havana, I: 140; Conf., 31, 61
Havard, Cdr. V., I: 420, XI: 342
HAVERFIELD, X: 288, 376
Haviland, Lt. J. W., III: 185
Havre M., VIII: 23
Hawaiian Is., defenses, III: 220, VII: 80, 91; expected invasion, III: 218–20; bases, VII: 88–9, 109, VIII: 159, 343, 348; Sea Frontier, IV: 70, 85–6. *See also* Pearl Harbor
Hawes, Cdr. F. W., XIV: 373

Hawes, Lt. R. E., III: 159
Hawes, Lt. R. K., XII: 383
HAWKBILL, XII: 406, XIII: 38n, 285, 287
HAWKESBURY, XIII: 261n
Hawkesworth, Maj. Gen. J., pic., IX: 203; mentioned, 271–3
Hawkins, Lt. W. D., VII: 166
HAWKINS, XI: 105, 161–2, 334
Hawkins Field, VII: 211, 287
Haworth, Lt. Cdr. R., XI: 342
Hawthorne, Maj. H. J., VI: 64
Hayakawa, Rear Adm. M., VIII: 416, XII: 431
HAYANAMI, VIII: 220, 416
HAYASHIMO, VIII: 416, XII: 431; sunk, 311
HAYASHIO, III: 163, 274, IV: 89, V: 84, 206
HAYASUI, VII: 417
HAYATAKA, VIII: 295n, XIV: 286n
Hayataka M., III: 179
HAYATE, III: 231n, 232
HAYDON, X: 261, 393, XI: 343
Hayes, Maj. C. H., V: 67
Hayes, Lt. Grace P., IX: xvi, XIII: 3, 214n
Hayes, Lt. Cdr. J. D., V: 56
Hayes, Lt. J. M., XIII: 306, XIV: 376
Hayes, Mr. J. R., VII: 334
Hayes, Lt. Cdr. W. C., XIV: 376
Hayford, Brig. Gen. B. F., VII: 104n, XIV: 157
Hayler, Rear Adm. Robert W., biog., XII: 237n; pic., VI: 195; mentioned, V: 296, 307–8, VI: 161, 181, 184, 189, VIII: 381, 409, 414, XII: 119–20, 199, 237, 417, 419
Hayman, Lt. R. W., X: 161
Haynes, Capt. H. J., XI: 342
Haynsworth, Cdr. W. M., I: 420
HAYNSWORTH, XIII: 317, XIV: 24, 384, 390
Hayo M., III: 161, 179
Hays, Maj. L. C., VII: 169–70
Hayter, Lt. Cdr. H. M., V: 309–10
HAYTER, X: 333, 353–4, 373, 376
Hayward, Lt. Cdr. J. T., VIII: 406
HAZARD, XIV: 377
HAZELWOOD, VII: 337, 344, 347, VIII: 227, XII: 244, 420, XIII: 317–18, XIV: 57, 249, 385, 391; pic., 295
Hazzard, Cdr. W. H., XIII: 285
HDML-1074, XII: 422, XIII: 306

Headden, Cdr. W. R., I: 420, II: 38, X: 267
Headland, Lt. Cdr. E. H., X: 343, 379
Headlee, Capt. C. D., IX: 390
Headley, Capt. J. G., VII: 239-40
Heald, Lt. Cdr. W. S., IV: 274
Healy, Cdr. H. R., IV: 57-8
HEALY, VII: 348, VIII: 414, XII: 319, 427, XIII: 318
Heap, Cdr. G. L., XIV: 382
Heard, Capt. W. A., V: 353
Heath, Lt. H. J. G., XI: 335
Heath, Capt. J. B., XIV: 384
Heavey, Brig. Gen. W. F., VIII: 52
Heber Creel, XIII: 324
Heckey, Lt. Cdr. A. R., IX: 389, XI: 341
HECLA, II: 173, 284
HECTOR, VIII: 420, XIV: 387
Hedding, Capt. T. J., VII: 197
Hederman, Capt. T. H., XIV: 382
"Hedgehog," I: 211-12, X: 52, 364; pic., I: 211
Hedrick, Lt. Cdr. R. R., XIV: 384
HEED, VII: 345, VIII: 410, XIV: 376; Class, XIV: 114
Heerbrandt, Lt. Cdr. P. F., VII: 335
HEERMANN, VII: 337, 347, VIII: 227n; Battle off Samar, XII: 244, 255-78 *passim,* 283, 304, 421, XIV: 248, 385; pic., XII: 279
Heffernan, Rear Adm. John B., I: xv, xvii, 76, 123, 418-20, II: x, 38, 77-8, 159, 170n, VIII: viii, 379, 419, XII: viii, 223n, 419, XIV: x, 147, 168, 227, 372
Heian M., VII: 325
Heideman, Lt. (jg) L. H., XI: 138n
Heimer, Cdr. R. C., II: 192, 195-6, 214, IX: 388; pic., frontispiece
Heineman, Capt. P. R., I: xv, 111, 119, 123, 226n, 228, 305, 322n, 337, 344, 388, X: 48, 362, XII: 428, XIII: 318, XIV: 373
Heinl, Col. Robert D., VIII: 198n, XIV: 41n; *Defense of Wake,* III: 223n; *Marines at Midway,* IV: 69n
Heisel, Lt. H. N., XIII: 305, XIV: 374
HELENA, III: 101-2, 116-17, IV: 276n, V: 150-294 *passim,* 326, 329, 345-6, VI: 106, 120, 156, 161-71, 178, 224, X: 212n; sunk, VI: 169-71; survivors, 172-4, 191-4, 227; pic., 170
Helfrich, Vice Adm. C. E. L., pic.,

III: 285; mentioned, 271-3, 297-8, 304-77 *passim,* XIV: 366
HELM, III: 97, 100, 213n, IV: 36, 272, V: 29-30, 41, 49-50, 52n, 81, VI: 39, 134, VIII: 413, XII: 319, 341-2, 428, XIII: 104, 305, 325, XIV: 161, 374
Helmick, Capt. G. B., XIV: 380
HELP, XI: 337
Helton, Chief Pharm. D. D., XI: 273n
Heming, Lt. Cdr. H. M., II: 40
Hemingway, Capt., XII: 121
Hemingway, Ens. B. T., XI: 299n
Hemingway, Ernest, XI: 135
Hencey, Watertender Clarence, VIII: 211
Henderson, Yeoman A. D., XIII: x, XIV: x
Henderson, Cdr. C. M., VIII: 416
Henderson, Rear Adm. George R., VI: 325, VII: 340, 350, XII: 420, XIII: 145, 305, XIV: 373
Henderson, Capt. H. P., XIV: 388
Henderson, Capt. Harry H., V: 353, 362, XIV: 384
Henderson, Maj. Lofton R., IV: 92, 110
Henderson Field, V: 14, 67-8, 101-49 *passim,* 169-269 *passim,* 285-369 *passim,* VI: 99, 120, 150n, 207, 290, 396, VIII: 164; Allied Squadrons at, V: 374-5; pic., 75; Battle for, 188-97
Hendren, Capt. Paul, II: 39, IX: 199, 204, 389
HENDRY, XIV: 381
Heneberger, Lt. Cdr. H. B., I: 418, V: 45-6
HENGIST, X: 257, 269, 381
Henke, Kaptlt. Werner, X: 282
Henkle, Capt. R. H., IV: 91, 272
Henley, Lt. C. L., XIV: 377
HENLEY, III: 104, 213n, IV: 35-6, 272, V: 52n, 81, VI: 39, 134, 269n, 272; sunk, 272-3
Hennecke, Ktradm., XI: 212
Henney, Lt. Col., II: 122, 129
HENRICO, XI: 137, 335, 339, XIV: 177, 375, 390
Henriques, Lt. Cdr. C. B., XIII: 308
Henry, Lt. Cdr. E. B., XIV: 386
Henry, Cdr. T. H., XIII: 320
Henry, Lt. Cdr. W. F., VIII: 412
HENRY A. WILEY, XIV: 49, 116, 376
Henry Bacon, Barnard, Broussard, Knox, Meiggs, X: 275n, 312-13, XIII: 313

Henry R. Mallory, I: 336
Henry T. Allen, II: 36, 118–21, VI: 131, VIII: 77, 135, 403
Henry-Martin, Gen., II: 67, 87n, 150–51
Hepburn, Lt. Andrew, II: 99n
Hepburn, Rear Adm. Arthur J., Report on bases, III: 32–4, 225, IV: 72, 163; on Savo battles, V: 17n, 32n, 62
Hepp, Oblt. Horst, X: 140, 168
HERALD, VIII: 410
HERALD OF THE MORNING, VIII: 410, XII: 416, XIII: 309, 313
HERBERT, I: 16n, 215, 420, VIII: 404, XI: 242n, XII: 417, XIII: 307, XIV: 376
HERBERT C. JONES, IX: 355, 396, XI: 343
Herbert-Jones, Cdr. G. B., IX: 392
HERCULES, VII: 95, VIII: 407, XII: 416, XIII: 308
Hering, Lt. Cdr. W. A., XII: 428, XIII: 305, XIV: 373
HERMANN SCHOEMANN, I: 169
HERMES, III: 382; sunk, 384
HERMIONE, I: 167
Hermle, Brig. Gen. Leo D., pic., XIV: 54; mentioned, I: 75
Hernan, Lt. E. J., VI: 232
HERNDON, IX: 388, XI: 105–6, 334, 342
HERON, III: 159, 197, 272, VIII: 49n, 50, 406, XIII: 312
Herr, Gen. T., IX: 279, 284
Herriman, Lt. Cdr. F. C., XIII: 304, XIV: 373
Herring, Cdr. G. G., II: 104n
Herring, Ens. J. W., VI: 61
Herring, Cdr. L. R., XI: 269, 341
HERRING, II: 39, VIII: 16, X: 87; sunk, VIII: 24
Herrmann, Capt. E. E., VIII: 413, XII: 99, 424, XIII: 316
Herrmann, Lt. George, XII: 423, XIV: 373
HERZOG, X: 380
HESPERUS, I: 326, X: 78
Hess, Cdr. F. G., XII: 429
Hess, Lt. Cdr. H. H., I: 208
Hessel, Lt. Cdr. E. W., XIV: 382
Hester, Maj. Gen. J. H., VI: 144, 155, 177–80, 198
Hetherington, Lt. Cdr. D. H. F., XI: 339
Hewitt, Lt. (jg) C. G., X: 124n
Hewitt, Lt. G. S., XII: 417, XIII: 307, XIV: 376

Hewitt, Adm. H. Kent, biog., II: 21n, IX: 14n; pics., II: frontispiece, 93, 164; mentioned, IX: 26, XI: 244; Comcrudiv 8, I: 83n; Comphiblant, 421, II: 21–3, 270; North Africa, 16–25, 30–33, 36, 41–50, 59n, 71n, 74, 80–82, 92–100, 107–15, 147–82 passim, 216, 245–6, 260, 273; Com Eighth Fleet & Navnaw, 255, IX: x, 33, X: 251–2, XI: 64n; staff, IX: 15; Moroccan-based air, X: 130; Sicily, II: 271, IX: 14–30, 61–8, 78, 93, 101, 104, 120–26, 141–82 passim, 190–91, 216n, 224, 385; Salerno, 246–51, 259, 273, 278, 290–97, 301, 391; Anzio, 350, 359; Southern France, XI: 222, 233–42, 247, 252–8, 274–91 passim, 311, 314, 338
Hewitt, Air Commo. J. E., VI: 65
Hewitt, Capt. J. G., XI: 342
Hewitt, Lt. Cdr. J. V., XIV: 379
Heyen, Lt. Cdr., VII: 151n
HEYWOOD, I: 76, IV: 273, 290, VII: 156, 159, 335–7, 347, VIII: 410, XII: 418, XIV: 308, 313
HEYWOOD L. EDWARDS, VII: 408, XII: 199, 221, 419, XIII: 304, XIV: 373
Hibbs, Cdr. W., III: 159, 272
HIBIKI, IV: 172, VIII: 417
Hibuson I., XII: 232
Hickam Field, III: 123–4
Hickey, Lt. (jg) H. W., X: 382
Hickey, Capt. R. F., XIII: 316, XIV: 384
Hickling, Capt. Harold, XI: 178n
Hickman, Ruben F., pic., VII: 319
HICKOX, VII: 349, VIII: 304, 413, XII: 319, 426, XIII: 63, 76–7, 317, 319, XIV: 383
Hicks, Lt. Cdr. C. O., XII: 419, XIII: 310
Hicks, Lt. Cdr. Harry L., I: 283
Hicks, Lt. J. R., XIV: 375
Hicks, Capt. R. L., XIII: 103, 304
HIDATSA, XIII: 306
Hie M., VI: 68
HIEI, III: 26, 87, 382, IV: 88, 179n, V: 82, 85, 206–59 passim, sunk, 260–61
Hieto, XIII: 91
Higashikuni, Gen. Prince N., XIV: 359
Higbee, Cdr. F. D., VIII: 404
Higgins, Lt. Cdr. E. M., X: 169–70, 375, XII: 422, XIII: 304, XIV: 374
Higgins, Capt. John M., III: 393, IV: 90,

Higgins, Capt. John M. (*cont'd*)
271, VI: 145, 182, VII: 350, XIII: 317,
XIV: 384
Higgins, Cdr. R. D., XI: 340
Higgins landing craft, II: 29, 35; PT
boats, 262-3
High, Cdr. P. L., VIII: 408, XII: 419,
XIII: 304, XIV: 383
Highfield, Lt. Cdr. C. F., XIV: 238,
373
High-Frequency Direction-Finders
("Huff-Duff"), (HF/DF), I: 105,
227-8, VIII: 251-4, 278, 285, X: 20, 53-
4, 143-4; mentioned, 58, 68, 77, 115,
119, 124, 139, 152, 168, 173, 187, 195,
210, 283-98 *passim*, 321-64 *passim*
Highland, Lt. Cdr. C. F., XII: 423
HIGHWAY, XI: 339
HILARY, IX: 150, 393
HILARY P. JONES, I: 76, 328, 354, 418, 420,
IX: 370, X: 258, 372, XI: 277-8, 282,
311, 342
Hilbert, Capt. W. E., II: 40, XIV: 327n
HILBERT, VIII: 411, XII: 429, XIII: 319
Hilger, Maj. J. A., III: 392
Hilken, Capt. T. J. N., XI: 342
Hill, Lt. Cdr. A. J., V: 366, VI: 161,
174, 181, 228, VII: 338
Hill, Cdr. B. C., XIII: 320
Hill, Col. Bruce C., airfield named aft-
er, XIII: 24, 34, 43, 48
Hill, Lt. Col. Charles W., VI: 145
Hill, Chief Boatswain E. J., III: 109
Hill, Lt. Cdr. H. D., X: 376, XI: 339
Hill, Vice Adm. Harry W., biog.,
VII: 152n; pic., 294; planner, I: 43n,
44; C.O. *Wichita*, 180, 419; Solomons,
V: 291, VI: 106, 146; Gilberts,
VII: 87, 90, 98-9, 114-16, 119, 145,
152-61, 171, 174, 182, 337; Marshalls,
225-8, 285-96, 300-304, 347; Marianas,
VIII: 186, 211, 256, 353, 356, 359, 407;
Iwo Jima, XIV: 7, 35, 50, 65, 166, 270,
309
Hill, Lt. Col. R. E., V: 145
Hill, Capt. Thomas B., VI: 11n,
VII: 105, 111, XIV: 165
Hill, Lt. W. E., X: 225
Hill, Col. W. H., IX: 327
HILL, X: 379-80
Hillenkoetter, Cdr. R. H., III: 106
Hilles, Cdr. F. V. H., XIV: 381
Hillman, Lt. F. M., XII: 423
Hills, Cdr. B. C., XIII: 282

Hillsinger, Cdr. L. B., XIV: 377
HILO, VI: 47, 53, 127
Hinckley, Cdr. R. M., XIV: 376
Hindman, Lt. Cdr. J. A. E., I: 420
Hindman, Cdr. S. E., VIII: 420,
XII: 26n, 420
Hinds, Cdr. W. B., XIV: 373, 375
Hine, Lt. R. K., VI: 129
Hinkle, Lt. T. B., XIV: 373
Hinnant, Cdr. J. R., XIII: 321
HINOKI, XIII: 102, 159; sunk, 116
Hinrichs, Ens. H. G., XIV: 56
HINSDALE, XIV: 155, 390
Hinton, Lt. Cdr. J. R., XIII: 319,
XIV: 375
Hirada, Lt. Gen. J., XIII: 240
HIRADO, sunk, XII: 400
Hiranuma, Baron, III: 36, XIV: 346,
350
Hirohito, Emperor, III: 10n, 69, 79,
V: 317, 373, VI: 16-18, XIV: 336-41,
344-5, 349-50, 353
Hirokawa M., V: 234, 283
Hirose, Rear Adm. S., III: 161-2, 174,
178, 275
Hiroshima, III: 26, VIII: 368, XIV: 344-
5
Hirota, Premier K., III: 13-14
HIRYU, III: 27, 87-8, 217, 245, 276, 296,
334, 382, IV: 83n, 88, 104-6, 110, 116,
123-5, 132-4, 138-9, 148, V: 214; sunk,
IV: 136-7
Hitachi, XIV: 314-16
HITAKA, VIII: 295n
Hitchcock, Cdr. N. R., V: 23
HITCHITI, XII: 429, XIII: 319, XIV: 388
Hitler, Adolf, naval and foreign policy,
I: 5-10, 34-8, 73, 95, 126, 127n, 161, 316,
400-401, X: 55; on radar, I: 266; Bra-
zil, 381; Iceland, 37, 57; Mediterrane-
an, II: 254, IX: 38, 46-7; France, II: 4-
5; Russia, 8; North Africa, 7, 18;
Sicily, IX: 45-7, 57, 69, 172, 195, 201-
2, 218; and Duce, 185-7, 201-2, 242;
Italy, 242, 307, 354, 361; not read
Clausewitz, 52; strategy, 304, X: 6-7,
58-60, 63, 230, 244; Normandy,
XI: 39-40, 43, 48, 159, 169, 173, 186;
Southern France, 217, 284; Channel
Is., 304-6; death, X: 358, XI: 324
Hitomi, Capt. S., XII: 431
HIWASSEE, XIV: 387
HIYO, V: 202n, 206n, 229, 234, 235n, 260,
266, 286, VI: 118, VII: 44, 54,

VIII: 217, 249, 264, 272, 294, 299, 307, 416; sunk, 295–6
HOBART, III: 261, 272, 308, 332*n*, 340, 365, IV: 19, 22*n*, 25, 38*n*, 272, 278, V: 29, VI: 39, 130, XIII: 234–5, 261, 264, 269, 323
Hobart Baker, XIII: 47
Hobbs, Capt. I. E., XIV: 373
Hobbs V., XIV: 166, 196, 386, 390
Hobby, Lt. Cdr. W. H., III: 110
HOBBY, I: 357, VI: 444, VIII: 112, 403, XII: 429, XIII: 316, 319
HOBSON, I: 420, II: 39, X: 376, XI: 95–6, 206, 209–10, 334, 337, 341, XIV: 237, 376, 391
Hoc, Pte. du, XI: 95, 105, 115, 119–29, 143, 158, 160; pic., 132
Hochuli, Lt. Cdr. E. S., XIV: 120, 377
Hodapp, Lt. Cdr. J. D. P., XIV: 372
Hodge, Maj. Gen. John R., VI: 364, 365*n*, 428, XII: 56, 113, 141, 153, 394–6, 418, XIV: 241, 379
Hodges, Lt. Gen. Courtney H., XI: 216, 323–4
Hodges, Lt. J. R., XII: 421, XIII: 306
HODGES, XIII: 125–6, 309, 326
Hodgson, Ens. E. R., X: 111
Hodnett, Lt. W. P., XII: 372
Hodson, Lt. N. D., X: 124, 379
HOE, XII: 405, XIII: 282–3
Hoeffel, Capt. K. M., III: 159, 201, 203*n*, 205
Hoel, Lt. Cdr. R. W., VIII: 268
HOEL, VII: 277, 296, 337, 347, VIII: 227–8, XII: 244, 255–63, 272, 313, 316, 421; sunk, 261
Hoey, Capt. G. B., I: 208
Hoffheins, Cdr. W. L., I: 421
Hoffman, Maj. C. W., *Saipan*, VIII: 5*n*; *Tinian*, 351*n*, 369–70
Hoffman, Lt. Cdr. G. D., X: 377, XI: 96, 334
Hoffman, Capt. H. D., VIII: 409, XIII: 304
Hoffman, Lt. Cdr. N. C., X: 377
Hoffman, Cdr. T. H., XIV: 387
Hoffner, Capt. C. C., XIV: 387
Hogan, Lt. (jg) G. G., X: 124, 128
Hogan, Lt. G. W., XII: 423
Hogan, Cdr. T. W., VI: 79–80, VIII: 217–18
HOGAN, I: 421, II: 39, 73, VII: 345, VIII: 82, 404, 409, 418, XIII: 306
Hoge, Brig. Gen. W. M., XI: 336

Hogg, Cdr. J. H., XII: 426, XIII: 316, 383
HOGGATT BAY, VIII: 227–8, XIII: 153*n*, 305
Hogland, Lt. E. D., XIII: 247–8
HOKAZE, IV: 172, VIII: 120*n*
Hokkaido, VII: 65, XIII: 158
Holcomb, Capt. Harold R., I: 111, III: 393, IV: 90*n*, 154, V: 86, 233
HOLCOMBE, IX: 393, X: 252–3; sunk, 253
Holden, Capt. C. F., VII: 349, XII: 426, XIII: 317
Holden, Capt. E. C., XIII: 310
Holden, Lt. Cdr. P. D., X: 378
HOLDER, X: 267
Holderman, A. L., X: 382
HOLLAND, III: 158, 193, 298, 303*n*, 320, IV: 222*n*, VIII: 26
Holland M., IV: 211
Hollander, Lt. F. H., VI: 341*n*
HOLLANDIA, XIV: 374
Hollandia, VI: 52; strikes on, VIII: 34–41; planning for, 9, 28, 61–5; Japs at, 65–7; captured, 45, 68–90; U.S. base, 50, 55, 96–7, 106, 123–45 *passim*, XII: 71, 82–3, 155; activity in Oct. '44, 114–16; Lingayen prelims., XIII: 6–8, 97, 144, 208; chart, VIII: 62; T.O., 403–6; pic., 88–9
Hollar, Capt. F. E., VI: 111*n*
Holler, Lt. Cdr. D. S., XII: 416, XIII: 309
Hollett, Lt. B. P., XII: 423
Holley, Lt. Cdr. G. M., III: 158, IV: 20
Hollingsworth, Lt. Cdr. A. F., XIV: 374
Hollingsworth, Cdr. J. C., XII: 411
Holloway, Capt. J. L., I: 420, II: 39, X: 49–50, XIII: 317
Holloway, L. A., I: 224
HOLLY, VIII: 419
Holm, Cdr. V. H. S., XIV: 386
Holmes, Machinist, V: 133
Holmes, Lt. Cdr. A. M., XIII: 309
Holmes, Cdr. E. P., VIII: 270, 409, XII: 426, XIII: 316
Holmes, Col. M. G., pic., VII: 167
Holmes, Cdr. R. H., VII: 333, 350, XIII: 102, 304, XIV: 373
Holmes, Lt. (jg) T. M., X: 196
Holovak, Lt. Cdr. C., XIV: 383
Holroyd, Lt. Cdr. W. W., XII: 422
Holsinger, Capt. R. W., XIV: 373
Holstrom, 1st Lt. E. W., III: 392

Holt, Chief Watertender A. H., V: 167
Holt, Lt. Cdr. E. R., XIII: 288
Holt, Lt. Cdr. P. C., XII: 377
Holt, Lt. (jg) S. B., X: 160
HOLT, XIII: 208
Höltring, Kaptlt. Horst, X: 127, 220
Holtz, Lt. Cdr. E. L., VII: 345
Holtz Bay, IV: 181, VII: 19, 41–8
Homann, Cdr. A. J., VIII: 411, XII: 428, XIII: 318, XIV: 387
Home, Lt. Cdr. J. W., XIV: 387
Homma, Lt. Gen. M., III: 161, 199, XIII: 32
Homonhon I., XII: 118–21
Hon Lon I., XIII: 161, 167
Hong Kong, III: 29, 155, 187, 191, VII: 80, VIII: 4, XII: 105, XIII: 157, 170–71, XIV: 355–6
HONOLULU, III: 31*n*, 119, 213*n*, IV: 83, 173; Tassafaronga, V: 291–309; later Solomons ops., 326, 329, 345, VI: 106*n*, 113*n*, 120, 156; Kula G. and Kolombangara, 161–3, 168, 178–90; N. Solomons, 363, 415; Aleutians, VII: 9*n*, 14; Marianas, VIII: vii, 181–2, 284, 326, 377, 393, 399, 409; Leyte, XII: 38–40, 80, 145–8, 419; pics., VI: 171, 194
Honolulu, III: 29, 142*n*; F.D.R.'s Conference, XII: 8–10
HOOD, I: 64, V: 165
"Hooligan Navy," I: 268, 274
Hooper, Lt. Cdr. A. M., XI: 298
Hooper, Lt. Cdr. Edwin B., V: 270*n*
Hooper, Cdr. S. G., XII: 426, XIII: 316, XIV: 386
Hooper, Rear Adm. Stanford C., II: 96*n*
Hoosier, I: 190, 191*n*
Hoover, Lt. Cdr. C. D., X: 212
Hoover, Capt. G. C., IV: 19, 90, V: 150, 155–7, 231, 253, 256, 258*n*
Hoover, Vice Adm. John H., I: 144, VII: 98, 118, 211–15, 250, 340, 350, VIII: 156–8, 242, X: 189–91, 197, XII: 43*n*, 49, 60, XIII: 82, XIV: 11, 307; pic., X: 185
Hoover, 1st Lt. Travis, III: 392
HOPE, XIV: 386
HOPEWELL, VII: 242, 273, 346, VIII: 228*n*, 404, XII: 417, XIII: 27*n*, 31, 37, 200, 304
Hopgood, Lt. (jg) R. B., I: 249

HOPI, IX: 284, 297–9, 388, 392, 396, XI: 340
Hopkins, Cdr. Harry RN, VIII: 210*n*, XIV: 102
Hopkins, Hon. Harry L., I: 36, 54, 69, II: 12, 15, IX: 7, X: 22*n*, XI: 9, 13–14, 232; pic., I: 70
Hopkins, Capt. Howard V., VIII: 49*n*, XIV: 374
Hopkins, Lt. R. H., VII: 333
HOPKINS, I: 15*n*, IV: 274, V: 57, VI: 145, 152, 156*n*, 297, VIII: 410, 418, XIII: 113, 306, XIV: 376
Hopman, Korvkapt. Rudolf, X: 165
Hopping, Lt. Cdr. H. L., III: 121, 262
HOPPING, XIV: 378, 391
Hoppock, Lt. (jg) H., VII: 341
HORACE A. BASS, XIV: 244
Horace Bushnell, X: 313
Horace Gray, X: 311
HORAI, III: 366*n*
Horaniu, Battle of, VI: 233–40; chart, 235
Hordern, Lt. Cdr. L. A., XI: 342
Horie, Maj. T., XIV: 67
Horii, Maj. Gen. T., IV: 18, VI: 33, 43, 267
Horn, Lt. Cdr. A. T., XIII: 313
Horn, Lt. Cdr. P. H., VII: 23*n*, 57, 335, 388
Horne, Vice Adm. F. J., biog., VII: 101*n*; mentioned, I: 114*n*, 116, VII: 101, 112
Horne, Cdr. K. F., XIV: 377
Horner, Lt. C. S., XII: 416, XIII: 306
Horner, Cdr. J. S., VIII: 404, XIV: 377
HORNET (1941), III: 31, 389*n*, 390–97, IV: 15, 62, 82–3, 91, 97, 101–3, 112–16, 120, 127, 130–31, 142, 148–52, 157, 182–4, 257, 276, V: 80, 110, 130–33, 136, 139, 148, 177, 201–5, 209–17, VII: xxvii, VIII: 176, 236*n*, XII: 91, XIV: 105; sunk, V: 219–22; pics., III: 394–5, IV: 100, V: 219
HORNET (1943), V: 222*n*, VIII: 32, 36, 174–5, 238–40, 250, 262, 272–4, 292, 297, 303–4, 311, 412, XII: 90, 106, 244*n*, 294, 304, 309, 424, XIII: 54, 316, XIV: 21, 199, 209, 300–301, 305, 382, 386
Hornkohl, Kaptlt. Hans, X: 184–6
HORNPIPE, IX: 396
Hornquist, E. R., X: 382

Horse race, GUARDFISH watches, IV: 209n
Horton, Lt. J. C., XII: 423, XIV: 230, 373
Horton, Lt. J. S., VII: 341
Horton, Adm. Sir Max, X: 8, 18, 24, 70, 149
HOSHO, III: 27, 130, IV: 89
Hosogaya, Vice Adm. B., pic., VII: 54; mentioned, III: 26, IV: 77, 169, 172, 175, 179–80, 184, VII: 4–8, 12–13, 18, 21–8, 32, 35
Hospital ships, Salerno, IX: 299–300
Hotchkiss, Lt. Cdr. S. T., XII: 304, 420, XIII: 307
Hottel, Lt. Cdr. M. P., IV: 92
Houck, Lt. Cdr. H. N., VII: 349, XIV: 385
Hough, Maj. F. O., *Assault on Peleliu,* XII: 30n
Houle, Cdr. D. J., XII: 428, XIII: 319
Hourihan, Capt. J. J., III: 160, 333, XIV: 378
HOUSATONIC, I: 422, II: 40, 263, XIII: 318, XIV: 387; pic., II: 149
House, Lt. A. C., I: 421
House, Brig. Gen. E. J., IX: 250, 277
House, Ens. F. W., X: 382
HOUSTON (1930), III: 152–4, 159, 193, 271, 284n, 299–302, 306, 312–17, 331–2, 339; Java Sea, 342–7, 351–4, 357; Sunda Str., 364–9; sunk, 369–70, 380; pics., 166, 285
HOUSTON (1943), VIII: 415, XII: 90, 95, 98–104, 117, 424–5; pic., XII: 102
HOVA, XI: 343
HOVEY, IV: 274, V: 169, 180, 236, VI: 297, VIII: 404, XII: 421, XIII: 106, 112, 306, 325
Howard, Lt. Frank T., XII: 237n
Howard, Rear Adm. Herbert S., I: 229n
Howard, Cdr. J. H., VIII: 410, XIV: 376
Howard, Col. Samuel L., III: 158, 204
Howard, Cdr. W. S., I: 418, VII: 341, XIV: 387
HOWARD, I: 422, II: 40, 139, VIII: 410, XII: 422, XIII: 306
HOWARD D. CLARK, XIII: 305
Howden, Capt. H. L., IV: 19
Howe, Cdr. C. M., VII: 350
Howe, Lt. G. H., IV: 291n

Howe, Cdr. H. W., I: 155, 355, 420, IX: 389
Howe, Ens. K. E., IX: 329n
HOWE, IX: 167, 236, XII: 61, XIV: 105, 388
Howers, Cdr. F. W., XII: 423
Howland, Lt. Col. John, V: x
Howland, Lt. (jg) R. H., X: 216
Howland I., VII: 96
HOWORTH, VIII: 404, XII: 417, XIII: 313, XIV: 191–2, 379, 390
Hoyo M., III: 263, IV: 18
Hoyt, Lt. Cdr. J. B., VIII: 408
Hozumi, Maj. S., VII: 6
Hryniewiecki, Cdr. S., X: 147–8
Hsu Yung-chang, Gen., XIV: 366
Hubbard, Lt. Cdr. Harry E., III: 393, V: 179
Hubbard, Capt. M. H., XII: 199, 202, 234, 420, XIII: 148, 151, 311, XIV: 375
HUBBARD, X: 332, 354, 373, 376
Hubbell, Capt. R. B., V: 375
Hube, Gen. Hans, IX: 172–3, 195–7, 202, 209, 215, 218
Huber, Cdr. Vernon, I: 420, II: 37, IX: 387
Huckaby, Lt. Cdr. W. F., VIII: 411, XII: 423, XIII: 308, XIV: 387
Huddleston, Lt. Cdr. J. C., XIV: 385n
Hudson, Capt. H. B., XIII: 266, 323
Hudson, Lt. Col. L. C., VII: 236n, 363
Hudson, Capt. L. J., III: 194, 337, 379, VII: 340, 349, VIII: 415
Hudson, Capt. R. C., XIV: 372
HUDSON, VI: 297, 342–3, 413–15, VIII: 329, 409, 415, XIV: 243, 381
Huebner, Maj. Gen., C. R., XI: 130, 142, 149, 152, 335
Huetter, Capt. J. J., XIII: 323
Huey, Lt. Cdr. Frederick, X: 333n, 353, 376
Huff, Lt. Cdr. E. H., XIII: 303
Huff, Lt. O. W., IX: 388
"Huff-Duff." *See* High-Frequency Direction-Finder's
Huffman, Lt. Cdr. Huston, XIV: 18
Huffman, Capt. L. J., IV: 226
Hüffmeier, Vice Adm. F., XI: 306, 328
HUGH L. SCOTT, I: 358, II: 38, 56n, 60n, 168, III: 213; sunk, 171–3, 284
HUGH W. HADLEY, XIV: 112, 256–8, 379, 392
Hugh Williamson, IX: 390

Hughes, Lt. (jg) Blake, I: 364–5, 375
Hughes, Hon. Charles E., I: xxxvi
Hughes, Capt. F. M., X: 279, 284, 289, 377
Hughes, Lt. Cdr. J. G., V: 256n, XII: 417, XIII: 309, XIV: 379
Hughes, Cdr. J. J., II: 36, III: 17
Hughes, Cdr. J. N., III: 272n, X: 377, XI: 339
Hughes, Cdr. Massie, IV: 92, 157
Hughes, Cdr. W. C., X: 213n, 227, XI: 252, 338
HUGHES, I: 75, 90, IV: 19n, 90, 153–5, V: 205, 219, 233, 345, VII: 141, 334, 337, 346, VIII: 405, XII: 383–5, 388, 416–17
Hughes-Hallett, Commo. John, XI: 19, 25
Huie, Cdr. B. S., XIII: 306
HULBERT, III: 104, IV: 183n, VII: 333
Hulings, Lt. Cdr. J. S., X: 382, XIV: 386
Hull, Hon. Cordell, I: 44–6, 68–70, III: 14, 35, 43, 47–9, 60, 65–70, 74–6, 79, 140
Hull, Maj. Gen. J. E., XI: 54
Hull, Lt. Cdr. J. L., IV: 92, 210
HULL, III: 104, 213n, IV: 274, VII: 61, 309, 335–6, 347, VIII: 413, XII: 429, XIII: 80–82, 319; sunk, 71–2
Hull spaces, VI: 169n
Hulme, Lt. Cdr. John, V: 375
HUMBOLDT, I: 390n, 420, X: 293
Humboldt Bay, charts, VIII: 62, 80; landing, *see* Hollandia
Hummer, Lt. Cdr. H. R., IX: 385, 388
Humphrey, Lt. J. B., XII: 423, XIII: 308
Humphreys, Elizabeth, VI: xii, XIV: xi
HUMPHREYS, I: 214, IV: 173, VI: 133, 261–3, 267, 269n, 374, 381, 436, VIII: 404, XII: 422, XIII: 112, 304, XIV: 376
Hunan, XIII: 291
Hunanagan Bay, XII: 290
Hundt, Capt. L. T., VII: 339, 349, 353
Hundley, Col. D. H., VI: 146
Hungerford, Capt. R. W., I: 123, 208, XI: 213n
Hunt, Cdr. C. B., IV: 273
Hunt, Lt. Col. L. P., pic., V: 130; mentioned, IV: 272, 286, 291
Hunt, Capt. R. B., XI: 62, 216n
Hunt, Cdr. R. B. A., XIII: 306

Hunt, Lt. W. T., XII: 421, XIV: 377
HUNT, VII: 349, VIII: 413, XII: 319, 426, XIII: 61, 317, XIV: 247, 383
Hunter, Lt. Cdr. E. N. W., X: 377
Hunter, Capt. George P., IV: 19, V: 86, XIV: 374
Hunter, Capt. L. L., VII: 337
Hunter, Lt. O. D., VI: 231
Hunter, Capt. R. N., XII: 420, XIII: 89n, 117, 306
HUNTER, IX: 250, 393, X: 40n, XI: 342
HUNTER LIGGETT, IV: 272–3, 285, V: 16, VI: 297, 304
Hunter-killer groups. *See* Escort Carriers
Huntington, Cdr. John, XIV: 162
HUNTINGTON, VIII: 236n
Huntoon, Capt. F. C., XIV: 387
Huon Gulf, VI: 258–9, 272–3, XIII: 96; opn., VII: 64
Hupfel, Lt. W. M., VIII: 410
Hurd, Lt. Cdr. K. C., III: 158
Hurff, Capt. J. E., II: 38, VI: 337, 415–16, 427, VIII: 409, 415, IX: 388, XII: 428, XIV: 373
Hurley, Maj. Gen. Patrick, XII: 6
Hurndall, Lt. Cdr. J. P., VI: 381, VIII: 403
Hurst, Cdr. A. M., III: 158, VII: 119, 337, 344
Hurst, Lt. J. Willard, I: xvii, 158n, 296n, 392n, 416
Hurt, Lt. Cdr. D. A., III: 158
Hurt, Capt. S. H., VII: 346, VIII: 409, XII: 223n, 419
HUSE, X: 320, 372, 378
Husted, Lt. C. L., XIV: 388
Hustvedt, Rear Adm. Olaf M., biog., X: 229n; mentioned, VII: 328, 349, 353, VIII: 415, X: 229–33
Hutchings, Cdr. C. S., X: 262–3
Hutchins, Lt. Charles H., pic., 169; mentioned, X: 163–7, 376
Hutchins, Capt. Gordon, I: 419, II: 37, 105n, 112, XI: 19
Hutchins, Col. Henry, VIII: 52
Hutchins, Seaman J. D., VI: 265
Hutchins, Cdr. T. B., VIII: 406
HUTCHINS, VI: 382, 385, 390, 436, 444, VIII: 66, 108–10, 127, 406, XII: 199, 218–20, 421, XIV: 229, 243, 379, 391
Hutchinson, Lt. Cdr. George, XI: 341
Hutchinson, Lt. L. L., XIV: 232
Hutchinson, Capt. M. W., II: 38

Hutchison, Cdr. C. K., VIII: 411, XIV: 387
Hutton, Capt. Charles L., VII: 334
Hutton, Capt. R. M. J., IX: 393
Huxtable, Lt. Cdr. E. J., VIII: 410, XII: 280, 421
Hvalfjordur, pic., I: 92; mentioned, 57-8, 77, 95, 117, 320
HYADES, X: 327n
Hyakutake, Lt. Gen. H., V: 70, 108-9, 123, 143-5, 149, 176, 190, VI: 118n, 425-31
Hyatt, Lt. B. M., XIV: 376
Hyde, Lt. B. D., XIV: 378
Hyde, Lt. Cdr. J. L., XII: 420
Hyde, Cdr. J. M., XIII: 284
Hydeman, Cdr. E. T., XIV: 292
HYDROGRAPHER, VII: 45, VIII: 420

Hydrography, New Guinea, VI: 32, 46; Solomons, 290, 298, 363; Green Is., 414; Attu, VII: 45; Tarawa, 153-4; Marshalls, 228, 286; Sicily, IX: 23; Naples, 311; Normandy, 68-9; Saipan, VIII: 184; Ulithi, XII: 49-50; Philippines, XIII: 218, 223; Tarakan, 260-61; Iwo, XIV: 72
HYDRUS, XIV: 378
Hyères, Island and Bay, XI: 250-53, 285
Hyland, Cdr. J. J., XIV: 385
Hylant, Capt. E. P., XII: 423, XIII: 308
Hyman, Lt. Cdr. W. M., IV: 19
HYMAN, XIV: 192, 381, 390
HYUGA, III: 26, IV: 89, XII: 90, 160n, 162, 191-2, 319-35 *passim*, 430, XIII: 158-76 *passim*, 284; sunk, XIV: 331

I

I-boats (Japanese submarines), *I-1*, V: 349-50; *I-2*, 169, VII: 57; *I-3*, V: 319; *I-4*, 207, 324n; *I-5*, 207, VIII: 222, 230, 417; *I-7*, III: 222n, V: 207, 235, VII: 56-7; *I-8*, V: 207, X: 299-300, XIV: 137, 243; *I-9*, III: 222n, IV: 168n, 173, V: 85, 106, 207, 235, VII: 57; *I-10*, III: 96-8, VIII: 229-30, 417; *I-11*, V: 85, VII: 224; *I-13*, XIV: 314; *I-15*, IV: 173, V: 85, 133, 207, 223, 235; *I-16*, V: 235, 292, VIII: 224-5; *I-17*, IV: 165n, 173, V: 85, 106, 235; *I-18*, 324n; *I-19*, III: 87, 222n, IV: 168n-9n, 173, V: 85, 131-3, 136, VII: 138, 144, XIII: 4n

I-20, V: 227n, 235, VI: 242; *I-21*, III: 87, IV: 18, 66n, V: 207, 215, 235; *I-22*, IV: 18, 66n, V: 207; *I-23*, III: 87; *I-24*, IV: 18, 66n, V: 207, 235, VII: 57; *I-25*, IV: 168, 173; *I-26*, III: 96-8, IV: 169-70, 173, V: 85, 111-12, 235, 257, XII: 432; *I-27*, IV: 66n, X: 277; *I-28*, IV: 18, 206; *I-29*, 18, 66n; *I-31*, V: 85, 235, VII: 44, 57; *I-32*, 308; *I-35*, 139; *I-36*, VI: 286, XII: 52, 432, XIV: 19; *I-37*, XII: 432; *I-38*, VIII: 417, XII: 432

I-40, VII: 144; *I-41*, VIII: 417, XII: 79, 347, 432; *I-42*, VIII: 30; *I-44*, XII: 432, XIV: 18-19; *I-45*, XII: 307, 342, 432; *I-46*, 342, 432; *I-47*, 52, 432, XIV: 160n, 317; *I-48*, XII: 53; *I-52*, X: 298-9, 372; *I-53*, VIII: 417, XII: 432, XIV: 317, 321; *I-54*, XII: 432; *I-56*, 301, 432, XIV: 248; *I-58*, XIII: 280, XIV: 19, 317, 321-2, 328-30; *I-70*, III: 98, 217; *I-73*, 258, IV: 74n

I-121, IV: 88, 93-4, V: 85; *I-122*, IV: 88, V: 235, XIV: 292; *I-123*, IV: 88, 93-4, V: 66-7, 85; *I-151*, X: 125; *I-155*, VII: 57; *I-156*, IV: 88; *I-157*, 88, VII: 57; *I-158*, *I-159*, *I-162*, *I-164*, *I-165*, *I-166*, IV: 88, 202

I-168, IV: 143, 155, VI: 68-70; *I-171*, 414; *I-172*, V: 227, 235; *I-174*, 85, 207, VI: 267; *I-175*, V: 85, 207, 235, VII: 139-41, 223-4; *I-176*, V: 182n, 207, VII: 188, VIII: 223-4; *I-177*, VI: 353n, 391

I-182, VI: 75; *I-184*, VII: 308, VIII: 222, 230, 417; *I-185*, VIII: 230, 417; *I-351*, XIII: 288; *I-361*, XIV: 244; *I-362*, XII: 305; *I-365*, 408; *I-368*, XIV: 18-19; *I-370*, 18; *I-371*, 289; *I-372*, 316, *I-373*, 294; *I-505*, X: 170

IBIS, II: 283

ICARUS, I: 155, 415

Ice Patrol, I: 60

ICEFISH, XII: 406, 429, XIII: 319

Iceland, occupation of, I: 57, 67, 74-9, 85, II: 9, X: 6; base, I: 37, 56, 82, 320, 359, X: 68-9, 77-9, 83, 148; conditions, I: 78, 95, 117-19; pic., 92, 128

Icenhower, Cdr. J. B., XII: 429, XIV: 293n

Ichiki, Col. K., V: 70-73

Ichimaru, Rear Adm. T., XIV: 14, 68

IDAHO, I: 57, 82, III: 57, 214, V: 236n, 325n, VI: 423, VII: 38, 43-4, 60, 258-60, 267, 334-6, 344, VIII: 180, 377, 409, XIII: 176n, XIV: 26-8, 31, 62, 148, 182, 229, 320, 329, 373

Iden, Capt. Ruben, V: 374

Identification, Friend or Foe (IFF), V: 93, 354, VI: 421, VIII: 242n, X: 173n, 197n, 261-3

Ie Shima, XIII: 182, XIV: 80, 83, 91, 136, 235, 240, 257-8, 271, 277-8, 359

Ihrig, Capt. R. M., III: 393, IV: 91, 272, VII: 104

Ijuin, Rear Adm. M., VI: 234-6, 244-7, 250-52, 306, 310

IJUIN, XI: 337

IKAZUCHI, III: 274, 334, IV: 172, V: 194-6, 207, 233, 254, VII: 24; sunk, VIII: 19

Ikeda, Capt. F., VI: 267

Ikuta M., VII: 214-15

ILEX, IX: 42, 394

ILFRACOMBE, XI: 333

Ilin I., XIII: 18, 29, 33, 40-41

ILLUSTRIOUS, III: 50n, VIII: 154n, IX: 251, 393, XIV: 105, 212-13, 249, 388

Ilocos Mts., XIII: 125, 185
Iloilo, III: 159, XIII: 13, 228–31
Ilsemann, Cdr. F. J., VIII: 411, XII: 428, XIII: 71, 318, XIV: 387
Ilu R., IV: 285*n*; Battle of, V: 69*n*
Imaizumi, Capt. K., III: 87
Imamura, Lt. Gen. H., III: 333, 366, V: 316, 342, VI: 49, 54, 63, 92, 118, 136, 233, 261, 265, 342, 348, 394, 403, 406–8
Imizu M., III: 275
Imlay, Capt. M. H., IX: 82*n*, 387, XI: 141, 164
IMPECCABLE, XIV: 376
Imperial Conferences, 1941, III: 12, 69; 1943, V: 342, 352; 1945, XIV: 340*n*
Imperial General Headquarters, described, VI: 17–20; strategy, 1943–44, 23–6, 117, VIII: 11, XII: 66–7, 70, VIII: 213–15; New Guinea, VI: 52, 136 233, 260, 284, 406, VIII: 65–7, Aleutians, VII: 18, 49–51, 54; Gilberts, 77, 136, 144, Marshalls, 222–3; Truk, 316; Marianas, VIII: 183, 324; cooperation with Germany, XI: 42; defensive tactics, XII: 35; Philippines, 13, 71, 149, 361, 394, XIII: 37, 240; Formosa Air Battle, XII: 108–9, 192; Iwo Jima, XIV: 13; Okinawa, 93, 101
IMPERIALIST, X: 157*n*
Imphal, VII: 83
IMPLICIT, XI: 313, 343
IMPROVE, XI: 313, 343
IMPULSIVE, I: 365*n*, X: 70
Inada, Gen., VIII: 67, 88
Inagaki, Maj. T., V: 341
INAZUMA, III: 274–5, IV: 172, V: 206*n*, 233–4, 273*n*, VII: 24; sunk, VIII: 217
INCESSANT, XI: 343
INCH, X: 283, 322, 378
INCONSTANT, IX: 40
INCREDIBLE, XI: 343
INDEFATIGABLE, XIV: 105, 212, 333, 388
INDEPENDENCE, VI: 330–35, 346, VII: xxvii, 85, 92–4, 117, 138, 142, 157, 339, XII: 90, 93, 133, 189–90, 195–6, 206*n*, 310, 317–20, 332, 359, 426, XIII: 54, 87, 165, 318, XIV: 248, 385–6
Indian Ocean, Jap. opns. in, III: 381–6; U-boats in, X: 274–8, 299–304, and chart, 301
INDIANA (1895), II: 286
INDIANA (1942), I: 419, V: 183, 291, 352, VI: 107*n*, VII: 228, 258, 339, 348,

VIII: 41*n*, 64*n*, 268–70, 415, XIV: 12, 21, 112, 307, 313, 382, 386
Indiana, VIII: 420
INDIANAPOLIS, pre-war, II: 21*n*, V: 88*n*; VI: 282*n*, IX: 14*n*, X: 345*n*, XI: 63*n*; XIV: 312*n*; war, III: 211, 215, 237, 266*n*, IV: 83, 173; Aleutians, VII: 9, 12, 18–23; Fifth Fleet flagship, 119, 207; Eniwetok, 288, 296, 301, 336–8, 343, 346; Marianas, VIII: 177, 197, 243, 308, 311, 332, 381, 400, 407–9, 414, 419; Palaus, XII: 39; Iwo, XIV: 21, 27, 34; Okinawa, 88, 372–3, 384; hit, 138, 390; sunk, 319–30, and chart, 323; casualties, 327; pic., III: 267
Indispensable Strait, V: 67, VI: 120, 160
Indochina, II: 9, III: 45, 61–2, 69, 153, XIII: 282–5
INDOMITABLE, III: 188, 382, IX: 167–8, XIV: 105, 212, 264–6, 388
Indonesia, XII: 68, XIII: 276–7. See Netherlands East Indies, Java
INDUS, XII: 423, XIII: 308
Ingerslew, Lt. Cdr. D. B., VII: 349, 352
Ingersoll, Adm. Royal E., biog., I: 206*n*; pic., X: frontispiece; Director of War Plans, III: 49; Cinclant, I: 115, 419, X: 7, 21–5, 272, A/S W, I: 206–7, 257–8, 382, X: 8, 47, 125, 169, 212, 251, 281–3, 296–8, 322, 325; North Africa, II: 41; Escort Carriers, X: 109–10, 128, 157; *Bogue*, 114; *U-505*, 293; Caribbean, 298; Comwestseafron, XIV: 157, 162
Ingersoll, Vice Adm. Stuart H., I: 85*n*, VIII: 413, XII: viii, XIII: x, 70, 80, 315, XIV: x
INGERSOLL, VII: 348, VIII: 414, XII: 319, 425, XIII: 318
INGHAM, pic., I: 230; mentioned, I: 305, 335, 343, 421, XIII: 323
INGLEFIELD, IX: 394, 396; sunk, 366
Ingling, Cdr. F. W., XII: 418, XIII: 305
Inglis, Rear Adm. Thomas B., III: 98*n*, V: xi, VI: 344, VIII: 409, XII: 95*n*, 103, 179–81, 427
Ingraham, Lt. Cdr. K. C., XII: 429
INGRAHAM (1941), I: 107*n*, 327, 420
INGRAHAM (1944), XII: 366*n*, XIII: 26, 304, XIV: 25, 254–5, 373, 391
Ingram, Lt. Cdr. C., VII: 340
Ingram, Lt. Cdr. J. C. A., X: 74–5
Ingram, Rear Adm. Jonas H., biog., I: 382*n*, X: 332*n*; pic., 224; men-

Ingram, Rear Adm. Jonas H. (cont'd) tioned, I: 83, 263, 276n, 377–8, 382–4, 388–90, 419; X: xv, 208–15, 220, 224–6, 293–5, 322–4, 343–5, 349, 355
Ingram, Lt. Cdr. W. T., XIV: 377
Inland Sea of Japan, XIV: 331–2
Innis, Cdr. W. D., V: 17n, XIV: 381
Inoguchi, Rear Adm. J., XII: 186, 430
Inoguchi, Capt. R., *Divine Wind*, XIII: 93n, XIV: 215n
Inoue, Lt. Gen. S., XII: 35–6, 42
Inoue, Capt. Y., XII: 431
Inouye, Vice Adm. S., III: 26, 165, 185, 244–5, IV: 11, 14, 17, 21, 44–5, 61, 255
Inshore Patrol, Atlantic, I: 266–7; Ellice Is., VII: 340
Inspection Service, I: 236–7
Intelligence, Naval, Pearl Harbor, III: 134–5; Coral Sea, IV: 13; Midway, 80, 96, 158; Aleutians, 170, 183; North Africa, II: 25–6, 237; Solomons, IV: 266–7, V: 83, 227–8, 272–3, 295; Gilberts, VII: 149; Marshalls, 255, 286, 291; Palaus, VIII: 28, XII: 32–3, 36; New Guinea, VIII: 34, 69, 72–5, 104, 116; Sicily, IX: 78, 212; Anzio, 336, 344, 347; Normandy, XI: 34–5, 71–2, 113–14, 121; Marianas, VIII: 168, 183; Philippine Sea, 237, 241, 247, 254, 274, 316; Southern France, XI: 234–5, 244, 268; Germany, 295; Leyte, XII: 71–3, 121; China, XIII: 289, 292–3; Okinawa, XIV: 119, 132
INTENT, IX: 101, 387, 393
INTREPID, VII: 208, 237–352 *passim;* bad luck, 321n; Leyte battle, XII: 90, 106, 125n, 175, 184–6, 244n, 318, 325, 425; hit again, 342, 358–60; near-miss, XIV: 94; hit again, 248; T.O., 385–6; casualties, 391
INTREPID, HMS, I: 196, IX: 394
Inveraray, II: 193, 204
Ionian Is., IX: 245
IOWA (1897), II: 286
IOWA (1943), VII: 208, 309, 326–9, 349, 353, VIII: 40, 270, 415, XII: 90, 318, 330, 345, 426, XIII: 54, 317, XIV: 314, 363; pic., 366–7; class, I: lviii, 28n, VI: 10
Iran V., XII: 83, 423, XIII: 308
IRENE FORSYTE, I: 285–6
Irish, Capt. E. W., VIII: 408, XII: 416, XIII: 309

IRO, IV: 18n, 29
Ironbottom Bay Club, VI: 103, XIII: 97
Ironbottom Sound, V: 4, 59, 81, 114, VI: 140, 178, 182, VIII: 172; pic., IV: 255
Ironclad, I: 191n, 373; pic., 170
IROQUOIS, IV: 71
Irvin, Cdr. W. D., VII: 119, 154, 342
Irvine, Ens. C. B., V: 208
Irvine, Cdr. G. W. A. T., XI: 79, 333
Irvine, Lt. Cdr. J. M., X: 333n, 376
Irving, Maj. Gen. F. A., VIII: 63, 75–9, 403, XII: 131, 137, 416
Irwin, Maj. D. D., V: 374
IRWIN, VIII: 409, XII: 179–83, 427, XIV: 135, 373
ISAAC SWEERS, II: 284
ISABEL, III: 159, 193, 272, 379
Isbell, Capt. Arnold J., biog., X: 109n; pic., 128; and hunter-killer group, 109, 117, 122–7, 159–63, 166–8, 171–3, 177, 281, 376; death, XIV: 98
Ischia, IX: 301
ISE, III: 26, IV: 89, XII: 91, 160n, 162, 191–2, 319–35 *passim*, 430, XIII: 158–76 *passim*, 284; sunk, XIV: 331; pic., XII: 326
Iselin, Lt. Cdr. Lewis, X: 357
Isely, Jeter A., *U.S. Marines and Amphibious War*, VII: 146n, VIII: 186n
Isely, Lt. Cdr. Robert H., VII: 338; death, VIII: 178; pics., VII: 198, VIII: 177
Isely Field, VIII: 209, 326–68 *passim*, XIII: 164
ISHERWOOD, XII: 419, XIII: 148, 188, 311, XIV: 244, 375, 391
Ishigura, Cdr. VIII: 298
Ishii, Capt. H., XII: 431
Ishikawa, Lt. (jg) S., VII: 122
Ishiwara, Capt. H., XII: 431
Ishizaki, Capt. N., IV: 18
Isigny, XI: 160, 167, 218n
Isitt, Air Vice Marshal Sir L. M., XIV: 366
Island Mail, VII: 341, 345
Islander, VI: 36
Ismay, Lt. Gen. Sir Hastings, IX: 7–8
ISOKAZE, III: 87, IV: 88, V: 85, 203, 206, 370, VI: 234–6, 244, 250, VIII: 416, XII: 272n, 431, XIII: 158, XIV: 202
ISONAMI, III: 276, IV: 89, V: 206n, VI: 75; sunk, 76–7

Isquith, Cdr. S. S., XIV: 378
Istria, XI: 227–30, 296
ISUZU, V: 173, 206, 234, 264–6, VI: 323, VII: 54, 137, 192, XII: 162, 319, 325, 430; sunk, XIII: 286; pic., VII: 199
Isuzugawa M., VI: 80
Itagaki, Gen., III: 37, 40
Itagaki, Capt., XIII: 203
ITALIA, IX: 35, 243
Italy, Air Force, IX: 35, 56–9; Army, II: 260, IX: 47–52, 90, 95, 119, 154, 160, 163, 171–3, 183, 195, 200, 260; coastal batteries, 88, 95–8, 106, 136, 156–7, 160, 169; Navy in 1922–43, I: lxi, IX: 34–9; armistice, 235; joins Allies, 242–4; submarines, I: 415, IX: 36, 40–43, 168, X: 64, 366, 370–73; midget, II: 254; MTBs, IX: 35–7, 78, 162–3, 190, 193, 244–5, 365–6, 376
Italian Campaign, preliminary landings, IX: 233–6. *See* Salerno, Anzio.
Itaya, Capt., III: 94, XII: 238n
ITCHEN, X: 143–5
Ites, Oberlt. Otto, I: 348–9
Ito, Col., VIII: 167
Ito, Capt. T., VII: 12
Ito, Vice Adm. S., XIII: 158, XIV: 129, 202–3, 206
Ito, Rear Adm. Y., VIII: 117–18, 122, 130
Itri, IX: 375–6

ITSUKUSHIMA, III: 162, 275, VIII: 119, 131
Ivaldi, Cdr. J. A., XIV: 388
Iverson, Lt. Cdr. Clifton, VI: 214–15, VII: 350
Iverson, Lt. Daniel, IV: 110
Ives, Capt. N. S., II: 43n, X: 87, XI: 215–16, 298; pic., II: 164
Ivigtut, I: 58, 334n, X: 69
Iwabachi, Rear Adm. S., XIII: 196–8
Iwagami, Capt. H., IV: 18, VII: 138
Iwagami, Cdr. J., XII: 431
Iwano, Maj., VIII: 380
Iwo Jima, strikes on, VIII: 238–40, 311–13, 354; strikes from, 328–9; description, XIV: 6–7; planning, XII: 17, XIII: 5, 175, 178, XIV: 3–9; logistics, XIII: 208, XIV: 8–9, 70; maps, 36, 71; pics., 46–7, 54–5, 71; preliminary poundings, 9–32; D-day, 32–46; conquest of, 47–75; U.S. base, 70–72, XIII: 162, 168–70, 75; controversies, 72–4; casualties, 44, 62, 75; ships lost or damaged, 389; air and naval gunfire support, 9–13, 27–35, 40–59, 62–6, 72–5; pic. of flag-raising, frontispiece
Izaki, Rear Adm. S., VI: 181–3, 190
IZARD, VII: 326, 338, 349, VIII: 413, XII: 425, XIII: 304
Izawa, Capt. I., IV: 18

J

J-967, X: 188
J. DOUGLAS BLACKWOOD, XIII: 307
J. FRANKLIN BELL, VII: 42–4, 47, 335–7, 344, VIII: 410, XII: 418
J. FRED TALBOT, I: 151n
J. L. M. Curry, I: 370
J. R. Williams, I: 417
J. R. Y. BLAKELY, X: 379–80
J. RICHARD WARD, X: 378
J. WILLIAM DITTER, XIV: 274, 377, 392
JACK, VI: 84, VIII: 21, 90, 416
Jack, I: 393
Jack Patrols, XIII: 58n
Jackson, Cdr. Alex, XIV: 374
Jackson, Lt. Cdr. J. L., XII: 369, 421, XIV: 376
Jackson, Lt. (jg) K. C., XIII: 309
Jackson, Lt. Cdr. P. W., XII: 420, XIII: 305
Jackson, Cdr. Paul, XIII: 307, XIV: 380
Jackson, Lt. Richard M., quoted, XII: 179–83
JACKSON, X: 327n
Jacksonville, X: 328
Jacksonville, Fla., I: 240–2, 248, X: 184
JACOB JONES (1916), V: 148n
JACOB JONES (1919), I: 16, 135, 215; sunk, 132
JACOB VAN HEEMSKERCK, X: 268
Jacobs, Lt. Cdr. T. D., III: 158, IV: 221
Jacobson, Capt. J. H., I: 390n
Jacobson, Lt. Robert, VII: 333
Jacques, Ens., II: 152
JAGUAR, XI: 183, 191
Jahnsen, Lt. L. M., XII: 429
JALLAO, XII: 333–4, 408, 429, XIV: 293n, 294
Jaluit, III: 215, 237, 240–41, 262–4, V: 340, VII: 74–5, 79, 97–8, 116, 122, 206–7, 213–14, 305–7, 314, VIII: 154n, 222, 230
JAMAICA, I: 366, II: 237, X: 237, 243
Jamaica, West Indies, I: 34, X: 201n
Jamata, King of Ailinglapalap, VII: 313
James, Lt. Cdr. H. A., II: 121n, 125n, IX: 259n
James, Capt. Jules, I: 83

James, Col. W. C., pic., V: 130
JAMES E. CRAIG, VIII: 406, XIII: 308
James Gordon Bennett, X: 145
James H. Breasted, XIII: 41
James Iredell, IX: 390
James J. Pettigrew, X: 382
JAMES K. PAULDING, X: 212n
James K. Polk, I: 388
James M. Gillis, X: 382
James Marshall, IX: 299
JAMES O'HARA, VIII: 408, IX: 143, 389, 392, XII: 366, 416, XIII: 309
James Rolph, XIII: 313
James Smith, X: 145
James W. Fannin, X: 381
James Whitcomb Riley, X: 382
James Woodrow, IX: 390
JAMESTOWN, V: 179–80, 290
Jamison, Capt. John W., II: 80, 82n, 159, VI: 131, VIII: 69, 404
JAN VAN BRAKEL, I: 349
JANAC, III: xi, XII: ix
Jane Addams, VII: 341
Janet L. Roper, X: 382
Jannotta, Cdr. A. V., XIII: 44n, 49, 322
Jansen, Cdr. E. A., XII: 419
Jansen, Ch. Boats. L. M., III: 107
JANSSEN, X: 354, 376
JANUS, IX: 344, 396
Japan, foreign policy, I: 159, III: 4–15, 36–42, 45, 64–70, 140; relations with Germany, 40–42, 45–8; influence on Atlantic war, I: 167; population, III: 5n; negotiations with U.S., 69–73, 76–8; war plans and strategy, III: 72, 82–4, 132, 164–5, IV: 4–6, 13, 255–6, V: 116–23, 188–9, 291–2, 316, 333, VI: 15–26, 90–93, 177–18, 183, 220, 275, 284–5, 394, VII: 4–18, 69–76, 136, 215, 283, 317, VIII: 10–14, 65–7, 145, 216, 219–21, 235, XII: 5–6, 66–71, 160–65, 336–8, XIII: 159–60, XIV: 16–18, 336–49; intelligence, VIII: 220, XII: 70–71; logistics, XIII: 159, 169, 285; projected invasion of, XIV: 356–8; submarine patrols off, IV: 199–206, 209–13, XII: 410–11, XIV: 91, 285–8,

291–6; surrender and occupation, 336–69

Army, Imperial, III: 162, 309, V: 143, 190, VI: 55, 274, 426–30, VII: 223, 283, VIII: 94, 118, 167, 324, 357, 373, XII: 35, 67, 354, 379, 409, XIII: 240, 251, XIV: 13; Army in government, III: 6–18; relations with Navy, VI: 19–20, 23

Army Groups, XIII: 196, 209; Southern Army, XII: 67; Second, VIII: 66, 143; Fourteenth, XII: 67; Sixteenth, III: 273n, 320; Seventeenth, V: 70, 79, 190, 334, VI: 425; Eighteenth, 54, 255, 408, VIII: 66; Thirty-first, 12–13, 167, 388; Thirty-fifth, XII: 135, 361; Army Air Force, III: 163, VI: 408, VIII: 66–7, 89, 120–22, XII: 68, 91, XIII: 14–15, 159, 240

Air Fleets, First, VIII: 218, XIII: 159; Second, 14; Third, 159; Fifth, XIV: 93; Eleventh, III: 163, 170, 361–2, V: 79–80, VI: 117–18, 284, 287, 330, 345; Twelfth, 286, VII: 65n

Aircraft, losses, III: 85, IV: 56, 140n, 293–5, VI: 403, VII: 145, 193, 198, 242, 287, 320, VIII: 38, 119, 122, 155, 174, 319–21, 367, XIII: 57–8, 89–90, 152, 156, 169–73, 179, 182–3, XIV: 22, 25, 59, 100, 250, 332, 352; pilots, V: 223, VIII: 11, XII: 69, XIII: 99; production, VI: 117, VIII: 13, XIII: 98–9, 159, XIV: 352; types, III: 94n, IV: xxiii, V: xxii, VI: xxix, 91, VII: xxv, VIII: xxiii, XII: xxv, XIII: xxxvii, XIV: xxv. *See also* Kamikazes

Air Search and Recce., III: 138, 222n, V: 20–21, VI: 307–10, 325, 351, 376, VIII: 124–6, 145, 219–20, 233–4, 256, 288, 312, XIII: 101

Coastal batteries, Solomons, V: 191, 329, VI: 110, 149, 152, 157–8, 302; Bismarcks, 420–22; Admiralties, 438, 441, 444–5; Kiska, VII: 11–12; Wake, 93; Gilberts, 119, 147, 156–7; New Guinea, VIII: 73, 108–10; Marianas, 169, 181–2, 211, 358, 362; Halmaheras, XII: 26; Leyte, 379, 391; Luzon, XIII: 114, 200; Tarakan, 262

Imperial Navy, III: 19–27, 58; big decisive battle concept, VIII: 11;

A/S W, IV: 234, VIII: 14, XII: 413–14; command, 161, III: 20; landing craft, 165–6, 180; radar & radar detectors, V: 154, 199, VI: 162, 166, 183, 220, 394, VII: 215, 283, 317, VIII: 235; submarines, IV: 195–8; motor torpedo boats, VI: 234, 241, 370, XIII: 226, 247–8, XIV: 135–7; in Jan. '45, XIII: 14, 158; Naval Base Forces, III: 162, XIII: 240; Special Base Forces, VII: 148, XIII: 196; Special Naval Landing Forces, IV: 89, VII: 122, 148, VIII: 168; torpedoes, III: 23, VI: 195. *See also* Kaiten

Merchant ship losses, IV: 5, VIII: 13, 16, 26, XIII: 281–8; cumulative, XII: 412–13

Navy, fleets, Combined, III: 25, VI: 23, 229, 286, VII: 136, 316, 319, VIII: 12, 27, 67, 94, 214, XIII: 158; T.O.s, IV: 87–9, V: 206–7, XII: 161n, 430–32, XIII: 158–9; Mobile, VIII: 214, 231, 242–9, 286–7; T.O., 216–17, 416–17, XII: 430–31; of Areas, VI: 93, 233, 394, VII: 65n, XIII: 37; First, III: 26; Second, 26, 160–61, IV: 76, VI: 323, 328, XIII: 158; Third, III: 26, 160–62, VI: 127, 284, 330, 347; Fourth, III: 25–6, 230, 244, 259–60, VII: 137, 148, 223; Fifth, III: 25–6, IV: 175, VII: 65n, XIII: 159; Sixth, III: 26, VI: 196, VII: 317, VIII: 222, XIII: 159; Eighth, IV: 256, V: 18, 79, 194, 200, VI: 92–3, 305, 426; Ninth, VIII: 67, 89

Japanese language officers, U.S. Navy, III: 30

Japara, VI: 36, 47

Jared Ingersoll, X: 266–7

Jarman, Maj. Gen. Sanderford, VIII: 332

Jarrell, Capt. A. E., VIII: 127–30, XII: 416, 427, XIII: 318, XIV: 110, 279–80, 373

Jarrett, Capt. H. B., IV: 10, VIII: 409, XII: 426, XIII: 316, XIV: 386

Jarvis, Cdr. B. C., XIII: 285

JARVIS (1912), V: 293n, VII: 37n

JARVIS (1937), III: 104, 243n, IV: 272, 295, 316, 39, 52, 55, 63n; sunk, 16

JASON, XIV: 388

Jaujard, Contre-Amiral, XI: 118–19, 215, 265–7, 282, 311–12, 316, 336, 340

JAVA, III: 273, 308, 322–57 *passim*
Java, IV: 246, XIII: 214, 276–7; invasion, III: 335–79; T.O., 333–4; chart, 374
Java Sea, Battle of, III: 342–58; charts, 348–50, 356; T.O., 333–4
JEAN BART, II: 89, 93, 96–8, 110–12, 162–5, 247–50, V: 279*n;* pic., II: 174
Jean Jadot, II: 205
Jean Nicolet, X: 299
JEANNE D'ARC, I: 30, IX: 306
JED, X: 75*n*
JEFFERS, IX: 100–21 *passim,* 191, 388, XI: 157, 161, 170, 334, 342, XIV: 225, 376
Jefferson Davis, XIII: 324
Jeffries, Lt. Cdr. J., XIV: 375
Jeffs, Capt. C. R., XII: 418, XIII: 307
Jellicoe, Capt. C. T., XI: 342
Jenkins, Lt. Cdr. C. M., XIV: 374
Jenkins, Capt. D. R., VI: 346
Jenkins, Cdr. H. L., XI: 339
Jenkins, Capt. P. H., VIII: 418, XII: 418, XIII: 309, XIV: 375
Jenkins, Chief Gunner S. G., XII: 284
Jenkins, Capt. Samuel P., IV: 91, 271, V: 86, 232, 242, 252, 255–6, XII: 417, XIII: 310–12, XIV: 378
Jenkins, Lt. Cdr. T. H., XII: 424, XIII: 315
JENKINS (1912), XIV: 88*n*
JENKINS (1942), II: 36, 91, 285, VI: 116, 145, 150, 153, 161–8, 181, 186, 190, 193, VII: 190, 339, VIII: 127, 404, XII: 416, XIII: 132, 261, 279, 309, 321–2
JENKS, X: 379
Jennette, Lt. C. R., XIV: 377
Jennings, Cdr. C. B., VIII: 409, XII: 418, XIII: 307
Jennings, Capt. R. E., VII: 352, VIII: 412
Jennings, Capt. William F., V: 270*n,* VII: 94*n*
Jensen, Lt. Cdr. C. M., I: 420, II: 37
Jensen, Ens. H. L., XII: 246–8
Jerome, Col. C. C., XIII: 194, 225, 241
JERVIS, IX: 344, 396
JERVIS BAY, I: 24
Jeschke, Col. R. H., V: 288
Jesselton, XIII: 266–7
Jester, Lt. Cdr. Maurice, I: 155
Jeter, Capt. T. P., VII: 353, VIII: 413
Jett, Lt. Cdr. C. M., IV: 271, V: 86
Jewell, Lt. N. L. A., II: 186*n,* IX: 128–9, 389

Jewett, Dr. F. B., I: 29, 222*n*
JICARILLA, XII: 429, XIII: 319, XIV: 388
Jim Bridger, XIII: 324
Jinei M., XII: 430
JINTSU, III: 26, 163, 177, 182, 274, 296, 315–54 *passim,* IV: 89, 142, V: 82, 85, 104, 295, 315, VI: 181; sunk, 184–7, 195; survivors, 190, 193–4
JINYO, sunk, XII: 409
Joans, Cdr. C. A., XIV: 380
JOBB, XIII: 322, 324
Jodl, Genoberst, IX: 173, 195, X: 356*n,* XI: 42
Joe Fellows, XIII: 313
Joe Harris, XIII: 313
Johannesen, Capt. J. R., XI: 336
Johannessen, K., VII: 334
Johansen, Lt. J. E., X: 289, 376
Johansson, N. P., X: 382
John, Mr. W. H., II: 37*n*
John Banvard, IX: 349, X: 382
John Barry, X: 302
John Bascom, IX: 319
John Burke, XIII: 44
JOHN C. BUTLER, XII: 244, 263, 268–9, 304, 421, XIII: 305, XIV: 374, 392
John Clayton, XIII: 48
JOHN D. EDWARDS, III: 160, 272, 298, 322*n,* 325–55 *passim,* 375, IV: 15*n,* XII: 140*n,* XIII: 290*n;* pic., III: 284
JOHN D. FORD, III: 158, 272, 284–5, 288–90, 322–4, 332–3, 375, XIII: 268; pic., III: 284
JOHN D. HENLEY, VIII: 411, XII: 428*n,* 429, XIII: 317, 318*n,* XIV: 374
John Dickinson, X: 382
John Dockweiler, XIII: 324
John F. Myers, X: 382
John H. Couch, VI: 328*n*
John H. Payne, IX: 390
John Hart, XIII: 313
JOHN L. WILLIAMSON, XIV: 66*n*
John La Farge, X: 312
JOHN LAND, VIII: 408, XII: 416, XIII: 308, 313
John Page, XIII: 313
JOHN PENN, I: 421, II: 26*n,* 36; sunk, VI: 229
John Penn, I: 364*n*
John Randolph, I: 172, 178
JOHN RODGERS, VII: 337, 344, VIII: 405, 418, XII: 416, XIV: 300, 332, 383
John Stevens, X: 382
John W. Griffiths, X: 382

JOHN W. WEEKS, XIII: 317, XIV: 384
John Witherspoon, I: 191*n*
Johns, Cdr. L. J., IX: 390, XII: 423, XIII: 308
Johnsen, Cdr. W. H., VIII: 230, 411, X: 375, XIII: 317
Johnson, Cdr. A. S., VIII: 411, XII: 423, XIII: 308, XIV: 387
Johnson, Rear Adm. Alfred W., I: 14-15
Johnson, Cdr. C. A., XI: 171-3, 334, XIV: 376
Johnson, Lt. C. Edwin, X: 382
Johnson, Lt. C. F., XIII: 306
Johnson, Lt. Cdr. C. V., XIII: 317
Johnson, Lt. Cdr. C. W., X: 378
Johnson, Col. Charles E., IX: 75
Johnson, Lt. Cdr. D. H., XIII: 313
Johnson, Ens. D. J., XII: 422
Johnson, Lt. Cdr. D. L., XII: 426, XIII: 317
Johnson, Capt. D. P., VIII: 409, XII: 421
Johnson, Maj. Gen. Davenport, VII: 66
Johnson, Lt. Cdr. E. A., XIII: 206, 306
Johnson, Capt. E. R., VII: 338, 346, VIII: 409
Johnson, Mr. Edwin E., I: 395
Johnson, Lt. Cdr. Elias, VII: 334, 348
Johnson, Cdr. F. J., VIII: 410
Johnson, Rear Adm. Felix L., V: xi, VI: xii, 297, XIV: 384
Johnson, Cdr. Frank L., V: 328*n*, XIV: 192-3, 381
Johnson, Capt. G. W., I: 79, 420, XIII: 310 12
Johnson, Maj. Gen. H. H., XIV: 360
Johnson, Capt. Henry C., XI: 249, 338
Johnson, Col. Howard R., XI: 90
Johnson, Lt. Cdr. Irving M., XII: 49, XIV: 72
Johnson, Chief Gunner J. D., IX: 362
Johnson, Lt. L. E., XI: 253*n*
Johnson, Lt. L. L., VI: 331, VII: 339, XII: 424
Johnson, Cdr. M. G., XIII: 316, XIV: 383
Johnson, Lt. Cdr. M. J., XIV: 387
Johnson, Lt. P. C., XI: 126
Johnson, Mr. P. H., X: 382
Johnson, Lt. Cdr. Raymond W., II: 39
Johnson, Commo. Robert C., XIV: 62*n*
Johnson, Lt. Cdr. Robert R., IV: 91
Johnson, Lt. Robert T., X: 227

Johnson, Lt. Cdr. Robert W., XIII: 305, XIV: 374
Johnson, Lt. (jg) Roscoe E., X: 214
Johnson, Capt. Roy L., VI: 331, VII: 339
Johnson, Lt. S. D., X: 104
Johnson, Capt. W. D., VII: 346, VIII: 405, 420, XII: 420
Johnson, Cdr. W. H., XII: 429
Johnson, Lt. (jg) William E., V: 208, 266*n*
Johnston, Col. E. S., II: 115*n*
Johnston, Cdr. Harry D., VI: 228
Johnston, Lt. Cdr. J. L., XIII: 307
Johnston, Lt. Cdr. Means, X: 379
JOHNSTON, VII: 245, 346-7, VIII: 223-4, 419; Battle off Samar, XII: 244, 255-7, 263, 266-8, 272-5, 278, 282-3, 421; sunk, 273-4; survivors, 313, 316; pic., 279
Johnston I., III: 33*n*, 84, 211, 216, 219-20, 242, 257, IV: 252, 276
Johnstone, Lt. O. P., X: 102
Johore M., VI: 70
Joint, defined, II: 23*n*, VI: x
Joint Assault Signal Companies, VIII: 325, 397*n*; pic., XIV: 70
Joint Board, II: 24, III: 52, 73*n*
Joint Chiefs of Staff, planning, VII: 9-12, 15, XI: 51; air controversy, I: 245; landing craft, II: 270; directives, IV: 260-61, VI: 7, 95-6, 132, 139, VIII: 9-10, 45, 61, 91, 95, 158, XII: 18, XIII: 5, XIV: 4-5, 80; beef up Pacific Fleet, VII: 85, 46; initiate Engineer Special Brigades, VIII: 2; and NEI oil, 140; and British Pacific Fleet, XIII: 256-7, XIV: 104; occupation of Japan, 354-6; Joint Strategic and War Plans Committees of, VII: 82, XI: 8-9. *See also* Strategy
Joint Intelligence Center, Pacific (JICPOA), XII: 32
Joint Munitions Assignment Board, X: 40
Jolly, Lt. Cdr. J. C., XIV: 261
Jolo, III: 163, 182-3, 335, XIII: 226-7; chart, 224
Jomard Passage, IV: 30-31, 41
Jones, Lt. Cdr. A. T., XIII: 307, XIV: 380
Jones, Cdr. B., XI: 175
Jones, Cdr. C. A., VII: 337
Jones, Capt. C. H., VII: 338

Jones, Lt. Cdr. Carl E., X: 124, 376
Jones, Cdr. Carlton B., XII: 426, XIII: 317, XIV: 383
Jones, Capt. Carroll B., XIII: 312
Jones, Mr. & Mrs. Charles, IV: 168, 181
Jones, Capt. D. M., III: 392
Jones, Lt. Cdr. E. K., VIII: 415
Jones, Cdr. Edward H., I: 215, XI: 333
Jones, Lt. Cdr. F. R., VII: 333
Jones, Cdr. G. M., VII: 344, VIII: 407, XII: 418, XIII: 308
Jones, Lt. Col. George M., VIII: 139
Jones, Cdr. H. M., XIII: 322
Jones, Lt. Cdr. H. R., X: 378
Jones, Rear Adm. J. Cary, I: 213, XIII: 317, XIV: 313, 316, 331, 384
Jones, Lt. Cdr. J. E., X: 212
Jones, Capt. James L., VII: 180–81, 225n, 227
Jones, Lt. Lawrence F., XI: 193
Jones, Brig. Gen. Lloyd E., VII: 18
Jones, Col. Louis R., VII: 246, VIII: 187, 199
Jones, Col. M. E., XIII: 306
Jones, Ens. P. H., XII: 422
Jones, Lt. Cdr. R. M., VIII: 409, XII: 421
Jones, Lt. Cdr. Robert E. C., V: 353
Jones, Lt. Cdr. W. F., XIII: 309
Jones, Cdr. Wilbur G., V: 205, 232, XIII: 307
Jones, Maj. William K., VII: 172–4, 227n
Joost, Mr. E., VII: 334
Jordan, Lt. Cdr. J. L., VIII: 415
Jordan, Lt. Cdr. R. A., XI: 340, 343
Jordan, Col. W. I., I: 77n, VII: 166, 172–3
Jordan, Lt. Cdr. William, VII: 348, VIII: 410
José Navarro, X: 276n
JOSEPH E. CAMPBELL, IX: 313n, X: 256, 372
Joseph G. Cannon, IX: 164
Joseph Henry, VII: 334
JOSEPH HEWES, I: 352, 421, II: 38, 79, 168, 172; sunk, 169, 283
Joseph Pulitzer, IX: 386
JOSEPH T. DICKMAN, I: 111, 421, II: 28n, 38, 58–62, 75, 84, 172, IX: 95–6, 259, 388, 392, XI: 102, 333, 340, XIV: 379
JOSEPH TOOLE, XIII: 313

Joshima, Rear Adm. T., V: 84, 151, 154, 169, VI: 98, VIII: 217, 249, 264, 416
Josiah Snelling, XIV: 272
Josselyn, Henry, VI: 192–3
Josselyn, Capt. J. W., XI: 334
Joubert, Air Chief Marshal Sir Philip, X: 12, 17, 27n, 88–9, 106
JOUETT, I: 15n, 84, 377, 390n, 420, X: 210, 213n, 220, 227–8, 370, XI: 275, 342
Joy, Rear Adm. C. Turner, pic., XIV: 167; mentioned, III: 387–8, V: 353, 358–9, VII: 334; Comcrudiv 6, VIII: 181, 378, 381, 399, 409, 415, XII: 424–5, XIII: 316, XIV: 119, 372; on *Laffey*, 237
Joyce, Lt. Cdr. G. P., XII: 425, XIII: 306
Joyce, 1st Lt. R. O., III: 392
JOYCE, X: 318–19, 372
Juan de Fuca, XIII: 35–6, 48
Juin, Gen. Alphonse, II: 9, 65, 87n, 186–7, 209, 217, IX: 333, 375
Jukes, Lt. H. L., IV: 174, 215
Jukka M., III: 275, 288n
Julia Ward Howe, I: 356–7
JUNEAU, I: 419, V: 80, 112, 205, 229–56 *passim*; sunk, 257
Junecrest, X: 382
Jungerheld, Lt. Cdr. E. L., XIII: 310
Junk battle, XIII: 300–301
Junker, Capt. A. F., VII: 341, VIII: 418
JUNYO, IV: 133, 172, 176–80, 184, V: 202, 206n, 209, 214, 218, 220–22, 234, 235n, 260, 267n, 286, VI: 118, VII: 6, 217, 249, VIII: 217, 249, 264, 272, 294–5, 416, XII: 161, XIV: 285
JUPITER (1913), X: 37
JUPITER (1942), VII: 341, VIII: 407, XII: 417, XIII: 309
JUPITER, HMS, III: 272, 333, 339–56 *passim*, sunk, 256
Jupp, Capt. S. D., IV: 20
Jurasevich, Chief Gunner Marko, I: 368
Jurewicz, Lt. Cdr. E. L., XIII: 318, XIV: 387
Jurika, Lt. Stephen, III: 391
Jushin, VIII: 340
Just, Lt. Cdr. F. W., XIII: 319
Justice, Boatswain, C. C., V: 120n
Justo Arosomeno, XIII: 313
Jutland, Battle of, XII: 159n, 241

K

K-gun, I: 210; pic., 344
K-7 through K-18, III: 273; K-7, 304; K-14, 191, 288n; K-18, 288n, 290
Kaafjord, X: 308n
Kabaena I., VI: 85
Kabakan, XIII: 244–6
Kabat, Lt. H. R., V: 167
Kabler, Lt. W. T., III: 159
Kachidoki M., III: 155, XII: 400
Kachosan M., VII: 14
KADASHAN BAY, XII: 244–6, 308, 420, XIII: 19, 117, 134, 306, 326
Kadena airfield, XIV: 83, 91, 135, 153, 171, 216, 243, 269–70
Kafka, Roger, VII: 163n
KAGA, III: 22, 27, 86–8, 276, 334, IV: xi, 88, 103, 106n, 115, 120, 123; sunk, 125–7
Kagawa, Capt. K., VI: 353–6
KAGERO, III: 87, IV: 89, V: 84–5, 104, 206, 234, 280, 297–8, 302, 307, 323; sunk, VI: 115
Kahili, VI: 90, 120, 128, 206, 230–31, 240, 245, 280–83, 291, 296, 426; mine field, 111–12
Kahoolawe, VII: 210, 252, VIII: 171, 180
Kaiser, Henry J., X: 41–2; class, VII: 141n
Kaiten (human torpedoes), XII: 51–3, XIV: 18–19, 160, 317–18
Kaitner, Cdr. W. E., VII: 338, 349, VIII: 413, XII: 425, XIII: 306
Kaizuka, Rear Adm. T., XII: 430
Kajioka, Rear Adm. S., III: 231–2, 245, 254, IV: 17, 45
Kajiwara, Capt. S., XII: 431
KAKO, III: 26, 245, IV: 18, V: 35, 47, 60; sunk, IV: 226, V: 61; pic., 43
Kaku, Capt. T., IV: 137
Kakuta, Vice Adm. K., III: 163, 276, IV: 94, 170–72, 175–84, V: 199–200, 206, 220, 234, VIII: 219n, 234, 260, 263, 289–90, 321, 357
KALININ BAY, VIII: 410, XII: 244, 273, 276–8, 282, 303, 313, 421
KALK, VI: 444, VIII: 111, 116, 132, 403
KALOLI, IV: 93
Kaltenbacher, Lt. Cdr. R. J., XIV: 380

Kamaishi bombardment, XIV: 312–13
Kamakura M., VI: 78
Kamen, X: 356
Kamikawa M., III: 338, IV: 18, 32, 42, 89, VII: 6–7
Kamikazes, origin and initial attack, XII: 101, 166, 244, XIII: 99; defense against, 53–8, 147–8; attacks off Leyte, XII: 300–306, 313, 342–5, 348, 358–9, 366–8, 374, 380–84, 388–92, XIII: 9, 52–3, 180–82; Mindoro, 21–6, 29–36, 43–8; Lingayen, 98–119, 125–6, 133, 137, 141, 143–52, 325–6; Iwo, XIV: 52–6; Okinawa, 93, 116, 124, 133, 154, 175–98, 216, 221–30, 233–9, 244, 247–50, 251–62, 267–82; on TF 57, 264–5; on TF 58, 94–102, 199, 209–14; no. expended and survived, 352; list of victims, 389–92; charts, 183, 234; pics., XII: 302, XIII: 36–7, XIV: 206–7, 294–5
Kaminsky, Lt. Cdr. Harold, III: 97
Kamiri, VIII: 135–6, 139
Kamo M., VI: 63
KAMOI, VI: 81–4
Kamoto, Capt. H., VIII: 89
Kanaoka, Capt. S., VI: 244–5
KANARIS, IX: 162
KANAWHA, IV: 273; sunk, VI: 121–2
Kanda, Lt. Gen., VI: 425, 428–31
Kane, Lt. H. J., I: 156
Kane, Capt. J. D. H., I: 420, VIII: 409n
Kane, Capt. J. L., XII: 420
Kane, Lt. Cdr. W. R., VII: 348, VIII: 297
KANE, IV: 174, VII: 42, 227, 288, 291, 335, 347, VIII: 404, 408, 419, XII: 422
Kanemitsu, Sgt. Maj., IV: 237–8, 240
Kaneohe Bay, III: 32, 122
Kangleon, Col. R. K., XII: 64–5
KANIMBLA, VIII: 77, 403, XII: 416, XIII: 265n, 272n, 310–12
KANKAKEE, VI: 324, 420, VIII: 411, XII: 428, XIII: 318, XIV: 387
Kanko M., II: 162, 263, III: 304
Kano M., VII: 12
Kanooka, Capt. E., XII: 233, 431
Kanoya, III: 27, XII: 90

KANSAS, VI: 282n, IX: 191n, X: 345n
Kansu Province, XIII: 294
Kaoe, VIII: 219
Kapa-Kapa Trail, VI: 42
Kapitzky, Kaptlt. Ralph, X: 195–7
Kaplan, Cdr. A. D., IX: 396
Kara, VI: 240, 280–81, 291
Karachi, I: 160
Karafuto, XIII: 159
Karanganjan, III: 370
KARANJA, II: 193, 195n, 220; sunk, 284
Karig, Capt. Walter, and W. Kelley, *Battle Report*, III: 98n
Karimata Strait, III: 297, 338
Karin, I: 384–5
KARLSRUHE, I: 4n
Karpe, Cdr. E. S., II: 38, III: 160, VII: 223, 338, 349, VIII: 413
Karsik, VI: 47
KASAAN BAY, XI: 342, XIV: 318
Kasba, II: 117–18, 121–26; pic., 130
Kase, Toshikazu, pic., XIV: 366–7; mentioned, 341, 365
Kasel, Lt. (jg) J. A., XIV: 187
KASHI, XIII: 37n, 159
KASHII, III: 276, XIII: 168
KASHIMA, III: 26, IV: 17
Kashima M., III: 263, VI: 79
KASKASKIA, IV: 157, 272, VIII: 411, XII: 428, XIV: 387
KASUMI, III: 87–8, IV: 89, 216, VII: 7, XII: 190, 431, XIII: 37, 158, XIV: 202
KATOOMBA, IV: 225, VI: 36
KATORI, III: 263, IV: 87, V: 85, 207, 235; sunk, VII: 328
Katschinski, Lt. Cdr. B. H., XII: 421, XIII: 310, XIV: 375
Katsukawa M., VIII: 23
Katsura M. No. 2, VII: 53
KATSURAGI, XII: 161n, XIII: 158, XIV: 331
Katsuragi M., IV: 227, V: 177
Katy, X: 344
Katz, Lt. Cdr. Benjamin, V: 353, VI: 181, 228, 244, VII: 338
Kauffman, Cdr. Draper L., VII: 134n, VIII: 166, 183n, 184, XIV: 117n, 121, 377
Kauffman, Vice Adm. James L., biog., I: 142n; mentioned, 76, 82, 135n, 142, 208, 250, 418, VII: 210, X: 16, XIV: 320, 328, 329n
Kavieng, V: 60, VI: 208, 292, 323, 369–

70, 383, 390, 410–34 *passim;* VIII: 8–10, 49n; pic., VI: 434
Kawabe, Lt. Gen. T., XIV: 359
Kawaguchi, Maj. Gen. K., V: 109, 123–9, 190–92
Kawakami, C. H., IV: xi, XII: viii
KAWAKAZE, III: 162, 275, 334, V: 81, 85, 206, 297–8, 302, 311, 367, VI: 214–16; sunk, 218–19
Kawasaki, Capt. H., XII: 431
Kawase, Vice Adm. S., pic., VII: 54; mentioned, 39–40, 43, 48, 51, 54, 57–9, 65n
KAWEAH, I: 422
KAYA, XIII: 37n, 159
KAZAGUMO, IV: 88, V: 85, 206, 234, VI: 112, 244, 247, 250; sunk, VIII: 120
KEARNY, I: 83, 92–3, 107, 420, II: 37, 285, IX: 371, 377–8, XI: 339
Kearon, R. S., X: 381
KEARSARGE, XIII: x
Keating, Cdr. G. R., XIV: 375
Keating, Capt. J. S., I: 215n, 420
Keating, Cdr. R. A., XII: 429, XIII: 320
Keefer, Lt. Cdr. J. R., XII: 421, XIII: 188, 199, 306
Keeler, Cdr. F. S., VIII: 410, XII: 426, XIII: 316, XIV: 386
Keeler, Cdr. Harry, V: 305, VII: 334
Keeling, Lt. Cdr. J. R., XIV: 196
Keeling, Lt. (jg) R. F., XIII: 40
Keene, Cdr. Campbell, III: 225
Keene, Lt. (jg) G. F., VII: 333
Kehl, Lt. G. W., I: 421
Keighley, Lt. Cdr. W. H., VIII: 410, XII: 421
Keijo M., IV: 18, VII: 53n
Keiko M., III: 162, IV: 224
Keise Shima, XIV: 127, 138, 180
Keisho M., VI: 275
Keitel, Feldmarschall Wilhelm, IX: 69
Keith, Lt. Cdr. H. H., III: 158, 196n, 272n
Keith, Lt. Cdr. L. W. J., XIII: 317
Keith, Cdr. R. T. S., VII: 338, VIII: 404, XII: 417, XIII: 404
KEITH, X: 354–5, 378
Keithly, Cdr. R. M., XIV: 286
Keiyo M., VIII: 175
Keizan M., VII: 14
Keliher, Capt. T. J., VI: 11n, VIII: 415, XIV: 382
Kelleher, Capt. D. A., VIII: 340n, 366, 369

Keller, Maj. Gen. R. F. L., XI: 181
KELLET, XI: 116, 335
Kelley, Capt. F. H., I: 111–12
Kelley, Col. G. W., VIII: 206
Kelley, Lt. Cdr. J. L., VIII: 410, XIV: 237, 379
Kelley, Cdr. L. E., IX: 386
Kelley, Cdr. R. B., XIV: 373
Kelley, Lt. Cdr. Stanley J., XIV: 63
Kelley, Capt. T. J., XIV: 384
Kellogg, Lt. Cdr. D. M., X: 279, 319, 377
Kellogg, Lt. Cdr. F. D., XI: 336
Kelly, Maj. B. T., VI: 192
Kelly, Capt. C. P., III: 180n
Kelly, Lt. J. C., VI: 331
Kelly, Ens. James J., V: 368
Kelly, Ens. M. L., X: 382
Kelly, Rear Adm. Monroe, II: 33, 36, 54, 117–19, 123–4, 132, IX: 351
Kelly, Lt. Cdr. Robert B., VI: 145, 151, 155, 213
Kelly, Cdr. T. D., XI: 339
Kelly, Capt. Thomas J., IV: 174, XIII: 308
Kelly, Cdr. W. D., VIII: 409
Kelsey, Capt. J. D., VII: 337, VIII: 407, XII: 419, XIII: 311, XIV: 378
Keltch, Ens. Rubin, X: 185
Kembu M., VI: 55–6
Kemp, Lt. E. L., XIV: 374
Kemp, Col. J. D., VIII: 165n, 183n
Kemp, Cdr. Peter K., XI: x
KEMPENFELT, IX: 396
Kendall, Cdr. C. H., XII: 426, XIII: 316, XIV: 383
Kendall, Lt. E. F., VIII: 261n
Kendall, Capt. H. S., VI: 146
Kendall, Lt. Cdr. J. E., XIV: 387
KENDALL C. CAMPBELL, XIII: 305, XIV: 374
Kendari, III: 293, 298, 307, 315–16, 361–2, 376, 382
KENDRICK, IX: 376–8, 389, X: 261, XI: 312, 316, 341
KENMORE, VII: 348, VIII: 410
Kennard, Lt. Cdr. R. A., XII: 428
Kennaday, Lt. Cdr. J. M., I: 418
KENNEBAGO, VIII: 411, XII: 104, 428, XIII: 318
KENNEBEC, I: 422, II: 37, 40n, 133, X: 158, 293
Kennedy, Lt. D. S., XI: 299n
Kennedy, Donald G., VI: 141–2
Kennedy, Lt. John F., VI: 211–12

Kennedy, Cdr. M. G., VIII: 409, XIV: 374
Kennedy, Thomas, X: 382
Kenneth A. J. Mackenzie, VII: 334
KENNETH WHITING, XIV: 279
Kenney, Lt. Gen. George C., pic., XIII: 276; Solomons, IV: 274, 279, 292, V: 115, VI: 90, 208; Pacific Mil. Conf., 7; New Guinea, 42–4, 125, 136–7, 255–6, 259–65, 373, VIII: 61, 66–7, 87, 220; Bismarck Sea Battle, VI: 57–9, 63–4; Rabaul, 275, 286–8, 292, 328, 332, 393–4; Cape Gloucester, 381–3; Com A.A.F. Sowespac, VIII: 46–9, 64n, XII: 60; Carolines, VIII: 156; Philippines, XII: 7, 72, 107, 136–7, 150–51, 354, 367, 376, XIII: 8–9, 21–2, 106, 156, 187; Labuan, 265; *General Kenney Reports*, VI: 27n
Kenney, Lt. R. L., XIV: 384n
Kenny, Capt. W. T., VII: 347, XII: 426, XIII: 317
KENOVA, XI: 333
KENTON, XIV: 380
Kentucky, I: 364n
KENWOOD, XIII: 307n, 308
Kenworthy, Cdr. J. L., III: 110
KENYA, I: 168
Kenyo M., IV: 88, VI: 73, VII: 222
KEOKUK, VIII: 329, 410, IX: 110, 385, XIV: 55–6, 377
KEOSANQUA, VIII: 420
KEPHART, XIII: 307, 321–4
Kepke, 2nd Lt. J. E., V: 374
KEPPEL, I: 179, X: 82, 143, 308
Kerama Retto, XIV: 117–19; chart, 84, 123; pic., 118; occupied, 58, 88, 112, 118–27, 360; casualties, 126; base, 117, 124–6, 161–4, 185–262 *passim*, 286–71, 295
Keravat, VI: 393, 406
KEREN, II: 193–5, 204, IX: 150, 156
Kernodle, Capt. M. H., XII: 427, XIII: 317, XIV: 382
Kerr, Col. J. E., XI: 102
Kesselring, Feldmarschall Albert, IX: 46–7, 51, 163, 171–2, 197, 201–2, 220–343 *passim*, 360–83 *passim*, XI: 228, 291, 295, 310–12, 320
Kessing, Commo. O. O. ("Scrappy"), V: 187, VI: 102, 181, 190, 279n, 365, 428, 431, XII: 49–52, 341, XIII: 183, XIV: 110
Kessler, 1st Lt., III: 232

Keswick, III: 159, 204-5
Ketcham, Commo. Dixwell, VII: 338, 346, VIII: 405, 420, XII: 46n, 49, XIV: 8, 381
KETE, XIV: 289
Kettenring, Lt. Cdr. J. C., XIV: 376
Kevern, Lt. Cdr. E. J., IX: 389
KEY, XIII: 248
Key West, I: 135-6, 240, 256, 260-64, 348; Sound School, see East Coast
Keyes, Cdr. C. M., XIII: 304, XIV: 274n, 375
KHEDIVE, XI: 342
Kibbe, Cdr. R. L., XII: 327n, 427
Kidd, Rear Adm. Isaac C., III: 101n, 108
KIDD, VI: 331, 334, VII: 190, 339, 348, VIII: 405, 410, 420, XIV: 210-11, 384, 391
Kido, Marquis, VI: 16, VIII: 340, XIV: 337, 341, 345-50
Kiefer, Capt. Dixie, XIII: 181, 317
Kieffer, Lt. de Vaisseau, XI: 185
Kiehl, Capt. Elmer, XIV: 177, 375
Kiel, X: 318, 341, XI: 326
Kieta, VI: 281-4
Kiirun, XIII: 91, 179, 182
KIJI, VIII: 120n
Kijima, Capt. K., V: 161, 169
Kikusui, XIV: 181, 233-9, 253-63, 274, 278-80
KIKUZUKI, IV: 17, 26
Kiland, Rear Adm. Ingolf N., biog., XIII: 93n; mentioned, IV: 273, V: 231, VI: 98-9, XIII: 93, 96, 125-7, 143, 310, XIV: 108, 118-21, 127, 375
KILAUTEA, I: 422
Kilduff, Lt. T. A., XIV: 98, 99n
Kiley, Lt. Cdr. J. C., X: 346, 378
Kili Atoll, VII: 312
KILLEN, XII: 153, 199, 218, 344, 421
KILMARNOCK, X: 372
Kilpatrick, Lt. Cdr. MacGregor, V: 360-62, XIV: 383
KILTY, VI: 145, 152, 156n, 228, 295, 381, 415, VIII: 404, XII: 417, XIII: 307, XIV: 374
Kimball, Dr. G. E., I: 224
Kimball, Lt. Cdr. W. F., XIV: 376
KIMBERLY, VII: 336, XI: 232, 247, XIII: 304, XIV: 124, 375, 390
Kimbrell, B. M., IV: 156n
Kimes, Lt. Col. I. E., IV: 92, 105
Kimihara, Maj. Gen., VI: 399-400, 403, 407-8

Kimikawa M., IV: 172, VII: 40, 43, 48
Kimmel, Adm. Husband E., III: 47, 61n, 74, 79, 89, 97, 101, 139, 210-15, 219-22, 225-7, 235-7, 241, 249-50; question of responsibility, 128-37
Kimmel, Cdr. M. M., VIII: 24
Kimmu Wan, XIV: 83, 277
Kimura, Rear Adm. M., pic., VII: 54; mentioned, VI: 55-8, VII: 57-9, XII: 431, XIII: 37, 40-42, 157
Kimura, Rear Adm. S., IV: 88, V: 85, 206, 233-4, 273-80, VIII: 416, XII: 272-3, 274n, 431
Kinai M., VI: 37
Kinaszczuk, Lt. (jg) Thomas, X: 180
Kincaid, Cdr. E. H., VI: 279n, XIII: 95
Kinch, Capt. R. E., VI: 145
Kindell, Capt. N. M., XIV: 385
Kindley Field, Bermuda, pic., I: 36
Kindley Field, Corregidor, XIII: 202
King, Lt. Cdr. C. A., I: 349
King, Hon. David W., II: 6n, 67
King, Cdr. E. R., VIII: 405, 419, XII: 418, XIV: 384
King, Flt. Adm. Ernest J., biog., I: 51n; pics., frontispiece, 36, 70, IV: 18, XIV: 366; Cinclant, I: 14, 215; Cominch and CNO, 114; staff, 116; "making the best," 52-3; defines Western Hemisphere, 61, 74; Op Plans, 74, 78-9, 82-3; reply to Gen. Marshall, 309-10; amphibious warfare, liv-lv, II: 20, 61n, VI: 131; AAF controversy, I: 241-6, 308-9, X: 27-31; detains battleships in Atlantic, I: 167; convoys, 95, 310, X: 9, 19, 88; volunteer efforts, I: 269, 275; Q-ships, 282; N. Africa, II: 12, 15, 41, 255; Pearl Harbor aftermath, III: 214, 257-8, 260-61, 265; Sowespac, 312, 387-90, IV: 249n; bases, III: 258, IV: 163, 248, 252; Coral Sea, 44n; Midway, 80, 143; torpedoes, 222; Guadalcanal, 245-8, 259-65, 268, V: 12, 62, 178, 183-5; Casablanca Conf., VI: 3-5, IX: 5-9; 1943 plans, 9, 12, 60, 93n, 130-31; numbered fleets, 97; logistics VII: 101, 110, XIV: 157; Saipan, VIII: 5-6; Scoffs at Kiralfy, 11; order to subs, 19; on "A.B.C.," IX: 14; Quebec Conf., 229-30; A/S survey board, X: 17n; Tenth Fleet, 21-5; "horse trade," 27-31; "1799" program, 33-5; orders A/S officers retained, 49;

relieves A/S submarines, 87; A/S aircraft controversy, 88, 91–5, 101–2, 106, 130, 186n; escort carriers, 19, 41, 307; Azores Command, 45; and Gen. Marshall, XI: 22; invasion of France, 13–14, 52–5, 66n, 222, 229, 238, 296; of Germany, 318, 325; Pacific strategy 1944–5, XII: 4–7, 11, 289, XIII: 3–5, 12, XIV: 4, 352; promoted Flt. Adm., XIII: 156; Lingayen, 170; and R.N., 257–8, 263, 386, XIV: 103–4; typhoon, 308; *Fleet Adm. King*, XI: xv; mentioned or quoted, I: 70, 205, III: 129, IV: 223, VII: 79–80, 85, 233, 281, IX: 29, X: 8, 251, 357, XIII: 58, 176

King, Lt. Cdr. F. R., XIII: 319
King, Cdr. G. C., XIV: 377
King, Lt. Cdr. J. D., XI: 339
King, Cdr. L. M., VII: 347, XIV: 381
King, Lt. Cdr. R. E., XIV: 387
King, W. L. Mackenzie, I: 32, X: 5, XII: 15
KING, IV: 174, VII: 333
KING GEORGE V, I: 165, 168, 171, VIII: 228n, IX: 167, 236, XIV: 105, 211–13, 264, 316, 333, 388; pic., I: 210
KING SALVOR, II: 251
KINGFISH, IV: 212–13, XIII: 319, XIV: 107, 286
KINGFISHER, VII: 341
Kingman, Rear Adm. H. F., VII: 243, 334, 337, 346, VIII: 197, 409, XII: 34
Kings Pt., I: 295
Kingsley, Lt. Cdr. M. P., I: 420
Kingston, I: 12
KINGSTON CEYLONITE, I: 417
Kinkaid, Adm. T. C., biog., V: 88n, XII: 55n–6n; pics., VI: 435–8, VII: 55, XII: 7, XIII: frontispiece; assistance, XII: 157; Comdesron 8, I: 111; Coral Sea, IV: 18, 59–60; Midway, 91; Solomons, 271, 280, V: 86, 95, 189; Sta. Cruz Battle, 201–4, 207–17, 220; Guadalcanal Battle, 227–8, 232, 259–62, 268–72, 291–4, 372; Comnorpacfor, 293n; Aleutians, VII: 17–20, 28, 34, 37–62 passim, 66, 333; Com Seventh Fleet, VI: 97, VIII: 45n, 46–9, 55, 64n, 217, XIII: 321; Cape Gloucester, VI: 385; Admiralties, 435–8; New Guinea, VIII: 63, 73, 91, 94, 122–6, 135, 403; Leyte, XII: 16, 55–6, 60, 72–4, 77, 113, 118, 122, 125, 138, 343, 346, 376, 393, 415; Leyte Gulf Battle, 174, 189n,

190–95, 198–9, 202–4, 234, 245, 285, 289–99, 304, 314, 329, 339–40; Mindoro, XIII: 39; Lingayen, 6–14, 18, 89, 98, 107, 111, 115, 118, 135, 145–8, 153, 156, 161, 303; and size of Seventh Fleet, 174–7; later Philippine opns., 184, 215; Borneo, 272; China occupation, 302, XIV: 355–7
Kinney, Cdr. S. H., X: 279, 377, XI: xvi
Kinposan M., V: 348
Kinryu M., V: 82, 85, 104
Kinsella, Cdr. W. T., I: 421, XIII: 288
Kinsey, Lt. (jg) P. A., X: 381
Kinsley, Lt. Cdr. F. W., XIII: 319, XIV: 374
Kintberger, Cdr. L. S., XII: 257, 262, 421, XIV: 227, 373
KINTYRE, XI: 339
KINU, VIII: 118–20, 125, 130, XII: 164, 169n, 431; sunk, 239
KINUGASA, III: 26, 245, IV: 18, V: 35, 40, 47, 50, 60, 85, 104–5, 150–264 passim; sunk, 61n, 266
Kinugasa M., IV: 172
Kinugawa M., V: 234, 283
KINZER, XIV: 220, 375
KIOWA, XI: 173, 337
Kip, Lt. (jg) R. F., X: 352
Kippen, Lt. R. F., XIII: 318, XIV: 383
Kiralfy, Alexander, VIII: 10–11, 173
Kircher, Cdr. J. J., XIV: 305n
KIRI, XII: 430, XIII: 159
KIRISHIMA, III: 26, 87, 378, 382, IV: 88, V: 82, 85, 100n, 203, 206, 214, 233–80 passim; sunk, 281
Kirishima M, VI: 79
Kiriwina. *See* Trobriand Is.
Kirk, Rear Adm. Alan G., biog., IX: 126n; pics., 130, XI: 52; assistance, IX: xi; staff conversations, I: 45; N. Africa, II: 16–17; Sicily, IX: 16, 28–31, 61, 64–5, 93, 124–31, 138–43, 144n, 224, 388–9; Normandy, 246, XI: 21, 29–30, 37, 52–4, 65, 69–71, 81–2, 126, 150–52, 155, 162, 168, 178–9, 196–7, 214–15, 333; French mop-up, 304, 309; invasion of Germany, 317, 326
Kirk, Cdr. F. S., VIII: 411
Kirk, Lt. Cdr. O. G., IV: 20, 224–5
Kirkby, Lt. G. J., XI: 336
Kirkenes, I: 166
Kirkpatrick, Cdr. C. C., IV: 201–2, 216, XIV: 255, 376
Kirkpatrick, Lt. C. E., XII: 33

Kirkpatrick, Cdr. C. S., I: 229, XIII: 104, 305, XIV: 374
Kirkpatrick, Lt. R. C., V: 135
Kirn, Lt. Cdr. L. J., IV: 270, V: 86, 95, 100
Kirtland, Capt. F. D., I: 76, 90, 418, VIII: 349, X: 6, 230
Kirvan, Cdr. W. H., XIV: 196, 376
KISARAGI, III: 231n; sunk, 234
Kishi, Rear Adm. F., IV: 89
Kishi, Capt. Y., XII: 430
KISHINAMI, VIII: 416, XII: 172, 431
KISHWAUKEE, XII: 82, 423, XIV: 387
Kiska I., IV: 168–70, 175, 215, VII: 8, 18, 40, 51; Japs. in, IV: 181–3, VII: 6, 13–15; air raids and bombardment, 5–6, 8–14, 39, 54–62; chart, 11; Jap. evacuation of, 56–9; U.S. invasion, 62–4; "Tales of K.," ballad, 64n
KISO, III: 26, IV: 172, VII: 58; sunk, XII: 356
Kita, Ikki, III: 10–12
KITAGAMI, IV: 89, XII: 239, XIV: 331
Kitazano, Maj. Gen., VIII: 67
Kitch, Cdr. W. L., XIII: 281, 320
Kitchen, Lt. J. S., XIV: 385
KITCHENER, XI: 337
KITE, I: 422, X: 93, 96, 151–2
KITKUN BAY, VIII: 360, 410, XII: 244, 253, 276–8, 281, 302–3, 308, 421, XIII: 117–19, 144, 305, 325
Kittaninny, X: 297–8
Kittredge, Capt. Tracy B., I: 38n, IV: xi, 245n
Kitts, Capt. W. A., V: 205, 219, 296, 306, 311, VII: 334
KITTSON, XIV: 380
KITTYHAWK, IV: 86
Kivette, Lt. Cdr. F. N., IV: 173
KIWI, V: 349–50
Kiyokawa M., IV: 18
KIYONAMI, VI: 181; sunk, 191n, 207
KIYOSHIMO, XII: 186, 356, 431, XIII: 37n, 42
Kiyosumi M., VII: 325, VIII: 17
Klain, Lt. D. P., XII: 146n
Klakring, Lt. Cdr. T. B., IV: 194, 209–10, V: 348
Klamano, VIII: 140
Klandasan, XIII: 271
Klare, Lt. Cdr. H. H., XIII: 317
Klein, Lt. Cdr. Millard J., IX: 42–3, 83, 312, 386; pic., 43
Kliewer, Lt. D. D., III: 231

Kline, Capt. E. C., XI: 337
Kline, Lt. Cdr. W. F., IV: 93
KLINE, XIV: 378
Klingman, Lt. R. R., XIV: 269
Klinker, Cdr. R. C., XIII: 319
Klinsmann, Cdr. G. O., X: 232, XIII: 317
Knapp, Cdr. R. A., I: 421
KNAPP, VII: 348, VIII: 414, XII: 319, 425, XIII: 318
Kneeland, Capt. O. A., XIV: 387
Kneupfer, Cdr. George, XI: 334
Knickerbocker, Cdr. H. P., VIII: 407, XII: 419
Knight, Cdr. A. V., VI: 382, VIII: 404, XII: 417
Knight, Lt. G. W., XIV: 377
KNIGHT, I: 420, II: 40, 143, 285, IX: 130, 191, 251n, 300, 389, 392
Knispel, A. W., X: 292
Knockerbocker, Cdr. H. P., XIII: 311
Knoertzer, Cdr. H. A., VI: 144, 243n, VII: 349, XII: 426, XIII: 317, XIV: 383
Knowles, Commo. Herbert B., IV: 273, 287n, VII: 155, 259–60, 335–7, 344, VIII: 407, 420, XII: 419, XIII: 310–12, XIV: 378
Knowles, Cdr. K. A., II: 167n, X: 24
Knowlton, Lt. Cdr. E. B., XIV: 377
Knox, Lt. Cdr. D. S., X: 291–2, 378–9
Knox, Commo. Dudley W., X: 28, XIII: xi, xvii–xviii; chap. on U.S. Navy between World Wars, I: xxxiii–lxii
Knox, Hon. Frank, biog., I: 29n; pics., 36, III: 190; mentioned, I: 29, 33, 41–6, 54, 65–6, 291, II: 7n, III: 58, 101n, 128, 140, 154, 250, 312, 338, V: 62, 178, 226, 344, X: vii, 9, 11n, 32–4
Knox, Hon. John C., II: 6n
KNOX, VIII: 408, XII: 418, XIII: 311
Knudsen, Mr. L. W., X: 382
KNUDSON, XIV: 120, 377
Kobayashi, Vice Adm. M., VII: 137
Kobayashi, Rear Adm. T., III: 162, 177
Kobe, Rear Adm. Y., XII: 430
Kobe, III: 394–6, XIV: 94, 331
Kobey, Cdr. T. H., VII: 349, XII: 418
Koch, Boatswain W. H., IX: 175
KOCHAB, XIV: 387
Kocorana, V: 364
Kodiak I., III: 32, IV: 163–7, 171–4, 182, VII: 4–5, 9–10, 13
Kodo-Ha, III: 10–12
Koehler, Lt. E. B., XI: 141

Koehler, Lt. Cdr. J. T., VII: 245, 252; VIII: 165*n*, 166; IX: 97*n*, 116*n*
Koei M., IV: 17
Koeltz, Gen., II: 87*n*
Koenig, Lt. Cdr. J. W., VII: 337, 350, VIII: 413, XII: 428
KOENIGSBERG, I: 4*n*
Koga, Adm. Mineichi, pic., VI: 103; C. in C. Combined Fleet, 23, 129; strategy, 24, 284-6, VIII: 12; Solomons, VI: 139, 156*n*, 207, 289, 305, 323, 347, 363; New Guinea, 271, 390; Aleutians, VII: 43, 49; Gilberts, 136-7; Marshalls, 210, 223; Truk raid, 319, VIII: 27; Z-plan, 173, 217; death, 13
Kogen M., XII: 404*n*
Koiso, Gen. K., VIII: 340, XIV: 172, 337
Kojima, Army Capt., VI: 202, 205
Kojima, Navy Capt., III: 308
Kokai M., VI: 403
Kokuyo M., IV: 88, V: 207, VIII: 18, 417
Kola Inlet, I: 159-61, 166, 359, 367-9, X: 311-13
KÖLN, I: 4*n*
Kolombangara, V: 4, 345, VI: 110, 114, 156, 213-14, 225, 227; Battle of, VI: 180-91, 194-7; T.O., 181-2; charts, 185, 240, pic., 194; evacuation, 239-43
Kolonie, Lt. A. P., VIII: 420
Komandorski Is., Battle of, VII: 22-36, 39, XII: 230-41; chart, VII: 26-7; pic., 31
Komatsu, Warrant Officer S., VIII: 269, 279
Komatsu, Vice Adm. T., IV: 87, 196*n*, V: 85, 235
KOMET, III: 50
Komura, Capt., V: 214
Komura, Rear Adm. K., IV: 129, V: 103*n*, XIII: 158, XIV: 202
Kona Kope, VI: 53, 60-61, 127
Kondo, Vice Adm. N., pic., V: 98; mentioned, III: 26, 160-61, 164, 178, 273, 276, 316, 333, 361, 376-8, IV: 76, 88, 132-49 *passim*, V: 83-4, 101-3, 199-285 *passim*, 363
KONGO, III: 26, 161, 276, 382, IV: 88, V: 173-5, 199, 206, 234, VII: 44, 137, VIII: 416, XII: 162-3, 248-81 *passim*, 311, 431; sunk, 410; class, III: 88
Kongo M., III: 389
Kongosan M., IV: 200
Konishi, Capt. K., III: 87

Kono, Lt. Gen., XIII: 232-3
Konoye, Prince, III: 14, 36, 44-6, 65-71, 77, XIV: 337, 341
Konrad, Cdr. E. G., VII: 350, XIV: 382
Kooistra, Cdr. A. H., VII: 347, VIII: 411
Kooken, Maj. J. D., VII: 280*n*, 292*n*
Koon, Col. R. E., VI: 65
Koonce, Capt. P. B., XIV: 387
KOPARA, V: 109, 191, 284*n*
Korako, VIII: 69
Korea, XIII: 160
Kornasoren, VIII: 135, 138-9
Korns, Capt. V. E., XI: 63, 216*n*
Koror Harbor, XII: 39
KORTENAER, III: 273, 322-3; sunk, 347, 357
Kosco, Cdr. G. F., XIII: 59*n*, 60-68
Kossler, Cdr. H. J., VIII: 280-81, 415, XII: 411
Kossol Passage, III: 182, XII: 32-3, 46, 78-84, 118, 204, 304, 307, XIII: 19, 23
Kota Bharu, III: 188, 297
Kota Nopan, I: 384, X: 40
Kotaki, Capt. H., XIV: 202
Kotohiro M., VII: 17
Koumac, IV: 279*n*
Kovar, Lt. (jg) I. M., XII: 232, 422
Kowa M., VI: 403
Koyama, Capt., III: 234
K.P.M. Ships, VI: 34*n*, 36-7, 46-7, 125-7, 130
Kra Isthmus, III: 49, 55, 130, XIII: 288
Kragan, III: 379
Kraiss, Gen., XI: 153
KRAKEN, XIII: 161, 320
Kraker, Capt. G. P., XI: 341
KRAKOWIAK, IX: 393
Kramer, Lt. (jg) Irving, XI: 333
Kramer, Mr. J., X: 382
Krancke, Vizeadm. Theodor, X: 56, XI: 46-9, 87, 107, 156, 169, 174-5, 183, 211, 244
Krapf, Cdr. A. E., VIII: 416
Kratky, Ens. H. R., X: 382
Krause, Capt. R. E., VIII: 419, XII: 418
Krause, Lt. (jg) W. B., X: 101
Kreisch, Kapt., IX: 40-41
Krick, Capt. H. D., VIII: 408
Krieger, Lt. Cdr. A. P., XIV: 377
Krieger, Capt. E. M., VII: 77*n*
Kroeger, Lt. Cdr. E. J., XIII: 316
Kroese, Lt. Cdr. A., III: 333
Krueger, Lt. Gen. Walter, CG Sixth Army, pic., XIII: 156-7; mentioned, VI: 15, 274, VIII: 46-8; Staff, 64*n*;

Krueger, Lt. Gen. Walter (*cont'd*)
New Britain, VI: 374, 380–81; New Guinea, VIII: 72–83, 94–6, 102, 133–6, 141; on Hollandia, 87; Leyte, XII: 15–16, 56, 141, 151, 156, 351, 362–3, 376, 385, 393, 415; Luzon, XIII: 6–8, 12, 135, 153, 156–7, 184–5, 193, 198, 303; *From Down Under to Japan*, xi
Kruz, Chief Boatswain W. C., X: 164
Kuantan, III: 189
Kruesberg, Lt. H. F., VI: 237*n*
Krulak, Lt. Col. V. H., VI: 296
Kubo, Rear Adm. K., III: 162, 181, 274–6, 307, 320–21, 329
Kuckens, B. G. F., X: 145
Kudat, XIII: 266
Kuhn, Lt. (jg) R. C., X: 80
Kukum, V: 16, 66, 124, 141
Kula Gulf, VI: 108–10, 115, 156, 209; mine fields, 113–16; Battle of, 160–75, 195–7; T.O., 161–2; chart, 164–5, 173; pic., 170–71
Kulizak, Coxs. H. B., II: 143*n*
Kullberg, Lt. C. L., VII: 352
KUMA, III: 161; sunk, VIII: 17*n*
Kumagawa M., V: 234
Kumakawa M., III: 161
Kumamba Is., VIII: 101; chart, 93
KUMANO, III: 26, 276, 308, 334, IV: 88, 143, V: 85, 206, VI: 207, 412, VII: 40, 137–8, XII: 162, 248, 256–8, 275, 408, 431; sunk, 311, 357, 409
Kummetat, Oblt. Günther, X: 116
Kummetz, Vizeadm. Oskar, X: 230, 236–7, 238*n*
KUNASHIRI, VII: 58
Kungnat Bay, pic., I: 61
Kunming, XIII: 91, 163*n*
Kuno, Capt. S., XII: 68
Kunz, Cdr. C. A., XIV: 374
Kupang, III: 282, 284, 315–16
Kure, III: 21*n*, 27, 88, 95, VII: 137*n*, VIII: 222, 298, XII: 52, 168, 312, 335, XIII: 158–9, 331, XV: 94; pic., 102
KURETAKE, sunk, XIV: 286
Kuretake M., III: 275, 289
Kuribayashi, Gen. T., XIV: 14–15, 31, 38, 45–8, 61, 67–78, 73
Kuriles, VII: 39, VIII: 8; raids on, XII: 107
Kurita, Vice Adm. T., pic., XII: 71; N.E.I., III: 334, 338, 341, 365, VIII: 216*n*; Midway, IV: 76, 88, 143–4; Solomons, V: 173–5, 206, 234, VI:

323–30, VII: 137; Philippine Sea, VIII: 249–50, 256, 263–5, 269, 288, 292, 298–300, 416, XII: 69; Leyte and Samar battles, 61, 119, 127, 160–62, 167–343 *passim*, 430; break off, 299–300, 312
KUROSHIO, III: 163, 274, IV: 89, V: 84, 206, 297–8, 302, 307; sunk, VI: 115
Kurokawa, Lt., VII: 122
Kurtz, Capt. T. R., I: 208
KURUMBA, XIII: 308
Kurusu, S., I: 80, III: 72–3, 76
Kusaie I., VII: 84, 201–2, 213, 287, VIII: 222
Kusaka, Vice Adm. J., pic., VI: 103; mentioned, V: 125, 149, 207, 234, 347, VI: 54, 92–3, 118, 136–54 *passim*, 207, 230, 233, 238, 261, 320–85 *passim*, 394, 408, 412, 416–17, VIII: 215–16, XII: 91
Kusaka, Rear Adm. R., IV: 88, 95, 125*n*, 143–4, 148–9
Kuter, Brig. Gen. L. S., VIII: 8
Kuter, Capt. P. E., XIV: 387
KUTTABUL, IV: 65
KUWA, XII: 430, XIII: 159; sunk, XII: 371–2
Kuykendall, Gunner C. W., VIII: 31
Kuzume, Col. N., VIII: 107–8, 118, 132–3
KWAJALEIN, XII: 428; XIII: 61, 64, 67, 69*n*, 70, 319
Kwajalein Atoll and Island, III: 26, 95, 261–3, IV: 87, 94, VII: 69, 74–5, 82–4, 98*n*, 105, 137–8, 203, 206–7, 223, XIII: 60; described, VII: 230–34; charts, 231, 253, 266; air raids on, 138, 191–3, 214–15, 218–21; pic., 198–9, 282–3; capture by Pacific Fleet (opn. FLINTLOCK), 230–81; T.O., 343–51; discussions, 278–81; unloading, 268; air and naval gunfire support, 234, 255–60, 265–7; as U.S. base, 288, 306, 308, 310–12, 329, VIII: 156, 172, 219, 260, 313, 343–5, 348, XIV: 158
Kweilin, XII: 5
Kyes, Cdr. J. E., I: 420, X: 174–5, 376
Kyle, Col. W. B., VIII: 408
Kyle, Maj. W. R., VII: 165
Kyle V. Johnson, XIII: 150, 313, 326
Kyllberg, Lt. V. H., IX: 387, 392
KYNE, XII: 429, XIII: 319
Kyokuei M., VI: 80
Kyokusei M., VI: 56–8
Kyokuto M., IV: 88, V: 207
Kyushu, XII: 344, XIII: 158
Kyushu M., V: 177

L

LA BOUDEUSE, XI: 343
Labomble, Capt. E. E. B., III: 333
LABUAN, X: 373
Labuan I., XIII: 264-5
LACHLAN, XIII: 260, 324
LACKAWANNA (1863), IV: 71
LACKAWANNA (1942), VII: 341, VIII: 411, 420, XII: 428, XIII: 318, XIV: 387
LA COMBATTANTE, XI: 193
Laconia, X: 57n-8n
LA CORTE, XIV: 380
Ladd, Cpl. F. B., VII: 79
Ladd, Ens. J. M., XII: 422
Lademan, Cdr. J. W., III: 159, 272
Lady Nelson, I: 145
LADYBIRD, III: 17
Lae, IV: 14, 17, 256, 260, VI: 31, 52-6, 60-63, 96, 136, 226n, XIII: 96-7; raid, III: 387-9; Lae-Salamaua opn., VI: 254-68; T.O., 261-2; pic., 263; chart, 264
La Farge, Lt. (jg) T. S., I: 62n
LAFAYETTE, II: 247
LA FERRIER, II: 252
LAFFEY (1942), IV: 271, V: 28, 151-3, 156-8, 162, 166, 232, 237, 251; sunk, 244-6
LAFFEY (1944), XI: 161, 206-8, 334, 337, XII: 379, XIII: 304, 312, XIV: 235-7, 372, 391; plan of kamikaze attack, 234; pic., 294
La Fleur, Lt. (jg) W. A., X: 170-71
LAFOREY, II: 279, IX: 42, 179, 277, 393, 396; sunk, 371
LAGAN, X: 78, 139
LAGARTO, XIV: 289, 296; sunk, XIII: 287
Lagens, Terceira, X: 45-6
LA GRACIEUSE, II: 108, 162, XI: 343
LA GRANDIÈRE, II: 108-9
LAGRANGE, XIV: 375
Lahaina, III: 221n
Lahaina Roads, III: 46
Laidlaw, Capt. J. S., XIII: 310, 313, XIV: 111n, 173, 379
Lair, Lt. C. E., X: 326
Lajeunesse, Cdr. R. W., VI: 237n, VIII: 408

LAKATOI, V: 67
Lake, Capt. Burton G., IV: 174, VI: 15n, VII: 334
Lake, Lt. Cdr. Richard C., IV: 228, V: 324, VI: 68
LAKE, XII: 429, XIII: 71, 319
LAKEHURST, II: 40, 137-9, 148, 151-2, 155, 267; pic., 149
Lakehurst, N. J., I: 250, X: 223n
Lakin, Lt. B. M., IX: 386, XIII: 304
Lakunai, VI: 393, 398, 402
L'ALCYON, II: 99, 107-8, X: 256, XI: 343
Lally, Lt. Cdr. W. F., XIV: 386
Lalor, Capt. W. G., XIV: 382
Lamade, Cdr. J. D., XII: 425, XIII: 316
LAMAR, VIII: 379, 419, XII: 418, XIII: 310, XIV: 380
Lamb, Lt. Cdr. R. S., III: 158, V: 284, 353, VII: 335
Lambe, Capt. C. E., XIV: 212, 388
Lamberson, Lt. Cdr. W. L., XIII: 315
Lambert, Lt. Cdr. George L., pic., IX: 43
Lambert, Lt. Cdr. V. G., VIII: 414, XII: 426
LAMBERTON, VII: 9n, 333
Lambrecht, Capt. J. O., XIII: 312
LAMERTON, II: 221, 265n
Lamkin, Lt. Cdr. H. C. M., XIII: 319
Lamon Bay, III: 162, 181-2
LAMONS, VIII: 411, XII: 429, XIII: 319
LA MOQUEUSE, XI: 343
LA MOTTE-PIQUET, XIII: 169
Lampedusa and Lampione Is., II: 280-81
Lampman, Lt. Cdr. L. R., I: 76, VI: 308, 317, VIII: 415
LAMSON (1910), X: 47n, 343n, XIV: 158n
LAMSON (1936), III: 210n, V: 296-7, 300, 307, 311, 326, 345, VI: 262, 382, 386, 390, XII: 344, 373-4, 380-5, 417; pic., 406
Lancaster, I: 178
Land, Seaman D. E., V: 284-5
Land, Rear Adm. Emory S., I: 291-2; *Merchant Marine at War*, X: xv
Landing and beaching craft, I: lv; types described, II: 29, 266-71, VIII: 53-4; distribution, June 1944, XI: 57; dis-

Landing and beaching craft (*cont'd*) pute over, 52–7. *See also each type indexed separately, below.*

Landing Craft, Assault, LCA, IX: 96*n*; N. Africa, II: 205; Sicily, IX: 96; France, XI: 57, 126–8, 134–6, 251–3

Landing Craft, Control, LCC, Kwajalein, VII: 261*n*, 280; Normandy, XI: 93, 98–100; Marianas, VIII: 190–92, 196, 383; Okinawa, XIV: 143–5; *LCC-20*, XI: 132; *–36, –38, –39*, VII: 344–5

Landing Craft, Flotilla Flagships, LC(FF), XIV: 379–80

Landing Craft, Gun, LCG, IX: 372; Salerno, 276; Normandy, XI: 100, 120–22, 184

Landing Craft, Headquarters, LCH, XI: 118, 141, 333–4, 341

Landing Craft, Infantry, LCI(L), described, II: 269–70, VIII: 55, IX: 32; distribution 1944, XI: 57; LCI flotilla one and two, II: 271; eight, XII: 387 *LCI(L)–1, –2, –5*, IX: 81–2, *–10*, 68, 75, 83, 386; *–12*, 366; *–20*, 395*n*; *–21, –22, –23*, VI: 228; *–24, –25, –27*, 294, 382; *–29, –30*, 381–2; *–31*, VIII: 111, 404; *–32*, IX: 85, 348, 387, 395*n*; *–34*, VIII: 100, 111, 114, 404; *–61, –62, –64, –65*, VI: 145, 228; *–68*, 228, 294; *–70*, 329; *–71, –72, –73*, 381, VIII: 100, 111, 404; *–74*, VI: 381; *–77*, VII: 344, XII: 52; *–78, –80*, 344; *–81*, XII: 52; *–82*, 346; *–85*, XI: 139–40; *–86*; IX: 78, 387; *–87*, XI: 141; *–88*, 97; *–90*, XIV: 392; *–91, –92*, XI: 139; *–95*, IX: 75, 387; *–96*, 387

LCI(L)–211, IX:341; *–213*, 194*n*; *–217*, 198; *–218*, 83*n*; *–220*, 99; *–221*, pic., 107; *–222*, VI: 145, 228; *–224, –226*, 381–2; *–232*, XI: 108; *–273* (HMS), IX: 395*n*; *–330, –334*, VI: 228; *–337, –338*, 381; *–339*, 263–4; pic., 263; *–343, –344*, 381; *–345*, VII: 346; *–349*, VIII: 393; *–365*, VII: 302, 344, VIII: 393; *–366*, VII: 344; VIII: 393; *–370*, XIV: 378; *–398*, 380 *LCI(L)–412*, pic., XI: 149; *–414*, 337; *–425*, XIV: 380; *–437, –439*, VII: 344; *–440*, 302, 344; *–441, –442, –449, –453, –455, –457*, 261*n*, 275*n*, 302, 344, 346; *–468*, VIII: 207, 418; *–490*, XI: 150, 159; *–496*, 171; *–543, –544*, VIII: 406; *–547*, XIII: 206; *–554*, XI: 141; *–588, –590*, 262; *–621*,

XIII: 48; *–627, –656, –657*, XIV: 375–8; *–725*, XII: 52; *–783*, 375; *–953*, XI: 339; *–988*, XIV: 378; *–993*, 387; *–994*, 380; *–1014, –1017, –1018*, XII: 373*n*; *–1080*, XIV: 11*n*

Landing Craft, Infantry (Demolition) LCI(D), *–228*, XIII: 323–4

Landing Craft, Infantry (Gunboats), LCI(G), XIII: 98, 104; described, VI: 295; VII: 202, 209; VIII: 55–6; *LCI(G)–70*, XIII: 104, 325; *–82*, XIV: 218, 390; *–365*, XIII: 140; *–409, –438, –441, –449, –450, –457, –466, –469, –471, –473, –474, –580*, 239, XIV: 29, 389

Landing Craft, Infantry (Mortar), LCI(M), Leyte, XII: 143–4; Lingayen, XIII: 129–30, 139; Iwo, XIV: 48, 63, 389

Landing Craft, Infantry (Rocket), LCI(R), New Guinea, VIII: 98–100, 120; Guam, 383; Morotai, XII: 22; Peleliu, 38; Leyte, 133, 134, 379; Mindoro, VIII: 31; Lingayen, 132; Zamboanga, 223; Cebu, 233; Balikpapan, 273–4; Okinawa, XIV: 29, 222; *LCI(R)–338*, pic., XIII: 261

Landing Craft, Medium, LCM, described, II: 29; distribution 1944, XI: 57; N. Africa, 81, 133, 147, 192, 205, 236–7; Pacific, IV: 285, VI: 300, 376, 446, VII: 95, 125–9, 135, 163, 167*n*, 239, 256, 263, 293; VIII: 52–3, 77–8, 99, 113, 137–9, 193, 196, 356, 361, 383, XII: 24, 50, 153, 156, 393; XIII: 47, 127, 142, 237, 245, 250; Iwo, XIV: 43, 127, 151, 153; Sicily, IX: 31, 106, 139–41, 152, 158; France, XI: 53, 57, 80, 102, 118–20, 139, 173, 241, 253, 263, 286; Rhine crossing, 317–23; pics., II: 82, XI: 317

Landing Craft, Medium (Gunboat), LCM(G), XIII: 244; pic., 260

Landing Craft, Medium (Rocket), LCM(R), XIII: 244

Landing Craft, Personnel, LCP, II: 20, 29, 192; LCP(R), 29, 63; Salerno, IX: 273; in Pacific, IV: 285, VIII: 54, 111–12, 192; XII: 120, XIII: 28, 190, 271; pic., II: 82

Landing Craft, Support (Large), LCS(L), described, II: 30, XIV: 37; in Pacific, XIII: 42, 202, 220, 235, 252, 256, 260, 270, 274, 280. *LCS(L)–15*, XIV: 244, 391; *–24*, 221; *–25*, 253; *–27*,

XIII: 202; *-28*, 271; *-33*, XIV: 223, 391; *-36*, 221; *-37*, 391; *-51*, 42, 237; *-52*, 260; *-57*, 223; *-64*, *-84*, *-87*, 187–90, *-88*, 392; *-111*, *-114*, 179; *-116*, 237, 391; *-119*, 392; *-121*, 259; *-122*, 275, 392

Landing Craft, Support (Medium), LCS(M), XI: 127

Landing Craft, Support (Small), LCS(S), IX: 129, 259

Landing Craft, Tank, LCT, described, II: 266–71, VIII: 55, IX: 30–31; number authorized and built, X: 35; distribution 1944, XI: 57; pic., 69; N. Africa, II: 220, 273; Pacific, V: 329, 364–6, VI: 122, 264, 376–7, 418, VII: 63, 134, 334, VIII: 54*n*, 55, 86–7, 106, 112, 120, 122, 125, 137, 171, 345, 349, 356, 363, XII: 22–4, 38, 50, 77*n*, 388, XIV: 127, 145, 173–4, 390; Mediterranean, IX: 33, 65–8, 75, 82–90, 106, 111, 124, 139, 144–395 *passim*; Normandy, XI: 53–98 *passim*, 102*n*–141 *passim*, 162–3, 177–8, 184–7; S. France, 239, 258, 262, 265, 269, 393; W. Europe, 302; pics., II: 273, VI: 133, IX: 83

Landing Craft, Tank (Rocket), LCT(R), XI: 100, 122

Landing Craft, Vehicle, LCV, II: 29; N. Africa, 63

Landing Craft, Vehicle Personnel, LCVP, IX: 31–2; pics., 131, 267, VI: 133; distribution 1944, XI: 57; Pacific, VI: 300, 376, 385, VII: 124–5, 129, 159, 163, 167, 170–71, 227, 237–63 *passim*, 293, 297, VIII: 52, 100, 113, 193, 211, XII: 50, 134, 142, 147, XIII: 127, 132, 261, XIV: 43, 120–21, 125, 136, 146, 153; Sicily, IX: 31–2, 80, 85, 88, 98–100, 129–31, 138–40, 143, 259; Anzio, 341; France, XI: 53, 57, 120, 134–6, 178, 258, 262, 301, 309; Rhine crossing, 317–22

Landing Ship, Dock, LSD, number authorized and built, X: 35; Gilberts, VII: 114–16, 127; Marshalls, 210, 239; elsewhere in Pacific, VI: 374, VIII: 54, 195, 383, XII: 22, 38; XIII: 134

Landing Ship, Infantry, LSI, IX: 29*n*; Sicily, 155–6, 206, 207*n*; Italy, 251, 258, 272, 323, 326, 334, 338

Landing Ship, Medium, LSM, XII: 142; Kwajalein, VII: 273–4; Leyte, XII: 142, 373–5, 379, 383–93; Philip-pines, XIII: 19, 28, 127–42 *passim*, 202–46 *passim*; Iwo, XIV: 38, 42, 51; Okinawa, 119, 122, 131, 141–74 *passim*, 256, 271, 279, 375, 389–92; pics., XII: 142, XIV: 158–9

Landing Ship, Medium (Rocket), LSM(R), XIV: 116, 125, 134–5, 224, 237, 253–5, 390

Landing Ship, Tank, LST, II: 234, 266–71, VI: 141*n*, IX: 30–31; number authorized and built, X: 35; pics., II: 273, VI: 102, 153, IX: 347, XI: 68–9, 173, 269, XIII: 37; as auxiliaries, VIII: 195*n*, 346, IX: 343*n*, 368, XI: 60, 263, XIV: 141, 162, 166; distribution, 1944, XI: 57; Flotilla 3, XIII: 144; Flot. 7, VIII: 56

LST-3, IX: 198*n*; *-6*, 75; *-16*, 343*n*; *-18*, *-22*, VI: 382; *-19*, *-20*, VII: 341, 408; *-23*, 313, 341, 345; *-26*, VI: 382; *-29*, VII: 344; *-30*, XI: 58; *-31*, VII: 337, 344; *-34*, 338, 344; *-38*, 345; *-41*, 344; *-42*, 347; *-65*, lost, IX: 234–5; *-66* to *-68*, VI: 382; *-69*, VII: 341; *-78*, 337, 344; *-84*, 341, 348, VIII: 207

LST-118, VIII: 404*n*; *-119*, VII: 347; *-122*, 345; *-126*, 347; *-127*, 344; *-128*, 347; *-134*, XI: 287; *-158*, IX: 387; *-168*, VI: 382; *-169*, VII: 341; *-170*, VI: 382; *-171*, 382; XII: 134; *-179*, VII: 127, 337; *-181*, XII: 134–5; *-202*, *-204*, VI: 382, 440; *-205*, VII: 341; *-218*, 341, 344; *-219*, XIII: 307; *-220*, VIII: 403*n*; *-221*, *-222*, VII: 345; *-223*, 347; *-224*, 344, XII: 52; *-226*, VII: 344–5; XI: 189; *-240*, VII: 341, 344; *-241*, 341, 347; *-242*, 338, 344; *-243*, 338, 344; *-244*, 341, 345; *-246*, 344; *-266*, XI: 337; *-268*, VII: 347; XIII: 151; XIV: 111*n*; *-270*, VII: 345; *-271*, 345; *-272*, 291, 344; *-273*, 344; *-274*, 347; *-276*, *-277*, 348; *-278*, 408; *-282*, XI: 341; sunk, 269–70; *-289*, 66. *See also* VIII: 408 for many of above and for *LST-40*, *-45*, *-120*, *-121*, *-124*, *-129*, *-130*, *-131*, *-166*, *-213*, *-225*, *-263*, *-269*, *-275*, *-278*

LST-305, IX: 395*n*; *-307*, XI: 189; *-311*, *-312*, IX: 107–8, XI: 61; *-313*, IX: 11, 109, 388; sunk, 101, 107–8; *-314*, sunk, XI: 174–5; *-318*, lost, IX: 203; *-331*, *-332*, XIV: 189; *-333*, lost, IX: 33; *-336*, 275; *-337*, *-338*, 106; *-339*, VI: 237; *-340*, *-341*, 140,

Landing Ship, Tank, LST (*cont'd*)
VIII: 408; *-342, -343,* VI: 145; *-344,*
IX: 106; *-348,* 84, 395*n;* sunk, 366,
X: 256; *-350,* XI: 189; *-353,* VI: 145;
lost, VIII: 171; *-354,* VI: 145, 228,
238-40, VIII: 408; *-359;* X: 331; *-366,*
IX: 349; *-375,* 252, 274-5; *-376,* sunk,
XI: 174; *-384,* 61; *-385,* IX: 274; *-386,*
274, 387; *-387,* 33; *-389,* 265; *-390,*
VIII: 408; *-395,* VI: 145, 228-30, 238;
-396, 145; sunk, 237; *-398,* 145, 238;
-399, 145, 228
   LST-410, IX: 342, 395; *-417,* 252*n;*
-418, -422, 348, sunk, 395*n;* *-446,*
VI: 417; *-447,* XIV: 381, 390; sunk,
195-6; *-449,* VI: 123; *-450, -451,*
VII: 334; VIII: 408; *-452,* VI: 382;
XII: 134; *-454, -456, -457, -458, -459,*
-465, -466, -468, -470, -474, -475,
VI: 382, VIII: 113, XII: 135, XIII: 309;
-460, 34; *-461,* VII: 334; VIII: 408;
-467, VI: 382, VIII: 119; *-471,* VI:
265-6; *-472,* 145; XIII: 30-31; pic., 37;
-473, VI: 265; *-476,* VII: 341, 347;
-477, 334, 341, 347, XIV: 56; *-478,*
-479, -480, VII: 341, 347-8, XIII: 35-6;
-481, -482, VI: 341, 344-7; *-483, -484,*
VII: 341, 345, VIII: 408; *-485,* 171,
408; *-486, -487,* 408; *-499,* XI: 173
   LST-507, -531, sunk, XI: 66; *-511,*
-515, 336-7; *-534,* XIV: 279, 392; *-538,*
XI: 175; *-599,* XIV: 177, 390; *-605,*
XIII: 33; *-700,* 148, 151, 326; *-708,*
307*n;* *-734,* XIV: 145; *-737,* XII: 385*n;*
-738, XIII: 30; *-739,* XIV: 196; *-749,*
XIII: 35-6; *-750,* 45; *-776,* XIV: 65;
-778, XIII: 150, 326; *-779,* XIV: 61;
-808, 392; *-884,* 128, 154, 390; *-911,*
XIII: 151; *-912,* 116, 325; *-925,* 140;
-950, XIV: 111*n;* *-1028,* XIII: 140;
-1122, XIV: 231; Memorial service to
F.D.R., 232
Landing Ship, Tank (Hospital),
VIII: 200, XI: 60, XIV: 162
Landing Vehicle, Tracked, LVT, amphtrac, described, VII: 89-90, 208-9;
North Africa, II: 84-5; Sicily, IX: 30*n;*
Cape Torokina, VI: 360; Gilberts,
VII: 114-18, 124-30, 133-4, 153, 159-
63, 165-7, 172-3, 177, 183*n,* 186, 202,
208; Marshalls, 209, 233, 237-9, 244-76
passim, 280, 285, 291-2, 296, 302, 310;
Marianas, VIII: 165, 190-95, 202, 209,
338, 349, 355-63, 383, 387-92; SW

Pacific, VI: 375, 445-6, VIII: 54, 77-8,
81-3, 106, 110-11, 138, 143, XII: 23,
34-8, 42; Philippines, 127, 142, 364, 393,
XIII: 127, 132; Palawan, 218-19, 223;
Panay, 230, 235, 261; Iwo, XIV: 37,
43; Okinawa, 145-6, 149-50, 154, 173;
pics., VII: 270, 279; XIV: 158
Landing Vehicle, Tracked (Armored),
LVT(A), VII: 209; Marshalls, 239,
245-7, 261, 275-6, 292; Noemfoor,
VIII: 138; Marianas, 190-92, 356-7,
364, 383; Peleliu, XII: 36-7; Leyte, 142;
Iwo, XIV: 38; Okinawa, 145, 149, 152,
172; pics., VII: 271, XIV: 158-9
Landis, Lt. Cdr. N. W., XIV: 386
Landrum, Maj. Gen. Eugene, VII: 48
Landrum, Lt. Col. J. E., VIII: 392
Lane, F. C., *Ships for Victory,* X:
xv
Lane, Lt. Cdr. W. J., VIII: 410
Laner, Ens. Daniel, XI: 213-14
Lang, Lt. Cdr. F. N., XIII: 318,
XIV: 387
LANG, I: 195-6, IV: 271, V: 28*n,* 87, 335*n,*
VI: 214-15, 219-21, VII: 353, VIII:
415, XII: 417, XIII: 309, XIV: 379
Lange, Oblt. Harald, X: 291
Lange, Lt. Cdr. J. R., XIV: 380
Lange, Brig. Gen. J. W., IX: 270
Langemak Bay, VI: 74
Langer, W. L., *Our Vichy Gamble,*
I: 31*n,* II: 4*n*
Langlan, King of Majuro, VI: 305-6
LANGLEY (1922), I: li-lii, III: 28-9, 159,
193, 272, 305*n,* 359-63, 378, VIII: 236*n*-
8*n,* X: 37, 42*n,* 197*n,* XII: 125*n,* 243*n;*
sunk, III: 363
LANGLEY (1943), VII: 208, 350, VIII: 37,
174, 238, 250, 265, 360, 414, XII: 90,
178-80, 318, 326-7, 427, XIII: 54, 70,
180, 317, XIV: 21, 385-6; pics., XII:
78, XIII: 84
Langley Field, I: 131, 223, 243
Lanham, Lt. Cdr. H. P., XII: 349*n,*
XIII: 315
Lanigan, Col. J. R., XIV: 38, 43
Laning, Cdr. C. B., VIII: 108-10,
XII: 421
LANING, X: 257
Lank, Cdr. T. S., X: 288, 375
Lankeneau, Capt. W. E., XIV: 381
Lannom, Capt. J. R., II: 36, VI: 144,
XIV: 379
Lanphier, Capt. T. G., VI: 124, 128

LANSDALE, I: 76, 90, 354, 418, 420, IX: 370; sunk, X: 268
LANSDOWNE, I: 154, 415, V: 132–3, 136, 205, 226–7, VIII: 405, 415, XIV: 363, 367
LANSQUENET, XI: x
Lantana, I: 242, 279
La Pallice, I: 22, X: 85, 259, 325, XI: 108
La Paz, Samar, XII: 153
La Plata, X: 232
LAPON, VIII: 21, XII: 406
LA PORTE, XIII: 307, 312
LA PROVENCE, XI: 287
LA PSYCHÉ, II: 98, 248
LAPWING, I: 15*n*, 84, 145*n*, 420; sunk, X: 313
LARAMIE, I: 330–31, 422
Larchbank, X: 138*n*
LARDNER, V: 182, 205, 226, 229, 232, 296–7, 300, 303, 307, 311, VI: 98*n*, VIII: 405, 415
Large, Lt. Cdr. J. M., XII: 180
LARGS, II: 105*n*, IX: 150, 166, 223, XI: 183, 278
Lark, Lt. Cdr. J. A., VI: 228, 297, 308, VIII: 408
LARK, III: 159, 194, 273, 379
LARK, HMS, X: 311
Larkin, Mr. I. E., IV: 174
Larkin, Capt. R. A., XIV: 114, 376
LARNE, XI: 339
Larner, Maj. E. L., VI: 59, 64
La Rochelle, XI: 308
Larranga, I: 160
Larry Doheny, III: 221*n*
Larsen, Cdr. A. C., XIV: 387
Larsen, Lt. H. H., IV: 270, V: 86, 101, 375
Larsen, Maj. Gen. H. L., VIII: 400
Larsen, Lt. Cdr. John, XIV: 386
Larsen, Lt. Col. S. R., V: 341
Larson, Lt. Cdr. F. W., XIV: 374
Larson, Capt. H. O., VI: 228, 242–7, 250, VII: 339, VIII: 405
Larson, Brig. Gen. Westside T., I: 242
LA SALLE, VII: 337, 346, VIII: 408, XII: 416, XIII: 309
Lascroux, Gen., I: 68; pic., 218
LASSEN, VI: 112, VIII: 346, XII: 21*n*, 429, XIV: 159, 167*n*, 386
Lasso, Mt., VIII: 359, 363–6
LA SURPRISE, II: 230
LAS VEGAS V., XIII: 307, XIV: 196, 386
Latham, Cdr. R. C., XIV: 292*n*

LATIMER, XIII: 307, 312, XIV: 380
Latin America, policy toward, I: 31–2
LATONIA, XIV: 386
Latta, Cdr. F. D., VII: 334, VIII: 22, XIII: 287, XIV: 289, 296
Latta, Lt. W. A., XIII: 306
Latus, Lt. Cdr. C. B. S., XII: 423
Laub, Lt. (jg) R. E., IV: 120*n*
LAUB, IX: 113, 146, 377, 389, X: 185, 261–3, 275
LAUDERDALE, XI: 343
Laughlin, Lt. (jg) H. L., I: 371
Laughon, Lt. W. R., I: 421
Laughton B. Evans, IX: 386
Laurel, José, XII: 67, XIII: 7
LAURENS, XIII: 307, 312, XIV: 380
Laurentide Park, X: 382
Laurin, Capt. de V., XI: 336, 340
Lautrup, Lt. Cdr. G. W., VIII: 30, 415
Laval, Pierre, II: 4, 11, 67, 185, 208, 217
LAVALLETTE, V: 353, 361–3, VI: 244, 251, VII: 190, 194–6, 245, 338, 345, VIII: 127, 404, XII: 373–4, 377, 387, 416, XIII: 27*n*, 200, 309
L'AVENTURE, XI: 336
LAWFORD, XI: 190
Lawlor, Cdr. F. L., XIV: 385
Lawrence, David, XIV: 273
Lawrence, Lt. Cdr. John C., X: 194, XIV: 383, 385
Lawrence, Lt. Cdr. S. J., VII: 340
LAWRENCE, I: 214
LAWRENCE C. TAYLOR, XII: 79, XIII: 319, XIV: 314, 374
LAWS, VIII: 410, XII: 319, 427, XIII: 318, XIV: 377
Lawson, Lt. Cdr. J. F., XIII: 306
Lawson, Lt. J. H., II: 40
Lawson, 1st Lt. T. W., III: 392
Lawton, Maj. C. B., VII: 310
Lawton, Lt. (jg) E. J., VIII: 302–3
Lawton, John, IX: xv, XI: xi, XIII: x
Laycock, Brig. R. F., IX: 272
Laysan I., IV: 85, 93–4
Layton, Capt. E. T., III: 130*n*, IV: xi, 5*n*, 6*n*, 77*n*, 89*n*, VI: 11*n*
Layton, Vice Adm. Sir Geoffrey, III: 53–4, 272
L-boats, IX: 212
LEA, I: 76, 121–2, 349, 418, 420, VI: 131*n*, X: 77, 375
Leach, Lt. Cdr. R. W., XI: 336
Leahy, Flt. Adm. William D., II: 4–11, III: 31, 49, VI: 3, VIII: 5–6, IX: 5, 228,

Leahy, Flt. Adm. Wm. D. (*cont'd*)
XI: 13, 22, XII: 7, XIV: 339, 347, 352;
pic., XII: 6
Leahy, Cdr. W. I., XI: 335
Leak, Chief Pharmacist, III: 106
Leal, 1st Lt. A. L., X: 96
LEAMINGTON, I: 71
Leamy, Capt. F. A., XIV: 379
LEANDER, IV: 255, V: 184, 330, VI: 178–
89, 190*n*
"Leapfrog" strategy, VI: 225–7,
VII: 85, 206, IX: 197–8
Learned, Lt. Cdr. Ebenezar, XIV: 375
Leary, Vice Adm. Herbert F., biog.,
X: 343*n;* mentioned, III: 260–61, 265,
277, IV: 15, 35, 39, 262*n*, 275*n*,
VI: 31–2, X: 343–5
Leary, Ens. Leo, VI: 390
LEARY, I: 15*n*, 225, 305, 420, X: 171–4,
376; sunk, 174–6; pic., 168
Leatham, Adm. Sir Ralph, X: 323–4,
XI: 63, 175
Leatherman, Lt. Cdr. F. J., VI: 262
Leavey, Maj. Gen. E. H., VI: 11*n*,
VII: 104–5
Le Barron, Lt. Cdr. H. E., XII: 419*n*
LeBoutiller, Lt. P., XIII: 304
LeBreton, Rear Adm. D. McD., I: 75–6,
78*n*
LeClerc, Gen. Jacques, XI: 101*n*,
XIV: 366
LEDBURY, IX: 393
Ledford, Yeoman Edward, XI: xi,
XII: viii, XIV: x
Lee, Lt. C. B., VII: 341, 345
Lee, Capt. C. L., XIV: 374
Lee, Capt. C. V., XIV: 378
Lee, Capt. Fitzhugh, XII: 420, XIII: 305
Lee, Lt. Cdr. J. M., VIII: 409
Lee, Lt. Cdr. James R., V: 204, 208, 233,
266
Lee, Lt. Gen. John C. H., XI: 50
Lee, Col. Richard H., X: 337*n*
Lee, Vice Adm. Willis A., biog.,
V: 270*n;* pic., 282; Cominch staff,
I: 116, XIII: 289–90; Solomons, V: 148,
182*n*, 197, 228, 352, 372, VI: 106; Santa
Cruz I., battle, V: 201–2, 205; Guadal-
canal battle, 233, 258, 261–2, 270–82;
285; Baker I., VII: 95; Combatpac,
111, VIII: 28–9, 37, XIII: 316; bom-
bardments, VII: 197; Mili, 309; Marshalls, 348; Truk raid, 353; Ponape
bombardment, VIII: 40–41; Saipan,

179; Philippine Sea, 242–5, 249–51, 258–
83 *passim*, 301–2, 305, 308, 415; Leyte
Gulf Battle, XII: 193–5, 241, 291, 294,
318, 322, 329–30, 427; anti-kamikaze
research, XIV: 281; Okinawa, 384
LEEDSTOWN (1942), II: 192–3, 195*n*, 198–
202; sunk, 212–13, 283
LEEDSTOWN (1943), VII: 268, 344,
VIII: 419, XII: 39–40, 416, XIII: 308
Leeper, Capt. J. E., I: 77, 420, XIV: 386
Lees, Capt. D. M., XI: 334
Leese, Lt. Gen. Sir Oliver, IX: 27*n*, 150,
374
Leeson, Ens. A. D., XII: 422
Leeson, Lt. Cdr. Robert A., VIII: 73,
XII: 204, 209, 395, 422
Leever, Cdr. L. C., XI: 336, XIV: 380
L'ESCARMOUCHE, XI: 336
LE FANTASQUE, IX: 306, 394, XI: 265*n*, 341
Leffler, Capt. C. D., I: 390*n*, X: 213*n*, 227
LE FORTUNÉ, XI: 343
LeFrancis, Capt. R. G., XIV: 324
Legaspi, III: 162, 177, XIII: 13; landing,
207–8
Legg, Lt. James C., IV: 93
Legg, Col. R. A., VI: 64
Leghorn, IX: 56, 260, 306, 365, XI: 310–
12
Legwen, Lt. Cdr. G. W., I: 283
LEHARDY, VII: 341, 345
Le Havre, XI: 20, 155–6, 175, 183, 191–4,
297, 302–3, 329
Lehigh, I: 38*n*
Lehlleitner, Lt. Cdr. C. H., XIV: 387
Lehman, Radioman D. G., XII: 246*n*
Lehman, 2nd Officer J. E., I: 398
Leide, Lt. Cdr. William, XI: 318*n*, 319–
21
Leigh, Squad. Ldr. H. DeH., X: 53
"Leigh-light" searchlight, X: 53, 83, 89,
96, 205, 349, 364
Leigh-Mallory, Air Chief Marshal Sir
Trafford, XI: xiii, 24, 29–30, 36–7, 69–
70, 82–3
LEINSTER, II: 195*n*, IX: 175, 299, 394, 397
LEIPZIG, I: 4*n*
Leith, Capt. Stanley, VI: 145, VIII: 170
LELAND E. THOMAS, XIII: 249
Lelet, Chief of Wotho, VII: 312
LE MALIN, II: 248, XI: 265*n*, 267, 278, 341
Le Mans, XI: 46
LeMay, Maj. Gen. Curtis E., XII: 55, 60,
XIII: 163–4, XIV: 87, 344
Lembang, III: 279, 312

Le Millier, Lt. de V., XI: 334
Lemly, Lt. Cdr. F. W., VI: 228, VIII: 404
Lemonnier, Contre-Am., pic., XI: 244; mentioned, 233, 255, 274, 289–90
Le Muy, XI: 248–9
Lend-Lease, I: 36–8, 158–61, 383, III: 61, X: 5, 33–4, 38, 314*n*; number of vessels built for RN, 35, XI: 344–5
Lennox, Lt. Cdr. F. H., XI: 339
Lent, Lt. Cdr. W. A., IV: 92
Lentz, Lt. (jg) V. E., X: 382
LEON, VIII: 408, XII: 417, XIII: 307, 312, XIV: 378
LEONARD WOOD, I: 110–11, 421, II: 26*n*, 37–8, 54*n*, 58–64, 168–9, 172, VII: 124, 288, 293–5, 300, 336, 347, VIII: 408, IX: 127–9, 389, XII: 416, XIII: 309, 313
Leonardi, Rear Adm. IX: 160–61
LEONIS, VIII: 410
LEOPOLD, X: 279*n*
Leopoldville, X: 334–7, XI: 304
LePage, Lt. Cdr., XI: 341
Leppert, Capt. J. H., II: 273, IX: 99, 388
LERAY WILSON, XII: 244, 421, XIII: 141, 310, 326
Leros I., IX: 245–6
Les Cazes, II: 88–9
Leslie, Lt. A. V., II: 37, 119
Leslie, Capt. Maxwell F., III: 392, IV: 90, 120*n*, 127–30, 133, 140, 271, V: 86, 99*n*, XIV: 379
Leslie, Cdr. N. H., IV: 173
LESLIE B. KNOX, XIII: 313–14
Les Miniquiers, XI: 304–8
Les Moulins, XI: 122, 145, 147, 149
Lester, Capt. J. C., VII: 344, VIII: 419, XII: 416, XIII: 308
LE TERRIBLE, IX: 306, 394, X: 191, XI: 265*n*, 277, 341
LE TONNANT, II: 110*n*
Letourneau, Lt. S. D., XIV: 377
Letts, Cdr. K. P., X: 379, XI: 333–4
LEUTZE, XII: 199, 221, 419, XIII: 105, 139, 304, XIV: 30, 182–6, 373, 390
Levant, Île du, XI: 251–3
Lever Brothers, VI: 35
Lever Hbr., VI: 209
Leverton, Lt. Cdr. J. W., VII: 17
LE VIGILANT, XI: x
Levin, Lt. Cdr. R. B., I: 420, II: 40
LEVIS, I: 71, 90
LEVY, XII: 429, XIV: 360

Lewellen, Cdr. B. E., I: 421, VII: 78, XIV: 293*n*
Lewin, Ens. R. H., VI: 418
Lewis, Lt. C. G., IX: 102–3
Lewis, Lt. Cdr. C. P., XIV: 381
Lewis, Edgar A., IX: xv
Lewis, Lt. F. G., XIII: 305
Lewis, Ens. Frank C., I: 249
Lewis, Lt. Cdr. G. A., IV: 92
Lewis, Lt. Cdr. J. H., I: 418, IV: 92
Lewis, Lt. Cdr. J. S., pic., VII: frontispiece; mentioned, X: 375, 378
Lewis, Lt. Col. Millard, VI: 64
Lewis, Cdr. R. P., XIV: 377
Lewis, Rear Adm. Spencer S., biog., XI: 242*n*; pic., 268; mentioned, IX: 15, XI: 242, 259, 268, 271–2, 341
Lewis, Capt. Thomas L., I: xv, 111, 218, VIII: 170, X: 22*n*
Lewis, Lt. W. F., VII: 334
LEWIS, XIII: 319
LEWIS HANCOCK, VII: 349, VIII: 413, XII: 319, 426, XIII: 317, XIV: 383
Lewis L. Dyche, XIII: 48
Lewis Morris, IX: 390
LEXINGTON (1927), I: xxxvii, lii, 52*n*, III: 28–9, 210–11, 215–18, 235–7, 240–41, 260, 265–7, 387–8, IV: 14, 19–56 *passim*, 63, V: 28, 92, 99; sunk, IV: 57–60; pic., 60–61; officers who served in, VIII: 238*n*, 263*n*, X: 77, 189*n*, 197*n*, XII: 243*n*–4*n*, XIII: 4*n*, 180*n*
LEXINGTON (1943), VI: 31, VII: xxvii, 85, 92–4, 97, 116, 141, 190–97, 309, 338, VIII: 32, 37–8, 174, 178–9, 243, 249–95 *passim*, 303, 308, 412, 414, X: 51*n*, XII: 86, 96, 180, 184–6, 196, 239, 291, 318–60 *passim*, 424–6, XIII: 54, 57, 66, 316, XIV: 21, 44; Phil. Sea battle chart, VIII: 275; pics., VII: 198–9, VIII: 232, 401
LEYDON, I: 323*n*
Leyte, island, history and descr., XII: 61–4; map, 62; planning and strategy, 7–18, 56–61; invasion of, command for, 55–6; preliminaries, 117–19, 122, 126–7, 131; landings, 130–56, T.O., 415–29; charts, 120, 132, 141; air and naval gunfire support, 106–8, 119–20, 123–4, 132–5, 142–3, 149–54, 349–54, 370; opns. ashore, 151–6, 361–5, 375–81, 392–7; chart, 152; Jap. counterattacks and reinforcement, 148, 164, 239, 343–6, 351–4, 380, 387–8, XIII: 13–15; logis-

Leyte (*cont'd*)
tics, XII: 74–85; unloading, 135, 139–
40, 155–6; resupply, XIII: 7; casualties,
XII: 365, 396–7; as U.S. base, 82–3,
XIII: 6, 24, 39, 43, 87, 98, 115, 144,
151–3, 187–9, 208–78 *passim*, XIV: 89,
106–63 *passim*, 212, 249, 307, 310, 320,
357; airfields, XIII: 25, 32–3, 59, 163,
349–50; operations around, XII: 339–
60; weather central, XIII: 83
Leyte Gulf, Battle for, XII: 159–338;
Jap. plans and movements, 158–69,
189–92; numbers engaged, 160*n;* Palawan Passage, 169–74; Sibuyan Sea,
176, 183–9; Surigao Strait, 190, 198–
241; Halsey's decision, 193–7, 289–93;
Samar, 242–316; Cape Engaño, 317–36;
kamikazes, 300–306; discussion, 336–8;
charts, 171, 185, 188, 200, 205, 214, 219,
225, 231, 247–9, 264–5, 277, 323; T.O.,
415–23; pics., 182–3, 190–91, 214–15,
222–3, 246–7, 278–9, 302–3
L'Herminier, Capit. de Frég. Jean,
IX: 305–6
Libby, Capt. R. E., VII: 335, VIII: 408
LIBRA, IV: 265*n,* 273, V: 229, 232,
VI: 144, 151, 297, VIII: 418, XIII: 307
Licata, IX: 20; landing, 26–30, 32–3, 42–
9, 58, 65–91; chart, 76–7; pics., 82–3
Liddell Hart, Capt. Basil H., XI: 5
LIDDESDALE, IX: 393, XI: 343
LIDDLE, XII: 383–5, XIII: 324
Lidstone, Cdr. N. A., VII: 141*n,* 337,
VIII: 223, 419
Liebenstein, Cdr. von, IX: 210
Lief, Lt. Cdr. S. A., VII: 348, VIII: 408
Likes, Lt. (jg) P. K., X: 382
Lillard, Capt. J. S., VII: 346, VIII: 408
Liloan Hbr., XII: 204
Limberis, Ens. G. P., IX: 136–7
Linchow, XII: 5, 105
Lincoln, Cdr. H. A., VII: 334, 341,
XIII: 316, XIV: 383
Lind, Lt. J. J., XIV: 376
Lindberg, Cpl. C. W., pic., XIV: front-
ispiece
Lindeman, Lt. J. E., X: 381
Lindemann, Prof. F. A., XI: 10
LINDENWALD, VII: 344, VIII: 196, 407,
XII: 148, 418, XIII: 311, 314, XIV: 380
L'INDISCRET, X: 339, 373
LINDISFARNE, XI: 336
Lindsay, Lt. Cdr. M. M., IV: 173,
VII: 334

Lindsey, Lt. Cdr. Eugene E., III: 392,
IV: 91, 120–22
Lindsey, Cdr. R. M., IV: 113*n,* V: 97–9
LINDSEY, XIV: 225, 376, 391
Lingayen Gulf, Jap. invasion, III: 159,
162, 178–81; U.S. operation, planning
and preliminaries, XII: 12, 17, 386,
XIII: 3–13, 89–90, 93–119; landings,
124–36; air and naval gunfire support,
7, 22, 109–14, 128–9, 135, 155–6; kami-
kazes, 325–6; progress ashore, 135–56;
unloading and resupply, 130, 133–4,
140–54; U.S. base, 229–30, 244; T.O.,
303–13; casualties, 129, 325–6; charts,
100, 124, 128–9, 131, 139, 154; pics.,
156–7, 165
Lingayen town, XIII: 112, 136
Lingga Roads, VIII: 117, 217, XII: 5, 61,
69, 119, 162–3, 170, 335, XIII: 38, 158–
9, 166, 176
Link, Lt. Cdr. E. M., VII: 348, VIII: 412
Link, Mr. F. S., III: 315, 319*n*
LINNET, I: 390*n,* 422
Linosa I., II: 280–81
LIOBA, XIV: 386
"Lion," IV: 252, VIII: 350
Lioy, Col. Vincenzo, IX: xvi, 57*n–*9*n*
LIPAN, VIII: 419, XIV: 387
Lipari, II: 248
Lippmann, Walter, VII: 199
Lipscomb Lykes, IV: 265*n*
Liri R., IX: 374
Lisbon, I: 16, IX: 238
LISCOME BAY, VII: xi, 337; sunk, 140–41
Lisianski I., IV: 85, 93–4
List, Cdr. F. V., XII: 417, XIV: 383
Litch, Rear Adm. E. W., VIII: 414,
XII: 426, XIII: 316, XIV: 373*n*
LITCHFIELD, III: 213
Little, Adm. Sir Charles, XI: xi
Little, Capt. J. K., V: 375
Little, Capt. M. N., XIV: 379
Little, Capt. Marion L., XI: 64
LITTLE (1918), IV: 273, V: 67, 109; sunk,
118–20; chart, 119
LITTLE (1944), XIV: 252; sunk, 253, 391
Little Creek, II: 22, 30, 58, 271–2, IX: 128
Littlefield, Cdr. G. A., XIV: 381
LITTORIO. See ITALIA
Livdahl, Lt. Cdr. O. L., V: 98
LIVERMORE, I: 83, 92, 232, 384, 420, II: 37,
285, XI: 339
Liverpool, XI: 131
Liversedge, Col. Harry B., VI: 103, 156–

8, 175–6, 180, 198, 202–3, 222, XIV: 39, 49, 61
Livingston, Lt. Stanley, XI: 286
LIVINGSTON, VII: 348, 410
Livingston, X: 328
Livinstone, Lt. Cdr. E. W., XIII: 310
Liuchow Peninsula, XIII: 171
Ljubljana Gap, XI: 23n, 225–30, 296
Lloyd, Ens. F. R., VII: 36
Lloyd, Air Vice Marshal Sir H. P., IX: 23, X: 252
LLOYD, XIII: 146n, 307, 321, 323–4
LOBELIA, I: 92, 335–6
Lobnitz pier, XI: 26, 166, 178; pic., 172
LOCH FADA, X: 339, 373
LOCH GLENDHU, X: 340
LOCH INSH, X: 313
Lockhart, Capt. R. G., XII: 428, XIV: 374
Lockwood, Vice Adm. Charles A., biog., IV: 223n; mentioned, 199n, 206, 223, 275, VI: 67, 75n, 82, VII: 54, 93, 222, 342, 351–3, VIII: 16, 19, 24, 158, 241–2, 252, 278, 415, XII: 168, 332–3, 398–400, 405–7, 429, XIII: 161, 284, 319, XIV: 292, 295–6, 327; *Sink 'em All*, 285
Lockwood, Cdr. R. E., XII: 425, XIII: 318
Lockwood, Cdr. R. H., XIII: 284
Lodge, Maj. O. R., *Recapture of Guam*, VIII: 371n
LOESER, XIII: 307
Loewith, Lt. Cdr. M. S., XIV: 381
Lofberg, Lt. Cdr. G. B., IV: 273, V: 120
Logan, Capt. D. N., XII: 428
Logan V., XIV: 166, 196, 386, 390
Logistics, Pearl Harbor, III: 46, 133; N.E.I., 303n, 330–32; Pacific 1941–43, VII: 100–113; Guadalcanal-Tulagi, IV: 254, 266, V: 108–9, 179–80, 334–5; Gilberts, VII: 110–11; Marshalls, 110–11, 210; Palau raid, VIII: 29; Sicily, IX: 19, 26; Salerno, 250; Anzio, 367; Marianas, VIII: 160, 341–50; Leyte, XII: 74–85; Okinawa, XIV: 156–69. *See also* Service Force
Logsdon, Lt. D. M., VIII: 380
Logsdon, Lt. Cdr. E. W., X: 173, 176, 376
Loker, Cdr. A. M., XIV: 388
Lombok I. and Strait, III: 285, 303, 329, 361, 364, 373, XIII: 164, 277, 288
Lomopog, XIII: 244

LONDON, I: 180–81
London, I: 223, II: 12, 16, 182, IX: 19, XI: 9, 14; Conference, III: 19; Naval Treaty, IV: 189
Londonderry, I: 53, 119, 262, 318–20
Long, Lt. Cdr. C. G., XIV: 387
Long, Capt. E. John, XII: viii, XIV: xi
Long, Gavin, XIII: 255n
Long, Cdr. J. W., XIV: 387
Long, Lt. Ralph W., X: 128
Long, Capt. V. D., XII: 428, XIII: 305
LONG, VI: 440, 444, VII: 9n, 335, 347, VIII: 82, 410, 419, X: 197n, XII: 422, XIII: 112, 306, 325; sunk, 106–7
LONG BEACH, VIII: 405
LONG ISLAND, I: 83n, IV: 83n, 276n, V: 73–4, X: 38
Longino, Lt. Cdr. J. C., XIV: 374
Longley-Cook, Capt. E. W. L., XI: 341
LONGSHAW, VIII: 410, XII: 319, 427, XIII: 318, XIV: 372, 392; sunk, 247
Longstaff, Cdr. J. B., I: 421
Longstreth, Lt. W. T., XII: 311n, XIII: 55n
Longton, Cdr. E. W., XI: 337
LOOKOUT, II: 281, IX: 179, 277, 281, 393, XI: 252, 316, 338
Lookout, Cape, I: 134, 155
Loomis, Alfred, X: 53
Loomis, Commo. D. W., VII: 207, 226, 285, 288, 291, 336, 347, VIII: 408, IX: 139, 389, XII: 139, 416, XIII: 134, 309
Loomis, Capt. F. Kent, XI: xi, XII: viii, XIII: x
Loomis, Lt. Cdr. Henry, VII: 324, 325n
Loomis, Lt. Cdr. S. C., VIII: 415
Loop Receiving Stations, I: 266n–7n
LOOSESTRIFE, X: 74
Loran, X: 53, XII: 54
Lorient, I: 22, 25, 156, 347, X: 85–6, 187, 319, 325–7, XI: 107, 218, 297, 302, 328
Lorrain, II: 121
LORRAINE, II: 252, XI: 238, 279, 284, 288, 309, 338
Los Negros I., VI: 432, 445–6, VIII: 164, 241, 260, 313
LOT, X: 116, 128
Loud, Cdr. W. R., VI: 297, 344, VII: 345, VIII: 410, XII: 118, 122, 166, 421, XIII: 98, 104–5, 112, 306, XIV: 376
LOUGH, XIII: 191–2
Loughlin, Cdr. C. E., I: 421, XII: 409, XIII: 297, 319, XIV: 291

LOUISIANA, X: 197*n*
LOUISVILLE, III: 212, 213*n*, 261, 264, IV: 83, 173, 257, V: 326, 353–9, VII: 9*n*, 14, 220, 233, 288, 301, 334, 346, VIII: 197, 200–201, 328, 409, X: 204*n*, 229*n*, XII: 34, 39, 118*n*, 122, 198–9, 223–4, 227, 234–6, 419, XIII: 39, 103, 304; kamikaze attack, and pic., 108–9, 325
Lounsbury, Lt. Cdr. R. E., XIII: 304, XIV: 176, 376
Love, Lt. Cdr. H. H., X: 377
LOVELACE, VIII: 405, XIII: 308
Loveland, Lt. Cdr. Kenneth, X: 376, XI: 334
Lovette, Capt. L. P., XIV: 385
Low, Rear Adm. Francis S., biog., X: 21*n;* pic., 32; mentioned, I: 116, II: 36, III: 389, V: 353, X: 21–6, 130*n*, 333, XIV: 307, 310, 385
Lowe, Capt. Frank L., IV: 91, V: 205, 231, 296, 305–6, 310
Lowe, Lt. Cdr. J. A., IX: 388, XI: 335
Lowe, Cdr. J. T., XIII: 315
LOWE, X: 257, 342, 373
Lowery, Cdr. S. J., XIV: 378
Lowestoft, Battle of, XII: 241
Lowrance, Cdr. V. L., XIII: 319
Lowrie, Cdr. N. W., XI: 216*n*
Lowry, Rear Adm. Frank J., biog., IX: 325*n;* pic., 346; mentioned, III: 212, IV: 18, 91, 270, V: 86, IX: 325–9, 332–50 *passim*, 355, 359, 370, 379–81, 395, X: 129, XI: 237, 242, 258–9, 339
LOWRY, XIII: 303, 313, XIV: 256, 260, 374
Lowther, Lt. Cdr. R. D., IX: 41, 388, 392
Lowther Castle, II: 178*n*
LOY, XIV: 378, 392
LOYAL, IX: 277, 281, 291, 393, 396
Lozica, Lt. A., XIII: 313
LSV (Jap.). *See* Transport
Luayon I., XIII: 249–50
Lucas, Lt. D. B., XII: 316
Lucas, Cdr. F. C., XIII: 320
Lucas, Air Commo. F. W. F., IV: 274
Lucas, Maj. Gen. John P., IX: 302, 325–30, 341–65 *passim*, 381, 395
LUCE, XII: 419, XIII: 311, XIV: 253, 375, 391; sunk, 253–4, 391
Lucier, Lt. Cdr. R. O., X: 379
Lucker, Lt. N., III: 158, IV: 20
Ludewig, Capt. J. W., XIV: 332, 383

Ludlow, Lt. Cdr. J. A., XI: 333
LUDLOW, I: 420, II: 38, 58–62, 74, 99, 110, 285, IX: 198, 203–4, 267–8, 280*n*, 348, 361–2, 386, 391, 396, X: 109, 253, 259–60, 372, XI: 278, 342
Luftwaffe, and U-boats, I: 7, 26*n*, 316, X: 59, 95, 172, 307–9; N. Russia, I: 161–92, 360–68, X: 237, 306; N. Africa, II: 212–14, 220–21, 242–3, 246, 252–4, 260*n;* Sicily, IX: 32–3, 56–8, 69, 85–9, 100–107, 119–64 *passim*, 190–94, 204, 217–18; Italy, 234, 248–9, 252, 261, 274–6, 319–20, 331, 341–6, 349, 355–76 *passim;* Medit., IX: 243, X: 261–73; Normandy, XI: 42, 46–8, 73–4, 156, 162–3, 170–74, 186, 190; S. France, 244, 257*n*, 270, 281–2; Rhine crossing, 319–20
LUIGI CADORNA, IX: 38
Luker, Cdr. G. R., XIV: 382
Lull, Cdr. E. E., XIV: 379
Lumsden, Lt. Gen. Herbert, XIII: 105
Lundeberg, Lt. Philip K., I: xvii, X: x, 198*n*, 352–3, XIV: x
Lundgren, Lt. Cdr. G. W., VII: 345, VIII: 410
Lundin, Lt. (jg) C. E., XIII: 309
Lunga, Pt. and Roads, pics., IV: 278–9, V: 16, 19, 335, VI: 100, 123
LUNGA POINT, XIII: 101, 304, XIV: 55, 250, 373
Lunt, Lt. Cdr. A. W., XIV: 375
Luosey, Cdr. M. J., XII: 419, XIII: 311
Lutong, XIII: 267
LÜTZOW, I: 4*n*, 161, 366, X: 57, 230, 237*n*
LUZON (1928), III: 16, 155, 159
LUZON (1943), VIII: 420, XIV: 388
Luzon, Jap. invasion of, III: 170–83; in strategy, VIII: 4, 157, XII: 4, 9, 68, XIII: 5, 12–16, 55; description, 11–12; map, 10; airfields map, 21; maps, 56; strikes on, XII: 100, 106, 341–57, XIII: 57–9, 84, 88–9, 106–7; liberation of, 184–210; maps, 186, 190; casualties, 209*n*, 210
Luzon Strait, VIII: 25, XII: 12, XIII: 161, 164, 172, 279–80
LYCOMING, XIV: 380
LYDD, XI: 335
Lyman, Cdr. C. H., VII: 349
LYMAN, XII: 429, XIII: 319
LYMAN K. SWENSON, XIII: 316, XIV: 382
Lyme Bay, XI: 65–6

Lynch, Lt. Cdr. J. J., V: 214, VII: 337, 344
Lynch, Cdr. R. B., VII: 98, VIII: 415, XIV: 292*n*
Lynch, Lt. Cdr. R. C., IV: 20, 275
Lynch, Ens. Robert F., VI: 48
Lynch, Capt. T. J., VI: 64
Lyon, Lt. Cdr. H. B., IV: 92

Lyon, Capt. John B., I: 419, X: 125–6, X: 209–12, 226, 227*n*
Lyon, Capt. R. D., I: 386
Lyon, Lt. Cdr. R. E., XIV: 375
LYON, II: 40, 139–42, 153–4, IX: 98, 388, 392, XI: 340; pic., II: 149
Lyons, Lt. E. P., VII: 345
Lyttle, Capt. G. H., XIV: 387

Mac and Mc

Mac and C.A.M. ships, X: 38, 321n
McAdoo, Lt. F. H., XIII: 275n
McAfee, Lt. Cdr. R., XI: 343
McAlister, 2nd Lt. J. A., III: 232
MacArthur, Gen. of the Army Douglas, pics., VI: 435, XII: 6, 70, XIII: 156, 276, XIV: 366–7; character and leadership, VI: 96, VIII: 40–48, 144–5; staff, V: 115, VI: 15, VIII: 46; campaign of 1942, I: 67, III: 50–56, 64, 168, 178–9, 182, 195, 203, IV: 249; Coral Sea, 13, 16, 20–24, 49; proposed raids, 254, 258; Guadalcanal, 260–65, 269, 274, V: 115–16, 185; Papua, VI: 41, 45, 50, 96, 255, 261, 269; New Britain, 372–4, 378; Admiralties, 433–8, 448; New Guinea, XIII: 45–8, 60, 78, 83, 91–6, 114, 135, 140–41; Morotai, XII: 19–23; Leyte, 13–16, 55–7, 60–65, 72, 113, 136–8, 149, 163, 198, 296, 337–94 passim, 415; Mindoro and Lingayen, 376, 386, XIII: 18–19, 55, 114–16, 153–5, 163; Luzon, 184, 189, 193–8, 207; arguments with Nimitz, XII: 354, 367, XIII: 174–9; Southern Philippines, 199, 205, 213–18, 233, 239–41, 249, 321; Java and Borneo, 214, 257–9, 268, 272–6, XIV: 104; Japanese surrender and occupation, 353–67; strategy, V: 115–16, 185, VI: 3–4, 95, 225–6, 254–5, 282–3, VII: 3–10, 91, XII: 3–18, 361–2, 397, XIII: 3–12, 18, 276, 289, 293, XIV: 4; sub. supply missions, VI: 85, XII: 64; and Navy, VI: 31, 42, 47; aid acknowledged, III: xi, VI: xi; quoted, on Pearl Harbor III: 14; naval raids, VI: 422; Buna, 46; "Leyte, then Luzon," XII: 11; "return," 137; Halsey, 343; Leyte secured, 394; "kept the faith," XIII: 198; on board *Missouri*, XIV: 365–8
McAuslan, Lt. (jg) A. C., X: 111–12
McBride, Col. A. C., III: 53n
MacBryde, Lt. Cdr. E. P., X: 379
McCabe, Lt. Cdr. F. M., IV: 173, X: 379
McCabe, Capt. G. E., VII: 344, VIII:
405

McCaffree, Lt. Cdr. B. C., I: 419
McCain, Lt. Cdr. J. S., Jr., II: 39
McCain, Vice Adm. John S., biog., XIII: 52n; pics., IV: 279, XII: 191, XIV: 166; Air A/SW, X: 28; Comairsopac, IV: 252, 264, 269–70, V: 184n, 374; Solomons, IV: 274, 279–80, V: 23–7, 32, 82–3; Morotai, XII: 22; strikes of mid-1944, 12, 86, 90–94, 101, 106; support of landings, Leyte, 108, 133, 150, 339–41, 348–9, 356; Leyte Gulf Battle, 175, 193, 294, 304–29 passim, 424; relieves Mitscher, 343; as CTF38, XIII: 22, 52–4, 88, XIV: 20, 87n, 266, 333–4; Dec. '44 typhoon, XIII: 66–8; South China Sea raid, 165, 170; June '45 typhoon, XIV: 299–301, 308–9; quoted, XIII: 58, XIV: 366–7
McCaleb, Cdr. W. R., I: 422; VIII: 418
McCall, Capt. H. W. U., XIV: 388
McCALL, VII: 9n
McCALLA, V: 151–3, 157, 162, 166–9, 205, 232, 236, 293, VI: 144, 151, 156n, 242, VIII: 415, XII: 425, XIII: 322
McCallum, Cdr. J. L. P., XIII: 286, 320
McCampbell, Cdr. David, pic. VIII: 177, 191; mentioned, 273, 276, 296–7, 414, XII: 177–8, 324, 426
McCandless, Lt. Cdr. Bruce, V: 247n, 252–3, XIV: 191, 198
McCandlish, Commo. B. V., X: 129n
McCann, Rear Adm. Allan R., biog., X: 345n; mentioned, 345, XII: 426
McCarry, Cdr. W. T., XIII: 309
McCarthy, Lt. E. E., VIII: 419
McCarthy, Capt. W. P., XIV: 388
McCarty, Capt. W. P., XIII: 304n, XIV: 378
McCauley, Cdr. J. W., XII: 420, XIII: 306
McCAWLEY, IV: 272–3, V: 14, 31, 34, 52, 64n, 148, 227, 231, 236, VI: 144, 147, 155; sunk, 151
McClain, Cdr. W. H., VII: 338, XIV: 383
McClaughry, Cdr. J. G., VII: 337, VIII: 407, XII: 419, XIII: 310

McClead, Lt. (jg) G. W., VII: 347
McClees, Lt. H. C., XIII: 307
McClintock, XII: 169–73, 429
McCloy, Hon. John J., VII: 62
McCloy, Ens. R. C., III: 96
McCloy, Lt. Cdr. W. M., XIII: 307, XIV: 380
McClure, Col. N. E., II: 29n
McClure, Brig. Gen. R. B., VI: 229, 233, 237
McClurg, Ens. D. W., IX: 121n
McClusky, Lt. Cdr. C. W., III: 392, IV: 91, 121, 127–30, 140
McColl, Capt. J. W., IX: 389
McCombs, Lt. Cdr. C. E., V: 232, 249
MacComsey, Capt. H. F., XIV: 386
McConnell, Cdr. R. P., III: 272, 360–62, VII: 338, 349, 353
McCONNELL, VI: 415, XII: 429
McCOOK, XI: 121, 124, 143–4, 158, 336, 343
McCool, Lt. R. M., XIV: 275
McCORD, VII: 276, 347, VIII: 227n–8n, XII: 244, 420, XIII: 318, XIV: 248, 385
McCorkle, Capt. F. D., I: 420, III: 38, IX: 389, XIII: 249, 323
McCormick, Cdr. G. W., XIII: 307
McCormick, Vice Adm. Lynde D., IV: 10, 11n, X: 230, XI: xi, XII: viii, XIV: 320, 329, 373
McCormick, Lt. (jg) N. C., I: 143
McCORMICK, I: 418, 422; X: 118
McCornock, Cdr. S. A., VIII: 120, 404; XII: 389
McCown, Capt. H. Y., I: 390n
McCoy, Capt. J. A., X: 70, 75n, 237–9
McCoy, Winfield, I: 333
McCracken, Lt. Cdr. A. R., III: 159, 205
McCRACKEN, XIV: 378
McCrane, Watertender J. C., XIII: 77
McCrea, Capt. J. L., VII: 349
McCrea, Cdr. V. B., I: 421, XII: 405
McCreery, Lt. Gen. Sir Richard, IX: 247, 271, 294, 392
McCreery, Cdr. W. A., XIV: 386
MacCrindle, Loretta I., I: xviii, XI: xi, XII: viii
McCroskey, Lt. Cdr. C. H., X: 377
McCullar, Maj. D. D., VI: 64
McCullough, Cdr. M. L., VII: 334, VIII: 409, XII: 418, XIII: 307, XIV: 385
McCullough, Lt. Cdr. R. J., XIII: 318, XIV: 383

McCune, Cdr. F. C. B., X: 356–7
McCurtain, Lt. Cdr. J. H., X: 377–8
McDaniel, Lt. Cdr. Eugene F., I: 232–3
McDaniel, Lt. (jg) J. G., X: 346n
McDaniel, Cdr. R. T., IX: 389
McDERMUT, VIII: 409, XII: 199, 212–18, 418, XIII: 307, XIV: 248; pic., XII: 222
McDill, Capt. A. S., III: 196n, 319n
MacDonald, Lt. Cdr. Donald J., VI: 161, 166, 181, 228, 244, 248–52
McDonald, Cdr. J. N., VIII: 406, XIV: 381
McDonald, William, X: 381, XIV: 238, 386
McDonnel, 1st Lt. W. S., X: 130
McDonough, Lt. Col. J. F., VII: 129–30
McDougal, Lt. Col. D. S., V: 141
McDOUGAL, I: 70n, 111, 420
McDowell, Lt. Col. E. II., XIII: 35, 309
McDowell, Cdr. L. R., XII: 415
McDowell, Capt. W. A., XIV: 380
McDowell, X: 205
McDuffie, Lt. W. K., XII: 421
McEathron, Cdr. E. D., X: 199n, XII: 377, XIII: 33, XIV: 220, 375n, 377
McElfresh, Lt. J. M., XII: 209, 213, 236, 422
McElligott, Capt. R. T., VIII: 410
McElrath, Cdr. R. W., VIII: 418, XII: 417, XIV: 383
McElroy, 1st Lt. E. E., III: 392
McElroy, Capt. John W., I: xviii, III: xiii, IV: xi, XIV: 176, 379
McElroy, Lt. R. Y., II: 128
McEntire, Cdr. F. E., XII: 428, XIV: 383
McEwen, Lt. A. G., XIV: 176
McFadden, Lt. Cdr. A. G. W., I: 217, 218n
McFadden, Lt. Cdr. J. F., XII: 52
McFall, Rear Adm. A. C., VI: 146
McFall, Cdr. E. A., IV: 174, VIII: 405, 419
McFarland, Lt. Cdr. A. R., XIV: 258, 381
McFARLAND, IV: 279, V: 23, 180–81, 317
MacFarlane, Sq. Ldr. H. M., V: 375
McFarlane, Lt. Cdr. R. N., I: 420, II: 39
McFeaters, Capt. C. P., IV: 273, V: 231
McGarry, Cdr. W. T., VIII: 409, IX: 388; XIV: 379
McGee, Capt. H. F., VI: 261, VIII: 55, 404, XIII: 208, 309

McGinnis, Lt. Cdr. R. D., VII: 339, 346
McGlaughry, Cdr. J. G., VII: 346
McGlone, Lt. Cdr. L. G., III: 160
McGoldrick, Cdr. J. A., XIV: 192, 381
McGoughran, Lt. Cdr. J. C., VII: 348
McGovern, Commo. John B., VII: 171, 335–7, 343, VIII: 405, 419, XIV: 37, 217, 381
McGowan, Lt. Cdr. Richard, XII: 426
McGOWAN, VIII: 409, XII: 199, 211n, 212–15, 418, XIII: 307, XIV: 53, 249, 385
McGowen, 2nd Lt. J. R. C., VI: 435, 439
McGrath, Roger, I: 331
McGrath, Lt. Cdr. T. D., XI: 335
McGraw, Lt. (jg) B. A., V: 208
McGregor, Capt. Donald, XIII: 307, XIV: 380
McGregor, Capt. E. G., XIV: 388
MacGregor, Lt. Cdr. E. J., II: 37
McGregor, Cdr. L. D., XIV: 285
McGregor, Lt. Cdr. R. R., V: 324
McGrigor, Rear Adm. R. R., II: 277–9, 280n, IX: 150, 155–6, 166, 206, 207n, 234, X: 311
McGuckin, Cdr. B. F., XII: 419, XIII: 310, XIV: 380
McGuire, Lt. W. E., VIII: 410
McGuirk, Lt. W. E., XII: 422, XIII: 306
McGurl, Capt. D. M., VII: 346, 352, IX: 389
McHale, Capt. W. A., VII: 345, VIII: 418, XII: 417
McIlhenny, Cdr. H. H., VI: 272, VII: 13, XIII: 317, XIV: 384
McInerney, Capt. Francis X., IV: 19, 65n, V: 86, VI: 110n, 161, 166–8, 171–4, 178, 181–8, 193, XIV: 384
MacInness, Lt. Cdr. D., XIV: 378
McIntire, Lt. (jg) J. O., VIII: 300n
McIntire, Rear Adm. Ross, pic., I: 70
McIntosh, Capt. H. D., XIV: 375
MacIntyre, Lt. Alexander, I: 418
McIver, Lt. Cdr. D. C., V: 309n
McKay, Cdr. B. M., VII: 333, XI: 341
McKay, Cdr. D. E., XIV: 379
McKean, Maj. W. B., IV: 267
McKEAN, IV: 273, V: 64, 124, VI: 145–6, 156n, 228, 294–5; sunk, 351
McKee, Lt. J. R., XIV: 381
McKEE, VI: 331, VII: 255, 274–5, 337, 344, VIII: 405, 418, XII: 416, XIV: 383
McKeesport, X: 67n, 68

McKellar, Lt. Clinton, IV: 93; VII: 16
McKelvy, Lt. Col. W. N., V: 125, 129, 190–91
MACKENDRICK, X: 321
McKenna, Capt. F. J., VIII: 409, XII: 302, 421
MacKenzie, Cdr. C. J., VIII: 415, XIII: 45, 306, XIV: 379
McKenzie, Capt. L. S., XIII: 308, XIV: 387
MacKenzie, Cdr. M. L., XIV: 385
MACKENZIE, IX: 378, 389, X: 275, 370, XI: 341
McKeon, Lt. J. P., XIII: 311
McKillip, Capt. J. C. S., XIII: 59n
McKinney, Cdr. C. G., X: 380
McKinney, Lt. Cdr. E. B., III: 158, IV: 220–21, VII: 93–4
McKinney, Cdr. J. D., VII: 347, XII: 426, XIII: 317, XIV: 383
McKinney, Cdr. J. R., II: 38, IX: 389
MacKinnon, Cdr. N. A., VIII: 405, XII: 421
McKnight, Lt. G. W., XIII: 306
McKnight, Lt. J. R., III: 159
McLain, Lt. Gen. R. S., IX: 140n
M LANAHAN, IX: 124, 385, 388, XI: 276, 341
McLaughlin, Cdr. C. H., VII: 337, VIII: 404
McLaughlin, Lt. J. B., XIII: 304, XIV: 377
McLaughlin, Capt. P. V., XI: 191, XIV: 388
MacLean, Cdr. C. R., XII: 418
McLean, Capt. Ephraim R., V: 353, VI: 158, VII: 238, 245, 346, VIII: 413, XII: 295, 419, XIII: 311
McLean, Capt. G. A., XIV: 126, 381
McLean, Capt. J. B., I: 420, II: 38, VII: 338, VIII: 127, 406, XIII: 43–6, 306, 311; "slow tow," 25–33
McLean, Lt. Cdr. J. L., VIII: 410, XIV: 380
MACLEISH, I: 418, 421, X: 118, 379
McLeod, Lt. Col. K. F., VII: 174
McLoughlin, Cdr. C. H., XIV: 379
McMahon, Cdr. B. F., VI: 69; XIV: 296
McMahon, Capt. F. W., V: 353; VII: 338
McManes, Capt. Kenmore M., pic., XII: 215; mentioned, VI: 382; VIII: 127–30, 406, XII: 199–202, 217–22, 229, 421

McMaster, Lt. F., I: 421
McMenemy, Cdr. E. H., VII: 334
McMillan, Cdr. D. G., VII: 341
McMillan, George, Old Breed, VI: 378n, 388–9, XII: 30n
McMillen, Lt. Cdr. W. N., XIV: 377
McMillian, Cdr. I. E., pic., XIV: 183; mentioned, XIII: 36, 304, XIV: 182, 373
McMillin, Capt. G. J., III: 184–6
McMinn, W. J., I: 333
McMonagle, Seaman T. B., IX: 100
McMorris, Vice Adm. Charles H. ("Soc"), biog., VII: 17n; pic., 30; mentioned, III: 129, 216n, 241n–2n, 251, IV: 271, V: 87, 150, 162, VI: 10–11; Komandorski battle, VII: 3, 17–35, 39, 334, XII: 9, 348n, XIV: 372
MacMurdy, Cdr. E. G., XIV: 380
McNAIR, VIII: 409; XII: 199, 418; XIII: 307; XIV: 385
McNarney, Lt. Gen. J. T., I: 45, IX: 228, X: 28
McNeil, Capt. D. C., VII: 345, VIII: 408, XII: 417, XIII: 309
McNeil, Lt. J. J., XIV: 185
McNider, Brig. Gen. Hanford, XIII: 208, 306

MacNish, Lt. Cdr. C. E., VIII: 411, XIII: 319
McNulty, Cdr. H. J., II: 40
McNulty, Lt. W. J., XIV: 378
McNULTY, XIII: 313
McPherson, Lt. Cdr. I. H., XII: 426, XIII: 316, XIV: 384
MacPherson, Cdr. J. I., XIII: 310, XIV: 380
MacPherson, Lt. Cdr. R. A., VII: 158, 295
McQuilkin, Ens. M. W. T., VI: 248
McQuiston, Cdr. E. I., XIV: 381
McRoberts, Lt. Cdr. J. F., XIII: 306
McVay, Capt. Charles B., XIV: 319–27, 372–3, 384; court-martial, 328
McVey, Cdr. J. B., VII: 336, 346, XIII: 308
McVickar, Lt. (jg) M., VIII: 419
McWhinnie, Cdr. C. J., VI: 144, 228, VIII: 408
McWhorter, Rear Adm. Ernest D., pic., II: 30; mentioned, I: 419, II: 31–2, 35, 39, 44, 90, 163, 247
McWhorter, Lt. (jg) J. F., X: 351
McWhorter, Lt. Cdr. J. H., X: 378
McWilliam, Capt. H. H., XI: 342

M

M. F. Elliott, I: 394
Ma Hung Kwei, Gen., XIII: 294
Maasdam, I: 77n
Mabalacat, XII: 302, 348, XIII: 102–3,
107
Mabilao, XIII: 135, 145
Mabley, Cdr. L. C., X: 333n, 376
Macajalar Bay, XIII: 249; chart, 242
Macauley, Lt. Cdr. Edward, VI: 343n
Macauley, Capt. W. S., I: 376n,
XIII: 304, XIV: 372
Macbeth, I: 364n
MACDONOUGH, III: 104, 213n, IV: 271,
V: 86, 111–12, 138, VII: 41, 124, 127–9,
224, 335–7, 345, VIII: 39, 178, 413,
XIII: 419, XIV: 319
Macharda, II: 192, 198n, 213
MACHIAS, XIII: 307n
Machinsky, Chief Carpenter, V: 135
Mack, Capt. A. R., XIV: 380
Mack, Lt. Cdr. B. D., XIII: 305
Mackensen, Gen. E. von, IX: 350, 361–
3, 366
MACKEREL, I: 421
MACKINAC, IV: 279, V: 23–4, 82, 205,
VII: 340, 350, XII: 46
MACOMB, I: 420, II: 37, X: 257–9, 372,
XI: 341, XIV: 236, 253, 376, 391
Macondray, Cdr. A., IV: 19
Macqueville, XI: 215
Mactan I., XII: 126, XIII: 235; pic.,
245
Maczkowski, Richard, I: 398
MAD. See Magnetic Airborne Detector
Madagascar, I: 167
Madang, VI: 96, 256, 261–2, 271, 383,
390–91
Maddalena, Sardinia, IX: 9, 37, 42, 243,
308, XI: 246
Maddaloni, IX: 329
Madden, Lt. Cdr. G. B., IV: 273,
V: 109–10
Madden, Capt. J. F., XIV: 378
Maddox, Cdr. W. S., VIII: 405, 415,
XIV: 385
MADDOX (1942), IX: 109, 388; sunk,
100–101

MADDOX (1944), XIII: 61–3, 181–2, 316,
XIV: 301, 382
Madeira, Capt. D. L., I: 111, 420, II:37,
117n, IX: 193, 388, X: 50
Madison, Maj. C. T., V: 374
MADISON, I: 90, 195, 328, 354, 418, 420,
X: 260, XI: 278, 311–12, 340–42, XIV:
326
Madson, Coxswain, III: 302
Maennle, Lt. Cdr. F. W., IX: 388
Maetsuycher, VI: 36
Maffin Bay, VIII: 92–4, 97, 102
Magaldan, XIII: 194
Magane M., IV: 172
Magann, W. P., X: 382
Magdala, X: 382
Magellan, Ferdinand, VIII: 149, XII: 61,
XIII: 235, 263; monument, pic., 245
MAGIC, XI: 192
Magicienne Bay, VIII: 183, 187, 210,
329; pic., 176
Maginnis, Cdr. J., VII: 348
Magly, Capt. A. V., XIII: 305, XIV: 374
Magnetic Airborne Detector, I: 224,
353, X: 95, 329
MAGOFFIN, XIV: 379
MAGOG, X: 329
Magzam, XIII: 241
Mahan, Rear Adm. Alfred T.,
VIII: 314, 318
MAHAN, III: 210n, V: 205, 223, VI: 260–
62, 267, 381–4, 390–91, 436, XII: 344,
380, 385, 417; sunk, 381–2
Maher, Cdr. A. L., III: 368n–9n
Maher, Lt. Cdr. E. H., XIII: 313
Maher, Cdr. J. B., II: 39, VI: 386, XIV:
373
Maher, Capt. James E., IV: 274, V: 87,
205, 218, VII: 338, 348
MAHOGANY, XIV: 377
Mahoney, Capt. J. J., VII: 334, 349,
VIII: 409
MAHRATTA, X: 308
Maiana Atoll, VII: 77
MAIDSTONE, IX: 33
MAIKAZE, III: 333, IV: 88, V: 85, 206,
370; sunk, VII: 328

MAINE, XIV: 86n
Mainguy, Capt. E. R., XIV: 388
MAINSTAY, XI: 343
Mainz, XI: 320
Maiori, IX: 271-2
Maizuru, III: 21n, 26, XIV: 331
MAJABA, V: 226, 227n
Majuro Atoll, VII: 206, 305-8, VIII: 154n, 219, 229; descr., VII: 225-6; chart, 225; occupation, 225-9; T.O., 347-8; U.S. base, 106, 218, 228-9, 304-5, 320, VIII: 29-41 *passim*, 343-5, 348, XII: 398
Makalapa, VI: 12; pic., 19
Makassar, III: 306-7, 320, XIII: 107; landing, III: 306-7
Makassar Strait, III: 281-5, 292, 299, 335
MAKASSAR STRAIT, XIV: 386
MAKI, XII: 326, 430, XIII: 159
MAKIGUMO, IV: 88, V: 85, 206, 222, 234; sunk, 367-8
Makin I., III: 262-4; raid, IV: 235-41; substituted for Nauru, VI: 12; plans, VII: 76-7, 82-5, 97-9, 121-2; capture of, 122-35; casualties, 134; chart, 128; pics., IV: 235, VII: 142; base, III: 240-41, VII: 203, 212, VIII: 156
MAKIN ISLAND, XIII: 99, 304, XIV: 250, 373
MAKINAMI, V: 206, 297-8, 302, 305, 318, 366-8, VI: 332-3; sunk, 356-7
Makino, Maj. Gen., XII: 67
Makua, VII: 252
Makushin Bay, IV: 176
Malabang, XIII: 243, 246
Malabang-Parang. *See* Mindanao
Malacca Strait, III: 385, VIII: 4-5, XIII: 256, 277
Malaita I., IV: 279, V: 4, 23-4
Malamaui I., XIII: 226
Malanaphy, Cdr. M. J., VII: 346, XIV: 26, 378
Malang, III: 281
Malangas, III: 159
Malantic, I: 342
Malaria, VI: 45, 49, 102
Malavergne, René, II: 129-30
Malay Barrier, III: 49-51, 55, 152, 270-80
Malaya, XII: 68, XIII: 169; Jap. invasion, III: 130, 187-92
MALAYA, I: 167, XI: 301
Malaybalay, XIII: 240, 250
Malcolm, Lt. (jg) I. D., XII: 422

MALCOLM, II: 207-8, 224
Mallard, Capt. J. B., VI: 261
Mallard, Lt. Cdr. P. W., XIV: 386
MALLARD, I: 421
Malo, Ens. J. K., I: 393
Maloelap, III: 261-3, VII: 74-5, 82-4, 97, 138, 203, 206-7, 223, 307-9, 314, VIII: 156; air strikes on, VII: 98, 118, 214-21, 229
Maloney, Lt. Cdr. J. L., XI: 273, 342
Maloney, Capt. James D., X: 156-7
MALOY, XI: 151, 299-302, 336
Malpass, Lt. Cdr. R. E., VII: 335
MALPEQUE, XI: 335
Malstrom, Capt. A. I., XIV: 373
Malta, I: 193-7, 396, II: 254, 279-81, IX: 23, 29, 69, 79, 101, 123-4, 142, 157, 236, 242-5, 251, 291-3, 297, 377, XI: 246, 318; relief, pic., I: 210; Conference, X: 338
Manakee, Lt. H. R., IX: 188n
MANATEE, XII: 428, XIII: 61, 318, XIV: 387
Manchester, Lt. R. C., VI: 246, 251
MANCHESTER, I: 181
Manchuria Incident, III: 11-12
Mancini, Lt. Emidio, IX: xiii
Mandalay, III: 381
Mandarich, Lt. Cdr. S., VII: 338, 346
MANDERSON V., XIII: 307; XIV: 386
Manees, Capt. L. J., III: 160, 272n; XIII: 313, 322
Mangarin Bay, XIII: 18, 26n, 31, 40-41, 46-7
Manggar, XIII: 268-70, 275
Mangrum, Lt. Col. R. C., V: 74, 104, 374
Maniagassa I., VIII: 182
Manila, III: 149-52, 167, 182, 195, XII: 67-8, 71, 91, 161n, 169n, 311, 351-2, XIII: 11-13, 16, 102, 157, 184-216 *passim*, XIV: 358-9; Conferences, III: 156, XIV: 355; pic., XIII: 197; chart, 190
Manila Bay, III: 33, 150, 158-9, 167; VIII: 51, XII: 239, 348, 356, XIII:11, 19, 103, 116, 215; cleared, 198-207; 1898 Battle, II: 286, XII: 241; chart, XIII: 190
MANILA BAY, VII: 304, 344, VIII: 209, 329n, 405, 411, XII: 244, 308, 420, XIII: 19, 103, 305, 325, XIV: 250
Manini, III: 221n
Manjome, Maj. Gen. T., XIII: 234-6

MANLEY, I: 15n, IV: 276n, V: 124, VII: 254, 277, 343, VIII: 408, XII: 422, XIII: 307, 374
MANLOVE, VII: 308, VIII 411, XIV: 381
Mann, Lt. Cdr. S. S., XIV: 289
Manners, Rear Adm. E., I: 86
MANNERS, X: 337
MANNERT L. ABELE, XIV: 49, 179, 373, 391; sunk, 223–4
Manning, Cdr. J. I., XIV: 237, 376
MANNING, VIII: 405, XIII: 308
Manokwari, VIII: 66, 86, 88, 107, 120n, 132, 143
Manon, II: 284
MANORA, VIII: 77, 403, XII: 416, XIII: 265n, 272n, 310, 312
Mansalay, XIII: 49
Manseck, Kaptlt. Helmut, X: 112–13
Mansergh, Capt. C. A. L., V: 330, VI: 181
Mansfield, Lt. Cdr. J. E., XIII: 304
Mansfield, Rear Adm. J. M., IX: 345–7, 359, 371, 396, X: 16, XI: 339
MANSFIELD, XIII: 316, XIV: 301, 382
Mantel, Oskar, X: 327n
Manteo, I: 279
MANUNDA, III: 317
Manus, VI: 432, 441; landing, 445; base, 446–7, VIII: 45, 49, 73–5, 96, 227, XII: 16, 76–148 *passim*, 304, 307, 366n, XIII: 60, 97, 115–17, 145, XIV: 104–6, 109, 388; pic., XII: 134
Mapia Is., XII: 53
Maples, Capt. H. L., III: 393, IV: 174, 272
Marable, Lt. Cdr. H. H., VII: 334
MARATHON, XIV: 176, 379
MARBLEHEAD, I: 390n, 419, III: 154, 160, 271, 284–5, 290, 298–306, 312, 375, X: 204n, 213n, 225–7, XI: 341; track chart, III: 302
Marcks, Gen., XI: 153, 163, 186
MARCUS, V: 325n
Marcus I., VIII: 172, XIV: 10, 360; carrier raids on, III: 268, VII: 92–3; bombardments, XII: 60, 87; surrender, XIV: 360
MARCUS ISLAND, XII: 243–4, 286, 420, XIII: 19, 29, 117, 145, 306, XIV: 120, 374
Mare, Cdr. A. L., XIII: 307, XIV: 380
Mare I. Navy Yard, III: 213, VI: 190n
Margetts, Lt. R. K., IX: 392
Marianas, III: 7, VIII: 3, 20; history and description, 149–54; charts, 153, 163; carrier strikes on, 154–5, 174–9
Marianas Opn., XII: 3–5, XIII: 162; planning, VIII: 157–66; logistics, 341–50; ammo. expended, 347; T.O., 407–16, 418–20; base development, 342, 348
Mariani, Capit. de Frég., II: 99
MARIAS, VIII: 411, XII: 428, XIII: 71, 318, XIV: 387
MARIE, XI: 337
Marinduque I., XIII: 50; chart, 27
Marine Corps, 1941 strength, I: 48n; Argentia, 69; Azores, 67; Iceland, 67, 75–8; Trinidad, 146–7; North Africa, II: 231; defense of P. I., III: 28–9, 155, 159, 204; Sansapor, VIII: 143; Southern France, XI: 289; Philippines, XII: 154, 351; Fleet Marine Force, I: liv, II: 20

Amphibious Corps, First, VI: 289, 348, 364; Third, VIII: 159, 170, 374, 379, XII: 32, XIV: 86, 89, 108, 171, 239, 266; Fifth, VII: 87–9, VIII: 159, 355, XII: 154, XIV: 7–8, 64

Divisions, First, I: 75, II: 21, IV: 259, 272, V: 12–14, 65–78, 123–30, 140–46, 188–98, 288, 334, VI: 131–2, 274, 289n, 378–88, 408, IX: 93, XII: 16, 34–43, XIV: 90, 171, 240, 378; Second, I: 75–7, III: 257–8, IV: 272, V: 334–5, 340–44, 352, VII: 89–90, 116, 152–86, 337, VIII: 170, 186–209, 330–69 *passim*, XIV: 90, 111, 217, 275, 381; Third, VI: 296, 337, 340, 352, 363–4, VIII: 160, 374–400 *passim*, 418, XIV: 8, 63–5, 68, 72; Fourth, VII: 167n, 232, 237–50, 273, VIII: 159, 170, 186–210 *passim*, 330–70 *passim*, 408, XIV: 8, 37–9, 49, 52, 72; Fifth, XII: 8, XIV: 37–42, 49, 62, 72–3; Sixth, 90, 171, 215, 240, 378; Provisional Brigades, I: 75–9, II: 20–21, VIII: 160, 374–6, 389–99, 416; Defense Bns., III: 227–35, 244–53, IV: 72, 93, 249, 263n, 272–3, VI: 428, VII: 78, 250, 347; Paratroops, IV: 273, 290; Raiders, 235–41, 272–3, 288–90, V: 118, 290, VI: 98, 102, 139, 142, 152, 156n; Engineers, 361, VIII: 399; pics., IV: 235, V: 130, 178, VI: 253, 388, VII: 166–7, 174, 246, 271, 278, 294, 310, VIII: 193, XII: 39, XIV: frontispiece (Iwo flag-raising), 47, 54
Marine Corps Air, planes, VIII: 156;

carrier-based, VII: xxix; Aircraft Wings, First, V: 228, 232; Second, IV: 92; Fourth, VII: 309, 340; Groups, Two, XIII: 272; Eleven, XII: 41; Twelve, 368, XIII: 23, 223–5; Fourteen, 223, 230; Twenty-two, IV: 92, XIII: 194, XIV: 271; Twenty-three, V: 74; Twenty-four, XIII: 194, 246; Thirty-one, XIV: 243, 374; Thirty-two, XIII: 190, 223; Thirty-three, XIV: 243, 374; Forty-five, XII: 51; at Zamboanga, XIII: 225; Fighter Squadrons, –111, VII: 97; –112, V: 375, XIV: 382; –121, V: 340, 374; –122, V: 375; –123, V: 375, VI: 230, XIV: 382; –124, VI: 230, XIII: 317; –211, III: 228, 246–7, XII: 380; –212, IV: 248, 263*n*, V: 375; –213, XIII: 317; –214, VI: 231; –218, XII: 380; –221, IV: 73, 93, VI: 150, XIV: 384; –223, V: 73*n*, 88, 374; –224, 374; –313, XII: 380; Night Fighter, –531, VI: 291*n*; –541, XII: 367; Observation Squadron, –155, VII: 335; Photographic Squadrons, –154, V: 375; –254, VIII: 164*n*; Scout Bombing Squadrons, –131, –132, –141, –142, V: 374; –151, VII: 350; –231, III: 210, IV: 72*n*, V: 374; –232, 73*n*, 374; –233, –234, 374; –241, IV: 92; –331, VII: 350

Marine Robin, XI: 340
Marion, Lt. G. T., XIV: 120, 378
Marion McKinley Bovard, IX: 390
Mariposa, I: 329
Maritime Commission, I: 291–4, X: 39–41
Marivcles, III: 155, 198, XII: 348, XIII: 14, 199; landing, 198–202
Marix, Lt. Cdr. G. E., XII: 306, 420
Mark, Lt. W. M., XIV: 377
MARKAB, VII: 334; VIII: 420; XIV: 387
Markham, Cdr. L. M., II: 38, IX: 387, X: 256
Markham Valley, VI: 261, 266–8, 271, 371, XIII: 96
Marks, Lt. D. A., VIII: 414
Marks, Lt. Cdr. J. A., XII: 429, XIII: 71, 319
Marks, Lt. R. A., XIV: 326
Markworth, Kaptlt. Friedrich, X: 122, 182–3
Marler, Lt. (jg) R. C., II: 211, 214–17
MARLIN, I: 421
MARMORA, XIV: 387
MARNE, I: 359

MARNIX VAN ST. ALDEGONDE, II: 195*n*, IX: 258, 392, X: 264
MAROCAIN, XI: 343
Maron, II: 192, 198*n*, 213
Marontate, Lt. Eugene, V: 340
Marpi Pt., Saipan, VIII: 168, 335, 338
Marquana Bay, VI: 244–6, 250–51
Marquand, John P., XIV: 29, 33
Marrakech, II: 150–51, IX: 327
Marron, Capt. R. V., VII: 346, VIII: 418
Marsala, IX: 45, 181
Marseilles, IX: 365, XI: 226, 232, 235–8, 275, 284–91; chart, 283; pic., 293
MARSH, XI: 340, 343
Marshall, Lt. C. B., XII: 425
Marshall, Maj. D. E., XIII: 317
Marshall, Gen. of the Army George C., pics., I: 70, VI: 18; assistance, XI: xi; pre-war negotiations and conferences, I: 39–40, 55, 70; III: 74–5; strategy, I: 46, II: 12–15, VI: 3, XI: 3, XII: 7, 11; Pearl Harbor, III: 128; A/SW, I: 240–46, 308–9, X: 27–8, 31, 88; Guadalcanal, IV: 245–6, 260–62; N. Africa, II: 16; Casablanca Conf., VI: 4–5, IX: 5–9; Admiralties, VI: 434; Aleutians, VII: 13; Marianas, VIII: 6; Conf. of May 1943, IX: 229; opns. after Sicily, 231; proposed as Supreme Commander Europe, XI: 22; invasion of France, 8–15, 18, 50, 54, 222–3, 226–9; Italy, 296; Rhine crossing, 318; Leyte, XII: 15; Jap. surrender, XIV: 339, 358
Marshall, Lt. Col. George C., II: 225
Marshall, Ens. H. M., X: 382
Marshall, Cdr. J. G., X: 375–6, XI: 146, 336
Marshall, Col. S. L. A., III: 389*n*, VII: 121*n*
Marshall, Capt. W. J., X: 157, XI: 148, 336, 418, XIV: 384
MARSHALL, VIII: 413, XII: 319, 426, XIII: 317, XIV: 383
Marshall Is., history and descr., III: 7, VII: 70–75; chart, 204–5; in pre-war plans, III: 55; Jap. fortification of, 60, VII: 71, 74, 222–3; Halsey's raid and air strikes, III: 261–4, VII: 75, 190–97, 211; capture of, plans and organization, 108–13, 201–8; air support, 218–21; chart, 216–17; numbers, 207, 351; T.O., 343–5 ; occupation of lesser

Marshall Is. (*cont'd.*)
islands, 310–14; chart. 311. *See also* Eniwetok, Kwajalein
Marston, Maj. Gen. John, I: 75, V: 340*n*
MARTE, I: 129
Martha's Vineyard, II: 28*n*
Martin, Maj. Gen. C. A., XIII: 241, 324
Martin, Brig. Gen. C. D., VI: 390
Martin, Capt. C. F., VIII: 409; XII: 419; XIII: 304
Martin, Donald R., I: xvii, II: 34*n*, III: xii, IV: x, V: x, VI: xii, VII: vii, VIII: viii, IX: xiv, X: x, XI: xi, XII: vii, XIII: x, 99*n*, XIV: x–xi
Martin, Cdr. F. B. C., XII: 387, XIII: 323
Martin, Brig. Gen. F. L., III: 128
Martin, Capt. G. D., XII: 429, XIV: 386
Martin, Capt. H. J., XII: 429, XIII: 305, XIV: 110, 372
Martin, Rear Adm. H. M., VIII: 414, XIV: 373
Martin, Cdr. J. C., XII: 406
Martin, Ens. J. J., II: 79*n*
Martin, Av. Radioman Jack W., VII: 212*n*, XIII: 99*n*
Martin, Lt. Cdr. L. H., V: 233
Martin, Capt. Lester, VII: 345, VIII: 418, XII: 416, XIII: 308, XIV: 380
Martin, Cdr. M. W., XIII: 307
Martin, Capt. W. A. P., I: xvi, X: xi, 11, XIV: 380
Martin, Lt. W. L., X: 382
"Martin, Maj. William," IX: 39, 45–7, 69, 129*n*, 167
Martin, Cdr. William I., VII: 324, 348, VIII: 176–8, 184, 414, XIII: 318, XIV: 383
Martin, Maj. William P., VI: 64
MARTIN, I: 359; sunk, II: 283
Martineau, Cdr. D. L., VII: 346, VIII: 210, 408, XIV: 374
Martinique, I: 30–33, IX: 306, X: 191
Martins, Adm. Dodsworth, I: 382–3
MARTS, X: 380
Marumo, Rear Adm. K., IV: 18, 22, 32, 39–40
Maruyama, Lt. Gen. M., V: 143, 188–90, 194
MARVIN H. McINTYRE, XIV: 378
Marvin-Smith, Lt. Cdr. H., XIII: 319
Mary Livermore, XIV: 272
Mary Luckenbach, I: 362–3, 364*n*

MARYLAND (1905), VII: 152*n*; XIV: 158*n*
MARYLAND (1921), III: 108–11, 145; IV: 82*n*, V: 291, VI: 106, VII: 103*n*, 116, 152–8, 164–8, 171, 337–8, 346, VIII: 180–82, 328–9, IX: 126*n*, XII: 80*n*, 132, 163, 199, 202, 224, 229, 295, 366–7, 416, XIII: 52*n*, XIV: 130, 197, 204, 372, 390; pics., III: 84, :10
MAS boats, XI: 277, 312*n*
Masaya, VI: 125
Masbate, XIII: 25
MASCOMA, VIII: 411, XII: 428, XIII: 67*n*, 68, 318, XIV: 387
Masina, Cdr. Leo, pic., IX: 43
Mason, Rear Adm. Charles P., V: 205, 212, 219–21, VI: 99*n*, 118
Mason, Ens. D. F., I: 154
Mason, Capt. L. Y., II: 36, IX: 389
Mason, Col. S. B., XI: 149
MASSACHUSETTS (1896), I: 208*n*
MASSACHUSETTS (1942), I: 419, II: 36, 43–4, 70, 91–106, 109–10, 113, 247, 285, V: 279*n*, VII: 258, 330, 339, 348, 353, VIII: 40, XII: 80*n*, 90, 318, 427, XIII: 19*n*, 54, 316, XIV: 21, 112, 307, 313, 382, 386; pic., II: 92
Massacre Bay, IV: 181
Massey, Lt. Cdr. L. E., IV: 90, 120–21, 127
MASSEY, XIV: 256, 279, 379
Massie, Lt. (jg) M. R., XII: 33*n*
Massmar, I: 178
Mast, Brig. Gen. Charles, II: 65–6, 184, 205, 216
Masters, Maj. J. H., XIII: 291
Masulis, Gunner A. A., XII: 372
MATACO, VII: 347, VIII: 420, XII: 429, XIII: 319, XIV: 387
MATAGORDA, I: 153, 420
MATAI, V: 349
Matanikau R., V: 68–9; actions, 140–46; map, 145; pic., 195
MATAR, XIV: 164, 386
MATCHLESS, X: 240
Mathenet, Gen., II: 116, 133
Mather, Capt. P. L., II: 38, IX: 389
Mathew Luckenbach, I: 343*n*
Mathews, Capt. B. C., XIV: 373
Mathews, Lt. Cdr. J. A., X: 376
Mathews, Lt. Cdr. J. C., XIV: 385
Matifou, Cape, II: 198–9
Matloff, M., *Strategic Planning for Coalition Warfare*, XI: xii

Matochkin Strait, I: 190
MATSU, VIII: 367
Matsuda, Maj. Gen., VI: 383, 387-8
Matsuda, Rear Adm. C., XII: 108, 192, 319-21, 325, 430
Matsuda, Capt. G., XII: 430
Matsue M., VIII: 19
MATSUKAZE, III: 161, VI: 181, 244; sunk, VIII: 24n
Matsumae, Col., XIII: 89n, 93n, 99
Matsumoto, Capt. K., VI: 56
Matsumoto M., XII: 404n
Matsunaga, Adm. S., VIII: 312
Matsuoka, Yosuke, III: 41, 44, 48, 61, 66
Matsushima, Capt. K., VIII: 187
Matsuyama, Rear Adm. K., V: 40n
MATTAPONI, I: 422; IX: 390
Mattera, Lt. A. A., XIV: 376
Matteson, Lt. Cdr. G. A., XIII: 313
Matthew Maury, IX: 40
Matthews, Lt. (jg) A. C., X: 183
Matthews, Hon. Francis P., III: xii, VI: xii, VII: viii
Matthews, Cdr. M. D., IX: 388, XI: 334, XIV: 376
Matthiesen, Lt. Cdr. H. O., VII: 348
Mattie, Cdr. D. L., VI: 145, 415, VIII: 404
MATTOLE, I: 422
Matulavich, Chief Gunner Sam, V: 305
Matuski, Lt. A. R., X: 196
Mauerman, Capt. R. J., XI: 333
Maui I., VII: 252, XII: 113-15
Maull, Maj. H. V., VI: 64
MAUMEE, I: 422, II: 176, 246
Mauna Kea, I: 172, 178
MAUNA LOA, VIII: 346, XII: 429, XIII: 319, XIV: 167n, 386
Mauna Loa, III: 314, 319
Maurer, Cdr. J. H., XII: 429
Mauretania, X: 133
Maurey, Lt. J. T., XIII: 308
Maurice, Maj. Gen. Sir Frederick, XI: 5
MAURITIUS, IX: 207, 276, 282, 361n, 393
Maury, Col. J. M., X: 316
MAURY (1918), VIII: 237n
MAURY (1938), III: 211n, IV: 91, 151n, 271, V: 28n, 86, 205, 294, 297-9, 310, VI: 98n, 182, 193, 214-16, 219-20, VII: 337, 350, VIII: 413, XII: 319, 428, XIII: 305
Maus, Kaptlt. August, X: 220
Maxon, Lt. (jg) W. F., VII: 94

Maxwell, Lt. M. M., VII: 348
Maxwell, Lt. P. W., V: 375
May, Cdr. C. W., III: 333, 349
May, Lt. Ernest R., IX: xvi
May, Cdr. L. G., VIII: 411, XII: 429
MAYA, III: 26, 161, 276, 333, IV: 172, V: 84, 177, 206, 234, 262, 266, VI: 323, 328, 335, VII: 24-31, 35, 43, VIII: 299, 309, 416, XII: 162, 172, 430
Mayazumi, Capt. H., XII: 431
Maye Shima, XIV: 115, 127n
Mayer, Capt. A. D., VIII: 409
Mayer, Capt. W. S., XIV: 375
MAYFLOWER, I: 208n, IX: 126n
MAYFLOWER, HMCS, I: 305
Maynard, Capt. G. E., IX: 388, XI: 339, XIV: 380
Mayo, Adm. H. T., I: xlix-l
Mayo, Lt. R. C., X: 192
MAYO, I: 76, 123, 328, 418, 420, IX: 341, 346, 391, 396
MAYRANT, I: 111, 181, 357, 420, II: 36, 91, 113, 285, IX: 191-3, 385; pic., II: 112
MAZAMA, VIII: 346, XII: 53, 83, 201n, 423
Mazza, Lt. Cdr. H. R., XIV: 384
Mead, Lt. (jg) R. J., VIII: 258n
MEADE, V: 283-5, 353, VII: 139, 156, 267, 335, 338, 344, XIII: 249
Meadors, Lt. W. W., XII: 259
Meadow, Capt. H. L., VII: 348, VIII: 405, 411
Meagher, Lt. W. J., XII: 423, XIII: 308
Medford, Lt. W. C., X: 382
Mediterranean Sea, charts, I: 194, IX: 398; opening of, I: 159, 352-3; command setup, II: 255; in strategy, IX: 3-11
MEDUSA, III: 114-16, VIII: 37n, XIV: 387
MÉDUSE, II: 104, 110n
Mee, Capt. F. J., XIII: 313, 324
Mee, Lt. (jg) J. L., XII: 423
Meehan, Lt. W. J., VIII: 408, X: 378, XII: 422
Meester, Cdr. J. B., de, III: 322, 325
Mehedia, II: 25, 33-4, 51, 54, 68; landing, 115-34, IX: 351; naval gunfire support, II: 117-18, 122-6, 130-31; chart, 114
Mehle, Lt. Cdr. R. W., VIII: 413, XII: 424, XIII: 315
Mehlman, Lt. Cdr. S. P., IV: 173
Meigen M., VI: 77
Meigs, III: 314-15, 319

Meister, Lt. C. S., X: 381
Meiyo M., IV: 89, 226, V: 18–19
Melanesia, VII: 69
Melbourne, VI: 380; Conference, IV: 262
MELBREAK, XI: 123, 336
Melgaard, Cdr. J. L., VII: 334, 353, VIII: 415
Melhorn, Lt. (jg) C. M., V: 320
Melichar, Lt. Cdr. G. H., VIII: 404, XII: 423
MELLETTE, XIV: 381
Mellies, Lt. Col. C. J., II: 237*n*
Mello, Vice Adm. A. V. de, X: 226
Mellu I., VII: 234–8
Melson, Lt. Cdr. C. L., IX: 389
Melville, Lt. Cdr. S. E., XIV: 381
MELVILLE, I: 382*n*, 390*n*, 420, IX: 191*n*
Melville, R. I., II: 263
Melville Stone, X: 202–3
Melvin, Lt. Cdr. D. J., VIII: 414, XII: 428
MELVIN, VIII: 230, 409, 420, XII: 199, 212–15, 418, XIII: 307, XIV: 385
MELVIN R. NAWMAN, XIII: 80, 319, XIV: 374
Mempakul, XIII: 266
MEMPHIS, I: 83–4, 142*n*, 377, 380–82, 390*n*, 419, II: 176, VII: 152*n*, X: 209, 213*n*, 225, XIV: 86*n*
Menado, III: 280–81, VIII: 122
MENARD, XIV: 380
MENDIP, IX: 276, 393
MENDOCINO, XIV: 143*n*, 380
MENEMSHA, X: 125
MENGES, X: 256, 342, 373, 379
MENIFEE, XIV: 378
Menocal, Cdr. G. L., I: 76, 418, IX: 385, 391
MENOMINEE, VI: 122, 415, XII: 420, 429, XIV: 387
Mentz, Capt. G. F., IX: 385, XIII: 44–6
Meola, Cdr. V. J., XII: 425, XIII: 318
Meonia, II: 233*n*
MERAK, I: 422
MERAPI, XIV: 386
Mercer, Capt. Preston V., VI: 11*n*, XII: 429, XIII: 73–5, 319, XIV: 385
Merchant Marine, Cadet Corps, I: 295; Seamen, 19, 84, 106, 164, 173, 182, 187–91, 298–300, 326, 331–99 *passim*, IX: 369–70, XII: 78–9; training, I: 295–6, 300; pay, 299*n*, 374
Merchant Vessels, arming of, I:9, 80,

296–302, 416; construction, 198, 290–95, 403–4; losses, 265, 337, 344–8, 367, X: 7–10, 65, 83, 363, 367; charts and tables of, I: 20–21, 59, 124, 140–41, 313, 404, 410–14, X: 14–15, 66, 136, 193, 294, 301, 365, 369; types, I: 293–5; no. at sea and convoyed, 301–2, 405
MERCURY, VII: 347, VIII: 329, XII: 418, XIII: 309, XIV: 159, 163
Mercury Sun, I: 139
MERCY, XII: 299*n*, 423, XIV: 267, 386
Meredith, Lt. W. C., X: 381
MEREDITH (1919), VII: 17*n*
MEREDITH (1941), III: 393; sunk, V: 179–80; pic., 178
MEREDITH (1944), XI: 162, 334; sunk, 170
Meridian V., XIII: 308
MERIWETHER, XIV: 380
Merker, O. H., X: 60
MERKUR, XII: 423
Merrill, Rear Adm. Aaron S. ("Tip"), biog., VI: 106*n*; pics., 195, 322; mentioned, I: 419, V: 314, 353, 372; VI: 106–10, 142, 146, 177–9, 203, 207–9, 213, 242, 290–92, 304–22, 337, 345–8, 363, 415, XIII: 39
Merrill, Cdr. S. D. B., I: 218*n*, XII: 426, XIII: 316, 318
Merrill, 2nd Lt. T. L., X: 196
MERRIMACK, I: 422, II: 40, 139, 142, XII: 428, XIII: 318, 387; pic., II: 45
Merrimack, I: 151
Merritt, Brig. Gen. L. G., VII: 340, 350
Mers-el-Kebir, II: 222, 238, 251, 254, 271*n*, IX: 167
MERTZ, VIII: 409, XII: 199, 418, XIII: 307, 314, XIV: 243, 248, 385
MERVINE (1921), V: 14*n*
MERVINE (1942), I: 420, II: 40, 144–5, 148, 285, IX: 136, 389, X: 261
Messe, Marshal, II: 260
Messina City and Strait, IX: 17–20, 26, 37, 47–51, 72, 151, 169–70, 180, 186–90, 202–20 *passim*, 233–4, 250, 383
Messmer, Cdr. W. L., IX: 187, 389, 392, XI: 340
Metcalf, Rear Adm. M. K., I: 206, X: 22*n*, 24
METCALF, XIII: 267, XIV: 374
METEOR, X: 306, XI: 316
Meteorology, XI: 79–83
METIVIER, XIII: 313–14
Metsall, John, X: 382

Mexico, merchant marine, I: 138–9
Meyer, Lt. Cdr. B. H., XI: 339
Meyer, Lt. Cord, VII: 299, 303
Meyer, Capt. John, VIII: 403
Meyer, Col. L. H., XIII: 194
MFP. *See* F-lighters
Miami, I: 135–8, 206*n*, 223, 231, 279
MIAMI, VIII: 415, XII: 90, 318, 345, 426, XIII: 54, 70, 317, XIV: 21, 58, 382, 386
MIANTONOMAH, II: 39, 78–9, 157, 172, 176*n;* sunk, XI: 303
MICCA, IX: 42
Michael, Cdr. F. D., XII: 420, XIII: 318, XIV: 385
Michael, Capt. S. J., I: 419, VII: 338, 347, VIII: 413, XII: 426, XIII: 316
Michaels, Pfc. J. R., pic., XIV: frontispiece
Michel, Lt. Cdr. E. A., XI: 172, 334
MICHEL, X: 275–6
Michelet, Lt. Cdr. W. G., I: 420, II: 40
Michelier, Vice-Admiral F. C., pic., II: 164; mentioned, 68–72, 87*n*, 98, 107–11, 162–5, 168, 216
MICHIGAN, V: 14*n*, XII: 80*n*
Michigan, I: 173–5, 178
MICHISHIO, III: 274–6, 329, IV: 88*n*, V: 234, 266, VI: 115, VIII: 416, XII: 190, 209, 219, 233, 431; sunk, 216, 220
"Mickey Finns," VIII: 24–5
Micronesia, VII: 69; chart, 72–3; in strategy, 69–70, 79–85
MIDAS, XII: 423, XIII: 308
Middleton, Capt. G. B., XI: 339
Middleton, Maj. Gen. Troy H., IX: 28, 64, 128, 138–9, 142–3, 195, 220, 356, 388, 391, XI: 298
Mid-ocean Meeting Point (Momp), I: 85, 96–7, 101–2, 120, 321, 327, X: 6
Midtlyng, Lt. Cdr. T. R., VIII: 405
MIDWAY, VIII: 409, XII: 27. *See also* ST. LO
Midway I., III: 32–3, 84, 87*n*, 210, 213, 219, 258, IV: 5, 276, VII: 16; chart, IV: 73; history, 70–74; reinforcement of, 85–6; Battle of, 74–87, 96–184, 205; charts, 94, 99, 108–9, 118–19, 123, 146–7; T.O., 87–93, 172–4; casualties, 140*n;* discussed, 157–9, VIII: 10; pics., IV: 100, 127, 152–3; as base, IV: 199, 210, 216, VII: 218*n*, XII: 33, 411
MIGNONETTE, X: 131, 337
MIGRANT, I: 267

Miike M., VIII: 20
Mikami, Cdr., VI: 160*n*
Mikawa, Vice Adm. G., pic., V: 42; Pearl Harbor, III: 87; Midway, IV: 88; Solomons, 255–6, V: 85, 126, 149–51, 169, 176, 200, 207, 234, VI: 22, 118; Savo I. battle, V: 18–22, 27–8, 34–46, 50–56, 59–65; naval battle of Guadalcanal, 259, 262–6, 270–71, 286; New Guinea, VI: 38, 55–8; Formosa Air Battle, XII: 91–2; Leyte Gulf, 161*n*, 233, 431–2; Mindoro raid, XIII: 37; assistance, V: 17*n*
MIKAZUKI, IV: 88, VI: 162, 174, 181, 186*n*, 187, 384; sunk, 190*n*, 208, 256
Mikkelsen, Cdr. H. M., XII: 428, XIII: 319, XIV: 387
MIKUMA, III: 26, 276, 308, 334, 365–8, IV: 88, 143–5, 149–52; sunk, 150; pic., 152
MILAN, II: 99, 106, 109–10, 248; pic., 174
Milazzo, IX: 58*n*, 207, 218, 249
Miles, Lt. Cdr. B. A., X: 376–7
Miles, Rear Adm. Milton E., biog., XIII: 290*n;* pic., 293; mentioned, 290–94, 297
Miles, Brig. Gen. Sherman, I: 45
Milford, Maj. Gen. E. J., XIII: 217, 268
Milford Haven, XI: 60, 77
Mili Atoll, III: 262–4, VII: 75, 79, 97, 122, 137, 206–7, 223, 226, 307–9, 314, VIII: 156; bombardments, VII: 116, 309; air raids, 98, 116–18, 187, 213–14, 229; surrenders, XIV: 360
Millard, Lt. R. C., I: 249
Miller, Lt. Cdr. A. J., X: 377
Miller, Capt. C. C., XII: 427, XIII: 318, XIV: 373
Miller, Cdr. C. H. K., XIV: 379
Miller, Lt. Cdr. C. L., VII: 340
Miller, Cdr. D. B., VIII: 409, IX: 389, XII: 427, XIV: 373
Miller, Lt. Cdr. D. C., XIII: 305
Miller, Cdr. E. S., XIII: 303; XIV: 374
Miller, Lt. Cdr. F. D., VII: 335
Miller, Pharmacist H. O., XII: 315
Miller, Cdr. Harry F., II: 36, VI: 145; 161, XII: 339
Miller, Cdr. Henry L., III: 391, VI: 325, XII: 340, 350, XIV: 384
Miller, Lt. Cdr. Herman E., X: 303
Miller, Cdr. J. A., VIII: 285*n*, 415; XIII: 312

Miller, Dr. John, V: x; *Guadalcanal*, 65*n*
Miller, Lt. Cdr. L. R., VII: 346, VIII: 405
Miller, Ens. Oscar, XI: 321
Miller, Lt. Cdr. R. F., X: 170, 375, XI: 339
Miller, Cdr. Shirley, VIII: 397-8
Miller, Capt. W. J., VII: 348, VIII: 414, XII: 425, XIII: 318
Miller, Lt. (jg) Wesley N., I: 361, 364
MILLER, VII: 349, VIII: 413, XII: 319, 426, XIII: 317, XIV: 383
Millett, Lt. Cdr. C. R., XIV: 381
Millett, Cdr. J. R., XII: 420, XIII: 317-18, XIV: 385
Millican, Lt. Cdr. W. J., IV: 207-8
MILLICOMA, XII: 428, XIII: 318, XIV: 307, 387
Milligan, Boatswain, III: 100
Milliman, Ens. R. D., IV: 91
Millington, Lt. Col. W. A., XIII: 317
Mills, Lt. Cdr. D., XII: 422
Mills, Lt. Cdr. R. E., IX: 385
MILLS, X: 266
Milne Bay, V: 25, 116, VI: 28, 34-40, 47, 52, 68, 124-7, 132-4, 261, 380-81, 390, 435-6, XIII: 97, 189*n*; chart, VI: 35; pic., 40
Milner, Samuel, VI: 41*n*, 50*n*
MILWAUKEE, I: 83, 377, 383-4, 390*n*, 419, VII: 283, IX: 126*n*, X: 213, 308, XII: 140*n*, XIV: 88*n*
MIMOSA, I: 153, VIII: 410
Minami Daito, XIV: 58, 307
MINAS, XI: 335
MINAZUKI, III: 161, VI: 181, VIII: 416; sunk, 220
Minckler, Cdr. C. H., XIV: 379
Mindanao, III: 167, 169, 182, 194, 198, 204, VIII: 7-9, 101, 118, XII: 68, 133, XIII: 240; description, 239-40; map, 242; projected invasion, VIII: 45, XII: 4-11, 14-15, 19; air strikes, 13, 108, 125-6, 149-50; landings, XIII: 217, 222-5, 239-43; T.O.'s 322, 324; charts, 224, 242
MINDANAO (1928), III: 155, 159, 172-3, 194, 205; sunk, 206; pic., 37
MINDANAO (1943), XIV: 388
Mindanao R., XIII: 243-6; pic., 260
Mindanao Sea, XII: 204, 238-9
Mindoro I., description, XIII: 17; map, 10, 27-8; in strategy, XII: 7, 376, 386;

the operation, plans and approach, XIII: 6-13, 17-26; landings, 26-33; chart, 28; pic., 36-7; Jap. air and surface attacks, 33-48; unloading, 21, 31; resupply, 34-6, 43-8; secured, 43-51; U.S. base, 102, 135, 144, 163, 199, 215-41 *passim*, 346
Mine fields and minelaying, East Coast, I: 126, 136-7, 417; N. Russia, 372; Philippines, III: 155, 177, 206; N.E.I., 355; N. Africa, II: 78-9, 157, 176*n*, IX: 65; SWPac., IV: 229-30, VI: 76, VIII: 32; Esp. Sto., V: 182*n*; Solomons, 367, VI: 110-16, 142, 308; Kiska, VII: 63-4; Sicily, IX: 40, 44-5, 78-9, 174; Salerno, 247, 266-8, 274; Anzio, 340-42, 346-8; Italy, 309; English Channel, XI: 43, 46; Normandy, X: 324, XI: 34-5, 41-6, 74, 96, 171-3, 190, 286, 303; S. France, 313, 372-3; Palaus, VIII: 32-3; Shimonoseki Strait, XIV: 101. *See also* Mines, Minesweepers, Minesweeping
Mine Squadron Two, XIII: 306; Six, I: 421; Seven, I: 421, II: 39, XI: 79, 198, 206; Eight, I: 422; Nine, 422; Eleven, XI: 313
Minecraft, light, XIV: 114
MINEGUMO, III: 162, 275, 334, 353, IV: 88, V: 138, VI: 107; sunk, 109-10; chart, 109
MINEKAZE, VIII: 19
Miner, Cdr. J. O., XII: 426
Minerd, Ens. R. E., X: 352
Mines, magnetic, VI: 111, XI: 171; pressure, 46-7, 173; sonic, 171
Minesweepers, described, I: 287*n*; XIV: 113-15; no. authorized and built, X: 35
Minesweepers, Jap., *No. 2*, III: 369; *No. 7*, 162, 315; *Nos. 8, 9, 10*, 162; *No. 10*, 176; *No. 12*, XIII: 286; *No. 15*, III: 161, 288; *No. 16*, 161; *Nos. 17, 18*, 162; *No. 19*, 161; sunk, 174; *No. 20*, IV: 18
Minesweeping, Cape Torokina, VI: 290; Admiralties, 445; Aleutians, VII: 45, 63; Tarawa, 158-9; Marshalls, 238, 257, 286, 289-90; Hollandia, VIII: 69, 82; Biak, 125; Marianas, 180*n*, 329, 368; Mediterranean, X: 250; Sicily, IX: 45*n*, 65-6, 93, 102, 110, 161, 174-5; Salerno, 259, 272-3; Anzio, 339-42, 348; Italy, XI: 312-13; Normandy, 78-

9, 94–100, 108, 116, 173, 198–200, 206–8, 217, 303; S. France, 255–6, 270–73, 285–7; Weser R., 328; Morotai, Palaus, XII: 23, 33–5, 42–4, 118; Ulithi, 50–51; Leyte, 117–19, 122, 131; other Philippines, 368–9, XIII: 26, 32, 104, 107, 111–13, 191, 199–201, 206–8, 219–23, 230, 233, 249, 264; Borneo, 260–61, 264–6, 269–70; Iwo Jima, XIV: 27–8; Okinawa, 113–17, 131, 134, 193–5, 218–20

Mingay, Lt. Cdr. J. I., VIII: 405, XIII: 308

Mini, Lt. Cdr. J. H., VIII: 414, XII: 426

MINK, XII: 423, XIII: 308

MINNEAPOLIS, III: 31*n*, 212, 215–16, 236, 242, 244*n*, 266*n*, IV: 18, 59, 60*n*, 91, 113*n*, 257, 270, V: 86, 112, 293–314 *passim*, VII: 93*n*, 190, 258–60, 275–6, 326–53 *passim*, VIII: 269, 409, 415, IX: 325*n*, XII: 122, 199, 227, 366, 419, XIII: 39, 177, 201, 304, 325, XIV: 122, 372; pic., V: 306

Minor, Cdr. J. O., XIII: 317

MINSTER, XI: 173

MINTAKA, XIV: 387

Mios Woendi I., VIII: 116, 132, 137, XII: 169, 204, 290, 304, XIII: 97; chart, VIII: 105

Mislicky, Lt. R. G., XII: 236, 422

MISOA, II: 234

MISSION BAY, X: 41, 201–3, 296, 345, 349, 355, 373, 379; pic., XIV: 310

MISSISSINEWA, XII: 51, 428

MISSISSIPPI, I: 57, 82, 208*n*, III: 57, 151*n*, 214, IV: 82*n*, V: 14*n*, 236*n*, 325*n*, VI: 282*n*, 423, VII: 37*n*, 55, 60, 124, 133, 258–60, 337, 344, VIII: 180, 238*n*, X: 51*n*, 189*n*, 200*n*, XII: 41*n*, 132, 199, 202, 224–6, 229, 241, 295, 343, 416, XIII: 132–3, 303, 326, XIV: 245; pic., VII: 142

Mississippi R. Passes, I: 138–9, 249

Misson, Capt. C. A., VII: 337, 347, VIII: 408, XII: 418

MISSOURI (1903), IX: 14*n*

MISSOURI (1944), XIV: 21, 45, 112, 169, 210, 299, 314, 333–5, 353, 361–8, 385–6

Mitchell, Rear Adm. Edward A., II: 22–4, 61*n*, 81*n*, XI: 30*n*, 37*n*, XIV: 373

Mitchell, Lt. Edward A., XIV: 378

Mitchell, Lt. F. K., XII: 28

Mitchell, Cdr. F. P., XIV: 376

Mitchell, Maj. J. W., V: 375, VI: 128

Mitchell, Lt. O. M., X: 184

Mitchell, Maj. Gen. Ralph J., VI: 350*n*, 395, XII: 368, XIII: 95, 194

Mitchell, Lt. Cdr. Samuel G., IV: 91

Mitchell, Ens., W. E., XIV: 232

Mitchell, Brig. Gen. William, I: xlv–li

MITCHELL, VIII: 411, XII: 429, XIII: 319

Mithois, Lt. de V., XI: 334

Mitscher, Vice Adm. M. A., biog., VIII: 236*n*; pics., III: 394, VIII: 232, XII: 102, XIV: 166; C.O. *Hornet*, III: 390–92, IV: 91, 117; CTF–17, 257; Comairsols, V: 369, VI: 99*n*, 128–9, 146, 169; Com. of Carrier Forces, Pacific, VII: 208, 331, VIII: 158, XII: 12; Marshalls, VII: 218, 348; Truk, 286, 320–21, 325, 352, VIII: 38–9; Hollandia, 85; Marianas, 154–5, 161, 172–9, 367, 378, 412; Battle of Philippine Sea, 233–316 *passim*; Bonins, 311; Formosa, XII: 86, 90, 95; Leyte, 57, 74, 125, 175, 196, 291, 318–27, 331–2, 339–40; CTF–38, 343, 424, XIII: 52; Iwo Jima, XIV: 7; Japan strikes, 20–24, 57, 94; Okinawa, 87, 91, 100–103, 112, 161, 203, 208, 263, 273, 382; quoted, VIII: 36–7

MITSCHER, XI: xvi

Miura, Capt. H., XII: 431

Miwa, Vice Adm. S., XII: 161*n*, 164, 432, XIII: 159, XIV: 19

Miyako Retto, XIII: 91, XIV: 106

MIZAR, IV: 265*n*, XII: 81, 423

Mizony, Lt. Col. H. I., VIII: 334

MIZUHO, III: 162, 197, 315; sunk, IV: 203

ML–304, XI: 127–8; –480, –483, II: 225, 228; –563, XI: 373

MOA, V: 349–50, VI: 121–2

MOALE, XII: 371, XIII: 30, 304, XIV: 25, 57

MOBERLY, X: 357, 373

Mobey, Lt. D. N., XIV: 385

MOBILE, VI: 341, 344, VII: 190, 220, 337, 346, 352, VIII: 37, 250*n*, 273, 413, XII: 90, 100, 318, 331, 425–7, XIII: 54, 318, XIV: 373

Mobile, I: 264, XIV: 163

MOBJACK, XII: 28, XIII: 275

Mobley, Maj. T. E., XIV: 382

MOCENIGO, X: 370

MOCHIZUKI, III: 231*n*, IV: 17, V: 227, VI: 162, 174; sunk, VIII: 49*n*

Mockrish, Cdr. J. J., VII: 337, 346, VIII: 407

MOCTOBI, XIV: 388
MODOC, I: 64n, 421
Moebus, Capt. L. A., XIV: 52
Moen, Capt. A. T., II: 36, 134n
Moen I., VII: 318–20, VIII: 38
Moffatt, Lt. G. G., XII: 417, XIII: 307
Moffett, Lt. Cdr. J. A., XIII: 313
MOFFETT, I: 33, 111, 377, 390n, 420, IV: 19n, X: 210, 213n, 220–21, 370–71
MOGAMI, III: 26, 276, 308, 334, 365–6, IV: 88, 143–55, VI: 323, 328, VII: 44, VIII: 264, 271, 294–7, 416, XII: 162, 168, 190, 207–9, 213, 219–40 *passim*, 431; sunk, 238; pic., 222
Mogmog I., XII: 49, XIV: 110
MOHAWK, I: 330, 421
Möhle, Kvtkapt. Karl, X: 58n
MOJAVE, I: 330, 421
Mokmer, VIII: 104, 107–8, 113–16, 132–3
MOLALA, VII: 347, VIII: 411, XII: 429, XIII: 319
Molla, IX: 84–6
Molokai, IV: 137
Molotov, V. M., II: 13, III: 61, XI: 11
Molotovsk, I: 159, 187n, 188, 364–6, 369, 373
Molucca Sea and Passage, III: 292, 296
Molumphy, Lt. Cdr. G. G., VII: 351
MOMI, XIII: 102
Momm, Cdr. A. O., XII: 415, XIV: 381
Momote, VI: 437–41, VII: 433, 436–8, VIII: 50
Momp. *See* Mid-ocean Meeting Place
Momsen, Capt. C. B., XII: 427, XIII: 318, XIV: 384
MONA ISLAND, XIV: 127, 377
Mona Passage, X: 191, 198n, 297–8
Monaco, XI: 278
MONADNOCK, II: 40, 139, 176n, XIII: 306, XIV: 377
MONAGHAN, III: 97, 104, 115, 213n, IV: 19, 91, 113n, 155, VII: 9, 23, 31–2, 35, 55–9, 335, 338, 346–7, VIII: 419, XII: 429, XIII: 80–82, 85, 319; sunk, 77
Monarch of the Seas, VII: 345
MONITOR, XII: 418, XIII: 188, 309, XIV: 379
MONOCACY, X: 204n
MONONGAHELA, VIII: 411, 420, XII: 428, XIII: 71, 318, XIV: 387
Monroe, Capt. Frank, XIV: 379–80
Monroe, Lt. H. S., IV: 218–19, XII: 429
MONROVIA, VII: 155, 337, 344, VIII: 407,

420, IX: 61–4, 93, 102, 105, 108, 123–4, 385–8, XII: 419, XIII: 311–12, XIV: 378; pic., IX: 26
Monsabert, Gen. de, XI: 236, 281
MONSSEN (1941), III: 393, IV: 91, 274, 289, 291n, V: 29, 89, 106, 112, 138, 141, 232, 237, 248–50, 253–4, XII: 212n; sunk, V: 256
MONSSEN (1944), VIII: 201, 409, 415, XII: 199, 211n, 212–17, 418, XIII: 307, 314, XIV: 243, 385
MONTANA, X: 204n
MONTCALM, II: 105, 240n, IX: 158–60, 306, XI: 118, 123, 149, 265, 280, 311, 336, 340
Montebello, III: 221n
Montecorvino, IX: 255, 271, 278, 281, 286
MONTEREY, VI: 411, VII: 117, 144, 197, 208, 339, 349, 353, VIII: 37–9, 174, 250, 258n, 260, 292, 298–9, 303, 413, XII: 90, 309, XIII: 54, 70, 73, 80, 315, XIV: 21
Monterey, X: 264
Montgomery, Cdr. A. R., V: 174; XIV: 375
Montgomery, Rear Adm. Alfred E., biog., VIII: 237n; Rabaul, VI: 71, 330–33, 336; Wake, VII: 92–4; Gilberts, 117, 138, 149, 156, 168, 339; Marshalls, 190–91, 196, 208, 218–19, 237, 242, 349; Truk, 321, 352; Palau, VIII: 32; Wakde, Hollandia, 37–8; Marianas, 154, 174, 178, 367, 378; Phil. Sea, 237, 243, 250, 258–60, 271–3, 276, 313–14, 413; Leyte, XII: 343, 346, 348; Luzon, XIII: 54, 315
Montgomery, Field Marshal Sir Bernard, pic., IX: 203; mentioned, II: 13n, 258; N. Africa, Sicily and Italy, IX: 3, 19–20, 24, 27–82 *passim*, 146–95 *passim*, 200–202, 206–7, 220, 233–4, 255–97 *passim*, 319, X: 358; Fr., Ger., XI: 24, 29–30, 65, 69–70, 154, 189, 216, 223, 228, 295–8, 318–27 *passim*, XII: 4
Montgomery, Capt. G. C., XII: 79, XIII: 319, XIV: 18, 373
Montgomery, Cdr. R. A., XIII: 129, 310
Montgomery, Lt. Cdr. R. J., X: 378
MONTGOMERY, III: 104, 213n, IV: 276n, V: 367, 368, XII: 51, 125
MONTGOMERY, HMS, X: 76
MONTICELLO, XIV: 88n
MONTPELIER, V: 353, VI: 106n, 107, 292,

307–8, 319–20, 363*n*, 415, VIII: 182, 183*n*, 276*n*, 335, 361*n*, 409, 414, XII: 366, XIII: 19, 115, 219, 243, 269, 274, 304, 321, 324

Montreal M., VII: 17

Montrose, Cdr. K. E., VIII: 415

MONTROSE, XIV: 231, 375

Montross, Cdr. K. E., I: 421, XIV: 288

Moody, Rear Adm. C., IX: 393

Moody, Cdr. D. L., XIV: 383

Moody, Lt. (jg) W. D., V: 216

Moon, Lt. A. E., V: 344*n*

Moon, Rear Adm. Don P., biog., XI: xv–xvi; pic., 53; mentioned, I: 168, 183–4, 420, II: 36, 91, XI: 29, 52, 56, 65, 77, 86, 93–5, 101–2, 109, 162, 215, 237, 333; death, 241–2

Mooney, Ens. W. R., VIII: 205

MOONSTONE, X: 290*n*

Moore, Cdr. A. W., VIII: 408, XII: 416, XIII: 310

Moore, Lt. Cdr. C. L., VIII: 414, XII: 428

Moore, Rear Adm. Charles J., pic., VIII: frontispiece; mentioned, I: 419, VII: ix, 80*n*, VIII: 10, 253*n*

Moore, Capt. E. P., VII: 338, 346

Moore, Ens. F. L., X: 299

Moore, Lt. Cdr. F. T., VII: 346, VIII: 420, XII: 420

Moore, Lt. Cdr. G. A., IX: 388, XI: 334

Moore, Cdr. H. C., XI: 339

Moore, Cdr. H. G., XIV: 210, 384

Moore, Vice Adm. Sir Henry and Lady, X: 19, 308, XIV: 369*n*

Moore, Col. Howard, X: 94

Moore, Lt. (jg) J. S., VIII: 291*n*

Moore, Cdr. John A., VIII: 17

Moore, Lt. Cdr. John R., IV: 20, 226, 275, V: 61

Moore, Capt. Malcolm A., VI: 64

Moore, Lt. R. C., X: 376

Moore, Lt. Cdr. R. D., XI: 337

Moore, Cdr. R. S., VIII: 180*n*, 410

Moore, Capt. Ralph, XIV: 115

Moore, Seaman Robert, XII: 284*n*

Moore, Lt. Col. Roy E., IX: 80

Moore, 1st Lt. Roy J., VI: 60

Moore, Capt. Samuel N., I: 15*n*, IV: 274, V: 29, 44–5

Moore, Pharmacist T. A., IV: 227

Moore, Lt. Cdr. W. B., XIV: 63–4

MOORE, X: 378

Moore-Cosgrove, Col. L., XIV: 366

Moosbrugger, Capt. Frederick, pic., VI: 333; mentioned, IV: 173, VI: 212–21, XII: 222, XIV: 193, 281, 375

MOOSE, XIV: 387

MOOSE JAW, I: 71

Moran, Commo. Edward J. ("Mike"), V: 150, 163–6, 170, VI: 209, XI: 26, XIII: 95

Moran, Cdr. Henry G., V: 213

Moran, Lt. J. H., XII: 422

Moran, Capt. Thomas, I: 148*n*

Moran, Lt. W. F., VIII: 419, X: 375, XII: 422, XIII: 304

Moranz, Lt. Cdr. V. J., XIV: 120, 378

Moray Firth, X: 339

Mordal, Jacques. See Cras, Med. en Chef

MORDEN, X: 144

Moreau, Lt. Cdr. R. H., VI: 228

Moreell, Rear Adm. Ben, V: 75, VII: 101

Morehouse, Capt. A. K., XII: 420, XIII: 305, XIV: 373

MORENO, IX: 284, 297, 387, 392, XI: 342

Morgan, Lt. C. F., VIII: 420, XII: 420

Morgan, Lt. Cdr. Charles C., VI: 144, 228, VIII: 404, 409, XII: 422, XIII: 307

Morgan, Lt. Cdr. E. V. St. J., III: 333

Morgan, Lt. Gen. Sir Frederick, XI: xi, 6, 18–20, 23–7, 34, 37, 69, 221; *Overture to Overlord*, XI: xv

Morgenthau, Hon. Henry, I: 37

Mori, Rear Adm. T., VI: 267, VII: 24*n*

Mori, Lt. Gen. T., XIV: 350

Morishita, Rear Adm. N., XII: 430

Morison, Lt. Elting E., I: 201*n*, 281*n*

Morison, Priscilla B., VI: xi–xii, VIII: viii, IX: xiii, X: xi, XI: x, 287*n*, XII: viii, XIII: x, XIV: ix

Moritz, Lt. (jg) J. T., VII: 341

Morlaix, XI: 301–2

Morland, Cdr. J. B., VIII: 415, XIII: 306, XIV: 384

Morlen, IV: 176*n*

Mormacland, X: 38

Mormacmail, X: 38

Mormacmar, I: 172

Mormacrio, I: 171*n*

Mormacsul, I: 178*n*

Morobe, VI: 136, 257, 262

Moroccan Sea Frontier, I: 223, 353, II: 246*n*, X: 16*n*, 88, 129–31

Morotai, VIII: 144, XII: 11, 65, 107, 127, 191, 311, 351–2, 368, 420, XIII: 163,

Morotai (*cont'd*)
241, 260–61, 264, 268, 272; landing and description, XII: 19–25; chart, 20
Morozumi, Lt. Gen. G., XIII: 240, 249
Morrill, Lt. Cdr. J. H., III: 159, 206*n*
Morris, Maj. Gen. E. L., I: 45
Morris, Capt. E. W., I: 390*n*, 419, X: 213*n*, 227
Morris, Cdr. R. L., VII: 339, 349, VIII: 413
Morris, Capt. Robert M., IX: 75, 84–5, 349, 386, XI: 269, 341
Morris, Lt. Cdr. S. F., X: 339
MORRIS (1919), XIV: 88*n*
MORRIS (1940), I: 82, IV: 19, 58–9, 60*n*, 90, V: 205, 214, 233, VII: 141, 334, 337, 346, VIII: 405, XII: 417, XIII: 309, XIV: 191, 390; pic., IV: 60
Morrison, Lt. D., XII: 419, 423, XIII: 308
Morrison, Capt. G. D., VII: 347, VIII: 407
Morrison, Lt. J. W., XIII: 313
Morrison, Cdr. W. J., XIII: 310
MORRISON, VIII: 410, XII: 180, 427, XIV: 136, 222, 243, 372, 391; sunk, 254–5, 391
Morrissey, Lt. Col. R. L., VI: 64
Morrissey, I: 62*n*
Morrow, Fort, VII: 5
Morse, Lt. Cdr. D. H., VII: 341
Morse, Rear Adm. John A. V., IX: 311, 359, XI: 311–12, 315
Morse, Dr. Philip M., I: 222–3, X: 22*n*
Morshead, Lt. Gen. Sir Leslie, XIII: 217, 259, 265–6, 274; pic., 276
Mortensen, Capt. Bernhardt, III: 154*n*, 281*n*, 336*n*
Mortimer, the Rt. Rev. R. C., Bishop of Exeter, XI: xi
Morton, Lt. Cdr. D. W., V: 324
Morton, Cdr. F. P., XI: 242*n*
Morton, Lt. J. L., XIV: 376
Morton, Dr. Louis, III: 154*n*
Morton, Lt. Cdr. R. C., VIII: 406, XII: 421
Morton, Lt. Cdr. W. B., XIV: 373
Moseley, Lt. Cdr. F. S., XIII: 306, XIV: 374
Moseley, Lt. Cdr. S. P., I: 421
Mosely, Lt. (jg) A. K., VII: 341
Moses, Capt. C. W., II: 216*n*
MOSLEY, X: 342, 349, 373, 379
Mostaganem, II: 273, IX: 16, 247

Motes, Lt. Cdr. J. H., VII: 337, 350
Moti I., XII: 29
MOTIVE, VII: 345, VIII: 410
Motobu Peninsula, XIV: 83, 91, 136, 171, 215, 266
Motor rafts, IX: 212–5
Motor Torpedo Boats (PT), development, II: 261–3; N. Africa, 261–4; defense of the Philippines, III: 201; Midway, IV: 86; their sailors, V: 369; described, VI: 61; Tulagi base, V: 369, VI: 102; New Guinea, VI: 47–9, 52–3, 136, 257–8, 273–4, 391, VIII: 56–8, 66, 73–4, 132, 136, 142–3; Guadalcanal, V: 174–6, 227, 263, 270–82, 290, 318–49 *passim*, 366–70; threatened brush with Lee, 273; Japanese tribute to, 368–9; Central Solomons, VI: 94, 145–6, 151–3, 209–12 (the Kennedy fight), 227–8, 296; Torokina, 341–3, 427–30; Green Is., 413–16; Bismarcks, 60–62, 372, 379, 383, 445–6; Aleutians, VII: 15–17, 54, 63; Sicily, IX: 78–9, 168–9, 187–90, 208, 213–17; Med. and Italy, 251*n*, 308–10, 358, 372–3, XI: 312–16; Normandy, 34, 66, 150, 163, 191–3, 214–15, 335; S. France, 239, 249–50, 273, 277–9, 282, 315–16; Port de Bouc, 286–7; W. Europe, 299–302, 306–7; Morotai, XII: 24–9; Leyte, 140, 191, 369–70, 377, 388, 391, 395–6; Surigao Str., 196, 202–12, 216, 232–3, 236–7; chart, 205; T. O., 422–3; Mindoro, XIII: 32–3, 39–43, 46–7, 50; Luzon, 149, 189, 203; Palawan, 221; Zamboanga, 223, 226; Patrols, 237–8; Davao Gulf, 247–8; Borneo, 265–6, 275; pics., VI: 262, IX: 282, XI: 316, XIII: 196
Motor Torpedo Boats, British, II: 264, IX: 41, 163, 168–9, 213, 234, 252*n*, 300, 316, X: 213, 373; XI: 314
Motor Torpedo Boats, German, *see* E-boats; Italian, *see* MAS boats
Motor Torpedo Boats Squadrons, One, IV: 93; Three, II: 263; Five, VI: 209; Nine, 209, XII: 28; Ten, VI: 209, 416, 418, XII: 28, XIII: 275*n*; Eleven, VI: 209, XII: 28; Thirteen, II: 262, VII: 54, 334, XIII: 265; Fourteen, II: 262; Fifteen, 261–6, 277–8, IX: 78, 187–90, 300–301, 309–10, 385, XI: 277, 339; Sixteen, XIII: 265; Eighteen, VI: 446, XII: 28; Twenty, VI: 428, XIII: 221; Twenty-one, VI: 446; Twenty-

two, X: 312, 316; Twenty-three, XIII: 221; Twenty-four, 247; Twenty-seven, 275*n;* Twenty-eight, 149, 313; Twenty-nine, XI: 311, 338; Thirty, 193, 299; Thirty-three, XII: 28; Thirty-four, XI: 299, 337; Thirty-five, 193; Thirty-six, XIII: 149, 313

Mount Austen, IV: 267, 286, V: 140, 290, 335–6

MOUNT BAKER, IX: 390, XII: 429, XIII: 319

Mount Desert Rock, I: 288, II: 330–31; X: 330

MOUNT HOOD, XII: 429

MOUNT MCKINLEY, XII: 34, 47, XIII: 187, 310, XIV: 117*n*, 118, 121–2, 375

MOUNT OLYMPUS, XII: 16, 34, 156, 415, 418, XIII: 6, 94–6, 117, 126, 146, 150, 303, 310, XIV: 369; pic., XIII: 157

MOUNT VERNON, I: 110–12, III: 359, 363*n*, X: 47*n*, XIV: 158*n*

Mountbatten, Adm. Lord Louis, pic., VI: 18; mentioned, II: 15*n*, 25, VII: 83, IX: 7, 323, XI: x, 11, 20, 224, 296, XIII: 257, 276, XIV: 356

MOUNTRAIL, XIV: 375

Mountrey, Lt. Cdr. R. W., XIV: 376

Moureau, Lt. Cdr. R. H., VI: 145, VIII: 408

MOURNE, X: 324

"Mousetrap," I: 211; pic., 211

Mowatt, Lt. Cdr. W. P., I: 420

MÖWE, XI: 183, 191

Moyer, Commo. J. G., XIV: 378

Mroczkowski, Cdr. R. E., XII: 417

Mroski, Yeoman John, VI: 333

Muara I., XIII: 264–5

Mucci, Lt. Col. H. A., XII: 119, 417

Mudaguchi, Capt. K., XII: 430

Mudge, Maj. Gen. V. D., XII: 130, 416, XIII: 193

Mueller, Maj. Gen. P. J., XII: 34, 45

MUGFORD, III: 104, 243*n*, IV: 272, 293, V: 52*n*, VI: 133–4, 262, 382, 386, 391, VIII: 408, 415, XII: 319, 373–5, 428

MUIR, X: 387

Mukai, Lt. Cdr. N., IV: 173

Muko Jima, VIII: 313

"Mulberrys," XI: 25–6, 165, 177–9, 188; pic., 172–3

Mulcahy, Maj. Gen. F. P., V: 374; XIV: 278

Muldrow, Lt. Col. H. L., IX: 287

MULGRAVE, XI: 335

Mullan, Capt. W. E. A., V: 47–9, XII: 426, XIII: 316, XIV: 385

Mullaney, Cdr. B. J., VI: 441, VIII: 405, XIV: 256–8, 379

Mullany, Capt. R. V., XIV: 386

MULLANY, VI: 382, 391, 440–42, VIII: 66, 97, 127, 405, XII: 415, XIV: 192–3, 381, 390

Mullen, Cdr. W. D., IX: 390

Mullinnix, Capt. A. P., II: 80*n*, XII: 425, XIV: 373

Mullinnix, Rear Adm. Henry M., biog., VII: x–xi; pic., 143; mentioned, I: 77*n*, 208, VII: 139–41, 337

Mullinnix Field, Tarawa, VII: 212, 260, 287

Mullins, Maj. Gen. C. L., XIII: 306

Mullins, Cdr. Henry, VII: 335, X: 289, 377

Mullins, Cdr. W. J., I: 33

Mulvihill, Lt. Cdr. T. P., XIII: 312

Mumma, Cdr. Morton C., III: 158, VI: 34*n*, 53, 61, 136, 370–72, VIII: 57*n*

Munda, V: 321–32, 345, 354, 375*n*, VI: 90–95, 99, 106–7, 116–20, 132, 147–50; fight for, 153–5, 177, 196–206; U.S. base, 222–4, 290–91, 296, 303, 350, 395–9, VIII: 156; chart, V: 327; pics., V: 338, VI: 116

Mundorff, Capt. G. T., XIV: 306, 386

Munger, Cdr. M. T., VII: 337, VIII: 409

Munholland, Lt. Cdr. John, VII: 139, 338

Munn, Col. J. C., XIV: 374

Munro, Signalman D. A., V: 141–2

Munroe, Cdr. F. A., VI: 47

Munroe, Rear Adm. William R., biog., I: 189*n;* mentioned, 135*n*, X: 189

MUNSEE, XII: 98–100, 429, XIV: 305, 387

Munson, Lt. Cdr. H. G., IV: 20, 226, 275, V: 18–19

Murai, Maj. Gen., XII: 43

MURAKUMO, III: 276, IV: 89, V: 118, 151; sunk, 169

MURASAME, III: 162, 275, 334, IV: 88, V: 84, 138, 206–7, 234, 239, 254, VI: 107; sunk, and chart, 109–10

Murdaugh, Capt. A. C., I: 121–2, XI: 170, 334, 342

Murdock, Lt. Cdr. J. F., VII: 346*n*, VIII: 405

Murmansk, I: 159–60, 366, 369–75, X: 233, 306, 309, 314–15

Muroran, XIV: 314

Murphey, Capt. C. D., XII: 417
Murphey, Lt. Cdr. W. B., XIV: 386
Murphy, Lt. (jg) C. H., XI: 315
Murphy, Lt. Cdr. C. L., I: 421
Murphy, Lt. E. J., XII: 425
Murphy, Lt. F. M., XII: 422, XIII: 306
Murphy, Capt. J. D., XII: 389, XIII: 226
Murphy, Cdr. J. E., II: 39, IX: 389
Murphy, Lt. Cdr. J. W., IV: 145
Murphy, Capt. M. E., VIII: 410, XII: 416, XIII: 310, XIV: 380
Murphy, Lt. Cdr. O. B., XII: 422, XIII: 112, 304, XIV: 376
Murphy, Hon. Robert D., II: 65–6, 184–7, 208, 215, 242; Weygand agreement, 5–6, 9–10
Murphy, Rear Adm. Vincent R., I: xvii, III: xii, 97, 131, IV: 86n, XII: 427, XIII: 316
MURPHY, II: 38, 58–62, 74–5, 110, 285, IX: 101, 141, 191, 388, XI: 203, 335–7, 342
Murphy, Camp, III: 171
Murray, Vice Adm. George D., III: 211, 392, IV: 90, 276, V: 139, 148, 177, 201, 205, 210, 215, 219, XIII: 83, 171, XIV: 308n, 327n
Murray, Cdr. H. Q., XI: 334, XIV: 376
Murray, Capt. J. E., V: 375
Murray, Rear Adm. L. W., RCN, I: 90, X: 20
Murray, Lt. Col. Raymond L., VII: 175–9, VIII: 193
Murray, Lt. Col. Roy A., IX: 104n
Murray, Capt. S. S., XIV: 362, 385
Murray, Lt. Cdr. T. O., XII: 420, XIII: 306
MURRAY, VI: 331, VII: 257, 337, 344, VIII: 405, 419, XII: 416, XIV: 57, 112, 383, 390
Murray-Smith, Capt. H. S., XI: 342
Murtha, Col. J. T., XIII: 24

MURZIM, XII: 423, XIII: 308
MUSASHI, III: 21, 31, VI: 284, VII: 44, 137, 317–19, VIII: 13, 27, 31, 131–2, 217–18, 299, 317–19, 416, XII: 162, 430, XIV: 200–202; sunk, XII: 186
Muse, Lt. Cdr. G. R., XIII: 317, XIV: 383
Musick, Lt. Cdr. K. F., VIII: 304, 413, XII: 425
MUSKALLUNGE, VIII: 415
MUSKETEER, X: 147, 240
MUSKOGEE, XII: 417
Mussett, Maj. E. P., VI: 64
Mussolini, Benito, I: 5, 34, II: 254, IX: 34–51 *passim*, 171–3, 184–7, 232, 237, 242, X: 5–7
MUSTIN, IV: 19, V: 133, 205, 221–2, 233, 262, 337, VII: 334–6, 346, VIII: 120–25, 405, XII: 366n, 417, XIII: 309, 312, XIV: 379
MUTINE, IX: 393
MUTSU, I: xxxvii, III: 26, IV: 89, V: 82–4
MUTSUKI, III: 231n, IV: 17, V: 85; sunk, 105
Mutty, Lt. J. B., II: 263n, IX: 189
MUZIO ATTENDOLO, IX: 39n
Myers, Lt. Cdr. Horace, VI: 145
Myers, Cdr. R. E., XII: 427, XIII: 318
Myers, Lt. R. F., VIII: 261n
Myers, Cdr. R. O., VII: 334
Myers, Lt. Cdr. W. G., IV: 92
Myhre, Lt. Cdr. Floyd B. T., VI: 144, 182
Myhre, Lt. Cdr. L. A., X: 333n, 354, 376
Myoho M., V: 348
MYOKO, III: 26, 274, 334, 371–2, IV: 17, 45, 88, V: 84, 105n, 138, 177, 179n, 206, VI: 305–6, 312–13, 321, VII: 43, VIII: 118–20, 130–32, 300, 416, XII: 162, 186, 431, XIII: 159
Myoko M., VI: 55n
Mystery ships. *See* Q-Ships

N

"NA" line, VIII: 223, 225; chart, 226
NABOB, X: 40n, 309n
NACHI, III: 26, 182, 274-5, 296, 334-71
  passim, IV: 6n, 172, 175, 179, VII: 24-
  35, VIII: 215n, XII: 103, 164, 168-90,
  230-36, 240, 431; sunk, 239, 348-9
NADAKAZE, V: 85
Nadzab, VIII: 34, 49, 61, 95, 107, 266,
  272
Nafutan Pt., VIII: 181-2, 208-9, 330-
  33
Nagaishsi, Capt. M., VIII: 234n
NAGANAMI, V: 206, 226, 297-8, 302, 311,
  VI: 306, 332, 341, VIII: 416, XII: 431;
  sunk, 353
Nagano, Adm. Osami, pic., III: 12; men-
  tioned, 82-3, IV: 75, VI: 17-18, 403
NAGARA, III: 162, 181, 274-6, 307, 320,
  329, IV: 88, 125, 132, V: 85, 206, 233-
  75 *passim*, VI: 208, VII: 137, 193;
  sunk, VIII: 17n
Nagara M., V: 234, 269n
Nagasaki, III: 29, XIV: 333, 345
Nagata M., III: 263
NAGATO, III: 26, 86, IV: 89, VII: 137, 222,
  319, VIII: 264, 294-7, 416, XII: 162-3,
  186, 248, 251, 259, 299, 308-11, 430,
  XIII: 158, XIV: 316
NAGATSUKI, III: 161, VI: 162, 168, 172;
  lost, 174-5
NAGAURA, VI: 403, 420
Nagle, Lt. R. A., XI: 314
Nagoya M., VIII: 16
Nagumo, Vice Adm. Chuichi, pic.,
  IV: 101; Pearl Harbor strike, III: 86-
  7, 92-3, 217-18; Rabaul, 260; in SW
  Pacific, 316, 334, 376-8; Indian Ocean,
  382-5; chart, 385; Coral Sea, IV: 11;
  Midway, 74-6, 88, 95-7, 102-7, 110,
  113-16, 125, 132, 138-9, 142, 148-9,
  155; E. Solomons, V: 82-4, 91, 100,
  200-203; Sta. Cruz, 206-8, 214, 219-21;
  Saipan, VIII: 167-8, 185; death, 335-7
Naha, XIV: 80-81, 83, 275
NAKA, III: 26, 162, 275, 284, 334-5, 340,
  345-7, 351-4, IV: 220, VII: 137
Nakagawa, Col. K., XII: 36, 43
Nakaguma, Col. T., V: 143-5

Nakagusuku Bay, VIII: 309, XIV: 83,
  220, 277-9
Nakahara, Capt. G., V: 297, 302
Nakajima, Cdr. T., *Divine Wind*,
  XIII: 93n, XIV: 215n
Nakamura, Capt. T., VIII: 182n, 201n
Nakano, Lt. Gen., VI: 55
Nakase, Rear Adm. N., XII: 328, 430
Nakashima, Col., VIII: 194
Nakayama, Capt. S., VI: 244, 251
Nako M., V: 234, 269n
Nam Kwan Bay, XIII: 298
Namatanai, VI: 422
Namber, VIII: 135
Namorik Atoll, VII: 312-13
Namu Atoll, VII: 312-13
Namur. *See* Roi I.
Nana M., III: 275, 284-6
Nandi, III: 259, IV: 252, 263n, V: 318,
  VII: 102
Nankai M., V: 323, VI: 37-8
Nanking, III: 16, 35
NANOK, I: 421
Nanomea I., VII: 94, 97-8, 118, 214n
Nansei Shoto, XIV: 79, 102
NANTAHALA,   XII: 428,   XIII: 318-19,
  XIV: 387
NANTUCKET, I: 296n
NAPA (1919), III: 159
NAPA (1944), XIV: 389
Napalm, VIII: 357-60, XII: 79, 356
Napier, Lt. (jg) C. E., VII: 340
Naples, City and Bay, IX: 39, 42, 194,
  215-97 *passim*, 302-83 *passim*, X: 271,
  XI: 237, 246, 311; clearing harbor, IX:
  311-12; pic., XI: 245
Naples M., VIII: 49n
NARCISSUS, X: 143
Narkunda, II: 284
NARRAGANSETT, IX: 194, 291, 389, 393,
  XI: 341
Narragansett Bay, I: 68, 254
Narsarssuak, I: 334n
NARUTO, IV: 89
Narvik, X: 308
NARWHAL, III: 104, 213n, IV: 92, 157n,
  190, VI: 85, VII: 42, 334, VIII: 22,
  XII: 27, 64, 401, XIII: 161n

Nash, Lt. (jg) D. F., X: 382
Nash, Capt. H. F., XI: 337
Nash, Lt. Cdr. W. V., XIV: 29
NASHVILLE, I: 57, 76, 83*n*, III: 31*n*, 57, 391–4, 397, IV: 83, 171–3, 177, V: 326–8, 345–6, VI: 106*n*, 113*n*, 116*n*, 320, 382, 436–7, 444, VII: 9*n*, VIII: 47, 78, 83, 97, 108, 123–4, 126*n*, 406, X: 204*n*; Gen. MacArthur embarked, XII: 14, 22–3, 136–8, 198, 343, 385, 415; hit, XIII: 19, 23–4, 34; Borneo, 264, 272–4; pic., 36
NASSAU, I: 419, V: 291, VII: 38, 43–4, 47–8, 86, 334, 338, 347, XII: 428
Nassau Bay, New Guinea, VI: 136–7, 254–6; pic., 133
Nasu, Maj. Gen. Y., V: 190–92
Nasugbu, landing, XIII: 189–92, 210; chart, 190; pic., 165
Natal, I: 83, 379, 386, X: 209, 212, 219, 227*n*
NATCHEZ, X: 36, 344, 373
Nath, Lt. Cdr. C. J., XIV: 375
Nathan Towson, X: 311
Nathanael Greene, I: 361–4
Nation, Lt. Cdr. M. A., II: 39
National Defense Act, III: 59
National Defense Research Committee, I: 29, 220, X: 5, 146
National Maritime Union, I: 298, 374
NATOMA BAY, VII: 348, VIII: 209, 329*n*, 405, 411, XII: 244, 310, 420, XIII: 19, 99, 305, XIV: 373
NATORI, III: 26, 161, 174*n*, 334, 365; sunk, VIII: 17*n*, XII: 160*n*
NATRONA, XIV: 375
NATSEK, I: 62*n*, 421
NATSUGUMO, III: 162, 275, IV: 88, V: 84, 151; sunk, 169
NATSUSHIO, III: 163, 274; sunk, 304, 307
Nauman, Cdr. H. K., XII: 407, 429, XIV: 293*n*
Nauru I., III: 257, IV: 10, 13, 62, VI: 12, VII: 77, 83–5, 307, VIII: 219; raids on, VII: 93, 117, 136, 197–8, 212
NAUSET, IX: 389, 393; sunk, 274
Naushon, I: 323*n*
NAUTILUS, IV: xi, 92; Midway, 111–12, 122–9 *passim*, 190, 212, 228; Makin raid, 235–41, V: 77; Aleutians, VII: 42; recce., 77, 97–8, 119; Tarawa, 154, 180–81, 187, 202, 334, 342; guerilla supply, VIII: 22, XII: 64
NAVAJO, IV: 154, V: 359–64

Navajo Indian "talkers," VIII: 376
Navajo V., XIII: 307
Naval Advanced Base Unit 5, XIII: 30; Unit 7, VI: 289*n*
Naval Air Arm, I: 49, 248–51
Naval Air Liaison Party, II: 128, 132
Naval Air Transport Service, I: 289, VIII: 349, X: 45
Naval Aircraft Radio Laboratory, I: 225
Naval Architecture & Engineering, pre-war development, I: lvii–lix
Naval Armament Limitations, I: xxxv–xl
Naval Armed Guards, I: 138, 160, 169–75, 180–92, 302, 331–3, 342, 345, 357, 361–4, 367–75, 392–9, X: 8, 68, 141, 145, 151, 182–3, 202, 207*n*, 211, 214, 265, 270, 277, 299, 302, 310–13, 327, 356, 381–2; tribute, I: 365; *Reports*, X: xiii
Naval Auxiliaries, defined, I: xxxvii–viii
Naval Base Unit 11, VI: 415
Naval bases in Pacific, I: xxxix
Naval Battalion, Bataan, III: 200–201
Naval Building programs, pre-war, I: lvi–lix, 27–8, III: 30–31, 59; 1799 Program, II: 267, X: 34–5; *see* Escort Carriers, Subchasers
Naval Coastal Frontiers, I: 71*n*
Naval Group China, XIII: 289–302
Naval Gunfire Control, VI: 195, IX: xi, 117, XII: 258
Naval Gunfire Support, N. Africa, II: 73–8, 91–8, 110–13, 117–49 *passim*, 161, 235, and chart, 94–5; Solomons, IV: 284–5, V: 138, 173, 182, 191, 226–7, 230, 284, 327–30, 337–47, VI: 294, 302–3, 361; Cape Gloucester, 386; Admiralties, 437–45; Attu, VII: 43–8; Gilberts, 124, 156–81 *passim*, 202–3; Marshalls, 227, 236–303 *passim*; New Guinea, VIII: 69, 76–100 *passim*, 108–16, 137–8; Sicily, IX: 82–104 *passim*, 110–19, 130–223 *passim*; Salerno, 249, 261–304 *passim*; Anzio, 341–84 *passim*; Normandy, XI: 55–6, 95–6, 104–7, 121–5, 142–9, 157–61, 166–9; British FOBs, 18–45; Cherbourg, 195–210; table of vessels, 56*n*; pic., 149; Marianas, VIII: 179–83, 192, 197, 203–5, 325–401 *passim*; S. France, XI: 257–89 *passim*; Italian Riviera, 312–13; Morotai, XII: 23; Palaus, 35–41, 44–5; Mapia

Is., 54; Leyte, 119–20, 123–4, 132–54 *passim*, 370, 379; Lingayen, XIII: 128–30; P.I. landings, 27–8, 203–50 *passim;* Iwo, XIV: 34–5, 40–44, 48–52, 62–6; Kerama Retto, 120–22; Okinawa, 147–53, 217, 221, 240, 245–7, 266; Tsugen Jima, 220; Borneo, XIII: 261–77
Naval landing battalions, XIV: 357
Naval limitation, I: xxxv–xl, III: 8–9, 19, 30–31
Naval personnel, III: 30–31
Naval Research Laboratory, I: 228
Naval School of Mil. Gov't. & Admin'n., XI: 325
Naval strength, 1922–41, comparisons, I: lx
Naval Torpedo Station, IV: 230–32
Naval War College, Newport, I: xxxiii, VI: 93, 226, XII: 213, 223; *Analyses, see* Bates, Commo. R. W.
Navarino, I: 191n
NAVARINON, XI: 342
NAVARRO, XIV: 379
Navy Language School, III: 30
Nazro, Lt. T. W., I: 347n, X: 378
Ndeni I., IV: 264, 279, V: 23, 83, 87, 201
NEAL A. SCOTT, X: 349–50, 378
Neale, Capt. E. T., VI: 47, XII: 428, XIII: 319
NECHES (1920), III: 242; sunk, 260
NECHES (1942), VII: 47n, 334, 340, XII: 428, XIII: 319, XIV: 387
Neely, Ens. E. S., I: 369
Neff, Lt. (jg) H. L., I: 16, 249, 325
Nefifikh R., II: 65; pic., 75
Negros I., XII: 57, 107–8, 126, 133, 149, XIII: 23, 25, 45, 228; pics., VI: 435, XIII: 36; landing, 231–3, and chart, 229; T.O., 323
NEHENTA BAY, VIII: 410, XII: 428, XIII: 67, 81, 172, 319
Nelms, Ens. K. S., VII: 341
Nelson, Capt. F. J., XI: 341
Nelson, Lt. (jg) G. I., VI: 382
Nelson, Lt. (jg) I. O., X: 381
Nelson, Cdr. N. W., XIII: 307
Nelson, Cdr. P. J., XII: 313
Nelson, Lt. Cdr. R. R., XIV: 379
Nelson, Lt. R. S., VIII: 290–91
Nelson, Cdr. Roger E., IX: 78, 86–8, 387
NELSON, I: 351, IX: 175, 191, 388, XI: 175, 335

NELSON, HMS, II: 189, IX: 167, 251, 393
Nemaha, I: 178
NEMASKET, XIV: 387
NEMESIS, I: 135
Nemeth, Fireman F. J., XIV: 185
NENOHI, III: 274, 276, 329, IV: 172; sunk, 216, VII: 7
Neocardia, X: 382
NEOSHO (1941), III: 111, 237, 240, IV: 19–34 *passim,* 63; sunk, 36; pics., III: 84, 111
NEOSHO (1942), VII: 47n, 341, VIII: 411, 420, XII: 428, XIII: 71, 319
NEREIDE, IX: 42, 168
NESHANIC, VII: 340, VIII: 345–6, 411, XIV: 387
NESHOBA, XIV: 380
NESTOR, XIV: 387–8
Netherlands East Indies, XIII: 169, 213, 257; Jap. conquest of, 270–380; Air Force, VIII: 47; Civil Admin'n. detachment, 140; defense batteries, III: 281
Netherlands Navy, 1941, III: 58; ABDA Command, T.O., 273; submarines, 304, 310, VI: 67n; motor torpedo boats, III: 322, 329
Netley, XI: 61
Nettuno, IX: 335–54 *passim,* 371; pic., 347
NEUENDORF, VIII: 406, XIII: 279, 308
NEUNZER, X: 353–4, 378
Neurath, Konstantin von, IX: 48, 182
Neutrality Acts, I: 80, III: 15, X: 4
Neutrality Patrol, I: 13–16, 51, 60, 83, XI: 3; pic., I: 60
NEVADA, III: 109–10, 118, 145–6, 250n, IV: 166n, 250n–51n, VII: 37n, 38, 42, 45–6, 334, X: 134, XI: 56, 86, 95, 104–6, 157–288 *passim,* 334, 337, 340, XIII: 19n, 176n, XIV: 26–30, 40, 64, 130, 133, 180, 240, 247, 372, 390; pics., III: 84, 110, XI: 292
NEVILLE, IV: 266, 273, VII: 129, 336, 347, VIII: 407, IX: 130, 389
Nevins, Cdr. J. H., VII: 339, 344, VIII: 418
Nevius, Lt. F. C., XIII: 309
New, Lt. Cdr. W. A., I: 421, III: 158, IV: 92
New Bedford, I: 323n
New Britain, VI: 96; described, 370; map, 29; strategy, 369–72
New Caledonia, IV: 6, 10, 248, 253,

New Caledonia (*cont'd*)
263*n*, 270, V: 14, VI: 90, 94*n*, 98, VII: 109, XIV: 89–90
New Georgia, V: 4, 7, 121; invasion, VI: 138–53, 155–9, 200, 203–4; opns. ashore, 175–80, 198–206, 222–4, VII: 20–21, 64; T.O., VI: 144–6; casualties, 203, 224; charts, 143, 201
NEW GLASGOW, X: 340
New Guinea, history and description, VI: 27–30, VIII: 59–61; conquest of, VI: 33–55, 125–7, 130, 137, 254, 275, 389–91, VIII: 45–145; maps, VI: 29, 134, VIII: 35, 62, 71, 76, 88, 93, 100, 105, 109, 121
NEW HAMPSHIRE, I: 51*n*, IX: 191*n*, X: 200*n*
New Hebrides, IV: 10, V: 108, VII: 112
New Ireland, IV: 256, VI: 418
NEW JERSEY (1906), VII: 37*n*
NEW JERSEY (1943), VII: 208, 289, 309, 326–9, 349, 352–3, VIII: 40, 187, 415, XII: 47, 86, 90, 190*n*, 193–5, 318–19, 329–31, 345, 424–6, XIII: 54, 60–77 *passim*, 183, 315, 317, XIV: 21, 112, 385–6
NEW KENT, XIV: 379
New London, Conn., I: 54, 421, II: 43, X: 51
NEW MEXICO (1918), I: 57, 82, III: 57, 214, 236*n*, VI: 423, VII: 55, 124, 139–40, 257, 336, 344, VIII: 180, 409, X: 47*n*, XII: 366, XIII: 19, 52*n*, 98, 101, 105, 177–8, 303–4, 325, XIV: 26*n*, 86*n*, 104, 138, 158*n*, 182, 229, 269, 373; pic., VII: 279
"New Operational Policy," VI: 284, VIII: 12, 213
NEW ORLEANS (1898), V: 236*n*
NEW ORLEANS (1934), III: 31*n*, 119, 212*n*–13*n*, IV: 18, 60*n*, 91, 113*n*, 257, 270, V: 86, 288*n*, 291–314 *passim*, VII: 190, 255, 258–60, 274, 326–53 *passim*, VIII: 181, 237*n*, 308, 361*n*, 399, 409, 415, 419, XII: 90, 318, 331, 428, XIII: 54, XIV: 373; pic., IV: 126
New Orleans, I: 242, II: 263
NEW YORK, I: 14, 75–6, 118, 137, 326, 355, 419, II: 39, 44, 139, 145, 148–51, 162–4, 172, 285, IV: 166*n*, VI: 131*n*, VII: 232*n*, X: 229*n*, 343*n*, XII: 21*n*, 118*n*, 244*n*, XIII: 176, XIV: 26, 130, 373
New York, I: 323
New York, N.Y., I: 134, 137, 159–60,

223, 256, 260–64, 354, III: 38, X: 116, 134, 184, 249, 281
New Zealand, coast watchers, VII: 77; bases, 109, 114; supplies from, VIII: 343, XIV: 163; Air Forces, V: 232, 290, 375; Army, VI: 239, 243, 289*n*, 294, 361, 413–15, VII: 78; Navy, V: 349–50, XIV: 388. *See also* Achilles, Leander
Newbegin, Lt. Cdr. R. G., IX: 82, 198, 386
Newcomb, Lt. Cdr. R. M., XIV: 317
NEWCOMB, VIII: 230, 408, XII: 199, 221–2, 234, 419, XIII: 36, 107–8, 304, 325, XIV: 182–5, 373, 390; pic., 206
Newell, Lt. Cdr. J. H., VII: 340
Newell, Lt. Cdr. James, VI: 325*n*, 328
Newell, Lt. R. T., VII: 343, VIII: 408, XII: 422
NEWFOUNDLAND, HMS (cruiser), II: 281, IX: 42, XIV: 313, 333
NEWFOUNDLAND, HMS (hospital ship), IX: 314, 394; sunk, 300
Newman, Col., VIII: 112–13
Newman, Capt. J. F., XII: 389
NEWMAN, XIII: 236, 307, 321, 323–4
Newport News, II: 119, 268
Newsom, Lt. Cdr. J., III: 158
Newsome, Lt. James H., IV: 174
Newton, Rear Adm. John H., III: 56*n*, 210, 215
Newton, Cdr. R. J., XIV: 379
Newton, Lt. Cdr. Roy A., VI: 214
Ngulu Atoll, VIII: 367, XII: 50–51
NIAGARA, I: 151*n*, III: 212, VI: 121–2; sunk, 139*n*
NIBLACK, I: 57, 73, 76, 94, 98, 123, 302–3, 418, 420, IX: 163, 303, 385, 391, 396, X: 252–3, 259–60, 372, XI: 312, 342; "incident," I: 73; pic., X: 264
Nichandross, Lt. Cdr. G. C., VIII: 415
Nichiei M., IV: 88, VI: 323, VIII: 417, XIII: 281
Nichiryu M., VI: 55*n*
Nichol, Capt. B. B., XIV: 373
Nicholas, Capt. G. A. G., XIII: 304
NICHOLAS, V: 172, 173*n*, 179–80, 190–91, 326, 342, 345–6, 364–7, VI: 107, 110*n*, 116*n*, 156–93 *passim*, 228, 234, VII: 190, 224, 338, VIII: 228*n*, 404, XII: 155, 295, 377, 387, 417, XIII: 202, 261, 304, 322; pic., VI: 117, 171
Nicholas Gillman, IX: 386
Nicholls, Lt. W. H., XIII: 323

Nichols, Maj. C. S., *Okinawa*, XIV: 170*n*
Nichols, Capt. Chester L., II: 192
Nichols, Col. F. H., VII: 105
Nichols, Lt. Cdr. F. M., I: 420
Nichols, Cdr. J. C., XIII: 319
Nichols, Cdr. P. G., I: 421
Nichols, Lt. Cdr. R. E., VIII: 416
Nichols, Capt. R. F., X: 381, XI: 342
Nichols, Lt. Cdr. S. G., I: 421
Nichols Field, III: 170–71, XII: 69, XIII: 14, 99, 125, 197
Nicholson, Lt. Col. G. W. L., IX: xv
Nicholson, Lt. Cdr. H. W., XIV: 382
NICHOLSON, I: 121–2, 420, VI: 443–4, VIII: 115, 403, IX: 42, 252, 387, XII: 319, 428
Nickeliner, X: 190
Nickelson, Lt. Cdr. W. R. D., VI: 335*n*
Nickerson, Capt. R. B., I: 215*n*, 420, II: 40
Nicobar Is., XII: 61
Nicolas Channel, X: 190
NIELDS, IX: 389, X: 252, 257–9, 370–72, XI: 341
Nielson Field, III: 171, XIII: 14
Nilon, Cdr. L. W., XI: 334
Nieuw Zeeland, II: 283
Nigaristan, I: 86
NIGERIA, I: 181
Night bombing, VII: 321–5; vision, V: 331*n*; fighters, XIII: 165, 171; recovery, VIII: 301–4
NIIZUKI, VI: 162–9, 172; survivors, 174
NIKE, I: 135, 139, 155*n*
Nikkai M., IV: 18
NIMET ALLAH, XI: 282–4
Nimitz, Fleet Adm. Chester W., biog., III: 255*n*; pics., 191, IV: frontispiece, XII: 6, XIV: 366; assistance, III: xii; Cincpac-Cincpoa, III: 250, 255–7, IV: 79*n*, 90, 250–52, 257–8, 276; staff, VI: 9–13; promoted, XIII: 156; strategy, VII: 8–9, 104–5, VIII: 11, XII: 4–10, 17–18, 57–8, XIII: 3–5, 9, XIV: 4–5; early opns., III: 260–61, 266, 390, IV: 235; sub. opns., IV: 189, 212, 217; Coral Sea, 13–16, 21, 27, 44*n*, 60; Midway, 68–9, 79–86, 94, 105, 141–3, 156, V: 22; Aleutians, IV: 166–7, 179, 182–4, 226–7, VII: 4, 9, 17, 21, 37–8; Guadalcanal, IV: 254, 260–61, 264–8, V: 14, 62, 115–16, 178, 181–4, 224, 344, 351, 370; Solomons, IV: 226–7, V: 137*n*,

298*n*, 313, 363, VI: 93–6, 123, 220, 289; Bismarcks, VI: 128–9, 413, 422, 423; Gilberts, VII: 69, 79–86, 97, 336; Marshalls, VII: 69, 82, 103–5, 201–6, 233, 281, 285, 343; Carolines, VII: 319; VIII: 10, 28, 34; New Guinea, VIII: 36, 63, 95; Marianas, VIII: 158, 341, 400, 407; Philippine Sea, VIII: 241; Morotai, XII: 3–4, 19, 22; Palaus, XII: 32; Formosa and Leyte, XII: 13–15, 55–60, 71–2, 109, 137, 346, 354, XIII: 58–9; Leyte Gulf battle, XII: 193, 291–4, 329; "Where is TF34?" XII: 292; fleet letter on typhoon, XIII: 84–6, XIV: 307; South China Sea raid, XIII: 87, 161, 170–72; Balikpapan, XIII: 272; Iwo, XIV: 7–13, 41, 68; Okinawa, XIV: 92, 101, 154, 157, 162, 198, 214–16, 250, 256, 273, 372; British Pac. Fleet, XIV: 102–4, 214, 250, 333; Japan strikes, XIV: 296, 310, 332; *Indianapolis*, 327; relations with Halsey, VIII: 161; and with MacArthur, XIII: 174–7; and A.A.F., XIV: 87–8, 327; occupation plans, 354–7; surrender ceremony, 361–7; quoted, IV: 188*n*, XIII: 81–6, XIV: 48, 252, 367
Nimitz, Cdr. Chester W., Jr., IV: 220, VIII: 416
Ninni Islet, VII: 252, 254, 257
NIOBRARA, VIII: 420, IX: 390, XII: 428, XIII: 319, XIV: 387
Nippon M., IV: 88, V: 73, VII: 58
Nira Luckenbach, IV: 87
Niscemi, IX: 104, 122
Nisewaner, Cdr. T. A., VIII: 409, XII: 222, 419
Nishida, Maj. Gen., VII: 294, 300
Nishimura, Vice Adm. S., III: 162, 176–8, 275, 283–4, 288, 334–5, 338–9, 340, 347, IV: 88, V: 85, 206, 234, 262–3, 270, VI: 207, XII: 127, 160–64, 167–8, 184*n*, 189–239 *passim*, 298, 312, 320, 337, 431; death, 229
Nishino, Cdr. S., XII: 207, 237
Nishiyama, Lt. Gen., XIII: 154
Nisida I., pic., XI: 245
Nissan M., IV: 172, 183, VII: 6
Nissan Atoll, VI: 413–14, 418–19
NISSHIN, IV: 89, V: 150–51, 171; sunk, VI: 207
Nisshin M., VIII: 21
Nissho M., VI: 323

Nisshu M., XIV: 14
Nissun M., VI: 69, XIV: 14
NITRO, I: 422, III: 224, XII: 429, XIII: 319
Nix, Lt. Cdr. J. J., III: 160
Nixon, Capt. E. B., III: 213, IV: 173
NOA, I: 138*n*, 139, 143–4, 420, VI: 381, VIII: 404, 408
Noble, Rear Adm. Alfred G., VI: 435, VIII: 64, 69–70, 96–8, 404, XII: 415, XIII: 215, 217, 241–8, 268, 272, 275, 324
Noble, Lt. Cdr. Christopher, V: 205
Noble, Capt. K. H., XIV: 385
Noble, Adm. Sir Percy, I: 53, 70, X: 8, 19
NOBLE, XIV: 378
Noel, Ens. H. W., IX: 338
Noel, Cdr. J. V., XII: 417
Noemfoor, VIII: 91, 132, 136, XII: 3, 22, 238, XIII: 97, 144, 105; description, VIII: 134; charts, 105, 137; landing, 135–40, 403–6
NOGAK, I: 421
Noguès, Gen. Charles, pic., II: 218; mentioned, 65, 68–71, 87*n*, 116, 164, 177–8, 216–18, 241
Nojima, Cape, XIV: 316
NOJIMA, VI: 55–6, 58
NOKAZE, XIII: 285
NOKOMIS, I: 206*n*
Nolan, Lt. James C., VI: 191
Nolan, Lt. Cdr. R. L., II: 37, IX: 386
NOMI, XIV: 291
Nomura, Adm. K., III: 60, 65–8, 70, 72–3, 78, 140
Nomura, Rear Adm. T., XII: 430
Non-recognition policy, III: 11
Nopby, Lt. Cdr. P. R., XIV: 382
Norcott, Lt. J. M., VIII: 406, XIII: 312
NORFOLK, I: 180, X: 237, 240–41
Norfolk, Va., I: 54, 223, 240, 264, 354, II: 22–3, 119, 129, 263, 270, V: 182*n*, X: 155, 181, 184–6, 249–51, 269, 343
Norgaard, Cdr. R. N., XIV: 192, 381
Norimitsu, Capt. S., XII: 431
Norman, Lt. Cdr. G. P., VII: 349
NORMAN SCOTT, VIII: 361–2, 409, XIII: 307, 314, XIV: 385
Normandy invasion, build-up and planning, IX: 3–4, X: 133–5, XI: 9, 12, 18–23, 27–34, 50–57, 62, 67–72, and table, 51; AS defense, X: 323–5; command and logistics, XI: 23–7; weather, 24–5,

79–83; defenses, 32–3, 39–49, and pic., 149; air and naval gunfire support, 35–6, 55–6, 95–6, 104–7, 121–5, 142–9, 157–61, 166–9, 184–5, 195–210; training and rehearsal, 64–7, and pic., 68; embarkation and crossing, 75–9, 83–8, and chart, 85; numbers engaged, 77; minesweeping, 78, 173; airdrops, map, 91; unloading, 150–51; British sector, 180–94; T.O., 333–7; charts, 31, 117, 133, 182; pics., 80, 100–101
Norness, I: 130
Norris, Maj. B. W., IV: 92, 111, 137
Norris, Capt. C. W. F., XI: 336
Norris, Watertender F. M., X: 175
Norris, Capt. S. H., XI: 339
North Africa, effect of occupation, I: 311, 324, 352, 365; French chain of command, II: 87; defenses, 46, 56–8; base, 244–52
North African Opn., diplomacy, II: 3–11, 184–8, 215–20, 255–8; plans and training, 15–18, 23–34, 182–4, IX: 12–16; T.O., II: 36–40; subs., 43, 167–74; chart, 172; crossing, 43–54; weather, 49–50; discussion, 177–8, 238; landings, air cover, 127–8, 149–52; cease fire, 164–5; vessels sunk, 283–4; expended ammunition, 285; summary, 286; charts, II *passim*; pics., 30, 44, 74, 82, 92, 112, 130, 148, 164, 174, 192–3, 218, 236–7. *See also* Algiers, Fedhala, Mehedia, Oran, Safi
NORTH CAROLINA (1908), VIII: 236*n*
NORTH CAROLINA (1941), I: 64, 151, 167, III: 31, IV: 257, 271, 280, V: 14, 28*n*, 86, 92–137 *passim*, 291, 352, VII: 339, 349, 353, VIII: 30*n*, 39–40, 269*n*, 415, X: 229*n*, XIII: 54, 176*n*, 180, 318, XIV: 21, 27, 34, 242, 314, 384–6
North Coast, VII: 334
North Pacific Area, IV: 250
North Pacific Force, IV: 83, 167, VII: 23, 37, 52, 66, 86
North Russia Run, I: 158–92, 358–75, X: 229–48, 304–16; charts, I: 162–3, X: 234–5; pic., I: 170–71
NORTH STAR, I: 61*n*, 421
NORTHAMPTON, III: 212, 261–3, 392, IV: 91, 113*n*, 257, 276, V: 205, 215, 219–20, 233, 291–326 *passim*, XI: 242*n*; sunk, V: 311
Northeast Greenland Sledge Patrol, I: 63

Northeast Providence Channel, X: 194, 198*n*
Northeastern Escort Force, I: 51*n*
NORTHERN FOAM, X: 143
NORTHERN GEM, X: 69
NORTHERN SPRAY, X: 71
NORTHLAND, I: 60–63, 64*n*, 155*n*, 421; pic., 61
Northland, I: 323
NORTHWAY, XI: 318
Northwest Atlantic Command, X: 20
Northwestern, IV: 177; pic., 167
Norway, X: 101, 230–35, 307–10, 323, 325
NOSHIRO, VI: 323, 328, 412, VII: 138, VIII: 131–2, 218, 416, XII: 162, 239, 248, 283, 431; sunk, 311
Noshiro Maru No. 2, IV: 17–18
Noto, Gulf of, IX: 20, 151, 157
Noto M., XII: 352
Nouméa, Japanese designs on, III: 265, IV: 12–15; South Pacific base, 246, 252–7, 279–80, V: 12, 17, 27, 59, 64*n*,

67, 107, 138–359 *passim*, VII: 102; conferences, V: 115–17, VI: 94; life at, V: 185–7; supply tangle, 334; Halsey's HQ., VI: 94*n*
Novaya Zemlya, pic., I: 170
NOWAKI, III: 333, IV: 88, V: 85, 207, 318, VII: 328–9, VIII: 131, 416, XII: 272*n*, 310, 335, 431; sunk, 330
Nowell, Lt. Cdr. B. H., VIII: 416, XII: 401
Noyes, Rear Adm. Leigh, IV: 257, 270–71, 280, 293, V: 14, 58, 83, 87, 102, 105, 131, 134–6
NUBIAN, II: 281, IX: 277, 282, 291, 393
Nukualofa Hbr., IV: 263*n*
Nukufetau I., VII: 94, 98, 118
Null, Lt. Cdr. R. S., X: 197
Numa Numa Trail, VI: 428
Nunn, Capt. I. H., VII: 338, 346, XII: 420, XIII: 318, XIV: 308*n*, 385
NÜRNBERG, I: 4*n*, X: 237*n*, XI: 328*n*
NUTHATCH, I: 422, XI: 333, 338

O

O-2, -3, -4, -6, -7, -8, -10, I: 421; -5, XIV: 86n
O-16, -17, -19, -20 (R.N.N.), III: 273
O. A. Knudsen, I: 133
O. L. Bodenhammer, XIII: 313
OAHU (1928), III: 17, 155, 159, X: 134n
OAHU (1943), XIV: 388
Oahu, III: 32, 44, 81; VIII: 371, 379; post-Pearl Harbor air raids on, IV: 69–70
OAK HILL, VIII: 196, 407, XII: 416, XIII: 310, 314, XIV: 379
Oakes, Maj. W. M., II: 209–12
OAKLAND, VII: 190, 195, 339, 348, 352, VIII: 413, XII: 90, 426, XIII: 54, 316, XIV: 385–6
Oakley, Cdr. T. B., VIII: 415, XII: 399–400, 411
OAKLEY, XI: 343
OAKVILLE, I: 249, 349, 415; pic., 374
O'BANNON, V: 232–57 passim, 326, 342, 345–7, VI: 107, 113n, 119, 156–8, 161–8, 181–2, 188, 193, 228, 234, 244–52, VIII: 228n, 404, XII: 377, 387, 417, XIII: 27n, 261, 278, 304, 321; pics., VI: 117, 252
Obara, Capt. Y., IV: 240–41
Obate, Lt. Gen. H., VIII: 12, 167, 373n, 388, 398–400
Obayashi, Rear Adm. S., VIII: 217, 247–8, 251, 263–5, 288, 416
OBDURATE, X: 305
Obeirne, Capt. Frank, XIV: 374
Obella, VII: 234, 239
Oberbroeckling, Chief Boatswain Edwin, XII: 96
OBERON, I: 421, II: 38, 60n, 159, 172, IX: 388, 392, XI: 339, XIV: 375
OBERRENDER, XII: 420n, 421, XIII: 311, XIV: 268, 375, 392
Oberwesel, XI: 320
OBORO, sunk, VII: 14
O'Brien, Lt. R. H., II: 265, IX: 309
O'Brien, Lt. Col. W. J., VIII: 336
O'BRIEN (1940), IV: 19n, V: 134; sunk, 135–7; pic., 138
O'BRIEN (1944), XI: 206–8, 337, XII: 379,

382, XIII: 31, 109, 304, 312, 325, XIV: 133, 373, 390
Observation Fighter Squadrons, XIV: 27, 44; VOF-1, XI: 280
Observation-spotter Squadrons, First and Second, XIV: 27, 373–4
O'Callahan, Lt. Cdr. J. T., XIV: 98
Ocean I., III: 257, IV: 10, 13, 61, VII: 77
Ocean Freedom, I: 190
OCEANUS, XIV: 270, 387
OCEANWAY, XI: 318
Ochiltree, Lt. Cdr. T. H., XIV: 380
OCKLAWAHA, XIV: 161, 387
O'Connell, Lt. Col. C. J., VII: 236n
O'Connell, Cdr. G. A., XIV: 376
O'Connell, Col. Geoffrey M., VIII: 333
O'Connor, Lt. Cdr. D. K., VII: 343; VIII: 408; XII: 422; XIII: 304
OCONTO, XII: 307, 313, XIV: 380
OCTAGON Conf. See Quebec, Confs., Sept. 1944
OCTANS, XII: 81, 423
OCTAVIA, XI: 339
O'Daniel, Maj. Gen. J. W., II: 204–5, XI: 236, 259, 262, 339
O'Donnell, Capt. J. J., XIV: 380
Odysseus, X: 382
OFFA, IX: 394, X: 70, 74
Office of Strategic Services, II: 66–7, 70, XIII: 293
Officers' Clubs, VI: 103, XII: 115–16, XIII: 97
O'FLAHERTY, XIII: 305, XIV: 374
Ofstie, Rear Adm. Ralph A., biog., XII: 253n; mentioned, III: x, VI: 331, VII: 349, 352, VIII: 287, 414, XII: 34, 39, 244, 253, 281, 302, 356, 421, XIII: 118, 305
Ogata, Col. K., VIII: 357–61, 364–6, 369
Ogden, Brig. Gen. David A. D., VIII: 52
Ogden, Cdr. S. B., VII: 341
Ogilby, Lt. J. D., IX: 81
OGLALA, III: 100, 109, 116; pic., 117
Ogle, Cdr. G. B., XIV: 380
O'Gorek, Torpedoman Jim, XII: 275
O'Gorman, Lt. Cdr. T. A., X: 378

Ogurasan M., VI: 81
O'Hara, Cadet Edwin, I: 398
O'Hare, Lt. Cdr. Edward H. ("Butch"), pic., VII: 86; mentioned, III: 267, IV: 14, VII: 339; death, VII: 143; O'Hare Field, Abemama, 213
Ohmae, Capt. T., III: xi, 380n, 395n, IV: xi, V: 17n, 182, 201–2n, 333n, VI: 19–37n, 118–327n passim, VII: 145n, 316n, VIII: viii, 17n, 215, 219n–292n passim, 298, 309n, 311n, 328n, 416n, XII: viii, 160n, 430n, XIII: ix, 37n, 98n, 158n, XIV: 160n, 202n, 209n, 244n, 314n
Ohnishi, Vice Adm. T., III: 83, XII: 68, 166, 432, XIII: 152, 159, XIV: 350
OI, IV: 89
Oie, Lt. Col. S., XIII: 232, 238
Oigawa M., III: 177, VI: 56, 61–2
Oikawa, Adm. K., III: 70–71, VI: 17n, XII: 161n
Oil, sources of, I: 253, X: 188; and Jap. econ., III: 15, 35–6, 62–4, 70–71, 77–8, VIII: 214–16, XII: 5; for Pacific opns., III: 133, 195, 330, 341, VII: 107–8, VIII: 344–5, XII: 75, 82–3, XIV: 129
Oilers, XII: 75–6
OITE, III: 231n, 232, IV: 17, VII: 319; sunk, 326
Oka, Col., VIII: 167, 333
Oka, Col. A., V: 193, 335–7, 341
Okada, Adm. K., III: 13, VI: 20
O'Kane, Cdr. R. H., VII: 353, VIII: 24, 155, XII: 401–5, 429; pic., 407
OKINAMI, VIII: 131, 416; XII: 308, 311, 356, 431
Okinawa Gunto, history and description, XIV: 80–86; chart, 84–5; Jap. base, VIII: 217, XII: 101, XIII: 160, XIV: 17; air strikes on, XII: 57, 90–91, XIII: 88–91, 172, 182, 257–8, XIV: 58, 101; defenses, 137, 180; beaches, 90; as U.S. base, 162, 276–82
Okinawa Opn., plans, XII: 17, XIII: 5, 176–8, XIV: 4–5, 86–92, 157; logistics, XIII: 208, XIV: 128, 156–69; kamikazes, 93, 116, 124–282 passim; air support, pics., 102; forces involved, 108–9; approach, 108–13; naval gunfire support, 112, 130–39, 147–53, 217, 221, 240, 245–7, 266; minesweeping, 113–17, 131, 134, 193–5, 220; suicide boats, chart, 125; ammunition expended, 138,

166, 245–7; landings, 140–45, and chart, 142, 150, and pics., 158–9; unloading, 154, 172–5; operations ashore, 170–276 passim; charts, 183, 189, 234; pics., 206–7, 294–5; casualties, 216, 221, 282, 390–92; T.O., 371–88
Okino Daito, XIV: 58, 307
OKINOSHIMA, III: 240n, IV: 17, 160n; sunk, 62
Okitsu M., VII: 222
OKLAHOMA, I: lii, III: 110–11, 143–4, IV: 251n, VI: 131n, XII: 237n, XIII: 93n; pics., 84, 102–3, 140–41
OKLAWAHA, VIII: 420
Okochi, Vice Adm. D., XIII: 13, 196–7
Okumiya, Cdr. M., III: 18n, IV: xi, 160n
Okuyo M., VIII: 16
Olch, Lt. Cdr. Isaiah, I: 109
Old, Capt. F. P., XI: 242, XIV: 382
Old Bahama Channel, I: 142–3, X: 190
Old Providence I., I: 151
Oldendorf, Vice Adm. Jesse B., biog., XII: 118n; pic., 214; Trinidad, I: 148; Wotje, Marshalls, VII: 220, 233–4, 288, 346; Carolines and Marianas, VIII: 40, 170, 180–81, 200, 210, 328, 356, 409; Peleliu, XII: 34–5, 43; Leyte, 83, 118, 121–7, 419; Surigao Strait Battle, 190, 197–245 passim; Samar Battle 293–8; Lingayen, XIII: 6n, 7, 12, 89–115 passim, 155, 178, 303–4; Combatron 1, 39n; injured, XIV: 109; Okinawa, 267n, 335; CTF-95, 310; quoted, XII: 202, XIII: 108
Oldenwald, I: 84
Oleron, Île d', XI: 308–9
Oliver, Commo. Geoffrey N., IX: 246–7, 271, 275–8, 294, 298, 392, XI: 181
Oliver, Brig. Gen. L. E., II: 223
Oliver, Capt. R. M., VIII: 406, XIV: 374
Oliver Ellsworth, I: 364n
Oliver Hazard Perry, IX: 390
OLIVER MITCHELL, XIII: 319, XIV: 374
Oliver-Bellasis, Capt. R., XIV: 388
OLIVINA, XI: 336
OLMSTEAD, XIII: 307, 312, XIV: 380
Olney, Capt. A. C., XII: 428, XIII: 319
Olongapo, III: 155, 158–9, 173, XIII: 188
Olopana, I: 187, 191n
Olsen, Lt. Cdr. A. R., XIV: 379
Olsen, C. N., XII: 429
Olsen, Lt. Cdr. E., IV: 92

Olsen, Cdr. H. B., XIII: 307, XIV: 378
Olsen, Cdr. H. S., XIV: 375
Olsen, Mr. J. G., III: 272
Olsen, Cdr. J. G., VIII: 411, XII: 428, XIII: 318, XIV: 387
Olsen, Cdr. K. J., XII: 418, XIII: 309, XIV: 379
Olsen, Lt. L. C., XII: 417
Olsen, Lt. Cdr. R. I., VIII: 21
Olsen, Capt. S. A., VII: 337, 347, VIII: 407, XII: 419, XIII: 310, XIV: 378
Olsen, Lt. T. E., VII: 341
Olson, Lt. Cdr. L. C., VIII: 410, XIII: 306
Olton, Lt. F. H., XII: 422
OLYMPIA, II: 286
OLYMPIC, planned opn. for Kyushu, XIV: 87n
OMAHA, I: 83–4, 377, 380, 390n, 419, VII: 101n, X: 212, 213n, 227–8, XI: 285, 339
Omaha Beach, chart, XI: 117, 133; pics., 132–3, 173; rehearsal, XI: 67, 110; terrain and defenses, 110–16; chart, 112–13; minesweeping, 116; crossing, 116–20; naval gunfire support, 121–5, 142–9, 152–3, 158–60; landings, 125–52; T.O., 130, 335–7; discussion, 152–4; operations ashore, 158; unloading, 160, 164–6
Omark, Lt. (jg) W. R., VIII: 296
O'Meara, Lt. (jg) H. J., XIV: 311n, 316n
Ominato, III: 26, IV: 175, VII: 6, 65n
OMMANEY BAY, XII: 244–5, 421, XIII: 19, 105, 305, 325; sunk, 101
Omori, Vice Adm. S., III: 87, IV: 169n, 172, 180–81, V: 206, VI: 304–14, 317, 321–3, 341
ONAMI, VI: 353; sunk, 356
Onderdonk, Lt. A. B., XIII: 304, XIV: 378
ONDO, XII: 356
Ondonga, VI: 331n, 396, 406
Oneida, X: 181n
O'Neil, Lt. G. L., XIII: 306, 323
O'Neill, Col. D. F., VI: 428, 431
O'Neill, Col. E. J., IX: 327
O'Neill, Lt. (jg) M. G., X: 127
O'Neill, Capt. Merlin, II: 38, VII: 336, 347, IX: 389
O'Neill, Lt. Cdr. R. A., XIII: 305, XIV: 374

O'NEILL, XII: 429, XIII: 319, XIV: 381, 392
Ono, Capt. T., IV: 172
Onoda, Capt. S., XII: 430
Onoe M., VI: 72
ONONDAGA, IV: 173, 176n
ONSLAUGHT, I: 359
Onslow, Capt. R. G., XIV: 388
ONSLOW, I: 365n, XIV: 381
ONTARIO, VII: 341, VIII: 420
ONTARIO, HMCS, XIV: 388
ONTONAGON, XIV: 387
ONYX, I: 138
Ooe, Capt. R., XII: 430
Oom, Cdr. K. E., XIII: 323
OPAL, I: 146
Opana, Oahu, III: 137, 214
Operational Research, I: 203; Training Command, X: 47–51, 245
Opie, Lt. Cdr. J. N., I: 420
Opp, Lt. Cdr. C. M., XII: 417
OPPORTUNE, X: 240
Oppenheim, XI: 319–20
O'Pry, Cdr. J. T., XII: 417, XIII: 309, XIV: 378
ORACK, VII: 288, 347, VIII: 410, XIV: 377
ORACLE, VII: 228, VIII: 410, XIV: 378
Oran, II: 17, 271n; landings, 222–38, 254; salvage, 251–3; as base, 251, IX: 42, 61, 64, 124, 142, 193, 247, 251, X: 257–9, XI: 246; pics., II: 219, 236–7; charts, 222, 227, 232
ORANGE, XII: 418
ORCA, VIII: 50, 123, XII: 25, XIII: 311, 325
Ord, Fort, VII: 38
Ordnance, advances in, V: 223–4, 329–30, VII: xxviii; Bureau of, XIV: 26
ORDRONAUX, IX: 78, 378, 385, XI: 271, 341
ORÉADE, II: 248; sunk, 98
O'Rear, Capt. G. M., XIV: 372
O'Regan, Capt. W. V., VIII: 24
OREGON, II: 4, 286, VIII: 349n
Oregon, I: 130n
Oregonian, I: 364n
Orella, Lt. Cdr. B., X: 381
Orem, Capt. H. E., I: 179n
Oren, Lt. Cdr. John B., I: 345n
ORESTES, XIII: 43, 46
ORIBI, X: 69, 74–5, 147
ORIOLE, IV: 173, VII: 334

ORION, IX: 276, 282, 345–7, 359, 361*n*, 393, 396, XI: 316
ORION, HMS, XI: 339
Orita, Capt. T., VI: 162, 174, 181
ORIZABA, I: 76, 111, IX: 108, 386
ORKAN, X: 161; sunk, 147
Orleck, Lt. Joseph, IX: 389, 393
Ormoc, XII: 63, 351–3, 361–72 *passim*, XIII: 9, 72, 249; landing, XII: 375–85; naval gunfire support, 379; resupply, 386–93; T.O., 377; pic., 406; chart, 378
ORMSBY, VII: 255, 268, 337, 344–5, VIII: 405, 419, XII: 416
Oro Bay, VI: 47, 124–5, 127*n*, 262, 380, 436
ORONTES, IX: 392
OROPESA, XIV: 114*n*
Oropesa gear, X: 199, XI: 272, XIV: 114
Orote Peninsula, VIII: 175, 262–3, 273–6, 283, 373, 377, 393–6; pic., 400
ORPHÉE, II: 110*n*
Orrell, Lt. R. W., XII: 422
Orth, Maj. R. C., VII: 333
ORTOLAN, V: 292*n*, VI: 123
Ortoli, Capt. de V., XI: 341
ORVETTA, VIII: 420
ORWELL, X: 147
Osborn, Capt. D. R., XIV: 305
OSHIMA, IV: 18
OSHIO, III: 274–6, 323–5, 328, IV: 88*n*, VI: 68; sunk, 69
Osler, Lt. Cdr. Paul G., V: 353, VI: 331, VII: 335, 340
Osmeña, Pres. Sergio, pic., XII: 70; mentioned, III: 203, XII: 136–8, XIII: 228
OSMOND INGRAM, I: 419, X: 77, 80–81, 111, 114, 168–70, 375, XI: 339
OSMUS, XIII: 319
Osorno, X: 172, 227
OSPREY, I: 422, II: 37, 118–20, 133, XI: 333; sunk, 79
Ostend, XI: 297, 327
OSTERHAUS, XII: 429
Ostrom, Lt. Cdr. Charles H., V: 375
Ostrom, Lt. Cdr. R. J., XIV: 374
Osugi, Rear Adm. M., VI: 306, 310–12, 321, 341
Oswald, Cdr. A. H., I: 420, II: 37
Otani, Cdr. T., XII: 280
Otis Skinner, XIII: 149, 313, 326
OTORI, sunk, VIII: 175
OTRANTO, II: 193

OTTER, X: 332–4, 376
OTTERSTETTER, X: 378
Ottinger, Cdr. G. M., XIV: 384
OTUS, III: 158, 193, 298, 303*n*, 306, 376
Ouessant (Ushant), II: 248
Ouistreham, XI: 185
Oujda, II: 50*n*, IX: 29
Outerbridge, Cdr. W. W., XI: 208, 334, XII: 383, XIII: 109, 304, XIV: 373
Outerson, Cdr. William, X: 263, XI: 336
Outlaw, Lt. Cdr. E. C., VII: 350, VIII: 414
Overesch, Capt. H. E., VII: 344, VIII: 409, XIII: 316
Overfield, Cdr. D. B., II: 39
OVERTON, I: 418, 421, VII: 254, 276, 343, VIII: 408, X: 118, 379, XII: 422, XIII: 304
Owada, XII: 299
Owen, Lt. Cdr. D. F., XIV: 380
Owen, Lt. (jg) D. H., XII: 208, 422
Owen, Lt. Cdr. E. M., VII: 388, 348
Owen, Cdr. G. R., I: 419
OWEN, VII: 349, VIII: 413, XII: 319, 426, XIII: 317, XIV: 383
Owen Stanley Mts., III: 388, V: 115–17, VI: 33–4, 42
OWEN SUMMERS, XIII: 313
Owens, Lt. (jg) D. W., XIV: 185
Owens, Lt. G. N., VII: 353
Owens, Lt. Grady, VII: 326
Owens, Cdr. H. A., XII: 419, XIII: 311
Owens, Sgt. Robert A., VI: 302
Owens, Cdr. Seymour D., VIII: 362, 369, 409
Owers, Lt. Cdr. J. E., X: 212
Ow, I., VIII: 50, 116
OWL, I: 15*n*
Owsley, Cdr. J. Q., V: 98
OXFORD, XIII: 307, 312, XIV: 380
Oya, Capt. G., VIII: 357, 369
Oyama M., VI: 69
OYASHIO, III: 163, 274, IV: 89, V: 84, 206, 234, 280, 297–319 *passim*; sunk, VI: 115
OYODO, VI: 412, VII: 44, VIII: 31, XII: 162, 191, 319, 325, 332–4, 430, XIII: 37
OYSTER BAY, VI: 446, XII: 28, 204, 422, XIII: 223, 247, 322
OZARK (1902), XIV: 86*n*
OZARK (1944), XIII: 127, 310, XIV: 141, 380

Ozawa, Vice Adm. J., pic., VIII: 217; East Indies, III: 273–6, 308–9, 334–5, 384–5; New Guinea, VI: 117, VIII: 117, 131; Bat. Philippine Sea, 185, 214–320 *passim*, 416; assistance in History, VIII: viii; Leyte Gulf plan, XII: 160–61, 167–8, 180; sortie, 191–4, 299; Bat. C. Engaño, 317–35; T.O., 430; *Yamato* sortie, XIV: 202

P

P-*48* (British submarine), II: 198; –*54*, 235
Pablo, I: 141
Pace, Lt. Cdr. J. E., XII: 262*n*, 421, XIII: 305, XIV: 374
Pace, Lt. Cdr. J. R., XIII: 309, XIV: 380
Pachino Peninsula, IX: 13, 20, 58, 145, 150, 155–6
Pacific Military Conf., VI: 7
Pacific Ocean, folding charts of, at end Vols. IV, V, VI, VII, VIII, XII, XIII, XIV; chart of Jap. bascs in, V: 13
Pacific Ocean Area, IV: 250, V: 12
Pacifist propaganda, I: xil–xlv
Packer, Capt. H. A., IX: 297
PADDLE, VII: 187, 342, VIII: 416; sinks *Shiniyo M.*, XII: 401
Paddock, Lt. Cdr. Merlin, XIV: 385
Padgett, Cdr. L. P., II: 38
Paer, R., X: 382
Paestum, IX: 255–8, 284–90, 314; landings, 259–70, 275; pic., 266–7
Pagan I., VIII: 152, 167, 175, 240
Page, Lt. Cdr. J. E., VIII: 224
Page, Radarman J. L., XI: 300
Pago Pago, III: 259, IV: 263*n*, VII: 102
Pahl, Capt. J. R., VI: 229, 415, 428–9, XIV: 387
Painter, Cdr. William, VI: 347
PAKANA, VIII: 420, XIV: 190, 236, 305, 387
PALADIN, X: 277
Palau Is., history and descr., III: 7, VIII: 27*n*, 32, XII, 30–32; chart, 31; Jap. base, III: 162–3, 166–7, VIII: 13, 20–74 *passim*, 167–8, 215–345 *passim*, 345, XII: 32; carrier strikes on, VIII: 28–32, 49, 174, 367, XII: 13; submarine patrols, IV: 233; invasion operation, planning, VII: 84, 201, VIII: 3, 9, 141, 157, 400, XII: 4, 32–4; minesweeping, 35; discussion, 46–7; logistics, 78; landings, *see* Angaur and Peleliu
Palawan, III: 159, XII: 107, XIII: 217, 222; landing, 217–21; chart, 219; T.O., 321–2
Palawan Passage, XII: 169–74, XIII: 282
Palermo, IX: 17–20, 37, 50, 58–60, 171–

203 *passim*, 244, 250–51, 281–308 *passim*, 346, XI: 246; pic., IX: 187
PALLAS, II: 252
Palliser, Rear Adm. A. F. E., III: 271, 363–4, 375–8
Palmer, Cdr. George G., I: 420, II: 40, 135*n*, 143–4, XI: 146, 336
Palmer, Lt. S. A., V: 375
PALMER, I: 421, II: 39, 78, VII: 345, VIII: 410, 420, XII: 422, XIII: 113, 306, 325*n*, 326
Palmi, IX: 217
Palmyra I., III: 33*n*, 84, 219–20, 257, IV: 252, 263*n*
Palo, XII: 153; landing, *see* Tacloban
PALOMARES, II: 190, IX: 251, 340, 391, 396, X: 157
Palompon, XII: 390, 393
PAMANSET, XII: 428, XIII: 319; pic., XII: 78
Pampanga R., XIII: 193
PAMPANITO, XII: 400, XIII: 284
Pampelonne, XI: 258–9, 264, 275; pic., 268–9
Pan-American Airways, I: 289, 379, III: 224–5, 229, IV: 72
Pan-American Conf., I: 61
Pan ships, *Massachusetts*, I: 135; *Atlantic, Kraft*, 191*n*; *Pennsylvania*, X: 318
Panam, X: 181
Panama, Act of, I: 14–15
Panama Canal Zone and Sea Front, I: 148–54, 263, 413, III: 219, X: 198–204; mine field, 374
Panama City, Fla., I: 279
Panama V., XIII: 313
PANAMINT, XIV: 241, 378
Panaon I., XII: 130, 140, 210, 236*n*
Panaon Strait, XII: 140
Panay, XII: 108, 126, 133, 149, XIII: 18, 25; landing, 217, 228–31; chart, 229; T.O., 323
PANAY, III: 16–18, 28, 35, 94*n*, XII: 21*n*; sunk, III: 17; pic., 36
Pancake Hill, VIII: 80
Pancoast, Cdr. L. W., VIII: 413, XII: 426, XIII: 317

PANDA, XII: 423, XIII: 308
Pandanan I., XIII: 221
Pandon I., XIII: 50
PANDORA, I: 138
PANGBOURNE, XI: 335
Pantelleria, II: 271, 275–80, IX: 20, 22*n*, 55, 101, 110, 185; chart, 276
PANTHER, II: 254
PAPAW, VIII: 420
PAPAYA, VIII: 420
Papua, IV: 260, 275*n*, V: 7, VI: 26–30; air raids, III: 388–9, VI: 118, 125–7; campaign, 27–65, 136–7; maps, 29, 135. *See also* Port Moresby
Paquet, Gunner Freeman, VIII: 33
Paracel Is., XII: 335
Param I., VII: 318–21, VIII: 38
Paramaribo, I: 263
Paramor, Cdr. H. R., X: 149
Paramushiro, IV: 162, 175, 183, VII: 4, 15*n*, 21, 34, 39, 43, 48–9, 58–9, 64–6
Paran M., VII: 220*n*
Paranaque R., XIII: 197
Parang landing. *See* Malabang
PARCHE, VIII: 23, 25, XIV: 291
Paré, Capt. E. E., VII: 108, 340*n*, VIII: 37, 345, 411, XII: 75
Parece Vela, VIII: 154, 285*n*, XIII: 83
Paret, Lt. R. S., VII: 341, VIII: 411
PARGO, VIII: 23, XIII: 284–5, XIV: 293*n*
Parham, Cdr. J. C., X: 213*n*
Parham, Cdr. W. B., XIII: 282, 320
Paria, Gulf of, I: 145, X: 190, 199; pic., I: 258
Paris, XI: 47–8, 303
Parish, Capt. E. W., I: 237*n*
Parish, Capt. Herman O., IV: 173, VII: 337, VIII: 405, 418, XII: 417, XIV: 383
Parish, Lt. W. W., X: 103
Parker, Cdr. Alton E., V: 309*n*, XIV: 179*n*, 223, 373
Parker, Cdr. C. W., VII: 338, 349, VIII: 413, XII: 425, XIII: 317
Parker, Cdr. Edward N., III: 160, 272*n*, 322*n*, 324–5, 333, V: 232, 241
Parker, Lt. Edwin B., V: 205, XIV: 383
Parker, Capt. Elton C., XIV: 26, 132
Parker, Maj. Gen. George M., III: 199
Parker, Cdr. H. R., I: 15*n*, XII: 423
Parker, Lt. Cdr. J. D., VIII: 415
Parker, Capt. R. E., XI: 340
Parker, Capt. Ralph C., III: xii, IV: xi, 160*n*, 165–6, 173, 179, VI: 279*n*, 305*n*,

VII: ix, 4*n*; Cincpac Monthly Intelligence Summary, XII: 336*n*, XIV: xii
PARKER (1913), VI: 211*n*
PARKER (1942), I: 355, II: 37, IX: 378, 389, XI: 341
Parkinson, Lt. Cdr. F. P., VIII: 411, XII: 428, XIII: 319
Parkinson, Capt. G. A., VII: 341, X: 343–4, 377
Parks, Maj. F. B., IV: 92, 104–5
Parks, Cdr. L. S., "Pirates," VIII: 25
PARKS, XII: 429
Parme, II: 233*n*
Parmenter, Lt. Cdr. Richard, I: 218*n*, 285
Parrish, Lt. J. A., VII: 334
PARROTT, III: 160, 272, 284, 288, 322*n*, 325, 328, 375, VIII: 237*n*, X: 125, 157, 200*n*, 377, XIII: 268, XIV: 158*n*
PARRSBORO, XI: 333
Parry, Capt. C. R. L., IX: 393
Parry, Rear Adm. William E., XI: 181
Parry I., VII: 283, 289, 294, 300–303, 307; landing, 300–304; chart, 295
Parsons, Cdr. Charles, VI: 85, XII: 64–5, 123
Parsons, Cdr. E. C., XIII: 307
Parsons, Lt. Cdr. F. W., VIII: 403
Parsons, Lt. Cdr. G. E. T., X: 379
Parsons, Wing Cdr. K. R. J., VI: 65
Parsons, Cdr W. S., XII: 377, XIII: 188–9, 307, 321–4, XIV: 344
Partridge, Lt. Col. R. C., II: 216
PARTRIDGE, XI: 175
Parylak, Lt. Cdr. B. J., XIV: 381
PASADENA, XIII: 54, 317, XIV: 21, 58, 313, 384, 386
Pasananca, XIII: 225
Paschal, Capt. J. B., XIV: 374
Pas-de-Calais, XI: 19, 40, 43–4, 49, 74–5, 89, 114, 159, 186, 190, 295
Pasig R., XIII: 191, 195
PASIG, XIV: 161
Pass Christian, I: 295
Pasteur, I: 329, X: 133
PASTORES, I: 422
Patch, Maj. Gen. Alexander M., IV: 253, V: 12, 334–51 *passim*, 364, 371–2, XI: 236–95 *passim*, 323; on PT sailors, V: 369
Patch, Capt. R. S., VI: 297
Paternoster Is., XIII: 275
PATHFINDER, I: 348, VI: 123, 363, X: 78, XIV: 268

Pati Pt., Guam, VIII: 398–400
PATOKA, I: 382, 390n, 422
Patriarca, Lt. Cdr. F. A., XIV: 383
Patrick, Cpl., V: 49
Patrick, Maj. Gen. Edwin D., VIII: 135, 139, XIII: 309
Patrick, Cdr. G. S., VIII: 419, XII: 427, XIII: 318, XIV: 373
Patrick, Lt. Cdr. W. W., X: 378
Patrick, Lt. Cdr. Willard T., XI: 318n, 322–3
Patrick Henry, I: 294–5, 364–5
Patrick J. Hurley, I: 350
Patrol Boats or Craft, Jap., pic., III: 225; *Nos. 1* and *2*, IV: 89; *No. 31*, VIII: 32n; *Nos. 32* and *33*, III: 231; *Nos. 34* and *35*, IV: 89; *No. 37*, III: 289; *No. 39*, VI: 69; *No. 105*, XII: 370
Patrol Bomber Squadron No. 18, XIV: 381; No. 20, XIII: 311; Nos. 21, 27, XIV: 381; No. 101, XIII: 312; No. 103, X: 340, 373; No. 106, VIII: 49–50; No. 112, X: 339, 373; No. 130, XIII: 311; No. 208, XIV: 381
Patrol Wing One, IV: 274; Two, III: 120, IV: 274; Three, I: 151–2, 419, XIII: 180n; Four, IV: 160n, 173, VI: 15; Five, I: 419; Seven, 77n, 419, VII: x; Nine, I: 419; Ten. III: 173, 194, 272, 282–3, 335, 338, VIII: 49n, 50; Eleven, I: 419; Seventeen, VIII: 49n
Patrol Squadron No. 12, I: 145n, V: 330–31, 375; No. 16, VIII: 242n, 415; No. 22, III: 257; No. 23, VI: 146; No. 25, XIII: 312; No. 31, I: 84, 110, 146, 419; No. 32, 419, X: 198n, 370–71; Nos. 33, 34, I: 15n, 419, VIII: 49, 406; No. 43, VII: 333; No. 44, VI: 146; No. 51, I: 15n, 33; No. 52, 15n, 69, 378–9, 419, VIII: 49, 406; No. 53, I: 15n, 351, 415, 420, VII: 340, 350; No. 54, I: 15n, 16, XIII: 311–12; Nos. 61, 62, VII: 333; No. 63, X: 95, 100, 372; No. 71, IV: 20; No. 72, VII: 340, 350; No. 73, I: 77, 249, 415–20, II: 131, 245; No. 74, I: 77, 227, 248, 386, 415, 420, X: 212, 370–71; Iceland camp, pic., I: 92; No. 81, 420; No. 82, 154, 248, 415, 420; No. 83, 379–81, 386, 390, 415, 420, X: 209, 212n; No. 84, I: 249, 325, 415, 420, X: 370; No. 92, I: 249, 415, 420, II: 245, X: 370; No. 93, I: 420; No. 94, I: 386, 390, 420, X: 212,
215, 370; No. 101, VIII: 49n; No. 130, X: 198n; No. 202, VII: 350; No. 203, X: 227n; No. 204, 198n, 371; No. 205, 195–6, 198n, 371; No. 211, 212
Pattee, Ens. Richard S., VI: xii, 66n, VII: viii, VIII: viii, 321n, XIV: x
Patten, Capt. S. F., VII: 343, VIII: 407, XII: 419
Patten, Lt. Cdr. W. F., VIII: 411, XII: 428, XIV: 387
Patterson, Lt. (jg) Harry B., X: 224
Patterson, Lt. Cdr. J. F., XIII: 305, XIV: 386
Patterson, 1st Lt. R. M., V: 374
PATTERSON (1911), XI: 242n
PATTERSON (1937), III: 104, 213n, 243n, IV: 272, V: 29–30, 34–63 *passim*, 106, VI: 242, VIII: 408, 415, XII: 319, 331, 428, XIII: 305, XIV: 373
Pattie, Lt. D. A., XIV: 385
Pattie, Cdr. S. H., IX: 80, 386, XIII: 206
Pattishall, Lt. Cdr. B. W., VI: 415, XIII: 319
Patton, Gen. George S., pics., II: 93, 164, IX: 26; N. Africa, II: 16–17, 23–83 *passim*, 108, 115, 155–77 *passim*, 216, 259; Sicily, IX: 16, 19–22, 27, 61–4, 108–47 *passim*, 171, 174–80, 184, 191–220 *passim*, 385; on Gen. Lucas, 328; Normandy, XI: 69, 74–5, 216; France and Germany, 228, 231–2, 295–8, 319–21, 324
Patton, Richard, VI: 273–4
PATUXENT, XII: 428, XIII: 71, 319, XIV: 387
Paul, Lt. Cdr. C. R., XIV: 386
Paul, Lt. D. N., XII: 423
Paul, Lt. Cdr. P. M., XIV: 374
PAUL G. BAKER, XIV: 379
PAUL HAMILTON, VIII: 411, X: 189n, XII: 385, 429, XIII: 305, XIV: 148, 372
Paul Hamilton, X: 268
PAUL JONES, III: 160, 272, 284, 288, 299, 331–3, 375, X: 21n, 125, 157, 212n, 377, XIII: 268
Paul Luckenbach, I: 171n
Paulus Potter, I: 187, 191n
Pavesi, Adm. Gino, II: 279
PAVLIC, XIV: 262
Pawka, Cdr. E. J., XIV: 383
PAWNEE, VI: 151, XII: 98–102, 429, XIV: 388
Payne, Lt. D. P., VIII: 418, XII: 306

Payne, Lt. (jg) F. W., III: 159, 272
Payne, Cdr. J. M., VIII: 418, XIII: 307
Payne, Lt. Cdr. J. N., XIV: 386
Payne, Lt. P. D., XIV: 376
Payne, Lt. R. M., X: 377, 380
Paynter, Lt. (jg) W. K., XII: 28
Payson, Cdr. Harold, VII: 353, VIII: 415, XII: 417
PCs, I: 230–31; Sowespac, VIII: 55; N. G., VIII: 135–7, 143; Sicily, IX: 66, 81, 87; Marianas, 192, 196, 209, 383; in A/S W, X: 35, 190; Caribbean, 203–5; Normandy, XI: 64n, 93, 98, 120, 131–2, 155–6; Southern France, 265; Channel Is. patrol, 304–8; Morotai, XII: 22; Cebu, XIII: 237; Okinawa, XIV: 143

  PC-451, -452, I: 230; -458, -460, 154, 415; -462–64, XIII: 307, XIV: 143–4; -469, X: 297, XIV: 143–4; -471, I: 230; -476, V: 320, XIII: 307n; -479, VI: 382; -484, XI: 102; -487, VII: 57; -490, X: 288n; -494, 216; -543, IX: 74n; -545, 366; -546, 73–4, 386; -550, 86; -552, XI: 134, 306; -553, 122; -556, 163; -558, 371–2; -564, 307–8, and pic., 133; -565, X: 181–2, 370, and pic., 184; -567, -568, XI: 121–2, 132; -574, pic., I: 231; -575, 387; -584, XIV: 116, 376; -591, IX: 136, 371; -592, I: 387, X: 211; -610, and pic., XIII: 261; -617, -618, I: 284; -619, X: 372; -621, IX: 388; -623, XII: 133, 314–16; -624, IX: 41, 259, X: 252, 371; -625, 388; -626, 372; -627, 366, 376, 388; -803, -804, XIV: 318

  PC-1119, VI: 382, XII: 314–15; -1120, VI: 382, VIII: 406; -1121, XIII: 307n; -1122, VI: 382; -1128, XIII: 307, XIV: 116, 376; -1129, sunk, XIII: 191; -1132, -1133, -1134, VIII: 406, XIII: 236; -1135, VII: 308; -1169, XI: 339; -1176, 98; -1179, XIV: 376; -1196, X: 196; -1261, XI: 108; sunk, 98; -1598, XIV: 376
PCEs, availability, X: 32; no. authorized and built, 35

  PCE-847, pic., I: 231; -851, XIII: 31; -872, XIV: 379; -873, 375; -877, 143, 380
PCE(R)-853, XIV: 376
PCS-1396, -1402, -1404, -1421, -1452, -1455, -1457, -1460, VIII: 192, 408, XIV: 143

Peacher, Cdr. R. M., I: 421
Peak, Lt. Cdr. C. O., XII: 428, XIII: 318, XIV: 387
Pearce, Cdr. H. A., IX: 386, XI: 342
Pearce, Lt. R. E., X: 205–6
Pearkes, Maj. Gen. G. R., pic., VII: 55
PEARL, XI: 337
Pearl and Hermes Reef, IV: 93
Pearl Harbor, chart, III: 105; time, 92n; base, I: 103, III: 46–9, 56, 75, 143–5, 219, 389, 397, IV: 14–5, 30, 81, 157, 199–276 *passim*, V: 25, 80, 106, 136, 200, 312, VI: 67, 74, 79, 190n, VII: 87–90, 97–8, 102–38 *passim*, 188, 197, 202, 210, 226–8, 233, VIII: 16, 24, 158, 172, 242, 252, 379, 400, XII: 59, 104, 398, XIV: 87n, 109, 158, 163–4; Jap. recce, III: 222n, 268n, VI: 286; ammo. explosion, VIII: 171; F.D.R.'s visit, XII: 8–9, XIII: 3–5; weather c'tr'l, XIII: 60–61, 69. *See also* Pearl Harbor Attack, Pearl Harbor Conference
Pearl Harbor Attack, III: 80–126; charts, 91, 99, 105, 136–7; pics., 102–3, 110–11, 116–17; Jap. plans and preparations, 82–6; sortie and movement, 88–94; phases, 102n; midget subs, 84–5, 95–8; search for Jap. force, 214–18; Jap. T.O., 87; casualties, 126; repairs, 143–5; effect, 209–10; discussion, 125–42, 143n
Pearl Harbor Conf., 1943, VI: 95; 1944, XII: 8–9, XIII: 3–5
Pearse, Lt. Cdr. C. H., XI: 273
Pearson, Capt. M. S., XI: 335, XIV: 381
PEARY, III: 158, 172, 196–7, 272, 314, 317, 332; sunk, 319; pic., 171
Peaslee, Capt. J. C., VI: 64
Peate, Lt. Cdr. H. B., XI: 339
Peatross, Lt. O. F., IV: 238
Peck, Brig. Gen. DeWitt, IV: 251, 262n, V: 115n, VI: 13, 93–5
Peck, Capt. S. E., VII: 340, 350, VIII: 411
Peckham, Cdr. G. E., VI: 244–6, 251, XIII: 317, XIV: 384
PECOS (1921), III: 159, 193, 272, 299, 330, 363n; sunk, 378
PECOS (1942), VII: 47n, 61, 341, VIII: 411, XII: 104, 428, XIII: 308, XIV: 387
Peddicord, 1st Lt. L. E., II: 58, 115n, 120–21

Pederson, Lt. N. E., V: 332
Pederson, Lt. Cdr. Oscar, IV: 19, 26n, 90
Peek, Lt. R. E., X: 376
Pegram, Vice Adm. Frank H., I: 383, X: 226
PEIFFER, XIII: 309
Peirce, Lt. Cdr. H. R., VII: 337, 345, XII: 369, 421, XIII: 306, XIV: 376
Peirse, Air Ch. Marshal Sir Richard, III: 271, 278, 336
Peleliu, VIII: 28, 174, 329, XII: 32, 36, XIII: 83, 216; landings, XII: 11, 16, 33–43; air and naval gunfire support, 35–41, 86; chart, 37; pic., 38. *See also* Palau Is., invasion operation
Peleus, X: 300
PELICAN, X: 75
Pell, Maj. F. S., III: 318
Pellam, J. R., I: 224
Penang, III: 191, X: 275–8, 288, 296, 301–2, 320
Penang M., VI: 76–7
Pendleton, Lt. Cdr. W. B., VIII: 224–5
PENELOPE, IX: 167, 291, 345, 361n, 396; sunk, 366, X: 256
Penelope Barker, X: 305
Penfield, Hon. James K., I: 58
PENGUIN, sunk, III: 184–5
Peniakoff, Lt. Cdr. V., IX: 235
Pennebaker, Lt. Col. E. P., VIII: 164n
Penney, Maj. Gen. W. R. C., IX: 329, 395–6
PENNSYLVANIA, II: 21n, III: 42, 103, 108–9, 117–19, 146, 250n, V: 14n, VI: 282n, VII: 38–9, 42–8, 87, 114–67 *passim*, 202, 258–60, 288, 301, 334–6, 344, VIII: 180–82, 238n, 328, 377–97 *passim*, 409, IX: 14n, 92n, X: 229n, 343n, XII: 41, 44, 118n, 122, 199, 202, 224, 295, 343, 419, XIII: 138, 304, XIV: 335; pics., III: 116, VII: 31, 279, XIII: 108–9
PENSACOLA, III: 212, 266n, IV: 91, 113n, 134–5, 153n, 257, 276, V: 148n, 205–312 *passim*, VII: 339, 350, XII: 87, 425, XIV: 11, 27–8, 62–4, 220, 373; class, III: 22
Pensacola, Fla., I: 248, 264
PENZANCE, I: 24
Perabo, Lt. (jg) Phil, X: 113
Peralta, Col., XIII: 230
Percée, Pointe de la, XI: 121, 127
PERCH (1936), III: 158; sunk, 304
PERCH (1944), XIII: 282, 320

Percifield, Capt. W. M., XI: 216n
Percival, Lt. Gen. Sir Arthur, III: 271, XII: 67, XIV: 365; pic., 366–7
Perida, VII: 39, 46, 335
Periès, Capit. de Frég., II: 99
Perkins, Fulton B., IX: xv
Perkins, Capt. H. C., VIII: 408, XII: 416, XIII: 309
Perkins, Lt. Cdr. Van O., VI: 345n
Perkins, Cdr. W. B., VII: 353, XII: 33
PERKINS, IV: 15, 19, 22, 28n, 65–7, V: 294, 297–9, 310, 337, VI: 260–62, 267
Perlman, Capt. Benjamin, IV: 18
PERMIT, III: 158, VII: 98n, 222, 351
Perry, Capt. Benjamin F., V: 205, 233
Perry, Lt. Cdr. F. C., XII: 426
Perry, Capt. John, IV: 174, VIII: 412, XII: 428, XIV: 382
Perry, Commo. Matthew C., XIV: 6, 81
PERRY (1902), VII: 152n
PERRY (1922), III: 104, 126, 213n, 276n, VII: 335, 344, VIII: 69, 404, 410, 419; sunk, XII: 35
PERSEVERANCE, I: 382n
Persian Gulf, I: 159, X: 158
Persons, Maj. Gen. J. C., XII: 21, 24
PERTH, III: 272, 333–70 *passim*; sunk, 368
Pescadores Is., XII: 92, 164, XIII: 5, 88, 170, 179
Pétain, Maréchal Henri, I: 30, II: 4–11, 67–70, 185–7, 208, 217–20, VII: 181
PETARD, IX: 123, 394
Peter Kerr, I: 191n
Peter Lassen, XIII: 307n
Peter Sylvester, X: 303
Peter Zenger, X: 381
Peters, Lt. Cdr. F. M., VI: 145
Peters, Capt. F. T., II: 225
Peters, Cdr. J. M., VI: 331, VII: 339, VIII: 412
Peters, Lt. Robeson, XIII: 108n
Peters, Kapt.-zur-See Rudolph, X: 230, 233, 236–8, 305–9
Petersen, Cdr. J. H., XIII: 322–3
Petersen, Capt. Wallis F., V: 205, 233, VI: 382, 420–22, 428, VIII: 410
Peterson, Cdr. C. A., VIII: 407, XII: 416, XIII: 310, XIV: 379
Peterson, Capt. C. H., VI: 382, XIV: 380
Peterson, Cdr. E. B., VIII: 411, XIV: 386
Peterson, Capt. George E., VIII: 23

Peterson, Lt. Cdr. H. A., XI: 334
Peterson, Capt. J. V., XIV: 374
Peterson, Lt. Cdr. M. R., I: 420
Peterson, Cdr. Mell A. ("Pete"),
VII: 111, XII: 350n, 372
Peterson, Cdr. R. W., XII: 429,
XIII: 319
PETERSON, X: 318–19, 372
PETO, VI: 72, XII: 408
PETREL, II: 286
Pétrel, II: 233n
PETROF BAY, XII: 244, 301, 304–5, 420,
XIII: 145, 306, XIV: 374
Petross, Cdr. L. C., VII: 349
Peyton, Maj. M. K., VI: 139
Pfaff, Capt. Roy, II: 36
Pfeffer, Kaptlt. Gunther, X: 343
Pfeifer, Lt. C. F., VI: 246
Pfeiffer, Col. O. T., I: 45, V: 115n
PGMs, Mindanao R., XIII: 245; Davao
Gulf, 247; *PGM-5*, 245n; *-9, -10, -11,
-17, -18, -20*, XIV: 194, 377, 391;
PGM-17, sunk, 220
Phal, Cdr. J. R., VIII: 410
PHAON, VII: 341, VIII: 211, 329, 411,
420, XIV: 388
PHEASANT, I: 422, XI: 206, 333, 337–8
Phelan, Cdr. G. R., IV: 91, VI: 242
Phelps, Lt. (jg) J. P., X: 215
PHELPS, III: 104, 116, 213n, 266n, IV: 19,
60, 91, 113n, 151n, 271, V: 86, 112,
VII: 42–4, 47–9, 124, 127–9, 224, 237–8,
244–7, 335–7, 346, VIII: 201, 210–12,
408
Phifer, Cdr. T. C., XIII: 311, XIV: 375
Philadelphia, I: 159–60, 254, V: 170
PHILADELPHIA, I: 57, 83n, 326, 355, 419,
II: 39, 138–9, 145, 148–9, 154, 285;
Sicily and Italy, IX: 28, 64, 125n, 131–
8, 141, 174–5, 191–9, 203–96 *passim*,
302–3, 362, 370–91 *passim*, X: 345n,
XI: 238, 257, 265, 278–80, 286–9, 340;
pic., IX: 42
Philip, Cdr. George, XII: 419, XIII: 305,
XIV: 44, 275, 372
PHILIP (1918), IX: 92n
PHILIP (1942), VI: 228–30, 237, 295, 337,
415, VIII: 408, XIII: 47, 139, 261, 310–
12, 322
Philippbar, Cdr. J. W., XI: 132n, 303n
Philippeville, II: 17, 252, X: 264
Philippine Islands, prewar, III: 64, 74,
130, 150–57; defense of, 33, 193–206;
T.O., 161–3; Jap. invasion of, 164–

83; chart, 175; in Allied strategy,
XII: 4–18; in Jap. strategy and defenses, 66–70, 165–6; Jap. naval forces
in, XIII: 14; opns. in, 1944–5, chart,
20; Jap. airfields, chart, 56; liberation
of, XIII *passim*
Philippine Sea, Battle of, preliminaries,
VIII: 212–56; air searches, 245–9, 285–
6; strength of opposing fleets, 233;
"Turkey Shoot," 257–78; submarines,
278–82; 20 June action, 282–304; pur-
suit, 305–9; discussion, 313–19; T.O.,
412–17; charts, 242–3, 248–9, 262–4,
270–71, 275, 288–9, 293, 306; pic., 233
Phillips, Lt. B., XIV: 374
Phillips, Lt. Cdr. G. L., IX: 85–6, 386
Phillips, Lt. Cdr. John L., VII: 143, 339
Phillips, Capt. John S., IV: 19, 35–6
Phillips, Torpedoman P. J., IX: 313
Phillips, Cdr. Richard H., VI: 375, 386,
VIII: 408, XII: 199, 212–18, 222, 418,
XIV: 385; pic., XII: 215
Phillips, Vice Adm. Sir Tom, III: 49,
156–7, 188–90
Phillips, Capt. W. K. ("Sol"), I: 123,
421, VII: 339, 348, 352, VIII: 413
Phillips, Capt. Wallace B., II: 40, 135n,
139, 143, 151n, 153, IX: 129, 140, 389
Phipps, Lt. Cdr. Peter, V: 350
PHOEBE, II: 189, IX: 358, 360–61n
Phoebus, Lt. Cdr. D. R., XII: 423
PHOENIX, III: 31n, 126, 212, 359, VI: 39,
130, 382, 435–7, 444, VIII: 47, 97, 108,
123, 126, 406, XII: 21, 135, 199, 223,
227, 343, 421, XIII: 39, 115–16, 200–274
passim, 304, 322; pic., VI: 435
"Phoenix," XI: 26, 165; pic., 172
Photographic Squadron One, VIII:
164n; Three, VII: 97, 340, 350, VIII:
164n; Four, 164
Piazze Marittime, IX: 49–50, 159–60
Pickens, Rear Adm. A. C., I: 14–16
PICKEREL, III: 158, 283, 304
Pickering, Lt. R. A., XIII: 245n
Picket destroyers, Philippine Sea,
VIII: 262, 268–70; Okinawa, XIV:
178–9, 180–91, 221–5, 233–5, 251–62;
chart, 189. See also Okinawa Opn.,
kamikazes
PICKING, XII: 295n, 304, 419, XIII: 188,
204, 311, XIV: 247, 375
PICUDA, XII: 399, 409, XIII: 297–8, 319,
XIV: 287
PIEDMONT, XIV: 387

Piegari, Lt. J. G., XIII: 317
Piening, Kaptlt. Adolf, X: 98
Pierce, Lt. Cdr. E. H., I: 76, 418; quoted, 123
Pierce, Cdr. G. E., XIV: 292n
Pierce, Lt. Cdr. John R., IV: 229, 235n
Pierce, Lt. (jg) T. P., XIII: 306
PIERCE, VII: 336, 344, VIII: 408, XII: 416, XIII: 309, XIV: 380
Pierre V., XIV: 386
PIET HEIN, II: 273, 322-4
Pietro Orseolo, X: 87, 104
Pietz, Lt. W. C., XI: 335
Pifer, Cdr. T. C., XII: 421
PIGEON, III: 159, 172, 193, 252; sunk, 206
Pigeons, carrier, IX: 144n
Pigman, Capt. N. M., VIII: 408, XII: 416, XIII: 308, XIV: 378
PIKE, I: 421, III: 158, 315, IV: 92, 213
Pikit, Fort, XIII: 244-5
Pilelo I., VI: 374
Pillenwerfer, I: 213, 322
PILLSBURY (1920), III: 158, 196, 272, 299, 322n, 325, 328-9, 332; sunk, 379
PILLSBURY (1943), X: 282, 290-92, 351-5, 378-9
PILOT, I: 421, IX: 340, 348, 392, 396
PILOTFISH, VIII: 22-3, 167, 415
Pilottown, I: 262
PINDOS, IX: 393, XI: 343
Pineau, Lt. Cdr. Roger, III: xi, IV: x, 87n, 292n, V: 17n, 20n, 84n, 182n, 229n, 333n, VI: 21n, 54n, 287n, VII: 74n, VIII: 213n, 230n, IX: 117n, X: x, XI: 287n, XII: vii, XIII: 92n, XIV: x
Pingley, Lt. Cdr. J. F., XII: 98, 429, XIV: 305
PINK, X: 70-71, 74; sunk, 324
PINKNEY, XIII: 310, XIV: 381, 391
PINNACLE, XI: 343
Pinnell, Lt. (jg) C. I., X: 293
PINON, XIV: 377
PINTADO, VIII: 22-3, 168, 415, XII: 333-4, 408, 429
Pinter, Ens. F. E., I: 249
PINTO, XI: 337, 341
PIONEER, I: 421, IX: 396, XI: 340
PIORUN, IX: 394
PIPEFISH, VIII: 415
PIPER, XIV: 293n, 296
"Pips, Battle of the," VII: 59-61
PIRANHA, VIII: 24, XIII: 319
Pirro, Ens. C. F., IX: 329n
Pisa, IX: 57, 307

PITT, XIV: 375
Pittman, Lt. S. L., XIII: 300-301
Pitts, Lt. Cdr. O. H., VII: 348, VIII: 410
Pitts, Cdr. R. M., VII: 338, 345, XIV: 259
PITTSBURGH (1905), IX: 325n
PITTSBURGH (1944), XIV: 97, 301, 304-5, 382, 386; pic., 311
Piva Forks, Battle of, VI: 352
Piva "Uncle" and "Yoke," VI: 365, 394-5, 398-9, 428-30
Plage, Lt. Cdr. H. L., XIII: 81, 319, XIV: 374
PLAICE, VIII: 415
Plain, Lt. Col. I. C., II: 231
Plander, Cdr. Henry, XI: 79, 206-8, 333, 337
Plane Recognition School, IX: 121n
Planning, strategic, VI: 3-26
Platt, J. W., XIII: 48
Platt, Capt. W. M., III: 247-8
PLATTE, IV: 91, 97, 155n, 272, VII: 334, 340, VIII: 411, XII: 428, XIV: 387
Platter, Fireman, IV: 227-8
Pleasants, Lt. Cdr. A. L., I: 76, 418
PLEIADES, XI: 246
Plumley, Lt. M. C., IV: 237
PLUNGER, III: 213, 258, IV: 92, 157n, VII: 79, 137, 187, 342, VIII: 415
PLUNKETT, I: 76, 92, 418, 420, IX: 193, 194n, 199n, 206-10, 313, 345-6, 385, 391, 396, XI: 206-10, 335-8
"Pluto," XI: 26-7, 218
PLYMOUTH, I: 13n, 234; sunk, X: 184-5
Plymouth, Eng., XI: 58, 62-3, 68, 78, 86, 160n, 161, 167, 197, 309
POCOMOKE, I: 420, VIII: 242n, 255n, XII: 46; pic., I: 258
Poehlmann, Capt. K. F., I: 420, II: 37, VII: 339, 350, VIII: 415, XII: 373-4, 428
Pogue, Forrest C., *Supreme Command*, XI: xiii
Pogue, Lt. Cdr. William G., IV: 19, 271, V: 86, VII: 18
POGY, VIII: 19, XIV: 293n
Poindexter, Lt. Cdr. W. L., XIV: 386
Point Breeze, X: 203, 298
Point Cruz, Battle of, V: 289-90
Poitou, II: 159, 246
Pola, IX: 244
POLARIS, I: 422
POLARIS, HMAS, VI: 46
Polenz, Hermann, XI: 282n

Poling, Rev. Clark V., I: 333
Polk, Ens. G. W., V: 67
Polk, Lt. W., XII: 423
POLLACK, III: 213, 258, VII: 78, VIII: 20, 23
Pollock, Lt. Albert D., V: 211
Pollock, Lt. Col. E. A., V: 71, VI: 381; pic., V: 130
Pollone, Rear Adm., IX: 244
POLLUX (1941), I: 422
POLLUX (1942), XII: 423
POLYANTHUS, X: 140, 143–5
Polynesia, VII: 69
Pomeroy, Capt. J. G., VII: 337, VIII: 405, IX: 389, XIII: 310
POMFRET, XIV: 296
POMPANO, III: 213, 258, IV: 203–4, VII: 79
Pompoon, X: 202
PONAGANSET, XII: 41, 84, XIV: 161, 387
Ponape, VII: 74, 84, 137, 201, 287, 315*n*, VIII: 8, 38–40, 156, 222, XIV: 10
PONCHATOULA, XIV: 387
Pond, Lt. Cdr. Hartwell, XII: 423, XIII: 306
Pond, Lt. Cdr. R. W., XIV: 378
Ponson I., XII: 395
Pont Blondin, Batterie, II: 56, 62, 72–6; pic., 75
Ponte Olivo, IX: 19, 58, 95, 117, 122, 205
Ponte Vedra, Fla., I: 200
PONTIAC, I: 422
Ponto, Cdr. A. R., VII: 336
Pontoon barges and causeways, VI: 417, IX: 31; Sicily, 90, 106–8, 111, 119, 152; Salerno, 265; Anzio, 342, 348–50; Leyte, XII: 134–5, 144; S. France, XI: 263; Lingayen, XIII: 134, 142; Cebu, 235; Normandy, *see* Mulberrys
Ponza, XI: 241, 300
POOLE, IX: 42, XI: 333
Poor, Lt. Cdr. R. L., VII: 348, XII: 313*n*
Poor, Lt. (jg) R. W., VII: 261*n*, 275*n*
Pootung, XIII: 301
Pope, Lt. A. J., XII: 94
Pope, Lt. Cdr. E. H., XIII: 313
POPE (1920), III: 158, 272, 284, 285*n*, 289, 322–5, 332–3, 342*n*, 364–5, 371–3, X: 204*n*, XII: 80*n*; sunk, III: 373
POPE (1943), X: 282, 378–9, XIII: 268
Popham, Capt. W. S., XIII: 307
"Popski's Private Army," IX: 235
PORCUPINE, XII: 423, XIII: 44–7
Poro I., XII: 395

PORPOISE, I: 421, III: 158, IV: 220, VII: 98*n*
Porquerolles, Île de, XI: 285
Port Arthur, I: 253, 264
Port Binanga, III: 199
Port Directors, I: 50*n*, 253
Port Etienne, X: 209
Port Lloyd, XIV: 5
Port Lyautey, I: 352, II: 17, 33–4, 88, 115–20, 129–33, 161–2, 245–6, X: 88, 102–3, 110, 129–31; pic., II: 131
Port Mahon, IX: 243
Port Melbourne, X: 382
Port Moresby, III: 265, 388, IV: 5, 10–14, 60–61, 74, 267–9, V: 109, 115–17, VI: 22, 30–35, 38, 42, 46, 56, 60, 124–6, 136, 266; pic., VI: 40
Port of Spain, I: 145–7, 388, X: 189–90, 196–7
Port Purvis, VI: 102–3
Port Royal, Jamaica, I: 153
Port Said, IX: 157, X: 158
Port Stephens, VI: 131, XIII: 189*n*
Port Sual, XIII: 138
Portal, Air Chief Marshal Sir Charles, pic., VI: 18; mentioned, II: 15*n*, IX: 6, 323, X: 90, XI: 36
Port-en-Bessin, XI: 115*n*, 146–8, 158, 289
PORTENT, I: 421, IX: 396; sunk, 342
Porter, Cdr. George E., VI: 80, XIV: 289
Porter, Lt. Cdr. J. A., XIII: 312
Porter, Lt. Cdr. P. W., XIII: 309
Porter, Capt. R. L., XIII: 317, XIV: 384
Porter, Cdr. R. N. D., IX: xvi
Porter, Cdr. W. B., VIII: 419, XIII: 307, XIV: 385
PORTER, III: 210*n*, 216, V: 205, XII: 140*n*; sunk, V: 215; class, III: 22*n*
PORTERFIELD, VII: 238–9, 242, 346, VIII: 410, XII: 319, 427, XIII: 318, XIV: 57, 133, 226, 373
Porthos, II: 163*n*, 248; pic., 174
PORTLAND, III: 56*n*, 210, 216, 237, IV: 18, 90, 133–5, 153–4, 257, 271, V: 86, 106, 205–56 *passim*, 309, VII: 55, 60, 190, 226–7, 288, 296, 338, 347, X: 343*n*, XII: 39, 119*n*, 199, 227–9, 236, 366*n*, 385, 419, XIII: 138, 177, 201, 304, XIV: 132, 373; pic., XIII: 108–9
Portland, Eng., XI: 48, 58, 62–3, 77, 81, 84–7, 102, 197–8, 211
Portland, Me., I: 68, 279–80

Portmar, III: 319
Porto Empédocle, IX: 39, 45n-6n, 69–70, 78–9, 125n, 174–7; pic., 186
Porto Maurizio, XI: 312
Portrero del Llano, I: 319
Portsmouth, Eng., XI: 67–8, 77, 182, 197
Portsmouth, N.H., IV: 233, X: 360
PORTUNUS, XIII: 324
Post, Lt. V. W., VI: 171n
Post, Cdr. W. S., VI: 77–8, XIII: 319, XIV: 287, 290
POTAWATOMI, XII: 420, XIII: 306, 309, XIV: 388
POTENTILLA, I: 325
POTOMAC, I: 69
Potsdam Conf. and Declaration, XIV: 340–43, 346–7
Potter, Maj. G. H., III: 248
Pound, Adm. of the Fleet Sir Dudley, pics., I: 70, IV: 18; mentioned, I: 44, II: 15n, IX: 6, 9, X: 17
Pound, Lt. Cdr. H. C., III: 158
Powell, Lt. Cdr. E. C., XI: 340, 343
Powell, Lt. Cdr. Edgar S., XI: 147, 336
Powell, Lt. G. G., XIV: 376
Powell, Lt. Cdr. H. G., XIV: 377
Powell, Lt. Cdr. M. A., XIV: 380
Powell, Rear Adm. P. P., XII: 16, 36n, 418
Powell, Lt. Cdr. W. T., VII: 344, VIII: 410
Power, Vice Adm. Sir A. J., II: 260n, IX: 236
Power, Capt. Harry D., IV: 273, V: 232, XIV: 267, 372
Powers, Lt. R. A., X: 224n
Pownall, Rear Adm. Charles A., VII: 92–3, 116, 120, 190–97, 203, 208, 338
Pownall, Gen. Sir Harry R., III: 271, 277
POYANG, XII: 83, 423
POZARICA, II: 190
Pozzuoli, IX: 41n, 312, 329, 332–3, XI: 236, 241, 246
Praia Bay, X: 46
PRAIRIE (1898), V: 325n
PRAIRIE (1940), I: 51, 225, 418, 420, VIII: 420, XII: 75, XIV: 387
Prange, Dr. G. W., VI: xi
Pratas I., XIII: 171, 287
Pratt, Maj. Gen. H. C., I: 147n
Pratt, Capt. J. L., III: 159, XIV: 55

Pratt, Lt. J. T., X: 379
Pratt, Lt. Cdr. M. S., XIV: 375
Pratt, Cdr. R. R., VIII: 409, XIV: 381
Pratt, Adm. William V., X: 37
Pratt, Cdr. William V., 2nd, VIII: 403, XII: 425
Prause, Lt. Cdr. J. H., VII: 341
PREBLE, III: 104, 213n, V: 367, VI: 112–14, VII: 350, X: 204n, XII: 421, XIII: 306
Pregari, Lt. J. G., XIV: 382
PRESERVER, VIII: 211–12, 411, XII: 420
PRESIDENT ADAMS, IV: 273, 291, V: 231, VI: 98n, 144, 297, VIII: 418, XIII: 307
President Coolidge, III: 213, V: 181n
President Fillmore, IV: 176n, VII: 334
President Grant, V: 335n
President Harrison, III: 155
PRESIDENT HAYES, IV: 273, 291, VI: 98, 144, 297, VIII: 418, XII: 418
PRESIDENT JACKSON, IV: 273, V: 231, VI: 98n, 144, 297, 300, VIII: 418, XIII: 307; pic., V: 243
PRESIDENT MONROE, VII: 181, 341, 347, VIII: 418, XIII: 307, 312
PRESIDENT POLK, VII: 255, 256n, 268, 341, 344, VIII: 419, XIII: 307
President Taylor, III: 265
PRESIDENT TYLER, IV: 264
PRESIDENT WARFIELD, I: 323n, XI: 60
Presley, Seaman S. D., V: 216
Pressey, Cdr. G. W., VIII: 403, XII: 429, XIII: 316, 319; XIV: 383
Preston, Lt. A. M., XII: 26, 237, 422
PRESTON (1936), IV: 276n, V: 205, 232–3, 259, 271, 283–4; sunk, 275–7
PRESTON (1944), VIII: 419, XII: 319, 427, XIII: 318, XIV: 373
Prestwich, Cdr. G. F., XII: 418, XIII: 308
PREVAIL, I: 421, IX: 346, 392, 396, XI: 340; XIV: 377
Price, Lt. Col. E. H., V: 128
Price, Cdr. G. C., X: 212
Price, Rear Adm. J. D., XIV: 295
Price, Lt. Cdr. R. H., VII: 338, 349, VIII: 415
Price, Cdr. Walter H., IV: 274, V: 29, 49, XII: 427, XIV: 372
PRICHETT, VIII: 408, XII: 427, XIII: 318, XIV: 179, 280, 372, 390
Prickett, Lt. Cdr. S. L., XII: 427, XIII: 316

Pride, Capt. A. M., VII: 339, 348, 352
PRIDE, IX: 313*n*, 256, X: 256, 342, 372–3, 379
Pridmore, Lt. Cdr. J. A., VII: 335, VIII: 409, 419, XIII: 304
PRIMAUGUET, II: 89, 99–101, 105–6, 109–10, 174, 248
Prime, Cdr. N. S., V: 353, VI: 229
Primrose IV, I: 274
PRINCE ALBERT, IX: 162, 272, 393
PRINCE BAUDOUIN, XI: 335, 339
PRINCE CHARLES, IX: 388, 393, XI: 136, 335
PRINCE DAVID, XI: 339
PRINCE GEORGES, VIII: 410
PRINCE HENRY, XI: 251, 339
PRINCE LEOPOLD, IX: 388, 393, XI: 335
PRINCE OF WALES, I: 69, 70*n*, 132, 157, III: 312; sunk, 188–90; pic., I: 70
PRINCE RUPERT, X: 372
PRINCESS ASTRID, IX: 276, 387, 393
PRINCESS BEATRIX, II: 221, IX: 347, 393, XI: 339
PRINCESS JOSEPHINE CHARLOTTE, IX: 387, 393
PRINCESS MAUD, XI: 335
PRINCETON, VI: 292, 324–32, VII: xxvii, xxix, 85, 92–5, 117, 137, 208, 340, 350, VIII: 37, 174, 248–50, 268, 271, 282, 303*n*, 310, 414, XII: 90, 187, 194, 321, 360, 426; sunk, 178–83; pic., 182
PRINGLE, VI: 228, 237, 320, 415, 428–9, VIII: 410, XII: 369, XIII: 46, XIV: 379, 391; sunk, 237–8
PRINS ALBERT, XI: 339
Printup, Cdr. C. A., VIII: 410
PRINZ EUGEN, I: 82, 161*n*, XI: 328*n*
Priok, III: 311
Prisoners of war and internees, Allied, VI: 397, VIII: 84, XII: 405–6, XIII: 184, 189, 193–6, 220, 258, 267, 292, XIV: 358, 361; Japanese, VII: 149, 178, 272, VIII: 83, 140, 339, 401, XII: 234*n*, XIV: 69, 276; German and Italian, IX: 90, 123, 142–4, 159, 176, 185, X: 110, 144–5, 150, 213–15, 249, 270, 274; pic., Italian, IX: 107
Privette, Lt. Cdr. W. G., VII: 349, XIV: 384
Prize crew, I: 84*n*
Probst, Lt. (jg) G. D., IV: 100*n*, 157
Procida, IX: 301
Proctor, Lt. Cdr. J., XIII: 307

PROCYON, II: 26*n*, 38, 159, 172, IX: 389, 392, XI: 287, 340, XIV: 379; pic., II: 175
PRODUCT, XI: 342
PROJECT, X: 327
PROMETHEUS, XIV: 387
Propper, Lt. Cdr. H. H. L., XI: 334
PROSPEROUS, IX: 346, 396
Prosser, Capt. A. L., XIV: 387
PROVENCE, II: 240
PROVO V., XII: 429, XIII: 308, 319
Proximity-influence fuze, V: 329–30, 356, VI: 99, IX: 79*n*
Prueher, Lt. Cdr. B. J., X: 212, 220–22
Pruett, Lt. (jg) S. R., XI: 272
PRUITT, III: 104, 213*n*, VII: 43, 335
Prusa, III: 221*n*
Pryce, Lt. R. F., III: 158
Pryor, Lt. Cdr. W. L., I: 421
PT Boats. *See* Motor Torpedo Boats
PUCKERIDGE, IX: 166
Puerto Castilla, Limon, I: 150, 153
Puerto Princessa, XIII: 216–21
Puerto Rican, I: 343, 369
Puerto Rico, I: 199, 248
PUFFER, VIII: 16, 218–20, XIII: 319, XIV: 287
Puget Sound Navy Yard, III: 213
Pulaski, Seaman, V: 99
Pullen, Capt. H. F., IV: 174, V: 353
Pullen, Lt. Weston C., XII: 395, 422
Puller, Col. Lewis B., V: 140–41, 144, 188*n*, 191, XII: 36
Pulo Anna, XIII: 83
Puluwat I., VIII: 156, 174
PUNJABI, I: 171
Purdy, Cdr. A. M., XII: 344, 415
PURDY, XIV: 192–3, 222–3, 381, 391
Purnell, Lt. F. V., V: 375
Purnell, Rear Adm. William R., III: 53–4, 55*n*, 129, 152, 158, 169, 205*n*, 278, 337
Pursell, Cdr. Ion, II: 38, IX: 388
PURSUER, X: 40*n*, XI: 342
PURSUIT, VII: 158–61, 171, 337, 345, XII: 368–9, 421, XIII: 306, XIV: 376
Puruata I., VI: 300, 340–41, 364
Purves, Lt. A. E., X: 381
Purvis, Capt. R. S., X: 350, 378
Purvis Bay, V: 10, 318, VI: 102–3, 203, 234, 292–364 *passim*, 418–22, VIII: 164, 170, 224, 227, XIII: 97

Pusan, XIV: 354
Putnam, Lt. Cdr. C. F., XIII: 320
Putnam, Maj. Paul, III: 228, 246–7
Putnam, Cdr. W. H., XIII: 308
Putnam, Cpl. W. H., XIV: 229
PUTNAM, XIV: 275, 381
Pye, Vice Adm. William S., biog.,
   III: 250*n;* mentioned, 101*n*, 111, 237,

241, 250–56, IV: 15, 82, 275, VI: 305*n*,
   358, VII: 31*n*
PYLADES, sunk, XI: 192
Pyle, Ernie, IX: 89; killed, XIV: 241;
   quoted, IX: 65–7
Pyne, Lt. Cdr. L. J. T., XI: 328
PYRO, XIII: 308
PYTHON, I: 111

Q

Q-ships, I: 281–6
Quackenbush, Cdr. R. S., VI: 104
QUAIL, III: 159, 205–6
QUAIL, HMS, IX: 394
QUALICUM, XI: 333
Quant, Lt. W. C., XIV: 377
QUANTOCK, IX: 393
QUAPAW, XII: 416, XIII: 104, 306, 322, 324
Quebec, I: 18, 322; Confs., August 1943, VI: 8, 84, VII: 84, 201, VIII: 8, IX: 233, 238, XI: 20–22, 27, 221; Sept. 1944, 296, 330, XII: 11–17, XIII: 257 XIV: 103
Queen Elizabeth, I: 329, X: 133
QUEEN EMMA, II: 221, IX: 164–5
Queen Mary, I: 329, X: 133
QUEEN OLGA, IX: 394
QUEENBOROUGH, IX: 394
QUEENFISH, XII: 399–400, 409, XIII: 297–8, 319, XIV: 287, 290
Queeny, Lt. J. F., XI: 299n; "The Far Shore," quoted, 71, 172, 302
QUENTIN, I: 348
Querqueville, XI: 200–203

Querville, Capit, de Frég., XI: 336
Quesada, Maj. Gen. E. R., XI: 70, 198
Quezon, Pres. Manuel, III: 203
Quiberon Bay, XI: 218, 231, 297
QUICK, I: 420, II: 40, 174, IX: 389
Quievercourt, Capt. de V. de, XI: 341
Quiggle, Lt. Cdr. L. C., I: 421
Quigley, Capt. W. M., II: 38
QUILLIAM, IX: 394
Quinby Capt. Charles F. M. S., XI: 216n
Quinby, Lt. (jg) W. C., VI: 61
QUINCY (1936), I: 14, 15n, 83, 110–11, 151, III: 31n, IV: 257, 274, 276n, 278–80, 284; Savo I. Battle, V: 29–30, 34, 41–6, 50, 63n; sunk, 46, 55–6; pic., 43
QUINCY (1943), XI: 86, 90, 95, 106, 157, 161, 167, 198–288 *passim*, 318–39 *passim*, XIV: 313; pic., XI: 204
Quirk, Cdr. P. D., VIII: 413, XII: 428, XIV: 384
Quonset, I: 248, 251, X: 185, 350
QUORN, XI: 192
Quynn, Commo. A. G., VII: 103, XII: 80n

R

R-boats, German, IX: 169, 308–10, XI: 174n, 191–3
R-class submarines, *Nos. 1–20*, I: 421; *R–6*, XIII: 161n; *–20*, VIII: 237n
R. H. Lee, I: 178
R. L. BARNES, III: 184
Rabat, II: 65, 68, 88, 115–17
Rabaul, history and descr., VI: 392–4; chart, 393; Jap. capture, 259–60; base, II: 259, IV: 11–61 *passim*, 256–9, 292, V: 18–88 *passim*, 105, 127–354 *passim*, VI: 30–93 *passim*, 117–420 *passim*, VII: 137–8; Allied strategy on, V: 117, VI: 6, 23, VII: 316, 331; carrier strikes, III: 266–8, VI: 323–6; T.O., 331, VII: 117; air raids, V: 323, VI: 90, 275, 286–92, 350, 370, 383–432 *passim;* bombarded, 419–22; pic., VI: 323
Rabenstein, Lt. H. B., VIII: 419
Raby, Lt. Cdr. John, II: 39, 88, VII: 339
RABY, VIII: 224–8, XII: 53
Race, Cape, I: 154
Radajkowski, Lt. D. T., XIII: 323
Radak chain, VII: 310, 313
Radar, invention and development, I: 220–21, 225; A/S warfare, 26, 224–6, 312; in navigation, II: 62, VI: 193, VII: 16, 54; overconfidence in, VI: 195; Fire Control, I: 356–7, VI: 184, 242, VIII: 244, XII: 224, 257–8; fighter-director, VI: 418, VII: xxviii, xxxv, xxxviii; air search, I: 357, IV: 83, 133, 176, V: 29, 30n, 34–5, 154, 216, 276, 296, 299, 347, VI: 118, 333, 384, VII: 41, 272–3, VIII: 143, 262, X: 173n, XII: 302; airborne search, I: 225–6, 244, 251, VI: 206, VIII: 262, X: 52–3, 83, 89, 99, 102, 130, 245–7, 266–8, 338, 364; plot, VI: 108n; repeating screens, V: 153n; scope, pic., VI: 61; surface search, I: 226, 356–7, II: 51, 119, 263, 266, V: 154–7, 276–9, 294, 299–300, VI: 161, 171, 183–4, 195, 213–15, 234, 245, 260, 273, 310, 343, 420, VII: 23, 140, IX: 131, X: 53, XII: 246, 257; submarine aircraft and surface detection, IV: 191, 210, 213, V: 348, VI: 80;

intercepters and detectors, X: 89, 329, 338. *See also* Germany, Navy; Japan, Navy
Raderman, M. W., V: 67n
Radford, Rear Adm. Arthur W., biog., VII: 95n; mentioned, I: 146, VII: 95, 117, 143–4, 193, 339, XI: xv$n$, XIII: 88, 91, 105, 165–6, 180–81, 200, 315n, XIV: 21, 25, 57–8, 94, 203–5, 249, 298–300, 306, 309–10, 385–6
RADFORD, V: 342, 345–7, 364–7, VI: 107, 110n, 112–14, 145–93 *passim*, 242, VII: 144, 190, 339, VIII: 127, 404, XIII: 105, 200–201, 304
Radio, ARC–5, VIII: 261; TBS, I: 106, VI: 250, X: 185, XII: 147; SCR–193, II: 30; countermeasures, VIII: 241, XI: 75; very-high-frequency, 261
Radio Marine Co., I: 103, 287
Radke, Quartermaster, V: 42–3
Raeder, Grossadm. Erich, I: 4, 6–9, 23, 34, 37–8, 73, 126, 165, 316, 381, X: 55–7
Ragan, Lt. Cdr. T. C., I: 420
Ragsdale, Rear Adm. Van H., VII: 168, 288, 338, 346–8, VIII: 68, 378, 381, 405, 420
Raguet, Lt. Cdr. C. L., XIII: 282
RAIDER, IX: 394
Raiders, German, I: 398–9, X: 213, 275–6
RAIL, III: 104, VI: 122, 148, XIII: 189
Railleuse, Batterie, II: 138, 144–5, 148–9; pic., 148
RAIMONDO MONTECUCCOLI, IX: 194, 243
"Rainbow" Plans, III: 49, 52, 77, 128–9, 132, 152, 219–20
Raines, Cdr. E. V., VIII: 411
RAINIER, VII: 112, VIII: 346, XII: 429, XIII: 319
Rakow, Cdr. W. M., VII: 344, VIII: 404, 418, XII: 417, XIII: 313
Rakuyo M., XII: 400
Raleigh, Ens. W. T., X: 224n
RALEIGH (1894), II: 286, IX: 325n
RALEIGH (1924), III: 113–14, IV: 276n, VII: 15, 18–20, 66, 334, IX: 191n, XII: 244n; pic., III: 102

Ralik chain, VII: 310, 313
RALL, XII: 429, XIV: 226, 391
Ralph T. O'Neill, XIII: 313
RALPH TALBOT, III: 104, 213*n*, IV: 93, 272, V: 29–30, 34–6, 47, 50–52, 58, 63*n*, VI: 144–57 *passim*, 182, 189, 242–4, VIII: 408*n*, 415, XII: 319, 428, XIII: 29, 305, XIV: 238, 326
Ramage, Cdr. D. B., IV: 21*n*, XIV: 238, 376
Ramage, Lt. Cdr. J. D., VIII: 414
Ramage, Cdr. Lawson P., VIII: 25
RAMAPO, III: 119, VI: 131*n*, VII: 17
Ramey, Lt. Cdr. J. W., VII: 337, 345
Ramey, Lt. Cdr. Ralph L., VI: 145, 228, 351; XI: 143–4, 336
Ramey, Col. Roger M., VI: 64
Ramey, Lt. Cdr. S. E., XIII: 303
RAMILLIES, III: 382, XI: 238, 253, 257, 284, 288, 323, 339
Ramirez de Arellano, Cdr. M. F., XIII: 319
Ramputi, Maj. F. R., VII: 333
Ramree Is., VI: 6, VII: 83
Ramsay, Cdr. Alston, VI: 308, XIII: 309
Ramsay, Adm. Sir Bertram, biog., IX: 148*n*; pic., 162; N. Africa, II: 182; Sicily, IX: 14–15, 28, 148–9, 157, 165, 323; Normandy, XI: 24, 27, 29–32, 37, 52–84 *passim*, 103–97 *passim*, 211, 215, 231, 326; *Assault Phase*, xiv
RAMSAY, III: 97, 104, 213*n*, IV: 276*n*, VII: 333, 350
Ramsey, Rear Adm. DeWitt C., I: 45, IV: 81*n*, 270, V: 83, 86, 111–12, 291, 352, VI: 106, 146
Ramsey, Cdr. Donald J., IV: 153*n*, 154, V: 62, 205, 233
Ramsey, Capt. Logan C., I: 419, X: 157, 279, 377
Ramsey, Lt. Cdr. Paul H., IV: 19
Ramu R., VI: 261, 271–2, 371
Ranau, XIII: 258
Randall, Lt. Cdr. H. E., XIV: 380
RANDOLPH, XIV: 21, 248, 264, 383, 386
RANGER, I: liii, 14–15, 83, 110–11, 419; N. Africa, II: 31–2, 39, 44, 51, 88–90, 98*n*, 106–10, 118, 123, 161–4, 167, 171; N. Russia, X: 231–3; officers who served in, VIII: 237, 238*n*, X: 42*n*, 51*n*, XI: 279*n*, XII: 125*n*, 244*n*, XIII: 52*n*, 161*n*; pics., II: 31, 165
Rangoon, III: 381
Rankin, Lt. D. W., VI: 232

RANSOM, XIV: 377
Ranta, Lt. Cdr. S. C., VIII: 410, XIV: 374
RAPIDAN, I: 422, IX: 390
RARITAN, I: 62*n*, 331*n*, 421
Rasmussen, Cdr. I. S., VI: 440
Rassieur, Capt. W. T., XII: 428, XIII: 319
Rassmussen, Lt. S. C., XII: 422, XIII: 306
RATHBURNE, I: 213, XII: 422, XIII: 304, XIV: 238, 391
Rathlin, I: 121*n*, 191*n*, X: 141
Ratliff, Lt. Cdr. W. K., XII: 428
RATON, VI: 71, VIII: 21, XII: 406–8, 429
RAVAGER, X: 40*n*
RAVEN, I: 422, II: 37, 118–20, 133, 173, XI: 333, 337–8
Ravenscroft, Lt. Cdr. V. D., XI: 336
Rawie, Lt. Cdr. W. E., XIV: 385
Rawlings, Vice Adm. Sir H. Bernard, XIV: 104–7, 211, 214, 231, 249, 264–6, 314, 333, 388
RAWLINS, XIV: 379
Rawson, Lt. R. W., X: 192
Ray, Cdr. C. C., XIV: 380
Ray, Capt. H. J., VII: 346, VIII: 409, XIII: 416
RAY, VI: 72, VIII: 16, 23, 218, XII: 408, XIII: 288
RAYMON W. HERNDON, XIV: 378
Raymond, Lt. Gordon, IX: 386
RAYMOND, XII: 244, 263, 266, 304, 421
Raysbrook, Sgt., V: 141
Raytheon Corp., VI: 273
RAZORBACK, XIV: 285–6
Read, Lt. Albert C., I: 1
Read, Cdr. H. T., I: 111, 420, II: 36, IX: 391
Read, Lt. Cdr. K. E., XIII: 309
Read, Rear Adm. Oliver M., biog., X: 212*n*; mentioned, I: 383–4, X: 212, 213*n*, 227–8
Read, Photographer R. F., V: 97
Read, Lt. R. R., XI: 335
Read, Capt. W. R., XIV: 380
Reade, Lt. (jg) Robert B., II: 264
Ready, Brig. Gen. Joseph L., VII: 270
REBEL, XIV: 377
Rebel's Rippers, XIII: 319
Recife, I: 83, 263, 378–9, 382, X: 212–13, 219
Reck, Lt. Cdr. Henry D., I: xvii, 400*n*, IX: xiii, 243*n*, X: x, XI: ix–x, XIV: x

Recreation, VI: 105-6, XII: 115-16
RECRUIT, XIV: 377
Redding, Fireman D. C., III: xii
"Reddy fox," XI: 241
Redfield, Capt. H. J., I: 111, XII: 416, XIII: 303
REDFIN, VIII: 19, 22, 221, 237, 416
REDFISH, XII: 161*n*, 399, XIII: 38, XIV: 285
Redhead, I: 273
Redman, Capt. J. R., VII: 105, XIV: 382
REDNOUR, XIV: 392
REDWING, II: 176
Reece, Lt. Cdr. F. A., XIII: 319
Reece, Lt. G., XI: 342
Reece, Lt. Cdr. M. K., XII: 423, XIV: 387
Reed, Lt. Allen, XII: 180
Reed, Lt. (jg) G. F., X: 382
Reed, Capt. Kendall S., II: 274, IV: 272, IX: 28, 386, XII: 426, XIII: 316, XIV: 385
Reed, Lt. Cdr. Walter C., V: 297
Reeks, Lt. (jg) E. H., XII: 423
Rees, Capt. J. F., VII: 105, VIII: 348
Rees, Lt. Cdr. Owen, XII: 423, XIII: 308, XIV: 387
Reeves, Rear Adm. John W., biog., VIII: 237*n*; mentioned, I: 194, VII: 4*n*, 208, 218-20, 242, 257, 333, 348, 352, VIII: 32, 37, 174, 178-9, 235-86 *passim*, 310, 367, 378, 414, XII: 43*n*, 52
Reeves, Adm. Joseph M., II: 20, 267, III: 13, 254, X: 35*n*, 37, 40
REEVES, XIV: 377
Refo, Cdr. M. P., XIII: 282-3
Regan, Lt. R. F., XIV: 382
Reggio, IX: 49, 52, 58
Regimental Combat Team, defined, II: 36*n*, IX: xvii
Register, Lt. Cdr. A. B., XIV: 381
REGULUS, III: 227
Reich, Cdr. E. T., XII: 400, 410
Reichmuth, Vice Adm. F. L., I: 421-2
Reid, Ens. Jack, IV: 98
Reid, Hon. W. Stafford, II: 6*n*
REID, III: 104, 213*n*, IV: 174, V: 335*n*, 341, VI: 265, 269-72, 381-2, 390-91, 436, 444, VII: 9*n*, 13, 82, VIII: 82, 114-15, 120-25, 404, XII: 385; sunk, 389
Reiffel, Lt. Cdr. S. J., XIII: 308
Reifkohl, Capt. Frederick L., I: 111, IV: 274, 285, V: 29-30, 41*n*, 47-9
Reifsnider, Rear Adm. Lawrence F.,

biog., XIV: 86*n*; mentioned, I: 421, IV: 266, 274, 285, VI: 297-8, 303-4, 313*n*, 423, VIII: 389, 400, 419, XIV: 86, 108, 240, 378
Reilly, Cdr. G. K. G., VIII: 419, XII: 418, XIII: 310, XIV: 380
Reilly, Lt. (jg) Thomas F., XI: 318*n*
REINA DEL PACIFICO, II: 233
Reiserer, Lt. R. L., VII: 352, VIII: 273, 412
Reith, Cdr. George, XIII: 311
Rekata Bay, V: 26, 177, 293, 323, VI: 90, 239
RELENTLESS, X: 278
RELIEF, VII: 341, VIII: 411, IX: 191*n*, XIV: 110, 386
Remage, Lt. Russell, XIV: 377
REMEY, VII: 345, VIII: 362, 409, XII: 199, 212-15, 418, XIII: 307, 314, XIV: 385
Remington, Lt. W. F., XIV: 376
REMLIK, X: 47*n*, XIV: 158*n*
REMO, IX: 42
Renard, Cdr. J. C., XIII: 312
RENARD, VI: 293*n*
Rend, Capt. C. J., I: 376*n*, XIV: 373
Rendahl, Lt. E. R., XIII: 76
Rendova I., V: 4, VI: 139; landing, 147-9, 154, and pics., 152-3; Jap. attacks, 150, 155-6; base, 199, 209-12, 227, 238
Renegar, Lt. Cdr. G. W., VIII: 411, XII: 428, XIII: 308, XIV: 387
Renfro, Cdr. E. C., VII: 340
Renken, Cdr. H. A., XI: 337
Rennell, Lt. P. T., VI: 446
Rennell Is., Battle of, V: 351-63; charts, 357, 361
Rennes, XI: 49
Rennie, Maj. Gen. R. G., XI: 181, 186
RENO (1920), X: 51*n*
RENO (1943), VIII: 414, XII: 90, 179-83, 318, 347-8, 427; pic., 406
RENONCULE, XI: 334
RENOWN, I: 195, II: 189
RENSHAW, VI: 228, 297, 308, 337, 351, 360, 415, VIII: 408, XII: 369-70, XIII: 310, 312
Rentz, Maj. J. N., *Bougainville*, VI: 279*n*; *New Georgia Campaign*, 138*n*
RENVILLE, XIV: 379
Reordan, Capt. C. E., III: 107
Republic, III: 212, V: 335*n*
REPULSE, III: 132, 157; sunk, 188-90

REQUISITE, VII: 158, 271, 310, 337, XII: 369, 421, XIII: 306, XIV: 376
Rescue opns., ships, I: 81, 121n, 191n, 249–50, 327–9, 334n, XIII: 81–2. *See also* Air-Sea Rescue; Sub. opns., Lifeguard
Rescue Squadron 3, XIV: 381
Research, pre-war, I: lix–lx
RESERVE, VI: 382, VIII: 404, XIII: 23
RESOLUTE, IX: 33, 393
Resolute, I: 152–3
RESOLUTION, III: 382
RESTIGOUCHE, I: 228, 305; pic., 374
RESTLESS, I: 13n
RESTORER, IX: 396
RETALICK, XI: 193
REUBEN JAMES (1920), I: 15n, 107, 418; sunk, 94, X: 6
REUBEN JAMES (1943), X: 343, 373
Reusek, Maj. J. P., VI: 64
REVENGE, III: 382, VII: 127, 135, 337, 345, XII: 368, 421, XIV: 376
Reykjavik, I: 77–8, 169–71
Reynolds, Cdr. Carroll D., IV: 272, V: 87, VI: 382
Reynolds, Chief Yeoman F. C., I: 218n
Reynolds, Capt. J. L., XIV: 380
Reynolds, Lt. Cdr. J. R. Z., IV: 20
Reynolds, Capt. L. K., VI: 308, 354, VIII: 223, XII: 287, 421, XIII: 318, XIV: 385
Reynolds, Capt. S. S., II: 37, XI: 334, XIV: 378
REYNOLDS, XII: 429, XIII: 319
Rhea, Capt. P. M., XI: 334, XIV: 372
Rheinberg, XI: 322
RHIND, I: 110–11, 181, 357, 420, II: 36, 91, 106, 285, IX: 197, 385, 391
Rhine crossing, XI: 317–23
Rhino ferries, XI: 118, 162, 187
RHODE ISLAND, XIV: 86n
Rhodes, Lt. F. A., V: 11n
Rhodes I., IX: 245, 326, XI: 22
Rian, Lt. (jg) G. R., VIII: 300
Ribbentrop, Joachim, I: 34, II: 18n, III: 48
Riccardi, Adm. Arturo, IX: 35, 45, 48
Rice, Cdr. R. H., VII: 342
Rice Anchorage, VI: 156, 158, 202
Rich, Lt. C. L., XI: 333
Rich, Col. Clyde, IV: 274
Rich, Lt. E. M., XIV: 318n
RICH, XI: 334; sunk, 171–2
Richard, Maj. R. H., V: 374

Richard Bland, I: 343, 369
Richard Hovey, X: 276–7
RICHARD M. ROWELL, XII: 27, 244, 305, 420, XIII: 306, XIV: 374
RICHARD MARCH HOE, VII: 334
RICHARD P. LEARY, XII: 146–8, 199, 221–2, 229, 344–5, 419, XIII: 105, 304, 325, XIV: 191, 246, 373
RICHARD S. BULL, XII: 244, 306–7, 314, 420, XIII: 306, XIV: 374
RICHARD W. SUESENS, XII: 244, 421, XIII: 146–7, 311, 326, XIV: 375
Richards, Cdr. A. E., XIV: 386
Richards, Cdr. Alfred H., IX: 259, 340, 392, 396
Richards, Denis, *Royal Air Force*, X: xv
Richards, Capt. F. G., XI: 207, 336
Richards, Lt. Cdr. G. H., X: 213n, 221
Richards, Ens. Ralph L., V: 368
Richards, Cdr. W. L., IV: 96n, 100n
Richards, Capt. W. R., XIV: 381
Richardson, Cdr. A. F., VII: 348, XII: 427, XIII: 318
Richardson, Mr. Adrian, X: 141–2
Richardson, Maj. Gen. Arthur A., IX: 15n
Richardson, Commo. C. G., II: 135n, VIII: 410, XII: 418, XIII: 143, 308, XIV: 380
Richardson, Lt. David C., V: 87–9
Richardson, Adm. James O., I: 14, III: 42–7
Richardson, Lt. Gen. Robert C., VII: ix, 90n, 184, 280, XII: 9; *Participation in Marshalls by U.S. Army*, VII: 199n
Richardson, Seth W., III: 127
Richebourg, II: 233n
RICHELIEU, II: 105–6, 240n, 250
Richer, Lt. (jg) J. B., XI: 100
Richmond, Lt. (jg) R. F., X: 119
RICHMOND, III: 213, VII: 19, 23–36, 66, 334, X: 47n, XII: 244n, 107n, XIV: 158n
Richmond, Fla., I: 250, X: 189
Richter, Lt. Cdr. W. J., VII: 335
Richtofen, Marshal von, IX: 57
Rickabaugh, Lt. Cdr. R. S., XIII: 310
Rickenbacker, Capt. Eddie V., VII: 79
Ricketts, Lt. C. V., III: 103–4, 106
Ricks, Ens. Robert B., I: 169–70
RIDDLE, VIII: 230, 411, XII: 429, XIII: 319, XIV: 230, 375

Rider, Lt. Cdr. E. C., VII: 346, VIII: 405, 415
Ridgway, Lt. C. D., VIII: 261n
Ridgway, Maj. Gen. Matthew B., IX: 94, 291, XI: 89–91, 106
Ridout, Cdr. Horatio, XIII: 313, 324
Riduka, Chief Quartermaster, V: 217
Riefkohl, Capt. Frederick L., III: 392, IV: 91, V: 29–32, 41, 47–9
Riera, Cdr. R. E., XII: 427, XIII: 316
RIGEL, III: 106, 119, IV: 254, VI: 133, 262, 381
Rigg, Lt. Cdr. J. F., XII: 426
Riggs, Rear Adm. R. S., biog., XIII: 187n; mentioned, VII: 23, 29–31, XIII: 187, 189, 216–19, 230, 243, 268–9, 304, 318, 321, 323–4
Riggs, Cdr. W. F., V: 304
Rigsbee, Cdr. E. O., XIII: 311
Riker, Cdr. M. M., VII: 336, VIII: 405, IX: 388
Riley, Lt. Francis C., V: 121
Riley, Capt. H. D., XIV: 386
RILEY, XIII: 313–14
Rimer, Capt. T. W., XII: 419, XIII: 311, XIV: 375, 378
Rimmer, Lt. Cdr. H. R., XII: 411
RINALDO, IX: 396, XI: 341
Rindskopf, Lt. Cdr. M. H., XII: 429
Rinehart, Dr. R. F., I: 224
Ring, Cdr. Stanhope C., III: 392, IV: 91, 116–17
RINGGOLD, VII: 153–4, 158, 168, 255, 260, 338, 344, VIII: 405, 419, XII: 417, XIV: 383
Ringle, Capt. Kenneth D., V: 308, XIII: 324
RINGNESS, XIV: 317, 326
RIO BRANCO, I: 387
Rio de Janeiro, I: 263, 382, 389, X: 212–14; pic., 388
Rio de Janeiro M., VII: 325
Rio Grande, X: 227–8
Rio Tercero, I: 200
Rippert, Lt. Col. J. K., IX: 116n, 122
Riseley, Col. J. P., VIII: 186n, 194
Risser, Cdr. R. D., VIII: 415, XIV: 292n
Ritchie, Lt. Cdr. Andrew E., X: 348, 378
Ritchie, Capt. O. H., VII: 337, VIII: 410, IX: 389, XII: 418
Rittenhouse, Cdr. B. N., XI: 341
Rittenhouse, Lt. Cdr. E. B., VII: 337, 346, VIII: 405, XII: 416

River Afton, I: 191n
Rivett-Carnac, Rear Adm. J. W., IX: 393
Rixey, Lt. Col. Presley M., VII: 164, 168; pic., 167
RIXEY, I: 421; VIII: 418, XII: 418, XIII: 309, XIV: 375
RO–boats (Jap. submarines), T.O., VIII: 417, XII: 432; *RO–15*, VIII: 222; *–30*, IV: 206n; *–33*, 18; *–34*, 18, V: 85, 235, sunk, VI: 119; *–36*, VIII: 417, sunk, 230; *–38*, lost, VII: 144; *–39*, sunk, 223; *–40*, sunk, 224; *–41*, VIII: 222, XII: 27, 432, sunk, XIV: 112, 243; *–42*, sunk, VIII: 229; *–43*, XII: 432, sunk, XIV: 18; *–44*, sunk, VIII: 229n; *–45*, sunk, 39; *–46*, XII: 50, 432, sunk, XIV: 291; *–47*, VIII: 417; *–49*, XIV: 243; *–50*, XII: 357n; *–55*, sunk, XIII: 279; *–56*, sunk, XIV: 243; *–61*, sunk, VII: 13; *–65*, sunk, 13n; *–68*, VIII: 417
  RO–101, VI: 154; *–103*, 140, 143, lost, 112; *–104*, *–105*, *–106*, *–108*, VIII: 417, sunk, 225–8; *–107*, sunk, VI: 179; *–108*, *–109*, XII: 432, sunk, XIV: 244; *–110*, sunk, X: 277; *–111*, sunk, VIII: 228–9; *–112*, XII: 432, sunk, XIII: 280; *–113*, *–114*, *–116*, *–117*, VIII: 417, sunk, 225–7, 230; *–115*, 417, XIII: 278–9, sunk, 280; *–501*, X: 372, sunk, 289
Roach, Cdr. J. P., XII: 333–4, 429
ROBALO, VIII: 24
Robards, Cdr. W. C. F., XIII: 309
Robb, Lt. B. W., VI: 228
Robbins, Cdr. B. A., XII: 419, XIII: 304, XIV: 30, 184n
Robbins, Capt. F. L., XIV: 387
Robbins, Cdr. J. A., XIII: 316, XIV: 383
Robbins, Cdr. R. C., IX: 355n, 395, XI: 343, XII: 429
Robbins, Rear Adm. Thomas H., IX: xvi, XI: xi, XII: viii
Robe, Pharmacist, IV: 228n
Robert, Rear Adm. Georges, I: 30–32, 33n, X: 191
Robert C. Tuttle, I: 417
Robert F. Hoke, X: 276n
ROBERT F. KELLER, XIII: 79, 81, 319, XIV: 314, 374
ROBERT H. SMITH, XIV: 377
ROBERT I. PAINE, X: 289, 377
Robert J. Walker, X: 302–3

Robert Rowan, IX: 83, 119–20, 141, 386
ROBERT SMITH, VII: 37n
Roberts, Capt. A. E., USA, V: 289n
Roberts, Lt. C. O., XII: 326–7
Roberts, Cdr. David G., III: 369, V: 205
Roberts, Maj. E. S., XIV: 384
Roberts, Cdr. H. B., XII: 417
Roberts, Lt. Cdr. Howard S., VIII: 413, X: 81, XII: 424
Roberts, Capt. J. S., I: 82, 420, VIII: 406, XII: 421
Roberts, Lt. Col. Jack, I: 244, X: 88, 129, 132
Roberts, Capt. John, IV: 41n
Roberts, Capt. R. H., VI: 416, VIII: 409
Roberts, Lt. Cdr. W. L., XIV: 379
ROBERTS, II: 190, 220, IX: 156, 276, 282, 290, 303, 393
Robertshaw, Maj. L. B., V: 374
Robertson, Ens., I: 390
Robertson, Capt. A. I., IX: 387
Robertson, Capt. A. J., VII: 345, VIII: 408
Robertson, Cdr. E. L., VIII: 403, IX: 78–9, 386
Robin Moor, I: 38n, 50, 63–4, 73, 296
Robin Wentley, VII: 341, 347
Robinson, Cdr. Allan M., XI: 313
Robinson, Rear Adm. Arthur G., biog., X: 204n; mentioned, III: 160, 299–303, X: 204–5, XI: 325, 328
Robinson, Lt. Cdr. C. F., XIII: 310
Robinson, Cdr. D. R., XII: 390
Robinson, Cdr. Hunter R., IX: 20n, 385
Robinson, Lt. Cdr. J. P., XIII: 312
Robinson, Lt. Cdr. K. G., XIII: 313
Robinson, Lt. Cdr. R. W., XIV: 374
Robinson, Col. Ralph R., VII: 201n, 203, 206
Robinson, Rear Adm. Samuel M., X: 33
Robinson, Capt. Stephan B., I: 208, III: 159, 284
Robinson, Walton L., IV: x, 87n, V: 84n, 372n
ROBINSON (1918), X: 204n
ROBINSON (1944), VIII: 409, XII: 199, 221, 419, XIII: 310, 313, 322, 324
Robison, Lt. Carl F., IX: 81
Robison, Cdr. H. C., I: 76, 420, II: 40
Roby, Cdr. A. B., VII: 331, VII: 339, 348, VIII: 405, 410
Rochefort, XI: 309
ROCHESTER, X: 131
ROCK, XIII: 161, 167–8, 320

ROCKAWAY, I: 420
Rockets, VI: 385; aircraft, VII: 209, X: 52–4, 364, XII: 79
Rockey, Maj. Gen. Keller E., pic., XIV: 54; mentioned, 8
Rockwell, Lt. D. L., XI: 132
Rockwell, Rear Adm. Francis W., biog., VII: 37n; pic., 55; mentioned, III: 158, 172, 195–8, 203, IV: 20, 220, VII: 37–40, 48, 51, 62, 334
Rockwell, Capt. J. P., XIV: 380
ROCKY MOUNT, VII: 87, 207, 256, 285, 343, VIII: 186, 202, 210, 242, 326, 377, 407, XII: 419, XIII: 222, 224, 264, 266, 310, 322
Rodee, Cdr. Walter F., IV: 91, V: 205, 209
Rodgers, Rear Adm. Bertram J., biog., XI: 237n; pics., XI: 268, XIV: 159; mentioned, VII: 23–33, XI: 237, 258, 264–7, 340, XIV: 26–31, 41, 130n, 267n, 372
Rodieck, Lt. Col. R. W., VII: 333
Rodimon, Cdr. W. S., XII: 417, XIII: 304
Rodman, Lt. Cdr. Hugh, IV: 71
RODMAN, I: 304, 359, 420, II: 40, X: 258, 372, XI: 203–4, 336, 340, XIV: 193–4, 376, 390
RODNEY, II: 189, 223, 235, 238, IX: 167, 393, XI: 300
ROE, I: 420, II: 37, 119–23, 285, VIII: 99, 404, IX: 78–9, 82, 386
ROEBUCK, X: 278
Roesch, Capt. H. O., VII: 179, 341, 345
Roessler, Cdr. A. C., IX: 388, 391
Rogers, Col. A. H., IX: 78
Rogers, Cdr. E. B., VII: 334
Rogers, Lt. Col. Francis M., pic., II: 164; mentioned, II: 23n, 71n, 96n, 99n, 101n, 104n, 109, IX: 124n
Rogers, Lt. Cdr. G. V., XIV: 381
Rogers, Maj. O. L., V: 141
Rogers, Lt. Cdr. Richard S., VIII: 409, X: 111, XII: 421
Rogers, Cdr. Robert H., IV: 19, VI: 144, 150
Rogers, Cdr. W. H., XIII: 304
Rogers, Lt. Cdr. W. K., XII: 428, XIII: 75, 319, XIV: 383
Rohwer, Dr. Jürgen, X: xi, 62n, 331n, 366n, XI: xi, 310n, 313n
Roi I., III: 262, VII: 138, 142, 230–36, 240–41, 286–7, VIII: 156; landings,

VII: 236, 240–50; charts, 235, 241; air and naval gunfire support, 236–7, 242, 246–8; air UDTs, VIII: 166; pics., VII: 246–7
ROMA, IX: 35–7; sunk, 243
Romberg, Lt. H. A., IV: 271, V: 87
Romberger, Lt. Cdr. W. M., XIV: 382
Rome, IX: 38, 48, 171, 186, 239–41, 331, 379, 383, XI: 22
Rommel, Marshal Erwin, II: 7–10, 18, 65, 242–4, 254, 258–9, IX: 260, 294, 304, XI: 40–44, 48–9, 159, 169, 211
ROMNEY, XI: 333
ROMOLO, sunk, IX: 42
Romoser, Lt. Cdr. W. K., I: 76, 418, VI: 114–16, 145, 154, 161, 167–9, 181
Romulo, Brig. Gen. C. P., pic., XII: 70; mentioned, 136
Roncador Reef, V: 101
Rongerik Atoll, VII: 79
Ronin, Col. A. J., X: 227n
RONQUIL, XII: 429
Rood, Capt. G. A., IV: 173
Rooke I., VI: 369, 379, 382, 384
Rooks, Capt. A. H., III: 159, 164, 314, 332, 364, 369
ROOKS, XIV: 192, 230, 381
Rooney, Cdr. C. W., XIV: 385
Rooney, Cdr. J. B., I: 420, II: 39, IX: 197, 388
Rooney, Lt. P. C., VII: 339
Rooney, Cdr. Roderick S., VII: 188, 342
Roosevelt, President Franklin D., pics., I: 70, VI: 18, XII: 6; assistance to History, I: xviii, 38n, II: 4n, V: xi, XIV: ix; Short of War period, I: 13–14, 27–37, 54–7, 67–8, 81; Atlantic Conference, I: 69–70; destroyer escorts, X: 32–5; frigates, 36; escort carriers, 38, 41; *Greer* incident, 80; subchasers, 230; PTs, II: 262; landing craft, 267; shipbuilding, I: 27–8, 200–221, 291, III: 30; Anglo-American staff conversations, I: 39–41, 44, 46; war outlook, Mar. 1942, IV: 3; strategy, 1943, VI: 3–7, 226; relations with Japan, I: 67, 81, III: 13–15, 62, 65–8, 72–3, 79, X: 6–7; Q-ships, I: 282; N. Africa, II: 7–15, 41, 42n, 70, 186–8, 208, 218–19; Mediterranean, 254; prewar in Pacific, III: 47, 49, 54, 64, X: 55, 202; relations with MacArthur, III: 202, XII: 7–11; Kimmel, III: 250; Mackenzie King, X: 5; Adm. King,

I: 116; Churchill, I: 70, 167, II: 11–14, IV: 3–4, VI: 4–6, XI: 23, 224; defense of N.E.I., III: 312; Lae-Salamaua raid, III: 389; Guadalcanal, V: 185, 263, 287; "Summit" Conferences, Casablanca, IX: 5–7, 13; Washington, May 1943, IX: 228–9; Quebec, Aug. 1943, VII: 201; Cairo, IX: 322; Quebec, Sept. 1944, XII: 15; Italian campaign, IX: 227, 382; surrender, 237–8; Aegean, 245; Cross-Channel invasion, XI: 9–16, 19–23, 54; S. France, 222–4, 229–32; Rhine crossing, 318; rejects idea of A/S "czar," X: 13; sea power, X: 55; message on return to Philippines, XII: 129, 137–8; Luzon, XIII: 3; peace, XIV: 338; death, XIII: 276, XIV: 231; memorial service, 232
Roosevelt, Lt. Cdr. Franklin D., Jr., II: 113, IX: 193, XIII: 104, 305, XIV: 111, 374
Roosevelt, Lt. Col. James, pic., IV: 235; mentioned, IV: 239, VII: 126
Roosevelt, Brig. Gen. Theodore, Jr., II: 223, IX: 93, 111, XI: 100–103
Roper, Capt. Clifford H., V: 296, 304
Roper, Capt. J. W., XIV: 385
ROPER, I: 155, 215, 415, 420, XI: 339, XIV: 379, 392
Rorschach, Lt. Cdr. A. L., IV: 271, V: 86, VII: 23n
Rosario, XIII: 154
ROSARIO, XI: 341
Roscoe, Theodore, *Submarine Operations*, VI: 66n, VIII: 15n
Roscoff, XI: 302
ROSE (Norwegian Corvette), I: 325; yacht, 272
Rose I., Samoa, III: 33n
Rosecrans, Col. H. E., VI: 387
ROSELYS, X: 143
Rosendahl, Rear Adm. Charles E., I: 250, V: 296, 304, 309
Rosendal, Lt. Cdr. H. D., IV: 271
Rosenthal, Joe, XIV: 61
Roskill, Capt. Stephen W., X: x, XI: x; *The War at Sea*, X: xv
Rosneath, II: 224, X: 87, XI: 52, 57–8, 326
Ross, Cdr. B. P., XIV: 385
ROSS, VIII: 409, XI: 335, XII: 80, 123, 419
Rosse, Lt. R. M., VIII: 419
Rosset, Capit. de V., XI: 288

Rossi, Gen. Carlo, IX: 50, 160
Rostand, Capit. de V. G., II: ix, IX: xv, XI: x
ROSTHERN, I: 305, 337, 341
Rota I., VIII: 149–51, 154–5, 233, 248, 271–4, 287–9, 324, 351, 378
ROTANIN, XIV: 387
Rotating Patrol Plan, VIII: 19–20
Roth, Lt. Cdr. E. A., III: 159
Roth, Lt. Cdr. E. B., X: 376, 381
Roth, Lt. Eli, V: 362
ROTHSAY, IX: 396
Rouelle, Col. Frank, XII: 65
Rouen, XI: 303
Routh, Lt. Col. R. C., IX: 143
Row, Brig. R. A., VI: 289n
Rowan, Col. G. R., pic., V: 130
ROWAN, I: 111, 180–81, 357, 420, II: 38, 162, 171, III: 285, IX: 314, 385, 391; sunk, 298–9
Rowbotham, Lt. W. E., VII: 350
Rowbothom, Cdr. W. B., War Diary, I: 17n
Rowe, Lt. Cdr. G. F., XIII: 32n
Rowe, Capt. Gordon, X: 232
Rowe, Lt. Cdr. H. A., V: 93n
Rowe, Capt. L. L., VI: 297, VIII: 418, XII: 417
Royal, Rear Adm. Forrest B., biog., XII: 140n; pic., XIII: 276; mentioned, I: 419, XII: 140–41, 144, 156, 419, XIII: 94, 96, 117, 125, 143, 146–7, 209; Southern Phils., 215–17, 222–3, 260–66, 310, 322
ROYAL OAK, X: 4
ROYAL SCOTSMAN, II: 195n, 231, IX: 393
ROYAL SOVEREIGN, III: 382, IX: 148n
ROYAL ULSTERMAN, II: 195n, 232, IX: 347, 393–5
ROYALIST, XI: 279, 342
Royan, X: 92, 108, 175
Royle, Adm. Sir Guy, VI: 51
Roys, F. G., X: 382
Rozendal, Cdr. H. D., VII: 335
Roziers, Capit. de Corv. de, X: 381
Rubber, X: 228
Rubinow, Lt. Cdr. S. G., X: 376
Ruble, Cdr. H. E., XIII: 319
Ruby, X: 202
Ruck-Keene, Capt. P., XIV: 388
Rucker, Cdr. C. G., II: 37, X: 293
Rudder, Lt. Col. James E., XI: 126–9
RUDDEROW, XIII: 322
Ruddock, Rear Adm. Theodore D.,

biog., XIII: 19n; mentioned, VII: 339, 348, VIII: 409, XII: 366, XIII: 19, 23–4, 29, 33
Ruddy, Cdr. J. A., II: 40, 151–2, X: 232
Rudowski, Lt. H. F., I: 214
RUDYERD BAY, XII: 428, XIII: 67, 71, 81, 319, XIV: 374
Rue, Contre-Am., XI: 309, 338
Ruff, Cdr. L. E., XII: 429, XIII: 316, 319
Ruge, Vizeadm. Friedrich, Report on Sicily, IX: 35, 46, 182, 214, 218; *Der Seekrieg*, X: xv, XI: xi
Ruhfus, Ktr. Adm., XI: 244, 284, 289
Ruhsenberger, Capt. J. R., X: 296, 345, 350, 379
Ruiz, Commo. J. A., X: 190n
Rujiyoru Islet, VII: 291
Rule, Capt. A. O., X: 197
Rumanian oil fields, IX: 44
Rummel, Lt. Cdr. W. K., XII: 419
Rumrunners, II: 262
Rundstedt. Feldmarschall G. von, XI: 39–45, 49, 159, 169, 186
Runquist, Cdr. E. R., XIV: 388
Runyan, Warrant Machinist D. E., V: 94–5
Runyan, Lt. Cdr. J. W., VIII: 412
Rupertus, Maj. Gen. William H., IV: 272–3, 279, 288, 291, V: 66, VI: 378, 385, XII: 34–5, 40, 43n
Ruppenthal, R. G., *Logistical Support*, XI: xiii
Rushing, Lt. (jg) R. W., XII: 177–8
RUSHMORE, XII: 419, XIII: 321
Russell, Capt. B. V. M., VII: 337, 344, VIII: 405, XII: 428
Russell, Cdr. G. L., I: 116
Russell, Philip T., I: 213n
RUSSELL, IV: 19, 24–5, 60n, 90, V: 205, 214, 219, 233, VII: 165, 338, 346, VIII: 120, 123–5, 405, XIII: 116, 146, 309, XIV: 379
Russell Is., V: 4, VI: 90, 94; landing, 97–100; as base, 120, 178, 199, 204, 231, 240, 294, XII: 34
Russia, supply routes to, IX: 4; lend-lease cargoes to, VI: 19, X: 314n; subs., 359; declares war on Japan, XIV: 345; occupation of Manchuria, 356. *See also* North Russia Run
Russillo, Cdr. M. P., VIII: 415
Rusteen, Lt. Cdr. M. A., XIV: 376
Ruth, Cdr. E. A., XI: 313, 341
RUTILICUS, VII: 348

Rutter, Cdr. J. B., VIII: 408, XIII: 139, 310

Rutter, Lt. Cdr. R. L., IV: 92

Ruud, Maj. Robert H., VII: 165

Ruyz, X: 264

Ryan, Capt. D. L., I: 57, 76, 418, XIII: 308, XIV: 380

Ryan, J. D., VII: 334

Ryan, Maj. Michael P., VII: 165, 169, 172

Ryan, Capt. Thomas J., VI: 144, 149, 181-2, 186, 193, 228, 234-6

Ryan, Capt. W. D., II: 39; XIV: 386

Ryan, Loch (Scotland), I: 53

Ryder, Maj. Gen. C. W., II: 17, 190, 202-3, 209

RYE, XI: 333

RYUHO, VI: 156n, VIII: 217, 249, 264, 272, 294, 297, 416, XII: 161, XIII: 158, XIV: 331

RYUJO, III: 27, 130, 163, 169, 182, 276, 308-84 *passim*, IV: 133, 172, 176-7, 184, V: 82, 85-91, 95, 102, 106, VII: 6; sunk, V: 89-90

Ryukyus, history and description, XIV: 3-4, 79-83; charts, 84-5, 201; in Jap. strategy, XII: 66

Ryuyo M., VIII: 16

S

S-boats, IV: 190, 224–6; *S–1*, XIII: 161*n*; *–4*, I: 52*n*; *–11* through *–17*, 421; *–18*, IV: 174, VII: 334; *–20*, *–21*, I: 421; *–23*, IV: 174, VII: 334; *–24*, I: 421; *–26*, sunk, 154*n*; *–27*, IV: 174, 176*n*, wrecked, 215, and pic., 206; *–28*, 174, VII: 53, 334; *–30*, 53, 334; *–31*, IV: 218, VII: 14; *–32*, *–33*, 334; *–34*, IV: 174, 214–15, VII: 334; *–35*, IV: 174, 214, 218–19, VII: 53, 334; *–36*, III: 159, sunk, 304; *–37*, 158, 304, 307, IV: 20; *–38*, III: 158, 178, 335, 338, 350, IV: 20, 226, 275, V: 18–19, 25, VII: 334; *–39*, III: 159, 177, 225, 304, IV: 20, 275; *–40*, III: 158, 179, IV: 20, V: 334; *–41*, III: 158, IV: 20, 275, VII: 53, 334; *–42*, IV: 17, 20, 62, 224; *–43*, 20, 275; *–44*, 20, 225–6, 275, V: 61, sunk, VII: 53; *–45*, IV: 20; *–46*, 20, 275; *–47*, 20, 225, VIII: 141; *–48*, I: 421; *–51*, 52*n*
Sabin, Ens. G. E., VIII: 230
Sabin, Capt. Lorenzo S., II: 272–3, IX: 68, 75, 81–4, 386, XI: 84, 118, 124, 132, 147, 164–5, 336
SABINE, III: 393, IV: 174, 272, VII: 341, VIII: 411, XII: 428, XIV: 333, 387; pic., III: 395
SACANDAGA, XIV: 387
Sackett, Cdr. E. L., III: 158, 194, 199
SACO, XIII: 289–302
SACRAMENTO, III: 104, 119
Sadau I., XIII: 261
Sadler, Ens. W. M., X: 382
Sado M., IV: 203, V: 234, 269*n*
SAFARI, IX: 72–3, 74*n*, 101, 386
Safi, II: 19, 33–4, 51, 54, 151, 245–6, 267; naval gunfire support, 145–9; unloading, 153–5; landing, 135–56, 162; chart, 136, 141; pic., 149
Sagami M., III: 276, 321, 329, IV: 224
Sagami Wan, XIV: 361
SAGE, VII: 224, 228, 347, XII: 421, XIII: 306, XIV: 376
SAGINAW, IV: 71
SAGINAW BAY, XII: 420, XIII: 145, 305, XIV: 374
SAGITTARIUS, VIII: 420, XIV: 377

SAGUENAY, I: 321
Saidor, VI: 289–90
Saigon, III: 61, XIII: 164, 168–9, 284–5
Sailer, Maj. Joseph, V: 318, 374
SAILFISH, III: 158, 304, VI: 53, VII: 189, VIII: 16*n*
ST. ANDREW, IX: 397
St. Blaise, II: 248
St. Croix, Cdr. B. de., XI: 336
ST. CROIX, X: 145; sunk, 142–3
ST. DAVID, IX: 368, 397; sunk, 346
ST. DAY, II: 210
St. Eval, I: 244, X: 99–100
St. George, Lt. Cdr. W. H., XIV: 386
ST. GEORGE, XIV: 268, 381
Saint-Grégoire batteries, II: 225
ST. JOHN, X: 339
Saint John's, Newfoundland, I: 18, 58, 319, 323, 331, 341, 344, X: 17, 70–71, 75, 184; pic., I: 71
ST. JULIEN, IX: 397
ST. KILDA, IX: 396
ST. LAURENT, X: 80–81
Saint-Laurent-sur-Mer, XI: 113, 150–51, 161–2
Saint Lawrence, Gulf and R. of, I: 314, 322, 330
ST. LO, XII: 27*n*, 126*n*, 244, 273, 276–8, 281–2, 303–6, 313, 421; sunk, 302; pic., 302. *See also* MIDWAY
Saint-Lô, France, XI: 216
ST. LOUIS, III: 31*n*, 97, 119–20, 212, 213*n*, 261, 264, IV: 83, 86, 173, V: 326, 329, 345, VI: 106*n*, 113*n*, 116, 120, 156–89 *passim*, 190*n*, 363, 415–16, VII: 9*n*, 12–14, VIII: 181, 409, 419, XII: 366–7, XIV: 132, 191, 226, 246, 372, 385
St. Lucia, I: 33–4; pic., 37
Saint-Malo, XI: 174–5, 300
Saint-Marcouf, XI: 97–8, 167, 174
ST. MARY'S, XIV: 375
Saint-Michel-en-Grèves, XI: 301–2
SAINT MIHIEL, VII: 334
Saint-Nazaire, I: 22–3, X: 85, 325, XI: 108, 297, 302, 328
St. Olaf, I: 361, 364
ST. PAUL, XIV: 313

Saint Paul Rocks, I: 315, 324, 385
Saint Pierre and Miquelon, II: 10
Saint-Raphaël, XI: 267, 270, 274
Saint Thomas, V. I., I: 84; pic., 37
Saint-Tropez, XI: 259, 264, 282
Saint-Vaast, XI: 96, 218n
Sainte-Honorine, XI: 113, 123
Sainte-Marguérite, XI: 276–7
Sainte-Maxine, XI: 264, 266, 277
Sainte-Mère-Église, XI: 91
Saipan I., IV: 89, VI: 433, VII: 74, 286, VIII: 17, 23, 174–8, 219, 222; history and description, 149–52; chart, 323; pic., 176; strategic importance, VII: 69, VIII: 5; carrier raids on, VII: 286, VIII: 154–5; Jap. defenses, 167–9, chart, 204; capture of, planning, 8–9, 157–9, 162; rehearsals, approach, 170–74; landing, 190–99; charts and diagrams, 188–91; pics., 192–3; air and naval gunfire support, 179–83, 186, 192, 203–5, 325–30, 333–5; opns. ashore, 199–212, 322–9, and chart, 204, 323; Jap. air attacks, 207–8, 328–9, 345, XIV: 10; unloading, VIII: 208; numbers, 339; discussion, 339–40; T.O., 407–12
Saipan ,I., as U.S. base, VIII: 26, 309, 344, 349, 360, 367, 397, XII: 75, 80, XIV: 4, 10, 89, 111, 162–4, 296
Saito, Adm., III: 13
Saito, Hon. Hiroshsi, III: 37
Saito, Lt. Gen. Y., VIII: 167–9, 183–7, 202–3, 208–10, 216, 319–21, 326, 334–7
SAKATONCHEE, XIII: 322
Sakishima Gunto, XIII: 88–91, 179, 182, XIV: 80; British attacks on, 106, 211–14, 249–50, 264
Sakito M., VII: 34, VIII: 17, 167, 373
Sakonju, Vice Adm. N., VIII: 118–20, 125–31, XII: 161n, 164, 169n, 239, 431
Sakura M., III: 366
Salamaua, III: 388–9, IV: 256, 260, VI: 31, 52, 63, 92, 96, 136–7, 255–8, 260–61, 268, VII: 316, XIII: 96
SALAMAUA, XIII: 152, 305, 326, XIV: 250, 307
Salamis, X: 260
Salamis, X: 382
SALAMONIE, I: 76, 422, IX: 390, XII: 82–4, 423, XIII: 308
Salawati I., VIII: 125, 130
Salazar, Dr. I: 66, X: 45–6, 87
Salé, II: 19, 115–17

SALEM, IX: 110, 385, XIV: 377
Salerno, Opn., IX: 227–313; planning, 232–3, 247–51; organization, 246–7; movement, 251–3; minesweeping, 259, 272–3; landings, 254–78; chart, 262–3; pics., 266–7, 282; air and naval gunfire support, 249–51, 265–8, 272–97 passim; opns. ashore, 279–314; chart, 288–9; German reaction, 252, 260–61, 274, 283–4, 296–300; unloading, 268–9, 276, 297–300; casualties, 285, 313; T.O., 391–4
Salerno, U.S. base, IX: 312, 332, XI: 236, 241
SALINAS, I: 422
Salinas, Ecuador, X: 201n
Sallada, Rear Adm. H. B., VII: 343, VIII: 326, 410
Sallenger, Lt. (jg) A. H., X: 123
Salm, 2nd Lt. Ernst, X: 131
Salmon, Lt. Cdr. N. D., XII: 418, XIII: 309
SALMON, III: 158, 179, IV: 220–21, XII: 406–7, 429
Salomon, Lt. Cdr. Henry, I: xv–xvii, 252n, 376n, III: xi, 147–293, notes passim, IV: x, 5n, 21n, 31n, 69n, 75n, 256n, V: 79n, 147n, 225n, 288n, 333n, VI: xi, 243–392, notes passim, 432n, VII: vii, 52n, 54n, 145n, 251n, X: ix, XII: vii, 202n, XIII: ix, XIV: x
Salomon, Lt. Cdr. Louis G., XII: 27
Salso and Salso R., IX: 71–2, 75, 86–9, pic., 82
SALT LAKE CITY, III: 217, 261–3, 271, 392, IV: 257, V: 87, 150–55, 158, 162–4, 170; VII: 22–40; Komandorski battle, in T.O.s, 339, 350, X: 204n, XI: 237n; XII: 87, 425, XI: 373; Iwo and Okinawa, XIV: 11–12, 27, 167, 180; ammo. expended 1942–5, 167; pic., VII: 31
Saltash, XI: 60
SALTASH, XI: 335
Saltmarsh, Lt. E. O., XIII: 306, 322
Saltonstall, Sgt. Peter B., VIII: 369
Saltsman, Lt. S. I., XI: 193
SALUTE, XII: 421, XIII: 207, 264, 267, 306
Salvage, N. Africa, II: 79–81, 133, 245–52, 274; Tarawa, VII: 170; Naples, IX: 311–12; Cherbourg, XI: 216–18; Fais, XII: 53; Manila, XIII: 198–207; Iwo Jima, XIV: 51
Salvage money, I: 84n
Salvesen, Mr. Georg J., I: 190–91

Salvia, Lt. Cdr. O. F., VIII: 410,
XII: 422, XIII: 306
Samah Bay, III: 187
Samar I., XII: 123; Battle off, 242–316;
casualties, 316; charts, 247–9, 264–5,
277; pics., 246–7, 278–9, 302–3; land-
ing, 153, 392
SAMARITAN, VIII: 411, XIV: 386
*Samdaring, -gallion, -harle, -kansa, -lea,
-fairy, -spelga, -penn,* X: 381–2
Samejima, Vice Adm. T., VI: 118–19,
210, 305–6, 323, 426
SAMIDARE, III: 162, 275, 334, IV: 88,
V: 84, 176, 206–7, 234, 239, 254, VI: 74,
119, 242–8, 306, 311, 315–17, 341, VIII:
125–6, 130, 416; sunk, 367n
Samoa Is., III: 216, 221n, 257, 261–2, IV:
6, 246, 251, 255, 263n, VII: 89, 116
SAMPHIRE, II: 213
Sample, Rear Adm. William D., biog.,
XII: 244n; mentioned, I: 419, II: 40,
150, VIII: 412, X: 24, XII: 34, 244,
420, XIII: 272–4, XIV: 132, 213, 374
Sampson, Cdr. N. J., X: 375, XIII: 303
Sampson, Lt. Cdr. R. D., XIV: 374
Sampson, Cdr. R. R., II: 40, VII: 346,
VIII: 410, 419, XIV: 274, 377
SAMPSON (1916), VIII: 237n
SAMPSON (1938), I: 83, VIII: 114, 406
Samsuva, X: 310
Samuel Adams, IX: 390
SAMUEL B. ROBERTS, in Battle of Samar,
XII: 244, 262–3, 266–8, 272, 313, 316,
421; sunk, 269–71
SAMUEL CHASE, I: 421, II: 191–5, 199–202,
212–15, IX: 61, 102, 117–19, 124, 251,
298, 387–8, 391–2, XI: 118–19, 335,
339; pic., II: 193
Samuel Chase, I: 182, 188–90, 191n
Samuel Huntington, IX: 355; *Parker,*
165; *Moody,* X: 381
SAMUEL N. MOORE, XIII: 316, XIV: 306,
383
SAMUEL S. MILES, VIII: 411, XII: 429,
XIV: 222, 373
Samuels, Lt. J. M., XII: 421, XIII: 304
Samuels, Lt. Cdr. W. T., X: 213n
San Augustin, Cape, XIII: 249–50
San Bernardino Strait, III: 177,
VIII: 202, 231, 241, XII: 189, 194–6,
290–93, 300, 317, 320, XIII: 207
SAN CARLOS, VIII: 50, XII: 313, 422
San Clemente I., VII: 233
San Clemente M., IV: 89

San Cristobal I., V: 4
SAN DIEGO, IV: 157, 257, 276, V: 205,
233, VI: 325, 329, VII: 190, 340, 349,
352, VIII: 154n, 415, XII: 90, 426,
XIII: 54, 316, XIV: 21, 58, 385–6
San Diego, Calif., III: 236, 242, IV: 81,
266, 279, V: 14, VII: 116, 210, 233, 239,
XII: 8; Sound School, I: 206n, 214–
15
San Fabian, XIII: 112
San Fernando, La Union, XIII: 12–14,
107, 154
San Fernando, Pampanga, XIII: 185
San Fernando Pt., III: 180; XIII: 105,
110
SAN FRANCISCO, I: 14, 15n, 206n, III: 31n,
212n–13n, 236, 242, 244n, 266n, IV:
257, 271, V: 87, 136, 148–257 *pas-
sim,* VI: 11, 17n, 23, VII: 60, 190, 194,
248–60, 271–6, 334–6, 344, 352,
VIII: 308, 409, 415, XIII: 54, 316,
XIV: 21, 34, 122, 135, 240, 280n, 372;
pic., V: 147, 243
San Francisco, Calif., I: 103, 112, III: 29,
IV: 275–6, VII: 38, 111–12, XIV: 163;
Conferences, Sept.–Oct. 1944, XII: 17,
XIII: 5, XIV: 4–5
San Isidro, XII: 63, 380
SAN JACINTO, VIII: 174, 178, 205, 250,
292, 298–300, 367n, 414, XII: 90, 318,
325–6, 341, 427, XIII: 54, 70, 317,
XIV: 21, 205, 306, 382, 386
San José, Luzon, XIII: 193
San José, Mindoro, XIII: 18, 26, 29,
34–41, 48–9, 149
San José, Panay, XIII: 25
SAN JUAN, I: 151, IV: 257, 274, 278, 289,
292n, V: 29–30, 52, 87, 205, 210, 216–
18, VI: 325, 329, VII: 190, 340, 350,
VIII: 413, XIII: 54, 317, XIV: 21, 382,
386; pic., V: 218
San Juan, P.R., I: 32–3, 240, 249, X: 189,
195, 205, 297
San Juanico Strait, XII: 63, 139, 151,
362, 368n, 370
San Mateo Cadet School, I: 295
San Miguel, I: 129
San Pablo, XII: 350, 364, 394
SAN PABLO, I: 420, VIII: 49n, 50, 406,
XII: 25, XIII: 312
SAN PEDRO, VIII: 405, XII: 417
San Pedro, Calif., III: 42, IV: 15n,
VII: 38
San Pedro Bay, Leyte, XII: 130, 190,

198, 203, 235, 306, 313–16, XIII: 215.
For landings, *see* Tacloban
San Pietro, II: 248
San Ricardo, landings. *See* Tacloban
San Roque, Cape, Brazil, I: 324, 380, 385, 388
San Roque, Mindanao, XIII: 225
San Stéfano di Camastra IX: 171–2, 192, 196–8
SANAE, VI: 75; sunk, 80
Sanagi, Capt. S., VI: 408*n*
Sanananda, VI: 41–5, 49
Sanchez, Lt. Cdr. Henry G., V: 205
SAND LANCE, VIII: 17–18, 22; pic., XIV: 367
Sandakan, Borneo, XIII: 258, 267
Sandel, Lt. Percy, XI: 307
Sanders, Cdr. E. R., VII: 340
Sanders, Rear Adm. Harry, IX: 360, 396, XI: 143, 147–9, 156, 174, 277, 335–7, 343
Sanders, Cdr. W. H., XIV: 251–2, 376
Sanderson, Lt. Cdr. E. G., XIII: 307, XIV: 385
Sanderson, Lt. W. B., XIV: 379
SANDOVAL, XIV: 272, 392
Sandoz, Ens. Edouard, IX: 23
SANDPIPER, I: 334, 420
SANDS, I: 214, 380, IV: 174, 251*n*, V: 359, 362, VI: 133*n*, 261–3, 267, 269*n*, 374–5, 381, 436, VIII: 404, XII: 121, 421, XIII: 304
SANDUSKY, XIII: 307*n*
Sanford, Capt. J. R., XIV: 387
Sanford, 1st Lt. W. L., X: 88, 129
Sangamo Electric Co., I: 216–17
SANGAMON, II: 37, 45, 90, 118, 123, 128, 132–3; III: 57, VII: 233–4, 288, 301, 338, 346–8, VIII: 405, 420, X: 40, XII: 26, 244, 301, 305, 420, XIV: 213, 250, 373, 391; class, II: 31, VI: 106, 141*n*, VIII: 29–30
SANGAY, VIII: 346, XII: 429, XIII: 319
Sanger, Cdr. K. J., XIII: 311
Sangro R., IX: 319, 324
Sanko M., VII: 24
Sansapor, Cape, VIII: 91, 143, XIII: 97; landing, VIII: 74, 140–44, XII: 3; T.O., VIII: 403–6; chart, 142; pic., 89
Sansonnetti, Vice Adm. L., IX: 35, 40, 45, 69, 242
Sant'Agata, IX: 198–9, 203
Sant'Angelo, Castel, Sicily, IX: 72, 85
Santa Catalina, X: 180–81

Santa Croce Camerina, IX: 94, 129, 144
Santa Cruz, Luzon, XII: 348
Santa Cruz Is., IV: 260–62, V: 7, 201; battle, 199–224, VI: 332; T.O., V: 204–7; discussion, 223–4; pics., 195, 218–19; chart, 210–11
Santa Elena, X: 264
SANTA FE, VI: 341, 344, VII: 39, 154, 190, 220, 334, 346, 352, VIII: 37, 413, XII: 21*n*, 51*n*, 90, 100–102, 318, 331–2, 425–7, XIII: 54, 318, XIV: 21, 34, 40, 45, 88*n*, 96–7, 267*n*, 334*n*, 383
Santa Isabel I., V: 4–5, 121
Santa Maria, Azores, X: 46
Santa Rosa, XI: 340
Santa Rosa, Mt., VIII: 398–400
SANTEE, I: 384, 419, II: 40, 89*n*, 90, 139, 150–52, 155, III: 57, VIII: 405, X: 40, 109*n*, 115–19, 176, 295*n*, 370–71, 379, XII: 26–7, 166, 244, 300–301, 304–6, 420, XIV: 213, 374
Santiago, Battle of, II: 286, XII: 241
Santiago I., XIII: 105–7, 135, 141, 148
Santmyers, Cdr. S. K., VIII: 413, XII: 428, XIII: 305, XIV: 382
Santo Tomás Prison, XIII: 194–5
Santore, I: 417; pic., 135
Sanuki M., *Sanyo M.*, III: 161, 176, 179, 275, 290*n*
SAPELO, I: 422, X: 65*n*, 67*n*, 69
SARANAC, VIII: 208*n*, 345, 411, XII: 82–4, 423, XIV: 387
Sarangani Bay, XII: 7, 12, 19, XIII: 98, 247–9; chart, 242; landing, 250
SARASOTA, XIII: 310, XIV: 380
SARATOGA, I: xxxvii, lii–liii, II: 31, III: 28–9, 211*n*, 213, 235–6, 241–4, 251–2, 260, 392*n*, IV: 10*n*, 81, 90*n*, 156–7, 182, 270, 280, 285, 293, V: 14, 27–113 *passim*, 210*n*, 291, 347, 352, VI: 106, 292, 324–32, VII: x–xi, xxvii, 91, 95*n*, 101*n*, 116–17, 137, 208, 220–21, 288, 340, 350, VIII: 154*n*, 218, 236*n*–8*n*, X: 37, 51*n*, 134*n*, XI: 279*n*, XII: 125*n*, 182, 243*n*–4*n*, 254*n*, XIII: 4*n*, 180*n*, XIV: 21, 52–6, 389
Sardinia, IX: 6, 9, 44–6, 55–9, 69, 101, 109, 215, 231, 242, 260, 304–5, 308
Sarenski, Machinist T., XIII: 76
SARGENT BAY, XII: 428, XIII: 319, XIV: 374
SARGO, III: 158, IV: 221
Sarmi, VIII: 36, 88, 92–7, 135. *See also* Wakde I.

Sarratt, Cdr. R. C., XI: 341, XIV: 378
Sarsfield, Lt. Cdr. E. S., I: 421, IX: 101, 388
Sasago M., III: 276, 323-4
Sasaki, Capt. A., VIII: 333
Sasaki, Maj. Gen. N., VI: 150, 177-80, 198-206, 222, 225, 242
Sasako M., V: 177
Sasebo, III: 21n
SATA, IV: 88
Satawan I., VIII: 38-40, 156, 174
SATINLEAF, XII: 423, XIII: 308
Sato, Capt. T., V: 297
SATSA, XI: 341
SATSUKI, III: 161, VI: 162, 168, 172, 181
SATTERLEE, XI: 121, 124-9, 143, 147-8, 277, 336, 343
SATURN, I: 422
SAUCY, I: 390n, X: 212, 220
Sauer, Capt. E. P., III: 393, IV: 91, 153n, 271, V: 86
SAUFLEY, V: 335n, VI: 228, 237n, 242, 337, 415, VIII: 410, XII: 367-9, XIII: 275, 310-12, 322
SAUGATUCK, VIII: 345-6, 411, XII: 428, XIII: 319
Saul, Cdr. T. N., XIV: 386
Saum, Motor Machinist I. R., X: 165
Saunders, Chief Quartermaster, V: 110
Saunders, H. St. G., *Royal Air Force*, X: xv
Saunders, Col. L. G., IV: 274; V: 150
Saunders, Capt. L. S., RN, I: 166n
Saunders, Capt. W. V., VIII: 227
SAUNTER, XII: 380, 421, XIII: 306
SAURY, III: 158, 179, 283, 338, IV: 223
Savadkin, Lt. Cdr. Lawrence, XII: 401n
Savage, Radarman, VI: 215
Savage, Lt. Cdr. A. M., XIV: 376
Savage, 1st Lt. F. S., VI: 65
SAVANNAH, I: 57, 83n, 384, 419, II: 36, 117n, 118-19, 122-8, 131-3, 285, II: 31n, 56n, 57, IX: 28, 93, 102-4, 110, 118, 122-4, 125n, 191-2, 197-8, 251, 266-7, 287, 295, 388, 391, XIII: 94n; bombed, IX: 283-4, and pic., 282
Savell, Lt. Cdr. W. L., XIV: 377
Savige, Lt. Gen. R. A. A., XIII: 95
Saville, Brig. Gen. G. P., XI: 233, 281
Savo I., IV: 282; V: 6; pics., IV: 255, V: 19, VI: 434; Battle of, V: 18-64; casualties, 60, 63n; discussion, 61-4; charts, 21, 24, 33-5, 42-3, 59-60; pic., 43

SAVO ISLAND, XII: 244, 310, 420, XIII: 19, 29, 103, 305, 325, XIV: 120, 373
Savoie, II: 248
Sawa, Capt. M., V: 161
Sawar, VIII: 36-7, 92-4, 102
SAWFISH, XII: 429
Sayre, Hon. Francis B., III: 152, 155, 203
SAZANAMI, III: 87, 334, IV: 18, 42n, 172, V: 84, VI: 68, 234-5; sunk, 73, VIII: 19
SCs, X: 32, 35; Caribbean, 202-3; Eniwetok, VII: 288; Sowespac, VIII: 55, 110; Sicily, IX:66, 87; Salerno, 251n; Normandy, XI: 65n, 131-2; Channel Is. patrol, 304; Okinawa, XIV: 143
SC-*449*, *-450*, I: 229-30; *-453*, 147, 229-30, 258n; *-505*, VI: 238; *-521*, 123; *-527*, *-528*, I: 421; *-530*, IX: 86, 194; *-539*, VII: 261, 293, 344; *-630*, XIV: 379; *-637*, VI: 382, VIII: 404; *-648*, 69, 404; *-651*, IX: 372; *-670*, VII: 345; *-688*, *-689*, 421; *-694*, IX: 388, sunk, 194; *-696*, sunk, 194; *-699*, VI: 375-6, 382, VIII: 114, 406; *-703*, VI: 382, VIII: 99-100, 404; *-704*, *-705*, I: 421; *-732*, XIII: 307n; *-734*, VI: 382; *-735*, XIII: 307; *-738*, VI: 382, VIII: 404-6; *-741*, XIII: 307n; *-742*, VI: 375; 382, VIII: 404; *-743*, VI: 376, VIII: 81, 404; *-760*, *-761*, VI: 229; *-770*, IX: 396; *-981*, VI: 382, VIII: 404; *-990*, *-994*, VII: 341; *-997*, 238; *-999*, 344
SC-*1012*, VII: 345; *-1028*, 347; *-1030*, XI: 271; *-1031*, VII: 347; *-1037*, pic., I: 230; *-1049*, XIV: 144; *-1066*, VII: 261, 290-91, 344, XIV: 144; *-1266*, VI: 237n; *-1270*, VII: 341; *-1272*, XIV: 380; *-1299*, X: 205; *-1312*, XIV: 144; *-1316*, *-1317*, VII: 341; *-1321*, XI: 333; *-1326*, VIII: 393; *-1329*, XI: 337
SC (Jap.). *See* Subchasers (Jap.)
SCABBARDFISH, XII: 408, XIV: 292
Scammell, Cdr. W. K., I: 111
SCAMP, VI: 69-73; sunk, XII: 411
Scanland, Capt. F. W., IV: 18, XIII: 285
Scanlon, Brig. Gen. Martin F., IV: 274
Scapa Flow, I: 359, X: 229
SCARAB, XI: 250, 282, 338
Scarborough Bank, XIII: 173
Scarfe, Lt. Cdr. G. O., XI: 339, XIV: 374
Scarpino, Cdr. W. J., VIII: 255n, 415
Schade, Cdr. A. F., XIII: 288

Schadewald, Lt. (jg) M. A., X: 327
Schaefer, Lt. Col. I. O., IX: 133
Schaefer, Lt. Col. William H., IX: 131–32, 140n, 145
Schaeffer, Lt. Heinz, X: 361n
Schaeffer, Commo. V. H., VIII: 412, XII: 415
Schanze, Cdr. E. S., V: 270n
SCHARNHORST, I: 4n, 161n, X: 230–31; sunk, 236–43, and chart, 242
Schatz, Lt. Cdr. O. C., VIII: 405
Schaum, Lt. F. L., pic., X: 328; mentioned, 359
Scheiber, Gen., IX: 173, 183–4
Schelling, Lt. Cdr. R. A., XIV: 383
SCHENCK, I: 335, 420, IX: 92n, 126n, X: 171–6, 376, XIII: 94n
Schetky, Capt. G. C., II: 38
Schiaffino, II: 248
Schieke, Capt. H. E., VIII: 418, XII: 418
Schiff–16, –36, –41, III: 50, 51n; *–45, see* KOMET
Schivley, Cdr. J. C., XII: 377
Schlel, Lt. J. B., XIV: 381
SCHLESIEN, SCHLESWIG-HOLSTEIN, I: 4n
SCHLEY, III: 104, 213n, IV: 276n, VI: 142, 145–6, 156n, VII: 243, 288, 345–7, VIII: 404, XII: 417, XIII: 307
Schlieben, Gen-Lt. Karl von, XI: 196, 211–12
Schlott, Lt. Cdr. A., VIII: 405
Schmalz, Col., IX: 163, 178, 296
Schmidling, Cdr. M. S., XIV: 384
Schmidt, Maj. Gen. Harry, VII: 247–50, 273, 345, VIII:187n, 338, 353–5, 369, 408, XIV: 7, 59, 64, 68–9, 73
Schmidt, Capt. J. W., I: 420; IX: 388, XIV: 379
Schmidt, Cdr. L. E., XII: 419; XIII: 311; XIV: 375
Schminke, Lt. Paul, XIII: 306
Schmitz, Lt. P. J., XIV: 195
Schnaars, Lt. Cdr. H. G., XII: 428, XIII: 318, XIV: 387
Schnable, Lt. A. G., I: 421
Schnechter, Cdr. G. E., XIII: 317, XIV: 382
Schneider, Lt. Cdr. E. C., X: 199
Schneider, Lt. Cdr. F. H., XII: 420, 429, XIII: 319
Schneider, Col. M. F., VIII: 390
Schneider, Col. Max, XI: 128
Schneider, Lt. Cdr. T. F., XIV: 385
Schnor, Sgt. W. A., XIII: 36

Schoeffel, Capt. M. F., VII: 349, 352
Schoeni, Cdr. W. P., VII: 342
Schoettel, Maj. J. F., VII: 159, 165, 171
Schofield, Yeoman R. F., IX: xiv, X: x, XIV: x
Schofield Barracks, III: 124
Schonland, Lt. Cdr. H. E., V: 252–3
Schotel, Lt. Cdr. P., III: 333
Schouten Is., VIII: 103–4
Schrader, Cdr. F. R., XII: 424
Schreder, Lt. R. E., I: 227–8, 248
Schreiber, Cdr. E. T., VII: 334, VIII: 409, XII: 427
Schrier, 1st Lt. H. G., pic., XIV: frontispiece; mentioned, 61
SCHROEDER, VII: 174, 269–71, 338, 344, 405, 418, XII: 417, XIV: 383
Schroeter, Kaptlt. Karl, X: 82
Schuirmann, Rear Adm. R. E., XI: 326
Schulke, Lt. (jg) R. C., VII: 341
Schull, Joseph, *Far Distant Ships*, X: xv
Schulten, Capt. L. B., II: 40, IX: 389, XI: 271, 335
Schultz, Lt. Col. D. E., VI: 175, 222–3
Schumann, Lt. R. W., VII: 348, VIII: 414, XIV: 384
Schumann, Ens. Ross E., IX: 259
SCHUYLKILL, VII: 340, VIII: 411, XII: 423, XIII: 308
Schwable, Lt. Col. F. H., VI: 291
Schwartz, Cdr. A. D., XIV: 381
Schwartz, Lt. Cdr. F. D., VI: 436, VIII: 404
Schweizer, Lt. Cdr. J. R., XIV: 379
Schweppenburg, Gen. Geyr von, XI: 41–2
Sciacca, IX: 18, 50, 58, 181
SCIESA, I: 415
SCIPIO AFRICANO, IX: 169
Scoggins, Capt. Olin, XIV: 378
Scoglitti, IX: 20, 49, 65; chart, 134–5; landing, 28–31, 61, 64–8, 78, 124–47; pic., 130
Scott, Maj. E. W., VI: 64
Scott, Cdr. J. A., VIII: 30, 415
Scott, Lt. Cdr. James, VIII: 224
Scott, Lt. (jg) L. W., X: 382
Scott, Rear Adm. Norman, biog., V: 148n; pic., 146; mentioned, III: 212, IV: 274, V: 29–30, 52, 87, 136; C. Esperance, 146–66, 170–71, 227–37; Guadalcanal Battle, 227–37, 252–3, 258, 300; killed, 243
Scott, Lt. Cdr. Peter, XI: 299

Scott, Sgt. Russell, VI: 351*n*
Scott, Lt. Gen. Winfield, XI: 5
Scott, Hon. Winfield, I: 129*n*
Scott-Moncrieff, Capt. A. K., IX: 394
Scott-Paine, Hubert, II: 262
SCOUT, III: 340, XII: 380, 421, XIII: 207, 306
Scout and Raider Group, IX: 81*n*, 85–7, 130, 152, 258–9
Scouting Force, III: 28–9
Scouting Squadron Two, IV: 19, XIII: 4*n*; Three, IV: 90, 270, V: 86; Four, 375; Five, IV: 19, 90, 271, V: 86, 375; Six, III: 121*n*, 392*n*, IV: 91; Eight, 91, V: 205; Nine, I: 249, 415; Ten, V: 204, 233; Forty-one, II: 39; Fifty-one, VII: 350; Sixty-one, XIII: 312; Sixty-two, X: 370; Sixty-five, Sixty-six, VII: 350; Seventy-one, IV: 271, V: 87, 375; Seventy-two, IV: 271, V: 87
Scrattin, Chief Boatswain J. T., III: 118
Screen, defined, I: 17–18
Scribner, Cdr. C. W., VIII: 411
SCRIBNER, XIV: 220, 375
SCRIMMAGE, XII: 422, XIII: 208, 306
Scruggs, Capt. R. M., VI: 382, 440–41, VIII: 56, 112, 404, XII: 23, 416, XIII: 309
Scuffle, Lt. Cdr. E. A., XIII: 306
SCUFFLE, XIII: 206, 221
Scull, Cdr. Gifford, XII: 427, XIII: 318
Scull, Capt. H. M., VII: 103*n*, 104–6, 341
SCULPIN, III: 158, IV: 226–7, V: 177, VII: 187, 342; sunk, 188–9
SCURRY, XIV: 377
SCYLLA, I: 360, II: 190, IX: 251, 293, 393, XI: 190
SEA DEVIL, XIV: 285, 291
SEA DOG, XIV: 292
SEA FOX, XIII: 319
Sea Frontiers, I: 71*n*, 207
Sea Gypsy, I: 273–4
"Sea Otter" design, I: 290–91
SEA OWL, XIII: 319, XIV: 291
SEA POACHER, XIII: 319
Sea power, tests and value of, I: 5–6, 35, 39, 68; X: 3–11, 361–7
Sea Roamer, I: 274*n*
SEA ROBIN, XIII: 281, 319
Sea Witch, III: 305*n*, 359–60, 363
Seabees (Naval Construction Battalions), organized, I: 300, V: 75–6; New

Zealand, IV: 252; N. Africa, II: 245; Azores, X: 46; Solomons, V: 75–8, 226, 290, VI: 98, 102, 222, 295, 361, 419, 429; Admiralties, 447; Aleutians, VII: 15; Baker Island, 94; Britain, XI: 58; Normandy, 177, 217; Europe, 303, 321–2, 326; Marianas, VIII: 209, 333, 350, 368, 399; Manila Bay, XIII: 206; Iwo Jima, XIV: 68–70, and T.O., 70*n*; Okinawa, 276–7; elsewhere in Pacific, VI: 447, VII: 15, 94, XII: 41, 49–53, 350; Battalions, third, IV: 263*n*; 6th, V: 76; 7th, IV: 252; 8th, XIV: 70*n*; 19th, VI: 387; 23rd, XIV: 70*n*; 24th, VI: 154; 31st, XIV: 70*n*; 33rd, 37th, VI: 415; 40th, 440–42; 47th, 153; 58th, 229, 238; 62nd, 90th, 95th, 106th, 133rd, XIV: 70*n*; 93rd, VI: 415, XII: 350; 113th, XIII: 30; 116th, XII: 28; Maintenance Unit, 629, XI: 322*n*; Detachment, 335
SEADRAGON, III: 158, 172, 304, V: 324, XII: 406, 429
SEAHAM, IX: 42, XI: 333
SEAHORSE, VIII: 17, 241–3, 415
Seakay, X: 318
SEAL, III: 158, 179, 338, VII: 187–8, 192, 207, 222, 342, 351–3
SEAL, HMS, X: 290*n*
SEALION (1939), III: 158, 172
SEALION (1944), XII: 400, 410, XIII: 320
SEARAVEN, III: 158, IV: 220, VII: 187, 222, 286*n*, 330, 342, 351–3, VIII: 155
SEARCHER, X: 40*n*, XI: 342
Searcy, Cdr. S. S., VII: 348, XIV: 385*n*
Searles, Lt. (jg) J. M., V: 174, 319
Searles, Lt. (jg) R. L., V: 174
Searles, Cdr. W. M., XII: 426, XIII: 317, XIV: 383, 385
Sears, Lt. Henry, VIII: 411, XIII: 319, XIV: 373
Sears, Lt. Cdr. Richard D., I: 286*n*
Sears, Ens. W. H., III: 126
Seattle, IV: 170, 174*n*, VII: 5, XIV: 163
Seattle Spirit, I: 171*n*
Seavey, Cdr. Morris, VII: 336, 344, VIII: 404, 408, XII: 419, XIII: 309
Seaward, Lt. Cdr. E. T., IV: 271, V: 87, 151, VI: 144
SEAWOLF, III: 158, 176, 320–21, 337, IV: 220, 223–4, VIII: 415; sunk, XII: 27
Seay, Capt. E. A., XII: 417, XIII: 152, 311, XIV: 380

Seay, Cdr. G. C., I: 421, XIV: 237, 373
SEBEC, XII: 428, XIV: 387
Sebou, R., II: 33, 116–17, 126–32, 246; chart, 114; pics., 130–31
SEDERSTROM, VII: 347, VIII: 410; XIV: 374
Sedgwick, Lt. Cdr. Ellery, XIV: 120
Seeadler Harbor. *See* Admiralties, Manus
Seehausen, Oblt. G., X: 284–6
Seeley, Lt. Cdr. E. B., X: 378
SEER, I: 421, IX: 68, 80, 259, 386, 392, XI: 340
Segi Pt., New Georgia, VI: 139–42, 152–3, 331
Segond Channel, V: 344
SEGUNDO, XIV: 285
SEID, XII: 52
Seidel, Cdr. H. E., XI: 339
Seidisfjordur, I: 359–60
Seidlitz, Lt. Cdr. G. R., XIV: 379
Seifert, Gunner D. R., X: 147
Seikai M., IV: 18
Seitz, Capt. G. A., XIV: 263, 384
Seiyo M., VIII: 231, 295, 417
Seki M. No. 3, IV: 18
Selby, Lt. Cdr. F. G., VIII: 218
Selden, Lt. C. B., VII: 126
Sele R., IX: 254, 267, 278–83, 286–90, 297, 302
Selective Service Act, I: 30
SELFRIDGE, III: 104, 213n, IV: 272, V: 52n, 87, VI: 39, 130, 244–52, VIII: 408, 420, XI: 237; pic., VI: 252
Seligman, Cdr. M. T., IV: 59
SELKIRK, XI: 335
Sellars, Lt. (jg) J. J., X: 285–6
Sellars, Cdr. R. F., IV: 218, XII: 429
Sellers, Adm. David F., II: 20n
SEMINOLE, V: 206; sunk, 196
Semirara I., XII: 311, XIII: 31
Semmes, Cdr. B. J., XII: 419, XIII: 311, XIV: 375
Semmes, Lt. Cdr. J. L., XI: 145, 335
SEMMES, I: 138, 421
Senda, Rear Adm. S., VIII: 107
SENDAI, III: 26, 276, 334, IV: 89, V: 234, 273–7, 281, VI: 220, 306, 310–11, 321–2; sunk, 315–17
SENECA, X: 216
SÉNÉGALAIS, IX: 313n, X: 256–7, 372
Senes, Capit. de V., XI: 340
Senger u. Etterlin, Gen. von, IX: xv, 51–2, 116, 216, 306–7

Senn, Capt. E. M., I: 390n, 419, XI: 334
SENNEN, X: 75
SENNET, XIV: 289, 296
Sentani, Lake, VIII: 60–63, 74–5, 78–81, 84–9, 94–5, 126, XII: 16, XIII: 7; pic., VIII: 88
SENTINEL, I: 421, IX: 85, 386; sunk, 85–6
SENTRY, XII: 422, XIII: 207, 306
Seoul, XIV: 355
Sepinggang, XIII: 268, 274
SEPULGA, VII: 341
SERAPH, II: 186, IX: 128, 389
SERENE, XIV: 377
Seriot, Capit. de Frég., XI: 250
SERPENS, XIV: 9n
SERRANO, XIV: 388
Serrat, Cape, IX: 65
Service Force, development of, I: lvi–lvii; Pacific Fleet, VII: 103–13, VIII: 341–50, XII: 74–80; Seventh Fleet, VIII: 47, XII: 80–85, 423; Service Squadron Two, XII: 80; Four, VII: 106–7, 228, 341; Six, XIV: 109, 160; Seven, I: 422; Eight, VII: 107–8, 340–41, XII: 75n, XIV: 9n; Ten, VII: 106–7, VIII: 343, 346, 350, 420, XII: 75, 80, 304, XIII: 84, XIV: 109; Twelve, VIII: 349–50, XII: 80
Sessions, Lt. Cdr. W. A., X: 318–19
Seton, C. W., VI: 296
Setoyama, Capt. Y., V: 234
Settle, Capt. T. G. W., VII: 347; XII: 419; XIII: 304; XIV: 373
"Seventeen-ninety-nine" (1799) emergency construction program, X: 35
Sever, Lt. Cdr. J. C., VIII: 411, XIV: 386
SEVERN, XII: 84, 423, XIII: 308, XIV: 161, 387
Sfax, II: 242, 259, 278, IX: 61, 65, 152
SHACKLE, XIV: 387
SHAD, II: 37, 119, X: 87, 104
SHADWELL, XIII: 308, 314
Shaefer, Cdr. L. G., XII: 291
Shafer, Lt. Cdr. D. W., I: 420
Shafer, Radioman Richard, IX: 133n
Shaffer, F. E., XIII: 36n
Shafroth, Rear Adm. John F., biog., XIV: 312n; pic., 366; mentioned, III: 265, IV: 250, V: 137n, VII: 229, XIII: 316n, XIV: 312–13, 382
Shafter, Ft., III: 124, 140
SHAH, X: 302
Shahjehan, IX: 40, 156

Shake, Lt. R. R., XIII: 313
SHAKESPEARE, IX: 253, 387, 391
Shambus, R. S., X: 298
SHAMROCK BAY, XIII: 117, 305, 374n, 386
Shands, Lt. Cdr. Courtney, IV: 271, V: 87
Shane, Lt. Cdr. L., III: 158
Shanghai, III: 11, 28–9, 39, 74, 151–2, 187, XIII: 160, 300–301, XIV: 17, 354–5
SHANGRI-LA, XII: x, XIV: 299, 386
Shank, Dr. L. S., III: 231n
Shannon, Lt. Col. H. D., IV: 85–6, 93–5
SHANNON, XIV: 252, 377
Shapley, Lt. Col. Allen, VIII: 390
SHARK (1936), III: 158, 198, 277; sunk, 304, VIII: 22n
SHARK (1944), VIII: 22–3, 168, XII: 429; sunk, 406
Sharkey, Chaplain Jack, VI: 189n
Sharp, Rear Adm. Alexander, I: 76, 419, XIV: 26, 113, 117n, 131, 376
Sharp, Lt. D. C., XIV: 377
Sharp, Cdr. G. A., I: 421, XII: 64
Sharp, Capt. L. D., XIV: 375
Sharp, Cdr. U. S. G., II: 39, VII: 339, VIII: 413, XII: 425
Sharpe, Ens. K. B., XII: 422
SHASTA, VII: 47, 112, VIII: 346, XII: 429, XIV: 8, 165–7, 386
Shattuck, Lt. Cdr. C. W., XIII: 317
Shaw, Cdr. H. H., VIII: 403
Shaw, H. I., *Okinawa*, XIV: 170n
Shaw, Capt. H. R., V: 292, VI: 297, XII: 416
Shaw, Rear Adm. James C., IV: x, V: ix-x, 225n, 304, VI: xi, 212n, 331–6, 410n, XIV: x; account of carrier ops., VII: xxvii–xxxix
Shaw, Col. James F., pic., XIV: 54
SHAW (1917), VI: 211n, VII: 17n
SHAW (1936), III: 118–19, IV: 276, V: 205, 215, 226, 232, 236, VI: 375, 381, 385–6, VIII: 211, 408, 420, XII: 54, 373–4, XIII: 116, 309; pic., III: 116
Shea, Lt. E. C., VIII: 408
Shea, Cdr. M. W., XII: 429
Shea, Cdr. W. H., VIII: 408, XII: 428, XIII: 305, XIV: 373
SHEA, XIV: 116, 248, 255, 376, 391
Sheela, Ens. B. C., X: 161
SHEFFIELD, I: 366, II: 190, 220, X: 237–41
Shelby, Lt. Cdr. E. E., I: 421, VII: 351–3, VIII: 155
Sheldon, Lt. Col. F. H., VII: 347

SHELDRAKE, VIII: 419, XIV: 114n, 376
SHELIAK, XIV: 378
SHELIKOF, XIV: 381
Shellabarger, Cdr. M. A., VIII: 408, XII: 428, XIV: 386
SHELTER, XIV: 377
SHELTON, XII: 27
Shemya, Aleutians, VII: 15n, 52
Shepard, Capt. A. G., VI: 308, VIII: 409
Shepard, Cdr. E. T., XIII: 319
Shepard, Lt. Cdr. L. M., XIV: 374
Shepard, Lt. Cdr. Richard D., VI: 244
Shepherd, Cdr. A. L., XIII: 304, XIV: 373
Shepherd, Maj. Gen. Lemuel C., VIII: 390–92, 395–6, 419, XIV: 378
SHEPPEY, IX: 396
Sherertz, Lt. H. J., XI: 299
Sheridan, Lt. Cdr. J. G., XIV: 383
SHERIDAN, VII: 170, 337, 346, VIII: 407, 420, XII: 419, XIII: 310, XIV: 380
Sherki battery, II: 73–5, 111–12; chart, 76
Sherman, Adm. Forrest P., biog., XIII: 4n; pic., 292; mentioned, I: 43n, 44, IV: 271, V: 58, 87, 131–6, VI: xii, 7, 10, 11n, VII: viii, 203, 206, VIII: 9, XI: 8, XII: 11, 57, 354, 376, XIII: 4, 8, 87, 165–6, 175, 180, XIV: 7, 256, 359, 366
Sherman, Rear Adm. Frederick C., biog., XIII: 180n; pic., VI: 389; C.O. *Lexington*, III: 210, 388, IV: 14, 19, 52–4, 57–9, 64; Solomons, V: 291, 352, 359, VI: 106, 292; Rabaul and Kavieng, 324–5, 411–12, VII: 117; Nauru, 136; Gilberts, 144, 339; Marshalls, 208, 218–21, 286–7, 349; Truk, 353; Marianas, VIII: 154; Philippine Sea, 238; Formosa Battle, XII: 12, 86, 90, 93, 103; Luzon strikes, 106, XIII: 54, 317; Leyte, XII: 108, 133, 150, 339–56 *passim*, 426; Leyte Gulf Battle, 175–82, 192–5, 291, 318–21, 325–7; Formosa and East China Sea, XIII: 91, 165–8, 180; Iwo Jima, XIV: 21, 34, 44, 52; Okinawa, XIII: 88–90, XIV: 199, 383, 386
Sherman, Col. H. B., IX: 75, 82, 174
Sherman, Lt. Cdr. P. K., VI: 331, VII: 340
Sherrod, Robert, V: 197n, VII: x, 50n, 52n, 93n, 171–3, XIII: xi, 184n, XIV:

47–8, 73–5; *Tarawa*, VII: 146*n*; *Marine Corps Aviation*, XIV: 215*n*
Sherwood, Cdr. G. B.., IV: 173, VII: 49, 334
Sherwood, Lt. (jg) H. B., XI: 71
Sherwood, Lt. Cdr. R. E., RN, X: 70–71, 74–5
Shevlin, Lt. W. A., X: 69
Shiba, Capt. K., XIV: 363*n*
Shibasaki, Rear Adm. K., VII: 148, 169
Shichisei M., VI: 63
Shifley, Cdr. R. L., VIII: 300, 413, XII: 425
Shigematsu, Maj. Gen. K., VIII: 373, 388
Shigemitsu, Hon. Mamotu, VI: 23*n*, VIII: 340, XIV: 343, 346, 359, 363, 366; pic., 366–7
Shigenaga, Rear Adm. K., XII: 431
Shigeyoshi, Vice Adm., VII: 74, XII: 164
SHIGURE, IV: 17, V: 214–20, 234–6, 238*n*, VI: 214–20, 234–6, 244–8, 306, 341, VIII: 118, 125, 130, 416; Surigao Str. Battle, XII: 190–91, 207–39 *passim*, 298, 431, XIII: 158, 281
SHIKELLAMY, XIII: 308
SHIKINAMI, III: 276, IV: 89, V: 85, 234, 274–6, 281, VI: 56, 62, VIII: 118, 125–6, 130–31; sunk, VI: 64*n*, XII: 400
Shima, Vice Adm. K., IV: 16–17, 22, 26, 61, XII: 103–4, 160–64, 167–8, 190, 207*n*, 210–348 *passim*, 431, XIII: 37, 159; pic., XII: 71
Shimada, Adm. S., III: 71, VI: 17, 20, 403, VIII: 214; pic., III: 13
Shimai, Capt. Y., VI: 181, 187–8
SHIMAKAZE, V: 85*n*, VIII: 131, 416, XII: 431; sunk, 353
Shimazaki, Rear Adm. T., XII: 431
Shimizu, Col., VIII: 136, 139–40
Shimizu, Vice Adm. M., III: 26, IV: 196
SHIMOTSUKI, VIII: 416, XII: 430; sunk, 411
Shimushu, Kuriles, VII: 39–40
SHIMUSHU, III: 276
Shinai M., VI: 56
SHINANO, XII: 161*n*, 411
Shinanogawa M., V: 269*n*
Shindler, Cdr. W. G., IV: 153*n*
Shinjiku M., VIII: 240
Shinkoku M., IV: 88
Shinoda, Rear Adm. T., XII: 431

Shinsho M., IV: 207
Shintani, Capt. K., XIV: 202
Shinyo M., XII: 401
SHIOKAZE, III: 163, IV: 172
Shionomisaki, XIV: 331
Ship Lane Patrol, I: 267–8; pic., 280
Shipbuilding, I: 205
SHIPLEY BAY, XII: 428, XIII: 319
SHIPPIGAN, XI: 333
Shipping Control System, XIV: 162
Ship-to-shore assault, described, II: 270–71
Shiraishi, Vice Adm. K., IV: 88, XII: 257, 308, 431
Shiraishi, Capt. N., XII: 431
SHIRAKUMO, III: 276, IV: 89, V: 109; sunk, VIII: 19
SHIRANUHI, III: 87–8, IV: 89, 216, V: 370, VII: 7, XII: 190, 239, 431; sunk, 312
SHIRATSUYU, IV: 17, V: 194–6, 207, 234, 238*n*, VI: 306, 312, 315–17, 341, VIII: 125–6, 130, 416; sunk, 231
SHIRAYUKI, III: 276, IV: 89, V: 151, 234, VI: 55–6; sunk, V: 169
Shoate, Lt. A. O., XII: 422
Shock, Capt. T. M., III: 261, IV: 18, 28, VI: 100–102
Shoei M., IV: 225, VII: 53, VIII: 22
Shoemaker, Capt. Harry E., I: 208
Shoemaker, Capt. J. M., XII: 94, 427
SHO-GO alert, XII: 91, 119, 167–9. *See also* Leyte Gulf, Battle for
SHO-GO plans, XII: 70
SHOHO, IV: 11–13, 18, 32, 40–42, 61–3, V: 82; sunk, IV: 42; pic., 52
Shoka M., IV: 206
SHOKAKU, III: 27, 83, 87–8, 334, 382, IV: 11, 17, 43, 48–52, 61–3, 202*n*, 276, V: 82, 85, 88–91, 206, 209, 213–15, 220, VI: 286, 332, VIII: 217–18, 249, 264, 271, 285, 307, 320, 416; sunk, 17*n*, 280–81; pic., IV: 53
Shomier, Cdr. J. E., VIII: 410, XIII: 307
SHONAN, XIII: 283
Shonan M., IV: 203; *No. 15*, VII: 328
Shook, Cdr. K. S., VIII: 419, XIII: 317, XIV: 383
Shore Fire Control Parties (sfcp), II: 30, IX: xi; Marianas, VIII: 197–8, 203, 206, 359, 393; Sicily, IX: 103, 119, 122–5, 142, 199; Salerno, 266–8, 276–7, 282, 290, 296; Anzio, 342–4, 351; Normandy, 105–6, 126, 143–6, 157–61, 167–8, 202–10; S. France, 241, 254, 272, 276;

Shore Fire Control Parties (*cont'd*)
Med., 313; Iwo Jima, XIV: 35, 41, 48;
Okinawa, 152
Shore Parties, II: 28–9, VIII: 53; School
for, II: 160; Vella Lavella, VI: 238;
Hollandia, VIII: 84; Sicily, IX: 107,
111, 119, 139, 222; Salerno, 276
Short, Capt. E. T., XIII: 311–12, XIV:
380
Short, Capt. Giles E., X: 77, 110–14,
375, XIV: 385; pic., X: 129
Short, Seaman L. V., III: 111
Short, Lt. Wallace C., IV: 19, 90, 136
Short, Lt. Gen. Walter C., III: 128, 133–
4, 140–42
Shortland Is., IV: 29, V: 4, 26*n*, 109, 139,
238, 259, 266, 282, 286, 307, VI: 99,
142, 207–8, 221, 240, 280, 283, 427
Short-of-war policy, I: 28–55
SHOSHONE, XIV: 381
Shoup, Col. David M., pic., VII: 167;
mentioned, 159, 164–7, 171–3
Shoup, Cdr. F. E., V: 56–7
Showa M. Nos. 7 and 8, IV: 89
Showa Restoration, III: 10–12, 17, 38,
44–5
Showers, Capt. H. A., IV: 272, XII:
421
Shoyu M., VI: 83
SHROPSHIRE, VI: 382–4, 444, VIII: 47, 73,
97, 126, 405, XII: 131, 199, 223, 227,
343–4, 421, XIII: 138, 201, 269, 275, 304
SHUBRICK (1919), XI: 119*n*
SHUBRICK (1943), IX: 97, 100, 103, 110,
113, 193, 388, XI: 95, 105, 214, 334, 342,
XIV: 261–2, 392
Shultz, Capt. J. H., XII: 418, XIII: 310
Shumaker, 1st Lt. G. L., IX: 264*n*
Shumaker, Capt. S. R., VII: 337
Shumway, Lt. Cdr. D. W., IV: 270,
V: 86, 89–90
Shupper, Lt. Cdr. B. H., XII: 419,
XIII: 319
Shuri, Okinawa, XIV: 83, 171, 240–43,
275
Shute, Cdr. C. C., VII: 346, 404
Siam Gulf, XIII: 286–8
Sibert, Maj. Gen. Franklin C.,
VIII: 142–3, XII: 56, 114, 130, 141, 362,
415, XIII: 217, 241–3, 246, 249, 324
SIBLEY, XIV: 381
Sibutu Passage, VIII: 217–18
Sibuyan Sea, XII: 339, 348; Battle of,
176, 183–9; pic., 190

SICARD, III: 104, 213*n,* VI: 297, 308, VII:
41, 335
Sicily, IX: 6, 9–13, 44, 47–52, 55–61, 383;
general map, 24–5; invasion of, planning, 10–30; training and rehearsal, 32;
approach, 61–70; chart, 62–3; motor
torpedo boats, 78–9; covering forces,
167–9; minesweeping, 174–5; landings,
71–169, and charts, 38–9, 73, 76–7, 96,
153, and pic., 82; Axis air raids, 81, 85–
6, 89, 100–204 *passim;* air and naval
gunfire support, 82–3, 87–90, 96–7,
100, 103–4, 110–19, 130–31, 136, 146,
156–7, 165–7, 174–6, 179, 191–2, 196–
9, 203–4, 207, 222; operations ashore,
119–25, 143–7, 170–209, and charts,
176–7, 196; unloading, 138–42; discussion, 169, 218–24; Axis evacuation,
200–201, 209–18, and chart, 209–18;
ammo. expended, 222*n;* casualties,
223; T.O., 385–90
Sickel, Capt. H. G., II: 168, 246
Sides, Capt. J. H., XIV: 376, 385
SIDI-FERRUCH, II: 110*n,* 168
SIDMOUTH, XI: 200, 337
Sidney Edgarton, XIII: 313
Siebel ferries, IX: 210–14, 305
Sieglaff, Lt. Cdr. W. B., VI: 76
SIERRA, XIV: 387
Sigel, Cdr. C. H., VII: 340–41
Sigel, Chief Torpedoman J. F., VI: 237*n*
Sigiura, Capt. K., XII: 430
SIGMA, XI: 337
SIGNET, XIV: 376
SIGOURNEY, VI: 297, 337, 351, 415, 429,
VIII: 410, XII: 199, 237, 370, 416,
XIII: 244, 311–12, 322–7
SIGSBEE, VII: 174, 255–6, 260, 267, 337,
344, VIII: 405, 419, XII: 417, XIV:
247, 383, 391
Silber, Lt. Cdr. S. L., VI: 331, VII: 339,
349
Sillers, Lt. (jg) C. B., XII: 290
SILVER CLOUD, XIII: 308
Silver Sword, I: 191*n,* 365
SILVERBELL, XII: 423, XIII: 308
SILVERSIDES, IV: 204, 227–8, VI: 70,
VIII: 22–3, XII: 407, 429, XIII: 319
Sima, Cdr. F. F., VII: 337, 345,
XIV: 193
Simard, Cdr. Cyril T., IV: 72, 85–7, 92–
5, 98, 105, 110, 137*n,* 145, 149*n,* 150
Simeon G. Reed, XIII: 48
Simms, Lt. (jg) R. L., XIV: 204, 208

Simon Bolivar, XIII: 313
Simonds, Maj. Gen. G. G., IX: 27*n*, 150
Simons, Capt. R. B., III: 114
SIMOUN, II: 108, X: 157, XI: 343
Simpler, Lt. Cdr. L. C., IV: 270, V: 86
Simpson, Dr. Albert F., II: 275*n*, III: xiii, VII: 158*n*, IX: xvi, 59*n*, 223*n*, XI: xi
Simpson, Cdr. H. S., XIII: 285
Simpson, Capt. R. S., VI: 420, 427
Simpson, Commo. Rodger W., V: 205; VI: 214–15, 218–22, 325, 364, 420, 427, XIV: 358, 361
Simpson, Lt. Gen. William H., XI: 321–3
SIMPSON, I: 15*n*, 90, 418, 421, XIV: 26*n*
Simpson Harbor, VI: 326–8, 392, 398, 407
Sims, Col. A. L., V: 140
Sims, Lt. (jg) C. A., VIII: 274
Sims, Capt. Gelzer L., IV: 91, 271, V: 86, 205, 297, VI: 182, 214, XIII: 303
Sims, Maj. Mitchell E., VI: 64
Sims, Lt. W. E., VIII: 404
Sims, Rear Adm. W. S., mentioned, I: 38; quoted, X: vii
SIMS (1939), IV: 19, 30*n*, 33, 63; sunk, 34
SIMS (1943), XIV: 271, 377, 381
Sinclair, Lt. Cdr. G. A., IV: 272, V: 29, 38
Sinclair, Lt. (jg) T. L., IX: 309*n*
Sinclair, Capt. V. R., XII: 419, XIII: 311, XIV: 380
Singapore, I: 41, 109–12, 167, III: 29, 49–51, 54, 57, 61, 152, 157, 187, 281, 297, 307, 311, 330, VII: 81, X: 278, 304*n*, XII: 163, 335, XIII: 157–9, 164, 168, 257, 265, 284; Conference, III: 53–5, 282
Singer, Cdr. W. T., VII: 138, 341
Singleton, Lt. Cdr. Charles T., IV: 174
Sintic, Lt. Cdr. A. J., XIV: 381
Sio, VI: 267, 389–91
SIOUX, VI: 297, 303, 321, 346, 415, XII: 429, XIII: 319, XIV: 160, 169
Sippin, Lt. Victor, XI: 287*n*
Sippola, Lt. (jg) J. C., X: 312–13
SIREN, I: 390*n*
SIRIUS, II: 189, IX: 167, XI: 339
Sitka, III: 32, IV: 174
SITKOH BAY, XII: 428, XIV: 374
Sizaire, Capit. de V., II: ix

'S Jacob, VI: 127*n*
Skahill, Cdr. B. J., XI: 337
SKATE, VI: 411, VII: 93–4, 319, 353, XIV: 292
SKEENA, I: 321
Skewes, Lt. Cdr. T. J., XIII: 319
SKILL, I: 421, IX: 174, 389, 392
Skinner, Lt. C. A., XII: 427
Skip bombing, VI: 57–60
SKIPJACK, III: 158, IV: 221, VII: 222, 351, VIII: 19, 155
SKIRMISH, XIV: 376
Skorcz, Lt. Cdr. J. C., XIII: 312
Skovfjord, I: 331–3
SKYE, XI: 336
SKYLARK, VIII: 418–19, XIV: 114*n*, 376, 390; sunk, 134
Slapton Sands, XI: 64, 67; pic., 68
Slaughter, Lt. Cdr. J. S., XII: 420, 429, XIII: 316, 319
Slawson, Cdr. P. S., VI: 145
Slayton, Cdr. Morgan, VII: 350, VIII: 405, XII: 418, XIV: 384
SLAZAK, IX: 393
Slessor, Air Chief Marshal Sir John, I: 45, IX: 213*n*, X: 17–18, 27*n*, 29–31, 86–106 *passim*, XI: 229
Sliney, Lt. Cdr. J. G., VII: 339, 349
Sloat, Cdr. F. T., VII: 338, 348
SLOAT (1920), XIV: 88*n*
SLOAT (1943), X: 378
Slocum, Capt. H. B., VIII: 409, XII: 419, XIII: 304, XIV: 372
"Slot," the Solomons', V: 4
Small, Rear Adm. Ernest G., IV: 271, V: 87, 150, 164, VII: 339, 350, VIII: 29
Small, Cdr. S. E., XIV: 386
Smart, Lt. (jg) C. A., XIV: 231*n*
SMARTT, X: 381
Smedberg, Lt. Cdr. William R., I: 154
Smeeton, Cdr. R. M., VIII: 301*n*
Smiley, Cdr. C. B., XI: 339
Smiley, Capt. C. S., III: 264, XII: 428, XIII: 319, XIV: 374
Smith, Lt. Cdr. A., I: 419
Smith, Lt. Cdr. A. W., XII: 421, XIII: 305
Smith, Rear Adm. Allan E., IV: xi, V: xi, VII: 338, 349, XII: 87, 113*n*, 425, XIV: 11–12, 129, 267*n*, 373
Smith, Ens. Allan E., XII: 77*n*
Smith, Lt. Cdr. B. H., XIV: 376
Smith, Lt. Cdr. C. C., III: 158, 304

Smith, Lt. (jg) C. D., VIII: 300*n*
Smith, Lt. Cdr. C. E., V: 348*n*
Smith, Cdr. C. H., VIII: 411, XIII: 317, XIV: 374
Smith, Lt. C. O., XII: 417, 423
Smith, Lt. Cdr. C. P., XIV: 374
Smith, Cdr. C. W., XII: 429
Smith, Lt. Cdr. D. E., III: 159
Smith, Cdr. D. F., XII: 427, XIII: 316
Smith, 1st Lt. Donald G., III: 392
Smith, Lt. Cdr. E. G., XII: 309, 314
Smith, Lt. E. R., VII: 107*n*
Smith, Rear Adm. Edward H. ("Iceberg"), I: 60–62
Smith, Cdr. F. T., XIII: 285
Smith, Lt. Cdr. H. I., X: 376
Smith, Lt. H. L., XIV: 223
Smith, Capt. H. P., III: 160, XII: 425
Smith, Rear Adm. Harold T., VII: 103*n*
Smith, Lt. Cdr. Harry, VII: 336
Smith, Lt. Cdr. Herschel A., V: 98
Smith, Lt. Gen. Holland M., pics., VII: 278, XIV: 46; Amphibious Force, Atlantic, I: liv, 67, 421, II: 21; Kiska, VII: 62; Makin raid, 77; Gilberts, 84–9, 132–3, 167, 183*n*; Marshalls, 206–7, 243, 257, 281, 343; Marianas, VIII: 159, 170, 186, 202, 206, 209, 324, 330–400 *passim*, 407; Iwo Jima, XIV: 7, 17, 48, 61, 64, 70, 73; *Coral and Brass*, VIII: 186*n*
Smith, Ens. I. H., X: 68
Smith, Lt. (jg) J. G., IV: 48–9
Smith, Cdr. J. MacDonald, VI: 145, 228, 294*n*
Smith, Cdr. J. T., XIII: 317, XIV: 384
Smith, Cdr. J. V., XIV: 383
Smith, Maj. John L., V: 74, 374
Smith, Maj. Gen. Julian C., biog., VII: 152*n*; pic., 167; mentioned, VII: ix, 89, 116, 146*n*, 152, 164–7, 171–4, 184–6, 337, XII: 34
Smith, Lt. Cdr. L. A., XII: 424
Smith, Lt. Cdr. L. J., RNR., IX: 234
Smith, Maj. Leo R., V: 374
Smith, Capt. R. McL., II: 38, 169
Smith, Capt. R. W., VIII: 404, XII: 417, XIII: 317, XIV: 384
Smith, Maj. Gen. Ralph C., VII: 90, 123, 133–6, VIII: 160, 171, 203, 330–33, 410
Smith, Capt. Robert H., IV: 272, XII: 369–70, XIII: 21, 310–12, 322
Smith, Robert R., *Approach to the Philippines*, VIII: 45*n*; *Triumph in the Philippines*, XIII: x
Smith, Cdr. T. A., VIII: 406
Smith, Chief Machinist W. A., V: 100
Smith, Lt. (jg) W. F., X: 219
Smith, Cdr. W. O. ("Wingover"), VIII: 303*n*
Smith, Maj. Gen. Walter Bedell, IX: xvi, 66*n*, 238–9, 324*n*, 327–8, X: 356*n*, XI: xi, 23, 27, 55, 69, 74–5, 82*n*, 178*n*, 231, 318
Smith, Capt. Walton W., XIV: 384
Smith, Vice Adm. William W., IV: 18, 27–8, 90, 135, VII: 4, 10–12, 17, XII: 74, XIV: 168
SMITH (1909), VII: 232*n*
SMITH (1936), V: 205, 217, VI: 260–62, 267, 272–3, 281–2, 390, 436, 443, XII: 344, 383–5, 389–92, 417, XIII: 274, 303, 322–3
SMITH THOMPSON, XII: 21*n*
Smoke, artificial, convoys, X: 267, 272–3; Leyte, XII: 147–8; Samar, 255; Lingayen, XIII: 137; Okinawa, XIV: 175
Smoot, Rear Adm. Roland N., pic., XII: 215; mentioned, III: 393, IV: 91, 274, V: 86, XII: 78, 79*n*, 199, 202, 221–3, 228, 234–5, 387, 419, XIII: 107, 304, XIV: 110, 185, 373
Smuts, Field Marshal J. C., IX: 362–3, XI: 229
Smyth, Col. G. W., XI: 213
Smyth, Lt. Cdr. J. B., XII: 428, XIII: 318, XIV: 387
Smythe, Cdr. L. W., XIV: 382
Snackenberg, Capt. J. A., XII: 418
Snafu, Camp, I: 77; pic., 92
SNAPPER, III: 158
Sneddon, Lt. (jg) J. B., XIV: 144
Snell, E. M., *Strategic Planning*, XI: xii
Snider, Lt. Cdr. L. L., VIII: 408
Snipes, Lt. R. F., XII: 420
SNOOK, XII: 406, 429
Snorkel, I: 317, 402, X: 317–18, 329, 338
Snow, Chief Watertender R. H., III: 143
SNOWBELL, XIV: 377
SNOWBERRY, I: 349
Snowden, Cdr. Ernest M., pic., VII: 198; mentioned, IV: 271, V: 87, VII: 338, VIII: 285, 414
SNOWDEN, X: 283–4, 320, 378
SNOWFLAKE, X: 68–9, 75
Snyder, Adm. Charles P., I: 236
Snyder, Lt. Peter M., XIII: 61*n*

Snyder, Lt. Cdr. W. H., XIV: 384
Soballe, Lt. Cdr. V. J., XIII: 318, XIV: 112, 249, 385
SOBIESKI, II: 195n, IX: 393, 396
SOEMBA, IX: 156, 396, XI: 105, 334
SOLACE, IV: 263n, VII: 341, VIII: 200, 389, 411, XIV: 110, 386
Sole, Monte, IX: 75, 83-6; pic., 82
Solent, the, XI: 67, 77, 182, 188
Solomon Is., history and description, V: 3-11; charts, IV: 9, VI: 91; air battles, Apr.-June 43, 139-40. See also Guadalcanal
Solomons, Cdr. E. A., VII: 337, VIII: 405, XII: 417
SOLOMONS, X: 295, 372, 380
Solomons I., Md., II: 22-3, 28, 271, IX: 128
Solon Turman, XIII: 307
SOMALI, I: 365, XI: 343
SOMERS, I: 83-4, 377, 383-4, 390n, 420, X: 213n, 215, 227, XI: 162, 252, 338
SOMERSETSHIRE, IX: 300, 394
Somervell, Lt. Gen. B. B., pic., VI: 18; mentioned, VII: 101, 112, IX: 7, XI: 54
Somerville, Adm. Sir James, III: 382-3, IV: 277, VIII: 154n, XII: 61
Sommer, Lt. Cdr. H. A., VIII: 406
Sommer, Kaptlt. Helmut, X: 321
Sonar, I: 212-19, X: 52
SONOMA, VI: 262, 270, 382, VIII: 114, 404, XII: 416; sunk, 148
Soprano, Monte, IX: 255-9
Sorenson, Cdr. T. C., IX: 388, XI: 340
Sorido, VIII: 104, 108, 133
Sorol Atoll, VIII: 367
Sorong, VIII: 37, 86, 89-90, 107, 117, 120-22, 125, 130, 141, 143, 219
Sorrento Peninsula, IX: 253, 271, 285, 302; pic., 266
Sorsogon Bay, III: 159, 177
SORYU, III: 27, 87-8, 217, 245, 276, 296, 334, 378, 382, IV: xi, 88, 116, 123-7; sunk, 127-9; pic., 127
Soter Ortynsky, XIII: 324
Sottane, Monte, IX: 255, 270
SOUBARISSEN, XIV: 161
Soule, Lt. Cdr. R. A., IX: 396, XI: 343
Sound Schools, I: 214-16
Sousa, Capt. B. H., IX: 376
Sousse, II: 242, 259, 264, 278, IX: 65, 151-2
South, Lt. Cdr. W. W., X: 351, 376

South Atlantic Force, I: 377, 390, X: 40; pic., I: 388
South Atlantic Patrol, I: 83
SOUTH CAROLINA, III: 255n, X: 197n, XI: 237n
South China Patrol, III: 28
South China Sea, III: 292, XII: 5, XIII: 58, 88, 111, 116, 161-74, 284-8; raid, 87, 157-8, 161, 164-74; chart, 166
SOUTH DAKOTA, I: 419, V: 80, 200, 204, 210, 215-18, 223-4, 233, 261, 271, 274-86, 352, VII: 85, 220, 338, 349, 353, VIII: 40, 269-70, 282n, 415, X: 230, XII: 90, 318, 427, XIII: 54, 188n, 316, 318, XIV: 21, 242, 312n, 313, 361, 384, 386; pics., V: 195, 218
South Greenland Survey, I: 60-61
South Pacific Area, IV: 250, VIII: 161
South Pacific Force, IV: 254, 270-74 V: 12, VI: 15, 89, 97, VIII: 86
SOUTHAMPTON, XIV: 381
SOUTHARD, IV: 274, V: 34-5, 180, 227, 235-6, VI: 297, XII: 422, XIII: 109, 306, 325
Southeast Pacific Area and Force, III: 265, IV: 250
Southerland, Cdr. J. J., XIV: 383, 385
Southern France Opn., planning and training, XI: 28-9, 221-2; loading and approach, 246-7, and chart, 245, and pic., 245; minesweeping, 255-6, 270-73; landings, 248-54, 258-74, and charts, 260-61, 283, and pics., 244-5, 268-9, 284, 292-3; air and naval gunfire support, 243-6, 257-9, 265-71, 276-9, 282, 285-9; unloading, 263-4, 275-6; opns ashore, 281-91; discussion, 291-2; T.O., 338-43
Southern Negros landing, XIII: 217, 237-8
Southland, I: 323
Southwest Pacific Area, IV: 249, V: 12, VIII: 45-8
Southwest Pacific Force, VI: 13-15, 130, VIII: 47-54; Amphibious Training Base, VI: 131, XIII: 189n
Southwick, Fireman D. F., X: 164
Southwick House, XI: 65, 79-81; pic., 80
Southworth, Capt. H. B., XIII: 307, XIV: 378
Sowell, Rear Adm. I. C., XIII: 133, 303, XIV: 373
Sowell, Lt. Cdr. J. C., I: 420, X: 269-71, 362, 381

Spaatz, Lt. Gen. Carl A., II: 277, IX: 16, 21, 120n, XI: 14, 35–8, 69
SPADEFISH,　XII: 399–400,　409–10, XIV: 289, 292n
Spahr, Lt. Cdr. O. W., IX: 385
Spain, II: 187–8, IX: 38; Spanish Morocco, 13
Spalding, Cdr. R. C., XIV: 387
Spanagel, Capt. H. A., VI: 382
SPANGLER, VIII: 227–8
SPANKER, XI: 341
SPARK, XIII: 286
Sparrow, Chief Photographer W. H., XII: 284n
SPARTAN, IX: 345, 358, 396; sunk, 355
Spatz, Sgt. H. A., III: 397
Spaulding, Capt. P. P., XIV: 378
Spaulding, Cdr. R. C., XII: 428, XIII: 319
SPEAR, XIV: 376
SPEARFISH,　III: 158,　206,　IV: 220, VII: 187, 207, 342, VIII: 23, XIII: 319, XIV: 18, 295
"Specific Operations for Defeat of Japan," VIII: 7–8
Speck, Cdr. R. H., VIII: 410, XII: 427, XIII: 318
SPECTACLE, XIV: 271, 377, 392
SPECTOR, XIV: 377
SPEED, I: 421, IX: 174, 389, 392, XI: 342
Spellman, Capt. F. T., VII: 339, 350
SPENCE, VI: 241, 308, 315–18, 322, 345, 357–8, 420, VIII: 415, XIII: 61–3, 80–82, 85, 316; sunk, 77–9
Spencer, Capt. D. A., XII: 424, XIV: 373
Spencer, Capt. Lyndon, XI: 333–4
Spencer, Lt. Cdr. Samuel, XII: 421, XIII: 311, XIV: 268, 375
SPENCER, I: 228, 322, 337–8, 341–6, 415, 421, X: 158, XIII: 246, 268, 321; pics., I: 344–5, XIII: 244
SPEY, II: 195, 209–12, 215, X: 75n
Spezia, IX: 39, 59, 242
SPICEWOOD, XIV: 377
Spielman, Lt. J. S., XI: 306
Spies and saboteurs, I: 128–9, 200, 282n, X: 326, 327n, 330, 344
Spigel, Capt. C. E. A., XIV: 380
SPIKEFISH, XIV: 294
SPIKENARD, I: 128
Spink, Ens. George, X: 382
Spithead, XI: 67, 77, 182
Spitkit Convoys, II: 176, 246, 271–4
Spitsbergen, I: 360, X: 230–31

Spooner, Maj. J. R., VIII: 398n, 400
SPOT, XIII: 319, XIV: 287–90
Sprague, Capt. A. T., VII: 334, XIII: 217, 233–6, 323
Sprague, Rear Adm. Clifton A. F., biog., XII: ix–x; pic., frontispiece; mentioned, VIII: 413, XII: 27; Battle off Samar, 243–330 *passim*, 421; quoted, 280, 297, XIV: 132, 373
Sprague, Ens. J. F., X: 123
Sprague, Rear Adm. Thomas L., biog., XII: 125n; pic., 246; mentioned, I: 419, VII: 349, 352, VIII: 420, XII: 22, 26, 121, 125–7, 237–9, 242–5, 251, 293, 300, 306, 312–14, 420, XIV: 310
Spratly Is., III: 38
Spring, Cdr. F. H., XIV: 381
Springer, Lt. Cdr. F. H., XII: 402
SPRINGFIELD, XIV: 313, 384, 386
SPROSTON, XII: 304, 419, XIII: 188, 311, XIV: 375
Sprow, Cdr. M. W., VIII: 404
Spruance, Adm. R. A., biog., IV: 82n; pic. 84, VIII: frontispiece; assistance, III: xii, IV: xi, V: xi, VII: ix, XIV: x; Com Ten, I: 32n; early opns., III: 211, 261–3, 392; relieves Halsey, IV: 82, XIII: 183, XIV: 20; Midway, IV: 84–5, 90, 94–8, 103, 112–16, 121–2, 130, 134–6, 141–3, 148–52, 157–8, 184, VIII: 254, 314–15; Chief of Staff to Nimitz, IV: 257, VI: 7; Com Fifth Fleet, VII: 86, VIII: 161, XII: 12; Gilberts, VII: 91, 99, 116, 119, 141, 336; Marshalls, 203, 206–7, 218, 227, 285, 343; Truk raid, 289, 320, 328, 352; Palau, Yap, Woleai raids, VIII: 28, 31; Marianas, 131, 158, 177, 202, 324, 332, 338, 345, 355, 371, 376–7, 381–2, 395, 400, 407; Bat. of Philippine Sea, 232–6, 240–45, 250–60, 264, 282–5, 290n, 301–2, 305–11; discussion, 313–19, 324, 412, XII: 3, 58–9; strategic plans, 17, XIII: 4–5, XIV: 4; logistics, XII: 76; Iwo Jima, XIV: 7, 73, 178; Japan strikes, 21, 55, 97; Okinawa, 87–8, 101, 138, 154, 162, 198, 203, 208, 217, 372, 384; and Royal Navy, 103–6, 214, 250, 266; *Indianapolis* sinking, 319; occupation of Japan, 356–7
SPRY, I: 390n
Spurgeon, Seaman L. F., V: 256n
Squadron 40–T, I: 16
"Squid," I: 212, X: 310

Stacey, Col. C. P., IX: xv, 35*n*
STACK, I: 109, IV: 271, V: 28*n*, 87, VI: 214-15, 219-21, 331, VII: 340, 349, VIII: 406, XII: 417, XIII: 309, 314, XIV: 379
Stadler, Lt. (jg) H., XII: 423
STAFF, I: 421, IX: 174-5, 389, X: 158, XI: 171-2, 333, 337-8
Staff conferences, III: 49-53, 152
Stafford, Seaman, III: 369
STAFFORD, XIII: 104, 305, 325
STAG, XIII: 308
STAGBUSH, XIV: 377
Stagg, Group Capt. J. M., XI: 79, 82
Staggs, Lt. Cdr. W. R., X: 379
Stagnone, IX: 58
Stahle, Lt. Cdr. J. H., VIII: 411, XIII: 319
Stalin, Marshal, I: 164, II: 15*n*, III: 61, IX: 6, XI: 23, 222, 230, XIV: 340-41
STALKER, IX: 250, 393, X: 40*n*, XI: 342
Stam, Capt., RNN, III: 386*n*
Standley, Adm. W. H., I: 164, 373
Standley, Cdr. W. H., Jr., IX: 391
Stanford, Cdr. Alfred, I: 268; *Force Mulberry*, XI: 24*n*, 165*n*, 176*n*
Stanley, Lt. (jg) E. L., X: 382
─ Stanley, Lt. Cdr. O. B., III: 267, VIII: 410   v.d+11
Stanley, Cdr. R. E., XIV: 381
Stanley, Quartermaster R. W., XII: 203*n*
STANLY, VI: 308, 421, VIII: 415, XIII: 24, 306, XIV: 225, 379
Stansbury, Lt. Cdr. T. R., XII: 422
STANSBURY, I: 422, II: 39, 173, VII: 346, VIII: 409, 418
STANTON, X: 267, 346-8, 378
Stanwood, Lt. Cdr. W. Reid, XIII: 79-80
Stapler, Capt. J. T. G., I: 208
Stark, Col. A. N., II: 235
Stark, Lt. (jg) H. B., III: 103
Stark, Adm. Harold R., biog., I: 39*n*; pics., 70, 170; CNO, 14, 27-8, 41-2, II: 12, III: 31, 43, 55-8, 61*n*, IV: 247*n*, XIII: 160; Anglo-American staff conversations, I: 40-41, 44; Memo. on National Policy, 42-4; strategy, 46, XI: 3-4; Support Force, I: 51; Iceland, 57, 74; Atlantic Conf., 70; Jap. negotiations, III: 65, 74-6; war warning sent, 77; Pearl Harbor, 128-30, 139-42; establishes Sea Frontiers, I: 207;

post-Pearl Harbor opns., III: 214, 219-20, 251; PTs, II: 262; N. Africa, 16, 193, 226; Guadalcanal, IV: 246; Comnaveu, X: 13, 18, 25, XI: 21, 30, 304; A/SW, X: 25, 325*n*; DEs, 33-4; subs in Europe, 87; escort carriers, 38; Cross-Channel invasion, XI: 14, 69; Rhine crossing, 317; occupation of Germany, 325-6; redeployment, 329; quoted, I: 56, X: vii
Stark, Capt. Harry, X: 211
Stark, Lt. Cdr. W. W., VIII: 404
Starkweather, Lt. M. W., II: 129
STARLIGHT, VIII: 419, XII: 418, XIII: 310, 313
STARLING, VIII: 418-19, XIV: 114*n*, 376
STARLING, HMS, VIII: 228*n*, X: 93, 151, 308
STARR, XIV: 218
States, Lt. L. A., XIV: 378
STAUNCH, XIV: 376
STAYNER, XI: 193
STEADY, I: 421, IX: 105, 388, 392, 396, X: 269, 381, XI: 342
STEAMER BAY, XII: 428, XIII: 305, XIV: 374
Stearns, Chief Machinist C. M., V: 132
Stearns, Lt. Robert L., X: 81, 121, 160
Stebbings, Lt. Cdr. H. E., XII: 180
Stebbins, Lt. Cdr. E. E., VII: 338, 348
Stebbins, Maj. L. R., VI: 145
Stedman, Lt. Charles H., VI: 145, XII: 420, XIII: 306, 309
Stedman, Lt. Cdr. G. W., VIII: 404
Stedman, Lt. Cdr. J. W., XII: 421, XIII: 311, XIV: 381
Steed, Lt. (jg) W. J., XII: 372
Steel, Lt. Cdr. F. P., XIII: 319, XIV: 375
Steel Voyager, X: 145
Steel Worker, I: 372
Steele, Capt. James M., VI: 10, 11*n*, VII: ix, 201*n*, 348
STEELHEAD, VIII: 25
Steen, Lt. Cdr. E. T., XIV: 384
Steere, Lt. (jg) J. W., X: 126
Steere, Lt. Cdr. R. C., II: 49, IX: 68*n*
Stefanac, Lt. Cdr. J. B., I: 418
Steffanides, Cdr. E. F., XII: 429, XIII: 282
Steffenhagen, Lt. Cdr. L. F., XIV: 382
Steiger, Lt. (jg) E. H., X: 118
Stein, Cdr. O. J., XII: 423
Steinbeck, Lt. Cdr. J. M., VII: 338, XII: 418

Steinhardt, Dr. Jacinto, I: 224, X: 208
Steinke, Cdr. F. S., VI: 113*n*, VII: 350, XIV: 376
Steinmetz, Cdr. E. H., XIV: 292*n*
Steinmetz, Cdr. J. L., XII: 417
STELLA, VI: 46
Stelter, Cdr. F. C., I: 420, II: 40, IX: 389
STEMBEL, VII: 347, VIII: 405, 418, XII: 418, XIII: 306, 311, XIV: 384
Stephan, Cdr. C. R., XII: 425
Stephan, Cdr. D. R., XII: 421, XIII: 316, 318, XIV: 385
Stephen, Lt. Cdr. E. C., V: 324, VI: 107
Stephen A. Douglas, X: 382
Stephen Hopkins, I: 398–9
STEPHEN POTTER, VII: 349, VIII: 39, 413, XII: 426, XIII: 317, XIV: 383
Stephens, Lt. (jg) R. E., X: 382
STERETT, I: 196, IV: 271, V: 28*n*, 87, 172, 173*n*, 226, 232–57 *passim*, VI: 214–15, 221, 331, VII: 340, 349, 353, VIII: 415, XIII: 309, 314, XIV: 197, 221, 379, 391
STERLET, XII: 91, 407, 429, XIV: 296
STERN, XII: 429, XIV: 375
Sternhell, C. M., *Antisubmarine Warfare*, X: xiii
Sterrie, Lt. N. A., VIII: 414
Stetson, Lt. T. H., XIV: 385
Steven Benet, XIII: 313
Stevens, Lt. Cdr. C. B., I: 421, VIII: 415
Stevens, Cdr. H. R., XI: 337
Stevens, Cdr. James E., IV: 174, X: 302, XIII: 282–3
Stevens, Capt. P. A., II: 36, VIII: 77, 403
Stevens, Lt. P. F., XIII: 38
Stevens, Cdr. R. R., VII: 111, XIV: 375
Stevens, Capt. W. I., XIV: 387
STEVENS (1918), VI: 131*n*, XI: 119*n*
STEVENS (1943), VII: 255, 274, 344, VIII: 404, 418–19, XII: 417, XIII: 271, 313, 323–4, 383
Stevenson, Capt. C. A., V: 72
Stevenson, Lt. H. F., XIII: 304
Stevenson, Robert Louis, VII: 76, 127, 179
Stevenson, Cdr. W. A., VII: 353
STEVENSON, VI: 436, VIII: 404, X: 158
Stewart, Lt. Cdr. A. V., XI: 334, 336
Stewart, Lt. Cdr. H. A., XII: 422, XIII: 313, XIV: 383
Stewart, Maj. J. L., VIII: 197
Stewart, Lt. Cdr. J. W., VIII: 410
Stewart, Ens. Jack, X: 124*n*
Stewart, Lt. W. K., XIII: 147

Stewart, Sgt. W. M., XIII: 298
STEWART, III: 160, 272, 298, 322*n*, 325, 328–9, 331, VI: 83*n*, X: 134*n*, XIV: 26*n;* wrecked, III: 378
Sticca, Capit. de Frég., II: 99
Stich, Cdr. F. S., VIII: 404
Stickell, Cdr. J. H., VII: 306*n*
Stickell Field, Eniwetok, VII: 306
STICKLEBACK, XII: 407*n*, XIV: 293*n*
Stickley, Cdr. D. P., XIII: 322–3
Stickney, Lt. Cdr. F. R., IV: 173
Stiesberg, Lt. Cdr. F. M., XI: 342
Stiff, Lt. Cdr. A. E., VIII: 411, XII: 428, XIII: 318
Still, Gunner H. L., VI: 237*n*
Stillman, Capt. C. F., XIV: 384
Stillman, Lt. J. H., XIII: 40–41, 192
Stilwell, Gen. Joseph W., XII: 6, 18, 55, 60, XIII: 163*n*, 293, XIV: 276
Stimson, Hon. Henry L., I: 29–30, 44–6, III: 11, 29, 75, 128, 136*n*, 142, X: xiv, 31, XI: 8, 11–13, XIV: 339, 347; *On Active Service*, X: 29, XI: xv
Stimson, Cdr. P. C., XIII: 281, 319
STINGRAY, III: 158, 179, 304, IV: 206–7, VI: 67, 79, VIII: 252–4, 278, 415
Stirling I., VI: 295, 395, 406
STOCKHAM, VIII: 262, 268–70, 409, 415, XII: 319, 426, XIII: 316, XIV: 58, 305, 383
Stockman, Capt. J. R., *Tarawa*, VII: 146*n*
STOCKTON, VI: 438, VIII: 114, 404, XIV: 136, 243
Stoker, Cdr. E. S., XIII: 307
Stokes, Lt. Cdr. E. C., XIV: 374
Stokes, Cdr. Thomas M., III: 393, V: 205, 232, 241–2
Stokey, Lt. Cdr. W. F., X: 380
Stone, Lt. Col. C. P., IX: 109*n*
Stone, Capt. E. E., XIII: 317, XIV: 385
Stone, Capt. E. S., I: 76
Stone, Lt. Cdr. H. L., III: 158
Stone, Cdr. L. T., VIII: 21
Stone, Ens. Merrill R., I: 395
Stone, Lt. Richard, I: 367–8
Store Ships (AF), VIII: 343–4, XII: 77, 81–2
Stores Issue Ships (AKS), VIII: 344
Storey, Lt. Cdr. F. G., VII: 341, XIII: 309
Storey, Seaman G. C., V: 256*n*
STORIS, I: 421

STORM KING, VIII: 408, XII: 417, XIII: 309, 313
STORMCLOUD, XI: 339
Stormes, Lt. Cdr. Max C., V: 205, 232
STORMES, XIV: 259, 271, 392
Storrs, Cdr. A. H. G., VII: 333, XI: 116, 335
Storts, Ens. H. A., II: 84-6
Stotsenburg, Ft., III: 179
Stott, Capt. G. W., XIV: 388
Stout, Capt. H. F., VI: 308, 354, XIV: 387
Stout, Capt. Richard F., IV: 274, V: 375, VIII: 97, 404
Stovall, Cdr. W. S., IV: 208, VII: 353
STRADTFELD, VII: 341
Strange, Lt. Cdr. J. C., VIII: 413
Strange, Cdr. R. O., VII: 338, 347
STRASBOURG, II: 239
Strategic Air Force Charter, XIV: 87-8
Strategic Plan for Defeat of Japan, VI: 7-8, VIII: 4
STRATEGY, XIV: 377
Strategy, Allied and U.S., basic I: 28; decisions, 138-49, II: 6-15, III: 48-56, 132, 218-22, 257, IV: 3-4, 245-63, V: 12, 116-17, 183, VI: 3-15, 89-97, 254-6, 281-4, 369-70, 412-13, 432-4, VII: 13, 17, 21, 65-6, 79-85, 201-6, 285, 319, VIII: 3-10, 19, 157, 313-16, IX: 3-11, 27, 227-33, 322-8, X: 22, 91, 249-50, XI: 3-18, 22, 221-30, 296, 317-18, XII: 3-18, 28, 60, 105, 223-5, 230, 336-8, XIII: 3-5, 163-4, 172-9, 213, 240-41, 256-9, XIV: 3-9, 17, 79-80, 92-3, 102-6; "leapfrog strategy," VI: 223-7, VII: 206, IX: 197-8
Strategy, Japanese, III: 82-4, 132, IV: 4-6, V: 117-23, 154, 333, VI: 15-26, 90-93, 183, 220, 394, VII: 4-18, 69-76, 136, 215, 283, 317, VIII: 10-12, 145, 216, 219-21, 235, XII: 5-6, 66-71, 160-65, 336-8, XIII: 159-60, XIV: 336-49
STRATFORD, VI: 121
STRATHALLEN, sunk, II: 254
Strathnaver, II: 195n, 221
STRAUB, X: 380
Straus, Lt. J. P., XII: viii
Strauss, Capt. E. B., XIV: 378
Strean, Lt. Cdr. B. M., VII: 338, VIII: 412
Street, Lt. Cdr. A. L., XIV: 291-3
Street, Lt. Cdr. G. M., XIV: 375
Streett, Maj. Gen. St. Clair, VIII: 50

STRENGTH, XIV: 377
Strickland, Lt. Cdr. B. W., XIII: 310, XIV: 380
Strickland, Lt. J. O., VII: 345
Strickland, Lt. Col. R. F., VI: 64
STRINGHAM, IV: 276n, V: 364, VI: 145, 228, 381, 415, VIII: 408, XIV: 381
STRIVE, I: 421, IX: 174, 187, 191-3, 348, 392, 396, XI: 273, 342, XIV: 377
Stroh, Cdr. R. J., VII: 97, 340, VIII: 164n
Strohbehn, Cdr. W. W., I: 218n, IX: 391
Strom, Lt. Cdr. C. G., XIV: 387
Stromboli I., IX: 190
Strong, Maj. Gen. George V., I: 40
Strong, Brig. K. W. D., IX: 238
Strong, Lt. S. B., V: 86, 208
STRONG, VI: 110n, 113n, 116n, 119, 179, 224; sunk, 156-8, 195-6; survivors, pic., 171
Stroop, Cdr. F. D., VII: 340
Strother, Cdr. J. A., V: 270n
Struble, Rear Adm. Arthur D., biog., XII: 119n; mentioned, XI: 30n, XII: 118-21, 127, 131, 375-84, 387, 416-17, XIII: 8, 18, 22-8, 31-2, 178, 184n, 187-8, 199, 202, 208, 215-17, 229-31, 249, 323
Struckey, Boatswain E. F., XIV: 231n
Strumm, Lt. Cdr. F. E., XII: 419, XIII: 311, XIV: 378
Stuart, Cdr. A. L., XIII: 307, XIV: 380
Stuart, Cdr. C. J., VI: 331, VII: 340
Stuart, Cdr. D. A., XI: 340-42
Stuart, Cdr. L. B., VII: 103n
Stuart, Col. W. J., VIII: 186n
STUART PRINCE, XI: 338
Stubbart, Lt. I. G., VII: 344, VIII: 410, 419
Stubbs, Lt. Cdr. H. K., XII: 420, XIII: 305
Stucker, Chief Yeoman, V: 49
Stump, Rear Adm. Felix B., biog., XII: 243n; pics., VII: 198, XII: 246; mentioned, III: 159, VII: 94, 196, 338, VIII: 326, 410, 420, XII: 243-5, 251-314 *passim*, 420, XIII: 21, 29, 33, 155, 177, 305, XIV: 132, 374
STURGEON, III: 158, 283, 304, 337, IV: 220, 227, V: 177, VIII: 23
Sturtevant, Radioman E. L., XIV: 325
STURTEVANT, I: 418; sunk, 136
Styles, Cdr. R. E., XIV: 285

SUAMICO, VII: 340, VIII: 411, XII: 82, 423, XIII: 116, 308, XIV: 387
Subchaser 2206 (Ger.), IX: 309n
Subchaser Training Center, I: 231–3, X: 9, 49
Subchasers (Jap.), –12, III: 275; –16, –17, –18, IV: 89; –22, VI: 37; –24, VI: 37, sunk, VII: 329; –53, sunk, XII: 370
Subchasers (U.S.N.), I: 229–31, 236. *See also* PCs; SCs
Subic Bay, XIII: 38, 198, 208, 215, 222, 260, 286; landing, 177
Sublette, Lt. Cdr. W. H., VII: 345, VIII: 409, 418
Submarine Force, U.S. Fleet, III: 28
Submarine operations, control, IV: 192; unrestricted warfare ordered, 190; Philippines, III: 166, 176, 179, 193–6, 205–6; N.E.I., 283, 303–5; in 1942, 258, IV: 198–234; Aleutians, 214–19, VII: 7–8, 52–4; Sowespac, IV: 270, VI: 66–85, VIII: 48, 120, XIII: 279–88; Solomons, V: 177–9, 270–71, 324, 348–50; in 1943, VI: 24, 63; Gilberts, VII: 187–9; in 1944, VI: 84–5, VIII: 15–26, 155, 167–8, XII: 398–411, XIV: 285–6; Marshalls, VII: 222; Truk, 319; Bat. Phil. Sea, VIII: 202, 231, 241–4, 250, 278–82, 316; Leyte G., XII: 332–5; in 1945, XIV: 91, 286–97; Sea of Japan, 292–3; recce., II: 37–40, 43, 54n, 139–40, VII: 98, 119, 141, 207–8, 222, 241–2, 250, 375, XII: 33, XIV: 18; lifeguard, IV: 213, VII: 22, 93–4, 187, 330, VIII: 30, 33, 39, XII: 91, 408–10, XIV: 91, 266, 294–7; guerrilla supply, VI: 78, 85, VIII: 21–2, XII: 27, 64; tonnage sunk by, XII: 412–13; casualties, IV: 194; discussion, XII: 412–14. *See also* under nationality; U-boats
Submarine Squadron One, Three, Seven, I: 421; Fifty, X: 87
Submarines, treaty limitations on, I: 8; "tame," 54, 119, 215–16; no. on 7 Dec. 1941, IV: 188; handicaps in early operations, 188; doctrine, 189–90; described, 190–95; conditions on board, 208; minelaying, 229–30
SUCCESS, XIV: 377
Sudest, Cape, VIII: 135
Suenaga, Col. T., VIII: 392
Suetsugu, Adm. N., VII: 69
Suez, I: 112, IX: 149–51
SUFFOLK, XIV: 375

Sugai, Cdr. T., VII: 148
SUGI, XII: 430, XIII: 37n, 159
Suguira, Capt. K., VI: 214–15, XII: 431
Suhren, Frgtkapt. Reinhard, X: 309–10
Suicide boats, XIII: 50, 138–40, 191–2, 202, XIV: 124, 217, 243; Okinawa, chart, 125, pic., 119
Suiyuan Province, XIII: 294
Sullivan, the five brothers, V: 257
Sullivan, Capt. D. J., XII: 251, 421, XIV: 374
Sullivan, Lt. Cdr. E. T. B., X: 378
Sullivan, Ens. H. P., XI: 134
Sullivan, Lt. J. C., XIV: 381
Sullivan, Hon. John L., III: xii, V: xi
Sullivan, Capt. John R., V: 231
Sullivan, Lt. (jg) T. L., X: 382
Sullivan, Lt. Cdr. W. W., XIII: 143, 322
Sullivan, Commo. William A., II: 247, 250, 274, IX: 32, 188, 311, 387n, XI: 179, 216–17, 303, 337, XIII: 206–7; pic., IX: 283
SULLIVANS. *See* THE SULLIVANS
Sultan, Lt. Gen. D. I., XIII: 163n
Sulu Sea, XII: 168, XIII: 12, 23–5, 99–101
Suluan I., XII: 118–21
Sumanoura M., III: 275, 288
Sumatra, III: 309, 322, XIII: 277, XIV: 104; chart, XIII: 294
Sumatra M., VI: 79
Sumiya, Col., VI: 383
Sumiyoshi, Maj. Gen. T., V: 190–91
Summers, Cdr. P. E., XII: 400, XIII: 284
Sumner, Lt. (jg) W. C., XIV: 111n
SUMNER, VII: 341, XII: 49–50, XIV: 72, 158n
SUMTER, VII: 236, 345, VIII: 408, XII: 417, XIII: 309, 312, XIV: 378
Sun Tzu, quoted, VIII: 187
Sunda Strait, III: 309, 331, 341; Battle of, 363–70, chart, 367
SUNFISH, IV: 212–13, VII: 222, 351–3, VIII: 155, XIV: 291
SUNFLOWER, X: 68, 75, 149
SUPERIOR, XIV: 377
SUPPLY, XII: 77
Supply Depots and Repair Bases in Britain, XI: 60–61
Support Force, Atlantic Fleet, I: 51, 54, 69; T.O., 418
Surabaya, III: 277–9, 283, 298–9, 303–79 *passim*, VIII: 154n, X: 302; Strait, III: 339

SURCOUF, I: 265
Suribachi, Mt., XIV: 6, 15, 29–30, 34, 37, 40–41, 44, 49–51, 61–2; pics., 47, 55
Surigao Strait, III: 177, VIII: 202, XII: 57, 160, 369, 374, 379, XIII: 44, 115; Battle of, XII: 198–241; charts, 200, 205, 214, 219, 225, 231; pic., 222–3
Surinam, X: 216
SURPRISE, I: 390n
Surrender ceremony, XIV: 362–7; pic., 366–7
SUSAN B. ANTHONY, II: 36, 120–22, 129, IX: 133, 141, 389; sunk, 171
SUSQUEHANNA (1851), XIV: 6
SUSQUEHANNA (1943), I: 422, XIII: 308
SUSTAIN, I: 421, IX: 388, 392, 396, X: 256, 269, 381, XI: 342
Susupe, Lake, VIII: 194, 199–200, 206
Sutherland, Lt. H. L., XII: 417
Sutherland, Lt. J. F., V: 260
Sutherland, Lt. Gen. R. K., III: 169, IV: 262, V: 115–16, VI: 7, VII: 319, VIII: 7–8, XII: 14–15, 136–7, XIII: 8–9, XIV: 366; pics., XIII: 156, XIV: 366–7
Sutphin, Chief Yeoman H. W., XIII: x
Sutton, Capt. F. C., XII: 420, XIII: 305, XIV: 374
SUTTON, X: 360, 378, XI: 335
Suva, III: 212, 259, IV: 246, 252, 263n, V: 335n, VII: 102
SUWANNEE, II: 39, 89–90, 168, 171, V: 353–4, 359, VI: 140, VII: 139, 153, 234, 288, 301, 308, 338, 346–8, VIII: 230, 238n, 405, 420, X: 40, XII: 166, 244, 301, 305–6, 420, XIII: 272, XIV: 213, 374; pics., II: 92, XII: 303
SUZUKAZE, III: 162, V: 85, 105, 206, 297–8, 302, 311, 325, VI: 162–72 passim; sunk, VII: 22, VIII: 19
Suzuki, Jap. planner, III: 77
Suzuki, Capt., V: 193
Suzuki, Adm. Baron, XIV: 172, 338–50, 359
Suzuki, Lt. Gen. S., XII: 135–6, 149, 361–4, 394–6, XIII: 15, 234–7
Suzuki, Vice Adm. Y., VIII: 416, XII: 431
SUZUKI, V: 85n
SUZUNAMI, VI: 332
SUZUTSUKI, XIII: 158, XIV: 202
SUZUYA, III: 26, 276, 308, 334, IV: 88, 143, V: 85, 206, 214, 234, 262, VI: 323,

412, VII: 137–8, XII: 162, 248, 279, 330, 431; sunk, 308
SVENNER, XI: 156, 183
Swafford, Cdr. C. A., VII: 341, VIII: 411, XII: 428
Swain, Capt. C. D., XIV: 387
Swain, Lt. J. B., I: 215
SWALE, X: 77
SWALLOW, VIII: 419, XIV: 114n, 244, 376, 391; sunk, 244
SWAN, III: 314, IV: 72, 263n, VII: 340
Swan I., I: 151
Swanson, Lt. Cdr. C. W., XIV: 384
Swanson, Hon. Claude H., II: 21n
Swanson, Lt. Cdr. L. V., VIII: 413
Swanson, Lt. Cdr. N. W., X: 378
SWANSON, I: 420, II: 38, 58–62, 74, 77, 100, 105, 174, 285, VI: 443–5, VIII: 403, IX: 68, 78–9, 82, 386, X: 180, XII: 319, 428
Swart, Lt. P. A., XIII: 40
Swartout, Lt. J. D., XIV: 376
Swasey, Capt. A. L., I: 229–30
SWASEY, X: 378
Swatow, XIII: 170
SWAY, I: 421, IX: 396, XI: 313, 341
SWEARER, VIII: 411, XII: 429, XIII: 81–2, 319, XIV: 375
Swearingen, Cdr. E. K., VII: 349
Sweeney, Cdr. E. J., VII: 336, 346, VIII: 408
Sweeney, Lt. J. J., XIV: 42
Sweeney, Capt. John B., V: 128
Sweeney, Cdr. John D., IV: 273, VI: 144–5, 193, 228, 381, 414, 415
Sweeney, Lt. Col. Walter C., IV: 93, 110, 137n, 159n
Sweet, Lt. Cdr. C. F., XIII: 319
Sweetser, Capt. W. M., V: 232, 297, VII: 349, VIII: 413, XII: 425
Swenceski, Lt. Col. A. B., VII: 164
SWENNING, X: 376
Swenson, Lt. Col. E. T., II: 207
Swenson, Lt. Lester V., VI: 404–5
Swenson, Capt. Lyman K., I: 111, 419, V: 205, 231
Swensson, Lt. R. M., VII: 339, 348, VIII: 412
Swentzel, Lt. Livingston, XIII: 300–301
SWERVE, I: 421
Swett, 1st Lt. J. E., VI: 122
Swift, Lt. Cdr. H. M. S., VI: 446
Swift, Maj. Gen. I. P., VI: 444, XIII: 97, 132, 146, 308; quoted, VI: 447

SWIFT, I: 421, X: 372, XI: 333, 337–8; sunk, 190

Swiftscout, X: 343

SWIFTSURE, XIV: 105, 388

Swigert, Capt. O. R., VII: 336, IX: 389, XII: 417, XIII: 314, 324

Swilly, Lough, I: 53*n*

Swinburne, Capt. E. R., XII: 399–400

Swing, Maj. Gen. J. M., XII: 379, XIII: 189

Swinson, Capt. D. H., XIV: 375

Switzer, Capt. W. G., XIV: 382

SWIVEL, XI: 337

Sworder, Lt. Cdr. E. R. D., XI: 273

SWORDFISH, III: 158, 191, 203, 303*n*, 304,

IV: 222, V: 348, VIII: 24*n*, 415; sunk, XIV: 288

SYBILLE, II: 110*n*, 168

SYDNEY, sunk, III: 51*n*

Sydney, Australia, III: 337, IV: 15, 20, 29, 279, V: 36*n*, 312, VII: 102, VIII: 135, XIV: 103; Battle of, IV: 65–8

Sydney, N. S., I: 18, 24, 160, 262, 319, 322, 330

Sydney M., VI: 82

Sykes, Capt. J. B., XIV: 382

Sylvester, Cdr. M. D., VIII: 407

SYMBOL, I: 421, IX: 392, 396, XI: 341

Syracuse, Sicily, IX: 18, 26, 49, 60, 151, 159–62

Syros, I: 172, 178*n*

T

T. A. Johnson, XIII: 324
TA-24, -29, sunk, XI: 316
T-25, -26, -27, -28, XI: 183; sunk, 35, X: 104
Taal Lake, XIII: 190, 209
Tabata, Lt. Cdr. S., VII: 139
TABBERER, XIII: 81-2, 319, XIV: 374
Tabitha Brown, IX: 386
Tablas Strait, XII: 175, 310, 339, XIII: 17
Tacey, Machinist R. C., XIV: 185
TACHIBANA, XIV: 312
TACHIKAZE, V: 324; pic., VII: 318
Tackney, Cdr. S. N., XIII: 317, XIV: 384
Tacloban, XII: 65, 124, 138, 151-5, 190, 238, 281, 299, 304-95 passim, XIII: 9, 18, 99, 175, 258; landings, XII: 130-40; chart, 132, 152; pic., 135
Tactics, Army vs. Marines, VIII: 330-31; Jap. island defense, XII: 35, XIII: 128-30, XIV: 18, 139, 170-71, 243
Tada, Rear Adm. T., III: 163
Tadena, Lt. A. F., XIII: 188
Tadji, VIII: 61, 69-70
TADOUSSAC, XI: 333
Taff, Cdr. C. O., V: 330, 375
"Taffies" (CVE group), XII: 125, 242-5; T.O., 420-21
Tagami, Lt. Gen., VIII: 97
Tagaytay, XIII: 192; chart, 190; ridge, 197
Tagg, Cdr. W. L., VII: 347, VIII: 405, 418, XII: 418, XIII: 306, 311
Taguchi, Capt. Taro, VI: 19n
Tague, Capt. J. R., X: 299, 322, 380
TAHOMA, I: 421
Tai Li, Lt. Gen., XIII: 290-93, 301
Taiei M., IV: 201
TAIHO, VIII: 217-18, 221, 249, 264, 269, 285-9, 307, 320, 416; sunk, 279-82
Taikyo M., XIII: 298
Taimei M., VI: 56
Tainan M., VI: 81
Taivu, Pt., V: 70, 71, 123n, 124
TAIYO, III: 27, V: 84
Taiyo M., IV: 203
Takagi, Vice Adm. T., III: 162-3, 177, 182, 274-5, 280, 293, 334-72 passim,

IV: 11-52 passim, 61, 88, V: 84, VIII: 167, 222, 229-30, 337n, 417
Takahashi, Vice Adm. I., III: 26, 156, 161-80 passim, 273-4, 283, 334-72 passim
Takahashi, Capts. K. and W., XII: 431
Takama, Rear Adm. T., V: 84, 207, 234
Takamatsu, Prince, XIV: 353
TAKANAMI, V: 206, 226, 297-301, 305-7, 314; sunk, 302-3
Takane M., XII: 430
Takao, III: 149, 162, XII: 94, 299, 405, XIII: 171, 179, 279
TAKAO, III: 26, 161, 276, 333, IV: 172, V: 84, 206, 234, 271-3, 278, VI: 323, 328, VIII: 162, 170-73, 416, 430, XII: 170, XIII: 159
Takao M., III: 177
Takaoka M., VIII: 23
TAKASAKI, VIII: 220
Takashina, Lt. Gen. T., VIII: 324, 373, 381n, 388
Takasu, Vice Adm. S., IV: 89, 149
TAKE, XII: 371, XIII: 159
Takeda, Lt. Col. H., VIII: 381-2, 401
Takeda, Rear Adm. I., VI: 426-7, 430-31
Takenaka, Rear Adm. R., III: 163
TALAMBA, IX: 158, 164
Talaud Is., XII: 15, 29
Talbot, Rear Adm. Arthur G., IX: 393, XI: 181-3, 186-8
Talbot, Capt. F. R., VI: 297, VIII: 418
Talbot, Cdr. Paul H., III: 158, 272n, 285-6, 289-90, XIII: 268
Talbot, Brig. Gen. Ralph, I: 147
TALBOT, I: 213, IV: 174, 176n, VI: 147, 156n, 228, 351, 415, VIII: 404, 409, XII: 422, XIII: 307, XIV: 158n
Taliaferro, Lt. Cdr. H. B., IX: 388
Talin Bay, XIII: 192
Talisay, XIII: 233
Talley, Col. B. B., IV: 164
Tallman, Capt. D. R., XIV: 379
TALLULAH, VI: 98n, VII: 341, VIII: 411, XII: 423, XIII: 307n, 308, XIV: 387
TALLY HO, VIII: 17n, X: 277

Talman, Lt. Cdr. B. L. E., IX: 388
Taloma Bay, landing, XIII: 247; base, III: 182
TALUGA, XII: 428, XIII: 319, XIV: 169, 387
TALYBONT, XI: 121, 126–7, 143, 336
TAMA, III: 26, IV: 172, VII: 24, 27–8, 35, 58, XII: 162, 319–21, 326, 335, 413n, 430; sunk, 334
Tama M., IV: 17, 26; *Nos. 3, 5*, 89; *No. 8, 17*
Tamagawa M., IV: 173
Tamai, Cdr. A., VIII: 394
TAMANAMI, VIII: 416
TAMBOR, III: 213, 241, IV: 144, 148, VI: 85, 92
Tami, VIII: 61, 87
Tamontaka, XIII: 244
TAMPA, I: 331–4, 421
Tanaga I., VII: 12–15
TANAGER, III: 205; sunk, 206
Tanahmerah Bay, VIII: 61, 63, 85, 94–6, XII: 114; chart, VIII: 62; landing, 37, 74–9, and chart, 76, pic., 89
Tanaka, Mrs. Lily Y., XII: viii
Tanaka, Rear Adm. R., pic., V: 306; mentioned, III: 163, 182, 274–5, 280, 296, 315, 334, 344–6, IV: 142, V: 82–5, 89, 104, 142, 206, 234, 259–61, 266–72, 280–85, 292, 295–8, 315, 318–20, 339, VI: 22, 181
Tanaka, Gen. S., XIV: 350
Tanambogo, landing, IV: 290–92, and pic., 289, 292; taken, V: 16
Tanapag, VIII: 152, 175, 187, 212, 346, XII: 333
TANATSIDE, XI: 122, 336
Tanauan, XII: 350
Tancred, Lt. Cdr. G. C., XIII: 324
TANEY, X: 268
TANG, VII: 319n, 353, VIII: 24, 30, 39, 155, XII: 401–4, 427; sunk, 404–5
Tangier, II: 65
TANGIER, III: 113, 159, 236, 242, 251, IV: 20, 30, 35, 73, 252–3, 263n, VIII: 49–50, 406, XII: x, 25, XIII: 312
Tanii, Capt. T., XII: 431
TANIKAZE, III: 87–8, IV: 88, 148, V: 85, 206, VI: 37, 162–3, 166–7, 171n, 172, VIII: 416; sunk, 220
Tanimbar I., XII: 107
Tanjong Priok, III: 339, 341, 355, 357, 363–5
Tankan Bay, III: 89

Tankers, sinking of, I: 130–33, 136–9, 186–8, 199, 309, 347–50, X: 8; Marianas, VIII: 344–5
Tanks, II: 13n, 126–30, 137, 147, 155; problem of landing, 137, 147, 155, IV: 291, V: 72, VI: 200, 204–6, 223, 430; German midgets, XI: 102, and pic., 101; DD amphibious, 98–100, 118, 132–8, 184–6, 262; in Gilberts and Marshalls, VII: 126–7, 133, 164, 173, 183n, 239, 245–8, 260–65, 268–71, 275–6, 280n, 292–3, 296, 299n, 303; Sicily, IX: 103–19 *passim*, 145–6, 223; Salerno, 265–7, 287–92; XII: 38; Manila, pic., XIII: 197
Tannenfels, I: 398–9
Tanner, Lt. R. M., VII: 347, 411
Tanner, Lt. W. P., X: 95
Tanuan, XIII: 18
Tanzola, Col. V. J., VIII: 390–91, XIV: 177
Taormina, IX: 59, 167, 207
Tapotchau, Mt., VIII: 152, 190, 197, 208, 330–35; pic., 192
Tappaan, Lt. Cdr. F. D., XII: 210, 422, XIII: 149, 313
TAPPAHANNOCK, VI: 123, VII: 341, VIII: 411, 420, XII: 428, XIV: 387
Tarakan, III: 154, 160, 214–16, 281–3, VIII: 119, 214, XIII: 262–3, 269; description, 259; landing, 217, 256, 259–64
Tarakan M., XIII: 281
Taranto, IX: 38, 42, 59, 235–6, 242, XI: 246; landing, 235–6
Tarawa Atoll, VII: 77–9, 84–5, 92, 97–9, 117–18, 146, 149, 156, 164, 211–12, 308; VIII: 156; described, VII: 146–7; and chart, 176; and pics., 102; capture of, plans, 149–53; hydrography, 153–4; landing, 155, 159–63, and chart, 160, and pics., 166–7, 174–5; opns. ashore, 163–79, and chart, 170–71; unloading, 167–9, 179; numbers, 153; discussion, 182–4, 202
TARAZED, I: 422, IX: 390
TARBELL, I: 418, 420
Taroa I., III: 263
Taroona, VI: 36
TARPON, III: 158, IV: 92, 213, VII: 207–8, X: 275–6
Tarr, Ens. Thomas, VIII: 277
TARTER, IX: 281, 393, XI: 175
TASAJERA, II: 234

Tashman, Boatswain N. W., XIII: 59*n*, 63*n*
Tasimboko, V: 124–6
Task Organizations, method of compilation, II: 34–5
TASKER H. BLISS: I: 358, II: 38, 168, 172; sunk, 171, 284; pic., 165
Tasman, VI: 36
Tasmania M., XII: 388
Tassafaronga, V: 70; Battle of, 293–313, VI: 195; chart, 290–91; T.O., 296–7; discussion, 313–15
Tate, Lt. (jg) B. C., VIII: 296
Tate, Cdr. Jackson R., IV: 174
Tate, Dr. John T., I: 222, X: 24
Tate, Capt. V. B., VII: 341, XIV: 380
TATE, XIV: 375
Tatekawa M., VIII: 218
TATNUCK, VII: 334
Tatro, Lt. Alfred, XII: 26
Tatsuhara M., III: 162
Tatsukami M., III: 275, 289
TATSUTA, III: 26, 231, 234, 245, IV: 18, V: 149, VI: 33, 37–9; sunk, VIII: 18
Tatsuta M., IV: 213
Tatsutagawa M., VIII: 239
TATTNALL, I: 151, X: 191, XI: 339
TATUM, XI: 343
Taussig, Cdr. E. D., III: 224, VIII: 150
Taussig, Ens. J. K., III: 109
Taussig, Capt. W. M., XI: 244*n*
TAUSSIG, XIII: 316, XIV: 383
TAUTOG, III: 104, 213*n*, 258, IV: 206, 229, VI: 76–7, 85, VIII: 19, 23–4, XIII: 319
TAWAKONI, XIV: 387
TAWASA, VII: 341, 345, VIII: 411
Tawes, Lt. Cdr. M. R., X: 65
Tawi Tawi, VIII: 94, 117, 131, 173, 185, 216–20, 235, XIII: 226, 269–71
TAY, X: 68–70
Taylor, Ens. A. C., II: 63
Taylor, Dr. A. Hoyt, I: 225
Taylor, Lt. Cdr. B., I: 420, XIII: 313
Taylor, Lt. B. E., XIV: 376
Taylor, Lt. Cdr. Brown, VIII: 408
Taylor, Col. Charles H., *Omaha Beachhead*, XI: xiii
Taylor, Cdr. E. A., I: 111, 420
Taylor, Cdr. E. B., V: 151, 158, 167, VI: 415, 421, 427, VIII: 409, 415
Taylor, Capt. F. N., XIII: 303
Taylor, Col. George A., IX: 98, XI: 130, 140
Taylor, Lt. Cdr. H. C., XII: 429

Taylor, Capt. H. W., VII: 337, 344, VIII: 405, 414, XII: 424
Taylor, Machinist Harold, V: 284–5
Taylor, Lt. Henry S., V: 174, XIII: 275*n*
Taylor, Capt. J. I., XIII: 152, 305
Taylor, Lt. James G. G., VI: 231–2
Taylor, Lt. Cdr. Jesse, X: 299, 376
Taylor, Cdr. Joe, IV: 19, 26, 49, XIV: 96
Taylor, Lt. Cdr. John B., V: 233
Taylor, Maj. Kermit A., V: 375
Taylor, Lt. Cdr. L., VI: 413, 416
Taylor, Maj. Gen. Maxwell D., IX: 240–41, XI: 89–90
Taylor, Lt. (jg) R. O., VI: 381
Taylor, Lt. Cdr. Robert L., VI: 244, VII: 338, 345
Taylor, 1st Lt. Roy L., VI: 65
Taylor, Lt. Samuel K., X: 225
Taylor, Ens. Thomas Hart, III: 109
Taylor, Capt. Thomas Herbert, X: 269, 381
Taylor, Lt. Cdr. W. A., XIII: 319
Taylor, Lt. W. R., XII: 426, XIII: 318
Taylor, Lt. W. T., VIII: 376*n*
Taylor, Cdr. Walter L., IV: 272
TAYLOR, V: 353, VI: 110*n*, 113*n*, 121, 179–81, 193, 228, 234, 242–4, VII: 190, 194, 338, VIII: 228, 404, XII: 366*n*, 417, XIII: 115, 261, 304, 322
Tazan M., IV: 221
TAZEWELL, XIV: 375
"TBS confusion," cartoon, I: 107
TEABERRY, XIII: 308
TEAK, XII: 423, XIII: 308
TEAL, VII: 353
Teall, Cdr. A. E., XIII: 317, XIV: 373
Tedder, Air Chief Marshal Sir Arthur W., IX: 10, 14–16, 101, 212–13, 246, 294, 323, 324*n*, X: 130, XI: 36–8, 69, 82
Tedder, Cdr. F. L., I: 420, VII: 347, VIII: 406, 414
Tegelberg, II: 233
TEHANA, XI: 337
Teheran Conf., XI: 23–4, 221–2, 230
Teihi M., VI: 80
Teihoku M., XIV: 294
Teison M., IV: 210
Teiyo M., VI: 55–6, 58, 172
TEKESTA, VII: 257, 345, VIII: 411, XII: 429, XIII: 319, XIV: 185, 375, 387
Telfair, XIV: 176, 375

Teller, Capt. Steadman, XII: 428, XIII: 305
TEMPÉTE, II: 108, XI: 343
Temple, Cdr. J. B. G., XI: 217
TENACE, IX: xiv
TENACIOUS, IX: 396
TENACITY, I: 13*n*, 387, 390*n*
Tenaru R., IV: 285*n*, 287, V: 66; Battle of, 69–73, and map, 72; pic., 74
TENBY, XI: 337
TENEDOS, III: 188, 340
Tenerife, I: 324
Ténès, II: 273
TENINO, XIV: 387
Tenjo, Mt., VIII: 386, 396
Tennant, Rear Adm. W. O., XI: 178*n*, 231
Tennent, Cdr. J. G., VII: 220, 338, 346
Tennes, Lt. Cdr. H. E., XIV: 382
TENNESSEE (1906), XIV: 158*n*
TENNESSEE (1920), III: 104–8, 145, VI: 423, VII: 37*n*, 165, 232*n*, 288–90, 301, 337, 346, VIII: 180–82, 187, 197–8, 360–62, 409, 419, X: 204*n*, XI: 207, XII: ix, 44, 163, 198*n*, 199, 202, 224, 226*n*, 228*n*, 295, 419, XIII: 19*n*, 176*n*, XIV: xi, 26–31, 127, 130, 133, 140*n*, 147–53, 168, 204, 227, 230–31, 335, 372, 391; pics., III: 84, 102, XIV: 158, 206–7
TENRYU, III: 26, 231, 234, 245, IV: 18, V: 19, 35, 40, 51, 234, 262, VI: 33, 37; sunk, IV: 228, V: 61*n*, 324
Teop Harbor, VI: 280–81
Tepuni, Ens. William, sinks first U-boat, I: 154
Ter Poorten, Maj. Gen. Hein, III: 53–4, 271, 278, 336–7, 379
Teraoka, Vice Adm. K., XII: 68–9, 161*n*, 432*n*, XIII: 159
Terauchi, Field Marshal H., III: 71, XII: 67, 165, 353–4, XIII: 13–15, 37
Terceira I., X: 349
TEREBINTH, XIV: 124, 127, 377
TERMAGANT, XI: 339
Termini, IX: 250–51
TERN, III: 104, XIV: 388
Ternasky, Lt. (jg) E. F., pic., VII: 198
Ternate I., XIII: 20, 29
Terpening, Lt. N. R., VIII: 419
TERPSICHORE, XI: 339
Terracina, IX: 329, 376, 381
TERROR, II: 39, 176*n*, VIII: 32*n*, XIV: 29, 113, 376, 391; pic., II: 174

Terry, Ens. H. L., XII: 422
Terry, Lt. L. E., XIV: 386
Terry, Capt. W. E., VIII: 410, XII: 418, XIII: 311, XIV: 380
TERRY (1910), I: 51*n*, XIV: 312*n*
TERRY (1943), VI: 242, 297, 360, 415, VIII: 409, 414, XIV: 63–4, 389
TERUZUKI, V: 206, 223, 233–4, 273*n*, 274, 278; sunk, 319–20
Teshima, Lt. Gen. F., VIII: 66–7
TETCOTT, IX: 162, 393, 396
Teteron Bay, pic., I: 258
Teters, N. D., III: 225, 228
TETON, XIV: 143, 379
TEXAS (1895), II: 286, VII: 101*n*
TEXAS (1914), I: 14, 73, 142*n*, 208*n*, 419, II: 36, 44, 118–19, 121*n*, 126, 132–3, 285, VII: 152*n*, XI: 56, 86, 116–18, 126, 129, 135, 148–50, 158–60, 168, 198, 205–10, 238, 265, 280, 284*n*, 336, 340, XIII: 176*n*, 187*n*, XIV: 26, 30, 130, 226, 246, 372; pic., XI: 204
Texas, I: 171*n*
Thach, Capt. John S., III: 267, IV: 14, 90, 120, 131, 267; Thach weave, XIII: 54
Thackrey, Capt. L. A., IX: 389, XI: 19
Thai R., XIII: 258
Thailand, III: 55, 81*n*, 130, 187–9, 381
THANE, X: 337
THATCHER (1919), VII: 37*n*
THATCHER (1943), VI: 308, 317–18, VIII: 415, XII: 429, XIII: 230–32, 316, 319, 323, XIV: 270, 392
Thäter, Oberlt. Ernst, X: 218
Thayne, E. P., X: 382
THE SULLIVANS, VII: 349, VIII: 413, XII: 319, 426, XIII: 317
Theater boundaries, VIII: 46*n*
Thébaud, Rear Adm. L. Hewlett, I: 92, VII: 350, VIII: 413, IX: 103–4, 235, 388, X: 6, 12–13
THEENIM, XIV: 381
Theiss, Commo. Paul S., IV: 272, VI: 140–41, 144, VII: 87, 202, VIII: 192, 409, XIV: 372
THEMISTOCLES, IX: 396, XI: 239*n*, 339, 343
Theobald, Rear Adm. R. A., biog., IV: 166*n;* pic., 166; mentioned, 83, 85, 160*n*, 166–7, 170–73, 177, 182–4, 215–16, 257, VII: 4–5, 9–12, 15–17
Theobald, Cdr. R. A., Jr., VI: 273, XIII: 317, XIV: 384
Theodore Dwight Weld, X: 140–42

THETIS, I: 138, 143, 415
Thew, Lt. Cdr. N. V. J. T., III: 333
Thieme, Capt. K. A., XIII: 313
Thieme, Lt. Cdr. R. I., XIII: 307
Thirkfield, Lt. B. A., XIV: 380
Thomas, Lt. Cdr. D. I., X: 375
Thomas, Plt. Sgt. E. I., pic., XIV: frontispiece
Thomas, Lt. Cdr. F. J., III: 109
Thomas, Capt. F. P., VII: 339, 349, VIII: 415
Thomas, Col. G. C., pic., V: 130
Thomas, Lt. Cdr. James A., V: 165, 204, 233, 268
Thomas, Ens. L. E., XII: 422
Thomas, Lt. Cdr. R. H., VII: 345, XIV: 388
Thomas, Capt. R. L., VIII: 420
Thomas, Cdr. T. C., VII: 341
Thomas, Cdr. W. D., VII: 337, 347, XII: 255, 258, 262, 421
THOMAS, X: 279, 319, 344, 373, 377
Thomas B. Robertson, XI: 334
Thomas Donaldson, X: 313
THOMAS E. FRASER, XIV: 49, 377
THOMAS F. NICKEL, XIII: 309
THOMAS JEFFERSON, I: 421, II: 38, 58-64, 77, 172, IX: 131-6, 259n, 389, 392, XI: 48, 119, 136-7, 335, 341, XIV: 378
Thomas L. Clingman; Thomas Nuttall, X: 382
Thomas Pinckney, X: 158
Thomas Scott, X: 311
THOMAS STONE, I: 421, II: 192, 195-202, 209-15, 254; pic., 192
Thomas W. Bickett, IX: 390, X: 382
THOMASON, XIII: 279, 308
Thompson, Capt. Edward M., VI: 341, 344, VII: 337, 344, VIII: 404, 418
Thompson, Mr. G. S., X: 214
Thompson, Col. George, XI: xi
Thompson, Cdr. Gerald, I: 285
Thompson, Lt. H. J., XIII: 313
Thompson, Cdr. H. L., VII: 335, 347-8, VIII: 410, XIII: 310
Thompson, Ens. Harold A., XII: 26-7
Thompson, Cdr. M. C., XIII: 307, XIV: 380
Thompson, Lt. R. W., V: 273n
Thompson, Capt. S. H., VIII: 407, XII: 419, XIII: 311
Thompson, Cdr. W., XII: 416
Thompson, Cdr. Wells, VIII: 404, XIII: 309

THOMPSON, XI: 121, 129, 147, 158, 333, 336, 343
Thompson Lykes, I: 265
Thomson, Lt. Cdr. H. P., III: 159
Thomson, Cdr. R. W. N., XI: 337
Thorburn, Lt. Cdr. J. G., XII: 423, XIV: 373
Thorn, Lt. Cdr. W. A., I: 420
THORN, VIII: 404, XII: 199, 420, 429, XIII: 319
Thorndike, Lt. Cdr. G. Q., XIII: 79n, XIV: 374
Thorne, Gen. Sir Andrew, XI: 329
Thornhill, Capt. H. E., IV: 273, VI: 297
Thornton, Capt. W. N., XIV: 379
THORNTON, III: 104, IV: 85, 93, XIV: 381
Thorsen, Mr. Hans, X: 277
Thorwall, Cdr. C. A., VIII: 224n, 227
THREADFIN, XIV: 200
THREAT, I: 421, XI: 171, 333, 337-8
THRESHER, III: 213, IV: 202-3, 207-8, 229, VI: 85, VII: 187-8, 342, VIII: 24; pic., IV: 207
Threshie, Capt. R. D., XI: 341
Thronson, Lt. (jg) H. A., XII: 236
Thronson, Lt. (jg) J. M., XII: 422
THRUSH, I: 15n, 380, 390n, 420
THRUSTER, II: 268n, IX: 392, 396
THUBAN, VII: 337, 344-5, VIII: 408, XII: 418, XIII: 308, 313
Thucydides, quoted, II: vii, 46, IX: viii, XIV: vii
THUNDER, XI: 335, 337
Thurber, Capt. Harry Ray, IV: 93, VI: 94, 226, VII: 9, VIII: vii, 409; C.O. *Honolulu,* XII: 38, 145-6, 419; as Halsey's planner, VI: 13
Thurman, Lt. R. K., XIII: 306
THURSTON, II: 38, 60n, 161, 172, IX: 98, 388, XI: 335, 339
Tibbals, Lt. C. B., XIV: 377
Tibbets, Lt. Cdr. J. B., X: 212, 218
Tibbets, Lt. Joseph, I: 386
Tibbets, Col. P. W., XIV: 344
Tiburon, Cape, I: 349
Tichenor, Capt. M. J., XIV: 372
TICONDEROGA, XII: 311, 357-9, 409, XIII: 54, 57, 180-82, 317, XIV: 301
Tidball, Ens. J. M., VI: 263-4
TIDE, I: 421, XI: 333; sunk, 173
Tides, Fedhala, II: 59, Normandy, XI: 102; "dodging" in Gilberts, VII: 151-2
Tidore I., XII: 20, 29

Tiemroth, Lt. Cdr. Harold H., III: 393, IV: 91, 271, V: 86, VII: 334
Tientsin, III: 39
Tiger, I: 133
Tilden, Lt. (jg) C. E., V: 338
TILEFISH, XIV: 286
Tillessen, Kaptlt. Hans, X: 200–206, 298
TILLMAN, I: 420, II: 38, 79n, 121n, 162, 285, IX: 113, 128–31, 146, 389, X: 261–3
Tillson, Capt. E. M., I: 76, XI: 339
Timberlake, Lt. J. H., VIII: 171n
Timboe, Lt. Col. A. C., V: 188n, 192
Timm, Kaptlt. Heinrich, X: 301–3
Timmers, Lt. Cdr. H. P., VIII: 411, XIII: 318, XIV: 387
Timor, III: 49, 55, 314–16, IV: 220, VI: 30, X: 46, XII: 107, XIII: 158, 164; chart, III: 295; Sea, 316
Timothy Pickering, IX: 164
TINGEY, VIII: 413, XII: 319, 426, XIII: 317, XIV: 383
Tinian, VIII: 8–9, 149–55, 158, 162, 167, 174–5, 208, 219, 234, 260, 311, 357; invasion of, 351–70; plans, 351–7; minesweeping, 368; landing, 161, 362–4; air and naval gunfire support, 325, 351–3, 359–62, 365–7; opns. ashore, 364–70; unloading, 368; discussion, 369; T.O., 407–12; as base, XIV: 22, 320, 344; chart, 352; pic., 176
Tinker, Maj. Gen. C. L., IV: 151
TINOSA, VIII: 22–3, XIV: 292
TINSMAN, XIII: 309
Tioga, I: 272
TIPPECANOE, IV: 19, 22, 24, VII: 334
TIRANTE, XIV: 291–3
TIRPITZ, I: 64, 81–2, 161, 165, 179–81, 185, X: 55, 230–31, 308n; sunk, 310
Tisdale, Rear Adm. Mahlon S., IV: 271, V: 86, 205, 231, 294–6, 308, 313, 326, 329
TISDALE, VIII: 410, XIV: 374
Titan, VII: 347
TITANIA, I: 421, II: 40, 139, 143, 148–50, 154, 171, VI: 297, VIII: 418, XII: 416, XIII: 310, 312
Tito, Marshal Josip, XI: 228
Titterton, Cdr. G. A., IX: xv
Titus, Capt. Jack C., I: 421, VIII: 22n, XII: 64, 198n, 203n, 236n, 401n
Tiverton, XI: 61
Tiyan, VIII: 282, 373, 399
Tizard Reef, XIII: 161
Tjeweri, Cape, VIII: 80

Tjilatjap, III: 298, 305–7, 322, 330–31, 337, 341, 359–63, 375–9, IV: 220; pic., III: 285
Tjisalak, X: 299
Toa M., IV: 89
Toal, Cdr. M., XII: 429
Tobago, I: 347
Tobelman, Lt. Cdr. P. H., IV: 174
Tobera, VI: 393
Tobin, Capt. Robert G., IV: 271, V: 87, 151, 155–7, 160, 182, 232, 248, 253, VI: 308
Todd, Capt. C. R., XII: 427
Todd, Cdr. D. W., XIV: 326
Todd, Cdr. H. C., XIV: 386
Toei M., IV: 89, V: 207
Toem, VIII: 92, 97, 102, 137, 143
Togo, Adm. Heihachiro, III: 93, XII: 223, 241
Togo, Hon. Shigenori, III: 71–2, XIV: 338, 341–5, 348
Toho M., IV: 17, 88, V: 207, VI: 78
Tojo, Gen. H., III: 44, 66–71, 77–9, V: 70, 333, VI: 17–20, 23–4, 33, 403, 421, VIII: 340, XII: 65, 412, XIV: 337–8; on why U.S. won, VI: 225–6
Tokashiki Shima, XIV: 119–20, 124–7
TOKEN, XII: 421, XIV: 377
TOKITSUKAZE, III: 162, 274, 334, IV: 89, V: 85, 206, VI: 55–6
TOKIWA, III: 263
Tokiwa M., XIV: 288
Tokuno, Lt. Cdr., VI: 109–10
Tokyo, VIII: 247, XIII: 91, 157, 162, 172, XIV: 334; Bay, VII: 44, 49, XIV: 360–63; Radio, VII: 197, 331, XII: 103, 109, XIII: 172, XIV: 51–2, 129n; Halsey-Doolittle raid, III: 389–98, IV: 75, 168, 199; pics., III: 394–5
"Tokyo Express," V: 81, 108, 113, 123, VI: 207, 210, 213–14, 239, 353, 411
"Tokyo Rose," IV: 158, VI: 231, 238, VIII: 187, XII: 117, 296, XIII: 172
Tollaksen, Lt. Cdr. L. B., IV: 173, X: 357
Tollberg, Watertender M. W., V: 362
Tolman, Cdr. Charles E., V: 366
TOLMAN, XIV: 116, 134–5, 376
Tolosa, XIII: 187, 215
TOLOVANA, XIV: 387
Tolten, I: 133
"Tom Cats," XIII: 54, 58, 181
TOMAHAWK, XII: 428, XIII: 319, XIV: 387

TOMICH, X: 378
Tominaga, Lt. Gen. K., XII: 68–9
Tomioka, Rear Adm. S., III: xi, VI: 18–19, XIV: 363n
Tomlinson, Capt. W. G., X: 45, XIV: 306, 382
Tomochika, Maj. Gen. Y., XII: 139, 149, 361, XIII: 251
Tomonaga, Lt. J., IV: 104, 107
Tomonari, Col., VI: 200–202, 205
TOMOZURU, III: 161
Tompkins, Capt. B. F., VII: 23n, 334, VIII: 409, XII: 426
Tompkins, Lt. Col. R. M., VIII: 334
Tonan M., VI: 82
TONE, III: 22, 87–8, 217, 245, 276, 382, IV: 88, 103n, 106–7, 114, 179n, V: 85–7, 90, 206–8, 214, 234, 259, VII: 44, XII: 162, 186, 248, 266–71, 276, 287–8, 308–9, 431, XIII: 158; sunk, XIV: 331
Toner, Cdr. R. J., XIII: 79, 374
Toney, Cdr. A. L., VII: 341
Tongatabu, IV: 15, 60, 246, 248–9, 251, 263n, V: 113, 136
Tonnage, defined, I: 292n
Tonolei Hbr., VI: 206, 280; pic., V: 179
Tooker, Lt. Cdr. Adin, XIV: 244, 386
Tooma, Capt. R., XII: 431
Topeka, X: 232
Topper, Lt. Cdr. J. R., V: 41–2, 56
Torgerson, George, VII: 334
TORNADE, II: 230
Toro, Mr. F. A., X: 381
Torokina, Cape, VI: 283–4, and pic., 253; airfields, 350, 361–2, 394–9, 405–6, 418, 428, VII: 319, VIII: 156, XII: 107, XIII: 95
Torpedo, acoustic, I: 312, 317, 402n, X: 63, 138, 142, 174, 256–7, 261, 279n, 282, 289, 305–6, 329; defects, IV: 191, 214, 222, 230–32; aërial, VI: 328n, 332, VIII: 299; submarine, 15–16; "Fido," X: 52, 118, 124, 127–8, 364; Mark VIII, XI: 312; Mark-18 electric, XII: 402
Torpedo School, II: 263
Torpedo Squadron, One, VIII: 412; Two, IV: 19, VIII: 412; Three, IV: 90, 271, V: 86, XIII: 315; Four, XIII: 317; Five, IV: 19, 49, VII: 338, 348, XIV: 383; Six, III: 392, IV: 91, V: 205; VII: 339, 349, XIV: 384; Seven, IV: 271, V: 87, XII: 425, XIII: 316; Eight, IV: 91–2, 122, 270, V: 86, 375, VIII: 413, XII: 425; Nine, VI: 331,

VII: 339, 349, XIV: 385; Ten, V: 204, 233, VII: 348, VIII: 414, XIV: 385; Eleven, XII: 424, XIII: 316; Twelve, VII: 340, 350, XV: 383; Thirteen, XII: 427; Fourteen, VIII: 413, XII: 424; Fifteen, VIII: 414, XII: 426; Sixteen, VII: 338, VIII: 414; Seventeen, VI: 331, VII: 349, 353, XIV: 382; Eighteen, XII: 425; Nineteen, XII: 426; Twenty, XII: 427, XIII: 316; Twenty-one, XII: 428; Twenty-two, XII: 424, XIII: 315; Twenty-three, VII: 340, 350, XIV: 385; Twenty-four, VII: 348, VIII: 412; Twenty-five, VII: 349, VIII: 415; Twenty-seven, VIII: 414, XII: 427; Twenty-eight, VIII: 413, XII: 424, XIII: 315; Twenty-nine, XII: 426, XIII: 316; XIV: 384; Thirty, VII: 349, XIV: 382; Thirty-one, VII: 349, VIII: 413; Thirty-two, VII: 350, VIII: 414; Thirty-five, Thirty-seven, 420; Forty-four, XII: 427, XIII: 317; Forty-five, 317, XIV: 382; Forty-six, Forty-seven, 384–5; Fifty, Fifty-one, VIII: 413–14, XII: 428; Sixty, VIII: 420; Eighty, XIII: 317; Eighty-one, XII: 349n, XIII: 315; Eighty-two, Eighty-three, Eighty-four, Eighty-six, Eighty-eight, XIV: 382–4, 385n
Torpedo Squadron, Night, Forty-one, XII: 426, XIII: 318; Ninety, 318, XIV: 383
TORRANCE, XIV: 375
Torres, Cadet A. M., X: 219
Torrey, Lt. Cdr. P. H., VI: 331, VII: 339, 349, XIV: 385
Torricelli Mts., VIII: 73
TORSK, XIV: 293n
Toshi M., IV: 17
Toth, Lt. Cdr. J. C., X: 212
Tothill, Lt. F. C., VII: 349, XIV: 382
Totsuka, Lt. Col., XIII: 230–31
Touchet, X: 207n
Toulon, II: 218, 239, 244, IX: 305, 365, X: 252, 256, 260, XI: 226, 234–8, 244, 275, 284–91; Fleet scuttled, II: 240; chart, XI: 283; pics., 292–3
Touve, Watertender R. R., V: 57n
Tovey, Adm. Sir John, I: 165, 168, 181
Toward, I: 121–2, 336
Towers, Vice Adm. J. H., VII: 91, 104, 208
Towner, Capt. G. C., XIV: 387

Townsend, Cdr. H. E., VII: 223, 350, VIII: 405, XII: 418
Townsend, Lt. N. A., XIV: 381
Townsend, Lt. P. J., X: 206
Townsville, IV: 14, 20, V: 25, VI: 133-4
Toyama, Capt. Y., IV: 100*n*, V: 298, 301
Toyoda, Adm. Soemu, biog., VIII: 13*n*; pic., 216; quoted, 221; and History, viii; For. Min., III: 66, 70–71; Chief Nav. Gen. St., VI: 17*n*; Com. Comb. Fl. VIII: 13; KON Opn., 120, 131; A-GO Opn., 94, 117, 132, 173, 215, 218–21; Philippine Sea, 217, 231, 290, 305, 309, 318; Formosa Battle, XII: 100–101; Leyte, 65–6, 160–61; SHO Opn., 69–73, 91–2, 119, 164–8, 187–9, 192, 206–7, 238, 321, 430; Mindoro raid, XIII: 38; Okinawa, XIV: 93, 181; Surrender, 345–51
Tozuka, Vice Adm. M., VII: 65*n*, XIV: 361
Tozzer, Dr. Alfred M., XIV: 79*n*
TRACKER, X: 39, 151–2, 176, 308
Tracy, Cdr. J. S., II: 37, XIV: 381
TRACY, III: 104, 213*n*, IV: 276*n*, V: 367, XIV: 377
Train, Rear Adm. Harold C., biog., X: 200*n*; mentioned, 200–201, 203–4
Training Squadron, III: 28
Trammell-Vinson Act, III: 30
TRAMONTANE, II: 228; sunk, 230
Transden, Mr. Chris, XII: 429
Transport loading, defined, II: 27
Transport Squadron, described, XIV: 90
Transports, *No. 6,* Japanese *Nos. 101, 102, 131,* XII: 431; *No. 9,* 352; *No. 11,* 387; *No. 14,* sunk, XIII: 171, XIV: 12; *No. 27,* VIII: 119, 131
Transports, shortage of, VII: 108–10, IX: 232; no. required to lift a division, VII: 108
Trapani, IX: 39, 45, 49, 58, 79, 168, 181, 291
Trapnell, Capt. F. M., VIII: 411
TRATHEN, VII: 96, 276, 296, 347, VIII: 127, 406, XII: 244, 420, XIII: 317–18, XIV: 385
TRAVIS, I: 421
Treasury Is., V: 4, VI: 280, 283, 293, 395, 416; landing, 294–6; chart, 294
Tredinnick, Lt. (jg) F. A., XIII: 41*n*
Trench, Lt. Cdr. A. W. P., XIV: 378
TRENCHANT, X: 302
Trent, Lt. J. M., XIII: 319, XIV: 375

TRENTON, I: 16, III: 213, 265, X: 204*n*, XII: 107*n*, 119*n*, XIV: 312*n*
TREPANG, XIV: 285, 296
TREVER, III: 104, 213*n*, IV: 274, V: 169, 194–6, 206, VI: 146, 156*n*
Trévières, XI: 158, 168
TRIANGULUM, VIII: 403, XII: 423
Tribble, Lt. Cdr. J. C., VII: 228
"Trickle movement" to Russia, I: 365–6
Trieste, IX: 260, XI: 227–9
TRIESTE, sunk, IX: 37
TRIGGER, IV: 92, 157*n*, 210–13, VII: 54, VIII: 20, XII: 335, 407, 429; lost, XIV: 289–90
TRILLIUM, I: 337, 341
Trimble, Cdr. F., XII: 429
Trincomalee, III: 381–5, IV: 277
Trinidad, I: 34, 145–8, 223, 240, 244, 248, 259, 314–15, 324, 347–50, 386, X: 189, 196
TRINIDAD, I: 166, XIII: 263
TRINITY, III: 159, 193, 272, 331
Tripartite Pact, III: 45, 48
Tripoli, II: 258, IX: 251, 252*n*
TRIPOLI, X: 283, 295–6, 380
Tripp, Capt. C. W. H., VI: 145
TRIPPE, I: 110–11, 357, 420, IX: 191, 217, 347–8, 360*n*, 385, 391, 396, X: 253, 371
Trippensee, Cdr. B. E. S., VII: 411, XII: 428
Tritchler, Ens. C. O., I: 396
TRITON (Coast Guard Cutter), I: 138
TRITON (Submarine), III: 213, 241, 249, IV: 88*n*, 201–2, 213, 216–17, VII: 7
TRIUMPH, XIII: 306, 376
Trobriand Is., II: 271, VI: 37, 62, 95–7, 254, 373; chart, 29; landing, 132–4; pic., 133
TROMBE, XI: 312
TROMP, III: 273, 299–300, 308, 322, 325, 328, XIII: 269; pic., III: 285
Trondheim, I: 161, X: 326
TROOPER, IX: 42
Troops, shortage of in Pacific, XII: 17, XIII: 3
Trosino, Cdr. Earl, X: 293
Troubadour, I: 180, 190, 191*n*, 373; pic., 170–71
Troubridge, Rear Adm. Thomas H., II: 17, 223, IX: 149–51, 157–62, 333, 338–41, 345, 351, 381, 396, XI: 239, 279, 342; pic., IX: 163
TROUBRIDGE, II: 281, IX: 394, XI: 342
Trousdale, Lt. J. H., VIII: 261

TROUT, III: 203, 213, IV: 91, 199–200, V: 271, VI: 85, VIII: 167, 373; sunk, 17

True, Cdr. A. E., IV: 19, 156*n*, V: 205, 233

True, Signalman D. E., IX: 137

True, Radioman E. J., IX: 102

Truesdell, Lt. Cdr. W. H., V: 42, 56

Truitt, Cdr. I. W., VII: 341

Truk I., III: 7, 26, IV: 12, 17, 25, 61–2, 150–52, 270, V: 70, 82, 104–228 *passim*, 238, VI: 6, 139, 143, 207, 284–5, 305, 347, 401–3, 411, 433, VII: 44, 49, 74, 84, 123, 136–8, 141–2, 201, 286, VIII: 9–10, 20, 29, 154*n*, 172, 219, 222, 263, 290, 324, 329, XIV: 10; strategic importance, VII: 69, 316–19; described, 316–17; lagoon, pic., 311; raid of Feb. 1944, 286, 315–31, VIII: 27; T.O., VII: 352; charts, 322–3, 327; pic., 318; air raids on, VIII: 38–40, 156, 174, 206, 313, 354, XII: 107; raid of Apr. 1944, VIII: 38–40

Truman, President Harry, XIII: 300, XIV: 339, 342–9, 355, 358

Trumbull, Robert, IV: 159*n*

TRUMPETER, X: 380

Truscott, Maj. Gen. Lucian K., II: 16, 25, 33, 36, 47, 116–18, 121–29, 133, IX: 28–33, 79–90, 173–7, 181–4, 196, 220, 300–315 *passim*, XI: 236, 266, 272

TRUXTUN, I: 15*n*, 418

TRYON, XIII: 307

Tsingtien, XIII: 300

TSUGA, XIII: 171

TSUGARU, IV: 18, VIII: 119, 131

Tsugen Jima, XIV: 220

Tsukahara, Vice Adm. N., III: 163, V: 80, 85

Tsukioka, Cdr., VI: 137

Tsukushi M., III: 274, XII: 432

Tsuruga M., III: 275, 290

TSURUMI, IV: 88

Tsushima Strait, Battle of, III: 93, XII: 223, 241

TSUTA, V: 85*n*

Tualatin, VIII: 420

Tucker, Dr. G. N., I: xvi; *Naval Service of Canada*, X: xv

Tucker, Boatswain H. W., XIII: 299

Tucker, Capt. T. T., X: 295, 380

TUCKER, III: 104, 213*n*; sunk, V: 182*n*

Tufi, VI: 48, 60–61

Tufts, Lt. Cdr. D. A., X: 378

Tuggle, Capt. R. B., IX: 390, XIII: 317, XIV: 384

Tugugarao, III: 170, 176, XIII: 133, 181

TUI, V: 349

TULAGI, XI: 239, 279–81, 342, XIII: 104, 305, XIV: 18, 196, 318, 374

Tulagi I., IV: 5, 12, 16–17, 22–5, 74, 252–4, V: 4, 10–12, 20, 35; pics., IV: 288, 292; base, V: 58, 114, 145, 169, 181, 187, 196, 255–369 *passim*, VI: 67, 73, 102, 113–94 *passim*, 213, 237, 295, VII: 102, VIII: 170, 219; Raid, IV: 25–8, chart, 23; landing, 287–90, V: 16, 66; casualties, 292

TULLIBEE, VIII: 30–31

TULSA, III: 155, 159, 194, 298, 379, VI: 47–8, 53

TUMULT, IX: 394, XI: 342, XII: 421

TUNA, IV: 203, XII: 333, 429, XIII: 282

Tungsha Tao, XIII: 287

Tunis, II: 260, 274, IX: 33, 101, 324–5, 362

Tunisian Campaign, II: 258–60; naval opns., 239–74; chart, 256–7; War Channel, IX: 65, 152

TUNISIEN, X: 381, XI: 343

Tunney, Cdr. J. J., XIV: 111

TUNNY, VIII: 30–31, 415, XII: 399, XIV: 292*n*

TUPELO, VIII: 420

Turkey, IX: 3, 6, XI: 22

TURKEY, III: 104, XIV: 388

Turkey Shoot, VIII: 257–78

Turnabout I. and Light, XII: 402; XI: 297

Turnage, Maj. Gen. A. H., VI: 289*n*, 296–8, 348, 360, 364, 365*n*, VIII: 383, 396, 418

Turner, Lt. Cdr. Blaney C., XIII: 191

Turner, Cdr. C. H., XIII: 315

Turner, Capt. E. C. L., IX: 329, 338, 342, 395

Turner, Lt. (jg) J. D., XII: 281*n*

Turner, Lt. Cdr. Renfro, X: 216, 224–5, 227*n*

Turner, Adm. Richmond Kelly, biog., V: 14*n*; pics., VII: frontispiece, XIV: 46; Cominch staff, I: 43*n*, 45, 116, III: 50, 134, VI: 9*n*, XI: 8; C.O. *Astoria*, III: 37; escort of convoy, I: 51; Guadalcanal, IV: 268, 272, 280–83, V: 4, 14, 36; Savo I. Bat., 22–64 *passim*; Sept. 1942, 114–16, 120–21, 130–31, 137–8; Oct., 140, 148, 172; Nov., 227–8;

Turner, Adm. Richmond Kelly (*cont'd*)
AA tactics, 230; Bat. Guadalcanal, 235–6, 259, 278–85, 295, 372; central Solomons, VI: 14, 97–100, 129, 138, 142–7, 150–52, 155, 177, 180, 189–90, 227, VII: 44; amphibious doctrine, VI: 131; Gilberts, VII: 86–8, 99, 111, 114, 118–23, 134, 142, 145, 152, 167, 336; Marshalls, 206–7, 210, 228, 232–3, 240, 251–2, 257–9, 260n, 272, 278–81, 285, 306, 343; Marianas, VIII: 158–90 *passim*, 200–202, 209, 242, 311–77 *passim*, 407; UDTs, 166; Iwo, XIV: 7, 32–5, 51–2, 65, 73; Okinawa, 87–9, 102, 108–11, 115n, 117, 140, 147, 161, 166, 175, 178, 195, 204, 215–73 *passim*, 372; Kerama Retto, 117–18; Occupation of Japan, 357; quoted, VII: 120; "Lessons Learned at Tarawa," 202
Turner, Capt. T. A., X: 129
TURNER, X: 158
Turney, Capt. H. W., XIV: 375
Turnquist, Cdr. W. H., VIII: 407, XII: 416, XIII: 308
TURQUOISE, I: 146
TUSCALOOSA, I: 14, 15n, 36, 69, 82–3, 168, 180–81, 359–60, 372, 419, II: 36, 43, 91–100, 104, 285, III: 31n, IX: 326n, X: 229–31, XI: 86, 106, 157, 161, 167, 197–276 *passim*, 334, 337, 341, XIV: 27, 30, 88n, 372; pic., II: 92
TUSCAN, XI: 342
TUSCANA, VIII: 420, XIV: 377
Tutu, Mr., VII: 177–8

Tutuila, IV: 263n
TUTUILA, III: 39, 155
TWIGGS, XII: 419, XIII: 305, XIV: 44, 239, 275, 372, 392; sunk, 275
Twining, Col. M. B., IV: 267
Twining, Maj. Gen. N. F., VI: 290–91
TWINING, VII: 409, 415, XII: 319, 426, XIV: 383
Twitty, Brig. Gen. J. J., VI: 11n
TWO STEP, IX: 396
Twomey, Capt. J. J., II: 36, IX: 390, XIV: 380
Two-ocean Navy, I: 27–8, III: 59, X: 5
Tyler, Cdr. C. L., II: 106n, 109n, XIV: 378
Tyler, Capt. M. A., IV: 92
TYLER, X: 337
Tyminski, Cdr. R., IX: 393
TYNE, XIV: 388
TYNEDALE, sunk, X: 252–3
TYNWALD, II: 190, 198, 212, 220; sunk, 221, 284
TYPHON, II: 229, 237, 252
Typhoon, VII: 347
Typhoon of Oct. 1944, XII: 77, 86; Dec. 1944, XIII: 59–84, chart, 62, 78, pic., 84; June 1945, XIV: 298–309, chart, 302–3, pic., 311
Tyree, Cdr. A. K., XIV: 292n, 296
Tyree, Cdr. D. M., VI: 204n
TYRIAN, IX: 394, XI: 342
TYRRELL, XIV: 380
Tyrrhenian Sea, IX: 189
Tyson, Cdr. I. J., X: 309

U

U. S. GRANT, VII: 46, 334
U-boat Subcommittee, War Cabinet, X: 17
U-boats, histories of individual. See under U-boats by number below
U-boats, in World War I, I: 125-6; no. at outbreak of World War II, 4-10, X: 3; production, I: 4-7, 128, 410, 60-63, 246-7, 366; charts and tables of sinkings by, I: 20-21, 59, 124, 140-41, 313, 404, 410-14, X: 14-15, 66, 136, 193, 254-5, 294, 301; bases, I: 22-3, 34-5, X: 85n, 105n, 252-60; tactics and strategy, I: 24-6 (wolf packs), 128-30, 199-200, 304, 318, 322, 325, 342-3, X: 58-60, 63, 81, 90-92, 150, 366; political restrictions, I: 35; deployment, 95; supply ships, 111, 129, 312, 317, 381; minelaying, 136-7; and aircraft, 142, 325-6, 402; rumors of Central American bases, 150-51; peak of achievement, I: 317, 344; nos. operating, 407, 410, X: 366; charts and tables of losses, I: 415, X: 179, 193, 217, 301, 366, 370-73, 382; average kill per U-boat, 407; weather patrol, X: 319-20, 331-2; midget, XI: 155, 192, 371-2; 1942 offensive, I: 126-56, 249, 311-18, 321-6, 330-37, 346-54, 385-6, IV: 247, 258, X: 7-8; N. Africa, II: 18n, 167-74, 246, chart, 172; 1943 offensive, I: 337-46, 355-8, 387-90; South Atlantic, I: 381-3, 386, X: 209-28, 298-9; Far East, IV: 197; Indian Ocean, VI: 16, X: 274-8, 299-304; Med., II: 195, IX: 38, 40-43, 152, 156, 312-13, X: 250-73, XI: 226, 284; 1944-45 operations, British waters, X: 297-8, 318-19, 325-9, 339-41, XI: 107-8, 155-6, 342-4; surrender, X: 359-61; Types, table of, I: 4n; X: 60-63, snorkel, I: 402, X: 317-19, 325-44. See also individual boats below, grouped by numbers.
U-30, I: 9, X: 3; -43, 371, and sunk, 119; -56, 373; -66, I: 417, X: 122-3, 181-3, 283, 288n, and sunk, 284-7,
372, and pic., 113; -67, sunk, 118, 370; -68, I: 151, and sunk, X: 283, 372; -69, I: 63, 417; -73, sunk, X: 253, 371; -81, IX: 41, and sunk, X: 371; -84, 192, 198n, and sunk, 127, 371; -85, sunk, I: 155, 415; -86, sunk, X: 168, 371; -87, I: 417; -88, sunk, 365n; -89, sunk, X: 78; -91, 82, 162-3; -94, sunk, I: 249, 348-9, 415; -98, 417
U-101, I: 93; -106, sunk, X: 98; -107, 187-8, 319, 374; -108, sunk, 372; -117, 122, 188n, and sunk, 123, 371, and pic., 113; -118, sunk, 113-14, 370, and pic., 112; -119, 184, 374, and sunk, 93; -123, I: 127, 283, X: 281; -125, sunk, 75; -126, -128, I: 134-5, X: 209, and sunk, 210, 370; -129, 180-81, 283; -130, I: 352, II: 171-3, and sunk, I: 358, 415; -132, 109; -134, X: 194, 198n, and sunk, 125; -135, sunk, 131, 370; -153, I: 153-5, and sunk, 153n, 154, 415; -154, X: 209, 297, and sunk, 322, 372; -155, 98; -156, 57n-8n, and sunk, I: 351-2, 415; -157, 143-4, and sunk, 155, 415; -158, 228, and sunk, 155, 249, 415; -159, 151-2, X: 198n, and sunk, 192, 370; -160, 275, and sunk, 118, 370; -161, I: 145, 152-3, II: 13n, X: 125, 180-81, 224, and sunk, 371; -162, sunk, I: 347-8; -164, 386, and sunk, 415; -166, 417, and sunk, 137, 249, 415; -168, and sunk, X: 302; -170, 224; -172, I: 152, X: 215, 218-22, and sunk, 169-70, 371; -173, II: 169-70, and sunk, I: 352, II: 174; -174, X: 188n, and sunk, I: 415, X: 180; -175, sunk, I: 415, and pics., 344-5; -176, sunk, X: 190-91, 370; -177, sunk, 293, 372; -178, 275, 304n; -180, 211; -181, 302, and sunk, 304n; -182, 210, and sunk, 274-5, 370; -183, X: 117, and sunk, 303, XIII: 286; -185, X: 92, 215, 220-22, and sunk, 127, 371, and pic., 113; -186, sunk, 78; -187, sunk, I: 335; -188, X: 278, 284, 288, 304n; -190, 181; -192, 69, and

U-boats (*cont'd*)
sunk, 74; *–193*, 207*n*; *–195*, 210–11, 296*n*; *–196*, 295; *–197*, 211; *–198*, sunk, 302; *–199*, 214–15, 219, and sunk, 371

U-200, sunk, X: 370; *–202*, I: 200; *–203*, 73; *–207*, 71; *–210*, 321, and sunk, 322, and pic., 375; *–213*, 417; *–214*, X: 126, 199, 283, 374; *–217*, 111–12, 370; *–218*, 82, 199, 297, 374; *–219*, 169–70, 296, 302; *–220*, 188, 374, and sunk, 157, 162, 371; *–223*, sunk, IX: 371; *–225*, sunk, I: 415; *–226*, X: 151–2; *–229*, 144; *–230*, 184, 374, XI: 285; and sunk, X: 373, XI: 284; *–231*, X: 80; *–232*, sunk, 130–31, 370; *–233*, 319, 372; *–234*, 360; *–238*, 140–42, 145, 168; *–248*, 332, and sunk, 333, 373; *–249*, 359, pic., 328, *–253*, I: 181*n*; *–254*, sunk, I: 325; *–255*, X: 279*n*; *–256*, 163; *–258*, 68–9; *–262*, 95, 123; *–264*, 159–60, and sunk, 317*n*; *–266*, 74, and sunk, 79; *–267*, 74–5; *–270*, 139, 144; *–271*, 162, and sunk, 371; *–274*, sunk, 151; *–275*, 174–6; *–279*, sunk, 147; *–286*, 313

U-302, X: 318; *–305*, 81, 173; *–307*, 236, and sunk, 313; *–309*, 339; *–311*, 318; *–314*, sunk, 306; *–325*, sunk, 340; *–327*, sunk, 339, 373; *–333*, 181*n*; *–336*, sunk, 146–7, 371; *–338*, 90, sunk, 142; *–340*, sunk, 157*n*; *–341*, sunk, 139; *–344*, sunk, 300; *–352*, sunk, I: 155, 415; *–354*, sunk, X: 309; *–359*, 198*n*, and sunk, 371; *–365*, sunk, 310; *–367*, I: 181*n*; *–371*, IX: 40, 313, and sunk, 313*n*, X: 256–7, 372; *–373*, I: 417, X: 119; *–375*, IX: 40, and sunk, 41, X: 252, 371; *–376*, 90; *–377*, 144; *–378*, 147, 161, and sunk, 161, 371; *–379*, I: 322, 326; *–380*, II: 214*n*, and sunk, X: 372; *–381*, 69; *–382*, 175; *–383*, sunk, 98; *–386*, 68, 142; *–387*, sunk, 310; *–388*, 370; *–389*, sunk, 147; *–391*, sunk, 103; *–392*, 372; *–394*, sunk, 309; *–399*, sunk, 340

U-402, X: 144, and sunk, 161, 371; *–403*, 119; *–404*, sunk, 96, 371; *–405*, sunk, 163–4, 371; *–407*, sunk, 260; *–408*, sunk, I: 249, 415; *–409*, sunk, IX: 40–41; *–410*, 366, and sunk, X: 372; *–415*, 173, 195, 199*n*; *–418*, 77, and sunk, 92; *–419*, sunk, 148; *–420*, sunk, 151; *–421*, sunk, 260, 372; *–422*, sunk, 159–60, 371; *–425*, 310, and sunk, 311; *–426*, 149; *–432*, I: 284, 288; *–435*, 365*n*, and sunk, X: 131; *–438*, 71, and sunk, 75; *–441*, 92; *–449*, sunk, 93; *–453*, IX: 40, 156; *–454*, sunk, X: 98; *–455*, I: 417, X: 159–60; *–456*, I: 332, sunk, X: 78; *–457*, sunk, I: 365*n*; *–459*, X: 222; *–460*, I: 381, and sunk, X: 159–60, 371; *–461*, 222, and sunk, 96, 371; *–462*, 222, 275, and sunk, 96; *–463*, 222; *–464*, sunk, I: 249, 415; *–466*, X: 218, and sunk, 373; *–467*, 222, and sunk, 370; *–468*, 80–82; *–470*, and sunk, 148; *–471*, 134–5, and sunk, 373; *–480*, sunk, 339; *–482*, 328; *–486*, 335–7; *–487*, sunk, 117–18, 370; *–488*, 112, 160–62, and sunk, 283–4, 372; *–489*, 222, and sunk, 320–21, 372; *–490*, sunk, 320–21, 372

U-501, I: 71; *–503*, sunk, 154, 248, 415; *–504*, 135, 152, and sunk, X: 96–8; *–505*, captured, 291–3, 372, and pic., 289; *–506*, sunk, 131, 370; *–507*, sunk, I: 415; *–508*, X: 128, and sunk, 103, 371; *–509*, 275, and sunk, 118, 370; *–510*, 216, 227, and sunk, 215; *–512*, sunk, I: 350, 415; *–513*, X: 213–15, and sunk, 218–19, 370; *–515*, II: 173, X: 186, 211–12, 290, and sunk, 282, 372; *–516*, 200–207, 298; *–518*, 199, 297, 327, and sunk, 349–50, 373; *–519*, sunk, I: 415, X: 88; *–521*, 181, 188*n*, and sunk, 182, 370; *–524*, sunk, I: 415, X: 129; *–525*, sunk, 124, 371; *–527*, sunk, 121, 370; *–528*, sunk, 105*n*; *–530*, 207*n*, 298, 360–61; *–531*, sunk, 75; *–533*, sunk, 75, 275; *–537*, 283, 329*n*, and sunk, 302; *–539*, 297–8; *–540*, sunk, 148; *–541*, 328; *–543*, 283, and sunk, 299, 372; *–544*, 371; sunk, 281–2; *–545*, 152*n*; *–546*, 351–3; sunk, 354–5, 372; *–548*, 343; sunk, 344, 373; *–549*, sunk, 289, 372; *–550*, sunk, 318–19, 372; *–552*, I: 133*n*; *–558*, sunk, X: 94, 370; *–561*, sunk, IX: 41; *–562*, I: 94; *–564*, sunk, X: 92; *–565*, sunk, 260, 373; *–566*, 184–6, 374; *–568*, I: 93; *–569*, X: 81, 370, and pic., 112; *–570*, I: 71*n*–2*n*, 290*n*; *–572*, X: 116, 198*n*, and sunk, 195, 371; *–574*, I: 133; *–575*, sunk, X: 317*n*, 372; *–576*, I: 249, 395–6, 415; *–578*, 132; *–584*, 200, 282*n*, X: 74, 143, and sunk, 162, 371; *–586*, sunk, 372; *–588*, sunk, I: 321; *–590*,

X: 215, and sunk, 370; *-591,* sunk, 219–20, 371; *-593,* IX: 33, and sunk, X: 252–3, 371; *-596,* sunk, 260, 373; *-597,* 306; *-598,* sunk, 216, 371

U-601, X: 238; *-603,* 111, 279, and sunk, 372; *-604,* 127, 220–21, and sunk, 222, 371; *-606,* I: 340, and sunk, 415; *-608,* 417; *-609,* sunk, 336; *-610,* sunk, X: 148; *-611,* sunk, I: 249, 325, 415; *-613,* X: 188n, and sunk, 119–21, 371; *-614,* sunk, 96; *-615,* 198n, and sunk, 195–7, 371; *-616,* IX: 313n, and sunk, X: 257–9, 372; *-622,* sunk, 371; *-624,* sunk, I: 337; *-630,* sunk, X: 71, 76; *-631,* sunk, 149; *-633,* sunk, I: 344; *-638,* sunk, X: 74; *-640,* 77; *-641,* 111, 143; *-642,* 131, and sunk, 372; *-643,* sunk, 148; *-645,* 148, and sunk, 174, 371; *-646,* sunk, 79n; *-648,* 121, 152; *-650,* 68; *-652,* I: 79–80; *-653,* X: 195, 198n, 216; *-654,* sunk, I: 415; *-656,* sunk, 154, 248, 415; *-657,* sunk, X: 370; *-662,* sunk, 216, 370; *-664,* 123–4, and sunk, 124, 371; *-665,* sunk, 90; *-666,* 144–5; *-671,* sunk, XI: 193; *-681,* sunk, X: 340, 373

U-701, I: 136–7, 155–6, 417, and sunk, 137, 247n, 415; *-706,* sunk, X: 98, 371; *-709,* sunk, 279, 372; *-716,* 238; *-731,* 147, and sunk, 372; *-732,* 192–3, 198n, and sunk, 157n; *-744,* 152n; *-751,* I: 417; *-752,* sunk, X: 52n, 82; *-753,* 78; *-758,* 90n, 112–14, 147; *-759,* 191, 198n, and sunk, 192, 371; *-760,* 95, 125n; *-761,* 372; *-772,* 337

U-801, sunk, X: 269–80, 372; *-802,* 326–8; *-804,* 322, 325; *-805,* 349, 355, 360; *-841,* sunk, 149; *-842,* sunk, 152; *-843,* 288, 304n; *-844,* sunk, 148; *-847,* sunk, 128, 371; *-848,* sunk, 225, 371, pic., 225; *-849,* sunk, 225–6, 371; *-850,* sunk, 170–71, 371; *-852,* 300–301; *-853,* 322; sunk, 321, 356–7, 373; *-855,* 325; *-856,* 372; *-857,* sunk, 343–4, 373; *-858,* 325, 355, 360; *-859,* sunk, 302; *-860,* sunk, 295, 372; *-861,* 302, 304n; *-862,* 301–3; *-863,* sunk, 329n, 373; *-866,* sunk, 342, 373; *-869,* sunk, 339, 373; *-870,* 331–2; *-872,* sunk, 372; *-873,* 360n; *-879,* sunk, 343, 373; *-880,* sunk, 348–9, 373; *-881,* sunk, 355, 373

U-921, sunk, X: 310; *-951,* sunk, 130, 370; *-952,* 143–5, sunk, 373; *-953,* IX: 40, X: 131; *-954,* sunk, 79n; *-960,* sunk, 259–60, 372; *-961,* sunk, 308; *-964,* sunk, 148; *-966,* sunk, 102–3, 371; *-967,* 257, sunk, 373; *-968,* 311; *-969,* sunk, 373; *-977,* 360–61; *-986,* sunk, X: 372

U-1003, sunk, X: 340; *-1006,* sunk, 329n; *-1014,* *-1018,* sunk, 339; *-1024,* captured, 340; *-1051,* sunk, 337; *-1053,* 331–2; *-1055,* sunk, 373; *-1059,* sunk, 280, 372; *-1062,* 288; sunk, 296, 329n, 373; *-1063,* sunk, 340

U-1107, X: 373; *-1172,* sunk, 337; *-1195,* sunk, 340; *-1199,* sunk, 337

U-1208, X: 339; *-1221,* *-1223,* 329; *-1224,* 289, sunk, 372; *-1228,* 360n; *-1229,* sunk, 326–7, 373, pic., 329; *-1230,* 330–31; *-1232,* 331; *-1235,* sunk, 348, 373; *-1274,* sunk, 340

U-1302, sunk, 340; *-2323,* sunk, 372; *-2501,* 61; *-2515,* *-2523,* *-2530,* *-3007,* sunk, 373

UIT-23, sunk, X: 277

UJ-2207, *-2216,* sunk, XI: 314–15; *-2223,* sunk, 373; *-6081,* sunk, 252

Uchida, Lt. K., III: 249

Ueg, King of Ulithi, XII: 49

Uehling, Dr. Edwin A., I: 224

Ugaki, Vice Adm. M., III: 86, IV: 87, VI: 129, VIII: 131, 221, 231, 241, 416, XII: 172, 184–7, 251, 260, 430, XIV: 93–4, 100

UGANDA, IX: 207, 276, 282, 290–91, 393, XIV: 388

Uhlig, Kaptlt. Herbert, X: 121

UHLMANN, XII: 319, 426, XIII: 316, XIV: 248–9, 386

Ujae Atoll, VII: 312

Ujelang Atoll, VII: 213, 314

Ulithi, history and description, XII: 48–9, and chart, 48; carrier strikes on, VIII: 367; occupation, XII: 11, 16, 47–9; base, 49–50, 75–81, 86, 104–5, 150, 341–9, 354–9, XIII: 9, 55, 83–4, 87–8, 93, 155–6, 161, 175, 182–3, 208, XIV: 8, 18–21, 41, 57–9, 89, 93, 101, 106, 109–11, 158–64, 357, 387; weather station, XIII: 83

"Ulithi Navy," XII: 52

Ulrich, Ens. C. M., I: 187

ULSTER, XIV: 212
ULSTER MONARCH, II: 195n, IX: 162, 393
ULSTER QUEEN, IX: 351, 355, 391, 396, XI: 339
ULTOR, IX: 307, 339, 397
ULVERT M. MOORE, XIII: 104, 278–9, 305, XIV: 374
Umezu, Gen. Y., XIV: 345–9, 363, 366; pic., 366–7
UMIKAZE, III: 162, 275, V: 85, 206, VI: 68, 332; sunk, 73, VII: 222, VIII: 19
Umnak I., IV: 164, 167, 170–71, 174–83, VII: 12
Umstead, Maj. F. G., VI: 237n
Umstead, Capt. Scott, I: 419, II: 39, 135n
Umurbrogol Ridge, XII: 41–2, and pic., 39
Unalaska, IV: 167
Underhill, Lt. Cdr. J. J., I: 420
Underhill, Brig. Gen. J. L., VII: 236, 345
UNDERHILL, XIV: 317; sunk, 318
Underwater Demolition Team School, Kameole, VIII: 166
Underwater Demolition Teams (UDTs), VIII: 165–6; Kwajalein, VII: 245, 252; Marianas, VIII: 183–4, 196, 208, 354–5, 359, 363, 383, 401; Normandy, XI: 101, 131, 138, 152, 164; France, 241, 256, 262; Palaus, XII: 33–5, 44; Leyte, 122; Lingayen, XIII: 112, 142; Zambales, 188; Borneo, 264, 270–71; Iwo Jima, XIV: 27–31; Okinawa, 120–25, 128, 132–9, 153, 240

Team Three, VIII: 380, XII: 422; Four, 422, XIV: 378; Five, XII: 422, XIII: 304; Six, XII: 422; Seven, 422, XIV: 378; Eight, Nine, XII: 422, XIII: 304; Ten, XII: 44, 422, XIII: 304; Eleven, XIII: 270–71, XIV: 378; Twelve, Thirteen, 377; Fourteen, XIII: 304, XIV: 377; Fifteen, XIII: 304; Sixteen, Seventeen, XIV: 378; Eighteen, XIII: 270–71; Nineteen, Twenty-one, XIV: 378
Underwood, Cdr. G. W., XII: 400, 409, XIV: 289
UNDINE, XIV: 107
Unger, Lt. Cdr. A. C., IX: 387
Unicoi, I: 249, 349, 395, 415
UNICORN, IX: 250, 393
UNIMAK, I: 420
UNITED, IX: 42

United States-Canadian Mutual Defense Pact, I: 32
United States Strategic Bombing Survey, *Campaigns of Pacific*, III: x; *Interrogations Jap. Officials*, x; *German Submarine Industry*, I: 4n
United V., I: 294n
Unmacht, Lt. Cdr. G. P., X: 377
UNRULY, IX: 42
UNRYU, XIII: 38, 158, XIV: 286; sunk, XII: 161n, XIV: 286
UNYO, VII: 189; sunk, XII: 399
Updegraff, Cdr. W. N., IV: 174
Upham, Capt. F. K., XII: 349n, XIII: 315, 317
UPROAR, IX: 340, 396
UPSHUR, I: 76, 86–7, 418, 420, XIV: 88n
Upson, Lt. Cdr. R., VII: 338, 348
Upthegrove, Col. F. R., VI: 64
URAKAZE, III: 87, IV: 88, V: 206, 339, VI: 37, 71, 332, VIII: 280–81, 416, XII: 272n, 431; sunk, 410
Uran, Lt. B. F., XIV: 378
URANAMI, III: 276, IV: 89, V: 85, 234, 274–6, 282, VI: 56, 62, VIII: 118, 125, 130, XII: 164, 431; sunk, VI: 63–4, XII: 239
URANUS, I: 422
URCHIN, IX: 396
Urquhart, Lt. Cdr. J. G., VIII: 410
Urquhart, Brig. R. E., IX: 150
URSULA, II: 235
Ushi Pt., Tinian, VIII: 325, 354, 357, 365–8
Ushijima, Lt. Gen. M., XIV: 102, 139, 170, 242–3, 266–7, 276
USHIO, III: 87–8, 334, IV: 17, 172, V: 84, XII: 190, 238, 356n, 431, XIII: 158
Ústica I., IX: 194
USUGUMO, VII: 43
UTAH, III: 113–14, XIII: 187n, XIV: 26n; pic., III: 102
Utah Beach, rehearsal and movement, XI: 65, 77, 80–81, 93; minesweeping, 94–100, 108; landing, 93–109, and chart, 99; naval gunfire support, 95–6, 104–7, 160–61, and chart, 99; opns. ashore, 156–7; unloading, 108, 162–4
UTE, VII: 334, XIV: 260, 387
Utgoff, Lt. Cdr. V. V., XII: 422
Utirik Atoll, VII: 313n
Utter, Cdr. H. T., XIV: 383
UVALDE, XIII: 307, 313, XIV: 380
UZUKI, IV: 17, V: 85, 105, 323, VI: 353, 356–8, VIII: 417; sunk, XII: 391

V

V-1, V-2, bomb and missile, XI: 43, 61
Vaenga Bay, I: 359
VALIANT, IX: 167, 293–7, 393
Valle, Adm. M. della, IX: xiv, 60n
VAMMEN, XIV: 381
VAMPIRE, III: 188–9, 384–5
Van Antwerp, Lt. Cdr. L. M., XII: 425
Van Arsdall, Cdr. C. J., VIII: 419,
XIV: 260, 381
Van Bergen, Capt. N. B., III: 298n,
XII: 419, XIII: 310, 378
VAN BUREN, XII: 418
Van der Poel, Lt. Cdr. P. A., I: 38n
Van Deurs, Capt. George, XII: 420,
XIV: 374
Van Eaton, Cdr. A. M., VII: 335–7
Van Every, S. A., VI: 376n
VAN GHENT, III: 273, 309
Van Heemskerk, VI: 36, 126–7
Van Heutz, VI: 36
Van Hook, Rear Adm. Clifford E.,
I: 149–54, XIII: 6
Van Lear Black, X: 381
Van Mater, Cdr. Blinn, VIII: 409, 414
Van Mater, Cdr. S., XII: 305
Van Metre, Cdr. M., I: 420, II: 39, XII:
427
Van Mook, Gov. H. J., XIII: 276
VAN NES, III: 273, 331
Van Orman, Lt. Col. E. G., VIII: 366
Van Outhoorn, VI: 126–7
Van Oyen, Maj. Gen. L. H., III: 271,
337
Van Sticklen, Lt. J. H., XIII: 221, 322
Van Straelen, Capt. P. B. M., III: 333
Van Swearingen, Lt. Cdr. E. K.,
IV: 272n, VII: 338
Van Valkenburgh, Capt. Franklin,
III: 108
VAN VALKENBURGH, XIV: 154, 259–61
Van Vollenhoven, VI: 82
Van Winkle, Lt. Robert, XII: 422,
XIII: 306
Van Wyen, Lt. A. O., "Air Operations
in Marianas," VIII: 164n
Van Zandt, Cdr. J. E., VIII: 405,
XIII: 309

Van Zant, Cdr. R. B., IV: 20
Vanasse, Cdr. R. B., XI: 335
VANCOUVER, VII: 333
Vancouver I., IV: 165n
Vandegrift, Gen. Alexander A., biog.,
V: 15n; pics., IV: 279, V: 130; Gua-
dalcanal, IV: 265, 269, 272, 279–80, 286,
289, V: 12, 15, 31–4, 65–8, 115–45 pas-
sim, 178, 198, 260, 273, 289–91, 334,
372; Bougainville, VI: 281, 282n, 289,
296, 304; Guam, VIII: 400
Vandenberg, Hon. A. H., III: 210
VANESSA, I: 326
Vangunu I., V: 323; landing, VI: 152–3
Vanikoro I., V: 201
VANOC, X: 372
Vanous, Cdr. W. W., VIII: 403
VANQUISHER, X: 148
Vargas, Pres. Getulio, I: 382, 386,
X: 208
Varian, Cdr. D. C., VIII: 409
VARIAN, X: 332–3, 354–5, 360, 376
Vasey, Maj. Gen. G. A., VI: 46, 266–7,
271–2
Veasey, Cdr. A. C., VII: 348, XII: 425,
XIII: 318
Veeder, Cdr. W. S., IV: 173, VIII: 403
VEGA, XIV: 26n
VEGREVILLE, XI: 333–5
Vejtasa, Lt. S. W., V: 211, 217
Vella Gulf, VI: 114, 190, 207; Battle of,
212–20; T.O., 214; chart, 217
Vella Lavella, V: 4, VI: 192–4, 221,
295, 303, 319, 416; occupation of,
227–39; U.S. expeditionary force
T.O., 228–9; casualties, 233; Battle of,
243–52, and chart, 249; Jap. evacua-
tion, 243–52, and chart, 240; Jap.
evacuation force T.O., 244
VELOCITY, XII: 421, XIV: 377
VELOX, II: 209–10
Vema, I: 273
Vendsen, S. S., X: 381
Venezia, X: 181, 213
Venice, IX: 260
VENOMOUS, II: 173
Venter, Lt. J. D., V: 310n

Ventimiglia, XI: 313
Ventotine I., IX: 251*n*
Verde Is. Passage, XII: 348, XIII: 17, 50, 209
Verge, Cdr. W. E., XIII: 266, 310, 322–3
VERITY, II: 254
VERMONT, VII: 232*n*
VERVAIN, I: 325, X: 339
Vesole, Ens. K. K., IX: 319
VESPER, XI: 336
Vest, Capt. J. P. W., X: 16–17, 130*n*, 283, 320–21, 356–7, 378
VESTAL, III: 108, V: 259*n*, 312, VII: 138, 341, VIII: 420, X: 200*n*, XIV: 387; pic., III: 84
VESUVIUS, XIV: 167*n*, 386
VETERAN, I: 71; sunk, 323
Vetter, Capt. J. P., VIII: 165*n*
Vian, Vice Adm. Sir Philip, IX: 150–55, 251, 293, 393, XI: 29, 52, 69–70, 180, 187, 190–91, XIV: 104–5, 211–14, 388; pic., IX: 163
VIBURNUM, XII: 50
VICEROY, X: 340
Viceroy of India, II: 195*n*, 283
Vickery, Rear Adm. Howard L., I: 291
VICKSBURG, XIV: 27, 42, 382, 386
Victor, Lt. Martin, XIV: 379
Victor Emmanuel III, IX: 186–7, 237
Victoria, II: 73
VICTORIOUS, I: 165, 168, 181, II: 189, XIV: 105, 265, 388; pic., I: 210
VIDETTE, X: 67, 75, XI: 336
Vienna, XI: 227–8
Viera de Mello, Vice Adm. A., X: 226
Vierville, XI: 113, 150
Vietinghoff, Gen. von, IX: 218, 260, 296, 302, 310, 382, XI: 312, 316
Vieweg, Capt. W. V. R., XII: 282–4, 421
Vigan, III: 176, XIII: 14, 57, 187*n*
VIGILANCE, XIV: 376
VIGILANT, I: 135
Vila, VI: 90, 93–5, 99, 106, 119, 210, 222–3, 227, 239–41; bombardments, V: 344–7, VI: 107–10, 115–16; action off, 107–10; charts, V: 327, VI: 109; pics., V: 116, VI: 61, 117
Villa, IX: 212
Villella, Lt. William, VI: 140
Viminale, IX: 189
VIMY, I: 335, 348, XI: 337
VINCENNES (1937), I: 14, 15*n*, 83, 111, III: 31*n*, 391–2, IV: 91, 113*n*, 134–5,

153*n*, 257, 274, 276*n*, 278–80; Savo I. battle, V: 29–30, 34, 38–41, 45–50; sunk, 49, 56; casualties, 63*n*
VINCENNES (1944), VIII: 415, XII: 90, 318, 345, 426, XIII: 54, 318, XIV: 21, 58, 382, 386
Vincent, Sydney A., I: 230
Vincent, Lt. Cdr. W. C., VII: 346, VIII: 420, XII: 420
VINDEX, X: 309
Vine, F. G., X: 381
Vinock, Lt. Cdr. E., XII: 425
VIRAGO, X: 240
Virden, Lt. Cdr. Frank, V: 353, VII: 334, 348
VIREO, III: 104, 112, IV: 93, 154–6, V: 179–80, VI: 123
VIRGINIA, VII: 232*n*, XIV: 88*n*, 312*n*
Virginia Beach, I: 157, II: 28
VIRGO, VII: 255, 256*n*, 337, 344, VIII: 404, 419, XIV: 9, 160, 380
Viru Harbor, VI: 139–41, 152–3; pic., 152
Visayan Attack Force, XIII: 19
Visayas, XII: 68–70, 125, 150; XIII: 21, 57, 238; carrier strikes on, XII: 13, XIII: 341; schedule of operations in, 207; chart, 229
Visser, Cdr. R. G., VIII: 406, XII: 220, 421
Vitiaz Strait, VI: 254, 257, 369, 378, 389
VITTORIA, XIII: 263
VITTORIO VENETO, IX: 35, 243
Vivian, Lt. D. D. E., XI: 336
Vivian, 1st Lt. J. M., X: 181
VIXEN (1898), II: 286
VIXEN (1941), I: 31*n*, 206, 419
Vladivostok, III: 396
Vlasich, Chief Carpenter, VI: 189
Voge, Capt. R. G., III: 158, XII: 332*n*
Vogel, Lt. R. M., XIV: 376
Vogeley, Cdr. T. R., XII: 417, XIV: 372
Vogelkop, New Guinea, VIII: 3, 6, 10, 141–2, 219, XII: 107; chart, VIII: 105
Volcano Is., VIII: 178
Volckmann, Lt. Col. R. W., XIII: 114, 210
Volk, Cdr. L. F., X: 377, XII: 426, XIII: 316, XIV: 386
Volturno R., IX: 302–4
VOLUNTEER, XI: 337
Von Heimberg, Capt. E. H., XI: 64
VON STEUBEN, VII: 101*n*

Von Weien, Lt. Cdr. H. C., VIII: 411, XII: 428, XIV: 387

Vorse, Cdr. A. O., XIII: 317

Vose, Lt. Cdr. James E., V: 205, 213, VI: 331–2, VII: 339

Vose, Capt. W. C., XIV: 382

Vosseller, Capt. Aurelius B. ("Abe"), biog., X: 51n; mentioned, I: 77, 218n, 237n, X: 51, 288–9, 298, 325–8, 376

Vouza, Sgt., VI: 103

VULCAN, I: 82, IX: 390

Vunakanau, VI: 393, 406

Vyn, Lt. (jg) Arend, XI: 139

Vytlacil, Capt. Nicholas, VII: 20

W

W-43, II: 79*n*
W. R. Chamberlin, Jr., IX: 390
WABASH, I: 422, XIV: 387
WACHAPREAGUE, XII: 204, 208, 422, XIII: 149, 313
Wacosta, I: 364*n*
Wade, Cdr. J. E., XII: 429, XIV: 386
Wade, Lt. W. L., XI: 142
Wadell, Cdr. R. P., VII: 346, VIII: 407
WADLEIGH, VIII: 230, 409, XII: 35
WADSWORTH, VI: 297, 303, 415, VIII: 409, 414, 419, XIV: 381
Waesche, Vice Adm. R. R., I: 58, 234*n*, 270
WAGER, XIV: 107
WAGGA, VI: 127
Wagner, Lt. Cdr. E. O., X: 95, 103
Wagner, Rear Adm. F. D., III: 159, 173, 180, 272, VIII: 50–51, XIII: 118, 311
Wagner, F. J., IX: xv, X: xi, XI: xi
Wahlig, Lt. F. N., I: 421
WAHOO, V: 324
Waianae, VII: 252
Waigeo I., VIII: 140
Wainwright, Lt. Gen. J. M., III: 179–81, 199–203, 206, IV: 32, 246, XIV: 365; pic., 366–7
Wainwright, J. M. V., IX: 299
WAINWRIGHT, I: 111, 168, 180, 183–4, 357, 420, II: 36, 91, 285, IX: 187, 194, 385, 391, X: 253, 371
Waisili, XII: 21, 26
WAKABA, III: 274–6, 329, IV: 172, VII: 24, 35, 58, XII: 431, XIII: 31; sunk, XII: 169*n*, 184*n*
WAKATAKA, III: 275, 334; sunk, VIII: 32
WAKATAKE, VIII: 32
WAKATSUKI, VI: 306, 328, 341, VIII: 282, 416, XII: 430; sunk, 353
Wakde I., VIII: 36–7, 50, 89–143 *passim*, 241; Wakde-Sarmi landings, 88, 91–101, XII: 3; charts, VIII: 93, 100; T.O., VIII: 403–6
WAKE, river gunboat, III: 155, 187
Wake Atoll, discovery, V: 6; as U.S. base, III: 32–3, 84, 211, 213; attacks on and surrender, 222–54; charts, 226, 232, 238–9, and pic., 224; strikes on, 268, VI: 286, VII: 92–3, 136, 218*n*; pic., 266, XIV: 10; decision not to recapture, VII: 201–2
WAKE ISLAND, X: 299, 322, 325, 372, 380, XIII: 305, XIV: 27, 179, 374, 390; pic., X: 41
Wakefield, Cdr. E. K., VIII: 409, XII: 426
WAKEFIELD, I: 110–11, 327–9, IV: 265, XIV: 99*n*
Wakelin, Lt. (jg) E. F., XII: 422
Wakita, Capt. K., XII: 430
Waldron, Lt. Cdr. A. L. C., VIII: 410, XIV: 376
Waldron, Lt. Cdr. E. M., I: 418
Waldron, Lt. Cdr. J. C., IV: 91, 116–17, 120–22
WALDRON, XIII: 317, XIV: 25, 384
Waldrop, Lt. L. E., XII: 273
Waldschmidt, Capt. T. M., I: 76, VII: 23, 334
WALKE (1911), VII: 17*n*
WALKE (1940), IV: 19, V: 233, 271, 283–4; sunk, 275–6
WALKE (1944), XI: 157, 334, XII: 381, XIII: 31, 105, 304, 312, 325
Walker, Sqd. Ldr. B. R., VI: 65, VII: 333
Walker, Lt. Bayard, XI: 286
Walker, Cdr. E. K., II: 36, 113*n*, IX: 385
Walker, Col. Edwin A., XI: 251–2, 338
Walker, Lt. Cdr. Francis D., VIII: 21
Walker, Capt. Frank R., IV: 272, V: 29, 34*n*, 38, 55, VI: 241, 244–52
Walker, Maj. Gen. Fred L., IX: 258, 391
Walker, Capt. Frederick J., RN, X: 93, 96–8, 151–2, 308, 317*n*
Walker, Capt. J. B., X: 231
Walker, Capt. J. P., XIV: 374
Walker, Lt. Cdr. P. A., VII: 341
WALKER, VII: 223, 350, VIII: 405, 420, X: 197, XII: 418, XIV: 249, 384
Wallace, Col. Clarence E., XIV: 275–6
Wallace, Col. Clarence R., VIII: 186*n*–7*n*
Wallace, Maj. Gen. Fred C., XIV: 277

Wallace, Lt. Cdr. H. K., XII: 423,
XIII: 308
Wallace, Lt. Cdr. J. B., XIII: 305,
XIV: 374
Wallace, Lt. Cdr. Lewis, III: 158, IV: 92
Wallace, Col. W. J., V: 75
WALLACE L. LIND, XIV: 384
Waller, Capt. H. M. L., RAN, III: 333
Waller, Capt. J. B. W., XI: 334
WALLER, V: 353-7, 362-3, VI: 110, 228,
237, 242, 337, 351, 415, 420, VIII: 410,
XII: 369-70, XIII: 310-12, 322
Wallin, Capt. Homer N., III: 143
Wallis I., IV: 253, 263n, VII: 89, 214
WALNEY, II: 224-5, 227, 230, 237, 251-2;
sunk, 228-9, 283
Walpole, Cdr. K. C., XI: 334
Walsh Capt. H. T., V: 270n, XI: 416,
XIII: 309, XIV: 380
Walsh, Cdr. J. A., RAN, V: 54
Walsh, Capt. J. F., I: 349, 420, VIII: 409,
414, 419, XIII: 319
Walsh, Cdr. Quentin R., XI: 213-16
Walter, Lt. Cdr. D. E., X: 355, 379-80
WALTER C. WANN, XII: 244, 421,
XIII: 311, XIV: 230, 381
Walter Forward, W. Ranger, IX: 390
WALTER S. BROWN, X: 381
Walton, Lt. Cdr. D. S., XII: 423,
XIII: 308
Wana Wana I., VI: 211-12
Wanigela, VI: 42
Wanless, Lt. Cdr. R. H., X: 378
War dogs, VI: 302, VIII: 376
War games, I: li-liii, III: 83
WAR HAWK, VIII: 407, 420, XII: 419,
XIII: 140, 148, 311-13
War Shipping Administration, I: 292,
295, VIII: 343, 347, XIV: 164
War warning message, III: 77
Warburton, Cdr. A. L., XI: 333, 340
Ward, Charles H., IV: x, V: x, VI: xii,
VII: viii
Ward, Lt. Cdr. D. W., XIV: 378
Ward, Capt. F. T., XIII: 305, XIV: 386
Ward, Lt. Cdr. Norvell G., VI: 73,
VII: 351
Ward, Lt. Cdr. R. E. M., VIII: 16n
Ward, Lt. R. L., VII: 347, XII: 429
WARD, III: 96-7, 115, 137, 240n, IV: 276n,
VI: 228, 295, 381, 415, VIII: 404,
XII: 380, 385, 417; sunk, 382-3
Warder, Lt. Cdr. F. B., III: 158, 321,
IV: 223-4

Ware, Capt., pic., VII: 167
Ware, Capt. J. G., I: 76
Ware, Lt. Cdr. Leonard, XI: ix
Ware, Lt. Cdr. R. M., XIV: 382
Ware, Cdr. W. L., XII: 429
Warfield, Lt. Cdr. T. G., III: 159,
VI: 428
Wark, Lt. (jg) R. C., V: 174
Warlick, Capt. W. W., I: 195, V: 87,
XII: 427, XIII: 316, XIV: 382
Warlimont, Lt. Gen. Walter, II: 260
Warner, Capt. Thomas D., IV: 272
Warrack, Capt. R. C., XII: 428,
XIII: 319
Warrack, Capt. Robert L., XIII: 61,
69n
WARRAMUNGA, VI: 440-42, VIII: 73, 97,
127-9, 405, XII: 148, 421, XIII: 106,
234, 261, 304
WARREGO, III: 314, XIII: 102, 306, 322-3
Warren, Cdr. J. T., XIII: 304n
Warren, Boatswain W. J., I: 368
WARREN, VII: 236, 345, VIII: 418,
XII: 417, XIII: 145, 307, 313
Warren Delano, X: 310
WARRICK, XIII: 307
WARRINGTON, VIII: 406, X: 327n
Warrior, I: 394
Warris, Cdr. J. F., XII: 418, XIII: 311
WARSPITE, III: 50n, 382, IX: 167-8, 179,
293-7, 393, XI: 183, 302
Warwick Castle, II: 284
WASAGA, XI: 335
WASATCH, XII: 22, 26, 133, 138, 156, 190,
279, 306, XIII: 6, 12, 118, 135, 153, 243,
261, 268, 303, 324
Washburn, Lt. G., XIV: 381
Washburn, Capt. G. A. T., XIII: 304,
XIV: 373
Washington, Father John P., I: 333
WASHINGTON (1906), XIV: 88n, 158n
WASHINGTON (1941), I: 64, 167-8, 171,
181, 185, 419, III: 31, V: x, 80, 137, 148,
182n, 197, 205; Naval Battle of Gua-
dalcanal, V: 223-82 *passim;* later opns.,
291, VI: 106, VII: 228, 255, 338, 348,
VIII: 244, 415, XII: 90, 193-5, 318, 427,
XIII: 54, 176n, 180, 318, XIV: 21, 27,
34, 48, 242, 384, 386; pics., I: 170, 210,
V: 283
Washington, I: 183, 186-91n
Washington Conferences, 1921, I: xxxvi-
xlii, III: 8, 19; Dec. 1941, XI: 4; June
1942, II: 13-14; May 1943, VI: 7,

Washington Conferences (*cont'd*)
VIII: 4, IX: 228–30, 231*n*, X: 28, XI: 19
WASMUTH, III: 104, 213*n*, IV: 276*n*, VII: 17
WASP (1940), I: 14, 83, 151, 168, 194–6, II: 31, IV: 81*n*, 257, 266, 271, 280, 293, V: 14, 28*n*, 58, 80, 83, 87, 102, 105–6, 110, 130–38, VIII: 237*n*, XIII: 4*n*, XIV: 105; chart Aug. 1942, V: 59; sunk, 136; pics., I: 92, 210, V: 138–9
WASP (1943), VIII: 174, 250, 271–3, 292, 295, 300–301, 308, 383, 413, XII: x, 12, 90, 106, 294, 304, 309, 349, 424, XIII: 54, 68, 87, 315, XIV: 21, 94–5, 382, 390
Wassell, Cdr. Corydon M., III: 379
Wassell, Lt. M., XII: 418
Watanabe, Gen., III: 13
Watanabe, Capt. Y., V: 17*n*, 173*n*, VI: 85*n*, 128*n*, 129, VIII: viii
WATCHMAN, X: 340
Water supply, Peleliu, Leyte, XII: 41, 84; tankers, 84, XIV: 161
Waterhouse, Cdr. J. W., XIV: 254, 375
Waterman, Lt. Cdr. J. R., II: 40
WATERMAN, VIII: 411, XII: 429, XIII: 319
Waters, Cdr. C. L., VII: 341
Waters, Lt. Cdr. D. W., RN, X: 6*n*, 44*n*
WATERS, I: 213, IV: 174, VI: 142–5, 148, 156*n*, 193–4, 228, 415, VIII: 408, XIV: 377
WATERWITCH, IX: 396
Watkins, Shipfitter C. C., V: 57*n*
Watkins, Rear Adm. Frank T., IX: xvi
Watson, Col. A. P., XII: 49
Watson, Maj. Gen. Edwin M. ("Pa"), XII: 7
Watson, Lt. G. F., VII: 341
Watson, 1st Lt. Harold F., III: 392
Watson, Capt. P. W., VIII: 420
Watson, Lt. R. B., X: 175
Watson, Maj. Gen. Thomas E., VII: 285, 288–96, 347, VIII: 186*n*, 335, 353, 407, XIV: 381; pic., VII: 294
Watt, Lt. Col. J. R., VII: 333
Wattengel, Pharmacist William, XII: 316
Wattles, Capt. T. L., I: 420, II: 39
Watts, Capt. Ethelbert, XIII: 311, XIV: 379
Watts, Lt. Henry, XI: 137*n*, 140*n*

Watts, Lt. J. A., X: 382
Wau, VI: 52–4, 136, 256, 258
Wauchope, Cdr. F. W., XIV: 380
Wauchope, Capt. G. M., VII: 346, VIII: 418, XII: 416, XIII: 308
Waugh, Lt. (jg) G. E., X: 216
Wavell, Field Marshal Sir Archibald, III: 271, 277, 282, 296, 312, 315, 336
Wawama, XII: 25
Way, Lt. G. L., XIV: 224*n*
Way, Lt. Cdr. J. F., X: 379
Waymouth, Capt. G. R., XI: 342
WAYNE, VII: 346, VIII: 418, XII: 416, XIII: 308, 312, XIV: 378
WEAR, X: 75*n*
Weasel, described, XIV: 50*n*
Weather, convoys, I: 95; forecasts, XIII: 60–61, 83–4; reports, V: 239, VII: 187, XIII: 289–92; Savo, V: 26; Vella Lavella, VI: 238; Rabaul strikes, 333; Philippine Sea, VIII: 257, 288; Sicily, IX: 67–8; Normandy invasion, XI: 24–5, 49*n*, 79–83, 176–9, 197; pic., 81; S. France, 249, 257, 275; Leyte, XII: 14, 118, 134, 322, 363; Surigao Strait, 206; Iwo, XIV: 50–51, 65; South China Sea strike, XIII: 88, 170–72, Japan strike, Feb. 1945, XIV: 57; Sakishima strike, 107; Okinawa, 111, 153, 174; Task Force 38 off Japan, Jul.–Aug. 1945, 332–4. *See also* Typhoons
Weather Centrals, XIII: 69, 83–4, XIV: 298–9
Weather ships, XIII: 84
Weather Stations, I: 62, VII: 312, XII: 54, XIII: 84, 171
Weaver, Maj. J. R., II: 61
Weaver, Lt. Cdr. P. L. F., I: 76
Weaver, Capt. W. H., VII: 344, VIII: 407, XII: 418
WEAVER, VIII: 411, XII: 429, XIII: 67*n*, 319
WEAZEL, IX: 396
Webb, Ens. Charles D., I: 249
Webb, Lt. Cdr. E. N., XIII: 153*n*, 305
Webb, Chief Carpenter J. R., XIV: 305*n*
Webb, Capt. R. C., VII: 344, XII: 418, XIII: 30, 313, XIV: 128, 375
Webb, Cdr. R. E., I: 94
Webb, Lt. Cdr. W. E., XIV: 379
Weber, Lt. J. A., VII: 348
WEDDERBURN, VIII: 419, XII: 319, 426, XIII: 316, XIV: 383

Wedemeyer, Lt. Gen. Albert C., IX: 7,
XI: 8–9, XIII: 163, XIV: 354–5
WEDGEPORT, XI: 333
Weeden, Capt. W. W., XIV: 379
WEEHAWKEN, IX: 110, 385, XIV: 377
Weekes, Lt. Cdr. A. D., XIII: 319
Weekes, Lt. Cdr. T. U., XIII: 307
Weeks, Lt. H. W., VII: 227
Wegforth, Capt. J. F., XII: 427,
XIII: 317, XIV: 385
Weiber, Capt. C. W., XII: 426
Weidner, Cdr. W. F., XII: 419,
XIII: 310
Weidorn, Capt. P. H., XIII: 310
Weiler, Cdr. J. B., XIV: 374
Weintraub, Cdr. D. J., XIII: 322, 324
Weitzel, Capt. C. W., IV: 273, V: 231,
VI: 144
Welch, Lt. Cdr. F. M., X: 379
Welch, Capt. P. P., IX: 389, XIII: 308,
XIV: 380
Welch, Lt. Cdr. R. L., XII: 422,
XIII: 304
Welch, Lt. V. W., V: 208
Weldin, Cdr. G. C., XIV: 387
WELFARE, XI: 339
Wellborn, Rear Adm. Charles C.,
I: 357, 420, II: 37, VI: xii, VII: ix,
IX: 187, 190, 385, 391
Weller, Lt. Col. D. M., XIV: 40
Weller, Capt. O. A., I: 419, VIII: 410,
XII: 424, XIII: 315, XIV: 94, 382
Welles, Capt. R. C., VI: 297, XIV: 381
Welles, Hon. Sumner, I: 14, 70
WELLES, VI: 436, 442, VIII: 404, XII: 199,
420, 428n, 429, XIII: 316, 318n, 319
Wellings, Capt. J. H., VI: 157–8,
XIII: 309, XIV: 379
Wellings, Cdr. T. F., II: 25
Wellings, Capt. Timothy A., XI: 30n
Wellington, N.Z., I: 112, IV: 265–6, 279,
V: 14, VII: 89–90, 102
Wells, Lt. (jg) John K., X: 381
Wells, Lt. Cdr. John K., IV: 173
Wells, Sonarman W. C., VII: 144
Welte, Lt. Cdr. C. R., XII: 425
Wemyss, D. E. G., *Walker's Groups*,
X: xv
Wenchow, XIII: 300
Wendelberg, Cdr. George, VII: 345,
XII: 390
Wendt, Cdr. W. F., VII: 346, XII: 429
Wenker, Lt. Wilton, XI: 318n, 319
Wensinger, Col. Walter, XIV: 38

WENSLEYDALE, XI: 193, 336
Wepman, Lt. E. R., X: 381
Weschler, Lt., III: 159
Wesel, XI: 322n
Weser R., XI: 327–8
Weserland, X: 227
Wesson, Cdr. J. H., XII: 426, XIII: 76,
317, 319, XIV: 383
WESSON, VIII: 411, XII: 429, XIII: 319,
XIV: 197, 373, 391
West, Lt. Cdr. C. R., XIV: 387
West, Lt. Cdr. R. L., XIII: 308
West, Lt. (jg) W. J., Ens. W. P.,
XII: 422
West Cactus, VI: 36
West Cheswald, I: 167n
West Madaket Maximus, X: 67n, 71,
74
West Negros, XIII: 217
West Palm Beach, Fla., I: 138
WEST POINT, I: 110–12; pic., 107
WEST VIRGINIA (1905), VIII: 237n
WEST VIRGINIA (1923), I: 39n, 64, III:
103–7, 126, 144–6, IX: 126n, X: 204n,
XII: 118n, 132, 199–295 *passim*, 366,
416, XIII: 19, 24, 133, 138, 180n, 187n,
303–4, XIV: 26n, 41, 154, 229, 312n,
373; pics., III: 84, 102, 110, 144–5
WESTBRIDGE, VII: 232n
Western Hemisphere, defined, I: 61, 74
Western Ocean Meeting Point, X: 71,
75, 82
Westhofen, Cdr. C. L., X: 146–7
Westholm, Cdr. R. E., V: 338, XII: 415,
XIII: 306, 311, XIV: 186–90, 381
Westlake, Cdr. N. W., XIII: 308
Weston, Lt. H. A., XIV: 387
Westover Field, I: 131
Westphal, Gen. S., on naval gunfire,
IX: 314
WESTRALIA, VI: 374, 382, VIII: 84,
XII: 417, XIII: 119, 265n, 272n, 312,
326
WETASKIWIN, I: 321
Wev, Cdr. B. N., XIII: 317, XIV: 374,
387
Wewak, VI: 52, 55, 256–9, 262, 383,
VIII: 10, 49n, 66–7, 73, 222
Weygand, Gen. Maxime, II: 3–10
Weyler, Rear Adm. G. L., VIII: 381,
409, XII: 124, 132, 199–201, 220, 223,
229, 343–5, 366, 416, XIII: 105, 303;
pic., XII: 214
Weyll, Lt. C. E., VI: 382

Weymouth, Lt. Cdr. Ralph, pic., VIII: 232, 274, 285n, 414
WHADDON, XI: 343
WHALE, IV: 212–13, XII: 406
Whale pontoon, XI: 26, 166
Whaley, Capt. W. B., XIII: 304, XIV: 373
Whaling, Col. W. J., V: 127, 144; pic., 130
Wharton, Brig. Gen. J. E., XI: 334
WHARTON, VII: 347, VIII: 418, XIV: 386
Wheately, Norman, VI: 147
WHEATLAND, II: 221, XI: 342
Wheeler, Capt. C. J., VI: 344, VII: 337, 346, 352; quoted, VIII: 316n–17n
Wheeler, Ens. J. B., II: 211, 216
Wheeler, Cdr. R. E., VII: 349, VIII: 406, XII: 417, XIII: 309
Wheeler, Cdr. R. V., VII: 347, VIII: 410, XII: 417, XIII: 309, XIV: 379
Wheeler Field, III: 123–4
WHEELING, XII: ix
Wheland, Cdr. K. R., XII: 429
Whelchel, Cdr. D. L., I: 421, VIII: 25
Whelchel, Capt. J. E., XIV: 372
Wheless, Capt. H. T., III: 177
WHIPPET, XIV: 387
WHIPPLE, III: 160, 272, 299, 332, 333n, 361, 375, 378, IV: 15n, 25
WHIPPOORWILL, III: 159, 172, 194, 273, 379, XIII: 23
Whitaker, Lt. Cdr. F. M., VI: 331, VII: 349
Whitaker, Lt. Cdr. T. A., VIII: 407
Whitcomb, Lt. (jg) R. S., X: 219
White, Lt. Cdr. A. F., VIII: 408
White, Cdr. A. J., IV: 59n
White, Brig. Sir Bruce, XI: 25
White, Lt. Cdr. D. C., IV: 92
White, Lt. Cdr. D. M., VII: 349
White, Cdr. Frederick H., III: 103, 106, VII: viii
White, Lt. Cdr. H. A., X: 378
White, Lt. H. J., XI: 333
White, Ens. Henry C., I: 249
White, Lt. W. D., XIV: 377
White House, IX: 228
WHITE MARSH, VIII: 408, 410, XII: 416, XIII: 308, 314, XIV: 379
WHITE PLAINS, VIII: 207, XII: 244, 252–3, 268, 276–8, 284, 302–3, 421, XIV: 374
WHITEHALL, X: 306, 309n
WHITEHAVEN, XI: 333

Whitehead, Brig. David A., XIII: 260, 262
Whitehead, Maj. Gen. Ennis P., VIII: 47, 64n, 123
Whitehead, Capt. R. F., VIII: 326, 407, XII: 133, 238, 246, 253n, 279, 286, 292–3, 299, 309, 415, XIV: 132
Whitehill, Cdr. Walter M., I: xviii, X: xiv; *Fleet Admiral King*, XI: xv
Whitehorn, Commo. I. W., X: 305n
WHITEHURST, XII: 307, 342, 423, XIV: 230, 373, 391
Whitemarsh, Capt. R. P., XIV: 376
Whiteside, Cdr. W. J., VII: 345, VIII: 408, XI: 317, 318n
Whitfield, Cdr. E. C., XIV: 378
Whitfield, Cdr. J. D., XIII: 304, XIV: 375
Whitfield, Capt. J. W., II: 40
Whiting, Cdr. C. J., I: 420, II: 40, IX: 389
Whiting, Rear Adm. F. E. M., I: 419, II: 36, 92, 97, XII: 426, XIII: 318, XIV: 58, 327n, 360, 382
WHITLEY, XIV: 389
WHITMAN, VII: 341, VIII: 411
Whitmore, Lt. Cdr. L. E., X: 378
Whitney, Capt. J. P., VIII: 410, XII: 421
WHITNEY, III: 104, XIV: 387
Whittier, Lt. Cdr. M. T., XIV: 386
Whorton, Lt. (jg) C. R., XI: 299n
WHYALIA, VI: 46
Whyte, Cdr. C. A., VI: 419
WICHITA, I: 82–3, 93, 168, 180–81, 419, II: 43, 48, 91–8, 107–10, 285, III: 31n, 36, V: 352–5, 357, VI: 106n, VII: 55, 60, 152n, 334, 349, 352, VIII: 181, 269n, 397, 409, 415, X: 21n, XII: 90, 96–100, 318, 331, 424, XIV: 132, 246, 372; pics., I: 92, 210, II: 112
Wichmann, Lt. C. J., IX: 389, 393
WICKES, XII: 419, XIII: 204, 290n, 311, XIV: 375
Wickham Anchorage, VI: 139, 146
Wickman, Lt. Cdr. C. L., XIV: 386
Wicks, Lt. Cdr. J. E., XIII: 309, XIV: 379
Wickstrom, Lt. K. W., X: 101
Widhelm, Capt. W. J., IV: 91n, V: 205, 209, 213–14, VI: 291, VIII: 285; pic., 232
Wieber, Capt. C. W., II: 37, XIII: 317, XIV: 383

Wiedemann, Torpedoman W. F., XII: 372
Wiedman, Cdr. W. A., XI: 340
Wiedorn, Capt. P. H., XII: 419, XIV: 380
Wier, Cdr. H. R., IX: 387, 396, X: 253, XI: 342
Wierzbicki, Lt. A. J., XIV: 237
Wight, Cdr. D. D., XIII: 293
Wight, Cdr. W. H., VII: 348
Wigley, Lt. Col. R. C., VII: 306n
Wilber, Cdr. D. T., VII: 344, VIII: 418, XII: 426, XIII: 316
Wilbor, Lt. Cdr. A. B., XI: 336
Wilbur, Col. W. H., II: 86-7, 109-10, 164
Wilcox, Lt. D. M., XIII: 294
Wilcox, Rear Adm. John W., I: 168
WILD GOOSE, X: 93, 373
Wilds, Thomas, VII: 78n, 121n, VIII: 374n
WILEMAN, VII: 347, VIII: 411
Wiley, Capt. H. V., III: 160, XII: 416, XIII: 304, XIV: 41, 373
Wilfong, Cdr. J. L., IV: 271, V: 87, VI: 214, 219, VIII: 419
Wilhelm, Cdr. Ralph A., VI: 144, 228, VIII: 404, 419, XIII: 307, XIV: 374
Wilhelmshaven, X: 341, XI: 326
Wilhoite, Ens. T. M., II: 88
WILHOITE, X: 269-71, 376, 381
Wilkes, Vice Consul C. D., II: 6n
Wilkes, Commo. Charles, VII: 76, 153
Wilkes, Rear Adm. John, biog., XI: 63n; pic., 205; mentioned, III: 158n, 179, 193, 283, 303n, 305, 321, IV: 199, 219-20, 223, IX: 386, XI: xvn, 52, 56-8, 62-5, 215-16, 218n, 299-303
WILKES, I: 420, II: 38, 58-62, 74, 77-8, 99-100, 105, 113-14, 161, 285, VI: 443-5, VIII: 78, 99, 115-16, 403, IX: 89n, 387, XII: 319, 428
WILKES-BARRE, XIII: 317, XIV: 21, 263, 313, 384, 386
Wilkins, Lt. Cdr. C. W., IV: 92
Wilkinson, Capt. E. R., V: 232, 245, 251, XII: 427, XIII: 318
Wilkinson, Lt. Cdr. R. C., XIV: 378
Wilkinson, Lt. Cdr. Robert H., VI: 145, 228
Wilkinson, Vice Adm. Theodore S., biog., VI: 282n; pic., frontispiece, XIII: 109; assistance to History, VI: xi, 138n, 279n; Director of Naval In-

telligence, III: 128, 134-5; Pearl H., 140-41; Dep. Comsopac, VI: 13-15; relieves Turner, 14, 97, 144, 227, VII: 87; Sols., VI: 144, 203, 204n, 212-13, 221, 227-30, 234, 241, 244-6, 281-4, 289-90, 293, 297-304, 329, 348, 414-19; longlance torpedo, 213; leapfrog strategy, 14, 226; Emirau, 423; Green Is. landing, 414-19; Yap, XII: 14-16; Palaus, 32-6, 41, 44; Ulithi, 47; Leyte, 56, 74, 82, 113, 117, 127-8, 135, 140, 146, 156, 415, 418; Leyte Gulf battle, 202-3, 290-91; Lingayen, XIII: 6n, 7-9, 12, 94-6, 115-19, 123-30, 134-5, 138, 145-50, 156, 184, 303, 310; XIV: 87n; occupation of Japan, 368; Pearl Harbor investigation, XIII: 160n; quoted, VI: vii, 340, VII: 179, XII: 4, XIV: 369
Will, Capt. C. R., XIII: 318, XIV: 385
Will, Lt. Cdr. H. R., XIII: 308
Willard, Cdr. C. S., XIII: 312
Willard A. Holbrook, V: 335n
WILLEM VAN DER ZAAN, III: 360
Willess, Acting Pay Clerk, V: 49
Willett, Ens. K. M., I: 398-9
Willey, Lt. Cdr. R. S., VIII: 415, XII: 51, 425
William B. Allison, XIV: 392
William B. Giles, X: 382
WILLIAM B. PRESTON, III: 159, 169, 272, 317-18, VIII: 49n; pic., III: 171
William Bradford, IX: 390
WILLIAM C. COLE, XIV: 379
WILLIAM C. MILLER, VII: 341
WILLIAM D. PORTER, XIII: 304, XIV: 274, 375, 392; sunk, 274
William Dean Howells, *William Few*, IX: 390
William H. Aspinwall, *William H. Moody*, X: 381-2
William Hooper, I: 184, 191n
William L. Thompson, VII: 334
William Mulholland, X: 382
WILLIAM P. BIDDLE, I: 76, 421, II: 26n, 38, 84, 161, 172, VII: 337, 345, VIII: 419, IX: 133, 389, XII: 419, XIII: 310, 313
William Patterson, X: 382
William Rockefeller, I: 156
William S. Colley, XIII: 47
William S. Ladd, XII: 388
William S. Thayer, X: 309
William Sharon, XIII: 44-5
WILLIAM SIEVERLING, XIII: 305, XIV: 374

William T. Coleman, IX: 164
WILLIAM WARD BURROWS, III: 225, IV: 276n, VIII: 420
William Wheelright, X: 310
William-Powlett, Capt. N. J. W., XIV: 388
Williams, Aircrewman, VIII: 177
Williams, Lt. C. H., XIII: 104n
Williams, Maj. F. H., III: 204
Williams, Capt. F. P., XIII: 310, XIV: 380
Williams, Lt. Cdr. G. B., XIV: 221, 377, 379
Williams, Cdr. H. G., IX: 385, XI: 343
Williams, Cdr. Harold N., IV: 93, 272, V: 29
Williams, Lt. Cdr. Henry, VII: 335, VIII: 405
Williams, Cdr. J. B., X: 376, 381
Williams, Lt. J. L., XIII: 309
Williams, Lt. Cdr. J. W., VII: 342
Williams, Lt. James R., VIII: 392
Williams, Col. L. O., XIV: 177
Williams, Lt. M., XIII: 323
Williams, Cdr. Mac. B., XIII: 315
Williams, Lt. Cdr. P. C., VII: 333
Williams, Cdr. P. D., VII: 350
Williams, Cdr. R. C., VII: 335, IX: 385, 396, XIV: 377
Williams, Capt. R. D., XIV: 378
Williams, Maj. R. H., IV: 290
Williams, Lt. R. R., I: 421
Williams, Lt. Cdr. Robert P., X: 118, 127, XIV: 373
Williams, Maj. Waldon, V: 375
WILLIAMSBURG, I: 82
Williamson, Cdr. F. T., VI: 214, VII: 337, XIII: 316, XIV: 382
Williamson, Lt. Cdr. J. A., VIII: 228n, XIV: 268, 373
Williamson, Cdr. Lindsey, XI: 339
Williamson, Lt. R. A., XIII: 322
Williamson, Capt. T. B., XII: 421
WILLIAMSON, IV: 173, VI: 107n, VII: 335, VIII: 180, 409, 419, XIV: 65, 381
Willidy II, I: 274n
Willingham, Capt. J. H., IV: 187n, 206
Willingham, Capt. S. D., I: 418, 420, II: 40, IV: 21n
Willis, Vice Adm. Sir Algernon, IX: 167–8, 251–2, 393
Willis, Capt. J. H., XI: 335, XIV: 375
Willis, Cdr. J. S., VI: 381, XIII: 181, 316; XIV: 190, 381

Willis, Col. W. A., XII: 368
WILLIS, X: 376
WILLMARTH, XII: 54, 423, XIV: 196, 373
Willoughby, Maj. Gen. Charles A., VI: xi, 27n, 259
WILLOUGHBY, XII: 204, 422, XIII: 221, 322
Willson, Lt. Cdr. R. C., XIII: 307, XIV: 380
Willson, Rear Adm. Russell, biog., I: 116n; mentioned, I: 116, 236, VIII: 8n
Wilmerding, Lt. Cdr. H. A., XI: 334, XIV: 377
Wilson, Lt. A. H., XII: 420, XIII: 306, 309
Wilson, Brig. Gen. Arthur, II: 175
Wilson, Lt. Cdr. C. F., XIV: 376
Wilson, Cdr. D. W., VIII: 405, XII: 418, XIV: 384
Wilson, Cdr. E. W., IX: 81, 386, XI: 334
Wilson, Cdr. F. E., I: 420, VIII: 404
Wilson, Cdr. George R., VI: 228, 244, 250, XIV: 186–90
Wilson, Lt. H. B., VII: 310n
Wilson, Gen. Sir Henry Maitland, IX: xii, 323, 324n, 326–7, 359, 363, 369, XI: 223–32, 236–7, 242, 311; pic., 244
Wilson, Lt. Cdr. J. C. G., XI: 342
Wilson, Capt. J. D., XIV: 372
Wilson, Lt. Cdr. J. Woodrow, III: 267, XIII: 319
Wilson, Cdr. R. L., XIV: 260, 374
Wilson, Cdr. Ralph E., V: 87, 151, 162, 232
Wilson, 2nd Lt. W. F., V: 374
Wilson, President Woodrow, I: 39, 70, 134; III: 7
WILSON, IV: 274, V: 29–30, 41, 49–50, 52n, 57, 343, VI: 213, 221, 331, VII: 340, 349, VIII: 415, XIII: 44–5, 47, 309, 314, XIV: 379
WILTON, II: 265n, IX: 396
Wiltse, Rear Adm. Lloyd J., VI: 11n, 325, VII: 340, 349, 352, VIII: 415, XII: 99, 424, 425n, XIII: 316, XIV: 382
Wiltsie, Capt. I. D., VII: 141, 337
Wimberley, Maj. Gen. D. N., IX: 150
Wimble Shoal, I: 134, 155
Winant, Hon. John G., XI: 325
WINCHESTER CASTLE, II: 205, IX: 395
Windeyer, Brig. J. V., VI: 269, 271–2
WINDHAM BAY, XIV: 161, 306, 386

WINDSOR, VII: 255, 268, VIII: 405, 415, XII: 417
Windward Passage, I: 134, 249, 315, 347–8, X: 192, 198*n*, 207*n*, 297
Winfield Scott, IX: 390
Winfred, I: 273
Wing, Maj. Gen. L. F., XIII: 308
Wingard, Cdr. W. C., VIII: 413, XII: 424
WINGED ARROW, VIII: 410, XIII: 307
Winkler, Lt. E. A., XIII: 308
Winn, Capt. W. C., I: 420, VIII: 409, IX: 389, XIV: 383
WINOOSKI, I: 352, 422, II: 39–40*n*, 169–72, IX: 390, XII: 82, XIII: 308
Winquist, Capt. E. E., XIV: 375
Winslow, Lt. Cdr. A., XIV: 377
WINSLOW (1915), VII: 37*n*
WINSLOW (1937), I: 111, 377, 390*n*, 420, X: 213*n*, 214, 227, XIII: 73
Winston, Cdr. F. L., VIII: 261*n*
Winston, Cdr. P. W., XII: 427, XIII: 318
Winston, Lt. Cdr. R. A., VII: 349, VIII: 413
Winston-Salem, I: 187, 191*n*
Winter Line, IX: 317, 324
WINTERBERRY, XIV: 377
Winters, Cdr. T. H., XII: 327, 331, 426
WINTLE, VII: 328, 341
Wirtz, Lt. Cdr. Peyton L., IV: 274, V: 195, VI: 144
WISCONSIN, XIII: 54, 317, XIV: 21, 112, 314, 385–6; pic., III: 141
WISHART, II: 209–10, X: 372
Wissinger, Lt. Cdr. R. J., XIV: 378
Withers, Rear Adm. Thomas, IV: 199
Witt, Lt. Daniel, X: 382
Witt, Kvtkapt. Hans, X: 180–81
WITTE DE WITH, III: 273, 333, 349, 352, 371*n*
WITTER, XII: 423, XIV: 190, 373, 390
Woelfel, Cdr. J. C., VII: 346, VIII: 410
Wogan, Cdr. T. L., IV: 174, 214, X: 275, XII: 168, 275, 429, XIII: 280, 320
Wolcott, Lt. Cdr. Theodore, VIII: 410
Woleai I., VIII: 33, 49, 156, 174, 215, 313, 354, XII: 53
Wolf, Lt. (jg) J. P., XII: 422
Wolfson, Lt. (jg) Morton E., I: 188–9
Wolseiffer, Cdr. Frederick, VIII: 403, IX: 387
Wolverton, Cdr. R. A., X: 377, XI: 335

Womble, Capt. J. P., XII: 426, XIII: 317, XIV: 383
Wood, Lt. Cdrs. A. C. and C. C., I: 420
Wood, Lt. E. E., VII: 349, VIII: 413
Wood, Lt. Cdr. E. W., VIII: 414
Wood, Lt. Cdr. Hugh, XIV: 382
Wood, Cdr. Hunter, V: 205, 217, VII: 337
Wood, Cdr. J. M., XII: 317, XIV: 374
Wood, Cdr. L. O., VIII: 410, XII: 427, XIII: 318, XIV: 372
Wood, Capt. Leighton, V: 353
Wood, Lt. Lester A., III: 318
Wood, Cdr. R. W., VII: 349
Wood, Lt. Cdr. W. W., XIV: 386
Woodaman, Cdr. R. J., IX: 385, XIV: 377
Woodard, Lt. Cdr. S. E., XIV: 376
WOODBINE, VIII: 420
WOODBURY, I: 138
WOODCOCK, I: 151
Woodhouse, Capt. C. H. L., IX: 167
Woodhouse, Lt. Cdr. E. W., XII: 421, XIV: 377
Woodke, Lt. F. A., XIV: 375
Woodlark I. *See* Trobriand Is.
WOODPECKER, X: 93
Woodruff, Capt. G. L., X: 158
Woodruff, Maj. Gen. R. B., XIII: 49, 241, 243, 246
Woods, Quartermaster D. E., VII: 196
Woods, Capt. E. E., XIV: 378
Woods, Maj. Gen. Louis E., V: 198*n*, 374, XIV: 278
Woods, Ens. P. O., X: 305*n*
Woods, Cdr. R. W. D., II: 25, 41
Woods Hole, Mass., I: 257
"Wood's Hole," Sicily, IX: 127, 138–9, 145–6; pic., 130–31
Woodson, Cdr. C. R., XI: 340
Woodson, Lt. W. E., XIV: 253
Woodville, Lt. Cdr. J. L. W., XI: 342
Woodward, Capt. D. C., VII: 344, VIII: 405, 418, XII: 417
Woodward, Lt. Cdr. S. E., XIV: 373
WOODWORTH, VI: 123, 144, 153, 156*n*, 182, XII: 98*n*, 425
"Woofus," XI: 241
Wooldridge, Capt. Edmund T., I: 85*n*; XIV: 385
Woollen, Lt. Cdr. W. S., XIV: 374
Woolley, Lt. Cdr. G. S., XI: 336

WOOLSEY, I: 420, II: 38, 171n, 174, 285, IX: 110n, 268, 387, 391, 396, X: 109, 253, 259–60, 371, XI: 270, 277, 312, 342
Wooster, Lt. F. S., XIV: 377
Wootten, Maj. Gen. G. F., VI: 267, XIII: 217, 263–4
Wordell, Cdr. M. T., XII: 327n, 427, XIII: 317
WORDEN, III: 104, 213n, IV: 19, 91, 113n, 151n, 271, V: 86, VIII: 237n; wrecked, VII: 18
World War II, length of, III: 101, XIV: 366
Worley, Lt. M. S., XIV: 374
Worth, Capt. D. F., X: 213n, XI: 339
Worthington, Lt. Cdr. J. M., III: 393, IV: 91, 271, V: 86
Worthington, Cdr. R. K. R., XIV: 290
Wotho Atoll, VII: 310–12
Wotje Atoll, III: 261–3, IV: 70, VII: 74–5, 82–4, 97, 138, 194, 203, 206, 223, 229, 234, 307–9, 314, XIV: 10; pic., III: 267; strikes on, VII: 194, 218–20
WRANGELL, XIII: 307, XIV: 8, 165–7, 386
WREN, X: 93
Wrenn, Capt. P. G., XIV: 378
Wrenn, Cdr. W. P., XIV: 377
Wright, Maj. B. C., XIII: 184n
Wright, Rear Adm. Carleton H., biog., V: 293n; mentioned, 86, 293–301, 308, 313, 318
Wright, Cdr. G. C., I: 76, 418, 420, X: 257–9, XI: 339
Wright, Capt. H. J., II: 38, XIII: 117, 309, 312, 380
Wright, Seaman Hugh P., I: 182

Wright, Lt. Cdr. J. D., XIV: 381
Wright, Capt. J. J., XIII: 309
Wright, Rear Adm. Jerauld, II: 182, 186, 252, III: xi, VII: 346, 352, IX: xiv, 15–16, 65n, XII: 427, XIV: 108, 111, 154, 175, 371, 381
Wright, Lt. (jg) K. L., X: 102–3
Wright, Lt. M. L., VII: 341
Wright, Lt. Cdr. T. K., II: 39
Wright, Lt. Col. W. C., V: 336
Wright, Capt. W. D., IX: 111n, 388, XI: 118, 141, 164
Wright, Cdr. W. H., VIII: 415
Wright, Lt. Cdr. W. L., III: 158, 283
Wright, Lt. Cdr. Whitney, XIII: 312
WRIGHT, I: li, 52n, VII: x, 101n, VIII: 50, X: 42n, XI: 279n
Wroten, Cdr. W. L., IX: 311
Wulish, Gen. von, II: 65
Wulzen, Cdr. D. W., XII: 427, XIII: 318, XIV: 373
Wunch, Lt. Cdr. E. W., XIII: 306
WYANDOT, XIV: 375, 390
Wyatt, Capt. Ben H., II: 37, V: 353–4
Wyatt, Capt. James L., VII: 110
Wyatt, Shipfitter W. J., V: 57n
Wyckoff, Lt. Cdr. J. M., VII: 345, VIII: 410
Wyckoff, Cdr. J. W., XIV: 377
WYFFELS, X: 381
Wylie, Cdr. J. C., XIII: 317, XIV: 384
Wylie, Cdr. W. N., XIV: 259
WYOMING, I: 14, III: 211n, X: 134n, XI: 242n
Wyrick, Ens. J. W., V: 99

Y

Yachts, converted, I: 234, 268–76; table of, 235

YAEYAMA, III: 162

YAEZAKURA, XIV: 316

YAHAGI, VIII: 218, 416, XII: 162, 248, 272–4, 282, 431, XIII: 158, XIV: 200–205; sunk, and pic., XIV: 207–8; chart, 207

YAHARA, XIV: 387

Yaka, I: 167n, 372

Yakabi Shima, XIV: 120–22, 125

YAKU, XIII: 285

YAKUTAT, XII: 46, XIV: 381

Yakutat, Alaska, IV: 174n

Yalta Conference, X: 338, XIII: 213–14

Yamada, Maj. Gen., VI: 270–72, 274

Yamada, Rear Adm. S., IV: 17, 256, 292, 294n–5n

Yamafuku M., IV: 89

Yamaguchi, Cdr. M., III: xi, XIII: 15n

Yamaguchi, Adm. T., IV: 76, 88, 132, 137

YAMAGUMO, III: 161, V: 84, 151, VI: 412, VII: 188–9, VIII: 131, 416, XIII: 190, 208–9, 233, 431; sunk, 216–18

Yamakawa, Sgt., V: 193

YAMAKAZE, III: 162, 275, 334

Yamamoto, Rear Adm. C., VI: 19, XIII: 159

Yamamoto, Fleet Adm. Isoroku, pics., III: 12, 26, V: 98, VI: 103; mentioned, III: 82–3, VI: 18; strat., III: 38–40, 45–6, IV: 6, V: 291, 352, VII: 74, VIII: 10; Pearl H., III: 61, 80–83, 86, 90–92; "Central Agreement," 71–2; Coral Sea, IV: 61; Midway, 11, 77–80, 87, 94, 132–3, 138–41, 144, 149, 152, 155–7; Aleutians, 177–9, 184, VII: 4, 8, 13; Solomons, V: 53, 61, 80–84, 123, 138, 199–203, 206, 225, 233, 258, 270, VI: 92–3; 117–20; New Guinea, 124–7; "peace in White House," 128n; death, 23, 128–9, XII: 138

Yamamoto, Capt. Iwata, XII: 430

Yamasaki, Rear Adm. S., IV: 173

Yamashiro, Capt. K., VI: 162–3, 166–8, 353

YAMASHIRO, III: 26, IV: 89, XII: 162–3, 190, 209, 213–21, 232–3, 241, 431; sunk, 222–9, 234; pic., 222

Yamashiro M., XIV: 24–5

Yamashita, Gen. T., XII: 67, 138, 353–4, 364, 387, 394, 397, XIII: 12–16, 37, 154, 184–5, 196–7, 209–10

YAMATO, III: 21, 31, IV: 80, 87–9, 94, 137–8, 144, V: 84, 199, 206, 233, VI: 410, VII: 137, 319, VIII: 131–2, 218, 221, 299, 416; Leyte Gulf, XII: 162, 172, 175, 184–6, 248, 251, 255, 259–63, 297–9, 312, 430, and pic., 190, XIII: 14, 38, 158, 177, 286; last sortie, XIV: 94, 199–205, 338; sunk, and pics., 205–9; charts, 201, 207

Yamatsuki, Yamaura M., V: 234, 283

Yamayuri M., VI: 400

Yamazaki, Col., VII: 43–4, 49–50

Yamazumi, Capt. C., XII: 431

Yanagi, Cdr., V: 173

YANAGI, XIV: 312

Yanagimoto, Capt. R., IV: 128

Yancey, Lt. Cdr. E. W., X: 375, 378–9

"Yangtze Raiders," XIII: 295–6, 302

Yangtze R. Gunboats, III: 28

Yano, Capt. M., VI: 38

Yap I., Carolines, III: 7, VII: 84, 201, 315, VIII: 219, 233–4, 245, 263, 290, 345, XII: 33, 49–53, 56, 74, 113–15, 127, 201; carrier strikes, VIII: 32–3, 367, XII: 13, 356–7; air raids, VIII: 174, 313, 354; projected invasion, XII: 11, 14–15, 47

Yards and Docks, Bureau of, *Building the Navy's Bases*, VI: 100n, XIV: 276n

Yarmouth, N.S., I: 319

YARNALL, VIII: 262, 268, 409, 415, 426, XII: 319, XIII: 316

Yarnell, Adm. H. E., III: 17n–18n, 151

YARRA, III: 379

Yashiro, Rear Adm., III: 263

YASOSHIMA, XII: 357

Yasuda, Capt. Y., VI: 39, 44, 50

Yatsui, Lt. Cdr. N., XII: 351

Yavorsky, Lt. Cdr. J. T., X: 376, 378
YAYOI, III: 231n, 234, IV: 17, V: 85, VI: 39
YDG-6, VIII: 420
Yeomans, Lt. Cdr. E. E., IV: 20, 219
YEW, II: 176
YG-17, III: 107
"Y-gun," I: 210, II: 147

YMS, number authorized and built, X: 35; SW Pacific, VIII: 55; Sicily, IX: 175; Salerno, 259, 272; Anzio, 340, 342, 348; Caribbean, X: 205; Hollandia, VIII: 84; Southern France, XI: 246, 256, 272; Mediterranean, 313; Ngulu, XII: 51; Leyte, 117, 131; Okinawa, XIV: 117, 220

YMS-8, *-10*, *-46*, *-47*, VIII: 404; *-19*, sunk, XII: 35; *-24*, sunk, XI: 272-3; *-30*, IX: 348, 396; *-39*, sunk, XIII: 270n; *-43*, IX: 144n; *-48*, VIII: 404, and sunk, XIII: 200; *-49*, VI: 384; *-50*, 376, and sunk, XIII: 269-70; *-51*, VI: 382, VIII: 404; *-52*, VI: 382, 384; *-63*, XI: 272-3; *-70*, VI: 376, 382; *-90*, *-91*, VII: 345; *-92*, *-103*, XIV: 391; *-104*, 377; *-176*, XII: 419; *-200*, XI: 272; *-262*, *-263*, *-283*, *-320*, *-383*, *-388*, VII: 345-7; *-287*, *-290*, VII: 341; *-315*, XIII: 24; *-316*, 306; *-365*, sunk, 270n; *-385*, sunk, XII: 50; *-409*, X: 327n; *-481*, sunk, XIII: 262
YMT-205, VII: 341
YOGURE, IV: 17
Yokohama, III: 29, XIV: 362, 369
Yokosuka, III: 21n, 95, VII: 54, VIII: 234, XIV: 316, 357-61
Yokoyama, Gen., XIII: 196-7, 209
Yokoyama, Rear Adm. I., VI: 21, XIV: 363n
Yokoyama, Col. Y., VI: 33, 44
Yonai, Adm. M., III: 40, VIII: 340, XII: 66, 338, XIV: 337, 341n, 346
Yontan, Okinawa, XIV: 83, 91, 135, 153, 171, 216, 243, 270
York, 1st Lt. E. J., III: 392, 396
Yorkmar, X: 148
YORKTOWN (1937), I: liii, 57, 83, II: 31, 214, III: 31, 57, 211n, 214, 257-66, 387-8, IV: 14-58 *passim*, 81-3, 90, 97, 101-3, 114-38 *passim*, 141, 151n, V: 28, 89, 92, 99, VI: 96n, VIII: 238n, XI: 279n, XII: x, 244n, 254n; sunk, IV: 153-6; pic., 153

YORKTOWN (1943), VI: 31, VII: xxvii, 85, 92, 116, 190-96, 208, 257, 321, 325, 330, 338, 348, 352, VIII: 37, 154, 174, 238, 250, 262-98 *passim*, 311, 383, 412, X: 109n, XIII: 54, 66, 315, XIV: 21, 94, 100, 310, 311n, 316, 334, 360, 385-6
Yorktown, I: 323
YOSEMITE, XIV: 387
Yoshida, Maj. K., VIII: 325
Yoshida, Capt. Masayoshi, XIV: 202
Yoshida, Ens. Mitsuru, XIV: 205, 209
Yoshida Maru No. 1, VIII: 20
Yoshimura, Capt. M., XII: 431
Yost, Maj. D. K., V: 374
Young, Lt. Cdr. A. L., VII: 335-6
Young, Capt. Cassin, V: 231, 247
Young, Lt. Cdr. D. E., XII: 422, XIII: 304
Young, Capt. E. W., IV: 272, XIV: 381
Young, Lt. H. G., XII: 423
Young, Capt. H. L., III: 121, 262, XII: 421, XIII: 101, 305
Young, Boatswain J., V: 44, 56
Young, Lt. J. A., XII: 420, 429
Young, Lt. James R., XIV: 204, 208
Young, Lt. L. A., XIV: 377
Young, Lt. L. V., VIII: 141
Young, Leo C., I: 225
Young, Lt. R. A., XII: 423
Young, Lt. Richard C., XIV: 375
Young, Cdr. Robert C., VII: 348, IX: 386
Young, Capt. Rufus C., X: 319n, 377
Young, Lt. (jg) Walter C., X: 219
YOUNG, VII: 103n, XIII: 188, 202, 204, 311, 324
Young America, VII: 341, 347
YP, described, V: 114n; Guadalcanal, V: 114; *YP-16*, *-17*, III: 184; *-63*, *-64*, I: 146; *-219*, I: 148; *-239*, V: 181; *-277*, IV: 70; *-284*, V: 206, and sunk, 196; *-289*, V: 124; *-346*, V: 124-5; *-389*, sunk, I: 156
YT-130, V: 284n
YUBARI, III: 26, 231-2, 245, IV: 17, 205, V: 19, 35, 40, 48, 51-2, VI: 68, 112, 155, 332; sunk, V: 61n, VI: 74-5, VIII: 17n
Yucatan Channel, X: 192, 207n
YUDACHI, III: 162, 275, 334, IV: 88, V: 109-10, 118, 197, 206-7, 234, 242; sunk, 254-5
YUGIRI, III: 276, IV: 89, V: 109, VI: 353; sunk, 356-7

YUGUMO, IV: 88, V: 85, 206, 234, VI: 244; sunk, 247-8, 250-51

YUGURE, V: 234, 238n, VI: 181; sunk, 191n, 207

YUKAZE, IV: 89

YUKIKAZE, III: 162, 274, 334, IV: 89, V: 85, 206, 233, VI: 55-9, 62-4, 181, 187, 189n, VIII: 417, XII: 272n, 431, XIII: 158, XIV: 202

YUKON, I: 422, VII: 334, XI: 246

YUMA, VIII: 406, XIV: 155, 375, 388

YUNAGI, V: 19, 35, 39, 51-2, 55, VI: 181, 244, VIII: 417; sunk, V: 61n

YUNNAN, XII: 83, 423, XIII: 308

YURA, III: 276, 308, 334, IV: 88, V: 84, 104-5, 138, 194-7, 202n, 207; sunk, 197

YUZUKI, IV: 17, 27, XII: 391

Z

"Z" Operation, VIII: 12–13, 173, 217, 253n

Z-24, XI: 175; -27, -32, -37, sunk, X: 104–5, XI: 175

Zaafaran, I: 191n

Zacharias, Capt. E. M., III: 392, VII: 336–7, VIII: 409

Zachary Taylor, X: 382

Zafaglione, Point, Sicily, IX: 127–8; pic., 130

Zahm, Cdr. J. C., XI: 334, XII: 371, XIV: 254, 373

Zaibatsu, III: 45, 66

Zamalek, I: 191n

Zambales Mts. and Province, XIII: 125, 135, 185, 193, 209, 271; landing, 178, 187–9, 278

Zamboanga, VIII: 118–19, XIII: 217, 240–41; landings, see Mindanao

Zamucen, Lt. (jg) B. C., XII: 51n

ZamZam, I: 38n, 63

Zanana, New Georgia, VI: 199, 202

Zandery, Surinam, I: 147, X: 189, 197, 218

ZANE, III: 104, 213n, IV: 274, V: 194–6, 206, VI: 144–8, VII: 344, 347, VIII: 410, 420, XIII: 187n, XIV: 388

ZAURAK, XIV: 66n

Zausmer, Dr. Otto, X: 247n

ZEAL, XII: 421, XIV: 377

Zebulon B. Vance, I: 171n

Zeigler, Lt. W. C., XIV: 376

ZEILIN, IV: 253, 273, V: 148, 229, 232, 236, VII: 156, 159, 255, 268, 274, 335–7, 344, VIII: 405, 419, XIII: 150, 307, 312, 326

Zelenka, Cdr. B. T., XIV: 381

ZELLARS, XIV: 227, 373, 391; pic., 206–7

Zern, Lt. Cdr. Richard D., V: 270n, 273n

ZETLAND, II: 198–9, 208, XI: 343

ZEUS, XIV: 388

ZH-1, XI: 175

Zhukov, Gen. Georgi, X: 345

Zimmer, Lt. Col. H. J., VIII: 366, 369

Zimmerli, Capt. R. M., II: 176, 274, IX: 298n

Zimmerman, Lt. Cdr. George, XII: 428, XIII: 318

Zimmerman, Maj. John L., V: x; Ars Longa, VII: 149n; Guadalcanal Campaign, IV: 278n, V: 65n

Zimmerman, Capt. W. E., I: 250, X: 224

Zimmerman, Col. Wayne C., VII: 49, 274–5

Zimmy, Lt. Cdr. S. M., XII: 428, XIII: 319

Zinn, Lt. Cdr. F. K., XII: 421, XIII: 306, XIV: 376

Zinser, Lt. E. J., XIII: 309, 322

ZIRCON, I: 234; pic., I: 259

Zittel, Cdr. K. O. A., XIII: 323

Zondorak, Lt. Cdr. C. J., II: 40

Zook, Seaman L. E., V: 257n

ZUIHO, III: 27, 274, IV: 88, 142, 179n, 184, V: 206–9, 213–14, 220, VI: 118, 286, VII: 6, 44, 137n, VIII: 217, 247, 263, 288, 294, 299, 416, XII: 91, 162, 319, 324–7, 335, 430; sunk, 328, and pic., 326

ZUIKAKU, III: 27, 87–8, 334, 382, IV: 11, 17, 43, 61–3, 179n, 184, 276, V: 82, 85, 88, 91, 179, 203, 206, 209, 214–15, 220–23, VI: 118, 286, VII: 6, 44, 137n, VIII: 217–18, 249, 264, 272–3, 285n, 287–9, 292–5, 298–300, 416, XII: 91, 162, 191, 319, 325–6, 335, 430; sunk, 327; pics., VIII: 233, XII: 327

ZUNI, VIII: 420, XII: 347–8, 429, XIII: 319, XIV: 388

Zurmuehlen, Capt. G. D., XIII: 324

Zursler, Lt. W. R., XII: 416

ZWAARDVISCH, X: 302

Zyo, Capt. E., XII: 430

ACHSE, Germany's Italian plan, IX

A-GO, Japanese counterattack, 1944, VIII

ANVIL, Allied plan for Southern France, same as DRAGOON, XI

AVALANCHE, Salerno, IX

BOLERO, U.S. build-up in U.K., X

CATCHPOLE, Eniwetok, VII

DRAGOON, Southern France, 1944, XI

FLINTLOCK, Kwajalein, VII

FORAGER, Marianas, VIII

GALVANIC, Gilberts, VII

HAILSTONE, Truk, 1944, VII

HOTFOOT, Submarines, Honshu, XIV

HUSKY, Sicily, IX

I, Japanese counterattack, 1943, VI

ICEBERG, Okinawa, XIV

KING II, Leyte, XII

KON, Japanese reinforcement of Biak, VIII

LANDCRAB, Attu, VII

LEADER, strike on German ships, 1943, X

MO, Japanese counterattack, 1942, IV

MONSTROUS, A/S in Med., 1943, X

NEPTUNE-OVERLORD, Normandy, 1944, XI

OBOE, Borneo, 1945, XIII

OVERLORD. See NEPTUNE-OVERLORD

POINTBLANK, air offensive, 1944, XI

RECKLESS, Hollandia, 1944, VIII

RO, Japanese defense of Rabaul, VI

ROUNDUP, proposed Normandy invasion, 1943, XI

SHINGLE, Anzio, IX

SHO-GO, Japanese Leyte offensive, XII

SLEDGEHAMMER, proposed French beachhead 1942, II, IX, XI

SWORDHILT, liberation of Brittany, XI

TA, Japanese offensive, Bougainville, VI

TEARDROP, antisubmarine barrier, 1945, X

TEN-GO, Japanese air offensive, 1945, XIV

TOENAILS, Central Solomons, 1943, VI

TORCH, North Africa, 1942, II

VICTOR, Visayas, 1945, XIII

WATCHTOWER, Solomons and Bismarcks, IV–VI

ZITRONELLA, Spitsbergen raid, X